Witnesses to Permanent Revolution

Historical Materialism Book Series

More than ten years after the collapse of the Berlin wall and the disappearance of Marxism as a (supposed) state ideology, a need for a serious and long-term Marxist book publishing program has risen. Subjected to the whims of fashion, most contemporary publishers have abandoned any of the systematic production of Marxist theoretical work that they may have indulged in during the 1970s and early 1980s. The Historical Materialism book series addresses this great gap with original monographs, translated texts and reprints of "classics."

Editorial board: Paul Blackledge, Leeds; Sebastian Budgen, London; Jim Kincaid, Leeds; Stathis Kouvelakis, Paris; Marcel van der Linden, Amsterdam; China Miéville, London; Paul Reynolds, Lancashire.

Haymarket Books is proud to be working with Brill Academic Publishers (http://www.brill.nl) and the journal Historical Materialism to republish the Historical Materialism book series in paperback editions. Current series titles include:

Alasdair MacIntyre's Engagement with Marxism: Selected Writings 1953–1974
Edited by Paul Blackledge and Neil Davidson

Althusser: The Detour of Theory, Gregory Elliott

Between Equal Rights: A Marxist Theory of International Law, China Miéville

The Capitalist Cycle, Pavel V. Maksakovsky, Translated with introduction
and commentary by Richard B. Day

The Clash of Globalisations: Neo-Liberalism, the Third Way, and Anti-globalisation, Ray Kiely

Critical Companion to Contemporary Marxism, Edited by Jacques Bidet and Stathis Kouvelakis

Criticism of Heaven: On Marxism and Theology, Roland Boer

Exploring Marx's Capital: Philosophical, Economic, and Political Dimensions, Jacques Bidet

Following Marx: Method, Critique, and Crisis, Michael Lebowitz

The German Revolution: 1917–1923, Pierre Broué

Globalisation: A Systematic Marxian Account, Tony Smith

The Gramscian Moment: Philosophy, Hegemony and Marxism, Peter D. Thomas

Impersonal Power: History and Theory of the Bourgeois State,
Heide Gerstenberger, translated by David Fernbach

Lenin Rediscovered: What Is to Be Done? In Context, Lars T. Lih

Making History: Agency, Structure, and Change in Social Theory, Alex Callinicos

Marxism and Ecological Economics: Toward a Red and Green Political Economy, Paul Burkett

A Marxist Philosophy of Language, Jean-Jacques Lecercle and Gregory Elliott

The Theory of Revolution in the Young Marx, Michael Löwy

Utopia Ltd.: Ideologies of Social Dreaming in England 1870–1900, Matthew Beaumont

Western Marxism and the Soviet Union: A Survey of Critical Theories and Debates Since 1917
Marcel van der Linden

Witnesses to Permanent Revolution

The Documentary Record

Edited and translated by

RICHARD B. DAY AND DANIEL GAIDO

Haymarket Books
Chicago, Illinois

First published in 2009 by Brill Academic Publishers, The Netherlands
© 2009 Koninklijke Brill NV, Leiden, The Netherlands

Published in paperback in 2011 by
Haymarket Books
P.O. Box 180165
Chicago, IL 60618
773-583-7884
www.haymarketbooks.org

ISBN: 978-1-60846-089-2

Trade distribution:
In the U.S., Consortium Book Sales, www.cbsd.com
In Canada, Publishers Group Canada, www.pgcbooks.ca
In the UK, Turnaround Publisher Services, www.turnaround-psl.com
In Australia, Palgrave Macmillan, www.palgravemacmillan.com.au
In all other countries, Publishers Group Worldwide, www.pgw.com

This book was published with the generous support of Lannan Foundation
and the Wallace Global Fund.

Printed in Canada.

10 9 8 7 6 5 4 3 2

Library of Congress Cataloging-in-Publication Data is available.

To Judith and Marielle

Contents

Preface

The year 2005 was the centenary of the first Russian Revolution. Over the past century, countless volumes have been written on this subject in every language and from every conceivable political viewpoint. One might well wonder what remains to be said. We have discovered that there are new perspectives to consider, and they come from having the foremost participants give their own accounts of the historical forces at work and the prospects they saw for a revolutionary victory that might affect the history of Europe and even the entire world.

The theme of our anthology is the rediscovery and elaboration of the concept of permanent revolution in the years 1903–7. In researching this project we have collected and translated into English for the first time a series of documents that bring fundamental issues to life in a way that no secondary account possibly could.[1] One of our principal discoveries is that Leon Trotsky, while certainly the most famous and brilliant proponent of permanent revolution, was by no means its sole author; indeed, several major contributions came from a number of other Marxists, some of whom – such as David Ryazanov – have rarely been mentioned in this connection, while others – Karl Kautsky in particular – have most often been regarded as pseudo-revolutionaries whose real commitment was always to parliamentary politics. The documents that we have translated demonstrate not only that

---

[1] The one document that has been fully translated previously is Kautsky 1983, pp. 352–403. We are grateful to Neil Harding and Richard Taylor (the translator) for kindly giving us permission to reproduce their work in this anthology. English versions of Kautsky 1905j and 'Old and New Revolution' (the latter under another title and without mentioning the source) appeared in pre-WWI socialist journals. In both cases the documents were checked against the originals and the first one was collated from two different versions printed before and after the Russian revolution of 1905. Two of the documents by Trotsky – 'Up to the Ninth of January' and 'After the Petersburg Uprising: What Next?' – have previously appeared in English but in highly abridged versions. We have provided the complete text of both.

Kautsky was a key participant in all discussions of permanent revolution, but also that in the years of the first Russian Revolution his thinking was often closer to Trotsky's than to Lenin's.

Historical research is inevitably a cumulative endeavour, and our work certainly owes much to the efforts of countless others. The task of historians is to clarify great issues first, but the very act of doing so poses new questions. Nuances have to be discerned, hypotheses have to be validated, and great events can only be fully examined when traced to the consciousness of the actors themselves. In rediscovering the debate over permanent revolution, we owe a special debt to Reidar Larsson and Hartmut Mehringer, whose books served as uniquely helpful bibliographical guides.[2]

We had hoped to complete this project for the centenary of 1905. We missed that target because documents had to be retrieved from numerous libraries in places as far apart as Great Britain, the United States, Canada, Germany, Finland, The Netherlands and Palestine/Israel. In translating the documents from German and Russian into English, we have divided the work equally and tried to reproduce both the letter and the spirit of the original texts. There is never a perfect substitute for reading a text in the original; nor can a neatly published translation ever reproduce either the thrill that comes from discovering an obscure insight or the frustration of having to translate it from some barely legible microfilm. We cannot share those experiences with readers, but we do hope that our efforts will generate deeper understanding of an important debate in Marxist historiography. To that end we have minimised the use of ellipses and provided extensive notations for those who may wish to pursue matters further.

Richard B. Day
Daniel Gaido

---

[2] Larsson 1970; Mehringer 1978, p. 201.

The Historical Origin of the Expression 'Permanent Revolution'

There is a story, possibly apocryphal, which says that Chou En-Lai (Prime Minister of China from 1949 to 1976) was once asked to comment on the long-run effects of the French Revolution. He is said to have replied that 'It is too soon to tell.' Those who debated the possibility of revolution in Russia from 1903 onwards certainly shared the same conviction, for they made continuous references to the French Revolution of 1789, often measured their own prospects by comparison with it, and adopted much of its political vocabulary, including the concept of permanent revolution or 'révolution en permanence'.

On 17 June, 1789, the representatives of France's Third Estate proclaimed themselves to be the National Assembly since they represented the overwhelming majority of the nation. King Louis XVI ordered the hall of the Estates-General to be occupied by armed men, forcing the people's representatives to meet in the Tennis Court of Old Versailles street where they adopted the following decree:

> The National Assembly, considering that it has been called to establish the constitution of the realm, to bring about the regeneration of public order, and to maintain the true principles of monarchy; that nothing may prevent it from

continuing its deliberations in any place it is forced to establish itself; and, finally, that the National Assembly exists wherever its members are gathered;

Decrees that all members of this assembly immediately take a solemn oath never to separate, and to reassemble wherever circumstances require, until the constitution of the realm is established and fixed upon solid foundations; and that said oath having been sworn, all members and each one individually confirm this unwavering resolution with his signature.[1]

The Tennis Court Oath denied the king's authority to dissolve the National Assembly and set a precedent for the Berlin and Frankfurt National Assemblies in 1848. After a reactionary Ministry had been formed in Prussia by royal order on 21 September, 1848, the *Neue Rheinische Zeitung*, edited by Karl Marx, cited a letter by a deputy that stated:

We have just learned beyond doubt that an entirely *counter-revolutionary Government* has been formed.... At tomorrow's session this same Government will read out a royal message wherein the *prospect of the disbandment of the Assembly* will be held out. The result of this is a *declaration of permanence* which will probably lead to a new and very bloody *revolution*. All parties of the National Assembly are consulting permanently in their usual premises.[2]

Half a century later, this expression reappeared in Franz Mehring's introduction to his anthology of writings by Marx and Engels in the *Neue Rheinische Zeitung*. Mehring described how, though the Prussian guard had been defeated by the Berlin proletariat in a fierce street battle on 18 March, 1848, the Frankfurt pre-parliament 'shrank before its own strength and failed to declare itself permanent [*sich für permanent zu erklären*] or to set up an armed force for its own defence'.[3] This reference has a linguistic connection with the theory of permanent revolution developed by Marx and Engels, but the class content is entirely different: in the case of Prussia in 1848, at issue was the permanence of the bourgeois-democratic revolution, whereas, for Marx and Engels, 'revolution in permanence' meant going beyond bourgeois democracy to the proletarian socialist revolution.

---

[1] Source: *Gazette Nationale, ou Le Moniteur universel*, trans. Laura Mason in Laura Mason and Tracey Rizzo, eds., *The French Revolution: A Document Collection* (New York: Houghton Mifflin, 1999), pp. 60–1.

[2] Marx and Engels 1848b, p. 448.

[3] Franz Mehring (ed.) 1902, p. 6.

Permanent revolution in the early writings of Marx and Engels

Marx and Engels referred to permanent revolution three times before writing their Address of the Central Committee to the Communist League in March 1850, on each occasion referring to the terrorist phase of the French revolution in 1793. The first instance occurred in 1843 in Marx's essay *On the Jewish Question*:

> Of course, in periods when the political state as such is born violently out of civil society, when political liberation is the form in which men strive to achieve their liberation, the state can and must go as far as the *abolition of religion*, the *destruction* of religion. But it can do so only in the same way that it proceeds to the abolition of private property, to the maximum, to confiscation, to progressive taxation, just as it goes as far as the abolition of life, the *guillotine*.... [I]t can achieve this only by coming into *violent* contradiction with its own conditions of life, only by declaring the revolution to be permanent.[4]

The second reference came in 1845 in *The Holy Family*, a polemic by Marx and Engels directed against their fellow left Hegelians, 'Bruno Bauer and Company':

> *Napoleon* represented the last battle of *revolutionary terror* against the *bourgeois society* which had been proclaimed by this same Revolution, and against its policy. Napoleon, of course, already discerned the essence of the *modern state*; he understood that it is based on the unhampered development of bourgeois society, on the free movement of private interest, etc. He decided to recognize and protect this basis. He was no terrorist with his head in the clouds.... He *perfected* the *terror* by *substituting permanent war* for *permanent revolution*.[5]

A third reference to permanent revolution, again concerning the terrorist phase of the French Revolution, occurred in an article on 'The Magyar Struggle' that Engels wrote for the *Neue Rheinische Zeitung* one month before publication of the *Communist Manifesto*:

---

[4] Marx 1844, pp. 155–6.
[5] Marx and Engels 1845, p. 123.

> Mass uprising, national manufacture of arms, issue of banknotes, short shrift for anyone hindering the revolutionary movement, revolution in permanence – in short, all the main features of the glorious year 1793 are found again in the Hungary which Kossuth has armed, organized and inspired with enthusiasm.[6]

When Karl Kautsky later wrote his *Class Antagonisms in 1789*, which first appeared in *Die Neue Zeit* as a series of articles commemorating the centenary of the French Revolution, he evidently drew from these sources (most probably from Marx's *Zur Judenfrage*) to describe the years 1793–4 in Paris, the time of the supremacy of the sans-culottes, as a period of '*Revolution in Permanenz*'.[7]

The Communist League and the Revolution of 1848–9

The Communist League – the first international proletarian organisation – originated in 1836 in the League of the Just [*Bund der Gerechten*], a utopian-communist group following the ideas of Gracchus Babeuf. In 1796, Babeuf had been executed for conspiring to provoke a plebeian uprising aimed at replacing the bourgeois Directory with a revolutionary dictatorship leading to 'pure democracy' and 'egalitarian communism'. The League of the Just held its first conference in London in June 1847, when Engels convinced its members to replace the motto 'All Men are Brothers' with Marx's slogan 'Working Men of All Countries, Unite!'

At the same conference, the organisation renamed itself the Communist League [*Bund der Kommunisten*]. New rules were drawn up by Marx and Engels and approved by a second congress, also held in London in December 1847. Article I read: 'The aim of the League is the overthrow of the bourgeoisie, the rule of the proletariat, the abolition of the old bourgeois society which rests on the antagonism of classes, and the foundation of a new society without classes

---

6 Engels 1849, pp. 227–38, pp. 227–8.

7 Kautsky 1889b, pp. 51–2. The relevant passages from this book were reproduced under the title 'Die Sansculotten der französischen Revolution' (Aus: Kautsky 1889b) in the Festschrift with the title *1649–1789–1905* (Berlin: Buchhandlung Vorwärts, 1905) pp. 11–12. In this anthology see, pp. 537–42.

and without private property.'[8] Marx and Engels were commissioned to draw up the organisation's programme, which became the *Communist Manifesto*.[9]

The policy followed by Marx and Engels during the revolutionary wave of 1848–9 involved much more than establishing new sections of the Communist League in Germany. In his article 'Marx and the *Neue Rheinische Zeitung*, 1848–49', Engels later pointed out that 'the German proletariat at first appeared on the political stage as the extreme democratic party', so that

> ...when we founded a major newspaper in Germany, our banner was determined as a matter of course. It could only be that of democracy.... If we did not want to do that...then there was nothing left for us to do but to preach communism in a little provincial sheet and to found a tiny sect instead of a great party of action. But we had already been spoilt for the role of preachers in the wilderness; we had studied the utopians too well for that....[10]

Declining the role of sectarian agitators, Marx and Engels joined democratic circles in Cologne and eventually took control of their publication, the *Neue Rheinische Zeitung*, which appeared from 1 June 1848 until 19 May 1849. They followed the tactics prescribed by the *Manifesto* for communists in Germany: 'they fight with the bourgeoisie whenever it acts in a revolutionary way, against the absolute monarchy, the feudal landowners, and the petty bourgeoisie', but 'they never cease, for a single instant, to instil into the working class the clearest possible recognition of the hostile antagonism between bourgeoisie and proletariat' so that 'after the fall of the reactionary classes in Germany, the fight against the bourgeoisie itself may immediately begin'. Marx and Engels believed that the bourgeois revolution in Germany, occurring at a more advanced stage of social development 'and with a much more developed proletariat than that of England was in the seventeenth, and France in the eighteenth century', would be 'but the prelude to an immediately following proletarian revolution'.[11]

---

8 Marx and Engels 1847, p. 633.
9 Marx and Engels 1848a.
10 Engels 1884a, p. 120.
11 Marx and Engels 1848a, p. 519.

Expecting the German bourgeoisie at first to lead the popular uprising against feudalism and absolutism along the lines of the French Revolution,[12] Marx and Engels referred to the *Neue Rheinische Zeitung* as the *Organ der Demokratie*, although it soon ceased to receive financial support from the democratic bourgeoisie. But the massacre of the Paris proletariat after the uprising of June 1848, and the capitulation of the German bourgeoisie before the monarchy and the nobility out of fear of the working class, soon persuaded them that no hope could be placed in even the most extreme bourgeois factions. In December 1848 Marx wrote:

> The German bourgeoisie developed so sluggishly, timidly and slowly that at the moment when it menacingly confronted feudalism and absolutism, it saw ... pitted against itself the proletariat and all sections of the middle class whose interests and ideas were related to those of the proletariat.... Unlike the French bourgeoisie of 1789, the Prussian bourgeoisie, when it confronted monarchy and aristocracy,...was not a class speaking for the whole of modern society.... From the first it was inclined to betray the people and to compromise with the crowned representatives of the old society, for it already belonged itself to the old society; it did not advance the interests of a new society against an old one, but represented refurbished interests within an obsolete society.[13]

Marx and Engels changed their tactics in February 1849.[14] Together with Joseph Moll and Karl Schapper, they concentrated their efforts in the Workingmen's Union of Cologne, which also had a representative in the District Committee of Democratic Societies. In April 1849, growing friction between workers and democrats led to a split in the latter organisation: the Workingmen's Union

---

[12] 'When the February Revolution broke out, all of us, as far as our conceptions of the conditions and the course of revolutionary movements were concerned, were under the spell of previous historical experience, particularly that of France. It was, indeed, the latter which had dominated the whole of European history since 1789, and from which now once again the signal had gone forth for general revolutionary change. It was, therefore, natural and unavoidable that our conceptions of the nature and the course of the "social" revolution proclaimed in Paris in February 1848, of the revolution of the proletariat, should be strongly coloured by memories of the prototypes of 1789 and 1830.' Engels, 'Introduction' to Marx 1850 pp. 506–24, 509.

[13] Marx 1848a, p. 163.

[14] Riazanov 1937.

recalled its representative, and Marx and his supporters resigned from the Committee. On 14 April 1849, Marx wrote:

> We consider that the present organisation of the Democratic Associations includes too many heterogeneous elements for any possibility of successful activity in furtherance of the cause. We are of the opinion…that a closer union of the Workers' Associations is to be preferred since they consist of homogeneous elements, and therefore we hereby from today withdraw from the Rhenish District Committee of Democratic Associations.[15]

A call was then issued to summon a General Workingmen's Congress in Leipzig, which failed to meet, however, due to mounting government repression.

The new tactics of the Communist League also led to a significant change of editorial policy at the *Neue Rheinische Zeitung*. The famous articles on *Wage Labour and Capital*, systematically expounding Marx's insight into the extraction of 'surplus value' through exploitation of wage-labour, appeared in April 1849. But the tactical move to the left was already too late, and on 18 May 1849, the Prussian government halted publication of the *Neue Rheinische Zeitung*. Reflecting in 1885 on the ensuing events, Engels declared that with the crushing of the Paris proletariat on 'June 13, 1849, the defeat of the May insurrections in Germany and the suppression of the Hungarian revolution by the Russians, a great period of the 1848 Revolution came to a close'.[16] The ensuing wave of repression saw most leaders of the workers' movement sent either to prison or into exile.

Engels on 'The Campaign for the German Imperial Constitution'

By the beginning of 1850, most of the old guard of the Communist League reassembled in London, where Marx and Engels resumed publishing the *Neue Rheinische Zeitung* as a journal [*Politisch-ökonomische Revue*] rather than a daily. Six issues appeared between January and November 1850, including Engels's 'The Campaign for the German Imperial Constitution [*Die deutsche Reichsverfassungskampagne*]'. Engels recounted how the Frankfurt National

---

[15] Anneke, Schapper, Marx, Becker, and Wolff 1849, p. 282.
[16] Engels 1885, p. 326.

Assembly had convened in May 1848, and by the following April it had produced a constitutional proposal that included civil liberties and national institutions within the framework of a constitutional monarchy headed by the Hohenzollerns. But the Prussian king, Frederick William IV, refused to accept a crown 'from the gutter', and most of the larger German states declined to recognise the constitution. Despite its limitations, however, the constitution remained as the sole achievement of the revolution, and many fighters rose to its defence. Engels himself participated in the Elberfeld uprising and fought against the Prussians (in June and July 1849) as the aide-de-camp of August Willich. He described the battles of Willich's volunteer corps in the last section of his work, 'To Die for the Republic!'. In the same section, he also summarised the logic of permanent revolution. From the political point of view, he wrote, 'the campaign for the Imperial Constitution was a failure from the very start' because of the compromising role of liberals and democrats. He concluded that the next revolution would have to transfer power directly to the proletariat:

> Ever since the defeat of June 1848 the question for the civilised part of the European continent has stood thus: either the rule of the revolutionary proletariat or…of the classes who ruled before February. A middle road is no longer possible. In Germany in particular the bourgeoisie has shown itself incapable of ruling; it could only maintain its rule over the people by surrendering it once more to the aristocracy and the bureaucracy. In the Imperial Constitution the petty bourgeoisie…attempted an impossible arrangement aimed at postponing the decisive struggle. The attempt was bound to fail: those who were serious about the movement were not serious about the Imperial Constitution, and those who were serious about the Imperial Constitution were not serious about the movement.
>
> This does not mean…that the consequences of the campaign for the Imperial Constitution were any the less significant. Above all the campaign simplified the situation. It cut short an endless series of attempts at reconciliation; now that it has been lost…. [T]he revolution can no longer be brought to a conclusion in Germany except with the complete rule of the proletariat.
>
> The [campaign for the] Imperial Constitution…contributed considerably to the development of class antagonisms in those German provinces where

they were not yet sharply developed…. The workers and peasants, who suffer just as much as the petty bourgeois under the present dictatorship of the sabre, did not go through the experience of the last uprising for nothing;…besides having their fallen and murdered brothers to avenge [they] will take care that when the next insurrection comes it is *they* and not the petty bourgeois who get the reins in their hands.[17]

The 'Address of the Central Committee to the Communist League' (March 1850)

In March 1850, the Central Committee of the Communist League in London issued a kind of second manifesto – a manifesto of *permanent revolution* – that was destined to play a central role in all the debates over the class character and political alliances of the Russian revolution in 1903–7. The 'Address of the Central Committee to the Communist League [*Ansprache der Zentralbehörde an den Bund der Kommunisten vom März 1850*]' began with the conviction that a new revolution was quickly approaching. Reflecting their own bitter experiences with even the most promising democratic circles in Germany, Marx and Engels now warned the workers against being deceived by the conciliatory preaching of petty-bourgeois democrats or allowing themselves to be degraded to the role of camp followers of bourgeois democracy: 'The revolutionary workers' party will cooperate with the petty-bourgeois democrats against the faction whose overthrow they both desire, but it will oppose them in all points where its own interests arise.'[18] Following the overthrow of feudal-absolutist reaction, the petty bourgeoisie was expected to use the revolution's success to reform capitalism, but the proletariat must continue to drive events forward. The workers' task was

> to make the revolution permanent until all the more or less propertied classes have been driven from their ruling positions, until the proletariat has conquered state power and…has progressed sufficiently far – not only in one country but in all the leading countries of the world – that competition between the proletarians of these countries ceases and at least the decisive forces of production are concentrated in the hands of the workers. *Our*

---

[17] Engels 1850a, p. 238.
[18] Marx and Engels 1850, pp. 277–87, 280.

> *concern cannot simply be to modify private property, but to abolish it, not to hush up class antagonisms but to abolish classes, not to improve the existing society but to found a new one.*[19]

Resolutely abandoning the former role of an 'extreme democratic party', the 'Address' urged workers to focus on their own party in opposition to the democratic organisations and to use every possible means to radicalise the revolution.

> ...[D]uring and immediately after the struggle the workers, as far as it is at all possible, must oppose bourgeois attempts at pacification and force the democrats to carry out their terrorist phrases. They must work to ensure that the immediate revolutionary excitement is not suddenly suppressed after the victory. On the contrary, it must be sustained as long as possible. Far from opposing the so-called excesses – instances of popular vengeance against hated individuals or against public buildings with which hateful memories are associated – the workers' party must not only tolerate these actions but must even give them direction. During and after the struggle the workers must at every opportunity put forward their own demands against those of the bourgeois democrats.[20]

If democrats demanded a ten-hour workday, the workers' party must demand an eight-hour day. If democrats called for expropriation of the large estates with compensation, the workers must insist on confiscation without compensation. 'Decisive, terrorist measures' had to be adopted from the very beginning to suppress any organised reaction, and every parcel of conquered territory had to serve further conquests until the last vestiges of class antagonism had been eradicated forever. As Marx wrote to Engels on 13 July 1851, the 'Address' of March 1850 to the Communist League was *'au fond* [ultimately], nothing less than a plan of campaign against democracy'.[21]

---

[19] *Ibid.* p. 281 (italics added).
[20] *Ibid.* pp. 282–3.
[21] Marx to Engels, London, 13 July, 1851, in Marx and Engels, *Collected Works*, Vol. 38: 383–5, p. 384.

Marxism, Blanquism, and revolutionary retreat

In the same month in which the 'Address' appeared, Marx also published in the *Neue Rheinische Zeitung* Part III of *The Class Struggles in France, 1848–50*. Here, he noted that while the petty bourgeoisie may identify with utopian socialism – rejecting class struggle and dreaming of peaceful change through state credit, progressive taxes, limitations on inheritance, state responsibility for large construction projects, and other such measures to slow the concentration of capital,

> the proletariat rallies more and more around revolutionary socialism, around communism, for which the bourgeoisie has itself invented the name of Blanqui. This socialism is the declaration of the permanence of the revolution, the class dictatorship of the proletariat as the necessary transit point to the abolition of class distinctions generally.[22]

One month later, in mid-April of 1850, Marx and Engels participated in creating a short-lived Universal Society of Revolutionary Communists [*Société universelle des communistes révolutionnaires, Weltgesellschaft der revolutionären Kommunisten*]. Article I of their Declaration of Principles stated: 'The aim of the association is the downfall of all the privileged classes and subjection of these classes to the dictatorship of the proletariat by maintaining the revolution in permanence until the realisation of communism, which is the final form of organisation of human society.'[23] The agreement to establish the new organisation was signed by two refugees in London on behalf of the

---

[22] Marx 1851, p. 203. Here we might note that Rosa Luxemburg, who during the Russian Revolution of 1905 opposed Lenin's organisational methods, would nevertheless defend the Bolsheviks against Plekhanov's accusations of Blanquism – perhaps because she had been accused herself of Blanquism by Georg von Vollmar during the debate on revisionism. See Luxemburg 1971, pp. 298–305. See also Tudor and Tudor (eds.) 1988, p. 29 and pp. 249–75.

[23] 'Le but de l'association est la déchéance de toutes les classes privilégiées, de soumettre ces classes à la dictature des prolétaires en maintenant la révolution en permanence jusqu'à la réalisation du communisme, qui doit être la dernière forme de constitution de la famille humaine.' Marx, Karl and Friedrich Engels 1977, pp. 568–69 and 1080–81.

Blanquists; by August Willich, Marx and Engels for the German communists; and by George Julian Harney, editor of *The Northern Star*, the central publication of the Chartist movement, on behalf of English communists. In 1928 David Ryazanov, the respected Marxist scholar who headed the Marx-Engels Institute in Moscow, compared this agreement with Section One of the Rules of the Communist League and noted crucial differences:

> The 'rule of the proletariat' is replaced by the 'dictatorship of the proletariat', while the revolution becomes a 'revolution in permanence' ('la révolution en permanence'). If the first change may be regarded as of an editorial nature, though it resulted from the experiences of the Revolution of 1848 (especially the events in Paris between February 24 and the June days), the latter formed an addition which was first resolved upon after 1848–49, although the expression appeared in Marx's early works on the lessons of the great French Revolution, particularly on the lessons provided by the Jacobins who supported the 'révolution en permanence'.[24]

In June 1850, the Central Committee of the Communist League issued a second circular reporting on the state of the organisation in Belgium, Germany, Switzerland, France and England. It also reaffirmed that the group's purpose was 'the revolutionary organisation of the workers' party', which must never 'subordinate itself to any other party'. By late 1850, however, Marx's study of the economic conjuncture convinced him that the industrial crisis of 1847, which had paved the way for the revolution of 1848, had receded, and that a new period of industrial prosperity had set in. He concluded that the revolutionary tide was ebbing and would not return until a new economic crisis created more favourable conditions. In the last section of *The Class Struggles in France*, published in the final issue (No. 5–6) of the *Neue Rheinische Zeitung* at the end of November 1850, he wrote:

> Given this general prosperity, wherein the productive forces of bourgeois society are developing as luxuriantly as possible within bourgeois relationships, a real revolution is out of the question. Such a revolution is possible only in periods when both of these factors – the modern forces of

---

[24] Riazanov 1928a, pp. 141–2. For a partial English version see Riazanov 1928b. The Universal Society of Revolutionary Communists did not survive a split in the Communist League in late 1850, after which Marx and Engels cancelled the agreement.

production and the bourgeois forms of production – come into opposition with each other.… A new revolution can only be a consequence of a new crisis. The one, however, is as sure to come as the other.[25]

Marx's opponents in the League of Communists insisted on forcing a new revolutionary uprising in Germany, which they claimed required nothing more than money and 'a number of daring individuals'.[26] In the heat of debate, Marx insisted on reading into the record another significant comment that maintained the spirit of permanent revolution but suggested a quite different timetable in view of changed circumstances:

> The point of view of the minority is dogmatic instead of critical, idealistic instead of materialistic. They regard not the real conditions but a *mere effort of will* as the driving force of the revolution. Whereas we say to the workers: 'You will have to go through 15, 20, 50 years of civil wars and national struggles not only to bring about a change in society but also to change yourselves, and prepare yourselves for the exercise of political power', you say on the contrary: 'Either we seize power at once, or else we might as well just take to our beds.' Whereas we are at pains to show the German workers in particular how rudimentary the development of the German proletariat is, you appeal to the patriotic feelings and the class prejudice of the German artisans, flattering them in the grossest way possible, and this is a more popular method, of course. Just as the word 'people' has been given an aura of sanctity by the democrats, so you have done the same for the word 'proletariat'. Like the democrats you substitute the catchword of revolution for revolutionary development.…[27]

Shortly afterwards, the remaining communists in Germany were rounded up, some were condemned to long sentences in prison, and, in November 1852, the Communist League was officially disbanded. Although Marx did not return to the subject of permanent revolution after 1851, mention should be made of his letter to Engels of 16 April 1856, which was not published until 1913. There he declared that 'the whole thing in Germany will depend on whether it is possible to back the proletarian revolution by some second

---

25 Marx 1850, p. 135.
26 Riazanov 1937. See also Marx and Engels 1850.
27 Marx 1853, p. 403.

edition of the Peasants' War' – *der deutsche Bauernkrieg*, a popular revolt in the Holy Roman Empire in 1524–5, involving hundreds of thousands of peasant insurgents. Given such a combination of urban and rural class forces, Marx thought 'the affair should go swimmingly'.[28] Lenin would later quote this paragraph as an accurate description of the class dynamics of the Bolshevik revolution of October 1917.[29]

Through participating in the Communist League's activities from 1847 to 1852, Marx and Engels bequeathed an array of tactics and concepts that would subsequently sustain the opposing views of Mensheviks and Bolsheviks alike. Which was the 'authoritative' Marx: the proponent of 'extreme' democracy who would fight together 'with the bourgeoisie whenever it acts in a revolutionary way, against the absolute monarchy, the feudal landowners, and the petty bourgeoisie'; the militant revolutionary who authored the call to permanent revolution in the 'Address of the Central Committee to the Communist League'; or the sober economic researcher who, in refuting a 'mere effort of will', anticipated a further '15, 20, 50 years of civil wars and national struggles' before the workers might be prepared 'for the exercise of political power'?

Engels on the danger of a democratic counter-revolution (1884–5)

Shortly after Marx's death, Engels returned in March 1884 to the theory of permanent revolution and appeared to resolve this confusion. In the *Sozialdemokrat* he published an article on 'Marx and the *Neue Rheinische Zeitung* (1848–49)', declaring that he and Marx had always used the publication to expose 'the parliamentary cretinism (as Marx called it) of the various so-called National Assemblies':

> When the 'Lefts' obtained the majority, the government dispersed the entire Assembly; it could do so because the Assembly had forfeited all credit with the people. When later I read *Bougeart*'s book on Marat, I found that in more than one respect we had only unconsciously imitated the great model of the genuine '*Ami du Peuple*' (not the one forged by the royalists) and that

---

[28] Marx 1856, p. 37.
[29] Lenin 1918a, p. 45.

the whole outburst of rage and the whole falsification of history, by virtue of which for almost a century only an entirely distorted Marat had been known, were solely due to the fact that Marat mercilessly removed the veil from the idols of the moment, Lafayette, Bailly and others, and exposed them as ready-made traitors to the revolution; and that he, like us, did not want the revolution to be declared closed, but in permanence.[30] We openly proclaimed that the trend we represented could enter the struggle for the attainment of our real party aims only when the most extreme of the official parties existing in Germany came to the helm: then we would form the opposition to it.[31]

Expecting that Europe would soon be convulsed by a new revolution in which bourgeois-democratic elements would again play a counter-revolutionary role, Engels also wrote to August Bebel on 11 December 1884, and predicted that the outbreak of proletarian revolution would incite all reactionary forces to coalesce under the banner of democracy:

> As to pure democracy and its role in the future…. Obviously it plays a far more subordinate part in Germany than in countries with an older industrial development. But that does not prevent the possibility, when the moment of revolution comes, of its acquiring a temporary importance as the most radical bourgeois party (it has already played itself off as such in Frankfurt) and as the final sheet-anchor of the whole bourgeois and even feudal regime. At such a moment the whole reactionary mass falls in behind it and strengthens it; everything which used to be reactionary behaves as [if it were] democratic.[32]

Finally, in November 1885, Engels reprinted Marx's essay from 1853, *'Revelations Concerning the Trial of Communists in Cologne'*. As an introduction he added a survey of the history of the Communist League, and as appendices he included the March and June 1850 'Addresses' of the Central Committee to the Communist League. Again, he warned of the danger of a democratic

---

[30] The usual English rendering of *'nicht für abgeschlossen, sondern in Permanenz erklärt wissen'* is misleading in that the word 'lasting' omits the conceptual significance of *'in Permanenz'*. Engels 1884. Reprinted in: Marx and Engels CW Vol. 26: 120–8, p. 126.

[31] Engels 1884a, p. 120. The book to which Engels referred is Bougeart 1865.

[32] Engels to August Bebel, London, 11 December, 1884, in Marx and Engels, CW, Vol. 47: 231–5, pp. 233–4. In the nautical sense, a sheet-anchor is an extra large anchor for use in an emergency.

counter-revolution and noted that the classical statement of the theory of permanent revolution might still alert workers to the impending danger:

> The Address [of March 1850], composed by Marx and myself, is still of interest today, because petty-bourgeois democracy is even now the party which must certainly be the first to come to power in Germany as the saviour of society from the communist workers on the occasion of the next European upheaval [which is] now soon due (the European revolutions, 1815, 1830, 1848–52, 1870, have occurred at intervals of 15 to 18 years in our century). Much of what is said there is, therefore, still applicable today.[33]

Eduard Bernstein and the revisionist controversy

Despite Engels's effort to fortify the workers' movement ideologically, the long spell of reaction that followed the crushing of the Paris Commune in 1871 led to a revival of bourgeois-democratic illusions in the socialist parties of the Second International. In October 1896, the 'revisionist controversy', provoked by Eduard Bernstein and his supporters, broke out within German Social Democracy. Originally a close friend of Engels, Bernstein had come under the influence of the Fabian Society during a period of exile in London and undertook to revise Marxism along reformist lines – first in a series of articles published in *Die Neue Zeit* and later in his book *The Preconditions of Socialism and the Tasks of Social Democracy*, published in 1899.[34]

Bernstein dedicated the second chapter of his book to 'Marxism and the Hegelian Dialectic', where he repudiated both 'the pitfalls of the Hegelian dialectical method' and the related theory of permanent revolution, which he regarded as a misguided concession to 'Blanquism' – meaning putschism. Convinced that the theory of permanent revolution resulted from infatuation with 'the Hegelian logic of contradiction', he offered the following example:

> In 1847, *The Communist Manifesto* declared that, given the stage of development reached by the proletariat and the advanced conditions of European civilisation, the bourgeois revolution, on which Germany was embarking, 'will be but the prelude to an immediately following proletarian

---

[33] Engels 1885, pp. 312–30.
[34] Bernstein 1993.

revolution.' In someone like Marx, who had already devoted serious study to economics, such historical self-deception – and a run-of-the-mill political visionary could hardly do better – would have been incomprehensible if it were not seen as resulting from a remnant of Hegelian…dialectics.[35]

Bernstein recalled how Engels, in his 'propaganda campaign in 1885 and 1887',[36] had included in the new edition of '*Revelations Concerning the Trial of Communists in Cologne*' the two circulars that he and Marx had written in March and June of 1850 to proclaim 'the revolution in permanence'. Engels had thought those tactics were still valid 'in principle', yet his projected new revolutionary upheaval had yet to occur. Bernstein attributed Engels's mistake to 'the dialectic taken over from Hegel' with its 'truly miraculous belief in the creative power of force'. Hegel's influence was said to be 'the treacherous element in Marxist doctrine' and the fundamental obstacle 'in the way of any logical consideration of things'.[37] Above all, Bernstein blamed dialectics for the fact that Marx and Engels had advocated revolutionary violence rather than recognising that steady economic progress would both dictate the need and ensure the possibility for peaceful social reform: 'Every time we see the doctrine which proceeds from the economy…capitulate before the theory which stretches the cult of force to its limits, we find a Hegelian principle.'[38]

Bernstein drew a link between Hegel's influence and Marx's apparent association with revolutionary Blanquism,

---

[35] Bernstein 1993, pp. 31–2. For an account of Marx's appropriation of Hegelian dialectics, see Day 2004. Bernstein totally misunderstood Marx on this account.

[36] By Engels's 'propaganda campaign of 1887' Bernstein meant his warnings about the inroads of reformism in the German Social-Democratic Party: 'Bourgeois and petty-bourgeois socialism is strongly represented in Germany down to this very hour; on the one hand by professorial socialists and philanthropists of all sorts with whom the wish to turn the workers into owners of their dwellings still plays a great role and against whom, therefore, my work is still appropriate; and on the other hand, in the Social-Democratic Party itself, and even in the ranks of the Reichstag fraction, a certain petty–bourgeois socialism finds a voice. This takes the form that while the fundamental views of modern socialism and the demand for the transformation of all the means of production into social property are recognised as justified, however, the realisation of this is declared possible only in the distant future, a future which for all practical purposes is quite out of sight. Thus, for the present time, one has to have recourse to mere social patchwork, and sympathy can be shown, according to circumstances, even with the most reactionary efforts for so-called "uplifting the working classes".' Engels 1887, pp. 424–33.

[37] Bernstein 1993, pp. 33–6.

[38] Bernstein 1993, p. 38.

the theory of secret leagues and the political putsch…the doctrine of the launching of revolution by a small, purposeful party acting in accordance with well-laid plans' and committed to 'revolutionary expropriation'.[39]

Marx's writings for the Communist League, and particularly his call to make the revolution 'permanent', were said to be permeated throughout by the spirit of Louis Blanqui and Gracchus Babeuf, with the result that

> All theoretical insight into the nature of the modern economy, all knowledge of the current state of the economic development of Germany, which was still far behind that of France at the time…all economic understanding vanishes to nothing before a programme so illusory it could have been set up by any run-of-the-mill club revolutionary.[40]

Proletarian terrorism, Bernstein added, would inevitably have reactionary and anti-democratic consequences: 'a policy modelled on the Terror of 1793 would have been the most senseless and futile imaginable', indeed, 'a crime for which thousands of workers would soon enough have to atone with their lives, and further thousands with their liberty'.[41]

At the instigation of English, Russian, and Polish leaders – Belfort Bax,[42] Plekhanov, Parvus, and Rosa Luxemburg in particular – Karl Kautsky, the foremost theorist of German Social Democracy, finally refuted Bernstein's challenge in *Die Neue Zeit*. Kautsky's articles were collected in 1899 under the title *Bernstein und das sozialdemokratische Programm, Eine Antikritik*,[43] and together with Rosa Luxemburg's famous pamphlet on *Social Reform and Revolution*,[44] they represented the major 'orthodox' Marxist response to Social-Democratic 'revisionism'.

Kautsky conceded that 'Marx and Engels made a mistake' when they initially supported German democrats, but he denied any connection between

---

[39] Ibid.

[40] Bernstein 1993, pp. 38–39.

[41] Bernstein 1993, p. 43.

[42] Belfort Bax, 1896a. Bernstein 1896. Belfort Bax, 1896b. A good selection of documents on the first phase of the revisionist controversy, i.e. before the publication of books by Bernstein and Kautsky, is found in Tudor and Tudor (eds.) 1988. Plekhanov's articles defending dialectical materialism against Bernstein and Conrad Schmidt appear in Plekhanov 1976.

[43] No English version is available, but a French one was issued in 1900 as Kautsky 1900. Available online at Gallica: (http://gallica.bnf.fr/).

[44] Luxemburg 1989.

permanent revolution and Hegelian dialectics. Instead, he pointed out that Marx and Engels had relied on the historical examples of the bourgeois revolutions in England in the seventeenth century and in France in the eighteenth century:

> Their starting point was the rising of the bourgeoisie against feudal absolutism, but they did not stop at that: they were the 'immediate prelude' to the terrorist regime of the petty bourgeoisie and to the beginning of plebeian revolutionary movements – in England the Levellers, in France the followers of Babeuf.

Those movements failed because neither the proletariat nor social conditions had sufficiently matured, but since the bourgeois revolution that Marx and Engels expected for Germany in 1847 was going to take place in more advanced conditions, Kautsky believed that the *Communist Manifesto* had correctly judged the potential for a proletarian revolution to follow. If Marx and Engels had made a mistake, it was in failing to see

> that every demonstration of force on the part of the proletariat pushes the bourgeoisie to the camp of reaction.... Their mistake was not to exaggerate the value of the proletariat, but that of the bourgeoisie.'[45]

One of the lessons Kautsky drew from this experience would have important implications for the Russian revolution. In the debate with Bernstein, he determined that a revolutionary seizure of power by the workers must be governed by the 'objective logic' of class interests. He developed this theme most extensively in his series of articles on 'Revolutionary Questions' (included in this anthology), which led Leon Trotsky to conclude in 1905 that once the workers' party took *political* power in Russia it must also pursue *economic* measures leading to a socialist republic.[46] As Kautsky wrote:

> The dictatorship in the factory will necessarily accrue to [the proletariat] once [it] has conquered state power. The position of the capitalists who still

---

[45] Kautsky 1900, Chap. La Méthode, b) La Dialectique, pp. 52–5. The whole discussion about the prognoses of the *Communist Manifesto* and the lessons of the revolutions of 1848–49 does not appear in the original German edition of Kautsky's book. He added it to the revised French edition, which appeared a year later.

[46] In this volume, see Trotsky's 'Foreword to Karl Marx, *Parizhskaya Kommuna*', pp. 497–520.

> remain after the nationalisation [*Verstaatlichung*] of the cartels and trusts must then become untenable.... Simply by the logic of class interests, the transition to socialist production will then necessarily impose itself on the victorious proletariat even if this was not its goal from the outset. In other words, capitalist production and the political rule of the proletariat are mutually incompatible.... [N]ecessity...will drive the victorious proletariat to replace capitalist by socialist production.[47]

An equally important scholarly response to Bernstein came from Franz Mehring, a widely respected historian of German socialism who meticulously corrected Bernstein's factual errors.[48] In the first place, Mehring pointed out, Marx and Engels had never advocated

> any putschist tactic, even when the temptation...was very great, for instance during the Cologne uprising of September 1848, as well as in May 1849, when the struggle for the Imperial Constitution began. They only called the workers to take up weapons in the Prussian crisis of November 1848 when the Berlin Assembly, which had adopted a decision calling for refusal to pay taxes, was dissolved by the sword; when the possibility of a great national uprising existed.... Just as little did Marx and Engels overestimate at that time the 'creative power of revolutionary force for the socialist transformation of modern society.' For them the only thing that mattered was to seize as many positions of power as possible from the counter-revolutionary powers; in that sense they opposed the cowardly philistine clamour for 'closure of the revolution' and demanded instead the 'revolution in permanence'.... Had the Berlin and Frankfurt assemblies followed their advice, they would not have perished so ignominiously as they did.[49]

The events that Mehring cited to explain the tactics of Marx and Engels in 1849–50 could just as well have been a script for the Russian Revolution. In both cases, the summons to permanent revolution came in response to bourgeois betrayal and the willingness of propertied classes to compromise with reaction rather than risk power passing to the proletariat. It was in these circumstances, Mehring pointed out, that the March 1850 'Address of

---

[47] Kautsky 1899, III. Die Taktik c) Selbständige oder unselbständige Politik?, pp. 180–1.

[48] Mehring 1899, pp. 147–54, 208–15, 239–47.

[49] Mehring 1899, p. 243.

the Central Committee' had given 'precise instructions, in the event of an imminent new outbreak of the revolution, for the Communists everywhere to mobilise the workers in order to make the revolution "permanent" '. Bernstein had accused Marx of ignoring economic conditions, yet Mehring noted that when conditions improved by the autumn of 1850, Marx and Engels changed course and 'actually preferred to accept the dissolution of the Communist League, rather than give in to Blanquist putschism, to belief in the "miraculous power" of violence'.[50]

Speaking for himself, Mehring thought

> The question of whether the political revolution is rightly or wrongly considered an indispensable precondition of socialism, of whether the triumph of the working class can be brought about with or without violent catastrophes, can ultimately be answered only by the actual course of history.[51]

Given the striking political similarities between Germany in 1848–50 and Russia in 1905, it was no surprise that, six years later, Leon Trotsky would publish in *Nachalo*, a newspaper that he briefly edited together with Parvus, a new article by Mehring entitled 'The Revolution in Permanence'. In that article, which we have included in this volume, Mehring frankly concluded that

> It is precisely by means of the revolution in permanence that the Russian working class must reply – and, judging by the news to date, has already replied – to the bourgeois cries of anguish for 'peace at any price'.[52]

Despite the critical responses of Mehring, Kautsky and others, the first practical application of the principles of revisionism occurred in 1899, when the French socialist deputy Alexandre Millerand joined the bourgeois 'government of republican defence' headed by René Waldeck-Rousseau (together with the butcher of the 1871 Paris Commune, General Gallifet) using as an excuse the Dreyfus trial. In *What Is to Be Done?* Lenin bitterly ridiculed Millerand's illusions:

---

[50] Mehring 1899, pp. 244–5.
[51] Mehring 1899, p. 245.
[52] Mehring 1905b, pp. 84–88. See this volume, pp. 457–64.

> …if Social-Democracy…is merely a party of reform…then not only has a socialist the right to join a bourgeois cabinet, but he must always strive to do so. If democracy…means the abolition of class domination, then why should not a socialist minister charm the whole bourgeois world by orations on class collaboration? Why should he not remain in the cabinet even after the shooting-down of workers by gendarmes has exposed, for the hundredth and thousandth time, the real nature of the democratic collaboration of classes? Why should he not personally take part in greeting the tsar, for whom the French socialists now have no other name than hero of the gallows, knout, and exile [*knouteur, pendeur et déportateur*]? And the reward for this utter humiliation and self-degradation of socialism in the face of the whole world, for the corruption of the socialist consciousness of the working masses – the only basis that can guarantee our victory – the reward for this is pompous *projects* for miserable reforms, so miserable in fact that much more has been obtained from bourgeois governments![53]

Bernstein's theories of peaceful reform were condemned in September 1903 at the Dresden Congress of the German Social-Democratic Party, as was Millerand's 'ministerialism' a year later at the Amsterdam Congress of the Second International. In the meantime, Mehring published in 1902 the third volume of his edition of early writings by Marx and Engels, covering the period from May 1848 to October 1850. In his introduction to the second part of the volume,[54] he commented that while Marx and Engels in 1848 had every right, historically and politically, to adopt a policy of driving the bourgeoisie forward, their subsequent change of course provided 'remarkable proof of how the elementary instinct of the workers' movement can correct the conceptions of even the greatest thinkers'.[55] By 1905, Mehring hoped the instincts of Russian workers would likewise correct the mistaken expectations of Plekhanov and others, who still ignored Marx's change of tactics in February 1849 and thought liberals and democrats would be necessary allies in the struggle against tsarist autocracy.

---

[53] Lenin 1902h, Chapter 1, Section 1: What Does 'Freedom of Criticism' Mean?, p. 354.
[54] Franz Mehring (ed.) 1902, 'Einleitung des Herausgebers', pp. 3–86.
[55] Franz Mehring (ed.) 1902, p. 82.

In *Vorwärts*, the official daily of the German Social-Democratic Party, Rosa Luxemburg reviewed the last two volumes edited by Mehring.[56] She, too, noted that Marx's plan had initially been '*to play the role of a left wing to bourgeois democracy*',[57] and that the policy was justified

> for a moment in which the modern bourgeoisie made its first debut on the political stage. At that time, to believe in the earnestness of its struggle against feudalism and in the possibility of pushing it forward through the resolute behaviour of a left, socialist wing was the right and the duty of every genuine revolutionary and practical politician.

Moreover, Marx could hardly do otherwise, for 'an independent socialist workers' party did not yet exist. German socialism was limited in the 1840s to a few exile colonies in Brussels, London and Paris, some short-lived socialist journals in Germany and some loose workers' circles in the Rhineland. The *Neue Rheinische Zeitung* could not therefore represent in the March revolution what actually did not exist: a separate class policy of the proletariat.'[58] As a result, 'During the revolution the *Neue Rheinische Zeitung* did not come to a *real* (therefore thoroughly socialist) opposition, that should have begun in the tricolor republic'.[59]

> With this in mind, the behaviour of the *Neue Rheinische Zeitung* appears as a well-considered, clever tactic, aimed at using the bourgeois uprising as a preliminary stage for the final proletarian one, to push it to its limits, where it would collapse and make room for a second, more radical cycle of the revolution. Seen from *that* point of view, the tactics of the *Neue Rheinische Zeitung* were not an abdication of socialism to help clear the way for the rule of the bourgeoisie but, on the contrary, a conscious utilisation of the rule of the bourgeoisie as a short preliminary stage, calculated at most to last a few years, for the proletarian victory.[60]

---

[56] See Luxemburg 1902, pp. 291–303.

[57] Luxemburg 1902, p. 300, emphasis in the original.

[58] Luxemburg 1902, p. 301.

[59] 'From the very beginning we did not consider it necessary to conceal our views. During a polemic with the judiciary here, we told you: "The real opposition of the *Neue Rheinische Zeitung* will begin only in the tricolor republic."' Marx 1849c.
Also in Rosa Luxemburg, *Gesammelte Werke*, p. 298, emphasis in the original.

[60] Ibid., p. 301, emphasis in the original.

Luxemburg's review spoke of 'the peculiar *conception* that Marx and Engels had of the March revolution, the "hope in a so-called 'revolution in permanence"'', but she did not yet recognise it as a distinctly new policy, necessitated by the betrayal of the German bourgeoisie and petty-bourgeois democrats. She did, however, link it with Marx's expectation 'that the bourgeois revolution would be only a first act, that it would be immediately followed by a petty-bourgeois and finally by a proletarian revolution'. Just three years later, she would herself interpret Russian events in terms of permanent revolution. The title of her article, which we include in this anthology, would be *After the First Act*.

Marxism and Russian populism

If the lines between orthodoxy and revisionism were clearly drawn in the West-European context, the same could not be said of Russia. It was obvious that Bernstein's belief in a peaceful parliamentary road to socialism had no relevance to a country that had yet to secure political representation or the most elementary constitutional rights. However, there was just as obviously no agreement on the question of how such fundamental changes could be forced upon the autocrat, Tsar Nicholas II. The documents in this volume reveal an array of opinions ranging from Plekhanov's conviction that a bourgeois revolution was pending – even if it must be led by the workers – to the opposite position shared by Ryazanov, Parvus and Trotsky, namely, that a permanent revolution would rapidly point beyond bourgeois democracy in the direction of socialism. And, just as Marx's changing tactics in 1848–50 helped to frame the West-European debates over revisionism, with regard to Russia Marx made equally controversial appraisals of the village commune and its potential to provide a basis for socialism without enduring the torment of primitive capitalist accumulation. Marxism emerged in Russia in a struggle against revolutionary *Narodnik* populism, but during and after the 1905 revolution the echoes of previous disputes with the Narodniks were still apparent in assessments of Russia's 'peculiar' characteristics given by Ryazanov, Trotsky, and even Lenin.[61]

---

[61] Trotsky thought Russian Marxism, through emphasising 'the identity of laws for all countries', developed a tendency 'to pour out the baby with the bath'.

The Narodniks held that Russian 'backwardness' provided a unique opportunity to reach socialism through traditional forms of land tenure.[62] The peasant commune (the *obshchina*) regulated social and economic life at the village level (the *mir*) by periodically redistributing strips of land according to family size, the number of able-bodied workers per household, or some other collectivist principle. Within each commune, a patriarchal assembly (the *skhod*), which included the head of each family and one or more village elders, decided how and when land repartition, planting, and harvesting would take place. While Russian Marxists regarded the commune as an archaic obstacle to modernity, the Narodniks emphasised its collectivist character, which distinguished Russia from capitalist Europe and created the prospect of bypassing capitalism on the way to a socialist future.

The most famous revolutionary populist organisation was the People's Will [Narodnaya Volya], formed in 1879 after the failure of previous attempts to radicalise the countryside through going 'to the people' with peaceful propaganda. Members of Narodnaya Volya succeeded in assassinating Tsar Alexander II in 1881, but the wave of repression that followed, and the failure of the expected popular uprising to materialise, resulted in a major

---

He acknowledged that his own conception of Russian history and permanent revolution owed much to Narodnik traditions: '…Narodism, with all its democratic illusions…rested upon indubitable and moreover deep peculiarities of Russia's development, understood one-sidedly however and incorrectly evaluated.' L. Trotsky 1977, Vol. 1, Appendix I, p. 471. Lenin made a similar remark in 1909: 'While fighting Narodism as a wrong doctrine of *socialism*, the Mensheviks, in a doctrinaire fashion, overlooked the historically real and progressive historical *content* of Narodism as a theory of the mass *petty-bourgeois* struggle of democratic capitalism against liberal-landlord capitalism, of "American" capitalism against "Prussian" capitalism.' Lenin 1909a. When Lenin in 1905 called for a 'revolutionary-democratic dictatorship of the proletariat and the peasantry', Plekhanov saw a Narodnik influence at work. In his notes to the 1905 Russian edition of Engels's *Ludwig Feuerbach and the End of Classical German Philosophy*, Plekhanov denounced Lenin's 'rather strange views' and 'the talk about the *seizure of power* by the Social-Democrats during the now impending *bourgeois* revolution. The supporters of such a seizure forget that the dictatorship of the working class will be possible and opportune only where it is a case of a *socialist* revolution.' According to Plekhanov, Lenin and the Bolsheviks were 'returning to the political standpoint of the late *Narodnaya Volya trend*.' Plekhanov 1920–7, Volume 3, p. 81. In his *History of Russian Social Democracy*, Julius Martov, one of the most prominent Mensheviks, also criticised *Nachalo*, the journal edited by Parvus and Trotsky in 1905, for 'a relapse into that Social revolutionary subjectivism which had been exhibited twenty five years earlier by L. Tikhomirov and other populists'. Martov and Dan 1926, p. 166.

[62] The standard history of Russian Populism is Venturi 2001.

ideological and organisational crisis. Narodnaya Volya split apart, and a rival group emerged, Chernyi Peredel' (or Black Repartition), whose more prominent members – Georgy Plekhanov, Pavel Akselrod, Lev Deutsch, and Vera Zasulich – in September 1883 founded Russia's first Marxist organisation, Osvobozhdenie Truda (the Emancipation of Labour Group).

According to Andrzej Walicki, in his excellent book on the controversy between populists and Marxists over the prospects of Russian capitalism, Marx and Engels were more impressed by the revolutionary Narodniks in the years just prior to Marx's death than by Plekhanov, who had been living in Geneva since January 1880 (and did not, in fact, return to Russia for another thirty-seven years):

> Since 1877 they had been convinced that Russia stood on the threshold of revolution and that this revolution would usher in a new revolutionary era in the whole of Europe. The founders of 'scientific socialism' were enthusiastic supporters of the 'Will of the People' and felt proud of their contacts with it; Plekhanov's party 'Black Repartition' was treated by them ironically, as a party that while preaching the need to work *among the people* went abroad and shirked real revolutionary activity. Even Plekhanov's conversion to Marxism was, at first, met by Engels (Marx was not alive by then) with a certain reserve and distrust. Plekhanov's criticism of the 'Will of the People' seemed to him premature and too doctrinaire.[63]

The first Russian thinker whom Marx took seriously was N.G. Chernyshevsky, an ardent 'westerniser' who simultaneously hoped his country would reach socialism without enduring the agony of capitalism. Criticising 'philosophical prejudices against the obshchina', Chernyshevsky projected the possibility that Russia might benefit from Europe's experience to 'skip all the intermediate stages of development or at least enormously reduce their length and deprive them of their power'.[64] In the preface to the first German edition of *Capital*, Marx made a nearly identical remark. He wrote that 'The country that is more developed industrially only shows, to the less developed, the image of its own future'. In the same place, he added that while no country could clear by 'bold leaps' or remove by 'legal enactments' the obstacles offered by 'the

---

[63] Walicki 1969, pp. 180–1.
[64] Quoted by Venturi 2001, p. 152.

successive stages of its normal development', it was nevertheless possible to 'shorten and lessen the birth-pangs'.[65]

These statements by Marx are frequently quoted in the documents we have translated. Moreover, the Russian proponents of permanent revolution often sounded remarkably like Chernyshevsky. Long before Trotsky, Chernyshevsky understood perfectly how history could be accelerated when a 'backward' country imports the experience of others that are more advanced in order to accelerate its own development:

> This acceleration consists of the fact that the development of certain social phenomena in backward nations, thanks to the influences of the advanced nation, skips an intermediary stage and jumps directly to a high stage.[66]

Comparing history to a grandmother 'very fond of its grandchildren', Chernyshevsky hoped Russia would fulfil the biblical saying that the 'last shall be first'.[67] In his notes to a translation of John Stuart Mill's work in political economy, he projected a socialist Russia economically organised through state-supported agricultural and industrial co-operatives.[68]

---

[65] Marx 1961, pp. 9–10.

[66] Chernyshevsky as quoted by Wada 1981, p. 134. Another Russian author with similar ideas was V.P. Vorontsov, who thought industrialisation, led by the tsarist state, could bypass capitalism to reach socialised 'popular production'. He wrote:
> The countries which are latecomers to the arena of history have a great privilege…consisting in the fact that accumulated historical experience of other countries enables them to work out a relatively true image of their next step and to strive for what the others have already achieved not instinctively but consciously, not groping in the dark but knowing what should be avoided on the way. To these peculiarly privileged countries belongs also Russia. (Quoted by Walicki 1969, p. 116.)

Leon Trotsky reformulated the same ideas in Marxist terms with the 'law of uneven and combined development':
> Unevenness, the most general law of the historic process, reveals itself most sharply and complexly in the destiny of the backward countries. Under the whip of external necessity their backward culture is compelled to make leaps. From the universal law of unevenness thus derives another law which, for the lack of a better name, we may call the law of *combined development* – by which we mean a drawing together of the different stages of the journey, a combining of the separate steps, an amalgam of archaic with more contemporary forms. Without this law, to be taken of course, in its whole material content, it is impossible to understand the history of Russia, and indeed of any country of the second, third or tenth cultural class. (L. Trotsky 1977, pp. 27–8.)

[67] Chernyshevsky quoted in Venturi 2001, p. 152.

[68] Ibid., p. 167.

In the afterword to the second German edition of *Capital*, Marx spoke highly of Chernyshevsky's work on Mill and referred to him as a 'master mind' and a 'great Russian scholar and critic'.[69] In 1875, Marx further specified that it was *West-European* countries that were seeing capitalist expropriation of the peasantry. When another Russian populist, N.G. Mikhailovsky, misinterpreted the section of *Capital* dealing with primitive accumulation to mean that the transformation of English peasants into wage earners portended the fate of all countries, Marx protested to the populist journal *Otechestvennye Zapiski* [*Notes on the Fatherland*]. He explicitly rejected the view that his 'sketch of the genesis of capitalism in Western Europe' was a supra-historical 'theory of the general path imposed by fate upon every people, whatever the historic circumstances in which it finds itself'. On the contrary, 'events strikingly analogous but taking place in different historic surroundings' often led 'to totally different results'. The question of whether 'Russia must begin by destroying the rural commune in order to pass to the capitalist regime', or whether it could instead 'appropriate all its fruits by developing its own historical peculiarities [*ses propres données historiques*]', could not be answered by reference to a universal scheme. By the late 1870s, Marx's study of Russian conditions led him to think that

> if Russia continues to pursue the path she has followed since 1861 [the year
> of the Emancipation Edict that abolished serfdom], she will lose the finest
> chance ever offered by history to a nation, in order to undergo all the fatal
> vicissitudes of the capitalist regime.[70]

But what if Russia did not continue along that path? What if revolution intervened? In 1881, Vera Zasulich, who, two years later, became one of the pioneers of Russian Marxism, again queried Marx concerning the role of the village commune. In one draft of his response Marx wrote that 'a Russian revolution is required if the commune is to be saved'; and

> If the revolution occurs in time…the rural commune…will develop…as an
> element in the regeneration of Russian society, as a point of advantage when
> compared to the nations enslaved by the capitalist system.[71]

---

[69] Marx, *Capital*, I, p. 15.
[70] Marx 1877, p. 199.
[71] Marx quoted by Wada 1981, p. 145. Georgy Plekhanov declined to publish Marx's letter to Zasulich, presumably on the grounds that it was not sufficiently Marxist.

A year later, Marx and Engels wrote a preface to a new Russian edition of the *Communist Manifesto* that represented Marx's final pronouncement on the subject:

> If the Russian revolution becomes the signal for a proletarian revolution in the West, so that the two can supplement each other, then present Russian communal land ownership can serve as a point of departure for a communist development.[72]

Marx became more responsive to populist ideas at the very moment when Plekhanov and his associates, in the name of Marxism, were parodying populist writers as reactionary utopians. In 'Socialism and the Political Struggle', written in 1883, Plekhanov ridiculed his former Narodnik comrades for fearing capitalist development, which was historically necessary in order to produce the modern proletariat as a real revolutionary force. Instead of recognising capitalism's inevitability, Russia's 'anarchists, Narodniks and Blanquists' expected 'old mother history to mark time while they laid new, straighter and better roads for her'.[73] Plekhanov replied that serious revolutionaries must turn away from the villages to concentrate on urban workers:

> The rural population of today, living in backward social conditions, is not only less capable of conscious political *initiative* than the industrial workers, it is also less *responsive* to the movement which our revolutionary intelligentsia has begun.... And besides, the peasantry is going through a difficult, critical period. The previous 'ancestral foundations' of its economy are crumbling, 'the ill-fated village commune itself is being discredited'.... [T]he process of Russian social development is creating new social formations by destroying the age-old forms of the peasants' relation to the land and to one another.[74]

While it is true that, after Marx's death in 1883, Engels tended to side with Plekhanov – by 1892 Engels regarded the *obshchina* as 'a dream of the past' that must give way in future to 'a capitalist Russia'[75] – the issue remained a focus of contention for at least another decade. In a monumental study of

---

Plekhanov believed Russia must pass through the capitalist stage, and the document was only finally published in 1924.

[72] Wada 1981, p. 147. For another study of Marx's views on Russia see Shanin 1981.

[73] Plekhanov 1883a, p. 61.

[74] Plekhanov 1883a, p. 105.

[75] Engels 1892, p. 383. See also Engels 1894, pp. 421–33.

The Development of Capitalism in Russia (1899),[76] Lenin supported Plekhanov with a plethora of statistical data intended to refute both Narodnik terrorism and *reformist* populists such as V.P. Vorontsov and Nikolai Danielson (translator of Marx's *Capital* into Russian), both of whom hoped revolution might be avoided through reforms initiated by the tsarist state. Like Chernyshevsky, Vorontsov saw the privilege of backwardness in Russia's ability to import foreign achievements. But fearing that private capital accumulation would further impoverish the peasant commune, he hoped for a painless transition to socialised labour through state-led industrialisation.[77] In 'The Heritage We Renounce', Lenin condemned Vorontsov for his 'idealisation' of the peasantry and his 'reactionary attitude'.[78] Narodism was 'the ideology of Russia's peasant democrats' and a manifestation of petty-bourgeois 'economic romanticism' – the same kind of romanticism that characterised all underconsumptionist theories that denied the possibility of capital accumulation on the grounds that ruin of small producers would eliminate the domestic market.[79]

By the time of the first Russian Revolution, however, the fate of the commune was becoming a secondary issue among Marxists and Lenin explicitly hoped for an 'American' style of capitalist agriculture that would accelerate class

---

[76] V.I. Lenin, *Collected Works*, Vol. 3.

[77] According to Vorontsov, industrialisation of Russia by private capital was impossible: 'The peculiar historical circumstance affecting our large-scale industry is that it must expand at a time when other countries have already attained a high level of development. Two things follow from this: first, our industry can make use of all the forms created in the West and does not have to crawl at a snail's pace from stage to stage; second, it must compete with the more experienced, highly industrialised countries, and competition with such rivals might utterly extinguish the weak sparks of our scarcely awakening capitalism.' V[orontsov] 1882, pp. 13–14.

[78] V.I. Lenin, CW, Vol. 2: 493–534.

[79] For a brief discussion of Lenin's anti–Narodnik essays and the issue of 'under–consumption', see Day 1981, pp. 29–31. For similarly 'romantic' responses to early capitalism in America see Gaido 2001, pp. 350–75 (on the doyen of the US Progressive historians Charles Beard) and Novack 1957, pp. 83–8. When Rosa Luxemburg later based her theory of imperialism on an under-consumptionist revision of Marx's schemes of expanded reproduction, claiming it is impossible to realise the whole of surplus value in the framework of bourgeois society without the presence of non-capitalist 'third parties', Lenin immediately saw in it a return to the mistakes of the populist economists. In a letter to Kamenev written in March 1913, Lenin said: 'I have read Rosa's new book *Die Akkumulation des Kapital*. She has got into a shocking muddle. She has distorted Marx. I am very glad that Pannekoek and Eckstein and O. Bauer have all with one accord condemned her, and said against her what I said in 1899 against the Narodniks.' Lenin 1974, p. 94. For a detailed account of Luxemburg's misinterpretation of Marx's *Capital*, see Day 1979–80.

differentiation and multiply rural allies of the proletariat. However, the question of abbreviating history remained, and the advocates of permanent revolution, Trotsky in particular, could draw upon another element of Russian historiography when emphasising the creative role of state power.[80] In a foreword to Marx's writing on the Paris Commune, Trotsky declared in December 1905 that

> The state is no end in itself. It is, however, the greatest means of organising, disorganising, and reorganising social relations. Depending upon whose hands control it, it can be either a lever for profound transformation or an instrument of organised stagnation.[81]

Lev Tikhomirov, the chief theoretician of *Narodnaya Volya*, had similarly argued that the tsarist state was an independent social force, the supreme organiser of social life, and for precisely that reason must be destroyed in order to fulfil the 'will of the people'.[82]

Notwithstanding the distractions posed by the commune, Russian Marxists from the outset did have one conviction in common with the Narodniks: the

---

[80] Andrzej Walicki writes:
The basic thesis of the 'etatist' school of Russian historiography, one of whose representatives was the eminent historian Sergei Soloviev, a leading Westernizer and a professor at Moscow University, was that in Russia the state had always been the leading organizer of society and the main agent of progress. This school argued that the emergence of the centralized Muscovite state was the decisive moment in the rationalization of social relations in Russia, and therefore also in the emancipation of personality from the fetters of traditionalism. It concluded that in the future, too, it must be responsible for the nature and implementation of reforms. (Walicki 1980, p. 149.)

[81] See p. 502 in this volume.

[82] Walicki 1969, p. 104. In his summary of the lessons of the 1905 revolution, *Results and Prospects*, Trotsky acknowledged that 'the autocracy played no small part in transplanting the factory system of production on to Russian soil'. Under the pressure of capitalistically more advanced Western Europe, 'a pressure that was transmitted through the military-state organization, the State in its turn strove to force the development of social differentiation on a primitive economic foundation'.
Thus, the Russian State, erected on the basis of Russian economic conditions, was being pushed forward by the…pressure of the neighbouring State organizations, which had grown up on a higher economic basis. From a certain moment – especially from the end of the seventeenth century – the State strove with all its power to accelerate the country's natural economic development. New branches of handicraft, machinery, factories, big industry, capital, were, so to say, artificially grafted on the natural economic stem. Capitalism seemed to be an offspring of the State. (See L. Trotsky 1969, Chap. I: The Peculiarities of Russian Historical Development: 37–45.)

impending revolution in Russia could not repeat the pattern of France in 1789. Plekhanov told a Paris Congress of the Socialist International in 1889 that 'the revolutionary movement in Russia will triumph only as a *working-class movement* or else it will never triumph!'.[83] Unlike previous bourgeois revolutions, in which artisans and proletarians provided shock troops for the bourgeoisie, the Russian working class would this time appear as an independent force with its own leadership and its own class consciousness. But, given the low level of development of the productive forces in Russia, Plekhanov also thought the strategic goals of this *sui generis* bourgeois revolution could not go beyond the framework of democratic civil rights and capitalist relations of production: it would be a bourgeois-democratic revolution based on an alliance between capitalists and workers against absolutism and the landlords. Although this element of Plekhanov's thinking was obviously incompatible with any notion of revolution in permanence, he also believed that capitalism in Russian would be much abbreviated compared to Western Europe: 'Our capitalism will fade before it has time to blossom *completely* – a guarantee for which we find in the powerful influence of international relations.'[84] The manifesto adopted by the first congress of the Russian Social-Democratic Labour Party in 1898, written by Pyotr Struve, expressed a similar conviction:

> The further to the east of Europe (and Russia, as we know, is the east of Europe) the weaker, more cowardly and baser in its political attitude is the bourgeoisie, and the greater the cultural and political tasks that fall to the proletariat.[85]

David Ryazanov on the Draft Programme of *Iskra* (1903)

The concept of 'permanent revolution' was first introduced into Russian Social-Democratic literature by David Ryazanov. In 1902–3 the *Bor'ba* [*Struggle*] group, the tendency within the Russian Party to which Ryazanov belonged, published three studies in Geneva under the general title *Materials on the Programme of the Workers' Party*.[86] The second document, a commentary

---

[83] Plekhanov 1889, p. 454.
[84] Plekhanov 1884, p. 379.
[85] Reprinted in Zinoviev 1973, p. 202.
[86] Ryazanov 1902; Ryazanov 1903a; Ryazanov 1903b.

on *The Draft Programme of 'Iskra' and the Tasks of Russian Social Democrats*, for the first time systematically interpreted Russian history with reference to an impending permanent revolution. Since Ryazanov's study was 302 pages in length, we have selected the most relevant sections for inclusion in this volume. Readers will be struck not merely by the scholarly depth of its analysis, but even more by the remarkable way in which it anticipates all of the arguments set forth by Trotsky three years later in his famous *Results and Prospects*.

For Ryazanov and Trotsky alike, the rise of Russian capitalism was an 'exception' to the West-European 'pattern'. Much of Russian industry had been recently financed from abroad and thus incorporated the latest technology. Large-scale industry meant the working class had better opportunities to organise, and the bourgeoisie was at the same time more vulnerable. These circumstances suggested that Russian liberalism would be politically ineffective and that Social Democracy would first lead the revolution against tsarist autocracy and subsequently move towards socialism – with support from the peasant masses and from rapidly ensuing revolutions in Western Europe, where economic conditions were already more highly developed. Ryazanov's prescience owed much to his knowledge of, and his evident respect for, the earlier Narodniks. He declared that 'the great ones of history are never "resurrected"', but they reappear in 'the activities of future generations, who are brought up on the experience of their great predecessors'.[87]

If Ryazanov understood Marx from within this 'exceptional' Russian context, Plekhanov did the opposite, interpreting Russia in terms of what he took to be Marx's *universal* laws of history. In the 1880s Plekhanov had struggled mightily and written volumes of scholarly and polemical literature to denounce Narodnik terrorist conspiracies and to initiate the organisation of a modern Social-Democratic workers' party. Since Plekhanov (together with Lenin) was a principal author of the new party programme being promoted by the journal *Iskra* in 1903, his prudential interpretation of Marx led him to write a blistering reply to Ryazanov's call for permanent revolution. In his article 'Orthodox Pedantry', also included in this collection, he denounced Ryazanov as a pretentious bookworm, an artisan of clever phrases and revolutionary fantasies that revealed a complete ignorance of Marx's method. While Ryazanov carefully explained how Marx and Engels had corrected

---

[87] In this volume see p. 86.

their tactical errors of 1848, Plekhanov denied that any such errors had ever occurred: Marx had always subscribed to precisely the tactic that Plekhanov insisted must also apply to Russia, namely, organising the workers to lead *a bourgeois revolution* that would enshrine the civil and constitutional rights needed for further growth of the Social-Democratic movement.

Plekhanov and Lenin succeeded in denying the *Bor'ba* group any official representation at the Second Congress of the Russian Social-Democratic Labour Party, which was held in London and Brussels in the summer of 1903. This congress resulted in the famous split between Bolsheviks and Mensheviks over organisational issues. On this occasion, Ryazanov denounced Lenin for his commitment to a centralised party of professional revolutionaries at the expense of a mass workers' party with internal democracy.[88] Though a detailed analysis of these organisational questions is beyond the scope of this volume, it is worth noting that *four* of the most prominent representatives of the theory of permanent revolution (Trotsky, Luxemburg, and Parvus, in addition to Ryazanov) were all opposed to Lenin's high-handed view of centralised party control.

The Russo-Japanese War of 1904–5

If the immediate cause of the Bolshevik Revolution in 1917 was the First World War, the revolution of 1905 was likewise the product of another imperialist carnage: the Russo-Japanese War, a conflict that grew out of the rivalry between Russia and Japan over Manchuria and Korea. The war was declared on 10 February 1904, and after a series of bloody land and naval battles it ended in crushing defeat for Russia. The Russian Pacific fleet was trapped at Port Arthur, which after a long siege finally fell to the Japanese on 2 January 1905. The Baltic fleet was also destroyed shortly thereafter in the Battle of Tsushima (May 27–28 1905). US President Theodore Roosevelt, fearing the strengthening of Japan, which could become a potential obstacle to America's own imperialist plans in Asia (e.g. the occupation of the Philippines, in which more than a quarter of a million Filipinos died, and the 'Open Door' policy in China), offered to mediate between Russia and Japan. Roosevelt's intervention led to the signing of a peace treaty at the US Navy facility of

---

[88] For an English version of the proceedings see Pearce (ed.) 1978.

Portsmouth, New Hampshire, on 5 September 1905. By then, the number of casualties had reached more than 72,000 deaths (of which more than 25,000 were Russians) and 300,000 wounded. Ironically, the prototypical imperialist Roosevelt, who led an aggressive American foreign policy in Panama and elsewhere, would earn a Nobel Peace Prize for his effort. By the terms of the Treaty of Portsmouth, Russia ceded the southern half of Sakhalin Island to Japan and granted it leasehold rights for twenty-five years in Port Arthur. Russia further agreed to evacuate Manchuria and to recognise Korea, which Japan later annexed in 1910 as part of the Japanese sphere of influence.

Shortly after the declaration of war, Parvus (Alexander Israel Helphand) published a series of articles in *Iskra* where he analysed its causes and possible consequences.[89] In a panoramic account of economic and geopolitical forces, he asserted that the war had begun as a dispute over Manchuria and Korea but had rapidly become a question of hegemony over the whole of East Asia. It therefore not only threatened a political crisis for the Russian autocracy but also entailed a radical alteration of the balance of imperialist forces. Since every developed capitalist country periodically suffered from lack of markets, all the great states of Europe, together with America, Russia and Japan, were engaged in a titanic struggle. Russia alone among these imperialist contenders, with its weakly developed economy, sought conquests for reasons other than the internal contradictions of the capitalist mode of production: 'The mindless quest of the Russian government for successes in foreign affairs is imperative in order to hide the empire's internal weakness'. With its poorly equipped peasant army, Russia had precipitated a conflict that would destroy 'the political equilibrium of the entire world'. The principal victim of the crisis would be its initiator, Tsar Nicholas II, whose overthrow by Russian workers would launch the permanent revolution that could open up world-wide perspectives for international socialism.[90]

Parvus and Trotsky on permanent revolution in Russia

The Russian Revolution of 1905 erupted on the 'Bloody Sunday' of 22 January (9 January by the Julian calendar, which was still in use at the time). When a

---

[89] Parvus 1904b.
[90] Mehringer 1978, p. 201.

peaceful demonstration by striking workers and their families arrived at the Winter Palace, intent upon delivering a petition of protest to the tsar, they were ruthlessly fired upon by the Imperial Guard. After decades of European reaction following the massacre of the Parisian Communards in 1871, the foremost theoreticians of Russian and West-European Social Democracy saw the prospect of a great revolution that would begin in St. Petersburg and then surge westwards. All Social Democrats eagerly awaited news of the tsar's overthrow,[91] but opinions differed widely as to who might replace him – liberals, petty-bourgeois democrats, or armed workers intent upon a socialist republic.

---

[91] For example, Rudolf Hilferding wrote to Karl Kautsky on 14 November, 1905, that 'the collapse of Czarism is the beginning of our revolution, of our victory, that is now drawing near. The expectation, which Marx had mistakenly expressed about the movement of history in 1848, will now, we hope, be fulfilled.' He believed that the key to the success of the Russian, and eventually also the European, revolution, would be the victory of Poland in its fight for independence. 'A free Poland would become a symbol to all the minority groups struggling for autonomy or independence within Germany and Austria. It would force Germany to intervene in Poland militarily to restore the old order, an action that would unleash a European-wide war and precipitate the outbreak of social revolution in Germany. Poland would provide the strongest, most effective impulse to the "permanent revolution".' Hilferding 1905, p. 9 and Smaldone 1998, pp. 28–9.

A year later, in *Results and Prospects*, Trotsky anticipated much the same chain of events concerning the international dimension of *permanent revolution*:

> The triumph of the revolution in Russia will mean the inevitable victory of the revolution in Poland. It is not difficult to imagine that the existence of a revolutionary regime in the ten provinces of Russian Poland must lead to the revolt of Galicia and Poznan. The Hohenzollern and Habsburg Governments will reply to this by sending military forces to the Polish frontier in order then to cross it for the purpose of crushing their enemy at his very centre – Warsaw. It is quite clear that the Russian revolution cannot leave its Western advance-guard in the hands of the Prusso-Austrian soldiery. War against the governments of Wilhelm II and Franz Joseph under such circumstances would become an act of self-defence on the part of the revolutionary government of Russia. What attitude would the Austrian and German proletariat take up then? It is evident that they could not remain calm while the armies of their countries were conducting a counter-revolutionary crusade. A war between feudal-bourgeois Germany and revolutionary Russia would lead inevitably to a proletarian revolution in Germany. (See L. Trotsky 1962, p. 241.)

Were France to intervene when revolutionary Russia repudiated the tsarist debts held by French bond owners, Trotsky likewise expected a proletarian revolution in that country: 'In one way or another, either through a revolution in Poland, through the consequences of a European war, or as a result of the State bankruptcy of Russia, revolution will cross into the territories of old capitalist Europe.' Ibid., p. 245.

For both Parvus and Trotsky, the issue was never in doubt. At the close of 1904 they entered a unique political and intellectual partnership that culminated in their leading roles in the St. Petersburg Soviet until its suppression in December 1905. Their collaboration began when Parvus wrote a preface, 'What was Accomplished on 9th January', to one of Trotsky's most famous early essays, 'Up to the 9th of January'. Both documents are included in this anthology along with several others that followed soon afterwards. Parvus and Trotsky rejected any artificial limitation of the Russian revolution to bourgeois demands and upheld the idea that a workers' government (and for Trotsky, even the dictatorship of the proletariat) could be established in backward Russia, where serfdom had only been abolished as late as 1861.

Both men believed that given the insipid character of Russian liberals and petty-bourgeois democrats, the workers alone, with the support of the poorest peasants, could dispose of the autocracy. Unlike Lenin, who advocated a 'revolutionary-democratic dictatorship of the proletariat and peasantry', they also denied any possibility of the peasantry becoming a coherent political force.[92] Following an argument already set forth by Karl Kautsky in his polemic with Bernstein and later in his essay 'Revolutionary Questions', Trotsky believed that the proletariat, once in power, would be compelled to go beyond democratic tasks and place collectivism on the order of the day, just as Marx and Engels had urged in their March 1850 Address to the Central Committee of the Communist League. The Russian revolution, Trotsky declared, could triumph only as a socialist revolution; and the survival of a worker's government, once confronted by armed counter-revolution,

---

[92] In 1898 Parvus had written of 'the reactionary nature of the peasantry in general' in Western Europe:

> The peasant is impelled to political action only with great difficulty.... Politically, the peasant is *passive*.... It is this unshakeable calm, this political detachment of the peasantry which underpins the myth of the peasant as a pillar of the political establishment by which he is governed.... Whenever, in the course of this century, the European peasantry took political action, it always did so as *an oppositional force*. It allowed itself to be made a fool of by adventurers and charlatans, from Napoléon le Petit down to Boulanger and Shlawrdt [sic], but that was precisely its way of protesting against the existing social order. (See Parvus 1898, p. 197.)

Despite these misgivings, Parvus and Trotsky hoped that in Russia the peasantry's land hunger would cause it to support Social Democracy rather than the liberals or Socialist Revolutionaries.

would, in turn, depend on the victory of socialist revolution in the West.[93] The central themes of Trotsky's writings on permanent revolution have long been familiar to English-speaking readers, but the series of documents that we have translated here make it possible for the first time to trace the origins and development of those ideas that eventually culminated in *Results and Prospects*, his most famous revolutionary statement from the years 1905–6.

It is important to add parenthetically that use of the expression 'permanent revolution' during 1905 was not confined to Social-Democratic circles. It was also used by the Socialist Revolutionaries, a party that regarded itself as heir to Narodnaya Volya. The SRs' work of agitation and organisation occurred mainly among the peasantry, and their tactics placed much emphasis on eliminating the most hated tsarist officials through acts of individual terrorism. But an article in the SR journal *Revolyutsionnaya Rossiya* (no. 70, dated 1 July 1905), attacked Bolsheviks and Mensheviks alike for assuming that the revolution would be bourgeois-democratic in character. According to the anonymous author – apparently Mikhail Rafailovich Gots, a leading member of the SR Central Committee and co-editor of the journal along with Victor Chernov – the working people of Russia should be encouraged not only to destroy the autocracy but also to prevent any ensuing bourgeois entrenchment:

> The forthcoming revolution [*perevorot*] will be achieved mainly by the efforts of the workers – the proletarians and peasants. They should take from this revolution all that the social conditions permit them to take – [and] the most important of these conditions is the extent of their own consciousness. They should not restrict the scale of this revolution in advance for the benefit of the bourgeoisie, but on the contrary they should turn it into a permanent [*permanentnyi*] one, oust the bourgeoisie step by step from the positions it has occupied, give the signal for a European revolution, and then draw new strength from there.[94]

---

[93] In this context it is worth mentioning that Trotsky explicitly refrained from emphasising Russia's *economic backwardness* as an obstacle to permanent revolution, specifying instead the threat of domestic counter-revolution supported by armed foreign intervention. The implications of this fact for economic policy after 1917 were elaborated in Day 1973.

[94] Quoted by Perrie 1973, p. 411.

Lenin on 'uninterrupted revolution'

The revolution of 1905 led to a programmatic break between the two main tendencies within Russian Social Democracy. While Mensheviks clung to the idea that the future of the democratic revolution depended on an alliance between the proletariat and the bourgeoisie, Lenin adopted an intermediate position between Plekhanov and Trotsky. For him, the aim of the revolution was to create the best possible conditions for the development of capitalism, and its central problem was the agrarian question. The bourgeoisie was incapable of resolving this task. Out of fear of the mass struggle, the capitalists were ready to reach a compromise with landowners and the tsar, which would lead to a slow and painful development of Russian capitalism along Prussian lines.

Lenin argued that the revolution could only triumph through an alliance between the proletariat and the peasantry, and that it would therefore be forced to make more serious inroads into private property than the classical bourgeois revolutions. These two classes, upon seizing power, would establish a joint 'democratic dictatorship' and proclaim the republic, the eight-hour workday and the most radical agrarian reform (including *land nationalisation*), which would enable Russia to embark on what Lenin called 'the American path of bourgeois development'.[95] Lenin almost certainly developed this idea from an article by Karl Kautsky on the agrarian question in Russia, which included long quotations from Marx's criticism of Henry George's single tax proposals as well as an explicit reference to the American homestead system.[96] Lenin praised Kautsky's work as a 'splendid essay' that 'sets forth the general principles of the Social-Democratic views on the subject'.[97] He expected nationalisation of the land to free the peasants from landlord exploitation; but, until a socialist revolution occurred in the West, the Russian revolution would stop short of full-scale nationalisation of all the means of production.

---

[95] For Lenin's analysis of the 'American path of bourgeois development' see his books Lenin 1902g and Lenin 1915.

[96] Kautsky 1905e, pp. 412–23. For further analysis of Lenin's theory see chapter two of Gaido 2006, pp. 28–48.

[97] Lenin 1906e, Section II: Four Trends Among Social-Democrats on the Question of the Agrarian Programme.

In the exhilarating atmosphere of the time, Lenin also occasionally made other statements that went beyond that schema. For instance, in September 1905 he famously commented that

> From the democratic revolution we shall at once, and precisely in accordance with the measure of our strength, the strength of the class-conscious and organized proletariat, begin to pass to the socialist revolution. We stand for uninterrupted revolution. We shall not stop half-way.[98]

But such remarks were outbursts of enthusiasm that contradicted official statements of Bolshevik policy as elaborated in Lenin's own subsequent writings. A few months later, in a note that was not published until 1926, Lenin worried that defeat of the Russian workers would be certain unless the West-European socialist proletariat came to their assistance:

> The second victory will be *the socialist revolution in Europe*. The European workers will show us 'how to do it,' and then, together with them, we shall bring about the socialist revolution.[99]

Kautsky, Lenin and Trotsky

Because Lenin ultimately led the Bolsheviks to victory in 1917, histories of the period often exaggerate his influence at the time of the first Russian Revolution. As the documents we have collected clearly demonstrate, no real understanding of the debate over permanent revolution is possible without first acknowledging the key role of Karl Kautsky. The centre of Marxist theoretical elaboration before the outbreak of the First World War was not Russia but Germany, the home of Marx and Engels and of the Sozialdemokratische Partei Deutschlands (SPD), which was the major party of the Second International. Even the leaders of the most extreme sections of Russian Social Democracy considered themselves faithful disciples of the SPD leaders Bebel and Kautsky. As Trotsky put it, up to 4 August 1914

> *Lenin considered Kautsky as his teacher* and stressed this everywhere he could. . . .
> Speaking of Menshevism as the opportunistic wing of Social Democracy,

---

[98] Lenin 1905f, pp. 236–7.
[99] Lenin 1906d, pp. 91–2, emphasis in the original.

Lenin compared the Mensheviks not with Kautskyism but with revisionism. Moreover he looked upon Bolshevism as the Russian form of Kautskyism, which in his eyes was in that period identical with Marxism.[100]

According to Trotsky, Lenin saw Bolshevik doctrine as 'only a translation into the language of Russian conditions of the tendency of Bebel-Kautsky'.[101] In the 1922 introduction to his book *1905*, Trotsky gave this assessment of Kautsky's role:

> The debate over the character of the Russian revolution had, even during that period, gone beyond the confines of Russian social democracy and had engaged the attention of the leading elements of world socialism. The Menshevik conception of bourgeois revolution was expounded most conscientiously, that is to say, most badly and candidly, in Cherevanin's book.[102] As soon as it appeared, the German opportunists seized hold of it with glee. At Kautsky's suggestion I wrote an analytical review of Cherevanin's book in *Neue Zeit*.[103] At the time, Kautsky himself fully identified … with my views. Like Mehring, now deceased,[104] he adopted the viewpoint of 'permanent revolution.' Today, Kautsky has retrospectively joined the ranks of the Mensheviks. He wants to reduce his past to the level of his present. But this falsification, which satisfies the claims of an unclear theoretical conscience, is encountering obstacles in the form of printed documents. What Kautsky wrote in the earlier – the better! – period of his scientific and literary activity (his reply to the Polish socialist Ljusnia,[105] his studies on Russian and American workers,[106] his reply to Plekhanov's questionnaire concerning the character of the Russian revolution,[107] etc.) was and remains a merciless rejection of Menshevism and a complete theoretical vindication of the subsequent political tactics of the Bolsheviks, whom thickheads

---

[100] L. Trotsky 1932, p. 132.

[101] Ibid.

[102] Tscherewanin 1908.

[103] Trotsky included his review of Cherevanin's book as an appendix to the 1922 edition to his book L. Trotsky, 1971a, 299–313.

[104] The reference is to Franz Mehring's *The Revolution in Permanence* (November 1, 1905). In this volume see pp. 457–63.

[105] Kautsky, *Revolutionary Questions* (February 1904). In this volume, pp. 187–249.

[106] Kautsky, *The American Worker* (February 1906). In this volume, pp. 609–61.

[107] Kautsky 1907a. In this volume, pp. 567–607.

> and renegades, with Kautsky today at their head, accuse of adventurism, demagogy, and Bakuninism.[108]

By 'the subsequent political tactics of the Bolsheviks' Trotsky obviously meant his own tactics of permanent revolution, which were adopted *de facto* by Lenin in the 'April Theses' of 1917.[109] But Kautsky was the first West-European Marxist to employ the theory of permanent revolution in connection with events in the Russian Empire. He helped to initiate the debate over permanent revolution with his article 'The Slavs and Revolution', published in *Iskra* on 10 March 1902. And his 1903 introduction to a Polish edition of the *Communist Manifesto* contained an explicit reference to the March 1850 'Address of the Central Committee to the Communist League' and to 'a bourgeois revolution that, in becoming permanent, grows beyond its own limits and develops out of itself a proletarian revolution'.[110]

After the outbreak of revolution in 1905, Kautsky also repeatedly employed the expression 'permanent revolution' in a series of articles published in July in *Die Neue Zeit* under the title 'The Consequences of the Japanese Victory and Social Democracy'.[111] This was the second mention of the phrase in the West-European Marxist press, following Rosa Luxemburg's article 'After the First Act'.[112] In December 1905 Kautsky published the article 'Old and New Revolution', where he stated that the Russian Revolution 'promises to inaugurate...an era of European revolutions that will end with *the dictatorship of the proletariat*, paving the way for the establishment of a *socialist society*'.[113] In the following month, he reprinted the section of his book on the French Revolution that described the policy of the sans-culottes in 1793–4 as one of permanent revolution. That document appeared in the *Festschrift 1649–1789–1905*, which was published in commemoration of the first anniversary of 'Bloody Sunday'.[114] Finally, in November 1906, he wrote his response to Plekhanov's inquiry on the character of the Russian revolution and the tasks of Russian socialists, 'The Driving Forces and Prospects of the Russian

---

[108] Leon Trotsky, 1971a, p. viii.
[109] Lenin 1917a.
[110] Kautsky 1904b. In this volume, pp. 169–85.
[111] Kautsky 1905f, pp. 460–8, 492–9, 529–37. In this volume, pp. 373–408.
[112] Luxemburg 1905f, pp. 610–14. See this volume, pp. 365–71.
[113] Kautsky 1905b, pp. 3–5. See this volume, pp. 529–36.
[114] Kautsky, 'Die Sansculotten der französischen Revolution' (Aus: Kautsky 1889b) in *1649–1789–1905*, pp. 11–12. See this volume, pp. 537–42.

Revolution',[115] which Trotsky called 'the best theoretical statement of my own views'.[116] All these articles by Kautsky have been included in the present anthology.

While Trotsky considered Kautsky's reply to Plekhanov to be an endorsement of his own theory of permanent revolution, Lenin also described it as 'a brilliant vindication of the *fundamental principles* of Bolsheviks tactics', which focused instead on the 'democratic dictatorship' of the proletariat and peasantry. Lenin commented:

> Kautsky's analysis satisfies us completely. He has fully confirmed our contention that we are defending the position of revolutionary Social-Democracy against opportunism, and not creating any 'peculiar' Bolshevik trend.[117]

Lenin also returned to this idea in his book *The Agrarian Programme of the Social Democracy in the First Russian Revolution, 1905–07*:

> The Bolsheviks,...ever since the beginning of the revolution in the spring and summer of 1905,...clearly pointed to the *source* of our tactical differences by singling out the concept of peasant revolution as one of the varieties of bourgeois revolution, and by defining the victory of the peasant revolution as 'the revolutionary-democratic dictatorship of the proletariat and the peasantry.' Since then Bolshevism won its greatest *ideological* victory in international Social Democracy with the publication of Kautsky's article on the driving forces of the Russian revolution.[118]

The fact that Trotsky and Lenin could both claim Kautsky's endorsement resulted from Kautsky's carefully phrased response to Plekhanov. Unable to read Russian documents in the original language, Kautsky had no wish to exacerbate differences between Trotsky and Lenin concerning the prospective role of the peasantry. He did make it clear, however, that given the correlation of class forces in Russian society, a bloc of the workers' party with the bourgeois-liberal Cadets, which Plekhanov contemplated, was out of the question. Agrarian reform was at the heart of the democratic revolution,

---

[115] Kautsky 1907a, pp. 184–90, 324–33. See this volume, pp. 567–607.
[116] L. Trotsky 1908. Quoted in Donald 1993, p. 91.
[117] Lenin 1906c, pp. 372–73.
[118] Lenin 1907e, p. 353.

and the bourgeoisie would never support confiscation of the landed estates without compensation. The urban petty bourgeoisie, in turn, was too weak to play the role it had assumed in the Paris Commune during the French Revolution. Accordingly, the Social-Democratic workers would be forced to seize power together with the peasants, and thereafter a whole series of possible variants would develop according to the extent of peasant war and the spread of revolution beyond Russia's borders. On the whole, it must be said that Kautsky's argument lent more support to Trotsky's formula of 'the dictatorship of the proletariat leaning upon the peasantry' than to Lenin's 'democratic dictatorship of the proletariat and the peasantry'. Whatever the case, there is no doubt that Kautsky was widely respected in all circles of Russian Social Democracy, and all were equally anxious to invoke his authority.

Karl Kautsky and Rosa Luxemburg during the first Russian Revolution

Kautsky's own radicalisation during this period partly resulted from the influence of Rosa Luxemburg, who was fluent in Polish and Russian and frequently endorsed permanent revolution together with use of the mass political strike both in Russia and in Western Europe. The nature of this influence can be gauged from the four items by Luxemburg included in this anthology, one of which, 'After the First Act', appeared in the West-European Social-Democratic press following Bloody Sunday,[119] while another, 'The Russian Revolution' (20 December, 1905), was published in the same collection as Kautsky's 'Old and New Revolution' to mark the first anniversary of that event.

A brief anecdote reveals how Kautsky and Luxemburg defended each other at the time not only against bourgeois enemies but also against the right wing of the German SPD, who resented Luxemburg's call for adopting the mass strike. In April 1906, Kautsky was forced to support Luxemburg, who was then leading the revolution in Warsaw and had been arrested together with Leo Jogiches on 4 March, 1906. According to one of the trade-union publications, the *Zeitschrift für Graveure und Ziseleure*, there were 'witnesses of

---

[119] Rosa Luxemburg 1905f, pp. 610–14. See this volume, pp. 365–71.

flesh and bone' to attest that 'comrade Luxemburg in a Berlin assembly [had] "drivelled" about the trade unions being an "evil"'. Kautsky replied that it was

> not comrade Luxemburg who undermined the relations between the party and the unions, but those union officials and editors that have taken Rexhäuser[120] as a model. The narrow-minded hatred of these elements against any form of the labour movement that sets itself a higher goal than five pennies more per hour is indeed an 'evil'.

Dismissing the union leaders' accusations, Kautsky furthermore protested:

> It is new in our movement, indeed unheard of, for comrades to hurl such nonsensical and frivolous accusations against a leader of the proletarian class struggle precisely at that moment when the hangman of all freedom has arrested her and made her defenceless because of her tireless work in the service of the proletariat. Even our bourgeois opponents, at least the more decent ones – to be sure they are not many – avoided attacking comrade Luxemburg.... [yet] a trade-union organ is going hand in hand with the most infamous and shameless press flunkies of capitalism and the aristocracy [*Junkertum*].[121]

Besides their shared expectations of revolutionary victory in Russia, Rosa Luxemburg and Karl Kautsky also had common misgivings concerning the increasingly conservative nature of German trade-union (and later, also party) officials. Kautsky raised the issue of growing bureaucratisation in September 1906 at the party's Mannheim Congress. The background to the congress was a bitter dispute between the leaders of the General Commission of Free (Social-Democratic) Trade Unions and the SPD executive over the political mass strike, which had been employed with crippling effectiveness in the struggles against the Russian tsar.

On 22–7 May, 1905, the fifth congress of the Free Trade Unions, which met in Cologne, directly opposed any use of the political strike. The General Commission's spokesman on this issue, Theodor Bömelburg, who was also

---

120 Ludwig Rexhäuser was editor of the *Correspondent für Deutschlands Buchdrucker und Schriftgiesser*, the organ of the printers' union (*Verbandes der Deutschen Buchdrucker*). Luxemburg 1907b, pp. 182–7.
121 Kautsky 1906d. Reprinted in Stern (ed.) 1961, Vol. 6, pp. 1548–9.

president of the construction workers' union, attacked not only the SPD left wing but even Eduard Bernstein (who saw in the general strike not a revolutionary means to overcome reformist parliamentarism but merely a way of defending parliament and democratic rights from reactionary attacks). Bömelburg proclaimed that 'in order to expand our organisation, we need peace and quiet [*Ruhe*] in the labour movement'.[122] The resolution adopted by the Cologne Congress rejected the mass strike as a political tactic and prohibited even the 'propagation' (i.e. propaganda or discussion) of this means of struggle. It also argued that the mass strike was being promoted by 'anarchists and persons without any experience in economic struggles' and warned workers 'to avoid being hindered in the everyday work of strengthening the workers' organisations by adoption and promotion of such ideas'.[123]

Nevertheless, on 17–23 September 1905, the Jena Congress of the German Social-Democratic Party approved in principle the use of the political mass strike. Against the decision of the Cologne trade-union congress, it adopted a resolution endorsing the strike in the fight for electoral and democratic rights, though, at the insistence of Bebel, the strike was also described as a defensive tactic against an expected assault by the bourgeoisie on the growing gains of the socialist movement.[124] But on 16 February 1906, the SPD executive and the General Commission held a secret conference that resulted in an agreement by which the party leaders pledged to prevent a mass strike, if possible, and to assume the sole burden of leadership should it break out. News of the secret agreement leaked out and provoked a scandal among the revolutionary wing of the SPD. It was against this background that Rosa Luxemburg published, in the same month as the Mannheim Congress (September 1906), her famous brochure *The Mass Strike, the Political Party and the Trade Unions*, which defended the tactic of the mass strike as the main lesson of the first Russian Revolution and emphatically contrasted the spontaneous revolutionary initiative of the masses with the conservative policies being endorsed by the trade-union leadership.[125]

---

[122] Referat Bömelburg 1905, pp. 115ff. Reprinted in Grunenberg (ed.) 1970, p. 353.
[123] Luxemburg 1905a, pp. 580–6.
[124] Kautsky 1905d, pp. 5–10. Luxemburg 1905g, pp. 595–604.
[125] On the Mannheim Congress of the SPD see Luxemburg 1906, pp. 171–6.

In his speech to the Mannheim Congress, Kautsky openly posed the question of the rising bureaucratisation of the party itself:

> Our own party, as it grew larger, has become in a certain sense a rather cumbersome apparatus. It is not easy to bring new ideas and actions into this apparatus. If now the trade unions want peace and quiet, what perspectives open up for us if they are fastened to the already cumbersome party body as brakes?[126]

The Mannheim Congress eventually produced a compromise between the SPD executive and the General Commission, which gave the union leaders *de facto* veto over any employment of the mass political strike. The radical *Lepiziger Volkszeitung* drew the bitter conclusion that ten years of struggle against revisionism had been in vain, 'for the revisionism we have killed in the party rises again with greater strength in the trade unions'.[127] The ability of the union leaders to impose their own line on the SPD derived from two main sources: the vast membership of the unions and their even larger financial resources vis-à-vis the party.[128]

The Fifth (London) Congress of the RSDLP (May 1907)

Rosa Luxemburg's essay on *The Mass Strike, the Political Party and the Trade Unions* sought to breathe the spirit of the Russian Revolution into the ossifying apparatus of German Social Democracy. By 1907, however, the Russian Revolution was in retreat at the same time as German Social Democracy suffered its own major setback. The Fifth Congress of the Russian Social-Democratic Labour Party met in London from 30 April to 19 May 1907 and

---

[126] SPD 1906. Selections reprinted in Stern (ed.) 1961, vol. 6, pp. 1762–3.

[127] Schorske 1970, p. 52.

[128] From 215,000 in 1892, membership in the Social-Democratic Free Trade Unions rose to more than 1.1 million in 1904 and to 2.5 million in the year before the outbreak of the First World War, leaving the liberal Hirsch-Duncker associations and the Christian unions trailing in their wake (with, respectively, 106,000 and 218,000 members in 1913). See Schneider 1991, pp. 70, 75. In 1906, when the SPD took its first census, it emerged that its membership was 348,327 as against 1,689,709 for the Free Trade Unions. In 1913 the ratio was still two and a half to one in favour of the unions. Moreover, the party income for the fiscal year 1906–7 was 1,191,819 marks; that of the trade unions was 51,396,784 marks, about fifty times larger. Not surprisingly, the proportion of trade union officials in the SPD Reichstag faction rose from 11.6 per cent in 1893 to 32.7 per cent in 1912. Schneider 1991, p. 92.

followed the infamous 'Hottentot Elections' in Germany, in which a wave of imperialist chauvinism resulted in loss of 38 Social-Democratic seats in the Reichstag.[129] The Russian Congress was attended by 336 delegates: 105 Bolsheviks, 97 Mensheviks, 57 Bund members, 44 Polish Social Democrats, 29 Latvian Social Democrats and 4 non-factional delegates. The Bolsheviks, with support from the Poles and Latvians, secured a stable majority.[130] As the prospect for 'permanent revolution' was evidently receding, in his 'Speech on the Attitude towards Bourgeois Parties' Lenin again emphasised the centrality of the peasantry and the agrarian question in Russia:

> The Bolsheviks…maintained unequivocally that in its social and economic content our revolution was a bourgeois revolution. This means that the aims of the revolution…do not exceed the bounds of bourgeois society. Even the fullest possible victory of the present revolution – in other words, the achievement of the most democratic republic possible, and the confiscation of all landed estates by the peasantry – would not in any way affect the foundations of the bourgeois social system. Private ownership of the means of production (or private farming on the land, irrespective of its juridical

---

[129] The ensuing debate on imperialism and colonialism resulted in the first book–length analyses of imperialism in Marxist circles. Parvus wrote *Die Kolonialpolitik und der Zusammenbruch* (Parvus 1907a) for the forthcoming Stuttgart Congress of the Second International (6–24 August 1907). See the review of this book by Hilferding 1907, pp. 687–8. Immediately after the congress Kautsky published his brochure *Socialism and Colonial Policy* (Kautsky 1907). The Stuttgart Congress adopted a resolution on militarism, whose concluding paragraphs, drafted by Luxemburg and Lenin, advocated the policy later made famous by the slogan: 'turn the imperialist war into a civil war':

> If a war threatens to break out, it is the duty of the working classes and their parliamentary representatives in the countries involved, supported by the coordinating activity of the International Socialist Bureau, to exert every effort in order to prevent the outbreak of war by the means they consider most effective, which naturally vary according to the sharpening of the class struggle and of the general political situation. Should war break out despite all this, it is their duty to intervene in favor of its speedy termination and to strive with all their powers to use the economic and political crisis created by the war to rouse the masses and thereby to hasten the abolition of capitalist class rule.

The Stuttgart Resolution on 'Militarism and International Conflicts', is republished in Joll (ed.) 1974, pp. 206–8.

[130] The agenda included 12 points (the activities of Social-Democratic representatives in the Duma; the relationship between the trade unions and the party; partisan actions; work in the army; the coming International Congress at Stuttgart, etc.) of which the most important point was the third, dealing with the attitude of the RSDLP towards the bourgeois parties. See Lenin 1907g.

owner) and commodity economy will remain. The contradictions of capitalist society – and the most important of them is the contradiction between wage-labour and capital – will not only remain, but become even more acute and profound, developing in a more extensive and purer form.[131]

For Lenin, the key to intensifying the revolutionary struggle in Russia was to seize the estates of the landlords and the royal family and to open the way for small-scale private farming in place of both feudal landlords and the atrophying village commune: 'confiscation of all landed estates and their equal division [would] signify the most rapid development of capitalism, the form of bourgeois-democratic revolution most advantageous to the peasants'.[132] A victory for the peasants presupposed 'the complete destruction of landlordism', and the proletariat alone was capable of consummating that victory by 'getting a large section of the peasantry to follow its lead'. Lenin repeated a familiar conclusion: 'The victory of the present revolution in Russia is possible only as the revolutionary-democratic dictatorship of the proletariat and the peasantry.'[133] With regard to Trotsky, who spent most of own speech criticising the Menshevik expectation of a bourgeois revolution, Lenin added this comment:

> A few words about Trotsky. I have no time to dwell here on our differences with him. I shall only note that in his book *In Defence of the Party* Trotsky expressed, in print, his solidarity with Kautsky, who wrote about the economic community of interests between the proletariat and the peasantry in the present revolution in Russia. Trotsky acknowledged the permissibility and usefulness of a Left bloc against the liberal bourgeoisie. These facts are sufficient for me to acknowledge that Trotsky has come closer to our views. Quite apart from the question of 'uninterrupted revolution', we have here solidarity on fundamental points in the question of the attitude towards bourgeois parties.[134]

Lenin's reference to Kautsky concerned the latter's essay, 'The Driving Forces and Prospects of the Russian Revolution', which was Kautsky's response to Plekhanov's earlier enquiry. Since Trotsky was in limbo between the Bolshevik

---

[131] Lenin 1907c, p. 457.
[132] Lenin 1907c, pp. 465–6.
[133] Lenin 1907c, pp. 457–8.
[134] Lenin 1907a, p. 470.

and Menshevik factions, the Congress organisers allotted him fifteen minutes to speak as the representative of a 'special tendency'.[135] Trotsky used the occasion to remind Plekhanov of his own past:

> I want to establish only one thing: if, as Plekhanov predicted, the revolutionary movement in Russia triumphs as a workers' movement, then the victory of the proletariat in Russia is possible only as a revolutionary victory of the proletariat – or else it is not possible at all.

In his book *The Permanent Revolution*, Trotsky recalled that on this occasion

> Lenin … did not forgive me my conciliatory attitude toward the Mensheviks – and he was right – [he] expressed himself upon my speech with a deliberately emphasized reserve … because I did stand outside the Bolshevik faction. In spite of that, or more correctly, precisely because of that, his words leave no room for false interpretations. Lenin established 'solidarity between us on the fundamental points of the question' concerning the attitude toward the peasantry and the liberal bourgeoisie.[136]

By the spring of 1907, Trotsky found himself in the increasingly awkward position of being neither Menshevik nor Bolshevik – the two factions that dominated the Congress – but on the question of the proletariat's relationship to other classes he declared his own solidarity with Rosa Luxemburg, whose address on the question of relations with the bourgeois parties we have also translated for the first time in this volume.[137] Conveying official greetings to the Russian Congress from the SPD, Luxemburg attributed both the recent electoral losses in Germany and the difficulties of the Russian revolution to the treachery of liberals who had become 'pathetic toadies of reaction'. Dismissing the Menshevik idea of revolutionary liberalism as 'an invention and a phantom', she also disputed Lenin's hope that the peasants could ever

---

[135] Trotsky's address, L. Trotsky 1971b, appears as the first annex to L. Trotsky 1971a, pp. 275–83.

[136] Trotsky, *The Permanent Revolution*, Chap. 4: 4. What Did the Theory of the Permanent Revolution Look Like in Practice?, 1962, pp. 94–5.

[137] Rosa Luxemburg spoke three times at the London Congress. Her first speech was translated into English by Raya Dunayevskaya and has recently been reissued in an anthology of her writings: Luxemburg 1907a, pp. 200–7. For this volume we have translated her second address and concluding remarks. See pp. 543–66.

produce a coherent party capable of joint action with the workers in some sort of 'left bloc'. The peasants could at best mount a spontaneous *jacquerie*, but

> peasant movements are completely unable to play an independent role and
> are subordinated in every historical context to the leadership of other classes
> that are more energetic and more clearly defined.[138]

For Luxemburg, as for Trotsky, the only genuinely trustworthy allies of Russian workers were comrades in other countries upon whose support the Russian revolution ultimately depended.

Centrism and Marxism: Karl Kautsky and Rosa Luxemburg after 1910

While Trotsky and Luxemburg linked the prospect for permanent revolution with events in Western Europe, there is also a passage in Trotsky's *Results and Prospects* which, though written in 1906, clearly anticipated the further decline of revolutionary commitment in the SPD once enthusiasm over the Russian revolution abated. Speaking of the danger of 'internal inertia', Trotsky worried that growing 'conservatism' in the German party might drain it of revolutionary purpose:

> As a consequence…Social Democracy as an organization embodying the
> political experience of the proletariat may at a certain moment become a
> direct obstacle to the open conflict between the workers and bourgeois
> reaction. In other words, the propagandist-socialist conservatism of the
> proletarian parties may at a certain moment hold back the direct struggle of
> the proletariat for power.[139]

When Trotsky wrote these lines, the last person he had in mind was Karl Kautsky. Nevertheless, within a few years, Kautsky succumbed to the enervating tendencies within the German Party about which he had been one of the first to sound the alarm. The war of attrition, waged for more than a decade by German trade unionists against the mass strike and the party's left wing, ended in a merger of interests between party officialdom and the

---

138 RSDRP 1907b, pp. 434–5. In this volume see p. 564.
139 Trotsky 1962, pp. 239–47.

trade-union apparatus. With its parliamentary caucus to protect, the Party became as anchored in the political *status quo* as the unions were committed to peaceful collective bargaining.

In *The Road to Power*, published in 1909, Kautsky was still writing of 'a new period of revolutions', possibly involving 'the *general strike*'.[140] On 26 September of the same year, he complained in a letter to Victor Adler about 'the overgrowth of bureaucratism, which nips in the bud any initiative and any boldness'. He wrote that 'only when the action comes from the masses can one reckon with the necessary impetus and enthusiasm', whereas 'in Germany the masses have been drilled to wait for orders from above', while those above 'have been so absorbed by the administrative needs of the huge apparatus that they have lost every broad view, every interest for anything outside the affairs of their own offices'. This bureaucratic paralysis had first emerged in the trade unions, but 'now we see it also in the political organisation'.[141]

Yet, despite these repeated misgivings – or perhaps because of them – in the following year Kautsky broke off his relationship with Rosa Luxemburg and emerged as the main spokesman of the SPD's prevailing 'centre' faction. According to Marek Waldenberg, his best biographer, Kautsky wrote to Ryazanov in June 1910 and attributed his break with Luxemburg to the need to distance himself from her extremely unpopular image in the union bureaucracy.[142] When Luxemburg submitted an article urging the strike as a means of securing universal suffrage in Prussia – while simultaneously posing the demand for a republic in the hope of provoking revolutionary action – Kautsky refused to publish it.[143] This resulted in a severing of his relations not only with Luxemburg but also with Franz Mehring (who was removed from the editorial board of *Die Neue Zeit* in 1912), as well as in a series of bitter polemics in *Die Neue Zeit* with several other leading representatives of Social Democracy's left wing. It was in the course of these debates that Kautsky developed his so-called 'strategy of exhausting the enemy [*Ermattungsstrategie*]' – as opposed to Luxemburg's call for 'defeating the enemy [*Niederwerfungsstrategie*]'. Whereas Belfort Bax had once labelled

---

[140] Kautsky 1972, p. 110, emphasis in the original English version. Kautsky 1909b.
[141] Adler (ed.) 1954, p. 501.
[142] Waldenberg 1980, pp. 673–4.
[143] The article was finally published as Luxemburg 1910d. English edition: Luxemburg 1910c.

Eduard Bernstein 'Our German Fabian Convert', now it was Karl Kautsky who found himself endorsing the strategy of Fabius Cunctator.[144]

With Anton Pannekoek, Kautsky quarrelled over mass action and the proper attitude towards parliamentarism, and with Paul Lensch and Karl Radek he debated the issues of imperialism and disarmament, which were assuming growing urgency with the approach of the First World War. On these issues, too, Kautsky was in full retreat, denying that imperialism was an economic necessity inherent in capitalism and recommending a solution to international conflicts through arms limitation agreements.[145] As Radek remarked, Kautsky was forced to revise his earlier theory that militarism is an inevitable outgrowth of imperialism, not because imperialism had changed its nature but because his Fabian strategy of 'wearing out the enemy' could not be sustained by his former analysis.[146] When Kautsky began to refer to members of the left wing as 'our Russians', Rosa Luxemburg called attention to the fact that just a few years earlier he too had been labelled both 'a Russian' and a preacher of 'revolutionary romanticism', whereas now his centrist politics involved 'nothing but parliamentarism'.[147]

At the outbreak of the controversy between the left and centre factions of the SPD, most Russian revolutionary leaders failed to take Luxemburg's side. In July 1910, Trotsky wrote to Kautsky that no one in the Russian Party, 'not even among the Bolsheviks', dared to side with Luxemburg, and that while he admired her 'noble impatience' he considered it absurd 'to raise it to a leading principle for the party'.[148] The most insightful comment on German factional disputes came from Parvus, who pointed out to Kautsky that 'the whole affair is an amusingly faithful copy of the discussion between the Bolsheviks and the Mensheviks before the Russian revolution'.[149] Although Lenin considered

---

[144] Kautsky 1910c, pp. 33–40, 68–80, reprinted in Grunenberg (ed.) 1970, pp. 96–121. See also Luxemburg 1910b, pp. 344–77. Kautsky 1910b, pp. 332–41, 364–74, 412–21, reprinted in Grunenberg (ed.) 1970, pp. 153–190. Luxemburg 1910a, pp. 378–420. Kautsky 1910d, pp. 652–67, reprinted in Friedemann (ed.) 1978, Vol. I. Quintus Fabius Maximus Cunctator (The Delayer) 275–203 BC, employed guerrilla tactics to wear down Hannibal's forces in the Second Punic war. This was also the origin of the name taken by the British Fabian Society.

[145] Ratz 1966, pp. 197–227. Petit 1969, pp. 325–37.

[146] Radek 1912a and Radek 1912b, pp. 156–207. Radek was following Luxemburg's lead: See Kautsky 1910–11, pp. 97–107; and Luxemburg 1911.

[147] Kautsky 1913, pp. 532–40, 558–68, 662–4. Luxemburg 1913.

[148] Trotsky 1910.

[149] Parvus 1910, pp. 183–84.

himself Kautsky's faithful disciple, for him the moment of revelation came when Kautsky failed to oppose war credits to the Kaiser in August 1914. At a special session of the SPD caucus, Kautsky instead recommended that approval of credits be made 'conditional on assurances as to the objectives of the war'.[150] As Lenin subsequently recalled, this was the moment when 'Kautskyism' finally revealed 'all its repulsive wretchedness'.[151]

1918: Karl Kautsky and the democratic counter-revolution

With the coming of the Bolshevik Revolution in 1917, the debate over permanent revolution and the dictatorship of the proletariat ended in two completely contradictory outcomes. In Russia, Lenin adopted Trotsky's view when he resolved to seize power from the Provisional Government; but, in Germany, Kautsky took exactly the opposite position – the same position that Marx and Engels had condemned in terms of democratic counter-revolution in 1849–50. To add to the irony, even Rosa Luxemburg expressed grave misgivings about the Bolshevik action.[152] The difference, of course, was that, in 1919, Luxemburg gave her life in the fight to carry the revolution to Germany, whereas Kautsky made peace with the Weimar Republic and devoted the remainder of his days to condemning Bolshevism as a betrayal of Marxism and a new tyranny from which Stalinist totalitarianism followed as a matter of course.

Faithful to the concept of permanent revolution, Luxemburg never accepted the counter-revolutionary argument that Russia was not 'ripe' for social revolution due to economic backwardness.[153] By 1918 she did, however, acknowledge that a proliferation of small-holding peasants would create 'insurmountable obstacles' to socialist agriculture;[154] she did worry that Bolshevik dispersal of the Constituent Assembly might end by replacing 'dictatorship of the *class*' with that 'of a party or of a clique';[155] and she did repeatedly warn that socialism was inconceivable without direct participation of the masses. 'Socialism in life,' she wrote,

---

[150] Kautsky as quoted in Salvadori 1979, p. 182.
[151] Lenin 1917b, Chapter VI, Section 3: Kautsky's Controversy with Pannekoek, pp. 381–492.
[152] Luxemburg 1918.
[153] Luxemburg 1918, p. 26.
[154] Luxemburg 1918, p. 43ff.
[155] Luxemburg 1918, p. 76.

> demands a complete spiritual transformation in the masses degraded by
> centuries of bourgeois class rule.... Decree, dictatorial force of the factory
> overseer, draconic penalties, rule by terror – all these things are but
> palliatives. The only way to a rebirth is the school of public life itself, the
> most unlimited, the broadest democracy and public opinion.[156]

Though she reproached Lenin and Trotsky, she also emphasised that 'even
the greatest energy and the greatest sacrifices of the proletariat in a single
country must inevitably become entangled in a maze of contradictions and
blunders'.[157] The duty of revolutionaries in other countries was therefore
perfectly clear – to make the revolution.

Kautsky, in contrast, assumed precisely the counter-revolutionary positions
he had repeatedly denounced in 1905–6. Although he had always believed
that the stages of development in Russia could only be shortened given
political rule by the workers in Western Europe,[158] he now denounced both
Lenin and Trotsky for Blanquism, for abandoning democracy by dissolving
the Constituent Assembly, and for provoking civil war through instituting
proletarian dictatorship as *a form of government*. Now he argued that Marx
and Engels, when speaking of the 'dictatorship of the proletariat', had in mind
only a *condition* of working class supremacy deriving from universal suffrage
(which presupposed a proletarian majority), not a governmental form in which
a single party repressed all others and systematically excluded one section of
the population after another from democratic political life.[159] By dispersing
the Constituent assembly on 6 January 1918, and concentrating power in
the Soviets instead, the Bolsheviks had escaped all political constraints and
embarked on reckless misadventures in which civil war became the sole

---

[156] Luxemburg 1918.

[157] Luxemburg 1918, p. 29.

[158] In this volume, see the introduction to Kautsky's 'Revolutionary Questions'.

[159] Kautsky 1964, pp. 42–58. It should be pointed out that Kautsky was always
ambivalent on this issue. As early as 1893 he wrote that 'by now it begins to be evident
that a real parliamentary regime can be just as well an instrument for the dictatorship
of the proletariat as an instrument for the dictatorship of the bourgeoisie,' and the
idea 'that the representative system is indissolubly linked with the domination of
the bourgeoisie is one of those myths that a single look at history suffices to destroy.
The representative system is a political *form* whose content can diverge widely.'
Kautsky 1911, pp. 121–2. First edition published 1893 as *Der Parlamentarismus, die
Volksgesetzgebung und die Sozialdemokratie.*

'remaining method of adjusting political and social antagonisms'.[160] In these circumstances, he decided that the Bolshevik commitment to the dictatorship of the proletariat was

> nothing but a grandiose attempt to clear by bold leaps or remove by legal enactments the obstacles offered by the successive phases of normal development. They think it is the least painful method for the delivery of 'Socialism', for 'shortening and lessening its birth-pangs'. But…their practice reminds us more of a pregnant woman, who performs the most foolish exercises in order to shorten the period of gestation…and thereby causes a premature birth. The result…is…a child incapable of life.[161]

With this single ironic comment, Kautsky encapsulated all of the themes that had preoccupied Russian revolutionaries, Narodniks and Marxists alike, since Marx first praised the work of Chernyshevsky in 1873. In the 1905 debate over permanent revolution, Kautsky had been the ally of Trotsky and Lenin in the struggle against Plekhanov and others who would limit the revolution to establishing a liberal-constitutional régime. By 1918, he committed the ultimate betrayal when he concluded that the Revolution had turned out be nothing more than a repetition of 1789:

> The Revolution has only achieved in Russia what it effected in France in 1789…. By the removal of the remains of feudalism…it has now made of the peasants…the most energetic defenders of the newly-created private property in land.[162]

In 1905 he had written that

> the breaking up of the great private landed estates will constitute a tie that will bind the peasants indissolubly to the Revolution…it is easily possible that differences may arise between the peasants and the urban proletariat, but the former will fight tooth and nail to defend the Revolution against anyone seeking to re-establish the old aristocratic landed regime, even by foreign intervention.[163]

---

[160] Kautsky 1964, p. 52.
[161] Kautsky 1964, pp. 98–9.
[162] Kautsky 1964, p. 116.
[163] In this volume see Kautsky, *'Old and New Revolution'* p. 534.

Yet, in 1918, he decided that the very act of abolishing feudal agriculture must inevitably set the peasantry against the proletariat and result in 'a peasant state'[164] committed to a bourgeois social order.

Kautsky wrote three books in defence of the democratic counter-revolution, the first two of which were answered by Lenin and Trotsky. In reply to Kautsky's *The Dictatorship of the Proletariat*, Lenin wrote *The Proletarian Revolution and the Renegade Kautsky*. Trotsky's *Terrorism and Communism* answered Kautsky's work with the same title. Kautsky's third book, *From Democracy to State Slavery: A Discussion with Trotsky*, has never been translated into English.[165] No one expressed the Bolsheviks' dismay better than Leon Trotsky in his 1919 preface to a new edition of *Results and Prospects*:

> Talking of the attitude of the Mensheviks to the Revolution, one cannot but mention the Menshevik degeneration of Kautsky…. [In 1905–6] Kautsky (true, not without the beneficial influence of Rosa Luxemburg) fully understood and acknowledged that the Russian Revolution could not terminate in a bourgeois-democratic republic but must inevitably lead to proletarian dictatorship…. Kautsky then frankly wrote about a workers' government with a social-democratic majority. He did not even think of making the real course of the class struggle depend on the changing and superficial combinations of political democracy….
>
> Now, when the prospects outlined 15 years ago have become reality, Kautsky refuses to grant a birth certificate to the Russian Revolution for the reason that its birth has not been duly registered at the political office of bourgeois democracy. What an astonishing fact! What an incredible degeneration of Marxism! One can say with full justice that the decay of the Second International has found in this philistine judgment on the Russian Revolution, by one of its greatest theoreticians, a still more hideous expression than in the voting of war credits on August 4, 1914.[166]

---

[164] Kautsky 1964, p. 127.

[165] See Kautsky 1964; Lenin 1918b; Lenin 1917b, Ch. II, Section 3 (December 1918 addition); Kautsky 1919; L. Trotsky 1920; and Kautsky 1921b; See also Radek 1995, pp. 35–75.

[166] Trotsky 1962, pp. 165–6.

But this was not Trotsky's final judgement. For that we must turn to the obituary that Trotsky wrote on the occasion of Kautsky's death in 1938. 'There was a time,' Trotsky recalled,

> when Kautsky was in the true sense of the word the teacher who instructed the international proletarian vanguard.... [I]n Germany, in Austria, in Russia, and in the other Slavic countries, Kautsky became an indisputable Marxian authority. The attempts of the present historiography of the [Stalinist] Comintern to present things as if Lenin, almost in his youth, had seen in Kautsky an opportunist and had declared war against him, are radically false. Almost up to the time of the world war, Lenin considered Kautsky as the genuine continuator of the cause of Marx and Engels.

Recognising that Kautsky 'leaves behind numerous works of value in the field of Marxian theory', Trotsky concluded that in the final analysis he was only 'half a renegade':

> We remember Kautsky as our former teacher to whom we once owed a great deal, but who separated himself from the proletarian revolution and from whom, consequently, we had to separate ourselves.[167]

Readers will find that Trotsky's judicious assessment of Kautsky's best years is fully confirmed by the documents we have translated for this anthology. By the 1930s, Trotsky had his own past to uphold in response to an endless torrent of Stalinist lies and vilification. Trotsky was exiled from the Soviet Union in 1929 and assassinated in Mexico by Stalin's agent in 1940. But in the intervening years he struggled tirelessly to clarify his own historical legacy and to deny that he and Lenin ever had irreconcilable differences concerning either the theory of permanent revolution or the political role it implied for the Russian peasantry. The comprehensive documentary record that follows will allow readers to make their own judgment. The theory of permanent revolution has been a focus of debate for decades, not only between Trotsky's followers and his critics but also amongst academic historians. But in the court of history, as Trotsky understood very well when judging Kautsky, fairness and decency require that participants be assured every opportunity to speak for themselves. With that conviction in mind, we have produced this anthology.

---

[167] Trotsky 1938, pp. 98–9.

Chapter One

'The Slavs and Revolution' (1902)

Karl Kautsky

At the time when this article appeared,[1] Karl Kautsky was regarded as the pre-eminent spokesman of Marxist 'orthodoxy' in Western Europe. His article on the revolutionary potential of the Slavic peoples introduces an important context for the documents translated in this volume. For the previous two decades, Russian Marxists had struggled against the heritage of the *Narodniks* and their commitment to revolutionary terrorism. In the Narodnik view, Russia was an exception to the West-European pattern of development and would establish a socialist society on the basis of the village commune, with its traditional collective tenure of the land and periodic redistribution based upon need and the ability to work. Yet, at the very moment when Russian Marxists were finally moving towards formal party organisation, with a seemingly coherent Social-Democratic programme authored principally by G.V. Plekhanov and V.I. Lenin, it was none other than Kautsky who cited the heroic Narodnik tradition in expounding Russia's current revolutionary potential.

---

[1] [This article originally appeared in *Iskra* No. 18 (10 March, 1902), a newspaper of the Russian Social-Democratic Workers' Party.]

The proponents of *permanent revolution* certainly shared neither the populist ideology nor the terrorist convictions of the Narodniks, but they did disagree profoundly with Plekhanov in their appraisals of Russia's revolutionary prospects. While they supported their arguments with citations from Marx, the spirit of their work was often closer to the revolutionary temperament of Narodniks than to the rigid economic determinism or 'revisionist' denials of socialist revolution that were increasingly prevalent among many West-European Social Democrats.

For advocates of *permanent revolution*, one thing was clear: the liberal bourgeoisie in Russia was a still-born political force and the revolution, even if it were 'bourgeois' in nature, would be accomplished mainly by the proletariat. To anticipate Russian workers overthrowing the tsar was one thing, but to explain the consequences was quite another. Would socialist workers lead a revolution in order to introduce capitalism, as Plekhanov expected, or would they immediately begin a movement towards socialism, as the theory of permanent revolution suggested? These questions recur continuously in this volume.

It is a remarkable irony that Karl Kautsky, who subsequently denounced the Bolshevik Revolution and was famously condemned by both Lenin and Trotsky as a traitor and a renegade,[2] in fact played a key role prior to 1905 in inspiring Russian Marxists. Kautsky's *gravitas* and undisputed authority lent unexpected support to a conception of Russian history that simultaneously confounded Plekhanov's view of 'orthodoxy' and breathed new spirit into Russian Social Democracy. In the spring of 1920, Lenin quoted this document in defence of the Bolshevik Revolution against Kautsky's criticism. Recalling how Kautsky believed in 1902, 'when he was still a Marxist', that the 'spirit of the Russian proletariat would provide a model to Western Europe', Lenin concluded: 'How well Kautsky wrote eighteen years ago!'[3]

* * *

---

[2] See Lenin 1918b and L. Trotsky 1920.
[3] Lenin 1993, pp. 15–18.

'The Slavs and Revolution'

A little more than half a century has elapsed since the revolutionary struggle of the March Days.[4] Although this is only a brief interval in the life of society, a whole world separates us from that epoch. The great transformation that has occurred since that time demonstrates even more clearly, perhaps, the relation between the Slavs and the revolution.

With very few exceptions, the Slavs in 1848 still comprised 'a single reactionary mass'. Apart from the minor gentry and intelligentsia in Poland, we could say that one part of the Slavs regarded the great struggle for the freedom of peoples with blind indifference, while the other part threw itself into the struggle with the aim of defeating the cause of freedom. The Slavs achieved this end with great success. The fate of the revolution was already decided in *Paris* at the time of the June days.[5] But if the revolution in Germany and Hungary was so utterly defeated and destroyed, if absolutism in Austria could so completely restore its domination, then that outcome was due to the intervention of the Czechs, the Croats, and the Russian armed forces. The fall of Vienna in the October days of 1848, and the surrender of the Hungarian army to the Russian General Paskevich[6] at Vilgos (on 13 August 1849), signified the same defeat of the revolution in the East as had occurred during the June massacre in the West.

It is no wonder that German revolutionaries, however strong their consciousness of international solidarity, were seized by such ardent hatred for the Austrian Slavs that they began to regard them as degenerate peoples; to Germans it seemed that the revolution would have to step over such degenerates. The Slavs appeared to be nations of slaves and peoples born to vegetate in servitude.

But the cause of the anti-revolutionary behaviour of the Slavs lay not in some hidden predisposition towards servitude, but, rather in the economic conditions in which they lived. With the exception of the Czechs, they were

---

[4] [The reference is to the struggle on the barricades in Berlin in March 1948. In this volume see Leon Trotsky, 'Introduction to *Ferdinand Lassalle's Speech to the Jury*'.]

[5] [In June 1848 the uprising in Paris was crushed by General Louis Eugène Cavaignac, whose use of artillery against the barricades cost at least 1,500 lives.]

[6] [Ivan Fedorovich Paskevich (1782–1856), Russian field Marshal and Viceroy of Poland, commanded the Russian troops sent to aid the Austrian Emperor in 1848.]

purely peasant peoples and were completely incapable of understanding the political and social requirements of bourgeois society. It is true that, in Bohemia, there was already a developed urban life and capitalist large-scale industry, but the Czech people consisted of peasants, a petty bourgeoisie, and proletarians who had no class consciousness and whose whole way of thinking followed at the tail end of the petty bourgeoisie. It is true that in 1848 the petty bourgeoisie was still a revolutionary class, yet even then it proved everywhere to be unreliable. The semi-bourgeois, the semi-proletarian, and the petty bourgeois leaned first one way and then the other, rushing first to the side of revolution and then to reaction, rising to revolutionary rage and then lapsing into humble submission, but never possessing any firm convictions. The Czech lower middle classes behaved the same way, first displaying their revolutionary and then their reactionary side, rising up in July against Windischgrätz, who bombarded Prague in response, yet in October sympathising with this same Windischgrätz when he marched against the hated Vienna.[7]

Apart, of course, from the unreliability of the petty bourgeoisie, such behaviour also reflected national antagonisms. For the Czech peasant, petty bourgeois, and proletarian, the German was the enemy, the exploiter, and the oppressor. Not only was capital in Bohemia German, but the same was also true of the upper layers of the bureaucracy, the priesthood, the army, and much of the nobility. Moreover, in Bohemia the revolution was a German product, its adherents were Germans, and its goal was to unify and strengthen the German nation! It is no surprise that, after a short period of revolutionary intoxication, the Czech people threw themselves into the embrace of the counter-revolution.

But how everything has changed today! Since 1848 capitalism has made its way through Germany and has reached the Slavs. It has already fully subordinated to itself a significant part of the Slavic world and is progressing rapidly not only in Germany and Poland, but also in Russia and among the Slovenes, the Croats, and the Serbs. Everywhere it is creating proletarians and giving rise to the antagonism between capital and labour, out of which sooner

---

[7] [Alfred Windischgrätz (1787–1862) was an Austrian Field Marshal and military governor of Bohemia in 1848.]

or later grows proletarian class consciousness and an independent proletarian politics that is necessarily a revolutionary politics.

The time has long passed, therefore, when the Slavs could be thought of as the embodiment of servile obedience: they have now joined the ranks of peoples with their own revolutionary classes, and there is now taking place among them a great cultural struggle for the emancipation of the working class and with it the whole of humanity.

But that is not all. This transformation of the Slavs has been obvious to everyone for quite some time, at least for a quarter of a century. Today, it seems not only that the Slavs have joined the ranks of revolutionary peoples, but even that they are more and more at the centre of revolutionary thought and action.

The revolutionary centre is moving from the West to the East. In the first half of the nineteenth century it was in France and occasionally in England. In 1848, Germany joined the ranks of revolutionary nations, from which England shortly afterwards departed. After 1870, the bourgeoisie in all countries began to lose its final remnants of revolutionary ambition. From that time onwards, to be a revolutionary also meant to be a socialist. It was during precisely this epoch that the events following the Franco-Prussian War moved the centre of gravity, both for socialism and for the European revolutionary movement, from France to Germany.

The new century is beginning with the kind of events that suggest we are now seeing a further movement of the revolutionary centre, namely, to *Russia*.

It has already happened once, in the late seventies and early eighties, that the heroic struggle of the Russian revolutionaries amazed all of Europe and exerted a most profound influence on the socialist movement of all cultured countries.[8] Along with the insurrection and heroic demise of the Paris Commune, and the incredible growth of German Social Democracy in its struggle against the 'great' Bismarck, nothing had such a fertile influence on the socialist movement of the seventies and eighties, and nothing gave it such

---

[8] [The reference is to Narodnik movements such as 'The People's Will', whose members hoped Russia would bypass the capitalist stage of development. In the absence of a revolutionary proletariat, 'The People's Will' turned to individual acts of terrorism against the autocracy and in 1881 stunned Europe with the assassination of Tsar Alexander II.]

encouragement and inspired such self-sacrifice, as the desperate struggle that a handful of Russian revolutionaries fearlessly, and at times with the greatest success, waged against the frightful force of autocracy.

This desperate struggle ultimately ended with the exhaustion of fighters who did not yet have the backing of a revolutionary class.

But, since that time, there has emerged among the Russian people a new generation of heroes, and now they are more than just individuals. Within the tsarist empire there is also growing up a powerful proletariat, which is producing its own heroes and providing the support that was previously lacking for revolutionary heroes from other strata of the people. This means that we are now entering a new epoch of revolutionary struggle in Russia – a struggle that is developing on a much wider basis than a quarter of a century ago but also one that, in terms of the zeal of its fighters, in terms of the brutal cruelty and meanness of the oppressors, and in terms of the heroism and devoted self-sacrifices of the revolutionaries, is just as impressive as the struggle of the Russian movement in earlier periods.

But the struggle that we now see beginning in Russia involves more than physically pitting force against force. The revolutionising of minds advances alongside the revolution of fists. The now-awakening strata of the people are being seized by a passionate thirst for knowledge and are attempting to clarify for themselves their historical tasks so that they might learn to resolve the most complex and difficult problems, rising above the small events of the daily struggle to survey the great historical goals that it serves.

And from this awakening of minds we can expect great deeds that cannot fail to influence Western Europe. Having absorbed so much revolutionary initiative from the West, Russia itself may now be ready to serve the West as a source of revolutionary energy. The revolutionary movement that is flaring up in Russia may become the most powerful means for overcoming the spirit of flabby philistinism and sober-minded politicking that is beginning to spread through our ranks; it may reignite the flame of commitment to struggle and passionate devotion to our great ideals.

In relation to Western Europe, Russia has long ago ceased to be merely a bulwark of reaction and absolutism. Today, the exact opposite is probably closer to the truth. Western Europe is becoming the bulwark of reaction and absolutism within Russia. The rotten throne of the tsars is falling apart and might have collapsed long ago had the West-European bourgeoisie not continuously reinforced it with its millions.[9] In 1848, the tsar lent his might to support Europe in suppressing the uprising of the European bourgeoisie; now that same bourgeoisie is sending its own powerful support to Russia to give the tsar the strength to suppress all the freedom-loving movements within his own country. The Russian revolutionaries might have dealt with the tsar long ago if they had not been compelled to wage a simultaneous struggle against his ally – European capital.

Let us hope that they will succeed this time in dealing with both enemies, and that the new 'holy alliance'[10] will collapse more quickly than its predecessors. But no matter what the outcome of the current struggle in Russia, the all too numerous martyrs that it produces will not sacrifice their blood and happiness for nothing. They will fertilise the shoots of social revolution throughout the entire civilised world and cause them to grow ever more rapidly and abundantly.

In 1848, the Slavs were the hard frost that killed the blossoms of the spring of peoples. Now, perhaps, they are destined to be the tempest that will break the ice of reaction and irresistibly bring a new, blessed springtime for the peoples.

---

[9] [Kautsky is referring to West-European loans to the Russian Empire. This theme of West-European capital's support for the Russian monarchy reappears several times in the documents translated in this volume.]

[10] [The 'Holy Alliance' was formed in 1815 by the Emperors of Russia and Austria together with the King of Prussia to support the post-Napoleonic status quo in Europe. Most European rulers eventually joined the alliance, and it became the symbol of conservatism and repression in Central and Eastern Europe.]

Chapter Two

The Draft Programme of *'Iskra'* and the Tasks of Russian Social Democrats (1903)

N. Ryazanov

David Borisovich Gol'dendakh (Ryazanov) was born in Odessa in 1870 and executed by Stalin in 1938. Although he played a secondary role in Social-Democratic politics, Ryazanov was without question one of the foremost Marxist scholars of his time. In *The Rise of Social Democracy in Russia*, the historian John Keep described him as 'an energetic and talented writer' who was 'Lenin's contemporary and more than his equal in Marxist scholarship'.[1] V.A. Smirnova, a Russian biographer writing in 1989, spoke of him as 'a brilliant individualist' who combined 'a thorough approach to scientific problems with the indomitable and volcanic temperament of a fighter, propagandist and fierce debater'.[2] His independence of mind was legendary: in his autobiography, Max Beer recalls Lenin's joking description of the Soviet Union as 'a dictatorship mitigated by Riazanov'.[3]

---

[1] Keep 1963, p. 85.

[2] Smirnova 1995, p. 144. The biographical information that follows comes from this article and from the following sources: Rogovin 1993, pp. 246–57; Rokityanskii 1991; Rokityanskii 1992; Yaroshevskii 1991, pp. 475–95.

[3] Beer 1935, p. 205.

Like most Russian revolutionaries of his generation, Ryazanov was either in prison (in the years 1887, 1891–6 and 1907) or in exile during much of the period prior to the revolution of 1917. In 1905–6, he was actively involved in organising trade unions and strikes, first in Odessa and then in St. Petersburg, where he worked closely with Parvus.[4] In 1907, he left Russia for Germany, where August Bebel introduced him to the archives of the German Social-Democratic Party, including the papers of Marx and Engels. At the time, the papers had never been systematically organised or catalogued, with partial exceptions such as Eleanor Marx's edition of her father's articles on the Crimean War[5] and Franz Mehring's edition of Marx and Engels's early writings.[6] Many papers had been borrowed and not returned; a substantial number were kept by Eduard Bernstein in his own home; others were held by Marx's daughter Laura and her husband Paul Lafargue in Paris; and numerous letters and other items were scattered in private libraries.

Following the deaths of Paul and Laura Lafargue in 1911, Ryazanov sorted their papers for the archive and added them to other documents found in libraries in London, Paris, Rome, Florence, Germany, Switzerland and Austria. From 1909 to 1917, he worked with the German Social-Democratic Party, collecting and editing the works of Marx and Engels from the 1850s and 1860s, which were published in German in 1917.[7] While conducting this research, writing for German and Austrian party journals, delivering lectures, and gathering material for another project on the history of the First International, Ryazanov discovered some 250 previously unknown articles and items of correspondence by Marx and Engels.[8]

Ryazanov was neither a Bolshevik nor a Menshevik prior to 1917. He participated in the Zimmerwald anti-war conference of 1915, and upon returning to Russia in April 1917 he briefly associated with Trotsky in the non-party Inter-District Organisation (the *Mezhraionka*) until both men joined

---

[4] Zeman and Scharlau 1965, p. 81. Zeman and Scharlau point out that Parvus first introduced Ryazanov to the leaders of German Social Democracy and that the two men had been pupils at the same school in the 1890s (p. 141). We have included two documents by Parvus in this volume: 'What was Accomplished on Ninth of January' and 'Our Tasks'.

[5] Aveling and Aveling (ed.) 1969. Reprint of 1897 edition.

[6] Franz Mehring (ed.) 1902.

[7] Rjazanoff 1917.

[8] Smirnova 1995, p. 146.

the Bolshevik Party in the summer of 1917.[9] From 1918–20, he was active both in trade-union work and in the Commissariat of Education. Although he was a regular participant at party congresses during the 1920s, he was principally committed to archival work and academic research.

From 1918–20 Ryazanov headed the new State Archive Administration and helped to establish both the Socialist Academy and the Marx-Engels Institute, where he served as Director from 1921 to 1931. During the 1920s, he acquired numerous library collections from abroad, and, by 1930, the Marx-Engels Institute possessed more than 450,000 publications in addition to 175,000 copies of documents, including the material by Marx and Engels from the German Social-Democratic archives. During his time at the Institute, Ryazanov published the collected works of Marx and Engels,[10] as well as those of Plekhanov and Hegel, together with numerous pre-Marxist classics of political economy. By 1930, the Institute had published 150 major works, almost all of them edited by Ryazanov.

This scholarly work ended when Ryazanov was arrested in February 1931 after being implicated in the trial of the so-called 'Menshevik Centre'. In a report to the Society of Militant Dialectical Materialists, called to denounce both 'mechanistic revisionism' and 'Menshevising idealism', M.B. Mitin, one of the most abhorrent of Stalinist 'philosophers', recalled Ryazanov saying in 1924: 'I am neither a Bolshevik nor a Menshevik, I am a Marxist.' According to Mitin, it was impossible 'to be a Marxist without being a Leninist, to be a Marxist without being a Bolshevik'.[11] On 8 March 1931, Trotsky responded to Ryazanov's arrest with an article entitled 'The Case of Comrade Ryazanov' in which he recalled Lenin's comments:

> Speaking of his strong side, Lenin had in mind his idealism, his deep devotion to Marxist doctrine, his exceptional erudition, his honesty in principles, his intransigence in defence of the heritage of Marx and Engels. That is precisely why the party put Ryazanov at the head of the Marx-Engels Institute which he himself had created.... Had Ryazanov alluded somewhere, even if only

---

[9] For an account of the Inter-District Organisation, written by an active member, see Iurenev 1924, 1, 24, pp. 109–39 and 2, 25, pp. 114–43.

[10] This collection had the title *Marx-Engels Gesamtausgabe* (abbreviated as MEGA), which was expanded and republished, beginning in the 1980s, by the Soviet and East German Communist parties.

[11] Yaroshevsky 1991, p. 478.

> in a few words, to the fact that Marx and Engels were only forerunners of
> Stalin, then all the stratagems of these unscrupulous youngsters would have
> collapsed.... But Ryazanov did not accept this.... Ryazanov fell victim to his
> personal honesty.[12]

Ryazanov was accused of 'wrecking activities on the historical front', expelled from the Party and exiled to Saratov, where he worked for six years in a university library. In 1937, he was arrested again and charged with involvement in a 'right-opportunist Trotskyist organisation'. On 21 January 1938, the Military Collegium of the USSR Supreme Court condemned him to death by firing squad. The sentence was carried out the same day. Neither in 1931 nor in 1938 did Ryazanov acknowledge any guilt. He was posthumously rehabilitated in legal terms in 1958, and in political terms by the Communist Party in 1989.

In the years prior to the 1905 Revolution, Ryazanov's most significant theoretical contribution came in 1902–3, when Lenin and Plekhanov were drafting a new programme for the journal *Iskra*. Ryazanov was associated with the Bor'ba [Struggle] group, which was formed in Paris in the summer of 1900 and took its name in May 1901. It included, besides Ryazanov, the prominent Marxist historian Yurii M. Steklov (Nevzorov) and E.L. Gurevich (V. Danevich, Y. Smirnov). Bor'ba published several volumes on programmatic issues. One of those, which we have edited and translated here, devoted 302 pages to an assessment of the *Iskra* programme and to criticism of Lenin in particular, from a point of view which Reidar Larsson, the historian who rediscovered Ryazanov and the Bor'ba tendency's role in the development of the theory of permanent revolution after a lapse of almost seventy years, described as 'revolutionary economism'.[13] At the time, Ryazanov considered Lenin to be not only ill-informed in terms of the history of Marxism but also inclined towards an 'opportunist' compromise with Russian liberalism.

Ryazanov's critique of the *Iskra* programme is remarkable because it anticipates in almost every detail the theory of *permanent revolution*, which is conventionally associated with Leon Trotsky's famous work *Results and Prospects*. For Ryazanov and Trotsky alike, the rise of Russian capitalism appeared to be an 'exception' from the 'pattern' of Western Europe. Much

---

[12] L. Trotsky 1931.
[13] Larsson 1970.

of Russian industry was financed from abroad and thus incorporated the latest technology. Large-scale industry meant the working class had better opportunities to organise and the bourgeoisie was more vulnerable. These circumstances suggested that Russian liberalism would be politically ineffective and that Social Democracy would lead the revolution against tsarist autocracy.

The theme of Russia's exceptionality was not new. In the 1840s, Slavophile writers had claimed that Russia was morally superior to capitalist Europe. Alexander Herzen, initially a 'westernising' critic of the Slavophiles, subsequently shared their interest in the village commune and, by the early 1850s, hoped that Russia might bypass capitalism and move directly to socialism. The emergence of Russian Marxism in the 1880s was a tale of struggle between revolutionary Narodniks, who thought terror would precipitate an immediate socialist transformation, and the Marxist group Osvobozhdenie Truda (the Emancipation of Labour group), which claimed Russia was subject to universal laws discovered by Marx and Engels.

Georgy V. Plekhanov, the principal leader of Osvobozhdenie Truda, had no doubt that Russia would follow the capitalist pattern of development. But in the 1883 programme of Osvobozhdenie Truda, he also emphasised certain peculiarities of the impending class struggle. In a country where capitalist production was not yet dominant, the 'middle class' was 'incapable of taking the *initiative* in the struggle against absolutism', meaning that Social Democracy must struggle not only against the state and the bourgeoisie, as in Western Europe, but also against remnants of serfdom:

> The working population of Russia is oppressed directly by the whole burden of the enormous police-despotic state and at the same time suffers all the miseries inherent in the epoch of capitalist *accumulation*.... Present-day Russia is suffering – as Marx once said of the West-European continent – not only from the development of capitalist production, but also from insufficiency of that development.[14]

Since the bourgeoisie was too weak to take the initiative against absolutism, the overthrow of the monarchy and creation of a democratic constitutional régime would fall principally to the organised proletariat. As he told the

---

14 Plekhanov 1974, p. 355.

International Workers' Socialist Congress in Paris in 1889, 'the revolutionary movement in Russia will triumph only as a *working-class movement* or else it will never triumph!'.[15]

In attempting to refute Narodnik theories of Russian 'exceptionalism', Plekhanov really succeeded only in rephrasing the question. This became evident when a new programme for the Russian Social-Democratic Labour Party was being prepared in 1902–3. In that context, Lenin added two new elements to the debate: first, he emphasised in *What Is to Be Done?*[16] the importance of a professional organisation of revolutionaries at the expense of 'economistic' preoccupation with trade unions; second, he methodically reworked Social Democracy's agrarian programme. Convinced that industrial workers would require support from the rural proletariat, Lenin believed that remnants of the serf-owning system must be abolished by returning to the peasants the land they had lost (the so-called cut-offs) at the time of the Emancipation Edict in 1861. By encouraging development of capitalist agriculture, Lenin hoped to accelerate class differentiation in the countryside, promote rural class struggle, and ensure peasant support for the workers' fight against autocracy.

Although the new programme was intended to unify Social-Democratic factions with a clear statement of principles and demands, Lenin himself did not escape the dilemma of Russia's apparent exceptionality. In 1901, he had written that Russian Social Democrats had abandoned Narodnik ideas of 'the *exceptionalist* development of Russia',[17] yet, in 1902, he premised the Party's agrarian programme explicitly on Russia's exceptional circumstances:

> we demand the complete and unconditional…eradication of the survivals
> of serf-ownership; we hold that the lands which the government of the
> nobility cut off from the peasantry, and which to this day still serve to keep
> the peasants in virtual bondage, are the peasants' lands. Thus, we take our
> stand – *by way of exception and by reason of the specific historical circumstances* –
> as defenders of small property.…[18]

---

[15] Plekhanov 1889, p. 400.
[16] Lenin 1902h.
[17] Lenin 1901, p. 79. Italics added.
[18] Lenin 1902g, p. 149.

Whereas West-European socialists were fighting to overthrow capitalism, Lenin also believed a Russian revolution would most directly benefit the emerging bourgeoisie. In 1901, he had written that Social Democrats and liberals would find common ground in the struggle against tsarist autocracy:

> The Russian Social-Democrats never closed their eyes to the fact that the political liberties for which they are first and foremost fighting will benefit *primarily* the bourgeoisie.... If the liberals succeed in organising themselves in an illegal party...we will support their demands, we will endeavour to work so that the activities of the liberals and the Social Democrats mutually supplement each other. But even if they fail to do so (which is more probable), we shall not give them up as lost, we will endeavour to strengthen contacts with individual liberals, acquaint them with our movement, support them by exposing in the labour press all the despicable acts of the government and the local authorities, and try to induce them to support the revolutionaries. Such an exchange of services between liberals and Social Democrats is already proceeding; it must be extended and made permanent.[19]

Ryazanov thought Lenin's solicitous attitude towards small property and bourgeois liberals was the antithesis of a proletarian-revolutionary programme. In 1850, Marx and Engels had declared that the battle cry of the workers must be '*The Permanent Revolution*'.[20] In his commentary on the *Iskra* draft programme, Ryazanov concluded the work we have translated here with a similar call for '*revolution in permanentia*'. He intended to submit his criticism to the Second Congress of the Russian Social-Democratic Labour Party, meeting in Brussels in the summer of 1903, but he was denied that opportunity.

Convened in the hope of unifying the Party, the Second Congress actually produced the irreconcilable split between Mensheviks and Bolsheviks. The immediate dispute concerned the definition of the responsibilities of a party member, but the greater issue involved two rival views of working-class organisation. The Mensheviks hoped for a mass movement similar to that in Germany and other West-European countries. In *What Is to Be Done?*, however, Lenin argued that

---

[19] Lenin 1901, pp. 78–9.
[20] Marx and Engels 1850, p. 330.

> The only serious organisational principle for the active workers of our movement should be the strictest secrecy, the strictest selection of members, and the training of professional revolutionaries.[21]

Ryazanov condemned the narrowness of Lenin's formulation. In his pre-congress commentary on the draft programme, Ryazanov protested:

> We must never forget that Social Democracy is the party of *a class*, not a *sect*; that it is a party of the *masses*, not of individuals; and that it aims to make *history*, not histories. *History* is made only by the *masses*.

Following Lenin's victory at the congress, Ryazanov wrote an account of the party split and denounced 'organisational fetishism', 'sectarianism' and an emerging '*Personencultus*'.[22] Like Rosa Luxemburg, he believed 'The "final goal" for Social Democracy is simultaneously the "starting point"'. Socialist *emancipation* could not begin with working-class *obedience*. In a party conceived as a conspiracy, 'the organisation will become an assembly of sheep, and the functionaries will transform themselves from its servants into its "dictators"':[23]

> Hitherto the [party] committees served the workers; now the workers serve the committees. Unconditional obedience is demanded of everyone: workers are to obey the committees, which in turn obey the Central Committee, and the latter, under supervision of the Central Organ [*Iskra*] – which is counting on working masses who are ready to be subordinated – prepares, orders, and produces the general armed uprising.[24]

Ryazanov's criticism of Lenin won him a notoriety among Bolsheviks that was endlessly recited from 1931 onwards and ultimately made him a victim of the party degeneration he had predicted more than a quarter of a century earlier. Although he never figured prominently as a political leader after the struggles

---

[21] Lenin 1902h, p. 480.
[22] Ryazanov 1904, pp. 16, 62, 77, 84–5, and 112–13.
[23] Ryazanov 1904, p. 84.
[24] Ryazanov 1904, p. 72. Compare this with Trotsky's remark in L. Trotsky 1904: 'In the internal politics of the Party these methods lead…to the Party organisation "substituting" itself for the Party, the Central Committee substituting itself for the Party organisation, and finally the dictator substituting himself for the Central Committee….".

of 1903, his scholarly contribution remains enormous and beyond dispute.[25] In the work translated below, he distinguished himself not only as a Marxist thinker, but as one who could respect Marx's accomplishments while also frankly discussing his tactical mistakes. Ryazanov's commentary on *The Draft Programme of 'Iskra' and the Tasks of Russian Social Democrats* provides unique insight into the principles at stake in early party debates. Addressing the issue of Russia's 'exceptionality', Ryazanov was the first Marxist to translate the burden of 'backwardness' into the historical possibility of *permanent revolution*. That insight alone earns him a place alongside Leon Trotsky as one of the outstanding visionaries of the first Russian revolution.

*   *   *

The Draft Programme of 'Iskra' and the Tasks of Russian Social Democrats[26]

Part I: Questions of theory

What must we demand of the programme? The party programme must be a brief, clear, and consistent exposition of principles. A programme is not the same as a manifesto, which is simultaneously an indictment of the existing order and a defence of 'the newly arising order of things'. A programme is a declaration of war against the existing system, one that takes into account, in advance, all the factors leading to victory while also showing the opponent a picture of his own future and his inevitable defeat. A programme is a kind of *credo* of the party and a *memento mori*[27] for its opponents. . . .

As a theoretical expression of capitalist society and a formulation of the material and intellectual elements of the socialist system it creates, as a diagnosis of its 'sickness' and a prognosis of its impending fate, the programme

---

[25] Ryazanov was awarded the Order of the Red Banner for his scholarship. For extensive and fulsome appraisals of his scholarly work, see the volume of essays (over six hundred pages) devoted to him on the occasion of his sixtieth birthday: *Na boevom postu: Sbornik k shestidesyatiletiyu D.B. Ryazanova* (Moscow: Gosudarstvennoe izdatel'stvo, 1930).

[26] [Ryazanov 1903a. The Programme of the Russian Social-Democratic Labour Party, which is the object of Ryazanov's commentary, was adopted in August 1903 and is translated in McNeal (ed.) 1974, pp. 42–5.]

[27] [A reminder of mortality.]

must be thoroughly international in content. But the general theoretical content of the programme is complicated by one element. However common the principles of Social Democracy may be, and however inevitable it is that the workers' movement will adopt them at a certain stage of its development, the actual process of adoption occurs in the context of diverse conditions that depend upon the particular development of the country in question and the combination of international economic and political conditions prevailing at a particular time.[28]

[…]

If we wish to emphasise the orthodox character of our programme, then we must not merely indicate our goal but also *underline* the means by which we Social Democrats, as distinct from all other socialist parties, attempt to achieve that goal. Bernstein's formula that the 'movement is everything, the final goal nothing' is meaningless nonsense in every respect. This is a formula devoid of content. A movement without a goal makes no sense.[29]

[…]

Collectivism, communism, socialism – this is the 'final goal' of the economic movement occurring before our eyes, whose laws of development were first discovered by Marx and Engels. The development of the capitalist system itself is preparing all the material and economic prerequisites for the socialist system. Socialism has *already* become an economic possibility. But how can the possibility be realised? Reality itself gives us the answer to this question too. And what does it say?

It says that history is the history of class struggles, that every major change of social relations results from the struggle of one class against another, and that the only idea with any prospect of being realised is the one with an organised class behind it. That class's revolutionary dictatorship is the necessary precondition for such realisation. But is there a class in today's society whose interest would be the realisation of socialism? In the opinion of *Social Democrats*, the answer is yes. That class is the proletariat….

---

[28] Ryazanov 1903a, p 13.

[29] [Ryazanov, 1903a, pp 48–9. The reference is to Eduard Bernstein (1850–1932), the most prominent German 'revisionist', who doubted the possibility of socialist revolution and instead advocated inter-class cooperation in pursuit of democracy and social reforms. Bernstein's most coherent statement came in Bernstein 1907.]

…[T]he 'final goal' of *Social Democracy*, that is, of the proletariat…is *social revolution* and *the revolutionary dictatorship of the proletariat*.… Such a 'final goal'…dictates with iron logic the form of 'movement' leading up to it, and it determines clearly and precisely every aspect of tactics. Social Democracy, consciously *aspiring to become and to remain the class movement of the proletariat*, comes out forcefully against any attempt to conceal the class struggle that is occurring in front of us. And regarding the class struggle of the proletariat against the bourgeoisie, when waged to its natural end, as the sole road to emancipation of the working class, it must energetically resist every attempt to replace that struggle with any form of 'collaboration' between the proletariat and the bourgeoisie. As Kautsky says, 'the goal and the movement of social democracy are closely tied together, and the one must not be separated from the other'.…

The 'final goal' for Social Democracy is simultaneously the 'starting point'. It is precisely because the contradictions of the *existing* system can be finally resolved only by socialism, that Social Democracy makes socialism the starting point of its 'direct revolutionary struggle' and the centre of gravity for all its propaganda and agitation.[30]

[…]

'If not in essence, then in form the struggle of the proletariat against the bourgeoisie is at first a national struggle. The proletariat of every country must first of all finish off its own bourgeoisie.'[31] But precisely because 'the great emancipatory movement of the proletariat' is a national struggle only in terms of 'form', the programme of Social Democracy must also express, by implication, 'the international functions of the working class' of the particular country.… [T]he most immediate *national* task of the Russian working class is at the same time one of the major tasks of the entire international proletarian movement. The overthrow of Russian absolutism, the main instrument of European reaction, will eliminate one of the greatest obstacles in the way of 'the great emancipatory struggle' of the international proletariat.… The Russian working class will derive renewed strength…from the knowledge that it is shouldering the task of emancipating all of Russia from tsarist

---

[30] [Ryazanov 1903a, pp. 49–51.]
[31] [The quotation is from *The Communist Manifesto* in Marx, Karl 1973, *The Revolutions of 1848*, p. 78.]

despotism, and also the entire international movement from one of its most dreadful enemies.[32]

[…]

Development of the capitalist mode of production has completely transformed both world trade and, together with it, the universal market.… As Parvus says,

> the national production of different countries is becoming interconnected with the result that it is losing its national character: in place of internationalism comes cosmopolitanism. National production is losing its independence. It is being subordinated as production activities in different countries become the interconnected and mutually conditioning parts of a single production whole: not located in any particular nation, it becomes precisely a universal market.[33]

[…]

It is precisely this development that creates in each country a proletariat whose interests are not merely *identical* in different countries but also *common*. Consciousness of this fact is spreading increasingly amongst the working classes of different countries, and the old utopian notion of the 'international brotherhood of peoples' is giving way more and more to the 'international brotherhood of the working classes in a common struggle against the ruling classes and their governments'.[34]

[…]

Orthodox Marxists have never claimed that the proletariat, the working class, already *comprises* an enormous majority of the population, only that it will *become* the majority.

When Russian Social Democracy first had to struggle for its right to exist, when it demonstrated that 'the revolutionary movement in Russia can triumph only as a revolutionary movement of the workers', it met with the objection that in Russia, 'out of a population of 100,000,000, *there are only* 800 thousand

---

[32] [Ryazanov 1903a, pp. 53–4.]
[33] [Ryazanov 1903a, pp. 58–9.] No one has shown the capitalist character of the contemporary world market as well as Parvus does in his famous articles on Parvus [1896a, pp. 197–202, 276–83, 335–42, 514–26, 621–31, 747–58, 781–8, 818–27], although he limits his task to the world market as it has already been *formed*.
[34] [Ryazanov 1903a, pp. 59–60.]

workers united by capital', and that 'the worker who is capable of exercising a class dictatorship hardly even exists'.

How did the theorists of Russian Social Democracy respond?…[T]hey appealed to the 'dynamic of our social life' and to the incontestable *growth* of the working class. This statement of fact was far more important to them than belabouring the question of the number of workers at any given moment.[35]

[…]

We are dealing with the programme of *Russian* Social Democrats. We have, therefore, the right to expect…an analysis of Russian reality. No one nowadays debates the question of whether Russia is or is not passing through the phase of capitalist development. That question was decided long ago. It is obvious not only that capitalism is becoming 'overpowering', but also that it is in fact already overpowering. This does not mean, however, that our capitalism is at the same stage of development as capitalism in Western Europe, and even there capitalism is not everywhere the same. What we find are different stages of capitalism, which develops in each country according to specific circumstances. All that is common are the characteristic features of capitalism and the tendencies of its development.[36]

[…]

Part II: Questions of practice

General issues facing Social Democracy

Social Democracy is the party of the proletariat that has become conscious of its class interests. It is a socialist party because it sees the principal cause of all the evils of the capitalist system in the existence of private property in the means of production, and it adopts the goal of abolishing these evils by transforming the means of production into social property. It is a democratic party because full democratisation of the state and the social system – a democratic republic –

---

[35] [Ryazanov 1903a, p. 63.] The representatives of legal Marxism, especially Tugan-Baranovsky, specialised in raising this question. They probably had in mind comrade Axelrod when he wrote the following lines: 'Meanwhile, the Marxist youths of the 80's…saw the only guarantee of our Social-Democratic movement's success in the numerical growth of the industrial proletariat' (*Rabotnik* 5–6, p. 16).

[36] [Ryazanov 1903a, p. 64.]

is the fundamental condition for free development of the proletariat's class struggle. It is a revolutionary party because it can only reach its goal through revolution.[37]

[…]

Even though it is not the majority of the population, the party of Social Democracy still represents the class that expands and develops with the growth of capitalism while other classes decline and disappear. Moreover, it is also the only party that, while directly involved in the present, is already *today* the *party* of the future.[38]

[…]

If Social Democracy puts forth the *principle* of class struggle, it is only in the sense that, being the party of the *proletariat*, it cannot help but be unconditionally opposed to all attempts to suppress the class struggle between the proletariat and the bourgeoisie and, in its place, to substitute peaceful coexistence or collaboration between these classes. If Social Democracy defends the interests of the oppressed classes better and more decisively than any other democratic party, that is simply because it is the party *exclusively* of the proletariat and represents its class interests *alone*. The simple reason for this is that only the interests of this class are those of 'progress' and social development. The class interests of the proletariat are the sole criterion that makes it possible to make our way in the labyrinth of the present. . . .

As the most advanced party, it must stand *at the head* and be the vanguard of the entire revolutionary movement against the existing system. For this purpose, however, it has no need to *recruit* other classes; it must attract them through example, through being the party of the most revolutionary class. . . . Any curtailment of the *class* demands of the proletariat, in order not to jeopardise a general consensus of the moment, is therefore a betrayal not only of the proletariat's cause but also of the interest of social development. Conversely, the emphatic expression of these 'narrow' class interests is at present the very best tactic for Social Democracy.[39]

[…]

How does . . . class consciousness emerge? 'Know yourself' – that is what Social Democracy never tires of saying to the working class. Close scrutiny

---

37 Ryazanov 1903a, pp. 83–4.
38 [Ryazanov, 1903a, p. 84.]
39 Ryazanov, 1903a, pp. 85–6.

of its own existence, of its conditions of life, leads the working class to consciousness of its historical mission, which is dictated precisely by those living conditions. Hand in hand with this must also emerge its grasp of the conditions of its emancipation, which is not possible without understanding the organisation of contemporary bourgeois society....

The objective precondition of this self-knowledge on the part of the working class is crystallisation of the different professional groups that make up the proletariat into a class that is united in the consciousness of its common interest, or in Marx's words, the conversion of the working class from a class *an sich* into a class *für sich*.[40]

[...]

[C]omrade Lenin...does not agree with these truisms.... [H]e is trying to 'push' us towards the following view:....

> Class political consciousness can be brought to the workers *only from without*, that is, only from outside the economic struggle, from outside the sphere of relations between workers and employers.[41]

[...]

'Bringing class-political consciousness to the working class *from without*' is just as absurd as 'attracting the masses into active political struggle'. *Les extrêmes se touchent.*

All the debates of recent years essentially come down to one main point: some people consider the working class to be a passive element that must be inoculated with Social-Democratic principles with the help of some homeopathic injection so that it might gradually be 'attracted' into active

---

[40] [Ryazanov 1903a, pp. 88–9. From a class *in itself* into a class *for itself*.]

[41] [Ryazanov 1903a, pp. 89–90. The reference is to Lenin 1902h.] The complete quotation is:

> Class political consciousness can be brought to the workers *only from without*, that is, only from outside the economic struggle, from outside the sphere of relations between workers and employers. The sphere from which alone it is possible to obtain this knowledge is the sphere of relationships of *all* classes and strata to the state and the government, the sphere of the interrelations between *all* classes. For that reason, the reply to the question as to what must be done to bring political knowledge to the workers cannot be merely the answer with which, in the majority of cases, the practical workers, especially those inclined towards Economism, mostly content themselves, namely: 'To go among the workers'. To bring political knowledge to the *workers* the Social Democrats must *go among all classes of the population*; they must dispatch units of their army *in all directions*. (Lenin 1902h, p. 422.)

political struggle, while others believe that the working class, by virtue of its circumstances, is the most revolutionary class in Russia.... The active protest of the working class arises just as inevitably from given social-political conditions as does the working class itself.

...Therefore, the view that socialism is brought to the proletariat from without, by the bourgeois intelligentsia, is just as mistaken as the view that Social Democracy grows up 'on its own' from within the proletariat. That kind of thinking accords the proletariat both 'too much honour and too much dishonour'.[42]

[...]

'People of science' were needed to work out the 'economy of the proletariat', and because of historical circumstances they are naturally recruited from the ranks of the intelligentsia.... [S]uch people are from the *intelligentsia*, but they are not *bourgeois*. In the great majority of cases they are representatives of the 'thinking proletariat',[43] who cannot tolerate a social system that converts science into an instrument of rule by the exploiters and subordinates arts and craftsmanship to their enjoyment.

Nor can one say that the class consciousness of workers develops outside of the relation between workers and employers.... The class consciousness of the working class develops when the *class* struggle begins between the proletariat and the bourgeoisie....

Despite all the 'pushing' by comrade Lenin, we...cannot understand the claim that 'The *only* sphere from which it is possible to obtain this knowledge is the sphere of relationships of *all* classes and strata to the state and the government, the sphere of the interrelations between *all* classes.'[44]

---

[42] [Ryazanov, 1903a, pp. 91–2. This was the expression that Marx used when the Narodnik Mikhailovsky accused him of interpreting social development in terms of universal laws that ignored the historical experience of particular countries. See Walicki 1969, p. 186.]

[43] [This was a term Plekhanov used in Plekhanov 1883a. See Plekhanov 1974, p. 100. Kautsky used the same term in Kautsky 1902–4, p. 109 of the English translation.]

[44] [The reference is to chapter three of Lenin 1902h. Contrary to so–called 'Economists', among whom he included Ryazanov, Lenin argued that production workers are too preoccupied with the immediacy of the trade–union struggle to comprehend, on their own, the *totality* of social and political relations, including Social Democracy's relation to the peasantry and the liberal bourgeoisie. At the same time, Lenin argued that Social Democrats must cultivate support among all classes of the population:

> We must 'go among all classes of the population' as theoreticians, as propagandists, as agitators, and as organisers. No one doubts that the

Comrade Lenin goes too far. *Social Democrats* cannot develop the consciousness of the working class without awakening consciousness of opposition between *its* interests and those of all other classes. Precisely because the proletariat is the sole *genuinely* revolutionary class, and precisely because it is the class of 'have-nots' that is deprived of private property, the starting point for Social-Democratic propaganda cannot be the '*interrelations between all classes*'. The fundamental condition for the success of Social-Democratic propaganda and agitation is, therefore, emphasis upon the specific class position of the proletariat. Only after emphasising what sets the proletariat apart can we enter without risk into 'the sphere of relationships of *all* classes'; only then can we refer to the points of contact between the working class and other social classes, particularly those in opposition, provided that we never fail to point out at the same time the *class* character of the state, which in turn alters attitudes towards it on the part of the propertied classes and those that are propertlyess.... I cannot understand, despite all the 'pushing' by comrade

---

theoretical work of Social-Democrats should aim at studying all the specific features of the social and political condition of the various classes. But extremely little is done in this direction as compared with the work that is done in studying the specific features of factory life. In the committees and study circles, one can meet people who are immersed in the study even of some special branch of the metal industry; but one can hardly ever find members of organisations (obliged, as often happens, for some reason or other to give up practical work) who are especially engaged in gathering material on some pressing question of social and political life in our country which could serve as a means for conducting Social-Democratic work among other strata of the population. In dwelling upon the fact that the majority of the present-day leaders of the working-class movement lack training, we cannot refrain from mentioning training in this respect also, for it too is bound up with the Economist conception of 'close organic connection with the proletarian struggle'. The principal thing, of course, is *propaganda* and *agitation* among all strata of the people. The work of the West European Social-Democrat is in this respect facilitated by the public meetings and rallies which *all* are free to attend, and by the fact that in parliament he addresses the representatives of *all* classes. We have neither a parliament nor freedom of assembly; nevertheless, we are able to arrange meetings of workers who desire to listen to *a Social-Democrat*. We must also find ways and means of calling meetings of representatives of all social classes that desire to listen to *a democrat*; for he is no Social-Democrat who forgets in practice that 'the Communists support every revolutionary movement', that we are obliged for that reason to expound and emphasise *general democratic tasks before the whole people*, without for a moment concealing our socialist convictions. He is no Social-Democrat who forgets in practice his obligation to be *ahead of all* in raising, accentuating, and solving *every* general democratic question. (Lenin 1902h, p. 425.)

Lenin, why Social Democrats, in order to bring class political consciousness to the workers, must go among all classes of the population.[45]

[...]

Comrade Lenin makes a cruel mockery of *our* movement with the following comment:

> At the present time...gigantic forces have been attracted to the movement. The best representatives of the younger generation of the educated classes are coming over to us. Everywhere in the provinces there are people, resident there by dint of circumstances, who have taken part in the movement in the past or who desire to do so now, and who are gravitating towards Social Democracy (whereas in 1894 one could count the Social Democrats on the fingers of one's hand). A basic political and organisational shortcoming of our movement is our *inability* to utilise all these forces and give them appropriate work....[46]

Alas, this is but a 'dream'.... Our problem is precisely the fact that...we have too few people capable of going to the workers with the *living* word of Social-Democratic propaganda. And *word-of-mouth commentary*...is far more important than anything in print.

At present, when our practical tasks are becoming all the more complex, when we must prepare the Russian working class for the decisive battle, we Social Democrats must ourselves 'go to the workers' and summon 'the best representatives of the younger generation'!

What exactly are the tasks we face?

The special characteristics of Russia and the tasks of Russian Social Democrats

There are many prejudices still circulating among Russian Social Democrats that should have been criticised long ago. These prejudices result from the fact that in our appraisals of Russian conditions, we were guided by the 'pattern' of Western Europe. This happened because in the debates with our proponents of 'exceptionalism'[47] we over-emphasised developmental similarities between

---

⁴⁵ [Ryazanov 1903a, pp. 94–5.]
⁴⁶ [This quotation is also from Lenin 1902h, p. 429.]
⁴⁷ [The reference is to the Narodniks, who thought Russia could reach socialism without passing through the capitalist stage.]

Russia and the West-European countries while setting aside or overlooking Russia's peculiarities.

The fact is, however, that Russia is developing in a very unique way. The activity of our party can only be effective *in historical terms* if, while following the general principles of scientific socialism, we also begin with an accurate analysis of all the peculiarities in Russia's historical development.[48]

[...]

All that is required is to keep in mind that we are talking about the *specific features* of Russia's historical development, which in no way prevent it, in general terms, from passing through all the same phases as 'Western Europe' did. But each of these phases, even apart from differences in duration, has its own specific features that are attributable to the equally powerful influences of international relations. The phase in which Russia presently finds itself is 'the eve of the bourgeois revolution', which the main countries of Western Europe passed through a long time ago, and the position of Russia is really quite unique.[49]

a) *The first peculiarity – capitalism under 'open surveillance' of socialism*

Not a single country in Western Europe, on the eve of its bourgeois revolution, had the same degree of large-scale industry as 'Holy Russia'.... Not a single West-European country experienced the same breakneck speed of capitalist development as our country.... In 'Western Europe', the technological and economic revolutions took place over hundreds of years, whereas in Russia they have been concentrated in a period of scarcely one hundred years.... [W]e can say that capitalism in Russia, once freed from serfdom, has completed in just four decades a greater work of 'destruction' and 'construction' than it did in England over a period of several centuries.

At the same time, a socialist movement has also been developing that in terms of intensity has no equal even in the history of the German revolutionary movement before 1848. Since the 1850s we have had an uninterrupted tradition not only of socialist thought, but also of socialist practice. By the 1880s, this movement gathered all its strength with the aim of giving Russia

---

[48] [Ryazanov 1903a, pp. 99–101. It is remarkable that the first chapter of Trotsky's *History of the Russian Revolution*, written almost thirty years later, carries the title 'Peculiarities of Russian History.']

[49] [Ryazanov 1903a, p. 104.]

the opportunity to bypass capitalism and move to socialism. Disregarding the laws of history, in the late 1870s the *narodovoltsy*[50] made an extremely audacious attempt to finish off absolutism and capitalism at one fell swoop. They were convinced that the collapse of absolutism would be a direct prologue to the collapse of capitalism. They were cruelly punished for their audacity, and today they are still sometimes being severely reprimanded for their sociological ignorance. But the fact is that were it not for their remarkable sociological practice and their bitter experience, we would hardly understand scientific socialism any better today than the 'pure' Marxists of the 1870s did.[51]

[…]

> The highly important circumstance that the socialist movement in our country began *already* when capitalism was *still* in the embryo must not be lost on us. *This* peculiarity of Russian social development was not invented by the Slavophiles[52] or the pro-Slavophile revolutionaries. It is an indisputable fact

---

[50] [Narodnik adherents of the group calling itself *Narodnaya Volya* (The People's Will).]

[51] [Ryazanov 1903a, pp. 104–7]. Our 'Socialist-Revolutionaries' are usually regarded as 'resurrected' *narodovoltsy*. This is absolutely untrue. They are no closer to the *narodovoltsy* than Bernstein is to Marx. The great ones of history are never 'resurrected', but they are *transformed* into the activities of future generations, who are brought up on the experience of their great predecessors. Only some small primitive tribe, who learned nothing and forgot nothing, could dream of vanquishing an enemy simply by putting in the front line the skeleton of its former chieftain who once brought it great victories. Do not disturb, therefore, the remains of dead warriors or complain if, in the heat of battle, a 'stray bullet' might strike them. Do not summon them up by wailing, by clattering clay pots, or by beating the drums. 'Was it you who dared to call on me? *You* are akin only to those whom *you* can comprehend, but not to me.' But you too, comrades, should not disturb the ashes of these fighters who are dear to us. In striking at your enemies, do not defame these great ghosts. You are dealing neither with 'vandals' nor with 'people who have been resurrected', just with people who have been 'awakened' by the sound of the battle of the proletariat and who, while still half asleep, have dressed themselves in someone else's feathers. [Ryazanov is portraying the original Narodniks of the 1880s as the 'great ghosts' whom Social-Democrats are still criticising for hoping to bypass capitalism, and whom Socialist-Revolutionaries are still imitating at a time when the development of capitalism has proceeded much further. His sympathetic appreciation of the *narodovoltsy* was related to his own expectation that capitalism in Russia had a short future.]

[52] [The Slavophiles were romantic conservatives, mainly from the educated aristocracy, who believed that Holy Russia must not be defiled by the materialism and secularism of the capitalist West. In principle, they regarded autocracy as appropriate in Russia – provided the government enacted reforms such as emancipating the serfs, ensuring civil liberties, and creating some limited political representation. The Slavophile movement was most active in the 1840s and 1850s, and many of its ideas

which we are all aware of and which will be of great benefit to the cause of our working class on the condition that the Russian socialists do not waste their energy building castles in the air after the style of the principality and *veche* epoch.[53]

Or, as we would now add, even in the style of the capitalist epoch.[54]

[…]

The process of laying the 'foundations' [of capitalism] in our country has always been exposed to socialist criticism. Russian Social Democrats have seen to this, and they will have to continue doing so all the more forcefully. Exposing all the methods of primitive accumulation, they will stigmatise every step that our capitalism takes in its 'peaceful' progress; they will also reveal the hypocritical reality behind all the talk about economic progress, civilisation and culture, with which it attempts to hide the rapacious exploits of capitalists of every category. Having at their disposal a wealth of experience in Western Europe, they will use these exploits to develop the class consciousness of the proletariat and to warn other exploited classes of the danger they face; they will also resist every attempt to speed up the development of capitalism with 'artificial means'. Struggling against every reactionary undertaking by the petty bourgeoisie, they must also avoid ever becoming advocates for the capitalists.[55] There is no need to defend the exploits of some particular groups of *capitalists* in order to show the historical importance of *capitalism*. That job, along with immediate concerns about 'economic progress', can be left to the capitalists themselves along with their toadies.[56]

---

and attitudes were later adopted in modified form by the Narodniks, who defended Russia's collective agriculture through revolutionary struggle against the tsarist state.]

[53] G. Plekhanov, *Nashi raznoglasiya* [Our Differences], p. 212. [See Plekhanov 1884, p. 274. The '*veche*' style refers to hopes of constructing socialism based on pre-capitalist communal land tenure. The *veche* was the medieval legislature of the city of Novgorod. The 'style of the capitalist epoch' refers to expectations that capitalism would have to evolve in the West–European 'pattern' before the socialist revolution would become practicable].

[54] [Ryazanov 1903a, p. 108.]

[55] [Ryazanov is referring to the view, prevalent among most Marxists prior to 1905, including Lenin, that the coming revolution would be of benefit principally to the capitalist class through creating a constitutional republic in place of the autocracy.]

[56] In our country, P. Struve served as just such a proponent when he was still introducing our capitalism to the people and attempting to secure its access to the salons of our intelligentsia. [Pyotr Berngardovich Struve (1870–1944) published Struve 1894. For a time he was associated with Plekhanov and Lenin, but in 1901 he abandoned

Only in this way will none of the responsibility for capitalism's development fall on the socialists even though that development works to the socialists' benefit. This is the only way in which Social Democracy can demonstrate to the entire toiling masses that in representing the interests of the proletariat, it simultaneously wages a struggle in modern society not just against the exploitation of hired labour, but also against every other form of exploitation and oppression.

That same unique feature also helps us in making propaganda for socialism, in which one of the most important conditions for success is the proletariat's understanding that the capitalist process of production has an historical, transitional character. In other countries, where capitalism has existed 'from time immemorial', its development was accompanied by formation of a kind of working class that, because of its education, tradition and habits, looks upon the demands of this mode of production as if they were obvious laws of nature. All the countless torments and suffering that are costs of development for this form of production, all the blood that was spilled in the history of primitive capital accumulation – all this is obscured by thick layers of dust built up over a history of many centuries.... An example can be seen in Holland, where capitalism developed very early. With the passage of time, social life in that country was moulded in certain stable forms, and Holland was transformed into a kind of bourgeois China. We can see the same thing in England. But today the tempo of industrial development is accelerating more and more, especially in young countries. 'Not only the development of capitalism in Russia cannot be as slow as it was in England, for example, its very existence cannot be so lasting as it has been fated to be in the "West European countries".'[57] It is also understandable that capitalism's more rapid tempo of development accelerates the development of its consequences. All

---

his academic flirtation with Marxism to embrace liberal demands for civil rights in a constitutional monarchy.] At every step of the way, he tries to show that capitalism is not generally responsible for the evils attributed to it. These kinds of solicitous melodies abound in the writings of our legal Marxists. Here is one example: 'Whence, indeed, does it follow that the efforts of our entrepreneurs to utilise the advantages of pre-capitalist methods of production should be charged to our capitalism, and not to those survivals of the past which retard the development of capitalism and which in many cases are preserved by force of law?' V. Ilyin, *Razvitie kapitalizma v Rossii*, p. 394. In the following pages, we shall have more occasions to refer to this writer. [Vladimir Ilyin was in fact Lenin, whom Ryazanov is comparing here to Struve and the legal Marxist 'toadies'. See Lenin 1899, p. 495.]

[57] G. Plekhanov, *Nashi raznoglasiya* [Our Differences], p. 299. [See Plekhanov 1974, p. 335.]

the 'fixed and fossilised relations' dissolve even more rapidly; and the result is that the people, including the proletariat, are *all the more* compelled to take a hard look at their own mutual relations and their conditions of life. These circumstances explain the more rapid growth of Social Democracy in Germany, Austria and Italy, and at the same time permit us to hope that in our country the development of Social Democracy will occur even more quickly.[58]

b) *The second peculiarity – the political sterility of our bourgeoisie*

> Political reforms are not the task of the Socialist-Revolutionary party. That whole business has to be left to the people who call themselves liberals. But those people are absolutely impotent in our country; for whatever reasons, they have turned out to be incapable of giving Russia free institutions or guarantees of personal rights. Such institutions are so vitally necessary that without them no activity is possible. For this reason, the Russian Socialist-Revolutionary party is obliged to take upon itself the responsibility for crushing despotism and giving Russia the political forms within which ideological struggle will become possible.[59]

That is how the *narodovoltsy* (mainly Zhelyabov) formulated their views at the Voronezh congress.[60]

[…]

[T]he *Osvobozhdenie Truda*[61] group also pointed out…the inability of our middle class to take any *initiative* in the struggle against absolutism. This thinking was set out in the first draft programme….[62]

---

[58] [Ryazanov 1903a, pp. 111–14.]

[59] E. Serebryakov, *Obshchestvo 'Zemlya i Volya'* [Land and Freedom Society].

[60] [Ryazanov 1903a, p. 114. Andrei Ivanovich Zhelyabov (1851–81), a leader of the narodnik organisation *Narodnaya Volya* (The People's Will), was executed for his part in organising the assassination of Tsar Alexander II in 1881. The early populist movements in Russia originally shunned 'political revolution', which they considered a bourgeois exercise, in favour of 'socialist revolution.]

[61] ['Osvobozhdenie Truda' (The Emancipation of Labour group) was founded in 1883 and was the first Russian Marxist organisation. The group translated and distributed Marxist works in Russia and became major critics of the populist ideology of *narodnichestvo* (narodism). Lenin later wrote that the group laid the theoretical foundations for the Social-Democratic movement. The group was followed by the League of Struggle for the Emancipation of the working Class in 1895, and by the Russian Social-Democratic Workers' Party in 1898.]

[62] [In the first draft programme, Plekhanov wrote: 'One of the most harmful consequences of this backward state of production was and still is the underdevelopment of the middle class, which, in our country, is incapable of taking the *initiative* in the struggle against absolutism.' See Plekhanov 1974, p. 355].

…The second draft was written in significantly different conditions.… [A] 'middle class' had irresistibly emerged along with the development of capitalism.… This reinforced the belief that in Russia…the Social-Democratic party would 'go along with the bourgeoisie because the latter is revolutionary in its struggle against absolute monarchy, feudal land holding and the petty bourgeoisie'.[63]

…[Comrade Axelrod wrote that] 'The Western pattern indicates that the overthrow of absolutism led to the rule of the bourgeoisie'; *ergo*, it 'was of benefit for the bourgeoisie above all'.[64] This same pattern suggests that the bourgeoisie raised the banner of struggle against the autocracy. But let us look at the issue more closely.

It is true that, in Western Europe, different strata of the bourgeoisie waged the struggle against autocracy; but, even there, it was waged more successfully when the proletariat actively participated in the struggle and drove the bourgeoisie on. The most resolute fighters for democracy were the petty bourgeoisie in the cities. The big and middle industrial bourgeoisie fought much less consistently. The only exceptions were England and France, where these strata of the bourgeoisie defended constitutional guarantees (a limited monarchy) in the struggle against absolutism, which was supported by the feudal landowners and the financial aristocracy.…

In Germany, it was already the case that 'the bourgeoisie had the misfortune to arrive too late'.[65] It failed even to win undivided power; and now, having secured for itself the political conditions necessary for free development of its passion for surplus-value, it has ceded power to the reactionaries.…It was frightened by the insurrection of the French proletariat, which did not herald particularly cheerful prospects for the bourgeoisie; and it was horrified to learn that the German proletariat – which in the 1840s had already expressed its dissatisfaction with what the bourgeoisie saw as mere imperfections in the political régime – was now ready to use revolution to secure the

---

[63] [Plekhanov 1887b, pp. 358–62.]

[64] [Pavel Borisovich Axelrod (1850–1928) was originally a member of the narodnik group *Zemlya i Volya* (Land and Freedom) but subsequently became a founding member of 'Osvobozhdenie Truda'.]

[65] [This had been Marx's conclusion in 1848. Marx 1848a, pp. 186–213.]

conditions needed for free development of its own *class* struggle *against the bourgeoisie*.…

…Someone might well ask: 'But doesn't this contradict *The Manifesto of the Communist Party* by Marx and Engels?'

The point is that Marx and Engels overestimated the progressive character of the German bourgeoisie. They only knew the experience of England and France, which suggested that…the historical mission of the bourgeoisie is the conquest of political freedom. They were convinced, therefore, that the coming revolution would result in the rule of the bourgeoisie, that the social and political conditions accompanying this rule would become a weapon in the hands of German workers against the bourgeoisie itself, and that this new struggle would *begin* immediately after the fall of the reactionary classes in Germany. In that case, the bourgeois revolution would necessarily serve as the immediate prologue to the workers' revolution.

The tactics that Marx and Engels adopted in 1848–9 logically followed from these views. They wanted to go along with the bourgeoisie, and they quite deliberately took a position on the extreme left wing of bourgeois democracy, differentiating themselves only by their more extreme political demands. During all of 1848 and the beginning of 1849, they helped the bourgeoisie to wage *its* political struggle, dictated its programme of action at each step of the way, energetically 'pushed' it in the direction of determined opposition, and themselves took the initiative in refusing to compromise.… But all the work and efforts of Marx and Engels were in vain. The fact is that the workers and the most radical strata of the petty bourgeoisie *made* the revolution. The bourgeoisie, as Engels said, only *endured* the revolution, and he and Marx soon understood that they had excessively idealised the bourgeoisie, which turned out to be completely incapable of fulfilling *its own* historical mission.

Moreover, while Marx and Engels were expending their energy in giving a push to the bourgeoisie, the *already* emerging workers' movement saw its turn to act. The League of Communists began its own activity too late, and it accomplished nothing in the sense of linking its 'final goal' to the workers' movement, which behaved perfectly 'spontaneously'. While the communists were fighting in the ranks of bourgeois democracy and providing it with leadership, the workers

> were busy with strikes, workers' unions, and production associations, forgetting that the main point at issue was to win for themselves, with the

> help of a political victory, the space without which the stable existence of such things was impossible.[66]

Marx and Engels soon recognised their mistake in light of the experience of the *Neue Rheinische Zeitung*. While 'inciting' the bourgeoisie, they were unable as devoted communists, despite their best intentions, to function merely as the extreme left wing of bourgeois democracy or to hide the fact that by 'pushing' the bourgeoisie they only ended up all the sooner 'at loggerheads'. As a result, they ended up 'pushing away' the bourgeoisie, who had no interest in continuing a revolution that had been foisted upon them.… It became obvious that the working class could not wait for a bourgeois victory as a precondition for taking up its *own* task.… But it was already too late. The bourgeoisie was already so frightened that it rushed to surrender itself to the wrath and mercy of absolutism at the expense not only of the workers but also of the peasants.

I have said that Marx and Engels '*made a mistake*'. But there are different kinds of mistakes. To use Marx's words, this was a mistake of world-historical character that was rooted in objective conditions. But if we want to avoid repeating that mistake, if we want to avoid making our own strictly 'subjective' mistake, then we must not close our eyes to one of Russia's 'special' characteristics, namely, the fact that our bourgeoisie has shown itself to be emphatically incapable of taking any revolutionary initiative whatever. […]

Our financial bourgeoisie is every bit as reactionary as its counterparts in Western Europe. All of its interests bind it to the autocratic system. Its purely political influence is attenuated by the fact that the Russian state controls the main reservoirs of the entire country's circulation of money and credit, and also by the fact that foreign loans play the predominant role in the system of state credit.

As for any active opposition role on the part of the big and middle industrial bourgeoisie in our country, it is practically non-existent. They do not even dream of carrying that role any further than so-called representation of the interests of industry. Only our commercial bourgeoisie is *liberally* inclined, along with that section of the landowners who have succeeded in becoming *industrial* capitalists, that is, who are concerned not only with the appropriation

---

[66] Engels, *Zur Geschichte des Bundes der Kommunisten*. [See: Engels 1885, pp. 312–30.]

of surplus value but also with its 'production'. It is around these people that the bourgeois intelligentsia are gathered. All of these elements are constrained under absolutism and would have no objection to 'limiting' it, but any such desires are poisoned before they can take root. Apart from that, the hen's flight of our liberalism is constrained by 'the indecisive mood of social strata that are not accustomed to political life'. If the German bourgeoisie could still gratify itself up to 1848 with the illusion that events such as the uprising of the Silesian weavers were due merely to imperfections of the political system, its Russian counterpart has already eaten so much from the tree of knowledge of good and evil that it is oblivious to any such illusions. It fears nothing so much as the mortal threat of *revolution*, even though, according to the pattern, it is supposed to benefit from the revolution *above all others*. It fears not merely the proletariat, but also the growing dissatisfaction of the petty bourgeoisie.

In other words, in Russia the ideology of the bourgeoisie – *liberalism* – 'has faded even before it blossomed'.[67] The growth of production in our country is being measured by hours rather than by days. The underdeveloped condition of the middle class has receded into legend, but they still resist any conscious awareness of their own emancipatory mission.

Our 'honest and incorruptible, wise and educated liberals', who 'truly sympathise with their suffering motherland',[68] are amazingly gracious when they compare 'Chernyshevsky, Dobrolyubov and others to flies fouling the picture painted by a great artist' (referring to the 'epoch of great reforms').[69] And our Russian radicals and constitutionalists, amongst whom, in comrade Lenin's words, there are 'many wise people', cannot even reason their way to the most fundamental 'basic right' – the right of every citizen to participate in the political life of the country. The 'general absence of people in the liberal

---

[67] [This was Plekhanov's expression in 1885. In *Nashi raznoglasiya* [Our Differences] he wrote: 'Our capitalism will fade before it has time to blossom *completely* – a guarantee for which we find in the powerful influence of international relations.' See Plekhanov 1884, p. 335.]

[68] Plekhanov, p. 174. [The reference is to a review by Plekhanov in *Zarya* no. 2–3.] [See also Plekhanov's reply to Ryazanov in '"Orthodox" Pedantry' in this volume.]

[69] [The reference is to the rule of Alexander II (1818–81), the 'Tsar–Liberator' who 'emancipated' the peasants by officially ending serfdom in 1861. The statement concerning Chernyshevsky appeared in a book that Plekhanov reviewed and that is discussed in the next document in this volume.]

camp', as comrade Martov[70] puts it, was never revealed as strikingly as it is now....

Comrade Plekhanov, along with *Iskra*, is still hoping for a rebirth of Russian liberalism. Comrade Plekhanov is convinced that when 'the idea spreads through the ranks of Russian liberals that the political awakening of the Russian proletariat is not a myth but an absolutely indisputable truth', then a serious liberal movement will emerge in our country. Inspired by this prospect, comrade Martov optimistically anticipates 'the men of the future, who will breathe new life into Russian liberalism', and he predicts that we shall have great figures in our own 'Johann Jacobys and [!] Lafayettes[71] where now we have only the depressing spectacle [as comrade Martov's voice becomes choked with "tears"] of knights of peaceful cultural development'.

'Abandon hope, all ye who enter'[72] into this world of people who are neither alive nor dead as they rejoice in the celebration of nonsense!

History has played a cruel trick on our liberalism. The reality is that a 'serious liberal movement' can only emerge where the political awakening of the proletariat is precisely a myth – and *not* an indisputable fact. The revolutionary struggle of the Russian proletariat is so spirited that it cannot have any other effect than to awaken people, even people as lethargic as our liberals. But even as they are just wiping their eyes, they begin to think to themselves: 'Is there not a "profit" to be made from this?' Our future Jacobys and (!) Lafayettes, preferring to hide under the tree of 'moderation', are already beginning to count the chestnuts that they will have others pull from the fire. Although they are 'devoted supporters of law and order', who 'oppose the

---

[70] [Julius Martov (1873–1923), originally a member of the Bund, a Jewish socialist group, joined with Lenin in 1895 to form the St. Petersburg League of Struggle for the Emancipation of the Proletariat. In 1903 Martov broke with Lenin over the latter's view that party membership should be limited to 'professional revolutionaries'. He subsequently became the principal leader of the Menshevik faction.]

[71] Only someone carried away by prophetic ecstasy and a 'wistful state of mind' – as comrade Martov obviously was when he 'composed' these inspiring lines – could explain the 'and' that connects Johann Jacoby, a really great and convinced democrat (and later a Social Democrat), with the petty theatrical hero of the Champ-de-Mars. [Johann Jacoby (1805–77) fought for a constitution in East Prussia in the 1840s and in 1848 supported a democratic–constitutional monarchy. In the 1860s Jacoby was a member of the German National Association and of the Progressive Party. As a *Landtag* deputy during the Prussian constitutional conflict, he called for a refusal to pay taxes and was sentenced to a term in prison. In September 1870 he protested the annexation of Alsace-Lorraine and subsequently joined the Social-Democratic Party.]

[72] [The sign over Dante's entrance to hell: 'Abandon hope, all ye who enter here.']

use of force by anyone, high or low', they also know perfectly well that a revolution *non olet*.[73] Together with their new leaders, they say to themselves: 'A moderate party with a clever tactic can profit from intensifying struggle between extreme social elements' – and as hard-headed realists in politics (and, of course, as idealists outside of politics), they are already becoming cretinous proponents of 'parleying a truce' with absolutism in anticipation of the time when they will be the 'cretins of parliamentarism'. . . .

But at this point I will be struck down by the author of the lead article in No. 16 of *Iskra* [Lenin, who says]:

> It is particularly in regard to the political struggle that the 'class point of view' demands that the proletariat *push forward* every democratic movement. . . . We will not forget, however, that if we want to push someone forward, we must continuously keep our hands on that someone's shoulders. The party of the proletariat must learn how to grab hold of any liberal at the moment when he contemplates moving by a *vershok* and force him instead to advance by an *arshin*.[74] And if he hesitates – then we will go forward without him and over him.[75]

. . . The party of the proletariat . . . may 'push forward' the liberals from time to time, but that only requires using the 'lash' of merciless criticism against every philistine banality of their 'non-committal moderation'. The experience of *Iskra* demonstrates the hopelessness of this business of 'pushing forward' the liberals. . . . However elegantly gloved is the 'hand that rests on the shoulders of the liberals', and however gently it deals with our 'wise and educated, honest and incorruptible liberals, who truly sympathise with the suffering of their motherland',[76] our 'future Jacobys and (!) Lafayettes' have enough of

---

[73] [When the Roman emperor Vespasian was asked to justify a tax on public urinals, he replied: '*Pecunia non olet*' (Money has no smell).]

[74] [1 vershok = 1 ¾ inches or 4.4 cm; 1 arshin = 0.71 m.]

[75] Evidently it is 'all the same' to Lenin, judging by how frequently he uses the expression 'push forward'. But *à la longue* all this 'pushing forward' and 'pushing against' ends up as 'pushing apart'. [For this quotation see Lenin's article in *Iskra*, no. 16, Feb 1, 1902 (Lenin 1902f and "The Class Point of View" ', CW Vol. 5: 337–343. There Lenin affirmed that 'The political demands of working–class democracy do not differ in principle from those of bourgeois democracy, they differ only in degree.', p. 342]

[76] On the other hand, it is delightful to see how *Iskra* deals with its 'comrades'. Instead of 'pushing them forward' it 'pushes against' them; instead of 'grieving', it 'crushes' them. 'What would you have us do, when these people don't understand a "subtle hint"! Taking off the gloves, it then 'gets out the hot iron, the nails and the

a class-based sense of smell to 'sniff out' anyone who, with his other hand, hopes to detect 'every falsifier of revolutionary Marxist theory on the plane of ideas'....

We are supposed to send greetings to...our new allies. [Lenin says] we are to help them:

> You can see that *they are poor*; they can only put out a small leaflet, issued in a worse form than the leaflets of the workers and students. *We are rich.* We shall publish it in printed form.... You can see that *they are weak; they have so little contact with the people* that their letter passes from hand to hand as if it were actually a copy of a private letter. *We are strong. We can and must circulate this letter 'among the people'*, and primarily among the proletariat, which is prepared for and has already commenced the struggle for the freedom of the whole people.[77]

With this kind of honeyed and unctuous language, *Iskra* 'encouraged' the 'old *zemtsy*' in connection with their letter of March 1902. And just two weeks later the 'poor' *zemtsy* were already revelling in the moderate voice of their 'own' man [Struve]. A new planet appeared on the horizon of illegal literature – not a *quasi*, but a real periodical – *Osvobozhdenie*.[78]

But *Iskra* was still not happy, having no wish to accept the liberals as they really are. It leaves that to the philistines. Sufficient unto itself, it retained its holy displeasure with life. It wasn't *you* that I 'pushed forward'; *you* are not the one I 'encouraged'. And with an angry hand it now 'pushes away' the liberal who appears before it in the flesh. 'Good riddance'! 'And he leaves without even receiving a greeting!'

But I, 'a secret and unconscious supporter of economism',[79] nevertheless greet *Osvobozhdenie* and wish it success with all my heart. I do so not merely because Mr. Struve 'cleared out' of the Marxist camp. Like many orthodox

---

oil' – in short, it boils wax [to pour into the victim's wounds] in order to drive out the devil!

[77] See the feuilleton in *Iskra*, No. 18. (Ryazanov's italics). [The article is by Lenin 1902d, p. 158. He is quoting and discussing a hectographed letter distributed at a session of the Zemstvo Assemblies.]

[78] [A journal edited by Struve but having no connection with the Marxist group 'Osvobozhdenie Truda'.]

[79] [In 1901 Ryazanov had attempted to mediate the dispute between *Iskra* and the so-called 'economists' in the conviction that the economic and political struggles were inseparable and that neither could be given primacy at the expense of the other.]

people, he only had a 'reputation' of being a Marxist. And we can only celebrate the fact that he 'cleared out' of the circle of our most 'influential' Marxists. A good quarrel is always better than a poor truce, especially with people who are 'moderate'.… There is one further reason why I welcome *Osvobozhdenie* and wish it success with all my heart: now that our liberals have finally shown their cards and spoken up clearly, they are no longer any threat. There is no need to tear from *this* bourgeoisie any ideological cover that they used in other countries to disguise their class interests. What we see before us is the 'naked interest' of the property owner and the 'heartless cash' of political calculation.[80]

[…]

…Every illusion is harmful, and this is especially true of class illusions, but the most harmful of all are illusions concerning another class. The sooner such illusions are abandoned, the better off we shall be.[81]

[…]

It is also time for *Iskra* to abandon its illusions. Of course, we ought not to take the liberals just as they *are*. We must take them as they *will become*, and in that context it is all the more urgent to get rid of illusions, especially when we have other means to do so than the use of 'honey'![82]

Nevertheless, however disgusting our liberal bourgeoisie may sometimes be, and expecting nothing from them for ourselves, we must always support, and we will always support, any 'ray of light' in this grey kingdom, any sparkle of political decency in their midst. But this support must by no means imply

---

[80] [Ryazanov 1903a, pp. 115–26.]

[81] [Ryazanov 1903a, p. 123.]

[82] The recent issues of *Iskra* demonstrate that it, too, is getting 'sick and tired' of our 'wise and educated' liberals. And, as usual, it is overdoing things. The incident in the Voronezh zemstvo turns out to be 'the exception that proves the rule', and the letter from Evreinov so disturbs its balance that it is falling into the embrace of *Moskovskie vedemosti*. From being a Jeremiah, it turned at once into an Isaiah: 'Oh, this zemstvo servility and the opposition lackeys!…What kind of Egyptian torture and Russian scorpions will still be needed in order, at last, to straighten the obsequiously bent spine of the liberal zemstvo man; in order to compel him to see himself not as an apprentice "representing the Russian government", but as a self-confident worker for the people's emancipation?!' (See 'The Bobchinskys in Opposition' in *Iskra*, No. 27 [Trotsky 1902, 48–50].) Poor *Iskra*! It is already weary of waiting for a liberal, but, taking heart, it 'dreams' of 'a worker for the people's emancipation'! [Ryazanov is referring to Trotsky, 1902. Pyotr Ivanovich Bobchinsky was a country squire in Nikolai Gogol's comedy 'The Inspector General'. The role in the play of Bobchinsky and Dobchinsky (another busybody landowner) was principally to spread gossip.]

that we will 'prepare ourselves so that the *proletariat*, in the event that *any* zemstvo *that is at all honest* is insulted by the tsarist government, will be able to reply with demonstrations against the pompadour-governors, the desperado gendarmes, and the Jesuit-censors'.[83] Here, too, *Iskra* is overdoing it. It is 'touched' by the miserable appearance of the 'poor' *zemtsy* and, like a good little mother, it has a duty to care for *all* its children and to be especially tender with those that are diseased or anxious. I would prefer it if the *honest zemstvos* responded *themselves*, not with demonstrations (they are too respectable for that) but at least with petitions against *the most egregious* insults to the proletariat and the peasantry. But – to borrow your energetic style, comrade Lenin – I have run out of patience waiting. So, what is to be done?

> 'You are an eminent Spartan,
>
> I am just a bourgeois doctrinaire.'

At the risk of 'passing for' an economist, or even being promoted to the higher rank of 'secret economist', may I be so bold as to inform you, with no intention of any offence or injury, that our support must go no further than pointing out to the working class the need for solidarity with liberal tendencies in one question or another, or in one task or another, in the struggle against absolutism. We will publicly stigmatise the vile swindles that our government perpetrates even on gentle liberals.

Our German comrades also wanted to have a different kind of bourgeoisie. But the party of the German proletariat never 'laid a hand' on the shoulder of the liberals. The Russian proletariat, likewise, has too much of *its own* work to do. We could, of course, along with Jeremiah Martov, 'grieve' as much as we want over the fact that there are no Jacobys and (!) Lafayettes in our country, but we have more rewarding things to do.

The point is that we must not be distracted by a pattern. And as comrade Lenin quite rightly said, we have no use for 'slavish (worse: apish) imitation'.[84] What we do need is an intelligent and critical attitude towards the experience

---

[83] *Iskra*, No. 18. The whole thing is an unctuous-sentimental feuilleton about the 'poor' zemstvos and the 'rich' proletariat. *Le jaurèsisme ou va-t-il se nicher!* Our *Iskra's* habit of 'roaming haphazardly and obliquely' is especially obvious when it roams into the question of demonstrations. Prove it to me right now that I am an 'unconscious economist'! This will give me a fine opportunity to discuss demonstrations with you. [Ryazanov is criticising Lenin's 'Letter to the Zemstvoists'.]

[84] [Lenin 1902h, p. 360.]

of Western Europe that will enable us to appraise it independently, while always setting our own course according to such reliable criteria as the principles of scientific socialism. History does not repeat itself. The only thing that is repeated is the sequence of the main phases of social development, but they occur each time in a *completely new historical* context depending on the unique course of the *historical* development of any given social 'organism'. And if we wish to avoid seeing something that first occurred as tragedy repeating itself as farce, we must closely study the *particular characteristics* of our own situation. Establishing the fact that our bourgeoisie is incapable of any resolute initiative in the struggle with absolutism, we must, I repeat, take matters into *our own* hands. This will be all the easier in view of the fact that our particular circumstances have already given birth to another uniqueness of Russian history that is becoming increasingly evident.

The point is that in the struggle for Russia's political emancipation, which, as the Hannibals of liberalism say,[85] is the impending task of our time, the socialist party has itself taken the initiative and has from the very beginning been actively supported by the working class. That was the everlasting contribution of Narodnaya Volya. And, in keeping with the Manifesto of the Russian Social-Democratic Workers' Party, we can say that: 'As a socialist movement and tendency, the RS-DRP continues the work and the traditions of all previous revolutionary movements in Russia. With the complete conquest of political power as its principal and most immediate goal, Social Democracy pursues the same objective that was *already clearly set out by the glorious figures of* Narodnaya Volya.'[86]

[…]

---

[85] Their only resemblance to the real Hannibal is in their Punic resourcefulness, or, as the 'straightforward' Roman 'narodniks' would say, their lechery. But there is another similarity. Having sworn his vow, Hannibal *did not yet* realise that he would have to depend on a Carthaginian bourgeoisie that was always ready to sell its freedom for a mess of pottage, always ready to make peace and have a truce. The unfortunate Hannibal died, but he died 'tragically'. And what can we say of our own Hannibals, who have yet to wage a war but are already shouting about peace and a truce? Leave Hannibal to rest in peace, and study instead 'The Life and Work of Count Camillo Benso Cavour'. [When Hannibal was nine years old, his father, Hamilcar, took him to a temple to vow 'never to be a friend of Rome'. The context for this reference is found in Lenin 1901.]

[86] [Ryazanov 1903a, pp. 129–32.]

Of course…the *narodovoltsy*….were merely a small band of heroes from the socialist intelligentsia and the working class. The peasants were indifferent to their struggle. But things have changed since then. Now we have a *class* that by virtue of its position is the implacable enemy of Russian absolutism – the kind of enemy that cannot be satisfied either by 'great' or 'not so great' reforms. This is the only social *class* whose *minimal* political demand is *universal suffrage*. It will settle for nothing less, and it has no choice but to stand at the head of the movement for emancipation of all the oppressed classes and strata of contemporary Russia. The task is difficult, but because of Russia's unique development the proletariat must shoulder it. This does not mean, of course, that it will complete this task *on its own*. Besides certain strata of the bourgeoisie mentioned previously, there are also other elements in our country that are capable of marching *side by side with the working class* in its struggle for political emancipation. Even in Russia, the political emancipation of the working class will only be completed with the help of all the various elements of the petty bourgeoisie. These helpers will come from both the urban and the rural petty bourgeoisie, that is, the peasants in the proper sense of the word.

We used the expression *side by side with the working class*, and these words actually summarise the whole difference between the position that Russia finds itself in on the eve of its bourgeois revolution and that of Germany in the corresponding epoch. There, the communists wanted to march side by side with the bourgeoisie; they assigned it the role of hegemon in the political struggle with the intention of beginning *their own* struggle and mounting their own opposition after *the bourgeoisie's* victory. But it turned out that the task was too difficult because the proletariat was unable to adapt to the 'slow pace' of the bourgeoisie and ended up getting ahead of it. In our case, the Social Democrats must from the very beginning *take upon themselves* the struggle against absolutism and leave it to the bourgeoisie either to move along *side by side with the working class* or else fall behind it.

In other words, the principal initiator and the most decisive and energetic fighter for Russia's political emancipation *cannot be anyone else* but Russian Social Democracy, which represents the interests of this class.

It *must* play this role. It is supported not just by the heroism of individual personalities but also by the heroism of the masses, which in *historical* terms is incomparably more fruitful. It is supported by all the objective conditions of social development. It is supported not just by practice but also by theory – by the most revolutionary theory that the world has ever known because it is the theory of the most revolutionary class that the world has ever known.

I have already said that the *narodovoltsy* waged their struggle reluctantly. Like all the narodniks of the 1870s, they were convinced that the task of a social-revolutionary party was not political reforms. An echo of this attitude could still be heard in the words of the first programme of the Osvobozhdenie Truda group. They considered the underdeveloped condition of the middle class to be one of the most *harmful* consequences of the backward state of production, and they believed this was the only reason why the socialist intelligentsia would have to take upon itself such an unusual role.[87]

Social Democracy has now abandoned this prejudice. Every class struggle is a political struggle. This means that the proletariat cannot help but take on political tasks. And if it does not have *its own* policy, other parties, bourgeois parties, will inevitably take it in tow.

> In the West-European countries the proletariat often fought absolutism under the banner and the supreme leadership of the bourgeoisie. Hence its intellectual and moral dependence on the leaders of liberalism, its faith in the exceptional holiness of liberal mottos and its conviction of the inviolability of the bourgeois system. In Germany it took all Lassalle's energy and eloquence merely to *undermine* the moral link of the workers with the progressivists. Our 'society' has no such influence on the working class, and there is no need or use for the socialists to create it from scratch. They must show the workers their own, working-class banner, give them leaders from their own, working-class ranks; briefly, they must make sure that not bourgeois 'society', but the workers' secret organisations gain dominating influence over the workers' minds. This will considerably hasten the formation and growth of the Russian socialist workers' party, which will be able to win for itself a place of honour among the other parties after having, in its infancy, promoted the fall of absolutism and the triumph of political freedom.[88]

---

[87] The *chernoperedeltsy* [members of the group Black Repartition], as comrade Plekhanov quite correctly noted, had nothing against political freedom and would have been very pleased if the liberals had won it. In their own view, the socialist intelligentsia was to devote itself to the task that it alone could complete.

[88] G. Plekhanov, *Nashi raznoglasiya* [Our Differences], p. 310. How fortunate for comrade Plekhanov that he wrote these lines at a time when comrade Lenin was

The last twenty years have demonstrated that historical conditions are now much more favourable for the creation of a Russian socialist workers' party to lead the struggle against absolutism. This means it is all the more important for us to get rid of the prejudice to the effect that *political freedom, for which Russian Social Democrats are the main fighters*, will be of benefit primarily to the *bourgeoisie*.[89] This harmful prejudice creates the illusion of *common* political

---

running 'with his mizzen sail down' and had not yet dreamed up a 'plan'. Otherwise, he would have been tried for 'demagogic activity', 'mercilessly beaten with the rod', and excluded from 'our' party! [The comment by Plekhanov is in Plekhanov 1974, p. 343.]

[89] N. Lenin, 'The Persecutors of the zemstvos and the Hannibals of liberalism', in *Zarya*, No. 2–3, p. 310. [Concerning the liberals, Lenin wrote:

The Russian Social-Democrats never closed their eyes to the fact that the political liberties for which they are first and foremost fighting will benefit *primarily* the bourgeoisie. Only a socialist steeped in the worst prejudices of utopianism, or reactionary Narodism, would for that reason object to carrying on the struggle against the autocracy. The bourgeoisie will benefit by these liberties and rest on its laurels – the proletariat, however, must have freedom in order to develop the struggle for socialism to the utmost. And Social Democracy will persistently carry on the struggle for liberation, regardless of the attitude of the various strata of the bourgeoisie towards it. In the interests of the political struggle, we must support every opposition to the oppressive autocracy, no matter on what grounds and in what social stratum it manifests itself. For that reason, we are by no means indifferent to the opposition expressed by our liberal bourgeoisie in general, and by our Zemstvo liberals in particular. If the liberals succeed in organising themselves in an illegal party, so much the better. We shall welcome the growth of political consciousness among the propertied classes; we will support their demands, we will endeavour to work so that the activities of the liberals and the Social Democrats mutually supplement each other. But even if they fail to do so (which is more probable), we shall not give them up as lost, we will endeavour to strengthen contacts with individual liberals, acquaint them with our movement, support them by exposing in the labour press all the despicable acts of the government and the local authorities, and try to induce them to support the revolutionaries. Such an exchange of services between liberals and Social Democrats is already proceeding; it must be extended and made permanent. But while always ready to carry on this exchange of services, we will never, under any circumstances, cease to carry on a determined struggle against the illusions that are so widespread in the politically undeveloped Russian society generally and among Russian liberals in particular. Paraphrasing the celebrated statement of Marx in regard to the Revolution of 1848, we may say of the Russian revolutionary movement that its progress lies, not so much in the achievement of any positive gains, as in emancipation from harmful illusions. We have emancipated ourselves from the illusions of anarchism and Narodnik socialism, from contempt for politics, from the belief in the exceptionalist development of Russia, from the conviction that the people are ready for revolution, and from the theory of the seizure of power and the duel–like combat between the autocracy and the heroic intelligentsia. (CW, Vol. 5, pp. 79–80.]

tasks for the Russian proletariat and the bourgeoisie, which is impossible because the political tasks of the bourgeoisie and the proletariat are not identical. Political freedom, for which *Social Democrats* are the main fighters, presupposes *universal suffrage*. Is this something that our liberal bourgeoisie wants?

This prejudice is also harmful because it implies a community of interest between economically opposing classes and creates the illusion of *all* classes marching against the main enemy of the Russian people, the autocracy. In reality, this illusion closes our eyes to the fact that the bourgeoisie might take from the proletariat the fruits of its victory unless we concentrate all of our efforts on preparing the worker masses for the political struggle that they face. That is why we must not be distracted by the struggle against the main enemy of the Russian people; we must not forget that the more prepared the working class is for the struggle against *the whole of* bourgeois society, the more it will gain from the fall of absolutism. At a time when other oppositional and revolutionary parties are more concerned with overthrowing the autocracy than with anything else, Social Democracy, representing the interests of the social class that is most opposed to the autocracy, must never forget that 'the more clearly the working class sees the connection between its economic needs and its political rights, the more profit it will derive from its political struggle'.[90] And for this purpose, all that is necessary is that Russian Social Democrats thoroughly absorb the principles of modern Social Democracy and, without restricting themselves to political propaganda, constantly make it known to their listeners that 'economic emancipation is the great end to which every political movement ought to be subordinate as a means'.[91]

No one among us can say when the revolution will break out. But even in the opinion of *Iskra* it is not that far off. And we must make every possible effort '*even in the pre-constitutional period to change the existing relation of*

---

[90] G. Plekhanov, *Nashi raznoglasiya* [Our Differences], p. 310. [Plekhanov 1884, p. 343.]

[91] G. Plekhanov, *Nashi raznoglasiya* [Our Differences], pp. 310–11. [Plekhanov 1884, pp. 343–4.] If I did not think that the correspondent of *Iskra* (No. 22) was merely bringing in his own opinion 'from the outside', then upon reading that 'one rarely hears in workers' circles any mention of "wages" or "surplus value" – it is the enemy of the Russian people who attracts all the attention of the proletarians', I would think, together with comrade Plekhanov, that our workers are already stranded between the Scylla of 'economism' and the Charybdis of 'politics'. Our correspondent, sounding like 'the siren call of a bird of paradise', was simply carried away in singing the praises of *Iskra* and *Zarya*, whose dissemination, according to him, is the most urgent task of the present moment. *C'est mon opinion, et je le partage!*

Russian social forces to the advantage of the working class', 'so that in the very opening period of the constitutional life of Russia our working class will be able to come forward as a separate party with a definite social and political programme'.[92] We will achieve this only when social democracy becomes the leading fighter of the most advanced class. Only if the proletariat is organised as a menacing revolutionary force before and during the revolution, will it become the backbone of the whole movement for emancipation and the main army to which supplementary detachments sent out by other social classes will be attracted.

Sooner or later, the day will come when Russia will see the dawn of political freedom. The more our party works for that great day, the more actively it participates *today* in every single event, the more closely it links its activity with every aspect of working-class life, the more rapidly and successfully will it develop 'on the day after the revolution', and the less will be the danger that in the arena of political life it will run into some bourgeois party that will rely on it for help and then drag along behind itself a part of the working class. We already see how actively our party is participating in a wide range of current events, and how favourable the conditions are in creating the possibility for it to take the lead in the movement to emancipate all the toiling and oppressed people of Russia. We shall also see now that a third special feature has already made it possible for our party to link all of its activities with every manifestation of the life of the working class, and that this opportunity will be all the greater if it only knows how to make use of it.[93]

c) *The third peculiarity: the gigantic growth of the workers' movement within the limits of the autocratic system*

We have already mentioned that not a single country in 'Western Europe', on the eve of its bourgeois revolution, had such a highly developed large-scale industry as Russia.[94] This also explains the fact that, even before the bourgeois

---

[92] Plekhanov, *Sotsializm i politicheskaya bor'ba* [Socialism and the Political Struggle], p. 73. [Plekhanov 1883a, p. 102.]

[93] [Ryazanov 1903a, pp. 134–9.]

[94] [In his *History of the Russian Revolution*, Trotsky made the same point when discussing the scale and concentration of Russian industry prior to the Bolshevik Revolution:

> At the same time that peasant land-cultivation as a whole remained, right up to the revolution, at the level of the seventeenth century, Russian industry in its technique and capitalist structure stood at the level of the advanced

revolution, the working class developed nowhere else with the same speed. Prior to the revolution in England, the proletariat appeared on the historical scene just 'as another class that suffered more than the rest'; even in the Leveller movement[95] it was completely lost among the petty bourgeoisie and the craftsmen at the time of the 'Glorious Revolution'. An independent movement of the proletariat only arose where capitalist relations originally formed, that is, in the village, but there it remained an isolated phenomenon. In France, the working class was a more active element – even before the revolution it made its presence felt in a whole series of strikes and rebellions that frequently broke out just before the revolution. Even in the mid-eighteenth century (1757), the working people produced from their midst an 'avenger' in the person of Damiens,[96] who, to the great horror and indignation of the encyclopaedists and philosophers of Enlightenment, wanted to remind the 'beloved' father of his people – by stabbing him – of the sufferings and torments of his children. In 1789, the urban workers already played the decisive role in overthrowing the 'old order'. The attempt by Babeuf's[97] followers, in alliance

------

countries, and in certain respects even outstripped them. Small enterprises, involving less than 100 workers, employed in the United States, in 1914, 35 per cent of the total of industrial workers, but in Russia 17.8 per cent. The two countries had an approximately identical relative quantity of enterprises involving 100 to 1000 workers. But the giant enterprises, above 1000 workers each, employed in the United States 17.8 per cent of the workers and in Russia 41.4 per cent! For the most important industrial districts the latter percentage is still higher: for the Petrograd district 44.4 per cent, for the Moscow district even 57.3 per cent. We get a like result if we compare Russian with British or German industry. This fact – first established by the author in 1908 – hardly accords with the banal idea of the economic backwardness of Russia. (L. Trotsky 1977, p. 31.)

[95] [The Levellers were the republican-democratic faction of Cromwell's army in the 'Glorious Revolution' against Charles I of England. See Bernstein 1963 [1895].

[96] [Robert François Damiens (1715–57), a domestic servant at the college of the Jesuits in Paris, unsuccessfully attempted to assassinate Louis XV of France in 1757. He was the last person to be executed in France with the traditional and gruesome form of death penalty used for regicides, which was drawing and quartering by horses.] Damiens died a hero after unbelievable torture and suffering. Even Voltaire, who showered upon this 'reckless fool' abuse as bad as we hear from many of our 'wise and educated, honest and incorruptible' gentry leaders, still had clear respect for this fanatic. Of course, the 'liberals' of the time made use of the 'memory' of Damiens. This curious episode from the history of XVIII century France has been completely forgotten. Nevertheless, it is time to cleanse the memory of this hero of the profanities and slanders that are still being repeated even today by learned historians. It is also time that someone wrote a history of the 'illegal' movement on the eve of the Great revolution.

[97] [François-Noel (Gracchus) Babeuf (1760–97) was a radical exponent of agrarian reforms and social egalitarianism. Imprisoned during the Reign of Terror, he was

with remnants of the revolutionary democrats, to win a better share of the spoils for the proletariat, ended in failure and served as one of the main factors in the formation of the Bonapartist empire, whose mission was to defend the bourgeois order in general against the proletariat.

Germany was better off in this respect as *The Communist Manifesto* already noted: 'The revolution is bound to be carried out under more advanced conditions of European civilisation and with a much more developed proletariat than that of England in the seventeenth century, or that of France in the eighteenth century.'[98] But Germany still did not have a workers' movement in the proper sense of the word. Large-scale industry was at a rudimentary stage. Most of the famous 'rebellions' and strikes were the affairs of handicraftsmen. It is true that there were others who took part in the revolutionary movement of the thirties and forties besides members of the 'intelligentsia', but right up to the formation of the League of Communists most of the workers were artisans. Germany had no organised strike movement before the revolution of 1848. The League of Communists was formed too late to sink deep roots among the workers. It hardly managed even to publish its *Manifesto* before the revolution broke out.

We have already seen how, by the time of the revolution, Marx and Engels, as the first theorists of the proletariat, attributed enormous importance to the economic struggle that had occurred up to 1848. They thought their task was only to be the vanguard of the *working class*; but to avoid ending up in the tragic position of Blanqui[99] and his followers, they had no choice but to serve as the vanguard of *democracy*.

While they were busy with the purely political struggle, allying with the democrats and devoting all their revolutionary passion to the attempt to win complete political freedom, the working class was busy with strikes

---

released after Robespierre's fall in 1794 but continued to attack the Thermidorian reaction and was briefly imprisoned again in 1795. In 1796 Babeuf took a leading role in planning an insurrection to restore the constitution of 1793. An informant revealed the plot, and Babeuf was executed in May 1797.]

[98] [Marx and Engels, *The Communist Manifesto*.]

[99] [(Louis-)Auguste Blanqui (1805–81) was a legendary French revolutionary who saw the rich as the aggressors in the class struggle and worked for revolution through the activity of a secret society that would overthrow the ruling class by means of a conspiratorial surprise attack. Although he was a socialist, Blanqui believed the revolution would have to establish a temporary dictatorship to educate the masses and reconstruct society in socialist forms.]

etc., mainly under the leadership of Born.[100] The mistake of Marx and Engels was compounded by the mistakes of Born and his comrades. A revolution requires organisation, but once the revolution has begun, the slogan of the revolutionary party is not organisation but struggle *à outrance.*

We, unfortunately, have no Marx or Engels among us, but we do find ourselves in much more favourable historical circumstances. There is no doubting the gigantic growth of the workers' movement even before 'the bourgeois revolution'. It began as early as the 1870s. And along with the growing numbers of revolutionaries from the working class, the strike movement is also expanding irresistibly....[101]

[...]

Obviously, this presupposed certain 'material' conditions, which, as we have seen, were not present during the corresponding periods in England, Germany, or France. But in addition to these 'material' conditions, the 'intellectual' conditions must also exist.

And they do exist in the form of Social Democrats. A characteristic peculiarity of Russia is the fact that the economic struggle and the trade-union movement are developing among the workers in direct proportion to the development of Social-Democratic propaganda. The full force of the idea of the emancipation of the working class was required in order to awaken among the workers a consciousness of their professional interests and thus to create a *conscious* strike movement. The trade-union movement in Russia is a direct offspring of Social Democracy, and the more effectively Social-Democratic propaganda is waged, the more rapidly and consciously will the economic struggle grow – a struggle that is so beloved but also so badly misunderstood by our 'economists'.

Let us consider the most talented among them, the author of *The Workers' Cause in Russia.*[102] Firmly convinced that the workers must initially appear as a

---

[100] [In Lenin 1905k Lenin discusses the role of Stephan Born. See also the footnotes to Vol. 9 of Marx and Engels Collected Works and Mehring 1935, Ch. 6.]

[101] [Ryazanov 1903a, pp. 139–41.]

[102] [Ryazanov 1903a, p. 142.] According to comrade Lenin, this author is a member of the *Iskra* group. [The author was Julius Martov, and the book, *Rabochee delo v Rossii,* was first published in Geneva in 1899. Five subsequent editions were published. See Getzler 1967, p. 39.] By now, of course, he has changed his views, and we hope that in the 'literary laboratory' of *Iskra* his pamphlet will undergo fundamental editorial revisions. Above all, it will be necessary to remove from it all the traces of 'the old dog'

class in 'economic' terms, he regards socialism only as a source of 'inspiration'. Then,

> when the working class has continuously developed in a free state, through class struggle and participation in state affairs and political life, and *senses itself to be strong enough, it will naturally assume the task of changing the very foundations of the system* that creates inequality between rich and poor and necessitates the class struggle between them.[103]

That Social Democrats must begin with this task even in 'the labour movement', that they must take it as their starting point – this is something that our 'economist' from the *Iskra* group cannot understand for the simple reason that for him socialism has never been anything but 'the final goal'. He cannot grasp why it is so important that the economic struggle be led by none other than Social Democrats, that is, by a party that aims *from the outset* to change the very foundations of the existing order.

Like any typical economist, the author of *The Workers' Cause in Russia* lives exclusively in the present. To think that the economic struggle of the proletariat can be used 'for the revolution' causes his flesh to creep and puts him in mind of Blanquism. He has no wish to impose an inappropriate task on the workers. He is patiently waiting until the working class matures of its own accord. He has only the vaguest idea of the great educational role of Social Democracy, which leads every manifestation of working-class activity and directs it towards a single goal – the development of class consciousness. [...]

Even under the 'autocratic regime', the working class is already waging the economic struggle despite the extremely unfavourable conditions imposed upon it in our country. And the duty of *Social Democracy* is to rush to its assistance – to whatever extent is possible under the autocratic régime. A political organisation of revolutionaries must make possible the new means of struggle that will come with political freedom.

But so long as Social Democracy is Social Democracy, it must also defend every 'small' need and every 'small' demand of the workers. There are no 'purely economic' demands – even if they only amount to 'adding a kopek to a

---

referred to with such indignation by A.B., author of the article 'What is the Lesson of the Kharkov May?' in *Zarya*, No. 1. [See also Lenin 1900, pp. 357–65.]

[103] *Rabochee delo v Rossii*, p. 73.

rouble'. Every such demand must be linked to general political conditions and used to awaken the political and class consciousness of the working masses. By defending these 'small' needs and being the sole advocate of the working class – an advocate with no 'interests on the side' – Social Democracy at the same time *clearly* demonstrates to the workers that even within the limits of the existing political conditions our party alone is the most resolute fighter for improvement in the position of the working class.[104]

[...]

Our proletariat has already begun its economic struggle; and the mass workers' movement, in the sense understood by practical people, will grow stronger in Russia the more quickly capitalism develops. We are not the ones who create it or call it forth, but we do have a duty to help it everywhere and in every way we can. It is precisely because we are *revolutionary* Social Democrats that we must respond now with 'economic' leaflets to every manifestation of the 'economic struggle'.[105] The important issue is not whether we put out leaflets that have a 'political' or an 'economic' character; it is more important, incomparably more important, that those leaflets be put out by *Social Democrats* whose task is to integrate every 'small' fact of the proletariat's life and activities into a single whole. Only *Social Democrats* are able to struggle successfully against every distraction that arises from various local, professional, and nationality differences. And since the best means of preventing the emergence and growth of various forms of a 'purely labour' movement is to lead the proletariat's economic struggle, we must never forget the words of the Bor'ba group[106] in its *Declaration* concerning publications:

> By ignoring the matter of organising the proletariat, or by leaving it exclusively to 'economists' of one type or another, revolutionary Social Democracy would also inadvertently help to promote the development of conditions in which the working class might fall under the political influence of non-socialist elements or even elements that are hostile to socialism. Moreover, by helping the working class to clarify and express its immediate demands, through drawing upon its own experience and the history and

---

[104] [Ryazanov 1903a, pp. 143–5.]

[105] [Lenin was more concerned with publishing political 'exposures' than with economic leaflets.]

[106] [Ryazanov was the leading figure of the *Bor'ba* group, which subsequently remained apart from both the Bolsheviks and the Mensheviks.]

practice of the West-European workers' movement, revolutionary Social Democracy must completely integrate immediate demands with the tasks of the movement as a whole, and do everything possible to make the mass workers' movement a Social-Democratic movement. Standing, so to speak, at the cradle of the workers' movement, carefully attending even to its smallest needs, and fearlessly defending its interests, revolutionary Social Democracy is creating traditions among the working class that will never allow bourgeois democracy, however revolutionary it may be, to take the workers' movement in tow.[107]

---

[107] 'Declaration' p. 9. Having received this 'declaration', *Iskra*, rather than dealing with essentials, in an act of 'reckless daring' kept things hidden in the mailbox. In that kingdom of dark shadows it saw, of course, the 'incomparable little word' *Personencultus*. If it ever glanced at the history of German and Austrian Social Democracy, it would certainly refrain from using this term, which only demonstrates its own 'incomparable ignorance'. Liebknecht, Bebel and Adler condemned any *Personencultus*. It is true that the first two had to deal with prominent people. Not everyone is so fortunate. When Adler protested against a *Personencultus* in the unification resolution at the Heinfeld congress, he was dealing with people whose names have already been forgotten by people who are less careless about such matters than *Iskra*. Ignorance is something that can be cured. But *Iskra* understood this little word 'subjectively'. In this case there is nothing that can be done. Poprishchin was also indignant when he protested against the cult of his own person. And *Iskra* cunningly 'winks' at the man of experience to hint that in the *Bor'ba* group 'the lump is right under the nose'. 'As a man of experience you will grasp what is at the bottom of it all from this one unparalleled and peerless little word.' (*Iskra* No. 18). A man of experience, inspired by a cult for the person of Ferdinand, king of Spain, now believes that in the *Bor'ba* group 'the lump is right under the nose'. What an interesting case of *folie à deux*.

[This note refers to Lenin's comment '*On the Bor'ba Group*', which was published in *Iskra* in March 1902. There Lenin wrote as follows:

> K.N. You ask what the *Bor'ba* group is. We know that several of its members have contributed to *Zarya* (two articles) and *Iskra* (3 reports, 2 articles and 1 commentary). Several articles they sent us were not published. They have now published a printed 'declaration', complaining of our 'undemocratic' attitude and campaigning even…against a *Personencultus*! As a man of experience you will grasp what is at the bottom of it all from this one unparalleled and peerless word. And when *Bor'ba* publishes its article against *Where to Begin?* about the rejection of which they also speak in the declaration – then even comrades who are absolutely inexperienced in Party affairs will understand why we did not receive these contributors with open arms. As for 'democracy,' see Lenin 1902h, IV, e): what is stated there about *Rabochee Delo* applies to *Bor'ba* as well. (See Lenin 1902e, pp. 493–7.)

The mention of Poprishchin is a reference to Gogol's *Diary of a Madman*, where Poprishchin was a schizophrenic suffering from the delusion that he was the King of Spain. By casting Lenin in the role of Poprishchin, Ryazanov is implying that Lenin's inflated notion of his own self–importance is what explains his refusal to publish the *Bor'ba* declaration.]

Social Democracy must make every effort to ensure that *now, before the downfall of the autocracy and on the eve of the revolution, the workers' movement becomes all the more closely aligned with socialism.* Only in this way will revolutionary Social Democracy ensure that at the time of the revolution the working class will use all its energy and all its revolutionary passion to demand complete political freedom, without being distracted from this, the main task, and without expending its resources in economic experiments. We must make every effort to ensure that the working class knows that the highest form of its *class* struggle is the political struggle, and this will only happen if we revolutionary Social Democrats lead the economic struggle.

Only in these circumstances can we assure ourselves of the most favourable circumstances for our activity on the day after the revolution. By significantly reducing the risk of a 'purely labour' movement emerging, we also reduce the risk of a split between the Social-Democratic workers' movement and the mass workers' movement.[108]

d) *Conclusions: what does the experience of German Social Democracy teach us?*

The practical tasks of Russian Social Democracy are complicated, as we can see, by all the special features of Russia's historical development that we have been discussing…. The tasks that even German Social Democracy could only accomplish incrementally now stand full-blown before Russian Social Democracy at a time when we do not yet have the corresponding political conditions.

But even if there is no single 'pattern', we must still be familiar with the experience of the West-European workers' movement. The colossal successes of German Social Democracy were in large measure due to the fact that they knew how to draw upon the experience of the English and French workers' movements. Coming onto the scene much later, the German workers'

---

[108] [Ryazanov 1903a, pp. 146–8.] This aspect of the question is dealt with at length in the article 'The Teachings of the Podkhalimovs and the Freedom of Workers' Unions' (see *Kalendar'*). Our Ozerovs, Wurms and other hangers–on of the autocracy dream about free workers' unions in Russia. This article demonstrates that there is not a single country in which legalisation of workers' unions occurred before the legalisation of socialist political associations. Comrade Lenin thinks, on the contrary, that this is not true of all countries. (See Lenin 1902h) I am still waiting with bated breath for him to show just which 'certain' countries he has in mind. If he is correct, then the conclusions of our learned Podkhalimovs will acquire *a certain degree* of validity.

movement, as Engels said, grew up on the shoulders of the English and the French movements and made use of their hard-won experience to avoid repeating their mistakes. Our movement appeared even later than the German movement, and for that reason it can and must take advantage of its lessons. That is why knowledge of the history, theory, and practice of German Social Democracy is so important to us.

Unfortunately, the case of comrade Lenin demonstrates that this knowledge is sadly missing even among our 'political chiefs'. [Lenin writes:]

> Let us recall the example of Germany. What was the historic service that Lassalle rendered to the German working-class movement? It was that he *diverted* that movement from the path of progressivist trade-unionism and co-operativism, towards which it had been spontaneously moving (with the benign assistance of Schulze-Delitzsch and his like).[109]

…Lassalle diverted the German workers' movement from the path of progressivist trade-unionism – just how can you take up your pen to write such nonsense?…

Poor comrade Lenin! How he struggles against this trade unionism! Marx, Engels, Lassalle, Liebknecht – all of them, of course, did nothing else but fight against trade unionism.

Lassalle's historic service lies in the fact that he laid the foundation for an independent workers' party. Perhaps he would have tried, like those who followed him, to divert the workers' movement from the road of trade unionism, had he not died before the appearance of a German trade-union movement.…

And Liebknecht? Do you know, comrade Lenin, just what historic service he and his comrades contributed? Of course, they fought against progressivist trade unionism; like you, they made a kind of 'bugaboo' of the word 'trade unionism'. Is that not so?

Alas! This too is just a 'dream'.… The fact is that Liebknecht and his comrades, far from *diverting* workers from this path, actually 'pushed them forward'. And how did they do that?

> They (Liebknecht and the other Eisenachers) decided to take an active part in the movement of craftsmen that began in the latter half of the 1860's. They

---

[109] N. Lenin, *Chto Delat'?*, p. 28.
[See Lenin 1902h, p. 385]

understood its enormous significance for the organisation of large masses of workers, and *fearing that, left to itself, it would attract the proletariat to the kind of palliatives sought in England, they took upon themselves the initiative in this matter and thus established a close bond between socialist propaganda groups and the craftsmen's organisation.* Thanks to their understanding of the principles and instruments of the workers' movement, the new socialist party succeeded in significantly raising the social consciousness and sense of self-worth among the masses of workers, and they saved the all-German union from demoralisation.[110]

[…]

For Liebknecht and Bebel, socialism was never merely a 'final goal'. The main point of all their activity, and the most urgent task of the present, to which all others were subordinated, was to change the foundations of an order that rests upon class antagonisms…. [F]or them, socialism absorbed the workers' cause. In other words, however important economic and political organisation of the proletariat may be in themselves, they must be subordinated to organisation in the name of social revolution, that is, to Social-Democratic organisation. The immediate interests of the proletariat, whether economic or political, are never self-contained; they are always subordinate to the interests of the future, to the interest of the social revolution; if they are merely immediate and self-contained, they will never reach beyond the limits of bourgeois society. The only class interest of the whole proletariat is the idea of the social revolution.

I say again, therefore, that … it is only in fighting for socialism that we can also fight properly for the workers' cause. The more resolutely and energetically we work as *Social Democrats*, the more resolutely and energetically we will also be struggling for 'immediate interests' and for improving the position of the working class. The only way we can improve its position in capitalist society is by *leading it towards* the 'final goal' of *that* society, which is socialism.

---

[110] [Ryazanov 1903a, pp. 148–51.] P. Axelrod, 'Results of the Social-Democratic Party in Germany' (*Obshchina*, No. 8–9). This article was written in 1878, when comrade Axelrod was still a Bakuninist, but a very unique one. It still contains a great many acute observations that comrade Axelrod would not disavow today. It would also be helpful to comrade Lenin because it would familiarise him with the main facts of the history of German Social Democracy in the 70's.

It is precisely because Liebknecht and Bebel were Social Democrats that they fought to shorten the working day, to raise wages, and to create conditions that would counteract the physical, mental and moral degradation of the working class. It is also precisely because Liebknecht and Bebel were Social Democrats that they fought for political freedom and a democratic republic. It is only in conditions of complete political freedom that the class struggle of the proletariat can freely develop, and it is only in a democratic republic that the proletariat can come to power.[111]

[…]

That is what the experience of German Social Democracy teaches us; that is what makes its policies the model for Social-Democratic parties in all countries.

However, the brilliant successes of German Social Democracy also had another side. They condemned German liberalism to a miserable life, as comrade Molotov quite justifiably noted in an article that I strongly recommend to comrade Lenin:

> …one of the reasons for the powerful development of German Social Democracy was undoubtedly the fact that the German workers at a comparatively early date organised themselves in an independent political party with a social-revolutionary programme. Of course, in doing so they simultaneously undermined the significance not only of bourgeois liberalism, but also, to an even greater degree, the significance of petty-bourgeois democracy, and drove both of them to the wall. The result was to unite the mass of workers, to enable them to stand on their own feet, and to awaken them to political life when otherwise they would have remained outside of politics in a state of indifference and apathy.[112]

We have already seen that the peculiarities of Russia's historical development have created the most favourable conditions possible for the organisation of an independent political party of the working class. It is time for us to forget about 'keeping a hand on the shoulder of the liberals'; it is also time to understand that if historical conditions have condemned our liberals to

---

[111] [Ryazanov 1903a, pp. 160–1.]

[112] Molotov, *Zarya* No. 1, 223–4. Later I shall have the opportunity to speak of our petty-bourgeois democrats. [P. Molotov was a pen name occasionally used by Parvus. See Katkov 1967, p. 78.]

sterility, then the organisation of a Social-Democratic party will diminish their significance even further. So stop grieving, comrade Martov, and shake off the 'miserable state of mind' that you are burdened with because of the 'general lack of people in the liberal camp'. Let's just get on with organising the Social-Democratic party and let it demonstrate that it is the most revolutionary party – and then our future Jacobys will appear only in order immediately to join the ranks of Social Democracy, just as Johann Jacoby did in 1871 after the heroic act of Liebknecht and Bebel.[113] And as for Lafayettes who will shoot people down in Kazan Square,[114] our liberalism will provide more than enough of them – without your tears comrade Martov, and without your 'pushing them forward' comrade Lenin!

Therefore, the tasks of the Russian Social-Democratic party are the following:

> *the organisation of an independent political party of the working class with a revolutionary Social-Democratic programme* for these purposes: *Social-Democratic education of the working class by means of exposing the class character of the whole of modern society and the state; development of class consciousness through propaganda and agitation; leadership of both the economic and the political struggle of the proletariat; coordination of its economic struggle against the bourgeoisie (the factory owners) and its political struggle against the government in a Social-Democratic struggle against class society and its class state; subordination of the economic and political organisation of the proletariat to its Social-Democratic organisation for the sake of the idea of social revolution, as the class interest of the proletariat, which inherently distinguishes it from all the other classes of modern society; and struggle of the Social-Democratic party against capitalism with the goal of diminishing the suffering that inevitably accompanies the expropriation of the toiling masses in such a system.*

---

[113] [In April 1872 Jacoby joined the Social-Democratic Party. Liebknecht had refused to vote for war credits, made an appeal to French and German workers to resist the war, opposed German annexation of Alsace–Lorraine, and expressed solidarity with the Paris Commune both in parliament and in the press. As a result, he was arrested and convicted on charges of 'treasonable intentions', leading to imprisonment for two years. August Bebel, having likewise refused to vote for war credits, was convicted along with Liebknecht.]

[114] [The square in front of Kazan Cathedral, St. Petersburg]

These are the tasks of Russian Social Democracy that are dictated by the peculiarities of Russia's historical development. They are the tasks that must determine both the organisation of the party and also the means it adopts for political struggle.

We must never forget that Social Democracy is the party of *a class*, not a *sect*; that it is a party of the *masses*, not of individuals; and that it aims to make *history*, not histories. *History* is made only by the *masses*. 'The more substantial any historical act, the greater will be the numbers of the masses involved.'[115] And since the masses *unite* mainly through action and struggle, it follows that the Social-Democratic party faces the question of the form of its organisation and the means of its struggle. But in this respect, it must always remember that its entire strength is in the working masses, that it must never isolate itself from the masses, that it must continuously expand its ties with them, and that it must adopt only those means that will not impede the development of class consciousness, obscure it, or contradict the practice of mass struggle.[116]

We must also never forget that precisely because Social Democracy wants to make *history*, it cannot be guided just by the demands of practice. Immediate successes in history do not always lead to final success. *Rira bien qui rira le dernier.*[117] And however difficult it may occasionally be to 'do' something, knowing that you are 'doing' nothing, there are a great many activities in which one must forgo any hope of *immediate success*. The cause of Social Democracy fits into this category. In setting out its demands, it must never diminish them to please 'practical people', for the latter lose sight of the basic

---

[115] [The quotation is from *The Holy Family* by Marx and Engels, Marx and Engels 1845, p. 82]

[116] An analysis of *Iskra's* 'organisational plan' will not be part this brochure. I have already shown the flimsiness of its theoretical basis in the text, and life has demonstrated quite well enough what a fantasy it is. I am convinced that comrade Lenin has already changed 'his method' in order 'to please the comrades'. To replace the 'primitive work' of committees with a capitalist form of domestic industry based on mutual confidence is far easier than to create an organisation with the 'totality' of Social-Democratic groups as its base, and with its highest instance in a congress that controls the activity of both 'the political chiefs' and the local committees. In the first case, the committees know only the 'local' work; in the second, they do only 'local' work and leave what is 'common' to mediation by an office; and in the third, they do the 'common' work within the local conditions. It is enough to read comrade Martov's foreword to 'A Letter to Comrade Propagandists' to see what absurdities can result when one sees the essential need of the proletariat in terms of political education conducted by way of political exposures.

[117] [He who laughs last, laughs best.]

condition of revolutionary activity and reduce it to merely a 'doctrinaire attitude': the work of revolutionaries is to aim as far as possible to the left; to make maximal demands upon reality 'within the limits of existing conditions'; and to leave it to the 'objective logic' of these conditions, which have already been strongly influenced by revolutionary activity, to determine the compromises that are permissible in view of the existing combination of social-economic relations. To anticipate this calculation – which is produced by reality itself and determined by the resultant of the maximum resistance of the given social-economic formation on the one hand, and the maximum of revolutionary forces that have formed within it, on the other – and to replace 'extreme' demands with the results of a 'subjective' calculation, would, of course, be very practical. However, to say it as gently as possible, it would also demonstrate nothing but the immaturity of revolutionary thought.[118]

[…]

Part III: Opportunism dressed up as orthodoxy

Let comrade Lenin speak for himself:

> For wage workers we demand such *reforms* as would 'safeguard them from physical and moral degeneration and raise their fighting capacity'; for the peasants, however, we seek only such *changes* as would help 'to eradicate the remnants of the old serf-owning system and facilitate the free development of the class struggle in the countryside'.[119]

---

[118] [Ryazanov 1903a, pp. 162–5.]

[119] [See Lenin 1902g. Lenin endorsed eventual nationalisation of all the land 'in principle', but his 'immediate' demand was for restitution of the land 'cut-offs' taken from the peasants at the time of the emancipation:

> And so, without harbouring any illusions about it being possible for the small producers to thrive or even to lead a tolerable existence in a capitalist society (such as Russia is becoming to a greater and greater extent), we demand the complete and unconditional revolutionary and not reformative annulment and eradication of the survivals of serf-ownership; we hold that the lands which the government of the nobility cut off from the peasantry and which to this day still serve to keep the peasants in virtual bondage are peasants' lands. Thus, we take our stand – by way of exception and by reason of the specific historical circumstances – as defenders of small property.... (Lenin 1902g, p. 149.)]

For the workers we *demand reforms*, for the peasants we *seek changes*?! Oh wise Oedipus, solve the riddle![120] He continues:

> ...in the workers' section [of the party programme] we have no right to go beyond the bounds of demands for social reform; in the peasants' section, however, we must not stop at social-revolutionary demands. In other words: in the workers' section we are definitely limited by the minimum programme; in the peasants' section we can and must produce a maximum programme.[121]

Evidently, the minimum programme walks on two legs: one is reformist, the other, revolutionary. In order to leave the reader in no doubt on this account, Comrade Lenin continues:

> What we set forth in both sections is not our ultimate aim, but our immediate demands. In both sections we therefore remain on the basis of present-day (= bourgeois) society. Therein lies the similarity between the two sections. However, their fundamental difference consists in the fact that the workers' section contains demands directed against the *bourgeoisie*, whereas the peasants' section contains demands directed against the *serf-owning landlords*.... We cannot present social-revolutionary demands among the immediate demands in the workers' section, since the social revolution which overthrows the rule of the bourgeoisie is the proletarian revolution which achieves our *final* goal. In the peasants' section, we present social-revolutionary demands as well, since the social revolution which overthrows the rule of the serf-owning landlords...is also possible on the basis of the existing order.... In the workers' section, we keep to our stand...in favour of social reforms, for what we are demanding here is only what the bourgeoisie can...concede to us without as yet losing its domination.... In the peasants' section, however, we must, *unlike the social-reformers*, also demand what the

---

[120] [The reference is to Oedipus and the Riddle of the Sphinx. On his way to Thebes, Oedipus killed Laius, the Theban king, not knowing he was his father. He then solved the riddle posed by the Sphinx, received the throne of Thebes as his reward, and ended up marrying his own mother, whom he also did not know. 'Wise' Oedipus unknowingly committed *two cardinal crimes*. In drawing this analogy, Ryazanov evidently has in mind the *two sections* of the programme being discussed by Lenin. The riddle posed by the Sphinx was: What is it that has one voice and yet becomes four-footed and two-footed and three-footed? Oedipus answered: Man, who crawls on all fours in infancy, walks on two feet when grown, and leans on a staff in old age.]
[121] [Lenin 1902g, pp. 117–18.]

feudal-minded landlords will not and cannot give us (or the peasants) – we must also demand what the revolutionary movement of the peasantry can take only by force.[122]

That is why the…criterion of direct and immediate 'feasibility' is applicable in general only to the avowedly reformative sections and clauses of our programme, and by no means to the programme of a revolutionary party in general. In other words, this criterion is applicable to our programme only by way of exception, and by no means as a general rule.[123]

It turns out that to achieve the demands in the agrarian part of the programme presupposes *revolution*, whereas achieving those in the workers' section is possible through *reforms*.[124]

[…]

The programme's authors are victims of 'the pattern'. In Western Europe the Social-Democratic parties have a 'final goal' together with 'immediate demands' that they present to the bourgeois state. But what makes sense in Western Europe is simply nonsense in our country.[125]

[…]

…If even in Western Europe factory laws are frequently nothing but a dead letter, if even there they are observed only when powerful worker's unions insist on the letter of the law, and workers are supported by a powerful Social-Democratic party that knows how to defend the immediate interests of workers, then one would have to be extremely naïve to think that in our country, where strikes are illegal, a factory law might provide a *legal* ground for the workers to present their demands….[126]

[…]

…It is the revisionist tendency [in Western Europe] that has provided our practitioners with the theory they are looking for. Whereas sober-minded Social Democrats in 'the West' [e.g. Eduard Bernstein] want to set aside the maximum programme and keep only the minimum programme (just for the time being, of course), what we are seeing in our own country is a unique

---

[122] [Lenin 1902g, pp. 118–19.]
[123] [Lenin 1902g, p. 119.]
[124] [Ryazanov 1903a, pp. 174–5.]
[125] [Ryazanov 1903a, p. 176.] A letter from a member of the southern group already pointed out this oddity (in No. 25) but *Iskra* did not understand his objection.
[126] [Ryazanov 1903a, pp. 180–1.]

attempt to make Western Social Democracy's minimum programme – the overthrow of autocracy – into our maximum programme, while simultaneously limiting our own minimum programme to political rights for the workers and economic reforms….

…All of this amounts to fear of telling the workers 'the truth, the whole truth': so long as the autocracy exists there is no possibility of any improvement in either the economic or the political position of the working class.[127]

[…]

No! What [must] be shown is that nothing but 'paper' reforms are possible under the autocracy…. *Carthaginem delendam esse!*[128] The issue is not reform or revolution, nor is it reform *and* revolution, it is simply revolution. No reform makes any sense whatever…so long as the autocracy exists…. Only a vulgar philistine could talk of improving the conditions of the working class within a system where 'unparalleled shame and infamy rule'![129]

[…]

…Whereas the programme of the Osvobozhdenie Truda group differed markedly from [Social-Democratic] programmes in other countries by *not including* any minimum programme…the construction of the new draft resembles foreign programmes just like two identical drops of water. Everything 'Russian' in it, everything that suggested we have a way of posing various questions that is different from the way they are posed abroad – all of this has just vanished. Now it turns out that we are nothing special. We have the same kind of minimum programme as our West-European comrades.

And what is a minimum programme? It consists of the *maximum* demands [that is, reforms] that can be made upon the existing system….

…[But] it is more likely the case…that even European Social Democracy will only succeed in achieving its *minimum* programme by way of revolution. That is why Kautsky doubts that any reform, such as the 8-hour working day, might be won by the proletariat prior to its seizure of political power.

With us, there is no point even in speaking of a minimum programme because we have yet to create the [constitutional] conditions in which such a programme might be put forth. The 'existing society and state', to which the

---

127 [Ryazanov 1903a, pp. 182–3.]
128 [Prior to the Third Punic War, Cato the Elder is said to have ended every speech by declaring that 'Carthage must be destroyed!']
129 [Ryazanov 1903a, pp. 187–8.]

minimum programme of West-European social democracy is addressed, is with us still *im Werden*.

The sole demand that we can make upon our existing régime is 'begone!' and do it quickly. Only when we have achieved this 'demand' will we present a whole series of political and economic demands to the régime that will emerge from the purgatory of revolution; not because they *promise* any tangible results, but only because their full and complete implementation will allow us to turn to the still more fundamental matter of destroying the foundations of the whole existing social system.

When we *conjecturally* formulate in our programme the demands that we will put forth at the time of revolution, we must never forget for a moment that our minimum programme has no *practical* significance and refers to no '*positive*' tasks. All it must do is answer the question of what we should demand during the revolution; its purpose is to present these demands to the working masses so that they will know, on the day of revolution, whose banner to gather around, and so that they will not be deceived by the 'honest and incorruptible, wise and educated liberals' of a Zemsky Sobor.[130] In that case the programme will have enormous educational significance.... But this programme...must always remind them that apart from revolution, and until such time as the autocracy is overthrown, there is no hope whatsoever for them of escaping from this hell....[131]

[...]

...The proletariat can never emancipate itself without first seizing political power. Only the dictatorship of the proletariat will put an end to class antagonisms and eliminate class society. That is why, while waging an uninterrupted struggle against the factory owners (the bourgeoisie), the proletariat, knowing its own class interests, sees political struggle as the highest form of its *class* struggle. Only through this kind of struggle can it win the political freedom without which it is impossible to defend its immediate economic interests. By virtue of its own *class* interests, it is the most determined fighter for democratisation of all forms of social and political life. A democratic republic is the form in which the class struggle of the proletariat

---

[130] [Ryazanov is anticipating that liberals will convene an estates-based consultative assembly of the land of the kind that tsars occasionally summoned in the sixteenth and seventeenth centuries.]

[131] [Ryazanov 1903a, pp. 190–2.]

against the bourgeoisie will freely develop. But it must be such in more than name. It must guarantee to every citizen the right to participate in the political life of the entire country, without excluding any class of the population. We have already said…that it is certainly not the working class alone that will overthrow absolutism. 'A state upheaval can be effected by the aggregate actions of many "forces" which, *though hostile to one another*, are nevertheless revolutionary in their attitude to the existing system.'[132] And we must never forget that overthrowing the common enemy is merely the first step, which will immediately be followed by the struggle between 'forces that are hostile to one another'.[133]

[…]

Is it possible for Social Democracy to enter into an *alliance* with bourgeois democracy prior to the fall of the autocracy? Comrade Lenin says yes:

> But an essential condition for such an alliance must be the full opportunity for the socialists to reveal to the working class that its interests are diametrically opposed to the interests of the bourgeoisie.[134]

I believe that such alliances are fraught with danger…. Even in countries that enjoy political freedom, such an *alliance* inevitably results in weakening the Social-Democratic point of view: Social Democracy becomes an appendage of bourgeois democracy and *its* extreme left wing.…

But Comrade Lenin tells us that 'The political demands of working-class democracy do not differ *in principle* from those of bourgeois democracy, they differ only *in degree*'.[135] Again, this is one of those prejudices that are the basis of all the sins of opportunism.[136]

[…]

The fundamental characteristic of democracy is sovereignty[137] of the people, but it is an empty word without the people's complete self-government. 'The people's sovereignty, i.e., concentration of supreme state power in the hands of a legislative assembly consisting of representatives

---

132 G. Plekhanov, *Nashi Raznoglasiya* [Our Differences], p. 246 [Ryazanov's italics. The reference is in Plekhanov 1884, p. 298].
133 [Ryazanov 1903a, pp. 223–4.]
134 [See Lenin 1902h, p. 362.]
135 [See Lenin 1902f, p. 342.]
136 [Ryazanov 1903a, pp. 224–5.]
137 [*Samoderzhavie*]

of the people',[138] as the first point says in the programme of *Iskra* and *Zarya*, must therefore be accompanied by the demand for complete self-government in the state, the provinces [*gubernii*], the cities and the villages [*obshchiny*].

Self-government in the state is a necessary condition in order that the people not become a plaything in the hands of the rulers, that is, *the bureaucracy*. Complete democracy is only possible where the existence of bureaucracy, as an organ independent of the people, is ended....

Every citizen in a democratic state, after reaching a certain age and regardless of sex, has the inalienable right to participate in every function of the supreme state power. The necessary guarantee for this is universal, equal, secret, direct, active and passive suffrage, both in elections to the legislative assembly and in every organ of self-government....[139]

Since bourgeois society by its very nature cannot guarantee equality *in fact*, it must at least provide full equality in all questions of *rights*. Inviolability of the person and the residence; freedom of movement and trade; unrestricted freedom of conscience, speech, the press and assembly; the complete equality of all citizens regardless of race, religion or sex – all of these demands are common to both workers' and bourgeois democracy. But the latter cannot go so far as complete democratisation of all civil and criminal law. Being tied up with the interests of the property owners, it ensures full protection only to those commodity producers who actually produce commodities, as distinct from their own human activity; hired workers, who sell their labour-power as a commodity, or sell themselves, have completely inadequate protection....[140]

[...]

...Only workers' democracy can guarantee to all citizens a secular school and universal free, obligatory, general and professional education. It alone can make education genuinely universal and provide every participating child with books, clothing and meals.[141]

Only workers' democracy can introduce complete democratisation of the entire national economy; only it can completely eliminate all indirect taxes,

---

[138] [The reference is to Lenin 1902a, p. 30.]
[139] ['Active' suffrage refers to the right to vote, 'passive' to the right to be elected.]
[140] [Ryazanov 1903a, pp. 227–9.]
[141] The *Iskra* draft speaks only of *poor* children, making a completely unnecessary distinction.

tariffs and duties, and establish progressive taxation of incomes, inheritances and capital....

But workers' democracy cannot be limited to making these general demands that affect all classes. Representing the class of propertyless workers, who are for this reason compelled to sell their humanity as a commodity, it must ensure for this kind of commodity producer circumstances that do not undermine the very source of his existence; it must oppose the physical, mental and moral degeneration that threatens the working class when the capitalists' 'freedom' to exploit is not restrained by law. And it can only do this by putting forth the demand for universal labour legislation that would embrace all categories of citizens who live, in one way or another, by selling their labour power (including urban and rural workers as well as every kind of servant). This is a demand on which Russian Social Democrats will have to focus their main attention in order to ensure that during the revolutionary period it will be fulfilled as completely as possible. Under the current political régime, any such reform is pure illusion. A partial improvement in the position of the working class can only be achieved and maintained through revolutionary struggle....

The two essential points of such legislation are: first, the complete and unconditional freedom of unions and strikes...and second, the 8-hour working day for every wage-worker without exception....[142]

[...]

If we once establish clearly the differences of principle between the demands of bourgeois and workers' democracy, then the question of how they relate to each other is easy to settle. In this respect, the experience of Marx and Engels is interesting.

Once they recognised their mistake and understood that *liberalism* had renounced its own historical mission, they expected, again relying on the experience of the English and French Revolutions, that the victory of reaction would only be brief and that the revolution would quickly break out again. But since they already believed that no social formation ever disappears until it has developed all its potential, they quite correctly concluded that the task of developing all the 'good' aspects of bourgeois society must be assumed by petty-bourgeois democrats. From the very beginning, however, they

---

[142] [Ryazanov 1903a, pp. 230–2.]

distrusted them and set out the main principles of tactics for the workers' party in the circular of the League of Communists (in March 1850).[143]

They had no wish, besides, to become an appendage of bourgeois democracy. They insisted on creation of an independent workers' party, drawn from the workers' circles, in which the position and interests of the proletariat would be discussed independently of any bourgeois influence. The workers had to organise, and their local organisations had to support the closest possible connections with all workers' societies. They now adamantly opposed any attempt to form a broader opposition party that would embrace all democratic elements because this would jeopardise the special interests of the proletariat. They took the view that even in the event of a struggle against a common foe there was no need for any special alliance. In this case, the interests of both parties would coincide, and cooperation would occur on its own when it became necessary. But during the entire period of struggle, and afterwards, the workers' party must always put forth *its own* demands.

Marx and Engels were again 'mistaken'. The revolution did not resume, yet Engels was correct when he reissued this circular in 1885 and wrote that 'one can still learn something from it even today'.[144] He believed that in the impending revolution the petty-bourgeois democrats might take the helm and Social Democracy would have to adjust its tactics accordingly. Personally, I think Engels overestimated the importance of petty-bourgeois democracy. But whatever the case, bourgeois democracy has yet to say its final word and may yet be the 'saviour' of bourgeois society.

Whereas, in the West, bourgeois democracy has been marginalised by Social Democracy, with us, as a political party, it has yet to utter even its first word.

---

[143] [Ryazanov is referring to 'Address of the Central Committee of the Communist League', where Marx and Engels spoke of the need for a *permanent revolution*:

> Although the German workers cannot come to power and achieve the realization of their class interests without passing through a protracted revolutionary development, this time they can at least be certain that the first act of the approaching revolutionary drama will coincide with the direct victory of their own class in France and will thereby be accelerated. But they themselves must contribute most to their final victory, by informing themselves of their own class interests, by taking up their independent political position as soon as possible, by not allowing themselves to be misled by the hypocritical phrases of the democratic petty bourgeoisie into doubting for one minute the necessity of an independently organized party of the proletariat. Their battle-cry must be: *The Permanent Revolution*. (Marx and Engels 1850, p. 330.)

[144] [Engels 1885, pp. 322–3.]

Meanwhile, the elements needed for emergence of such a party do exist. How should we relate to it *if* it should take shape?

We will extend no 'political credit' to such a party even then. Preserving our own clearly distinctive position, Social Democracy, for its part, will support them if, of course, in addition to universal suffrage, they include in their programme the demand for freedom of unions and strikes. Steady support and temporary joint action, where and when the conditions of battle demand it, together with merciless criticism of all the illusions of bourgeois democracy – that is the policy of Social Democracy in this regard.

For its own part, Social Democracy must strive to retain and continuously fortify its own position as the most decisive and advanced fighter in the struggle to emancipate all oppressed classes and the entire exploited masses. This brings us to the question of the peasantry.[145]

[...]

...Comrade Lenin...thinks that 'There is hardly any need to prove at length that an "agrarian programme" is essential to the Russian Social-Democratic Party.'[146]

...[Yet] he still feels somewhat uncomfortable. He is prepared to support the workers directly, without any reservations or conditions, but he is much more cautious in relation to the peasants:

> ...in our draft programme the inclusion of the 'peasant' demands hinges on two *highly circumscribed conditions*. We make the legitimacy of 'peasant demands' in a Social-Democratic programme dependent, firstly, on the condition that they lead to the eradication of remnants of the serf-owning system and, secondly, that they facilitate the free development of the class struggle in the countryside.[147]

---

[145] [Ryazanov 1903a, pp. 233–5.]

[146] [Lenin 1902g, p. 109.]

[147] [Ryazanov 1903a, p. 244. The quotation is from Lenin 1902g, pp. 111–12. The demands that Lenin proposed on behalf of the peasantry were the following:
    1) abolition of land redemption and quit-rent payments, as well as of all services now imposed on the peasantry as a taxable social-state;
    2) annulment of collective liability and of all laws restricting the peasant in the free disposal of his land;
    3) restitution to the people of all sums taken from them in the form of land redemption and quit-rent payments; confiscation for this purpose of monasterial property and of the royal demesnes, and imposition of a special land tax on members of the big landed nobility who received land redemption

[…]

…The *raison d'être* of Social Democracy is recognition of private property in the means of production as the source of every affliction in modern society. If Social Democracy were to take upon itself the defence and strengthening of one or another form of private property, it would be committing suicide because this would dull the class consciousness of workers and help to preserve the illusions of petty producers. This would undermine all the moral prestige that Social Democracy enjoys as the most far-sighted and truthful of all the parties. That is why 'orthodox' Marxists unconditionally reject any agrarian programme that would have the goal of assisting the peasants as a 'class of modern society'.

---

loans, the revenue thus obtained to be credited to a special public fund for the cultural and charitable needs of the village communes;

4) establishment of peasant committees

a) for the restitution to the village communes (by expropriation, or, when the land has changed hands, by redemption, etc.) of the land cut off from the peasants when serfdom was abolished and now used by the land lords as a means of keeping the peasants in bondage;

b) for the eradication of the remnants of the serf-owning system which still exist in the Urals, the Altai, the Western territory, and other regions of the country;

5) empowerment of courts to reduce exorbitant rents and to declare null and void all contracts entailing bondage.

Anticipating revolution rather than reform, Ryazanov replied that Social Democrats must demand expropriation of *all large estates*: 'This is the minimum demand that a revolutionary party can put forth during a revolutionary period.' Instead of renting this land from the nobility, the peasants might then rent it from the state, which would promote collective farming by associations of agricultural workers (Ryazanov 1903a, pp. 292–3). This was also the view of Marx and Engels in their 'Address of the Central Committee to the Communist League': 'The workers…must demand that the confiscated feudal property remain state property and be used for workers' colonies, cultivated collectively by the rural proletariat with all the advantages of large-scale farming and where the principle of common property will immediately achieve a sound basis in the midst of the shaky system of bourgeois property relations', Marx and Engels 1850, p. 328. On land currently in the peasants' possession, Ryazanov thought the village commune might continue in operation, although individual peasants should have the right to leave. He concluded:

It might happen, of course, that the expropriated land will not remain in the hands of the state, that the peasants will simply divide the seized land amongst themselves, or that the state, guided by the idea of a free turnover of the land, will put the land up for sale as at the time of the great French revolution, and that we will not be able to prevent this. But this is not so terrible. Even in this worst case, this will be the only way to create a real divide between the past and the future and, with a single revolutionary blow, to abolish all remnants of feudalism…(Ryazanov 1903a, p. 293).

> We Russian Social-Democrats [says Lenin, with all the satisfaction of a new Columbus], will try to make use of the experience of Europe, and begin to attract the 'country folk' to the socialist working-class movement *at a much earlier stage and much more zealously* than was done by our Western comrades, who after the conquest of political liberty continued for a long time to 'grope' for the road the industrial workers' movement [?] should follow: in this sphere we shall take much that is ready-made 'from the Germans', *but in the agrarian sphere we may perhaps evolve something new.*[148]

The 'something new' is the discovery that 'There are two sides to all things in the world'.[149] Whereas in the 'West' an agrarian programme that proposed to 'multiply small farming and petty property' would violate the principles of Social Democracy, in the 'East' we have an 'exceptional case'. We support multiplication of small holdings in the interest of eliminating the remnants of serfdom and promoting the free development of class struggle in the countryside, in other words, *in the interest of the development of agrarian capitalism.*

That kind of agrarian programme is truly something 'new'. 'It is clear,' says Kautsky, 'that promoting the economic development of agriculture in a capitalist sense cannot be the purpose of a socialist agrarian programme.' But, when Kautsky adds that such an idea 'never entered anyone's head', he is mistaken: he did not yet know that a 'new' orthodoxy, which has discovered 'something new' concerning agriculture, is coming from the East.... He hadn't yet discovered that Social Democrats have to 'push' capitalism forward or that there are 'exceptional' cases when Social Democrats must 'multiply small holdings' because this will promote the development of capitalism....

Marxism has never assumed the task of promoting the development of class struggle or of introducing it, for this would mean promoting the development of capitalism. Capitalism is developing in the village and in the city, in industry (in the proper sense of the word) and in agriculture. In every case it replaces the

---

[148] One can just imagine what satisfaction this remark gave to the honourable Olenin, who, as we know, is the happy possessor of the greatest collection of quotations from the transcripts of German party congresses in the entire world, showing irrefutably that Social Democrats thought about the peasants much too late and never dealt with this question with sufficient commitment. [The quotation cited in the main text is from Lenin 1902g, p. 136.]

[149] [Lenin 1902g, p. 134.]

struggle between social strata with the struggle between and within classes. In this process the development or introduction of class struggle simply does not involve us as revolutionaries…. Our task is to clarify the uniformity of basic tendencies in capitalist evolution, both in the city and in the village, to show that class antagonism becomes increasingly acute, and to expose mercilessly all illusions concerning an identity of interests between the different classes of toilers. We must show that in both the city and the village, regardless of all variations in the form of capitalist evolution, independent producers are condemned to inevitable destruction and the number of proletarians steadily increases. Condemning any attempt to moderate the struggle between classes, both in the countryside and in the city, we must fulfill our main positive task: the organisation of the proletariat.

The idea of 'introducing the class struggle into the countryside' is just as absurd as introducing class struggle into the city….[150]

[…]

The secret to all the 'obvious absurdities' of *Iskra's* agrarian programme is simply that it is *practically oriented upon the period prior to downfall of the autocracy.*[151]

[…]

> Our agrarian programme [continues Comrade Lenin] is, therefore, calculated in practice mainly for the immediate future, for the period *preceding* the downfall of the autocracy. A political revolution in Russia will at all events lead inevitably to such fundamental changes in our most backward agrarian system that we shall unfailingly have to revise our agrarian programme.[152]

[…]

…Comrade Lenin assures us that after the autocracy has fallen we will have to take another look. But what shall we do in a revolutionary epoch, at the time when autocracy is being liquidated? This is what is being asked by the Social-Democratic agitators we have sent to the countryside.[153]

[…]

---

[150] [Ryazanov 1903a, pp. 246–9.]
[151] [Ryazanov 1903a, p. 277.]
[152] [Ryazanov 1903a, p. 278. Lenin 1902g, pp. 120–1 footnote.]
[153] [Ryazanov 1903a, p. 279.]

How do we move ahead?

…When the authors of the Breslau agrarian programme defended it by saying that it imparted a proper concreteness to the Erfurt Programme, Kautsky quite justifiably called this desire to stuff the programme with 'concrete means' *Detailkramerei*. When they, like Comrade Lenin, referred to the need to 'push forward' the development of agriculture, Kautsky replied that…Social Democracy

> has no part of its task to place even the true interests of agriculture – those in harmony with the interests of society as a whole – in the forefront of its efforts, just as it does not perceive its role as expending its energies in advancing the interests of industry and commerce. This is not because it places a low value on these interests, but rather because it is certain that they have ample opportunity to express themselves in the modern state, and that the state will do everything it can to foster them.

It must act in positive ways and 'push' things forward only when dealing with the interests of the proletariat:

> Social Democracy, whose duty is to be active and positive in the interests of the proletariat, should adopt a basically negative, defensive, posture when it comes to protecting the interests of society at large under present-day circumstances. The positive elements must take a back seat as long as it lacks a real determining influence on political life.[154]

This refers to the Social-Democratic Party at a time when it already enjoys political freedom and has numerous representatives in parliament and in municipal and rural councils. And what can we say of Russian Social Democracy? What can it accomplish in the way of something 'positive'? What 'concrete' means can it devise without incurring the risk of playing into the hands of all the knights of primitive accumulation, without obscuring the class consciousness of the workers, without creating illusions concerning the possibility of partial improvements in the condition of the toiling masses even within the limits of the autocratic system? The answer is: exactly nothing – nothing on behalf of the peasants, and nothing on behalf of the workers.

---

[154] Karl Kautsky, *Die Agrarfrage*, pp. 385–386. [Kautsky 1988, Vol. II, p. 391.]

That is why it is equally senseless to adopt any *minimum* programme that is oriented upon *practical* tasks in the period *preceding* the fall of autocracy, whether we have in mind helping the workers or the peasants. In this sense, there is no difference *in principle* between the demands we make on behalf of the workers or the peasants. Every attempt to conceive such a difference *in principle* between the demands made on behalf of one or the other will lead, and can only lead – as we have seen in the agrarian programme of *Iskra* – to abandonment of *every principle* of international Social Democracy.[155]

[…]

Let us assume that the revolution has already broken out. A Constituent Assembly is summoned, in which the 'wise and educated, honest and incorruptible' liberals will probably be the majority. Social Democrats must know in advance that the arena of their practical activity will not be parliament but the street, that even within parliament their only role will be as conduits for the pressure being put on parliament by their comrades and the workers they have influenced. Their main task will be to prevent the revolutionary tempest from cooling, to drive the revolution forward, and to lead it to its final consequences. The slogan for Social-Democratic activity is *revolution in permanentia* – not 'order' in place of revolution, but revolution in place of order.

The stronger the revolution is in the countryside, and the more the party of order is compelled to dissipate its forces in search of countless enemies, the more successfully will Social Democracy complete its revolutionary work in the cities. This means that the more revolutionary are the demands made by Social Democracy, the more forcefully it intrudes *in fact* upon all the sacred and inviolable rights, the more the people *in fact* seize all their rights and freedoms, and the more numerous the circle of people who have an interest in preserving the revolution's accomplishments – the deeper will be the divide between past and future, and the more favourable will conditions be for the further development of Social Democracy.

The outcome of the revolution itself will to a great extent depend upon the attitude of the peasantry. If we are concerned for the revolution's success, if we hope to secure a social-political victory for the revolutionary party, then we must put forth a whole series of measures in the interests of the peasantry,

---

[155] [Ryazanov 1903a, pp. 285–6.]

who have been unfairly treated by the entire existing regime. This does not mean that we will 'promise' them blessings that we ourselves don't believe can be realised. In the words of the programme of the Osvobozhdenie Truda group, we can say that 'the triumph of the Russian revolutionary movement will be of primary benefit to the peasantry'. And, if we are speaking of material benefits to come from the revolution, there is no doubt that in this respect the peasantry will gain more than the working class. But, even during the revolution, when we are making maximum revolutionary demands on behalf of the peasantry, we must still tell them that if private property in *all* the means of production continues, along with commodity production, then their eventual entry into the ranks of the proletariat will be just as inevitable as it was before, albeit with less torment.

Not wishing to encourage any illusions with respect to their position, we must also avoid deceiving ourselves by overestimating the possible political role of the peasantry. The very conditions of their existence mean that they are an element that is generally incapable of joint political activity. So-called peasant wars have become an important political factor only where the peasant movement has temporarily merged with an urban movement. The peasants are an element of the population in which there is an *identity*, but by no means a community, of interest. They rise up 'like one man' only when, throughout the entire country, they are struck by a series of spontaneous calamities that result from the existing social system and represent the final drop in their cup of misfortune. Local interests continue to prevail, so that whatever their capacity to resist at a particular moment, the peasantry is easily caught with petty bait. The initial outburst soon evaporates, and one village after another abandons the 'common' cause to settle for minor concessions....[156]

[...]

To this point I have been assuming that the Russian revolution will remain an isolated event that will not extend beyond the limits of the Russian Empire. Personally, I consider this most unlikely. In my opinion, it is much more probable that a revolution in Russia would serve as the signal for the West-European revolution. The fate of Russia is today so tied up with the fate of Western Europe that such a fundamental upheaval cannot help but serve as a powerful impetus to the revolutionary movement of the European proletariat.

---

[156] [Ryazanov 1903a, pp. 288–90.]

The position of the latter is today unique. Reaction, supported by the entire bourgeoisie, has prevailed for many years and compelled the proletariat to be extremely cautious. The issue is not so much one of winning new freedoms as of preserving old ones that the bourgeoisie is prepared to give up. German Social Democracy, for example, despite extremely favourable circumstances, is taking no decisive step out of fear that everything won with such hard work will be lost through an ill-conceived outburst. The conditions of the Russian proletariat are different. It has literally nothing to lose and everything to gain. Because of its circumstances, it is also the most revolutionary force in the ranks of the European proletariat. For this reason, we agree completely with Kautsky when he says:

> Having absorbed so much revolutionary initiative from the West, Russia itself may now be ready to serve the West as a source of revolutionary energy. The revolutionary movement that is flaring up in Russia may become the most powerful means for overcoming the spirit of flabby philistinism and sober-minded politicking that is beginning to spread through our ranks; it may reignite the flame of commitment to struggle and passionate devotion to our great ideals…. In 1848 the Slavs were the hard frost that killed the blossoms of the spring of peoples. Now, perhaps, they are destined to be the tempest that will break the ice of reaction and irresistibly bring a new, blessed springtime for the peoples.[157]

This outcome will be all the more likely, the more flaming becomes the spirit of revolutionary protest that has made the proletariat the most revolutionary class of present-day Russia….

And if the revolution of the Russian proletariat becomes the signal for the European proletariat, if the Russian revolution merges with the West-European revolution, if it genuinely 'breaks the ice of reaction' that has frozen the revolutionary energy of the European proletariat, then our revolution will be the immediate prologue of the social revolution.

Whatever happens, if we wish to give faithful voice to the most revolutionary class of present-day society, we Russian Social Democrats must work in such a way that the impending revolution, which will unquestionably occur on the basis of bourgeois relations of production and in that sense will certainly

---

[157] [Kautsky 1902b. See above, pp. 64–5].

be 'bourgeois', will also, from beginning to end, be *proletarian* in the sense that the proletariat will be its leading element and will make its class imprint on the entire movement. We must avoid diminishing the scope of our own revolutionary work in advance by persuading ourselves that our victory will benefit mainly the bourgeoisie. Instead, we must continuously broaden and deepen our efforts to create even now the conditions that will shorten the period of transition from the coming 'political' revolution to the ensuing social revolution. We must work to convert the political into the direct prologue of the social revolution. For this purpose, we must repudiate revisionism in all its forms. In all our activity, we must place the question of *revolution* on the order of the day. We must prepare, and prepare ourselves, *for the revolution.*

Regardless of what various philistines may say, and no matter how hard various 'critics' try to argue on behalf of 'peaceful' progress, the words of Marx are every bit as true today as they were fifty-five years ago:

> It is only in an order of things in which there are no more classes and class antagonisms that social evolutions will cease to be political revolutions. Till then, on the eve of every general reshuffling of society, the last word of social science will always be:
>
> *Le combat ou la mort; la lutte sanguinaire ou le néant. C'est ainsi que la question est invinciblement posée.*[158]

---

[158] [Ryazanov 1903a, pp. 295–8. See Marx 1847, p. 212. Marx is quoting from the novel Jean Žiska by George Sand: 'Combat or death: bloody struggle or extinction. That is how the question is inexorably posed.']

Chapter Three

'Orthodox' Pedantry (1903)

G.V. Plekhanov

The fundamental theme of Plekhanov's reply to Ryazanov is stated near the end of this essay:[1] 'The real question is how to achieve the triumph of a democratic republic.' Whereas Ryazanov anticipated movement *beyond* a bourgeois revolution, Plekhanov believed Russia was about to win a constitutional order that would finally eliminate remnants of serfdom and establish a law-governed régime of private property and civil liberties. In *Plekhanov: The Father of Russian Marxism*, Samuel H. Baron summarised Plekhanov's thinking this way:

> In keeping with his long-held strategy, Plekhanov was most preoccupied during the revolutionary crisis of 1904–6 with the question of the relations between the bourgeoisie and the proletariat. In his estimation, the developing upheaval could only be a bourgeois revolution, and, inevitably, the bourgeoisie would have a prominent part in it; but the proletariat was destined to strike the decisive blows. Provided each played its prescribed role, absolutism would be overthrown, the bourgeoisie would become the governing power in a democratic regime, and

---

[1] Plekhanov 1903, pp. 371–410.

> the proletariat would be in possession of the rights which would enable it
> to prepare for its economic emancipation later on.[2]

Plekhanov's position, adds Baron, was 'a logical consequence of an unshakable attachment to Marx's theory of an economically determined sequence of historical stages. In that context, Russia's upheaval could be only a "bourgeois" revolution'[3] (with, of course, all the reservations already pointed out in our introduction to Ryazanov's criticism of the *Iskra* programme).

The background to Plekhanov's expectations can be traced through his successive drafts of a Social-Democratic programme for Russia. Although he believed the Russian empire was subject to general laws of history, in the *Programme of the Social-Democratic Emancipation of Labour Group*[4] (1883) Plekhanov had written that all socialist parties must take into account the specific circumstances of their respective countries. In Russia, where 'rising capitalism' coexisted with 'obsolescent patriarchal economy', this meant socialists must simultaneously

> organise the workers for the struggle against the bourgeoisie and wage war
> against the survivals of old pre-bourgeois social relationships, which are
> harmful both to the development of the working class and to the welfare
> of the whole people.[5]

With a proper constitutional order, all the bourgeois freedoms would be established (including democratic elections and freedom of conscience, speech, the press, assembly and association). At the same time, Plekhanov wrote, a 'radical revision of our agrarian relations' would put an end to the peasants' redemption payments for land acquired in 1861, thereby facilitating the extension of private agricultural property in place of traditional communal organisation.

Just four years later, in the *Second Draft Programme of the Russian Social-Democrats* (1887), Plekhanov used similar language but elaborated his comments on agriculture. Capitalism was still 'striving to become dominant' in the country as a whole, but the village commune remained a means of 'enslaving the peasant population to the state' and hindering 'their intellectual

---

[2] Baron 1963, p. 263.
[3] Baron 1963, p. 265.
[4] The Osvobozhdenie Truda group.
[5] Plekhanov 1883b.

and political development'. Victory of the revolutionary movement 'would be first and foremost profitable to the peasants', and genuine emancipation of the peasants would accelerate class struggle: 'The disintegration of the village commune is creating…a new class of [the] industrial proletariat.... [T]his class responds to the call of the revolutionaries more easily than the backward rural population.' The proletarian ejected from the commune would 'return there as a Social-Democratic agitator'.[6]

Although Plekhanov and Lenin had numerous differences over details while drafting the new *Iskra* programme in 1902–3, for the moment the two men were in fundamental agreement. All the themes embraced by Lenin in 'The Agrarian Programme of Russian Social-Democracy'[7] were easily reconciled with Plekhanov's statements. Both men agreed that capitalism had finally become the dominant mode of production; both stressed the urgency of eliminating 'remnants' of serfdom; and both anticipated that the revolution would bring new 'juridical institutions' compatible with political liberty.[8] Plekhanov's proposals for the *Iskra* programme laid particular emphasis upon the need for coherence between the capitalist mode of production and its legal institutions:

> As the most outstanding of all survivals of our serf-owning system and the most formidable bulwark of all this barbarism, the tsarist autocracy is wholly incompatible with political and civil liberties, which have long been in existence in the advanced countries of capitalist production, as the natural legal complement to that production. By its very nature it must crush every social movement and is bound to be the bitterest enemy of all the proletariat's emancipatory aspirations.
>
> For these reasons, Russian Social-Democracy advocates as its immediate political task the overthrow of the tsarist autocracy and its replacement by a republic based on a democratic constitution....[9]

---

[6] Plekhanov 1887a, pp. 81–4.

[7] Lenin 1902g.

[8] See Lenin 1902b, pp. 19–27; see also Lenin 1902a, pp. 27–33; and Lenin 1902c, pp. 37–57.

[9] Quoted by Lenin 1902a. In the final draft of the *Iskra* programme, adopted at the Party's second congress in 1903, this section was abbreviated to read as follows:
> In Russia, where capitalism has already become the dominant mode of production, there are still numerous vestiges of the old pre-capitalist order, where the toiling masses were serfs of the landowners, the state,

In the final version of the *Iskra* programme, adopted at the Party's Second Congress in 1903, Plekhanov's reference to political and civil liberties as the 'natural legal complement' of capitalist production was excised – after Lenin complained that the word 'natural' 'smacks, reeks, of a sort of liberalism' – but the fact remained that, for Plekhanov, the appropriate response to Russia's peculiar development was to make it conform with the West-European 'pattern' as expeditiously as possible. The job of the proletariat in the bourgeois revolution was to ensure the final 'triumph of a democratic republic' and only thereafter to begin the struggle for socialism as the final goal.

Plekhanov saw in Ryazanov's critique of the *Iskra* programme an echo of Narodnik utopianism. Ryazanov expressed a clear respect for the Narodnik revolutionaries, notwithstanding their populist limitations, that contradicted the new view that the Social-Democratic Party should be promoting the advance of rural capitalism. Whereas Plekhanov and Lenin attributed peasant distress to 'remnants' of serfdom, Ryazanov answered that the real problem lay in the 'rudiments' of capitalism. If 'remnants' of serfdom were the issue, Plekhanov and Lenin thought the task of Social Democrats was to *promote* a consistently capitalist form of agriculture, which, in turn, would accelerate class struggle in the countryside. But if the peasants' afflictions were attributable to 'rudiments' of capitalism, then Ryazanov insisted that the task of Social Democrats was first and foremost to *forestall* further capitalist development by way of *permanent revolution*. This was one major source of disagreement.

The other was closely related and concerned the role of liberals in the impending revolution. In the original programme of Osvobozhdenie Truda, written in 1883, Plekhanov had denied any significant role to liberals saying they were 'incapable of taking the *initiative* in the struggle against absolutism'.[10]

---

or the sovereign. Greatly hampering economic progress, these vestiges [or 'remnants'] interfere with the many-sided development of the class struggle, help to preserve and strengthen the most barbarous forms of exploitation by the state and the propertied classes of the millions of peasants, and thus keep the whole people in darkness and subjection. The most outstanding among these relics of the past, the mightiest bulwark of all this barbarism, is the tsarist autocracy. By its very name it is bound to be hostile to any social movement, and cannot but be utterly opposed to all the aspirations of the proletariat toward freedom.

[10] Plekhanov 1883c, pp. 55–8. In *Our Differences (Nashi raznoglasiya)* Plekhanov wrote: 'Our capitalism will fade before it has time to blossom *completely* – a guarantee for

The 1887 draft still spoke of 'the powerlessness and timidity' of 'educated sections of the higher classes'.[11] But the *Iskra* programme of 1903 declared that in pursuit of its 'immediate goals' the party would 'support any opposition or revolutionary movement directed against the existing social and political order in Russia'.[12]

Plekhanov's response to Russian exceptionalism was to make Russia *less exceptional*. Ryazanov, on the contrary, thought an exceptional past pointed to an exceptional revolution, a *permanent revolution*, in which an entirely new *socialist* 'pattern' would be established both for Russia and for Europe. While Plekhanov looked for allies among the 'upper classes' of Russia, Ryazanov said

> it is much more probable that a revolution in Russia would serve as the signal for the West-European revolution. The fate of Russia is today so tied up with the fate of Western Europe that such a fundamental upheaval cannot help but serve as a powerful impetus to the revolutionary movement of the European proletariat.

In terms of the role of liberals, Ryazanov was quite correct in saying that in 1902–3 Plekhanov had abandoned his own programme of twenty years earlier. At the same time, however, Plekhanov could point to equally clear elements of continuity, particularly on agrarian issues. In his reply to Ryazanov, which we have translated here, Plekhanov denied any change of his own views and, by implication, any possibility that Lenin had played the role of 'serpent-tempter' in manipulating his thinking. As the 'father' of Russian Marxism, Plekhanov was outraged by Ryazanov's critique and interpreted it as a personal insult. Giving the title '"Orthodox" Pedantry' to his response, Plekhanov contemptuously dismissed Ryazanov in an essay that was as condescending as Ryazanov's was insightful. While it provided little insight of its own, Plekhanov's response strikingly clarified the differences between these two opposing appraisals of the 'peculiarities' of Russian history and the impending consequences.[13]

---

which we find in the powerful influence of international relations.' See Plekhanov 1884, p. 335.

[11] Plekhanov 1887b.

[12] Mc Neal (ed.) 1974, p. 45.

[13] Despite Plekhanov's dogmatism regarding the bourgeois character of the Russian revolution, clearly evident in the present document, his 1914 *History of Russian Social*

* * *

'"Orthodox" Pedantry'

N. Ryazanov has devoted all of 302 pages to criticising our draft programme of the Russian Social-Democratic Workers' Party.[14] This is very fine, of course, and I would be the first to commend him for his diligence and thank him for paying us so much attention if only his critique shed just a little new light on questions concerning our programme. Unfortunately, this is exactly what it does not do. Ryazanov clarifies nothing and confuses a great deal. His critique is about as pointless as a virgin dedicating herself to God. Moreover, it is insufferably petty and pretentious. It cannot help but bring to mind Molière's '*précieuses ridicules*'.[15] The reader can imagine, therefore, just how delightful

---

Thought – Plekhanov 1926 – was much more nuanced so that Trotsky thought it provided a suitable background for his own analysis. This is what Trotsky wrote in 1922:

> It is perfectly true that a few years later (in 1914) Plekhanov formulated a view of the peculiar features of Russia's historical development which was very close to the one put forward in [my book]…*Our Revolution*. Plekhanov quite rightly dismisses the schematic theories of both the doctrinaire 'Westerners' and the Slavophile Narodniks on this subject, and, instead, reduces Russia's 'special nature' to the concrete, materially determined peculiarities of her historical development. It is radically false to claim that Plekhanov drew any compromising conclusions from this (in the sense of forming a bloc with the Kadets, etc.), or that he could have done so with any semblance of logic.
>
> The weakness of the Russian bourgeoisie and the illusory nature of Russia's bourgeois democracy undoubtedly represent very important features of Russia's historical development. But it is precisely from this, given all other existing conditions, that the possibility and the historical necessity of the proletariat's seizure of power arises. True, Plekhanov never arrived at this conclusion. But then neither did he draw any conclusion from another of his unquestionably correct propositions, namely: 'The Russian revolutionary movement will triumph as a working class movement or it will not triumph at all.' If we mix up everything Plekhanov said against the Narodniks and the vulgar Marxists with his Kadetophilia and his patriotism, there will be nothing left of Plekhanov. Yet in reality a good deal is left of Plekhanov, and it does no harm to learn from him now and again. (See L. Trotsky 1971a, Ch. 27, 'On the Special Features of Russia's Historical Development: A Reply to M.N. Pokrovsky'.)

[14] See his book: Ryazanov 1903a.

[15] [In Molière's play of the same title, the *précieuses ridicules* are pretentious but foolish young women who fall in love with their suitors' valets thinking they are wittier than their masters.]

it is to read this new work from Ryazanov and what pleasure comes from exploring it! It is pure torment and about as bothersome as a toothache.

But please do not think, dear reader, that I am speaking ill of Ryazanov's book just to take revenge because he criticised me: 'There now, you criticise us, and we laugh at you.' No, not at all! Even if we were vindictive and able to take revenge on a party comrade because of his criticism, the essay by Ryazanov would still not lead us to think in such terms: the kind of criticism that he makes is no threat to us because every reader with the least sense will probably see at once that it makes absolutely no serious or thoughtful contribution to the subject matter. Moreover, speaking for myself, even if I were biased in my literary reviews, I would be more inclined to praise Ryazanov's book than to censure it. He frequently refers to my writing most approvingly, and in one place he even ranks me among the most accomplished theoreticians of modern socialism. This is obviously a very great compliment; so great, indeed, that I hesitate and fear to ask myself whether I am so deserving. After all, have I never written anything pedantic? Do I not myself remind people of Molière's *prècieuses ridicules*? Nevertheless, I take some consolation from the thought that Ryazanov by no means approves of me completely. To be precise, he praises only my older works, whereas the things that I have written in *Zarya* and *Iskra* do not warrant his approval. Speaking honestly, I must say that I am not indifferent to my own past work, and I would be very upset to think that my book *Our Differences*, for example, or my articles in *Sotsial Demokrat*, suffered from the same kind of ridiculous literary pedantry that blossoms so luxuriously on the pages of Ryazanov's book. But eventually I consoled myself with at least one thought; I told myself that if Ryazanov felt obliged to praise my older work but could only shrug his shoulders in bewilderment at the most recent things I have done, the truth of the matter is that his view had nothing to do with the *content* or the *merit* of either.…Ryazanov approves of my past works not because he thinks they are good, but only because he *must* do so for certain reasons that are completely extraneous…in character. There is no reason, therefore, for me to be distressed by his praise.[16]

* * *

---

[16] [Plekhanov 1903, pp. 371–2.]

What he wants to show, you see, is that the precursor of Russian Social Democracy, the Osvobozhdenie Truda group,[17] had the correct point of view until Lenin, the serpent, led it into temptation. He laments the fall into sin, but at the same time he understands that there were mitigating circumstances and – as if to shake free of the serpent's coils – he is even prepared to wipe things clean. He proposes that our party reject the draft programme worked out by the editors of *Zarya* and *Iskra* and adopt instead the older draft of the Osvobozhdenie Truda group with some modifications. He obviously considers his suggestion to be extremely flattering to the members of that group and hopes they will support it. That kind of 'music' would be very pleasing to Ryazanov, but we do not have the slightest intention of accommodating him.

In the first place, Ryazanov is terribly mistaken in thinking that the current draft programme, of which he is so critical, was imposed upon us, the former members of Osvobozhdenie Truda, by the serpent-tempter. The serpent-tempter never imposed anything but always acted in complete ideological agreement with us[18] as a like-minded comrade who understood just as well as we did the enormous importance for our work of a correct theory, and who had no intention whatever of sacrificing theory to *practice*.[19] And if the draft programme that we are now proposing to Russian Social Democracy is flawed in some way, then the flaws are just as much our responsibility – mine, P. Axelrod's and V. Zasulich's – as they are the responsibility of Lenin or any other member of our editorial collective.[20] It is high time for Ryazanov and other penetrating 'readers', who so love to gossip about *Iskra* and *Zarya*, to memorise my categorical statement on this matter once and for all. The legend of the serpent-tempter, which is being so zealously cultivated nowadays by certain lovers of poetic fiction, must be disposed of for good.

In the second place, our present draft programme is, in fact, simply the *old draft of the* Osvobozhdenie Truda *group* re-issued with the appropriate changes. Ryazanov does not accept the changes, but we are convinced that they are

---

[17] [The Emancipation of Labour group.]

[18] [See Lenin's frequent criticism's of Plekhanov's draft in Lenin 1902a].

[19] [Plekhanov is implying that Ryazanov, supposedly an 'economist', attached greater importance to trade-union work than to political 'theory'.]

[20] [Members of the *Iskra* editorial collective were G.V. Plekhanov, P.B. Axelrod, V.I. Zasulich, Y.O. Martov, A.N. Potresov, and V.I. Lenin.]

necessary. Indeed, if our party assigned us to write up a new programme, taking the older draft of our group as the starting point, we would not hesitate in the least to put forth, paragraph by paragraph, exactly the draft that is now associated with the editors of *Iskra* and *Zarya*. We could not possibly write up any other draft, and the reason is simply that no other draft could possibly represent our views more accurately.[21]

* * *

...Let us consider the *practical* tasks of our party.[22] According to Ryazanov, *Iskra* resolves these tasks wretchedly: here the opportunism of our editorial board reaches a climax; here the pliability of the former Osvobozhdenie Truda group is such that the 'old revolutionary programme of Russian Social Democracy' has been relegated completely to the archive. This is truly horrible. And if this horror is not just something thought up by our merciless critic, then one must acknowledge that the former Osvobozhdenie Truda group, which produced the 'old revolutionary programme of Russian Social Democracy' and then relegated it 'to the archive' at the insistence of the serpent-tempter, is directly guilty of *betrayal*.

But why does the prosecutor not frighten us?

Let us look at the grounds for the accusation. Ryazanov is most distressed, for example, by that part of our draft programme that says capitalism in Russia, while it has already become the prevailing mode of production, still encounters at every step remnants of the old precapitalist social order, which are hindering economic progress and preventing a comprehensive development of the proletariat's class struggle. As is customary for him, at this point Ryazanov resorts to irony.

'What's Hecuba to him?'[23] – he exclaims –

---

[21] [Plekhanov 1903, pp. 372–3.]

[22] [Here the translation resumes on Plekhanov's page 387. The omitted pages deal mainly with overproduction and the theory of crises. Ryazanov did discuss these topics in Ryazanov 1903a, but neither he nor Plekhanov contributed anything original and what they did say was not related to political tactics or to the issue of permanent revolution.]

[23] [The reference is to Shakespeare's Hamlet. Ryazanov was comparing the authors of the *Iskra* programme to the actor observed by Hamlet: they were making a show of their grief over the lack of 'economic progress'. In his soliloquy in Act 2, Scene 2, Hamlet comments on the actor's portrayal of passionate grief:
What's Hecuba to him, or he to Hecuba,
That he should weep for her?

> How does economic *progress* find its way into a Social-Democratic programme? And can it really be the case that we must promote economic *progress* in order to facilitate the comprehensive development of proletarian class struggle?[24]

It seems to Ryazanov that the word *progress* is not merely excessive but even completely impermissible in a Social-Democratic programme. He reminds us that Marx 'never spoke of economic *progress*, only of economic development'.[25] In our eyes, of course, the example provided by the author of *Capital* will always be very instructive; however, without dwelling on *words*, and preferring instead to detect their hidden *meanings*, we invite Ryazanov to recall the preface to the first edition of Volume I of *Capital* where it is said, among other things, that Germany, along with all the rest of continental Europe, suffers not only from the development of capitalist production but also from the inadequacy of its development.

> Alongside of modern evils, a whole series of inherited evils oppress us, arising from the passive survival of antiquated modes of production, with their inevitable train of social and political anachronisms. We suffer not only from the living, but from the dead.[26]

Is it true, as Ryazanov supposes, that Marx saw no need to help in overcoming these relics of the past? And if Marx did see such a need, then how does it happen that we are guilty of betraying Marxism when we aim to abolish the

---

What would he do
Had he the motive and the cue for passion
That I have? He would drown the stage with tears
And cleave the general ear with horrid speech,
Make mad the guilty and appal the free, Confound the ignorant, and amaze indeed
The very faculties of eyes and ears.]

[24] [Ryazanov 1903a] p. 211. Ryazanov pointed out in this connection that the 1887 programme, although written at a time when Plekhanov thought 'modern capitalist production' was 'as yet only striving to become dominant', gave not the 'slightest hint' that the task of Social Democrats, in the name of progress, was 'to eliminate the obstacles standing in the way of its development': 'Even in *Our Differences* comrade Plekhanov ridiculed L. Tikhomirov, who fancied that a Russian Social Democrat would have to "take up the cause" of capitalism's development.'].

[25] Ibid., p. 212. [Ryazanov's italics. In other words, Marx did not consider capitalism to represent unqualified 'progress', nor did he urge socialists to promote such 'progress', whereas Plekhanov thought Social Democrats must help in achieving a coherent capitalist order as a precondition for an effective struggle for socialism.]

[26] [Marx, preface to the first German edition of *Capital*, Marx 1976.]

countless fragments of the precapitalist order that still survive in Russia? How can it be that a task regarded as necessary and inevitable in the programme of Marx and his West-European comrades has become inappropriate and even a matter that compromises us when it appears in the programme of *Russian* Social Democrats?

But why must you speak of economic *progress*? – exclaims an agitated Ryazanov – Why not speak simply of *development*?

We reply: Calm down your Honour! Remember that we take a *dialectical* point of view, and from this point of view *the process of development has two sides: emergence and destruction*, in other words, *progress* and *regression*. Not being *reactionaries*, we necessarily side with *progress* and consider ourselves obliged to struggle against every phenomenon and every institution that delays the *progressive movement of social relations*. If we thought otherwise, then we would resemble those 'true' German socialists of the forties, who were so sarcastically mocked by the *Manifesto of the Communist Party* and with whom you have so much in common. Like them, you have a pedantic love for clever expressions but are completely incapable of *dialectical thought*, without which it is impossible either to resolve or even to formulate properly the revolutionary tasks of our time.

The real extent of Ryazanov's inability to abandon the point of view of *metaphysics*, which reasons according to the formula 'Yea is yea; nay is nay; whatsoever is more than these cometh of evil', is obvious in the following example.In a review that I wrote and that was published in *Zarya* concerning *Russia on the Eve of the Twentieth Century*, a book by an anonymous author, I characterised a certain type of Russian liberals by using the words 'wise and educated, honest and incorruptible'. Ryazanov apparently finds this description extremely amusing. He continually returns to it and each time, so to speak, rolls about in laughter. What seems especially comical to him is the fact that I also included among this kind of liberals the unknown author of the work I was reviewing, who referred quite negatively to Chernyshevsky[27] and his co-thinkers. Obviously, Ryazanov is firmly convinced that such an attitude towards our great enlighteners could only be adopted by people who

---

[27] [Chernyshevsky, Nikolai Gavrilovich (1828–89) was a revolutionary socialist and forerunner of the Narodniks. Marx regarded Chernyshevsky as a 'great Russian scholar and critic'. See Marx 1961, p. 15.]

are stupid, uneducated, dishonourable and corrupt. That kind of conviction on his part shows what great respect he has for people who genuinely deserve such respect. But it also demonstrates his truly childish naïveté and his complete inability to understand the dialectic of feelings and attitudes that emerges from *social struggle*. Chernyshevsky himself understood this dialectic very well, and that is why he would regard his infantile and naïve defender with real pity.

Ryazanov is very disapproving of our general attitude towards liberals, in which he sees one of the clearest proofs of our opportunism. He eagerly emphasises this presumed evidence, knowing that this aspect of our tactical views is not yet fully understood by those Russian Social Democrats who *have yet to overcome fully the prejudices of 'economism'*.[28] Here, as elsewhere, Ryazanov does not explain the question but merely confuses it. For that reason, I think it will be of some interest to pause and deal with it.

Our relation to the different political parties that exist in Russia today can be defined by the words of the *Manifesto of the Communist Party*, which says: *'the Communists everywhere support every revolutionary movement against the existing social and political order of things'*.[29] It is obvious that the more profound and serious its *revolutionary* significance, the more we sympathise with any particular social movement. But it is *only the party of the proletariat, only Social Democracy*, that is revolutionary in the most complete and most profound sense of the word. By comparison, all other parties can be recognised as revolutionary *only to a degree, only within certain limits that are sometimes very restrictive.* Unable to take the proletarian point of view, the revolutionaries of other parties cannot help but include in their social-political propaganda and agitation *an element of narrowness and narrow-mindedness.* Insofar as this element contradicts our own *propaganda and agitation*, confuses the minds of workers, or is *conservative* or even *reactionary*, we consider ourselves compelled to enter a life-or-death *struggle against* it, allowing no confusion to result from reproaches levelled against us in this regard by certain naïve readers or listeners. This is the reason for our *'passion for polemics'*, which everyone is aware of and which causes such indignation. But precisely because this

---

[28] [In other words, those who preferred to struggle against capitalist employers rather than support political liberals.]

[29] [Marx and Engels 1848a.]

'passion' is conditioned by our extreme revolutionary point of view *and by that alone*, we give their due even to our most stubborn and committed political opponents whenever they take any resolute steps in the struggle against the existing order, provided they *do not attempt to obscure the class consciousness of workers*, and we do so without being confused by any 'dogmas' or 'schemes'. And this is why we appear to be *'opportunists'* to certain irrationally zealous defenders of 'orthodoxy'. That, in general terms, is our relation to other parties. And as for *liberals* in particular, we regard them as representatives of the bourgeoisie and relate to them in exactly the same way as Marx and Engels related to the German liberal bourgeoisie in the late forties of the last century. The *Communist Manifesto* says:

> In Germany the communists fight with the bourgeoisie whenever it acts in
> a revolutionary way against absolute monarchy, the feudal squirearchy and
> the petty bourgeoisie. But they never cease, for a single instant, to instil into
> the working class the clearest possible recognition of the hostile antagonism
> between the bourgeoisie and the proletariat.[30]

Ryazanov himself knows very well that in this respect we are faithfully following the example of Marx and Engels, and that is why he declares that *Marx and Engels were mistaken in their understanding of the prospective political role of the German bourgeoisie at that time*. Without getting involved in an examination of this historical issue, I will limit myself to three brief observations.

In the first place, if our relation to the liberal bourgeoisie is mistaken, then it turns out that we are in pretty good company, namely, *with the authors of the Communist Manifesto*.

Secondly, it is worth noting that in order to prove our *deviation from orthodoxy*, Ryazanov had *to accuse Marx and Engels themselves of being in error*.

In the third place, the error that our critic attributes to us could not possibly be of any practical significance even if it were a fact. To use Ryazanov's words, this error consists of *overestimating* the progressive role of our bourgeoisie. Suppose we really are overestimating them. What are the practical consequences of such overestimation? Do we cease, as a result, to develop in the minds of workers a consciousness of the opposition between their interests

---

[30] [*Ibid.*]

and those of the bourgeoisie? Do we strive even in the least to curtail the class struggle that is occurring in our country? Anyone who is familiar with our publications and wants to keep a clear conscience will say that nothing of the sort has ever occurred and that we always clearly and resolutely defend the proletariat's class point of view. *Our supposedly exaggerated expectations of the bourgeoisie do not cause us to diverge even by a hair's breadth from the line that we would follow if we had no such expectations at all.* It follows that to reproach us for them merely means to encourage a completely futile argument over a question of 'expectations', for which there is no possibility of finding any exact way of coming to a conclusion. I am aware that it is precisely these 'expectations' that explain our supposed heresy of wanting, as comrade Lenin put it, to go out *among all classes of society*.[31] It is precisely this wish that suggests to certain of our critics a betrayal of the proletariat. But here again we see that people are dealing with *words* without clarifying for themselves what their *meanings* are. When the ideologists of the French bourgeoisie in the XVIII century 'went' among the aristocracy, recruiting fighters for a new social order, did they betray the *point of view of their own class*? Not at all. No such betrayal occurred, only a perfectly correct political calculation (or, if you will, instinct), which led to an even more consistent affirmation of exactly the same point of view. And will there be any betrayal if ideologists of the proletariat go among the 'upper' classes with the goal of finding means and resources that might serve the interests of Social Democracy? It would appear that in this case, too, there will no betrayal; here again, the 'reaching out' will be a matter of political

---

[31] [The reference is to chapter three of Lenin 1902h. Lenin argued that Social Democrats must cultivate support among all classes of the population:

> We must 'go among all classes of the population' as theoreticians, as propagandists, as agitators, and as organisers.…The principal thing…is *propaganda* and *agitation* among all strata of the people. The work of the West European Social-Democrat is in this respect facilitated by the public meetings and rallies which *all* are free to attend, and by the fact that in parliament he addresses the representatives of *all* classes. We have neither a parliament nor freedom of assembly; nevertheless, we are able to arrange meetings of workers who desire to listen to *a Social-Democrat*. We must also find ways and means of calling meetings of representatives of all social classes that desire to listen to *a democrat*; for he is no Social-Democrat who forgets in practice that 'the Communists support every revolutionary movement', that we are obliged for that reason to expound and emphasise *general democratic tasks before the whole people*, without for a moment concealing our socialist convictions. (Lenin 1902h, p. 425.)

calculation. There is, therefore, nothing here to debate from the standpoint of *principle*. All that remains is a question of *practical opportunities*. Do there exist among Russia's 'upper' classes such means and resources as might render some service to our movement? Yes, they *still do exist* to a considerable degree, and it would be a very, very great pity for us not to make use of them. Furthermore, do there exist within our own midst such people, and even whole groups of people, who are not able to work among the *proletariat* but who could establish lasting and beneficial relations for us with so-called *society*? There is no doubt that such people do exist, so that this part of the question can be solved quite simply: a 'reaching out' to all classes of society – within the limits we have noted – is both possible and necessary. Let there be no confusion among us regarding any betrayal of our principles in this matter. A betrayal can happen for completely different reasons. It is possible to betray the proletariat *without departing even for an instant from its midst.* All that is needed is to lose clear sight *of the dividing line that separates its interests from the interests of other classes.* But as far as this kind of loss is concerned, it cannot be encouraged by the propaganda either of *Iskra* or of *Zarya*. The fact is that we are famous for our 'passion for polemics' precisely because we have always, everywhere, decisively, and ruthlessly defended the *proletariat's class point of view.*

From all of this, the reader can see just how far *Iskra* and *Zarya* are from any intention of consigning to the archive 'the old revolutionary programme of Russian Social Democracy'. If such a programme ever existed – and it certainly did exist – then *Iskra* and *Zarya* must have been its best and most reliable defenders. They fearlessly defended it during the dismal period when *real* opportunists from all sides raised an outcry against it, and they are doing so now, when thanks to these same organs the efforts of these opportunists have completely failed. To accuse them today of betraying 'orthodoxy' at a time when, thanks again to *Iskra* and *Zarya*, a *revolutionary* direction has finally triumphed in our Social Democracy, can only be an act of displaying one's own mental poverty or of speculating on the mental poverty of other readers for some sort of reasons that are *purely personal.*

Nothing further needs to be said on this matter.

After lecturing us on the theme that there is 'no place' in a Social-Democratic programme for struggle against the remnants of precapitalist social relations, Ryazanov then undertakes to demonstrate for us that the institutions – he speaks of 'phenomena' – that we take to be *remnants* of the old social order, must in fact be regarded as *'rudiments'* of a new order, of *capitalism* to be precise.[32] The proofs that he adduces in this case are so typical of this would-be critic that I cannot resist the temptation to reproduce at least a few of the more remarkable ones.

He says:

> Meanwhile, there is an even greater question as to whether all those phenomena that are cited in the *Iskra* programme as being due to 'remnants' should really be attributed to 'remnants' rather than to the 'rudiments' of capitalism. Would there be any need for us to be concerned with 'a radical review of the conditions of the peasants' emancipation' if this 'emancipation' was prepared not by 'popular production'[33] but instead by 'capitalism based upon *corveé* labour', that is, by landlords who were already tempted by the practice of squeezing out 'surplus-value' together with the state, which was just as interested as they were in the development of capitalism?[34]

These lines were written, as the reader will see, in an extremely awkward manner, and for that reason it is no easy matter to understand just what they mean. But to the extent that any understanding is possible, they have to be

---

[32] [If, as Ryazanov claimed, exploitation was more a result of capitalist 'rudiments' than the 'remnants' of serfdom, the obvious implication was that Social Democrats must fight against capitalism rather than promoting its development in the name of economic 'progress'.]

[33] [The 'legal populist' V.P. Vorontsov hoped to avoid capitalist primitive accumulation by moving to socialised labour on the basis of the peasant commune. Andrzej Walicki writes: 'In historical development of economic relationships he saw…three stages: (1) the pre-industrial popular production, (2) the 'socialization of labour' in the process of industrialization, and finally (3) the socialized 'popular production', i.e. socialism (the word 'socialism' was avoided for the sake of Tsarist censorship).' See Walicki 1969, p. 120). Ryazanov also used the term 'popular production' with reference to the traditional system of communal land tenure in Russia and non-market, pre-commodity production. His point was that the cut-offs were retained by the landlords in order to continue extracting peasant labour for market-oriented production. In other words, pressures from 'rudimentary' capitalism distorted the conditions of emancipation from the outset.]

[34] Ryazanov 1903a, p. 215. [Ryazanov claimed it was the business of liberals, not of Social Democrats, to struggle against pre-capitalist remnants in agriculture. Liberal historiography associated capitalism with progress and enlightenment, dismissing pre-capitalist society as backward, whereas Marx had far greater respect for the communal character of pre-capitalist social formations. Communism itself, wrote Ryazanov, would mean a return not merely to a *non-market* economy, but to *'natural economy…en grand'* (Ryazanov 1903a, p. 218).]

interpreted to mean that if the abolition of serfdom had been prepared by so-called popular production (as they say in the Narodnik literature), and not by capitalism on the basis of *corveé* labour, then there would be no need for us now to be demanding a radical review of the conditions of the peasants' emancipation. But we have to ask ourselves whether 'popular production' really could create conditions in which the abolition of serfdom would become a real economic necessity. Not a single reader with a head on his shoulders will hesitate to answer: No, over the course of time this 'production' itself came to be the most solid basis for our serfdom in all its forms and variations.[35] On this matter, there is no room for any doubt whatever. And once we are convinced of that fact, then we face a new question: just why did Ryazanov need his ridiculous hypothesis concerning the 'preparation' of the peasant reform of 1861 by popular production? Apparently, he needed it only to give greater emphasis to the idea that if the peasants were emancipated in conditions extremely unfavourable to them, then this was due to none other than the development of capitalism itself even if it continued to be based on *corveé* labour. And this idea, apparently, must lead us to the inevitable conclusion that the position in which the Russian peasant was placed by legislative act of 1861 was itself 'prepared' by the development of capitalism.

The only correct part of this conclusion is the fact that economic development, moving in the direction of capitalism, did make it imperative for the landowners to have such conditions of emancipation as would convert the peasant into a semi-proletarian who would be forced to sell his labour-power. To the extent that the peasant became a seller of labour-power, he fell into the same position that capitalist society requires for the working class as a whole, and that position will only be abolished *by the socialist revolution.*[36] Naturally, that position is neither a remnant of antiquity nor is it the focus of those paragraphs in our programme that deal with struggling against vestiges from the old precapitalist order. The real point is that the common position of both the small-holding peasant and the proletarian *is complicated by the existence of a*

---

[35] [This, of course, was precisely the issue that provoked Plekhanov's break with and subsequent criticism of the Narodniks in the early 1880s.]

[36] [This was exactly Ryazanov's conclusion. If *capitalism* was responsible for the conditions of the peasants, then *socialist revolution* was the solution – not, as Lenin and Plekhanov were claiming, some legal reforms of the terms of the 1861 emancipation, which Lenin hoped would promote the capitalist development of agriculture.]

whole number of such institutions, thanks to which our seller of labour-power is bound hand and foot and compelled to sell his only commodity in circumstances even worse than he would face in the legal position of a proletarian in modern bourgeois society. These kinds of institutions are survivals of our ancient order of serfdom; and it against them that the part of our draft – the part that provoked Ryazanov's confusing discussion of 'rudiments' and 'remnants' – calls upon revolutionaries to struggle. If Ryazanov thought these institutions – for instance, the fastening of the peasant to the land and other similar ones – are rudiments of capitalism, then he would have to support his opinion with something more serious than the comical hypothesis suggesting that we would not need to demand a radical review of the peasant's emancipation had it been prepared by popular production. But he did no such thing for the simple reason that he had nothing more serious to say, and what he did say resulted from considerations that have nothing to do with the tasks of a Social-Democratic programme.

'Is it not the case that the period from the epoch of the great reforms to the present time – continues Ryazanov – a period of capitalism's uninterrupted development, has created a whole series of rudiments that are preventing the comprehensive development of the proletariat's class struggle?'[37]

Let us suppose this is the case. Does it follow that the remnants discussed in our draft do not exist, or that there is 'no place' to point them out in a programme of revolutionary Social Democracy? It seems that this does not follow at all.

But Ryazanov is still not finished.

> Is it not the case that this period [i.e. the one just mentioned] has created a whole series of rudiments that are not only helping to preserve and strengthen the most barbaric forms of exploitation of the multi-millioned peasantry, but are also creating new ones that are less barbaric but incomparably more refined? Has it not created a whole array of rudiments that are keeping the entire people in a condition of ignorance and deprived of any rights, and doing so to no less degree than the remnants of pre-capitalist customs? Is it possible that protectionism, the system of taxes, militarism, etc., etc. are all the results of serfdom?[38]

---

[37] Ryazanov [1903a] p. 215.
[38] *Ibid.*, p. 216.

How does one respond to this? If the period mentioned by Ryazanov has really created new, less barbaric but, at the same time, more refined forms of exploiting the peasantry, then this can be due to one of two things: either these *new forms* rest upon *old legal institutions* bequeathed to us by our previous serfdom, or else they are based on elements of our civil law whose content corresponds fully with the production relations of the most modern capitalist society. In the first case, any serious struggle against them is a struggle against 'remnants' and is noted in the corresponding points of our programme. In the second case, the struggle against new forms of exploitation is just one element of the Social-Democratic struggle against capitalism. The tasks involved in this latter struggle are also quite clearly discussed in our programme, and that is why new, less barbaric but more refined forms of exploiting the peasantry are neither surprising to us nor do they represent any argument whatsoever against any part of our programme.

As for the Russian system of taxation, even to this day it is based partly on the peasants' lack of any rights as an estate, and in that respect it doubtlessly rests upon 'remnants'. And so far as protectionism is concerned, militarism, 'etc., etc.' (whatever that means), such phenomena are essential characteristics not only of our conditions but also of Western Europe, and in that sense, of course, they cannot be attributed to any 'remnants'. But I ask once again: So what? The only implication is that the answer to the question of how to struggle against them is not to be found in that part of our programme that deals with 'remnants'. That is all there is to it. The reader will surely have no difficulty in agreeing that this is absolutely no basis for confirming Ryazanov's view, namely, that 'there is no place for remnants in a Social-Democratic programme'.

Ryazanov continues:

> The best that Social Democrats can do is to leave it to bourgeois democracy to struggle against the remnants of precapitalist orders, while simply pointing out for their own part that destruction of such remnants is inevitable wherever capitalism has already become the prevailing mode of production, and that within a commodity economy they are transformed from a source of prosperity into one of calamity.[39]

---

[39] *Ibid.*, p. 216.

Now pedantry, like everything else, has its own logic. Remembering only the *terminology* of orthodox Marxism and being unable to grasp its content, Ryazanov naturally arrives at conclusions that represent a most malicious parody of Marxism. We are to leave it to bourgeois democracy to struggle against remnants of our old order, and we will limit ourselves merely to *showing* that destruction of such remnants 'is inevitable wherever' and so forth! No, Mr. Ryazanov. If we were to behave that way, we would thereby demonstrate once and for all, and with irrefutable clarity, that the Narodniks and subjectivists were correct when they accused Marxists of *quietism*; if we behaved that way, then we would leave it completely to bourgeois democracy to play the role of the revolutionary factor in the contemporary social life of Russia, reserving to ourselves only the miserable role of *armchair pedants*.

The importance of this matter is evident in the fact that our peasantry, which in legal terms also includes the majority of industrial workers, is thus far in its struggle for better living conditions running up continuously against obstacles resulting from the existence of 'remnants' that provide a skilful agitator with a multitude of irreplaceable opportunities for political propaganda. To dismiss these opportunities on the grounds that some thinker might regard 'remnants' as 'rudiments' would amount to following the example of the famous metaphysician who, sitting in his pit, hesitated to use the rope lowered to him on the grounds that it was 'simply a rope' and insisted on trying to think of 'something else' instead.[40] If our party claims the honour of being the most energetic and decisive bearer of revolutionary ideas, then it is also *obliged* to struggle more energetically and more decisively than all other parties against remnants of precapitalist relations. Otherwise, its claim will be groundless and thus ridiculous.

Ryazanov notes that

> The precapitalist social order was not always based on serfdom.[41] As Marx
> says, we must never forget that it is very easy to be 'liberal' at the expense

---

[40] [The reference is to a fable by Ivan I. Khemnitser (1745–84), in which a father sends his foolish son abroad to study. When the son returns, he is still a fool, but now a learned fool. One day the son, in a metaphysical dream, wanders off the road and falls into a pit. His father throws him a rope, but the son, instead of pulling himself from the pit, first wants to reflect on the question: What is the real 'essence' of a rope? See: <http://www.moskvam.ru/2000/03/kolagin.htm>.]

[41] [In other words, some pre-capitalist orders involved communal agriculture (primitive communism) but not serfdom, the implication being that communal

of the middle ages.[42] And in a country such as Russia, where 'capitalism has already become the prevailing mode of production', we must destroy all the legends concerning precapitalist systems.[43]

It is perfectly true that not every precapitalist order was based on serfdom. But in our draft we deal with a quite specific and very well-known precapitalist order that really was based upon enserfment of the toiling masses by the highest estate, by the government or by its head. Just how would we describe this order if not as one based on serfdom? As for the ease of being liberal at its expense, I don't see the point. Under the influence of Narodnik propaganda, for a very long time the Russian reader was inclined, *on the contrary*, to idealise our precapitalist order – at least in economic terms – with the result that with us *it was much easier to 'be liberal' to its benefit than at its expense*. And although capitalism really has become the prevailing mode of production in our country, in the first place not everyone recognises this, and in the second place, the capitalist mode of production with us still does not have its corresponding *legal superstructure*. We now have a deep contradiction between *the economy* and *the law*, whose abolition must be the first great accomplishment of our socialist movement. And since our *legal superstructure* – insofar as it contradicts the demands of modern society – was inherited from our precapitalist order, *it is not possible for any thinking Russian to be too 'liberal' at this order's expense*. It is also ridiculous to compare our relation to this order with that of today's citizens of Western Europe to the 'Middle Ages'. Here, again, Ryazanov has put his foot into it. He wanted to sound like Marx when

organisation is not self-evidently objectionable and that socialists will themselves eventually promote communal agriculture.]

[42] [In a footnote to Chapter XXVII, Volume I of *Capital*, Marx wrote: 'Japan, with its purely feudal organisation of landed property and its developed *petite culture*, gives a much truer picture of the European middle ages than all our history books, dictated as these are, for the most part, by bourgeois prejudices. It is very convenient to be "liberal" at the expense of the middle ages.' See Marx 1976, p. 878.]

[43] Ryazanov [1903a] p. 217. [Ryazanov was referring to the 'legends' of bourgeois historiography, which from the time of the eighteenth–century enlightenment painted all pre-capitalist agrarian relations as exploitative. In this connection he quoted the 'vulgar' Marxism of Struve, who wrote:

> The economic history of our Russian peasantry convincingly shows that even in the epoch of natural economy, when – we are told – the means of production belonged to the producer, there occurred an enormous process of enslaving the direct producers by a particular type of 'capital' and especially with the help of *credit*.]

speaking of social relations that *Marx himself, had he encountered them, would probably have described quite differently.*

Ryazanov is also very displeased by the fact that we describe tsarism as the greatest and most harmful remnant of our precapitalist order. Our critic attributes this to the 'enlightened' historiography peculiar to bourgeois democracy.[44] 'Historically – he says –

> our autocracy really is rooted in the past, but this is a condition that it shares with numerous other aspects of social life. Unlike other 'remnants', it is not a *holdover* or some accidentally preserved fragment of the past. Alas, it is very much part of the *present*. And if the authors of our draft did not divide the whole of history into two periods – one being pre-capitalist and the other capitalist – they would see how much the character of our autocracy has changed since the time of Ivan III.[45]

Neither in our draft, nor in any of the commentaries on it, is there a single line suggesting that we attribute an *unchanging character* to Russian autocracy. We know perfectly well that its character has changed along with the development of our social relations. But the undisputed fact of such change does not in the least prevent our autocracy from being a *'remnant'* and *'holdover'* from the past. Is it really the case that the only institutions that figure on the historical scene as 'holdovers' or 'remnants' are ones distinguished by their unchanging character? That really would be news! And why does Ryazanov think that we regard the autocracy as an *accidentally* preserved fragment of the past? Indeed, in this case too, there is not the slightest hint, either in our draft or in the commentaries, that would lead to such a thought. There is,

---

[44] Ryazanov [1903a] p. 219. [In this connection Ryazanov cited the exchange between P.N. Tkachev and Engels:

> The view of tsarist autocracy – as a *remnant* of the pre-capitalist order – is the fruit of the same 'enlightenment' historiography that is characteristic of bourgeois democrats: 'Our social forms,' P. Tkachev wrote when instructing Engels, 'owe their existence to the state, which hangs, so to speak, in the air and has nothing in common with the existing social structure and is rooted entirely in the past, not in the present.' And how did Engels respond? He listed for Tkachev all the classes with an interest in preserving the Russian state. He came to the conclusion that it was not the Russian state that hangs in the air, but rather Tkachev himself, and he could only marvel that such talk could come from anyone over twelve years of age. (See Engels 1874, pp. 39–50.)

[45] [Ryazanov [1903a] p. 220.]

however, such an *unchanging character* in Ryazanov's method of 'criticism': it consists of attributing absurdities to his opponents, which never entered their minds, and then triumphantly refuting these imagined absurdities. It goes without saying that this kind of method greatly facilitates Ryazanov's effort at 'criticism'.

We furthermore learn from Ryazanov the interesting news that our autocracy was always an instrument in the hands of one social class or another.

> It underwent especially noteworthy changes in the period from the end of XVIII century up to the epoch of the great reforms, when 'popular production'…finally gave way to capitalism based upon *corveé* labour. And we will be much closer to the truth if we say that in its contemporary form our autocracy is a product of the rudiments of capitalism. Historical legends of the time when it was an instrument solely of the nobles are long gone, even though they recede only 'stubbornly' in face of the vigorous and forceful shoots of capitalism. It is still trying to maintain an equilibrium between the landlords and the bourgeoisie, but the growing contradictions between its two sources of support, which result from the development of capitalism, must lead to its destruction despite all its attempts to adapt to the changing class structure.[46]

So, the autocracy will perish because it is incapable of adapting to the changed 'class structure'. Why can it not make the adjustment? Is it not because autocracy is the kind of political institution that does not correspond to a capitalist society that has already reached a significant degree of development? And, if that is the case, does it not mean that autocracy is a political institution that represents *a relic from the old social order*? Certainly, that would appear to be the case! Even Ryazanov senses that this is true, but he does not relent. He declares the autocracy to be a product of capitalist rudiments on the grounds that it has long ceased to be an instrument solely in the hands of the nobility and has begun simultaneously to serve the bourgeoisie in achieving its goals. But this conclusion would only be convincing if Ryazanov were to demonstrate that the bourgeoisie never wished, or was never able, to bend to its needs one or another holdover from the old order. And, since he provides no such proof and never will, his whole argument once again falls apart like a house

---

[46] *Ibid.*

of cards. In reality, every newly emerging social class always endeavours, often successfully, to use for its own purposes institutions that have grown up on the basis of the old social order, and it enters into conflict with those institutions only when, with their help, it has already reached a certain level of development. There was a time, for example, when the bourgeoisie tried to transform *feudal institutions* into instruments for achieving its goals. But only someone who is incapable of 'adapting' to the most elementary demands of logic could conclude, on these grounds, that such institutions were a product of the 'rudiments' of bourgeois development.

Ryazanov is also very displeased by our idea that the autocracy, by its nature, is hostile to all social movements.

'How did this wisdom end up in a Social-Democratic programme? – Ryazanov menacingly exclaims – Were those who prepared the draft unaware that the autocracy is hostile by nature not to *all* social movements but only to *certain ones*, not to the social movements of *all* classes but only to those of *certain* classes?'[47]

We have already heard from Ryazanov that our autocracy has always been an instrument in the hands of one social class or another. If that is the case, then it is clear that even in the reign of Nicholas Pavlovich there was some social class that knew how to make the unrestrained power of the tsar into its own instrument.[48] We will not squabble with Ryazanov over the question of precisely which class the autocracy served at that time: for us, it is enough to know that if our initial premise is true, then it invariably had to serve one or several of them. Starting from that conviction, we ask Ryazanov to show us exactly which social movement, of which specific class, did not face the hostility of the Tsar-Sergeant Major's government. We openly admit that we are 'unaware' of any such movement.

The more that duty requires me to scrutinise Ryazanov's book, the more I am reminded of the exclamation that Engels once directed to certain critics of historical materialism: these gentlemen know nothing of dialectics! As I have already mentioned, what is beyond Ryazanov is precisely dialectics. He is a born metaphysician. And when a metaphysician is set loose to theorise, nothing good can be expected. For a metaphysician – as for the nihilist portrayed by

---

[47] *Ibid.*, p. 222.
[48] [The reference is to Nicholas I, emperor of Russia from 1825–55.]

Count Tolstoy – every movement is awkward and every teaching is coarse. And Ryazanov hands out his coarse teaching to us as the most orthodox orthodoxy. What fun!

But our metaphysician turns out to be even more clumsy and coarse in his criticism of our *agrarian programme.*

In his article on the agrarian programme of Russian Social Democracy, Comrade Lenin observed that on matters concerning the industrial workers' movement, we acquire a great deal ready-made 'from the Germans', but in agrarian matters we may succeed in working out something new.[49] Having barely finished reading these words, Ryazanov, as they say, is all ears: 'Hmmm! New! That means something not covered in the works of Marx and Engels. And anything that is not covered in the works of Marx and Engels cannot be orthodox. That means Lenin is a heretic and must be treated as such.' But Ryazanov's orthodox jealousy is even more aroused when he hears from Lenin that 'not everything that is appropriate in the West is also appropriate in the East'. In that connection, Ryazanov lets loose the following spiteful tirade:

> The 'something new' is the discovery that 'There are two sides to all things in the world.' Whereas in the 'West' an agrarian programme that proposed to 'multiply small farming and petty property' would violate the principles of Social Democracy, in the 'East' we have an 'exceptional case'. We support multiplication of small holdings in the interest of eliminating the remnants of serfdom and promoting the free development of class struggle in the countryside, in other words, in the interest of the development of agrarian capitalism.[50]

From the point of view of dialectical materialism, everything in the world really does have two sides. A particular principle that is important when applied to one place or time stands a good chance of proving false when applied to another place or another epoch. But a metaphysician does not understand this, and that is why his jaw drops in astonishment when he hears that a principle that was acknowledged to be true in the circumstances

---

[49] [See Lenin 1902g, p. 136.]

[50] Ryazanov [1903a] p. 247. [Here, of course, Ryazanov was not presenting his own views but paraphrasing those of Lenin, whom he bitterly opposed for endorsing, together with Plekhanov, the growth of capitalism in the countryside.]

of one place and time is declared untrue in others. He sees inconsistency in this, contradictions, betrayal. The great founders of scientific socialism had no sympathy for metaphysicians. The *Manifesto of the Communist Party* was a work, by the way, that waged war against metaphysicians. The reader will probably remember the place where it speaks of German wiseacres, philosophers and semi-philosophers, who eagerly pounced upon French socialist literature but happened to forget that 'when these writings immigrated from France into Germany, French social conditions had not immigrated along with them'.[51] These wiseacres, philosophers and semi-philosophers were pure-blooded metaphysicians. The authors of the *Manifesto* could not excuse their ignorance of the fact that French socialist criticism, of which they were merely a silly echo, 'presupposed the existence of modern bourgeois society, with its corresponding economic conditions of existence, and the political constitution adapted thereto, the very things whose attainment was the object of the pending struggle in Germany'.[52] Ryazanov is just as much a pure-blooded metaphysician, trying to disgrace us by pointing to West-European Marxists who have no wish to 'multiply petty property'. Ryazanov is forgetting that the agrarian views of these Marxists, of which he is merely a silly echo, apply to modern bourgeois society and the corresponding economic and legal position of the peasant, *that is, the very conditions whose attainment is still only being talked about in our agrarian programme*. When our peasant finds himself in the same position as West-European peasants are in today, then we too will take a stand against any attempt to 'multiply' private property. But presently, when our peasant finds himself in completely different circumstances, the example of West-European Marxists cannot be convincing for us: being in different social circumstances, we must also reason differently. Of course, this does not mean that we must invariably multiply private property. No, that matter also depends upon circumstances, but it is obvious that when we are discussing private property we must take into account the specific aspects

---

[51] [Marx and Engels 1848a. Marx and Engels were criticising the 'True' socialists of Germany who applied French revolutionary literature to their own circumstances in denouncing liberalism: 'While this "True" Socialism thus served the government as a weapon for fighting the German bourgeoisie, it, at the same time, directly represented a reactionary interest, the interest of German Philistines.' Plekhanov is implying that Ryazanov is likewise a reactionary in applying to 'backward' Russian circumstances ideas that may be appropriate in more 'advanced' Germany.]

[52] [*Ibid.*]

of our position and not satisfy ourselves with some completely pointless reference to West-European Marxists.

Just what are the circumstances that give rise to our talk about multiplying private property?

They are of two kinds.

In the first place, some multiplication of the private property of the peasants can result from the return to them of the famous cut-offs, that is, the land that they once used but was taken from them with the abolition of serfdom.[53]

In the second place, a significant multiplication of private property will result from giving the peasant the right to dispose freely of his land, that is, from the internal stratification of communal land tenure.[54]

Let us first consider the cut-offs. What is their significance in the economic life of the peasant? They are the source of his enslavement. Here, for example, is what we learn about them from someone so familiar with our village life as A.N. Engelhardt:

> With the peasant allotments, any land that exceeded their entitlements was cut off, and this cut-off land, which was vitally important to the peasants, became someone else's property and constrained them simply by its location. Usually it is a narrow strip that surrounds their land and borders all three fields, so that wherever the cattle might leap they invariably end up on the master's land. At first, when the landlords did not recognise the importance of the cut-offs, and wherever the peasants where more pragmatic and placed less hope on the 'new freedom', they managed to obtain ownership of the cut-offs for money or for some other kind of 'payment', and such peasants are now relatively prosperous. But nowadays everyone understands the importance of the cut-offs,[55] and every buyer of an estate, every lessee,

---

[53] [The Emancipation of 1861 abolished serfdom on private lands. The peasants received much of the land they had used to date and were to pay for it over a period of 49 years. Often they overpaid for the land and received the least productive parcels. The 'cut-offs' were parcels that were previously used by the peasants but now reverted to the nobility. Estimates of the amount of land involved in the 'cut-offs' range from 4–15 percent. The land that the peasants received continued to be periodically redivided within the rural communes (the *obshchiny*) and was paid for collectively through taxation.]

[54] [The peasants only gained the right of private land tenure with the Stolypin reforms that followed the 1905 revolution as Plekhanov hoped they would.]

[55] In this observation Engelhardt was not completely correct; the significance of the cut-offs is not apparent to many of our critics, to Ryazanov for example.

even the German who can't speak Russian, first of all looks for cut-offs, how they are situated, and to what extent they constrain the peasants. Here the peasants universally work the landlords' land for the cut-offs – they work in a circle [i.e. are back where they started] because they use their own horses and their own implements to produce, and just as in the case of serfdom they fully till all three fields. These cut-offs, often worthless, are valued not according to the land's quality or productivity but only by the degree to which they are *indispensable* to the peasants, by the extent to which they *constrain* them, and by how much can be squeezed out of the peasants for these cut-offs.[56]

That is what the cut-offs mean to the peasant. Would their return be beneficial to the peasants? Clearly, the answer is yes. And if the answer is yes, then why should we not include it in our programme? Because – our critics reply – this would amount to supporting private property and its multiplication. And why is support and multiplication of private property detrimental? Because it delays the economic development of society. There are no other grounds for saying it is detrimental. This means that wherever it would not delay society's economic development – for whatever the reasons – but would rather accelerate it, there are no possible grounds for objection. But that is precisely the situation in the case that concerns us. All the researchers unanimously recognise that the 'squeezing' of the peasants as a result of the cut-offs – so vividly described by Engelhardt – is a powerful obstacle to the success of agriculture in Russia. Accordingly, returning the cut-offs to the peasants would significantly stimulate the economic development of our country. And since economic development in our country, as everywhere else, will ultimately lead to the triumph of socialism, i.e., to elimination of private property in the means of production, it follows that return of the cut-offs serves the interests of socialist revolution and that support for *private* property and its expansion, in this case, will accelerate transformation of the means of production into *social* property. Therefore, we *not only may but are even obliged* to stand for return of the cut-offs to the peasants. To a metaphysician, of course, such a conclusion will seem to be a logical trick.

---

[56] A.N. Engelhardt, *Iz Derevni* [Letters from the Countryside], p. 415. [See Lenin's 'Story of Engelhardt's farm' in Lenin 1899, pp. 215–19. Lenin also discusses Engelhardt in Lenin 1897, pp. 491–534.]

But it is not our business to convince *metaphysicians*: we are concerned with people who are able to adopt the *dialectical method* of modern socialism.

Let us note in passing that when Ryazanov attributes to us the intention to *purchase* all of the cut-offs (pp. 264–5), he is seriously misrepresenting our thoughts. We provide for purchase only where the former landowner's estates have already passed into someone else's hands. But even in this case, *purchase must take place – according to our demand – not at the expense of the peasants or of the state, but rather of all the landlords who will on this account be subject to a special tax.* The reader can judge for himself how such a purchase compares to the 'notorious purchase operation' described by our profound, wise and resourceful Ryazanov.

And now we come to the *village commune*.[57] There is no doubt that elimination of communal land tenure would mean significant support for private property and its multiplication. Even more important, the result would be that numerous Russian peasants would for the first time acquire land as private property. Can socialists agree to this without betraying their programme? We believe they can; and with that belief we find ourselves once again in very good company. In March of 1850, the 'Address [*Ansprache*] to its members from the Central Committee of the Communist League' – evidently written by Marx's own hand – categorically stated that *the party of the proletariat can least of all [am allerwenigsten] accept perpetuation of communal property [Gemeindeeigentum], which is a backward form even compared to modern private property and must everywhere and inevitably be transformed into the latter.*[58] As we see, Marx did not in the least regard an expansion of private property, resulting from dissolution of communal property, as a factor that would impede the movement of modern society towards socialism. Nor could he possibly regard it in that manner.[59] As a powerful dialectician, he saw better than anyone else the truth of the view that there are two sides to everything,

---

[57] [The *obshchina*.]

[58] [See Marx and Engels 1850.]

[59] [This is not true. In the preface to the second Russian edition of the *Communist Manifesto*, Marx and Engels said: 'If the Russian Revolution becomes the signal for a proletarian revolution in the West, so that both complement each other, the present Russian common ownership of land may serve as the starting point for a communist development. In a draft reply to Vera Zasulich (March 1881), Marx also 'expressly' limited the 'historical inevitability' of 'the expropriation of the agricultural producer' to Western Europe. CW, Vol. 24, p. 346. For reasons why Marx's letter to Zasulich was not published by Plekhanov and *Osvobozhdenie Truda*, see Walicki 1969, pp. 187–8.]

and that support for private property and its expansion – which is harmful and reactionary in the context of a bourgeois society that is already moving *more or less* rapidly towards *socialist revolution* – might still be a necessary and useful measure in cases where the issue is one of freeing bourgeois society from the fetters of 'the old regime' and destroying backward forms of property that have become obsolete.

But the *Address* that I have just quoted also demands confiscation of 'the land of feudal property owners' and its conversion into *state* property to be used for *workers'* colonies.[60] Here, the programme that Marx and his co-thinkers supported at that time appears to part ways with our draft, and Ryazanov seems to be really orthodox after all because his draft of an agrarian programme seems in this respect to correspond with Marx's programme. But this only appears to be the case, for, here again, Ryazanov is trying to speak like Marx in the context of social relations that Marx himself would have addressed quite differently.

If Marxism can really be called the *algebra of revolution*, then a programme that is true to the spirit of Marxism must be *a revolutionary programme* from beginning to end. But, in a revolutionary programme, each separate demand is judged in terms of *how it promotes the success of the revolutionary movement*. If it turns out that implementation of any given demand would have the effect of strengthening the forces of counter-revolution, then it must be rejected regardless of the fact that on its own it might promise certain benefits to the

---

[60] [In this context Marx and Engels wrote:
The first point over which the bourgeois democrats will come into conflict with the workers will be the abolition of feudalism. As in the first French revolution, the petty bourgeoisie will want to give the feudal lands to the peasants as free property; that is, they will try to perpetuate the existence of the rural proletariat, and to form a petty-bourgeois peasant class which will be subject to the same cycle of impoverishment and debt which still afflicts the French peasant. The workers must oppose this plan both in the interest of the rural proletariat and in their own interest. They must demand that the confiscated feudal property remain state property and be used for workers' colonies, cultivated collectively by the rural proletariat with all the advantages of large-scale farming and where the principle of common property will immediately achieve a sound basis in the midst of the shaky system of bourgeois property relations. Just as the democrats ally themselves with the peasants, the workers must ally themselves with the rural proletariat. (See *CW*, Vol. 10: 277–87.)]

revolutionary class. Let us consider the demand to transform the land into state property from this point of view.[61]

With us in Russia, the state has been accustomed since ancient times to regard the land not as belonging to so-called private owners but rather *as its own property*. The communal land tenure of the peasants actually meant that *both the land and the peasants attached to it belonged to the treasury* and were treated according to the 'treasury interest'. That is why our communal land tenure has been the most stable economic foundation of tsarism. *In order to bring down tsarism, it is necessary to destroy its economic foundation, and for that purpose the peasants must be placed in conditions of modern private property, and the Asiatic form of state land tenure that has been established in our country must be eliminated.* That is why all projects for nationalisation of the land or for transforming gentry land into state property *are for us essentially reactionary despite their revolutionary appearance.*[62] That is also why Marx would likely

---

[61] [Ryazanov explicitly cautioned against transforming *'all* the land' into state property. He did, however, call for *'expropriation of all the large estates'*, which would then become state property that the peasants would pay to use: 'Moreover, Social Democrats will generally insist that the land be leased mainly to associations of village workers, or to the peasants who now possess it, who would work it on behalf of the state.' If it happened that the expropriated lands were sold, as in the French revolution, it would still be possible 'with a single revolutionary blow to eliminate all the remnants of feudalism' and to prepare conditions for a 'final decisive battle between the proletariat and the bourgeoisie'. In this case the only surviving 'remnant' would be the village commune, which would continue untouched, although individual peasants would be given the right to leave (Ryazanov, 1903a, pp. 292–4).]

[62] [On this point, there were furious debates between Plekhanov and Lenin after the latter began to advocate land nationalisation in the aftermath of the 1905 revolution. Plekhanov saw in this a danger of restoration of the Asiatic mode of production on which the Russian autocracy was historically based. On this issue Lenin wrote:

> In his *Dnevnik*, No. 5, Comrade Plekhanov warns Russia not to repeat the experiments of Wang Hang-che (a Chinese reformer of the eleventh century who unsuccessfully introduced nationalisation of the land), and tries to show that the peasants' idea of land nationalisation is of reactionary origin. The far-fetched nature of this argument is only too obvious. Truly *qui prouve trop, ne prouve rien* (he who proves too much, proves nothing). If twentieth-century Russia could be compared with eleventh-century China probably Plekhanov and I would hardly be talking either about the revolutionary-democratic character of the peasant movement or about capitalism in Russia. As for the reactionary origin (or character) of the peasants' idea of land nationalisation, well, even the idea of a general redistribution of the land has undoubted features not only of a reactionary origin, but also of its reactionary character at the present time. There are reactionary elements in the whole peasant movement, and in the whole peasant ideology, but this by no means disproves the general revolutionary-democratic character of this movement as a whole. That being so, Comrade Plekhanov by his exceedingly far-fetched argument

judge such projects to be in contradiction with the fundamental demand of our pending revolution. If he held a different view in Germany, it is because conditions there were also completely different.

It is true that Ryazanov and the so-called Socialist-Revolutionaries – from whom he has borrowed his agrarian project – say that after the revolution the land taken from the big landowners will no longer belong to our current police state but instead to a free democratic republic, which will have a completely different approach both to the land and to agriculture. But when they speak that way, Ryazanov and his 'social-revolutionary' teachers turn the question that we have been considering upside down. The real question is *how to achieve the triumph of a democratic republic. If we simply assume* that this question has already been *resolved*, then, of course, we also resolve all the difficulties associated with it – but at the same time *we abandon the viewpoint of scientific socialism and transform ourselves into utopians.* In reality, a democratic republic will triumph and become stable only in the event that the revolutionary movement destroys the economic basis of tsarism; that is, the very *state land tenure* whose stabilisation and expansion the Socialist-Revolutionaries (read: reactionaries) and our poor Ryazanov are attempting to promote.

I have just a couple more comments to make. Ryazanov says that, by working for return of the cut-offs to the peasants, we thereby acknowledge that the rest of the land is a perfectly legal possession of the gentry.[63] This argument resembles that of the anarchists like two drops of water; they never tire of telling us that by demanding a shortening of the working day, say to eight hours, we are thereby acknowledging the legitimacy of any bourgeois exploitation that does not exceed the eight-hour limit. There is no point in discussing these kinds of arguments.

Ryazanov reminds me that, in my commentary on the draft programme, I recognise that, at some stage of the revolutionary movement, we might have to put forth the demand for complete expropriation of the gentry's land. I understand this point perfectly well. However, I do not see here any

---

has not proved his thesis (that Social-Democrats cannot, in certain political conditions, put forward the demand for nationalisation of the land) and has, indeed, weakened it very considerably. (Lenin 1906e, Chap. II: Four Trends among Social-Democrats on the Question of the Agrarian Programme, Note 4.)]

[63] [See Ryazanov 1903a, p. 266.]

contradiction with the demand for return of the cut-offs. There is *no qualitative difference* between these two demands, only a *quantitative one* – just as there would be only a quantitative difference between two draft laws, one of which might demand shortening of the working day to ten hours, and the other, say, to six hours. Which of these demands we are inclined to support at the current moment depends solely upon the balance of social forces. Presently, when the revolutionary energy of the peasantry is *very modest*, we naturally confront it with more modest demands; but if the time should come when our peasantry displays much greater revolutionary energy, then, of course, we shall not hold it back. That is not our affair. We are showing them the way to a greater revolutionary goal. But, in this case, too, we shall remain true to the spirit of our programme and *not become supporters of the reactionary utopia* that Ryazanov has adopted from the Socialist-Revolutionaries. *That is the whole issue* and the principal distinction of our programme.

To conclude my conversation with Ryazanov, I cannot help but recall an observation by Catherine II. The royal empress once wrote:

> Disagreements often result, unfortunately, from the fact that some people discredit the efforts of others, however beneficial they might be, solely because they did not accomplish them themselves, and they do so even when they would never be capable of accomplishing them themselves.

The same applies to Ryazanov. It seems to me that our draft displeases him precisely because he did not write it himself. On his own, our strict critic is 'capable' of producing only an unintelligible medley of his own poorly understood Marxism; and he is, unfortunately, much too impressed by the reactionary-utopian demands of the socialist-'revolutionaries'.

Chapter Four

'To What Extent Is the Communist Manifesto Obsolete?' (First edition: 1903 – Revised edition: June 1906)

Karl Kautsky

This essay was originally written as an introduction to the Polish edition of the *Communist Manifesto*, first published in Cracow in 1903 and reprinted in Warsaw two years later.[1] The German version appeared in July 1904 in the *Leipziger Volkszeitung*, one of the main organs of the SPD's left wing.[2] A Russian translation of that version was printed in 1906.[3] The present version is a corrected edition of the English translation that appeared in the journal *Social Democrat* on 15 March 1905.[4] It was checked against the first German version, as reprinted in December 1904 in the journal *From the Arsenal of Socialism: A Compilation of Old and New Propaganda Writings*,[5] as well as against the revised edition of June 1906, which appeared as a preface to the seventh German edition of the *Communist Manifesto*.[6] Note the explicit reference to the March 1850 'Address of the Central Committee of the Communist League' and to 'a

---

[1] Krakau, Prawo Ludu, 1903, and Warsaw: Bibl. Naukowa, 1905.
[2] Kautsky 1904b.
[3] St. Petersburg: Epoch, 1906.
[4] Kautsky 1905j, pp. 155–64.
[5] Volksstimme (Frankfurt) (Hrsg.) 1904, Bd. III, pp. 96–105.
[6] Marx and Engels 1906. Reprinted in Hamburg by E. Dubber, 1907.

bourgeois revolution that, in becoming permanent, grows beyond its own limits and develops out of itself a proletarian revolution'.

Although Kautsky made reference to the theory of permanent revolution, in terms of the debates within the Russian party the implications of his essay were studiously ambiguous. Like Ryazanov in his criticism of the *Iskra* draft programme, in the original 1903 edition of his essay Kautsky affirmed that 'Now there is only *one* class of the population that, with all its strength, stands for social progress, and that class is the proletariat.' He added that 'Today we can nowhere speak of a revolutionary bourgeoisie,' and he cited Marx's 'Address to the Central Committee of the Communist League' to argue that the proletariat must consistently raise its own independent demands against those of bourgeois democrats in order that its revolutionary potential could not be exploited for bourgeois purposes. Such remarks corresponded perfectly with the themes set forth by Ryazanov.

At the same time, however, Kautsky was clearly of two minds concerning the possible revolutionary potential of the *Russian* bourgeoisie. The events of 1848, he noted, had brought the era of bourgeois revolutions to an end in Western Europe, and 'The Russian bourgeoisie…has already adopted the reactionary turn of mind of the bourgeoisie in the West'. Yet, he added in the original version of his essay that this conclusion might not hold for Russia, 'where the peasantry and the intellectuals play an entirely different role than in Western Europe'. Whereas European workers' parties might have occasion to co-operate with liberals for the purpose of defending rights already won, in this respect, Russia was also an 'exception', implying that Russian workers might co-operate with the bourgeoisie even for revolutionary purposes. Such remarks would have encouraged Plekhanov in his quarrel with Ryazanov, although Plekhanov would have been dismayed by the prospect of 'a bourgeois revolution' that becomes 'permanent' and grows over into 'a proletarian revolution'.

Even more perplexing were the revisions Kautsky made to his essay when it was republished in June 1906. By that time, the Russian Revolution was in retreat following the dispersal of the Petersburg Soviet, the brutal suppression of the Moscow insurrection, and the ensuing Duma elections. Although the Kadets won the largest number of seats in the First Duma and hoped for a parliamentary monarchy, the tsar insisted upon his prerogative to dismiss the Duma at will and did so in July 1906, shortly after Kautsky's revised essay appeared. Writing on the eve of this catastrophe, Kautsky obviously hoped for a more progressive outcome and hedged his comments accordingly. While the proletariat alone stood for social progress, on this occasion he added that 'this rule does not apply to Russia'. And, while it was no longer possible to speak of a revolutionary bourgeoisie in general terms, he also added in this context that Russia might be a 'possible exception'.

In short, both in its original and in its revised version, Kautsky's introduction to the *Communist Manifesto* could be cited in support of diametrically opposed positions within the Russian Party. Kautsky had helped to initiate the Russian debate over permanent revolution with his article on 'The Slavs and Revolution', yet his cautionary remarks in this essay, and his simultaneous reference to the *Communist Manifesto* and the 'Address to the Central Committee of the Communist League' – without pointing out clearly the change of tactics that intervened between them[7] – served better to echo and even amplify divisions among Russian Marxists than to assist in resolving their differences. All sides in the Russian debate could therefore claim to speak with Kautsky's authority while Kautsky himself avoided any definitive conclusions on the grounds that events in Russia might ultimately be determined as much by international circumstances as by domestic class struggle.

*   *   *

'To What Extent is the Communist Manifesto Obsolete?'

The following remarks were written, at the invitation of the Polish comrades, as a preface to a new Polish edition of the Communist Manifesto and were therefore first published in Polish.[8]

Almost sixty years have passed since the *Communist Manifesto* was written, sixty years of a mode of production that consists, more than any preceding one, of a constant overturning of the old and a continual hurrying and hunting after the new. They have been sixty years of thorough political and social revolutionising, not only of Europe but of the whole globe. Naturally, these sixty years could not pass without leaving their mark on the *Communist*

---

[7] Ryazanov 1928a, pp. 141–2. For a partial English version see Ryazanov 1928b.
[8] [Kautsky's introduction to the 1903 ed. Removed from the 1906 preface to the *Communist Manifesto*.]

Manifesto. The more correctly it comprehended and corresponded to its time, the more it must necessarily grow obsolete and become an historical document that bears witness to its own time but can no longer be definitive for the present.

But this, it should be emphasised, is true only regarding some points, namely, those where the *practical politician* speaks to his *contemporaries*. Nothing would be more erroneous than to stamp the whole of the *Communist Manifesto* as simply an historical document. On the contrary, the *principles* developed by it, the *method* to which it leads us, and the *characterisation* it gives in a few strokes of the capitalist mode of production, are today more valid than ever. The whole actual development, as well as the whole theoretical investigation of the period since the writing of the *Manifesto*, is nothing but an unbroken line of confirmations of its fundamental conceptions. Never was the principle more universally accepted that the history of all hitherto existing (civilised) society is the history of class wars; and never has it been clearer that the great driving force of our times is the class struggle between the bourgeoisie and the proletariat.

But neither the proletarians nor the bourgeoisie are any longer quite the same as they were six decades ago. Sharp and accurate as the *Manifesto*'s portrayal of them is, and although it constitutes even today the most brilliant and profound description possible within so narrow a framework, in some respects it does not any longer tally.

At the time when the *Communist Manifesto* appeared, the most striking characteristics of the proletariat were its degradation, the lowering of its wages, the lengthening of its working hours, its physical and often its moral and intellectual decay; in short, its misery. Of the three great classes that made up the bulk of the people – the peasants, the petty bourgeoisie and the wage-workers – the latter then stood, in every respect, at the bottom. They were poor, oppressed, and helpless; both in numbers and in economic importance (with the exception of England), they ranked below the two other classes. For most disinterested spectators, the working class was only an object of pity. It therefore required all the economic and historic knowledge and all the acumen of a Marx and an Engels to detect in the class struggle of the proletariat the strongest motive force in the social development of the coming decades at a time when the successors of the great utopians still regarded the proletariat as a helpless mass to which relief could come only from the upper classes. At the time, revolutionists expected everything from what was called the 'people', that is, essentially from the petty bourgeoisie and the peasants; the mass of wage-workers was an appendix of the petty bourgeoisie and peasants and was intellectually, socially, and often economically dependent upon them.

Today, the position of the proletariat is entirely different. True, it is still subjected to the pauperising influence of capital, as it was sixty years ago, and capital even today strives to lower wages, lengthen the hours of labour, supplant the worker with the machine, displace the working man by the woman and the child, and thus degrade the proletariat. But 'the revolt of the working class, a class always increasing in numbers, and disciplined, united, organized by the very mechanism of the process of capitalist production itself', is also growing ever stronger.[9] The resistance of the proletariat continuously intensifies as its strata learn, one after the other, to overcome the degrading effects of capitalism.

The situation of the peasantry and the petty bourgeoisie is quite different. While, for decades, growing numbers of proletarians were shortening their working time and increasing their wages, the working time of the craftsmen and small farmers remained the same or was extended even to the limits of physical endurance; the intensity of their labour grew, and their standard of living is approaching more and more the level of subsistence. Moreover, while the working class knows how to erect an ever-stronger defence, an ever-greater protection for women and children employed in the great industries, the craftsmen and farmers are increasingly forced into extensive exploitation of their own women and children as well as those of others.

Hand in hand with this economic transformation goes an intellectual and political one. A hundred years ago the small tradesmen far surpassed all other classes of the people in intelligence, self-reliance, and courage; today, the proletariat vigorously develops those virtues while the small tradesman has become the prototype of narrowness, servility and cowardice. A hundred years ago, the petty bourgeoisie still formed the heart of democratic opposition and bourgeois radicalism, which declared war upon the castles, thrones, and altars, and peace to the cottages. Today, the petty bourgeoisie have become the élite troops of reaction, the bodyguard of those in the castles, thrones and

---

[9] Marx 1976, Part VIII: Primitive Accumulation, Chapter XXXII: Historical Tendency of Capitalist Accumulation: 927–30.

altars, to whom they look for salvation from the misery into which they have been thrown by economic development.

A similar thing happened to the peasantry.

Now there is only *one* class of the population [in the capitalistically developed nations – this rule does not apply to Russia –][10] that, with all its strength, stands for social progress, and that class is the proletariat. But all these transformations are, fortunately for social progress, accompanied by a complete shift in power relations. When the *Communist Manifesto* was written, the great majority of the population (in France and Germany, from 70 to 80 per cent) still lived in the countryside. In the cities, the petty bourgeoisie was dominant. Today, the urban population constitutes the majority in all the industrially developed states of Europe, and in the cities the proletariat is predominant. Moreover, its economic importance has grown still more than its proportion to the whole population. A hundred years ago capitalist industry, especially on the European continent, still served above all to satisfy the demands of luxury, producing silk stuffs, rugs, porcelain, paper, etc. Sixty years ago, economic life rested mainly upon handicrafts and husbandry. At present, the economic significance and the wealth of a country depend in the first place upon its great capitalist industries, which produce no luxuries but rather articles of mass consumption and the necessities of life. A modern state can exist without peasants and handicraftsmen, as is shown by the example of England, but it cannot exist without capitalist industries and the corresponding means of transportation.

[The proletariat also grows along with large-scale industry and the means of mass transportation. It is already the strongest stratum of the population in purely numerical terms. In German industry, the wage-workers were in 1882 for the first time 66 per cent, i.e. *two thirds*, of the gainfully occupied persons; in 1895, they were already *three fourths* of the gainfully occupied persons.

Today, the entire economic life of the country depends on them. Within their ranks there are even growing numbers whose conditions of life and work surpass those of the small artisans, merchants and peasants.

---

[10] [Added to the 1906 edition (preface to the sixth German edition of the *Communist Manifesto*).]

The situation of many strata of the propertyless workers is today better than that of wide circles of propertied people, i.e. those who possess their own means of production.][11]

One can no longer say, as the *Manifesto* did, that

> The modern labourer…instead of rising with the process of industry, sinks deeper and deeper below the conditions of existence of his own class. He becomes a pauper, and pauperism develops more rapidly than population and wealth.[12]

Thus the proletariat occupies today a position quite different from that of sixty years ago. To be sure, one must look at things in a peculiar way to think that, as a consequence of these changes, the *antagonism* of the proletariat toward *capital* has been moderated. Quite the contrary. On the one hand the proletariat, like every other class, today has at its disposal greater access to the advantages of culture than in former centuries or even past decades. The enormous increase in the productive forces, which have been unchained by capitalism, has not passed by the working class without leaving its mark. We may speak of an amelioration of the condition of many proletarian strata if we compare them with the condition of the *petty bourgeoisie* and the *small peasants*, but the situation of workers is decidedly and rapidly worsening vis-à-vis the situation of their exploiters, the *capitalist class*. The productivity of labour has grown enormously under the rule of capital, the social wealth has enormously risen, but what the proletariat gets from it is very meagre compared to the riches appropriated by the capitalist class. The condition of the proletariat is deteriorating compared with the living standards of the capitalist class and the accumulation of capital; its share in the product of its toil is decreasing, and its exploitation is steadily increasing. All the progress that it has nevertheless made has been won only by fighting against capital, and the workers are able to maintain it only through a continuous struggle. In this way, not only the degradation of the proletariat but also its elevation, not only its defeats but also its victories, become sources of a continuous and growing anger against the enemy class. The forms of the struggle change and become more acute. Isolated acts of wild despair are replaced by the

---

[11] [Also added to the 1906 edition.]
[12] Marx and Engels 1848a, Chapter 1: Bourgeois and Proletarian, pp. 482–96.

planned acts of great organisations, but the antagonisms remain and become ever more acute.

Like the proletariat, the industrial bourgeoisie has also undergone a transformation during the last sixty years. When the *Communist Manifesto* appeared, that class had only just done away with the Corn Laws, the final obstacle to its domination in England, and on the continent of Europe it was confronted with the necessity of a revolution to subordinate political power to its own aims.

It stood in hostile opposition to the powers that most clearly oppressed the bulk of the population – the clergy, the nobility, the monarchy, and high finance. It was still cherishing great political aims and ideals that even gave it a sort of ethical idealism. It still believed that only the debris of feudalism stood in the way of general prosperity and that after it was cleared away, there would begin an era of general happiness.

The revolution of 1848 brought the great disappointment and unveiled the class antagonisms that economic development, as we have seen, steadily intensified. Thus the industrial bourgeoisie and its followers were driven into the camp of reaction. It was unable to attain absolute power anywhere in Europe. It tried to obtain political power with the help of the petty bourgeoisie and the proletariat, and to preserve its domination with the help of those social powers against which it had mobilised the democracy. To this should be added the fact that industry has more and more surrendered to high finance through the stock exchange, which has always been anti-democratic and has favoured absolute power in the state.

The *Communist Manifesto* could still declare:

> In Germany the Communist Party fights with the bourgeoisie whenever it acts in a revolutionary way, against the absolute monarchy, the feudal landowners, and the petty bourgeoisie.[13]

Today we can nowhere speak of a revolutionary bourgeoisie [with the possible exception of Russia].[14]

---

[13] Marx and Engels 1848a, Chapter 4: Position of the Communists in Relation to the Various Existing Opposition Parties, pp. 518–19.

[14] [Added to the 1906 edition (preface to the sixth German edition of the *Communist Manifesto*).]

However, not only are the bourgeoisie and proletariat in some respects differently disposed today from what they were at the time of the *Communist Manifesto*, but the course of development has also not turned out quite as had been expected. To be sure, the basic economic development has moved entirely along the path that the *Manifesto* outlined so clearly; and what it says in this respect remains classic to this day. But the political development has proceeded differently from what one could foresee at that time.

Marx and Engels were well aware of the fact that the working class, in its condition at that time, especially in Germany, was unable to conquer political power and keep it. But they expected the impending bourgeois revolution, which they believed would take place in Germany sooner than elsewhere, to take a course similar to that of the English Revolution of the seventeenth and the French Revolution of the eighteenth century. They expected it, from the outset, to be a movement of the revolutionary bourgeoisie against absolutism and feudalism, but they hoped that in its further development the proletarian elements would more and more recognise and develop their antagonism towards the bourgeoisie, and that the revolution would strengthen the influence of the proletariat and cause it rapidly to intensify and mature. For, during a revolution, every development proceeds at a most rapid pace; a revolutionary class advances as far in five years as it would otherwise do in a century. Thus, the bourgeois revolution would be followed immediately by a proletarian revolution, and the conquest of political power by the proletariat would be won not as the result of a coup, but through years, perhaps decades, of revolutionary struggles.

The *Communist Manifesto* says in this respect:

> The Communists turn their attention chiefly to Germany because that country is on the eve of a bourgeois revolution that is bound to be carried out under more advanced conditions of European civilization, and with a much more developed proletariat than that of England was in the seventeenth and of France in the eighteenth century, and because *the bourgeois revolution in Germany can be but the prelude to an immediately following proletarian revolution.*[15]

---

[15] Marx and Engels 1848a, Chapter 4: Position of the Communists in Relation to the Various Existing Opposition Parties, pp. 518–519. (Italics added by Kautsky.)

This expectation did not materialise, as we all know; it did not materialise just because the revolution of 1848 happened 'under more progressive conditions of European civilization' than those of 1640 and 1789.

It was war that drove the proletarian, the semi-proletarian, and semi-petty-bourgeois elements of the English and French Revolutions to the forefront and enabled them temporarily to seize political power – a life-and-death war that the revolution had to wage and in which it could only endure through the workers' characteristic disregard both for their own lives and for the property of the moneyed classes. In England it was the long war of Parliament against the feudal armies of Charles I, and in France it was the war against the allied monarchs of Europe, which likewise lasted for years.

But the revolution of 1848 kindled no war. The governments were not brought down by a protracted civil war; the barricade battles of a single day were sufficient to cause their collapse in Paris, Vienna, and Berlin. And, since the revolution extended over the whole of Europe, there was no foreign power to proclaim war against it. Absolutist Russia at first kept very quiet.

But, while the feudal-absolutist opponents of the revolution of 1848 were much weaker than in the seventeenth and eighteenth centuries, the proletariat was much stronger. During the days of February, it immediately gained a dominant position in Paris. In place of a life-and-death struggle against the monarchy and nobility, for which it would have been necessary to call the proletariat to arms and ultimately to submit to its influence, the bourgeoisie was immediately forced to begin a life-and-death struggle against the proletariat itself. For this purpose, the bourgeoisie turned for help to the only recently subdued power of the state and its army, and thus it ultimately submitted once more to its yoke.

The battle of June was the catastrophe of the revolution of 1848. It inaugurated a new historical epoch. It marked the moment when the bourgeoisie completely ceased to be a revolutionary class in political terms, and it brought to a close the era of bourgeois revolutions, at least for Western Europe. I will not discuss here how far this holds good for Russia, where the peasantry and the intellectuals play an entirely different role than in Western Europe. Since June 1848 a bourgeois revolution that could become the prelude to a proletarian revolution is no longer possible in Western Europe. The next revolution can only be a proletarian one.

And, in Russia, too, the initiative for a revolution can only emanate from the industrial proletariat, even if it does not as yet lead to its exclusive domination.

But all this has given the labour movement a totally different role from the one it had at the time when the *Communist Manifesto* was written.

The strengthening of the working class, and its elevation to a position that would enable it to conquer and retain political power, can no longer be expected from a bourgeois revolution that, in becoming permanent, grows beyond its own limits and develops out of itself a proletarian revolution. This maturing and strengthening must take place *outside* of the revolution and *before* it. The proletariat must have reached a certain degree of development before a revolution is at all possible. The revolution must take place through methods of peace, not of war – if one may express oneself so paradoxically as to distinguish between warlike and peaceful methods of class struggle. Protection of the workers, trade unionism, organisation of co-operative societies and universal suffrage now gradually assume a significance quite different from that of the period before June 1848.

That which sixty years ago was still enshrouded in the utmost darkness is today as clear as daylight. Thanks to this fact, many a short-sighted mole, diligently digging for earth-worms, thinks himself far superior in range and clarity of vision to the masters of the *Communist Manifesto* and even looks down with pity upon their intellectual errors. But the fact is that there were no socialists and revolutionaries who comprehended the new situation sooner than Marx and Engels.

They were the first to recognise that the era of revolution, for the near future at least, had come to an end. It was the International[16] that first systematically sought to promote trade-union organisations on the continent of Europe. Marx's *Capital* first offered a theory for the legislative protection of the workers, and in the 1860s the International participated energetically in the movement for universal suffrage in England.

Not only the *methods* by which the working class becomes mature, but also the *pace* of development had to change as a consequence of the new situation.

---

[16] [The International Workingmen's Association, or First International (1864–1876).]

The place of rapid revolutionary impetus was taken by the snail-like movement of peaceful and legal evolution, which is too slow for a fiery soul.

Thus some things have reached a different outcome from what the authors of the *Communist Manifesto* expected at the time of writing. But they were the first to recognise the new situation, and they did so because of the principles and methods they had developed in their *Manifesto*. The new situation was itself a confirmation of those principles, though in a different form from the one they foresaw. If the legislative protection of the workers and the trade-union organisations acquired during the following decades an importance that was still impossible to recognise in 1847, this was only due to the fact that a few months after the appearance of the *Manifesto* the class antagonism between bourgeoisie and proletariat already affected the bourgeoisie in a manner that nobody suspected before February 1848. It was also due, therefore, to the fact that the delineation of this antagonism in the *Communist Manifesto* already proved to be truer for its own time than its authors had assumed.

Very few of those who play the part of 'critics' of the *Manifesto* suspect these kinds of connections. From the fact that a rapid and stormy development was replaced by a 'peaceful' and gradual one, and that revolutionary methods of class war were replaced by legal ones, they conclude that an antagonism between bourgeoisie and proletariat either does not exist at all or is constantly diminishing. They preach co-operation between the liberal bourgeoisie and the proletariat and, in so far as they are socialists, they refer to the sentence of the *Manifesto* that states:

> In Germany the Communist party fights *together with the bourgeoisie* as long as it acts in a revolutionary way, against the absolute monarchy, the feudal landowners, and the petty bourgeoisie.[17]

[This sentence, it is claimed, sanctions the policy of forming a democratic bloc in order to capture the government (*die Politik des demokratischen Regierungsblocks*) and the policy of socialist ministerialism that is practiced by some socialist factions in France and Italy and preached everywhere by the representatives of the 'new method'. Here we have a Marxist 'dogma'

---

[17] Marx and Engels 1848a, Chapter 4: Position of the Communists in Relation to the Various Existing Opposition Parties, pp. 518–19.

defended with truly dogmatic fanaticism precisely by the champions of 'critical' socialism.][18]

But we have seen that insofar as we may speak of a 'mistake' in the *Manifesto* and consider criticism to be necessary, this must begin precisely with the 'dogma' that the bourgeoisie is revolutionary in political terms. The very displacement of revolution by evolution during the last fifty years grows out of the fact that a *revolutionary bourgeoisie* no longer exists. Besides, Marx and Engels understood by the term 'fighting with the bourgeoisie' something different from what the supporters of contemporary socialist ministerialism understand.[19] The 'Address of the Central Committee to the Communist League' of March, 1850, deals with the attitude of the communists towards bourgeois democracy, which, it was assumed at the time, would place itself at the helm of the state during a new revolutionary eruption. To quote:

> At the moment, while the democratic petty bourgeois are everywhere oppressed, they preach to the proletariat general unity and reconciliation; they extend the hand of friendship, and seek to found a great opposition party which will embrace all shades of democratic opinion; that is, they seek to ensnare the workers in a party organization in which general Social-Democratic phrases[20] prevail while their particular interests are kept hidden…and in which, for the sake of preserving the peace, the specific demands of the proletariat may not be presented. Such a unity would be to their advantage alone and to the complete disadvantage of the proletariat. The proletariat would lose all its hard-won independent position and be reduced once more to a mere appendage of official bourgeois democracy. This unity must therefore be resisted in the most decisive manner.…In the event of a struggle against a common enemy a special alliance is unnecessary.

---

[18] [This paragraph appears in the 1903 edition but was removed from the 1906 preface to the *Communist Manifesto*. By 'the representatives of the "new method"' and 'the champions of "critical" socialism' Kautsky means the Revisionist followers of Eduard Bernstein.]

[19] [Another reference to the revisionist right wing of the Second International. 'Ministerialism' means support for the policy of socialist politicians joining bourgeois governments, after the precedent set by Alexandre Millerand (1859–1943), a French socialist member of the Chamber of Deputies who in 1899 joined the bourgeois cabinet of René Waldeck-Rousseau as Minister of Commerce.]

[20] What was then called Social Democracy was not a proletarian class party but a petty-bourgeois-proletarian mixture without a definite class character, but with predominantly petty bourgeois aspirations.

As soon as such an enemy has to be fought directly, the interests of both parties will coincide for the moment and an association of momentary expedience will arise spontaneously in the future, as it has in the past. It goes without saying that in the bloody conflicts to come, as in all others, it will be the workers, with their courage, resolution and self-sacrifice, who will be chiefly responsible for achieving victory.…During and after the struggle the workers must at every opportunity put forward their own demands against those of the bourgeois democrats. They must demand guarantees for the workers as soon as the bourgeois democrats set about taking over the government. They must achieve these guarantees by force if necessary, and generally make sure that the new rulers commit themselves to all possible concessions and promises – the surest means of compromising them. They must check in every way and as far as…possible the victory euphoria and enthusiasm for the new situation which follow every successful street battle, with a cool and cold-blooded analysis of the situation and with undisguised mistrust of the new government.…In a word, from the very moment of victory the workers' suspicion must be directed no longer against the defeated reactionary party but against their former ally, against the party which intends to exploit the common victory for itself.[21]

This, then, was the form of common struggle of the bourgeoisie and proletariat against absolutism and feudalism, as Marx and Engels regarded it when they wrote the *Communist Manifesto*. It is something quite different from what the present-day socialist ministerialists [*Ministeriellen*] in France and Italy aim for.

Of course, one may object that what took place at that time were revolutionary struggles. But a common revolutionary struggle is the most favourable case for a united action of the bourgeoisie and the proletariat. The danger that the political power of the proletariat may be exploited by the bourgeoisie, that the proletariat may lose the political power that emanates from its political independence, together with the need to distrust a bourgeois-democratic government, are evidently much stronger in circumstances where the bourgeoisie can no longer be anything but conservative than where it still aims for the revolutionary conquest of new positions.

---

[21] Marx and Engels 1850.

But wherever co-operation of bourgeoisie and proletariat may today become necessary, it is, with the exception of Russia, not for revolutionary but for conservative purposes – for the preservation and security of the existing meagre rudiments of democracy against the onslaught of reaction. In these struggles against reaction, the proletariat also has to stand its ground; here, too, its lot is to take on the most difficult work and it sometimes has to cooperate with the liberal bourgeoisie. But, even more than in the revolutionary struggle, there is a danger here that the proletariat may be betrayed by its allies. The proletariat must therefore face them with open distrust and above all retain a completely independent organisation. By virtue of its class position, the proletariat is a thoroughly revolutionary class, and today it is the only revolutionary class. For a time, circumstances may force it to participate in a conservative response to reaction, but its forces can never be fully spent in that task. It must always give practical proof of its revolutionary character, which will break through even where, for the moment, it acts in a conservative manner. Its powers can only develop and increase through revolutionary action and revolutionary propaganda, and it destroys the sources of its strength if it limits itself to the role of a conservative guardian of the ruling liberal bourgeoisie against the onslaught of the clergy, the landed aristocracy and the mercenaries.

[Of course, these are questions that concern the socialists of Western Europe more than those who are active in the Russian Empire. The latter live under political and economic conditions that still greatly resemble those of Germany on the eve of the revolution of 1848. For that reason, the *Manifesto* is still far more valid for them than for the socialists of Western Europe, not only as regards its fundamentals, its methods and its description of the general character of the capitalist mode of production (all of which today still constitute the unshakeable foundations for every conscious proletarian movement in every country) but also in many details that for Western Europe have become obsolete.

With the modern conditions of international intercourse, however, no country, and least of all a capitalist country, moves along the path of its domestic development solely as a result of its own internal driving forces. Outside influences, and above all the effects of class wars in foreign countries, become almost equally important for its class struggles.

The revolutionary battle of June 1848 in France proved decisive not only for the course of the French revolution, but also for that of the German Revolution and for the labour movement in England. Likewise, the relation between the proletariat and the bourgeoisie in Western Europe affects the relation between these classes in Russia as they face a political and economic situation that corresponds to the time of the *Manifesto* but also embodies all the experiences accumulated over two generations of uninterrupted economic revolution since the *Communist Manifesto*.

The political relation between bourgeoisie and proletariat, between liberalism and socialism, is for that reason a much more complex and difficult one in Russia than in Western Europe. To comprehend it correctly, the socialists active under Russian absolutism will have to take into consideration the more primitive conditions of their own country just as much as the more highly developed conditions of other countries. The Russian bourgeoisie still has a revolutionary task to fulfil, but it has already adopted the reactionary turn of mind of the bourgeoisie in the West.][22]

Russian socialists will find their best and most reliable guide in the *Communist Manifesto*. [To be sure, there can be no single model for all the forms that the class struggle of the proletariat has assumed in every country, and the *Communist Manifesto* must likewise not be regarded in this way. The circumstances under which the proletariat has to conduct its political and economic struggles today are extremely diverse and complex. In every country many of these conditions are completely unique. Nowhere do they correspond perfectly to the conditions that influenced the writing of the *Communist Manifesto*. Nevertheless, it remains the proletarians' best and most reliable guide on their way to emancipating their own class and therefore the human race.][23]

The *Communist Manifesto* is no Gospel – no Bible, as it has been called, whose words are holy – but a historical document that should be subject to criticism; to criticism, however, that does not limit itself to stating how some sentences and turns of phrase no longer fit the case; and to criticism, furthermore, that endeavours to comprehend the work itself as well as those sentences that today are obsolete, thereby deriving new knowledge from them.

---

[22] [1903 edition. Removed from the 1906 preface to the *Communist Manifesto*.]
[23] [Added to the 1906 edition (preface to the sixth German edition of the *Communist Manifesto*).]

To those who study the *Communist Manifesto* in this manner it is a compass upon the stormy ocean of the proletarian class struggle. A compass to which the socialist parties of all countries are indebted for the fact that, despite all contrary currents, despite fogs and cliffs, they are always headed in the right direction. A compass that proved reliable by pointing out, for sixty years, the direction of economic development, and which all the facts have corroborated again and again. There is no historic document more gloriously confirmed by the decades following the time of writing than the *Communist Manifesto*.

Chapter Five

'Revolutionary Questions' (February 1904)

Karl Kautsky

This essay[1] was Karl Kautsky's response to criticism of his 1902 book *The Social Revolution*[2] by Michał Luśnia (Kazimierz Kelles-Krauz). Luśnia was a leading theorist of the Polish Socialist Party (PPS), which was the main rival of the Social-Democratic Party of the Kingdom of Poland and Lithuania (SDKPiL), headed by Rosa Luxemburg and Leo Jogiches. Kautsky's work was published in Russia at least twice in the aftermath of the 1905 revolution.[3] Luśnia gave the title 'Unarmed Revolution?'[4] to his critical review, which appeared in *Die Neue Zeit* with this prefatory note by Kautsky:

> Outside the circle of party comrades engaged in direct struggle with the tsars, the views developed here, insofar as they relate to a violent revolution, may be valid for special circumstances in which international Social Democracy is not strongly represented. In German Social Democracy I know of nobody who holds similar views. But I feel that I am

---

[1] Kautsky 1904a. Literally the title of the article series reads 'Revolutionary Allsorts' or 'Various Things Revolutionary'. Kautsky reprinted *Allerhand Revolutionäres* in the final part of his book Kautsky 1914, pp. 67–103.

[2] Kautsky 1902–4.

[3] Kautsky 1906l; Kautsky 1907c.

[4] Luśnia 1904, pp. 559–67.

not entitled, as editor, to suppress a criticism directed at me, and for that reason I agreed to publish the article of our Polish comrade. One will understand, however, why we delayed until now the publication of this article, which reached us almost a year ago. During the period of the election campaign for the national and state legislatures, as well as of the debate about the vice-president, it did not seem appropriate to us also to place on the order of the day a discussion over the question of the revolution. With the consent of its author, we have therefore postponed until now publication of the following article. A reply follows in the next issues of *Die Neue Zeit*.[5]

Luśnia began his article by praising Kautsky for having raised the issue of the concrete forms that the next social revolution would assume: 'Thanks to him we will be able to speak again about those things without being looked upon as lunatics by the fanatics of purely "practical" work.'[6] Luśnia then proceeded to criticise Kautsky's description of the first economic steps that the future proletarian government would be forced to take, such as unemployment relief, concentration of the workers in the largest and most efficient enterprises, and so forth. He then presented a scenario of the future revolution that proved, with the benefit of hindsight, to be much closer to actual revolutionary events of the coming decades than Kautsky's more 'pacifist' outlook. The following excerpt will provide readers with the essential ideas of Luśnia's article, 'Unarmed Revolution?':

> In yet another respect my views about the period of struggles [i.e. the period of transition from capitalism to socialism] diverge from those of Kautsky, and here we come to the principal difference of opinion between us, which appears with an interrogation mark in the title of this article. I think that it is not a purely subjective feeling when I say that the chapter of Kautsky's brochure on the *Forms and Weapons of the Social Revolution*[7] is fragmentary and gives an impression of indecision, of diffidence, which is unusual in Kautsky. One perceives here the latent influence of the continuing and yet to be overcome condition of the proletarian movement, in which one can think about the revolution, about the decisive struggle, only reluctantly and

---

5 Kautsky 1904c, p. 559.
6 Kautsky 1904c, p. 560.
7 [Kautsky 1902–4, Vol. I: *The Social Revolution*, Part 7: Forms and Weapons of [the] Social Revolution. In the 1902 English edition see pp. 84–102.]

with anxiety. For that reason, people tend to persuade themselves that the revolution can and must be unarmed. But I think that, *precisely considering that frame of mind of the majority of the fighters, it is much more useful to draw all the consequences and also to destroy those illusions* without, of course, adopting in the least a ridiculously heroic pose.

Kautsky is surely correct when he thinks that the coming revolution will be very different from previous ones. For the first time a revolution will be carried out making use of democratic forms and will not be directed against an isolated government but rather will lead to a struggle by part of the people, to be sure a larger and more energetic part, against perhaps a fairly large part of the people – many petty bourgeois and small peasants together with the capitalists and the large landowners. Kautsky is very sagacious when he writes: 'the coming revolution will be much less a sudden uprising against the authorities than a long *drawn out civil war'*, but he is totally mistaken, I think, when he adds: 'if one does not necessarily associate with these last words the idea of *actual wars and slaughter*. We have no reason to assume that *armed insurrections* with barricade battles and similar warlike occurrences can still play a decisive role even today.' Why? Kautsky answers: 'The reasons for this have been given so often that I have no need of dwelling on them further.'[8] And he counts only on the mass strike (a still unknown method of struggle), on a war, and finally on the unreliability of the military. Let's take a closer look at those issues.

Naturally, we have no wish to speak about means that are today unknown and unforeseeable. As regards the mass strike, it is certainly a prejudice for people to reject that means of struggle in principle, indeed, a harmful prejudice when the partisans of the mass strike, due to certain historical circumstances, employ the incorrect expression general strike. One must only free this idea absolutely from all the misunderstandings and fallacies that cling to it and reduce them all to the single delusion that the mass strike is a magic means that replaces all others. Kautsky rightly protests against the idea that the mass strike can make parliamentary tactics superfluous,

---

[8] [Kautsky 1903, Vol. I: *The Social Revolution*: Forms and Weapons of Social Revolution. The passage had to be retranslated, as the mention of armed insurrections has been deleted from the English version of Algie Simmons.]

but does he really believe, along with Allemane[9] and many others, that the revolution of 'crossed arms' can replace the revolution of clenched fists, or rather of armed fists? In other words, can a decisive struggle of the people against the exploiters and the government, involving vital political demands, be fought by means of the mass strike without inevitably leading to clashes with the military? One has only to consider the demonstrations and assemblies that are unavoidable in a mass strike, especially a political one; the intense agitation that must possess the people in such life-and-death struggles, the provocations of the government, and most especially the strike-breakers. The organised workers are everywhere the minority, and whoever cherishes hopes that the organisation of the proletariat in capitalist society will be able to encompass the majority of the workers, or even the entire class prior to the triumph of the revolutionary movement, has to think about the unemployed. Is it not highly probable that if the strike lasts for some time, the unorganised, and especially the unemployed, will be invited to work in place of the strikers? Even given all the discipline and all the illusions about peace, would the strikers then be able to preserve legality? Would they be able to refrain from attacking the traitors when they become really noxious? The replacement of certain workers by soldiers, or the militarisation of certain categories of workers, which has already been attempted against the railway employees in Italy, could also easily lead to clashes in which the workers would confront the military. What then? Is all lost?

All the arguments against the probability of a new popular insurrection are only correct to the extent that today, in view of modern military technique, neither the greatest courage nor barricade struggles and so on can save the people from defeat when the unarmed or badly armed people confronts the military *and the military does not shrink from carrying out the most horrible slaughters*. To that extent, Kautsky is also correct when he says: 'Militarism

---

9 [Jean Allemane (1843–1935) was a French worker and Communard. Deported to New Caledonia, he returned to France after the amnesty. In 1890 he broke with the *possibilistes* to form the *Parti ouvrier socialiste révolutionnaire* (POSR), with positions close to those of revolutionary syndicalism. In 1905 it joined with other parties to form the Socialist Party (SFIO). Allemane was for a long time a leader of the socialist left, and his supporters where known as 'allemanistes'. A well-known anti-militarist and *maximaliste*, he supported the revolutionary general strike. During the First World War he followed the 'national unity' policy of the SFIO. When the French Communist Party was formed in 1920, he was sympathetic to it but did not join it. In 1906 he published his *Mémoires d'un Communard* (Paris: Librarie Socialiste).]

can only be overthrown by rendering the military itself disaffected with the rulers, not through its being defeated by popular uprisings.'[10] But the military must appear disaffected in the action itself, not in the consciousness of the rulers. Only when it goes through that test will one know what to expect from it. In its action, a part of the military can pass over to the side of the people. I say explicitly *a part*, because it seems to me impossible to expect that response from the whole military or even from its majority. The army is today an image of society; it consists of members of all classes. On the one hand there will be among the officials some friends of the people, but on the other hand there will be also very many soldiers, including soldiers of peasant and petty-bourgeois extraction but also some from the working class, who, unnerved by clericalism, will be ready to take part in the repression of the revolutionary movement. Whether the military will for the time being repress the movement or join it will therefore depend on the composition of each army division in question, and also naturally on the strength of the popular movement in each particular place, on the moral impression that it is able to make on the minds of the soldiers. It is therefore improbable that the revolution will be victorious throughout the whole country at once. But is it not certain that the assailed regime will strain every nerve, with the help of the loyal part of the army, in order to wrest victory from the hands of the rebels and crush the rebellious troops? For the latter there would be no way back; they would have to help the masses arm themselves and set up a fighting organisation, which would be made much easier by universal conscription. And so *two armed camps* would confront each other: the revolution and the forces of order. If the situation reaches that point, they would have to start a *real* civil war with actual battles and sieges. Let us recall the *Paris Commune*: then, too, a part of the troops passed over to the side of the revolution and fought, together with the armed population, against the troops of order. Only that prototype would be augmented a hundred times: hundreds of 'communes' would arise, and the victorious ones would come to the help of the others. To

---

[10] [Kautsky 1902–4, Vol. I: *The Social Revolution*, Part 7: Forms and Weapons of the Social Revolution. In the English edition see p. 88.]

conceive the coming revolution in some other concrete form seems to me impossible.[11]

Luśnia concluded his article with an analysis of the 'outward, international aspects of the revolution',[12] where he developed the idea that Russia would continue, as in the nineteenth century, to be the bulwark of reaction in the event of a revolutionary outbreak in Europe – an erroneous perspective that led him to conclude that 'a war *on European soil* is highly improbable'.[13]

In his biography of Luśnia, Timothy Snyder commented upon the reactions of the leading Marxists of the time to this exchange:

> As Plekhanov pointed out, Kautsky was unable to meet Kelles-Krauz's challenge to provide a credible scenario for socialist revolution in Germany [Plekhanov to Kautsky, 28 September 1904, cited in Waldenberg's Polish book on Kautsky (Timothy Snyder's note, p. 182)].... Rosa Luxemburg seized the occasion of this debate to attack Kelles-Krauz for the first time. By this time, she and her allies had gained control of the SDKPiL [the Social Democracy of the Kingdom of Poland and Lithuania], and she chose its organ *Przeglad Socjalistyczny* as her forum. In her own inimitable style [she wrote in Vol. 2, No. 2, 1904]: 'This "professor" of "retrospective sociology," "doctor," baron, knight of three titles, having striven vainly for years with the help of two pseudonyms to gain a name for himself, has finally attained his goal. He has received for his troubles a few kicks in the back from Kautsky, but that's how it goes, that's just part of the European acclaim that in Mr. Elehard Esse's opinion Mr. Michał Luśnia has now gained.... [Elehard Esse was one of Kelles-Krauz's two pseudonyms]. One has to hand it to the social patriots: they have indeed nationalized Polish socialism in the full sense of the word. For such Luśnias are the incarnation, in the world of socialism, of our own particular type of Warsaw publicist, who gains his notoriety by stomping on the corns of the famous in the street.[14]

Rosa Luxemburg and Kautsky were both dismayed by the way Luśnia minimised the role of Russian workers in the coming revolution. When, in February 1905, Luśnia submitted to *Die Neue Zeit* an article calling for a

---

[11] Luśnia 1904, pp. 563–5.
[12] Luśnia 1904, p. 565.
[13] Luśnia 1904, p. 566.
[14] Snyder 1997, pp. 182–84.

separate Polish movement to break away from the larger Russian issues and seek Polish independence, Kautsky rejected the article with these words:

> I am little edified by the politics put forward by you in your article. You wrote the unbelievable sentence that Poland certainly is ripe for democracy, *but perhaps not Russia*. This statement is the worst betrayal of the Russian revolution that one can think of and simultaneously reveals the most short-sighted parochialism. The PPS seems still not to know that the history of all nations living in the Russian empire will be decided in Petersburg, not Warsaw, that the destruction of tsarism is the precondition of the independence of Poland, that today it is a question of combining all the forces of revolution against the tsar. You think [you will] be able to win Polish democracy before the Russian is won, therefore you separate the Polish revolution from the Russian and you make a struggle of the Poles against Russians out of the struggle of the Polish and Russian proletariat against the tsar. I cannot co-operate in that.[15]

It was certainly Kautsky's defence of the Russian proletariat as the future revolutionary vanguard of Europe, rather than his advocacy of the mass political strike as opposed to the armed insurrection, that led Trotsky to praise and quote extensively from Kautsky's article in his book *Results and Prospects*. But Trotsky appears also to have adopted from Kautsky a line of economic argument that reappeared in his own essay late in 1905 on the Paris Commune (included in this volume) and again in chapter eight of *Results and Prospects*; namely, the claim that once a proletarian party seized political power, the objective logic of its situation would compel it to begin implementing a socialist programme. In the document translated here, Kautsky cited the case of unemployment relief, which any workers' party would be compelled to initiate even if it did not *intend* immediate socialisation of the means of production. Kautsky reasoned that 'If every unemployed person were guaranteed a minimum living wage, every strike would be irresistible and the workers would be the true masters of the factory'. He concluded that

> wherever the proletariat has conquered political power, socialist production follows as a natural necessity even where the proletariat has not arrived at

---

15 Kautsky to Michał Luśnia, February 4, 1905. Quoted in Steenson 1978, p. 137.

> a socialist consciousness. Its class interests and economic necessity force it
> to adopt measures that lead to socialist production.... [I]f the proletariat has
> political power, then socialism follows as a matter of necessity.

In his essay on the Paris Commune, Trotsky followed similar reasoning to claim, as Ryazanov had done in his earlier criticism of Lenin and Plekhanov, that any distinction in Russia between a 'minimum' and a 'maximum' programme would vanish in the practice of *permanent revolution*. Whereas Kautsky spoke specifically of unemployment relief, Trotsky declared that a workers' government in Russia would have no choice but to legislate an eight-hour day, which would precipitate lock-outs and necessitate socialisation of the factories.[16] Although Kautsky specifically noted that 'A revolution in Russia cannot establish a socialist régime at once', in *Results and Prospects* Trotsky insisted that a workers' government in Russia would immediately have to 'take the path of socialist policy':

> It would be the greatest utopianism to think that the proletariat, having been raised to political domination by the internal mechanism of a bourgeois revolution, can, even if it so desires, limit its mission to the creation of republican-democratic conditions for the social domination of the bourgeoisie.... The workers cannot but demand maintenance for strikers from the revolutionary government, and a government relying upon the workers cannot refuse this demand. But this means paralysing the effect of the reserve army of labour and making the workers dominant not only in the political but also in the economic field, and converting private property in the means of production into a fiction. These inevitable social-economic consequences of proletarian dictatorship will reveal themselves very quickly, long before the democratization of the political system has been completed. The barrier between the 'minimum' and the 'maximum' programme disappears immediately the proletariat comes to power.[17]

In 'Revolutionary Questions', Kautsky left the door ajar for Trotsky's interpretation of his argument. While he personally expected a Russian revolution to produce only a democratic government from which an

---

[16] In this volume, see pp. 519–20.
[17] Trotsky, *Results and Prospects*, Chapter 8, 'A Workers' Government in Russia and Socialism', in L. Trotsky 1962, pp. 233–4.

'impetuous and progressive proletariat…would be able to demand important concessions', he also observed that

> The political rule of the proletariat in Western Europe would offer to the proletariat of Eastern Europe the possibility of shortening the stages of its development and artificially introducing socialist arrangements by imitating the German example.

Kautsky further explained how a Russian revolution might trigger a revolution in Europe when the upheaval in Poland was transmitted to Austria and Prussia. In chapter nine of *Results and Prospects,* dealing with the topic 'Europe and Revolution', Trotsky again followed Kautsky's line of thought: if the German and Austrian governments attempted to suppress the revolution in Poland, war would follow between Germany and revolutionary Russia and 'would lead inevitably to a proletarian revolution in Germany'. If a revolutionary government in Russia repudiated the tsarist debts, it would also precipitate a crisis in France that could only end with French workers seizing power. 'In one way or another,' Trotsky wrote, 'either through a revolution in Poland, through the consequences of a European war, or as the result of the State bankruptcy of Russia, revolution will cross into the territories of old capitalist Europe.' In that case, Kautsky's own proviso in 'Revolutionary Questions' would become operative: a workers' government in Russia would be able, as Kautsky himself said, to shorten the stages of its own development by following the example of socialist Germany.

Although Kautsky endorsed the mass political strike in 'Revolutionary Questions', in February 1910, under pressure from the conservative party apparatus, he refused to publish an article by Rosa Luxemburg that called for using the strike in order to achieve universal suffrage in Prussia and for raising the slogan of the republic as a transitional demand in order to turn the issue of electoral reform into a channel for revolutionary action.[18] This resulted in a furious round of polemics in the course of which Kautsky became the leading theoretician of the SPD centrists and developed the so-called 'strategy of exhausting the enemy [*Ermattungsstrategie*]' as opposed to the 'strategy of defeating the enemy [*Niederwerfungsstrategie*]', which was

---

[18] The article was finally published as Luxemburg 1910d. English edition: Luxemburg 1910c.

advocated by Rosa Luxemburg.[19] In her polemics against the centrists in the SPD, Rosa Luxemburg referred to 'Revolutionary Questions' as an example the revolutionary positions that Kautsky endorsed in 1904 but repudiated just six years later. In 'Theory and Practice' she wrote:

> Comrade Kautsky has proved yet another superfluous thing. If the general economic and political conditions in Germany are such as to make a mass strike action like the Russian one impossible, and if the extension which the mass strike underwent in the Russian Revolution is the specific product of Russian *backwardness*, then not only is the use of the mass strike in the Prussian voting rights struggle called into question but the Jena resolution as well. Until now, the resolution of the Jena party convention [of September 1905] was regarded both here and abroad as such a highly significant announcement because it officially borrowed the mass strike from the arsenal of the Russian Revolution and incorporated it among the tactics of German Social Democracy as a means of political struggle. Admittedly, this resolution was formally so composed, and by many exclusively interpreted so that Social Democracy seemed to declare it would only turn to the mass strike in case of an attack on Reichstag voting rights. But at one time, in any case, Comrade Kautsky did not belong to those formalists; indeed, in 1904 he emphatically wrote: 'If we learn one thing from the Belgian example, it is that it would be a fatal error for us in Germany to commit ourselves to a specific time for proclaiming the political strike – *for example, in the event of an attack on the present Reichstag voting rights.*' ['Revolutionaries Everywhere', *Die Neue Zeit*, Vol. 22, No. 1, p. 736. Rosa Luxemburg's emphasis].[20]

Rosa Luxemburg returned to this reference in the final part of her article. She remarked that 'comrade Kautsky quite rightly reminds us that "even before the Russian Revolution" he gave an exact description of the working of a political mass strike in his article "Revolutionary Questions"', but she added that this only made his centrist turnabout even more evident:

---

[19] Kautsky 1910b, pp. 332–41, 364–74, 412–21. Luxemburg 1910a, pp. 378–420. Kautsky 1910d, pp. 652–67. Kautsky 1913, pp. 532–40, 558–68, 662–4. Luxemburg 1913.

[20] Rosa Luxemburg, 'Theory & Practice [A polemic against Comrade Kautsky's theory of the Mass Strike]', Part 3 [Kautsky: the mass strike is incompatible with Germany]'. In this English version (at http:www.marxists,org/archive/luxemburg/1910/theory-practice/ch03.htm) *Allerhand Revolutionäres* is referred to as 'Revolutionaries Everywhere'.

The more Comrade Kautsky turned to broad theoretical generalizations to justify his position in the Prussian voting rights struggle, the more he lost sight of the general perspective of the development of the class struggle in Western Europe and in Germany – which in previous years he never tired of pointing out. Indeed, he himself had an uncomfortable sense of his present viewpoint's incongruence with his earlier one, and was therefore good enough to completely reproduce his 1904 article series "Revolutionary Questions" in the final, third part of his reply to me. The crass contradiction is not thereby done away with: it has only resulted in the chaotic, flickering character of that article's last part, which so remarkably lessens one's pleasure in reading it.[21]

* * *

'Revolutionary Questions'

I. Considerations against the consequences of a proletarian régime

The criticism that Comrade Luśnia offered of my two brochures dealing with the social revolution is, in some respects, a welcome occasion to complete what I said there and to correct some mistaken opinions that have been expressed regarding those writings.[22]

People have put into them conceptions that are not mine, especially in the second part, *On the Day after the Social Revolution*. I refrain here from answering the criticisms levelled at them by people like Mr. von Bülow[23] and

---

[21] Ibid.

[22] [Kautsky 1902–4.]

[23] [Bernhard von Bülow (1849–1929) held several diplomatic posts before he was appointed secretary of state for foreign affairs (the same office his father had held) in 1897. As foreign secretary Bülow was chiefly responsible for carrying out the policy of colonial expansion (or *Weltpolitik*) with which the emperor had identified himself. In 1899 Bülow was raised to the rank of Count after bringing to a successful conclusion the negotiations by which the Caroline Islands were acquired by Germany. On the resignation of Prince Chlodwig von Hohenlohe in 1900 he was chosen to succeed him as chancellor of the empire and Prime Minister of Prussia. His first conspicuous act as chancellor was a defence in the Reichstag of German imperialism in China. His foreign policy encouraged the formation of the Triple Entente. On October 28, 1908, Kaiser Wilhelm II gave an interview to the *Daily Telegraph* where he revealed his

other bourgeois elements, who carry around our 'green guidebook [*Bädecker*] for travels to Utopia' and complain that, in spite of that fact, they have been unable to find their way to our 'state of the future'. Whoever does not feel at home in the Swiss mountains will be unable to climb a high summit even if he carries his travel guide. Instead, he will probably break his neck. In the same way, a member of the bourgeois classes will be unable to understand our views of the future if he doesn't feel at home in our entire literature. There is no Nuremberg Funnel[24] for journalists, members of parliament, and state chancellors that will allow them to speak with authority about socialism without having studied its fundamental works, and I have no intention of providing them with one.

The following statements are therefore directed only against those critical considerations that have been voiced about my brochures in party circles. Many people saw in them a utopia, the construction of a socialist state of the future, whose model I built for future generations. But I had no intention of prescribing rules of conduct for a time that will see all social issues much more clearly than the sharpest seer can do today, for it will have at its disposal the experiences of the entire period from today to the epoch of the revolution. My intention when I wrote the brochures was very practical. I wanted to intervene in the struggles that have taken place in our ranks during recent years.

I don't see in the antagonism between revisionism and consistent or 'orthodox' Marxism any contradiction between pessimism and optimism, or between the expectation of a slow or a rapid pace of development, or between far-sighted theory and practical routine work. One can, indeed, find a bit of all this in the great antagonism, but that is not what defines it historically.

---

desire for a larger navy. Bülow assumed the official responsibility and was blamed for the arms race that followed. Bülow held office until July 14, 1909, when he was forced to resign after losing support in the Reichstag and was replaced by Theobald von Bethmann-Hollweg. Bülow later served as ambassador to Italy (1914–15) and published a book on foreign policy called *Imperial Germany*.]

   [24] [*Nürnberger Trichter*: A legendary funnel device to fill knowledge into the head.]

The antagonism arises from our historical situation. It is a product of the advance of Social Democracy, which in most of Europe has overcome the first stage of a revolutionary party's growth, when it has to struggle in order for its existence to be tolerated. Social Democracy has become a force. And that fact now raises the great question: should we remain a powerless party, as we have been until now, or does this new position of strength impose upon us new aims and new tactics? Until now we have said that we could emancipate the proletariat only through the conquest of political power. Should we also let that basic principle be our guide in the future? That would mean entering the practical struggle for political power when we have become so strong that our striving for power cannot be regarded any longer as purely Platonic. But if we have become strong enough to claim political power in theoretical terms, we are still not strong enough to conquer it in practice. This is an extremely difficult situation. Is there no means to escape from it by renouncing the struggle for political power? Can one not, perhaps, manage without it? And will we not finally reach practical results more quickly if we fit into the existing state organism as one of the government parties and thereby share in the benefits it can offer instead of eating the dry bread of opposition until the day of the revolution?

That is revisionism's line of reasoning. Against it I attempted to show in the first part of my brochures that the proletariat cannot emancipate itself without the conquest of political power; all the practical results that have been reached by means of social reforms and the organisation of the proletariat make it more fit for the struggle but do not attenuate its antagonism towards the capitalist class, which instead grows continuously until those classes clash in a decisive battle for political power.

In the second part, I tried to show that wherever the proletariat has conquered political power, socialist production follows as a natural necessity even where the proletariat has not arrived at a socialist consciousness. Its class interests and economic necessity force it to adopt measures that lead to socialist production.

The *conquest of political power* – that is the alpha and the omega of both brochures: without the possession of state power, we cannot advance in the abolition of classes and class interests; if the proletariat has political power, then socialism follows as a matter of necessity.

To prove that was the task of my brochures. If they have succeeded in doing so, they have accomplished a highly topical task. That has also been noticed by the revisionists; for that reason their criticism has been dismissive enough, and from their point of view rightly so. To be sure, their dismissal is in many cases instinctive; it is not always based on a clear understanding.

For instance, a contributor to the *Münchener Post* commented in its panegyric on the brochure of Steinigans[25] that it pursues

> always the same method: to reveal Kautsky's contradictions by means of facts; in which task he does not lack a sense of humour at the right opportunity. Thus, for instance, he lets Kautsky refute himself by pointing out that the *reformist* proposals in *On the Day after the Social Revolution* are nothing but what the revisionists of ill repute actually *already* want *now*: a [social] transformation.

It is certainly nice of the revisionists to accept completely my 'reformist proposals': expropriation of the capitalist class, reduction of the hours of work to five hours a day with the simultaneous doubling, even tripling, of wages, etc. And the fact that they do not want to wait for the revolution but want to have all that at this stage proves clearly that the revisionists are actually more radical than I am. However, they not only want these good things at this stage but also earnestly believe that they can achieve them *before the revolution* and therefore under a *bourgeois* government. That is truly the most humorous self-refutation of my remarks and the most devastating revelation of my contradictions by the facts that has ever fallen to my lot.

More serious is the criticism that Luśnia levelled at the second part of my book. But it also proceeds from the erroneous assumption that my book should have developed the revolutionary program of Social Democracy and stated the demands that our party intends to implement after victory. In this regard, it compares the comments of my brochures with the revolutionary programme of the *Communist Manifesto*. But I had not the slightest intention of delineating a programme of that character. What Social Democracy wants it has already explained in its programme. The way in which it will succeed in carrying out its demands as soon as it seizes state power is partially given there too. Until that happens, [the realisation of its demands] depends on a

---

25 [Steinigans 1903.]

series of factors that are today still impossible to recognise and about which it would be idle to ruminate and speculate.

As I already mentioned, what I wanted to point out was something completely different. I wanted to examine what consequences *necessarily* follow from the political rule of the proletariat by virtue of its class interests and the necessities of production, whatever the theoretical convictions prevailing at the moment of its victory. I also abstracted from any influence of socialist ideas on the proletariat. I expressly placed at the beginning of my investigation the question: What will the triumphant proletariat begin to do once it seizes power? 'Not how it *would* begin upon the grounds of this or that theory or opinion, but how it *must* begin, driven thereto by its class interests and the compulsion of economic necessity.'[26]

However, it seems that I did not make my intentions sufficiently clear because almost all my critics are astonished by them. Some of them, like Gaylord Wilshire in his monthly,[27] were even disappointed or indignant because, for instance, I place in the forefront of economic transformations the need for the triumphant proletariat to undertake, whatever the circumstances, not socialisation of the means of production but rather adequate unemployment relief, which entails that socialisation. They have evidently overlooked the fact that I myself said: 'It is well recognised that the Social Democrats when they came into control would strive consciously for this solution (the socialisation of the means of production).'[28] But my objective was not to elaborate what Social Democracy wants; I assumed that to be known. I wanted to show that a triumphant proletariat, even when its does not have a socialist consciousness, will be forced by the logic of the facts to make arrangements that will lead to socialism.

In order to provide a basis for my assumption of a non-socialist proletariat I had to go outside the sphere of the German, Latin and Slavic proletarian movements. Only the Anglo-Saxons offered me some foundation for my

---

[26] [Kautsky 1902–4, Vol. II: *On the Day after the Social Revolution*, Part 1: The Expropriation of the Epropriators. In the English edition, p. 107.]

[27] *Wilshire's Magazine*, May 1903. [Henry Gaylord Wilshire (1861–1927) a millionaire socialist, made his money in real estate speculation in Southern California. Wilshire was a close friend of Upton Sinclair and converted him, along with Jack London and many others, to socialism.]

[28] [Kautsky, 1902–4. Vol. II: *On the Day after the Social Revolution*, Part 1: The Expropriation of the Expropriators. In the English edition, p. 114.]

presuppositions. To be sure, it is unlikely that a non-socialist proletariat may conquer political power, for how can the proletariat seize power without coming into collision with the bourgeois parties, and how can it get rid of bourgeois conceptions without acquiring a socialist consciousness?

However, let us suppose that we have in England a non-socialist, radical labour party – something along the Australian pattern – and that it wins a majority in the parliamentary elections, whereupon the bourgeois parties immediately and offhandedly abdicate. In short, historical development takes place in such a way that Messrs. Barth and Naumann[29] cannot raise the slightest objection against it. What will the new régime be forced to do before anything else?

Surely, it must give adequate support to the unemployed? That cannot be denied by anyone with any knowledge of the English worker. Being foreign to all theory, the English worker is interested only in the most immediate demands and usually even in a *single* demand. Recognising this situation, for two decades, English socialists have already striven to win over the workers to socialism through 'practical policy', i.e. by raising one or the other particular demand. But neither political demands such as the general suffrage and abolition of the House of Lords, nor economic ones, such as nationalisation of the railways and mines, nor even the legal eight-hour workday, were able to shake the English worker out of his political lethargy. Only once, in the years 1885 to 1890, did socialism win significant influence over the proletariat of England. It was a period of high unemployment when socialists stood at the forefront of the struggle for national and municipal relief for the unemployed.

It is also noteworthy that Gaylord Wilshire, in America, expected conversion of the mass of the workers to socialism as a result of the growth of unemployment, which had to result from the crisis that was incipient there. Unemployment – that is the frightful lash that must whip even the most thoughtless worker into bitter opposition to the present regime when his energy

---

[29] [Friedrich Naumann (1860–1919) was a liberal politician and Protestant theologian. He founded the *Nationalsozialen Verein* and the magazine *Die Hilfe* to promote social liberalism. Theodor Barth (1849–1909) was also a liberal politician and long-time Reichstag member. From 1883 to 1907 Barth was editor of the 'left' liberal weekly *Die Nation*. During the late 1890s and early 1900s he and Naumann worked closely in the *Freisinnigen Vereinigung* (Liberal Union).]

is not completely consumed, for the present regime proves to be absolutely incapable, even unwilling, to fight energetically against unemployment. And if unemployment hits the unorganised, badly-paid workers the hardest – there is an intimate connection between lack of organisation and low wages – it also threatens the unionised workers, even the unions themselves, with heavy sacrifices. No trade union can pay an amount even approximately approaching a full wage as unemployment relief; none can support the unemployed beyond a certain period; all are forced to increase substantially the workers' dues with the growth of unemployment. And, in this way, high unemployment threatens to break the unions' power of resistance vis-à-vis the bosses.

The struggle against emergency situations caused by unemployment is therefore the point where even the *reapolitisch* worker, who does not see beyond the most immediate tasks, gets rid of bourgeois conceptions and goes beyond the boundaries of bourgeois society, which can and will do nothing in earnest to relieve him of this distress.

We must be confident that a triumphant proletariat, even if it is still averse to any socialism, will exert itself to the utmost in order to provide adequate unemployment relief.

Luśnia eventually comes to the same conclusion when he declares:

> On the day after the conquest of political power the party of the proletariat must carry out one task unconditionally and immediately: the abolition of misery and the guarantee of a minimum of existence to those who cannot work, such as the invalids.

That is also my opinion. When Luśnia remarks polemically against me that it is impossible to abolish unemployment as long as production is not organised by the state, and that this organisation must precede the abolition of unemployment, I agree with him totally. But in the section under consideration I spoke about 'adequate *support* to the unemployed', not about the *abolition* of unemployment. Those are two completely different things. Support for the economically active unemployed can only exist as long as it is impossible to abolish unemployment.

Satisfactory state support for the unemployed, even if implemented by a triumphant proletariat, seems, when considered on its own, perfectly innocent and totally compatible with bourgeois society. But the bourgeois parties know very well why they do not implement it – because it has far-reaching consequences. If every unemployed person were guaranteed a minimum living wage, every strike would be irresistible and the workers would be the true masters of the factory. Therewith, however, private property in the means of production would lose all meaning for the capitalist; it would burden him with the responsibility and risk of his enterprise without granting him the possibility of controlling and exploiting it. Socialisation of the means of production would be a necessity that the capitalists, under these conditions, would perhaps feel even more strongly than the workers. Continuation of production on capitalist foundations would then be impossible.

But adequate support for the unemployed has yet another consequence. If the unemployed were guaranteed a minimum living wage, that would cause a considerable rise in wages and a reduction in hours of work if the workers are to have sufficient incentive to ensure the continuation of production.

At present wages generally rise but little above the minimum living wage if they rise at all. More frequently they coincide with it, and sometimes they even drop below it. Continuation of production with adequate support for the unemployed thus requires not only socialisation of the means of production but also a considerable rise in the present wages with a simultaneous reduction of working hours. But that is only possible if outmoded and inefficient small businesses are abandoned as rapidly as possible and production is concentrated in the most efficient enterprises in every branch where large-scale production is technically possible. If a certain development of large-scale businesses is a precondition for rule of the proletariat, this rule must, in turn, lead to the complete replacement of small-scale enterprises in most areas of production.

We thus see that the foundations of socialist production must follow naturally from the political rule of the proletariat even if the triumphant proletariat itself has not yet attained a clear socialist consciousness. The only difference would be that after numerous experiments and under the compulsion of necessity, perhaps even of hardship, it would indirectly reach the point that a Social-Democratic régime would have aimed for at the outset.

Luśnia raises a series of considerations against the necessary rise in wages.

I believe that such an increase is only possible with a considerable growth of production. It seems to me that the most effective means to achieve this growth is abandonment of the numerous irrational, inadequately equipped enterprises and concentration of the workers in the best equipped and most productive enterprises, where two or three times the current number of workers can be employed with a corresponding change in shifts (without night work and with a significant reduction in the hours of work).

Opposing this argument, Luśnia asks first of all: 'How would such a concentration, such a transfer of millions of workers to a small number of great factories, be feasible in practice?'. He refers to my example of the concentration of textile production from the 200,000 enterprises it presently involves into 3,000 great enterprises and remarks:

> The 3,000 great textile factories are located in a much smaller number of places than the total number of enterprises of that industry. What an enormous and complicated problem of transportation and housing! We are talking about many hundreds of thousands for the textile industry alone!

Undoubtedly, we face a problem. However, Luśnia does not want to assert that it is an unsolvable problem. If one considers what masses capitalism even today sets in motion every year; if one thinks about the migratory workers, the influx of Polish workers to the coal mines of western Germany, the emigration, etc., then the problem raised by Luśnia loses much of its enormity.

One must also keep in mind that large-scale and small-scale enterprises of the same branch of production often co-exist in the same region, so that in those places the workers of the small businesses can reach the large ones without great migrations. For instance, in Reuss alterer Linie[30] we find in the textile industry, within 300 square kilometres, 44 per cent of the workers (5,371 out of 12,165) in the 20 largest enterprises with more than 200 workers; 33.4 per cent (4,061) in 39 enterprises with 50 to 200 workers; and 22.5 per cent (2,733) in 956 small enterprises. Within that small state, it would be neither a formidable nor a complicated transportation and housing problem

---

[30] [The two principalities of Reuss were the smallest states of the German Confederation. They were located in central Germany, east of Thuringia, along the western boundaries of the former Kingdom of Saxony. Their combined area was only 440 square miles. Reuss alterer Linie (Reuss Senior Line), also known as Reuss-Greitz, was the smaller, with 122 square miles and a population of around 70,000 people in 1905. Reuss jüngerer Linie (Reuss Junior Line), or Reuss-Schleiz, had 318 square miles and approximately 145,000 inhabitants. In the aftermath of the First World War both principalities were incorporated into Thuringia.]

to concentrate the 56 per cent of the workers (6,794) of the 995 enterprises with fewer than 200 persons in the 20 largest enterprises.

The lion's share of these enterprises is in wool weaving. They comprise 9 large enterprises (over 200 workers) with 3,366 workers, 32 medium-sized enterprises (50 to 200 workers) with 3,406 workers, and 421 small enterprises with 1,843 workers.

In a similar way, in most industrial areas small-scale and large-scale enterprises are intermixed, so that one can often transfer the workers of the first category to the second without more ado.

At any rate, a large number of the workers in the most backward enterprises can be absorbed without difficulty by the more advanced ones, and that would immediately mean a considerable increase in labour productivity. The more distant workers of the backward enterprises could certainly be recruited gradually into the most rational ones as soon as housing units were built for them in the proximity to the latter.

Luśnia's objections, therefore, do not prove that a rapid growth of labour productivity is impossible in the ways I adduced. They only show that this growth will be most rapid and extensive, all other conditions being equal, the closer the workers of the small, backward enterprises reside to the large, more advanced enterprises, and the more the different categories of enterprises are concentrated in a few industrial centres.

That economic development continuously requires this concentration is well known.[31]...The more the industrial population concentrates, the easier it is to transfer it from a series of establishments to others in the same branch of production, and the more insignificant become the apparently enormous housing and transportation problems pointed out by comrade Luśnia.

But he offers an even more substantial consideration against the increase in labour productivity:

> Even if such an immediate increase in production were possible, that would only bring about an increase in wages...in those branches of production where consumption can double in reality – in the first place in the production of foodstuffs, where precisely the method of concentration can only be applied to a limited extent. As far as the textile industry is

---

[31] [We omit here the statistical data Kautsky cites to illustrate the point.]

concerned, the consumption of its products can indeed increase, but whether a production twice as great as the present one can be consumed, especially in the countryside, seems to me doubtful. So to produce a rise in wages the amount of [textile] exports must grow, which is also true of other branches of production. But Kautsky does not refer to the question of foreign trade.

Again, there is problem here, but not where Luśnia is looking for it.

Suppose the productivity of labour in the textile industry doubles as a result of the concentration of workers in the most advanced enterprises. Would consumption [of textile products] double as well? Very probably that would not be the case. The mass of the population even today does not lack clothes, to mention only the category of textile products that is undoubtedly most important. The clothing problem often lies in the poor quality of the fabrics consumed rather than in an insufficient quantity. A rise in wages will therefore probably produce not so much an increase in the demand for textile products as an increase in demand for high-quality products and a simultaneous decrease in demand for shoddy articles. Since good fabrics last considerably longer than trashy ones, and since the artificial stimulation of fashion by private entrepreneurs will disappear in a socialist society, causing fashion to change less rapidly, it is very possible, indeed, that consumption of clothing fabrics will not keep pace with a doubling in the productivity of labour. Under these circumstances, the growth of labour productivity would entail reduction of the number of workers [in that branch of production].

The situation must not be very different with the production of foodstuffs – assuming that the community will produce most of its foodstuffs itself, which, even for Germany, would only be possible, without changing the mode of production, if it became a single economic area with Austria. But there is no doubt that, apart from the poorest of the poor, the masses of the population already fill their stomachs now, even if they have long been inadequately nourished. Likewise in this case, a rise in wages would cause a change less in the quantity than in the quality of foodstuffs consumed. The demand for potatoes and turnips would decline; that for rye and wheat would rise. Simultaneously the demand for horses would drop as a consequence of abolishing the standing army, reducing the number of private luxury vehicles, introducing electric engines in agriculture, etc. For this reason, the cultivation of oats would also decline. In contrast, the demand for milk and meat products would increase.

Whether all these and similar changes in consumption will increase the manpower employed in agriculture, especially with the advancing application of machines, remains an open question.

On the other hand, a good deal of additional manpower will be required for the construction industry.

The living conditions of the masses of the population are today much worse than their food and dress. Even the 'aristocrats' of labour are quite resentful about that. There are few wage-workers, even petty bourgeois and small peasants, whose housing corresponds to the demands of modern culture or even of the most primitive hygiene. And living conditions under the capitalist mode of production worsen constantly, not only in relative but also in absolute terms. To find rapid relief from this situation is one of the most important tasks of a proletarian régime. To that should be added the housing problems caused by local displacements of population. We have seen that the new régime must strive to concentrate workers in the best organised enterprises. Alternatively, it must attempt to transfer industry to the countryside or to the small towns and to distribute the population uniformly over the entire territory of the state in order to abolish both the physical degradation generated by the great cities and the mental atrophy resulting from peasant isolation.

To this should be added the growing need for public buildings – schools, hospitals, theatres – resulting from a proletarian régime. This must generate enormous building activity, and since precisely in that area the machine often does not prevail, the demand for workers must grow considerably.

These few examples are enough to show that, in general, a change in the mode of production must also cause a change in consumption habits, which in turn must react back on production. The relations between the different branches of production will shift considerably, and great changes will be necessary in the number of workers employed in particular branches.

That is surely a major problem that will present numerous difficulties, but definitely not those stressed by Luśnia. He argues that wages can be doubled, with the corresponding increase in labour productivity, only in those branches of production where domestic consumption or else exports can be doubled. That would be correct if the workers of each enterprise were not paid with money – i.e., with vouchers for some of the products of the social production process – but instead with their own production, if the number of workers in each branch of production were fixed and immutable, and if labour productivity had to increase to the same degree in each branch of production.

The rise of wages in a socialist society will be determined by the growth of labour productivity in general, not in each particular case. It may happen that through concentration of production in the most efficient enterprises labour productivity will multiply tenfold in many branches, for instance in the footwear industry, while in others it will remain unchanged, for instance in the building industry (in the narrow sense). But, if average labour productivity grows, wages in all branches of production could be increased accordingly, those of the construction workers as much as those of the footwear workers.

The productivity of labour varies enormously in particular branches of industry: in one place, production is still carried on by hand, while elsewhere workers produce a thousand times more with machines. In other branches, the product can only be manufactured from the outset with the help of machines. But wages always show a tendency to equalisation, much like wants and living standards within a social class. The level of wages, when it exceeds bare subsistence, is a product of social circumstances as a whole, and therefore the wage level in each particular branch of production also depends on the productivity of society as a whole, not of the branches of production in question.

Deviations from the average wage level among a particular stratum of workers are caused partly by special costs of production of their labour-power (training), partly by the special living standards of the social stratum from which they are recruited, partly by exceptional conditions of supply and demand, etc., but they never stand in any relation to the specific productivity of their own labour.

And there is no reason why that should change in a socialist society.

Therefore, Luśnia's objection that the rise in wages would find its limits in the impossibility of increasing consumption is invalid. The consumption of products of particular branches of production can have its natural limits beyond which it may not advance. But the needs of mankind, and therefore its consumption capacity, are in general unlimited: they grow with the productivity of labour. This fact was already recognised by the classical political economists, who believed they could conclude from it that overproduction was impossible. That is not true for capitalist society, whose consumption is determined not by needs but by the aggregate purchasing power of consumers. But it does hold true for a socialist society, where general overproduction would be impossible and where, to the extent that labour productivity increases, new needs would be added to the old ones. But to refute the idea that a doubling or tripling of wages must founder on the impossibility of increasing consumption accordingly, it is not necessary to refer to some newly acquired need. The tripling of the average wage with constant prices would for the first time bring the average living standard of the workers to approximately the level that today characterises a modest bourgeois existence. It would only offer the possibility of satisfying in one way or the other needs that proletarians are already experiencing. It would still offer no inducement for extravagances.

From whatever angle Luśnia's considerations are viewed, they prove to be unsound. I know of no other considerations that weigh against the consequences of a proletarian régime as set out in *On the Day after the Social Revolution*.

II. Revolutionary centres

The considerations against unemployment relief and the rapid increase of production are just subsidiary matters for Luśnia. The most serious fault of my brochures seems to him to be the complete overlooking of the Polish question. How can someone speak about the revolution and say nothing about Poland! Comrade Wilshire, on the other hand, reproaches me for behaving as if the United States didn't exist.

Each reproach nullifies the other. I could not include Poland in an analysis of the revolution in the United States or America in a presentation of the Polish question. But I never had the intention of dealing with either of those countries because that would not have corresponded with the aims of my writing. What I attempted to do was to analyse the problems of the future that are vital for our present work as well as the ways to solve them insofar as they are accessible to scientific analysis. I did not want to slip back from the scientific into the utopian point of view, i.e., I wanted to guard myself against the danger of describing desirable scenarios rather than pointing out discernible and necessary processes. Therefore, I had to limit my analysis to the simplest tendencies, common to all the capitalist nations, and their consequences. Only they can be distinguished with any degree of accuracy over a long period of time from the facts already at hand. By contrast, if we go beyond them to the concrete forms that the trend of development assumes in particular nations, we then come across such complicated phenomena that it is impossible to foresee with any degree of accuracy, even for the immediate future, which results the interaction of the innumerable factors under consideration will yield.

In springtime I can say with complete security that at the end of the year there will again come another winter. But I can only forecast with a certain degree of probability the weather of the following day, even if I am a very learned and experienced meteorologist and well acquainted with the latest meteorological data. It is impossible for me to forecast the weather of the coming months.

Something similar happens with politics. If I find that class contradictions are becoming more acute in all the capitalist countries, that the proletariat cannot emancipate itself without conquering political power, that this conquest, regardless of all the purposes and aspirations by which it may be accompanied, leads necessarily to the development of socialist production, I do no overstep the boundaries of scientific analysis. Naturally, that still doesn't prove that these conclusions are correct; that depends on the correctness of the method and the observations by means of which they were obtained. But the possibility does exist of reaching a scientifically grounded conclusion concerning these questions.

That possibility diminishes the more we engage in analysis of the special development of particular nations. Each nation follows a different course of development, stands at a different stage, is influenced by its neighbours, etc. If the general tendency of development in all nations is and must be the same, the particular course of development followed by each nation is different, and each faces the most diverse eventualities. That doesn't prove that we don't have to concern ourselves with these questions and that we can gain no insight into them. Every politician who does not simply drift with events but rather exerts a determining influence upon them must attempt to take stock of the probabilities and alternatives of the special course of development of the nation in which he operates; his work will only succeed if his aspirations go in the same direction as this particular developmental path, which is just as necessary as the general tendency of development of all nations even though this necessity is not so easily discernible. Nothing is more baleful than to sneer at every far-sighted policy, at each prediction, as the fanatics of present-day politics and exclusively routine work are so gladly doing today. The practical politician, if he wants to be successful, must attempt to see into the future just like the theoretical socialist. Whether this foresight assumes the form of a prophecy will depend on his temperament. But he must, at the same time, always be prepared for the appearance of unexpected factors, which will frustrate his plans and impart a new direction to development, and he must therefore always be ready to change his tactic accordingly.

To analyse the general tendency of the impending social and political development in capitalist society and the special course of development of particular lands – these are two totally different tasks. Study of the latter presupposes solution of the former. Therefore, any attempt to mix the two and perform both tasks simultaneously can only lead to confusion.

That is why my chapter on the 'Forms and Weapons of Social Revolution',[32] as Luśnia put it, 'is fragmentary, and gives the impression of indecision, of diffidence, which is unusual in Kautsky'. He is totally mistaken when he thinks he detects here 'the latent influence of the continuing and yet to be overcome condition of the proletarian movement, in which one can think about the revolution, about the decisive struggle, only reluctantly and with anxiety'.

Analysis of the questions raised by Luśnia was beyond the framework of my writing, but I have no reason to avoid them. It can do no harm if one occasionally deals with them. But one must not forget that in doing so we are no longer dealing with developmental tendencies that can be identified as *necessary*, only with those that are *contingent* and more or less *probable*.

Luśnia seems to assume that the Polish question is necessarily given in any revolution and, furthermore, that it is always posed in the same terms. His position on this issue is that of early democracy (formerly defended also by Marx, Engels and Liebknecht), according to which a revolution in Western Europe would face a reactionary Russia. The first task of any revolution was therefore to paralyse Russia, which could be done best by establishing an independent Poland. The restoration of Poland and the European revolution

---

[32] [Kautsky 1902–4. Vol. I: *The Social Revolution*, Part 7: Forms and Weapons of Social Revolution. In the English edition, pp. 84–102.]

thus implied each other, they were inseparably connected, and each Polish patriot was also a fighter in the European revolutionary army.

This conception was self-evident and necessary as long as there was no revolutionary Russia and no fighting proletariat in Poland. The emergence of the latter has substantially cooled off the enthusiasm of most of the non-proletarian classes of Poland for the European revolution. On the other hand, strengthening of the revolutionary movement in Russia has opened up the possibility of giving battle to tsarism on its own terrain, and for this reason the possibility that Russian absolutism could again, as in 1848, strangle a Western-European revolution has simultaneously diminished dramatically. Today, tsarism resists the assault of its beloved subjects only with difficulty and thanks to the support of West-European capitalists. If a victorious revolution in the West puts the proletariat in power instead of those capitalists, then support for autocracy will not only vanish but be replaced by vigorous support for the revolutionary opponents of tsarism. Then absolutism must irremediably collapse – if it does not meet that fate even earlier. What need would there be then of restoring Poland in order to save the revolutionary cause?

Consequently, the Polish question today has an entirely different significance from what it did a generation ago. Socialism, even democracy, includes the principle of popular sovereignty, of the self-determination and independence of each people. It goes without saying that a victorious European revolution would provide the impulse for establishment of an independent Polish republic. But, for the revolutionary cause, that is no more important than any other national question that the bourgeois régime bequeaths to the proletarian one; such as, for instance, the creation of a Czech national state augmented by Slovaks, the union of the Serbs in a single state, or the union of Trentino with Italy.

To be sure, German Social Democracy has no less reason to strive for a friendly understanding with the Polish comrades on this account. It must pay attention not only to their national feelings but also to their national susceptibilities. It is characteristic of small, dismembered nations, whose very existence is under threat, to go beyond national feelings and to develop a certain national oversensitivity even among proletarians, who readily see oppression even in circumstances where, with full equality of rights, it is merely a question of the preponderance of the majority over the minority. Unpleasant situations sometimes result, but the proletariat of a nation as great and solid as the German one should go beyond theoretical imperatives and show, according to the principle of *noblesse oblige,* some indulgence for the national susceptibilities of its weaker and more oppressed neighbours, though certainly it should not go so far as to let them interfere with the unity of organisation and action.

However, the exceptional position that the Poles occupied as the protective barrier of the revolution vis-à-vis Russia no longer exists, and with it has disappeared every reason for including the Polish question in a general analysis of the coming revolution.

But there is also a further reason why the Polish question falls beyond the scope of my brochure. Luśnia's remarks on the topic spring from the assumption that the next revolution will have its starting point in Germany, maybe especially in Berlin. That is surely not impossible, but it is only one of numerous possibilities and not the most probable among them. Today, at any rate, a whole series of states stand closer to the revolution than Germany despite the rapidity of its economic development and the growth of its Social Democracy. The German government is today the strongest in the world. It has at its disposal the strongest, most disciplined army and bureaucracy, and it faces a population that is prosaic and peaceful and lacks any revolutionary tradition. Of course, one can also imagine in Germany a government that mismanages the country to the point of disorganising the army and the bureaucracy, and of driving the masses to desperation while at the same time embroiling the country in useless and costly, perhaps even humiliating adventures; those would be factors that could drive even the German people to rebellion. Rudiments of such a situation can already be found, occasioned by the growing greediness and distress of the bankrupt Junkers, the growing fear of rising Social Democracy, the sharpening of class contradictions between capital and labour, as well as the growth of imperialism in all nations – and with it the growing danger of military conflicts. But those rudiments would have to grow considerably for the German people to take the initiative in the next revolution.

Its Eastern neighbour is much closer to revolution than Germany. Luśnia warns us not to overestimate the revolutionary force of the Russian proletariat, but one must also not underestimate it. Luśnia should be especially wary of that danger because the presupposition of his views on the Polish question is an unshakeable, vigorous Russian absolutism, and they would be untenable without it.

There is no doubt that the economic development of Russia lags far behind that of Germany or England or that its proletariat is much weaker and less mature than the German or the English. But all things are relative, including the revolutionary power of a class. More than anywhere else the proletariat in Russia today is the advocate of vital interests of the whole nation so that in its struggle against the government it faces almost no opposition from other classes. On the other hand, in the whole of Europe there is no weaker government than the Russian, with the possible exception of Turkey, because it has no support in the state other than a thoroughly corrupt bureaucracy and an army that already shows signs of disorganisation and discontent. There is no other government whose conditions of existence stand in more irreconcilable contradiction with the living conditions of the nation or whose moral and economic bankruptcy is more evident. Until the 1880s, Russian absolutism found its firmest support in a vigorous peasantry. This support no longer exists; the Russian peasant is ruined, starved or rebellious. Tsarism avoided impending bankruptcy with the help of West-European capital, which enabled it to develop, as if in a hot-house, an expanding large-scale industry. Now this industry is collapsing and, instead of providing absolutism with rich revenues, it confronts it with a revolutionary proletariat. The Russian workers plunge into the struggle undaunted by death because they find themselves in a state in which they have nothing to lose but their chains.

The more completely Western Europe withholds help from absolutism, the sooner it will be overthrown. To bring this about, to discredit tsarism as much as possible, is today the most important work of international Social Democracy. And socialists everywhere have grasped this fact. How they see to it in each country must depend on particular conditions. But whether one stigmatises tsarist barbarism in popular assemblies, as our comrades in Vienna did during the latest visit of the tsar, or chases its representatives back into their hiding places by threatening to jeer them, as our Italian comrades managed to do, or whether one declares war against it in parliament, as Bebel succeeded so stunningly in doing during the budget debate – everywhere the comrades have done their duty according to their situation, with the exception of the ministerial socialists of France.

Meanwhile, despite all his valuable friendships in Western Europe, the Autocrat of the Russias grows visibly less powerful. The war with Japan may greatly hasten the progress of the Russian revolution if it does not result in a quick and mighty victory of the Russian army. Even in the case of a decisive Russian victory, absolutism can be badly hurt and become totally exhausted if the war should last, for example, as long as the Boer War.[33]

What took place after the Russo-Turkish war[34] will be repeated on a broader scale: a great flare-up of the revolutionary movement. Not only is the government weaker and the revolutionary movement stronger than they were then: the war against Turkey to liberate the Slavic brothers was popular, it was a struggle for freedom against the barbarians – at least that was the illusion of the combatants and initially served to enhance the Russian government's prestige at home. The war against Japan is an entirely different case: it is a war against a freer and more highly developed country in whose defeat the Russian people does not have the slightest interest. That can be seen clearly if one compares the war fever that raged through Russia in 1875, when the uprising in Bosnia and Herzegovina broke out, and that lasted until the declaration of war in 1877, with the indifference with which, even a few weeks ago, the threatening war was received in Russia as contrasted with Japan.

A revolution in Russia cannot establish a socialist régime at once. The economic conditions of the country are not sufficiently developed for that. The best it can do is to bring about a democratic government behind which would be a strong, impetuous and progressive proletariat that would be able to demand important concessions.

Such a régime would react powerfully upon the neighbouring countries of Russia: first, by reviving and inspiring the proletarian movement itself, thereby

---

[33] [The Boer War or South African War (1899–1902) was waged against Great Britain by an alliance of the Boer (white settlers of Dutch descent) governments of Transvaal (South African Republic) and the Orange Free State. It ended with a British victory. The Boer War played a central role in the elaboration of Hobson's theory of imperialism, which had a major influence on Lenin. See Hobson 1902]

[34] [The last Russo-Turkish War (1877–8) came as a result of the anti-Ottoman uprising that broke out in 1875 in Bosnia and Herzegovina. On Russian instigation, Serbia and Montenegro joined the rebels in their war on the Ottoman Empire. After securing Austrian neutrality, Russia openly entered the war in 1877. The Treaty of San Stefano in 1878 resulted in large territorial gains for Russia and Russian-influenced Bulgaria.]

giving it the impulse to attack the political obstacles to real democracy – in Prussia, for example, primarily the 'three-class' electoral system; secondly, through releasing the manifold national questions of Eastern Europe.

It seems beyond any doubt to me that a Russian revolution must revive Panslavism in a new form. In its previous form Panslavism is pretty decrepit. It was a revolutionary means towards reactionary ends: to spur on the Slavic peoples of Austria and Turkey to rebellion in order to conquer, as those peoples fancied, their national independence under Russian leadership, but, in actual fact, in order to extend the domain of Russian despotism. But the times are past when reactionary governments were allowed to play with impunity with the revolutionary liberation struggles of the peoples; when Napoleon conspired with Kossuth (1859), Bismarck organised a Hungarian legion against the Habsburg régime and met half way the revolutionary aspirations of the Czechs (1866),[35] Rieger went on a pilgrimage to Moscow as an agent of panslavism (1868), and general Ignatiev, as Russian envoy in Constantinople, could arrange the overthrow of the Turkish Empire according to all the rules of conspiracy (1864–77).

Since then, governments everywhere have grown more cautious and apprehensive. The government of a capitalist country only still dares to use revolutionary methods to serve its needs in places like South Africa or Central America. The Russian government is no exception to this rule. The rebellious Macedonians of 1903 totally deceived themselves when they thought that the tsar would help them as much as he helped the Bosnians and Bulgarians three decades earlier.

On the other hand, the situation in Russia has become so desperate that, at least among the Slavs of Austria, the longing for union with the Russians,

---

[35] 'How little satisfied the Slavs were (with the government of [Count Richard] Belcredi in Austria in 1866) is shown by … the jubilation with which the Czechs greeted the Prague proclamation of the *Prussian general* Rosenberg-Gruczynski "To the People of the Glorious Kingdom of Bohemia" (which was believed to have been inspired by the police director Stieber) because it held out a prospect of fulfilling their national aspirations. Not the fortunes of war at [the Battle of] Königgrätz [on July 3, 1866] marked the climax of the hard times that befell Austria, but that moment in which the Czech newspapers, under the protection of the *black-and-white banner* waving at Hradschin, threw dirt at the German-Austrian one, and said openly to the face of Count Belcredi that *count Bismarck* would give them what he had not dared to grant them out of fear of the [Austrian] centralist clique.' Rogge 1872, Vol. II, p. 335).

which during the reform era of Alexander II was very strong, has disappeared completely. Thus the roots of panslavism have withered from both sides.

A democratic Russia must tremendously rekindle the aspiration for national independence among of the Slavs of Austria and Turkey, as well as their endeavours to win the help of the great Russian people for that purpose. The Polish question will also become acute again, but not the way Luśnia thinks. The Poles will point their bayonets not against Russia but against Austria and Prussia, and to the extent that Poland serves the revolution, it will become a means not to defend the revolution against Russia but to carry it to Austria and Prussia.

Austria will then burst open, because the collapse of tsarism will disintegrate the iron ring that to this very day keeps together the disparate elements [of the Austro-Hungarian Empire]. If that happens, the German empire will be forced to include the German-inhabited regions of the Habsburg monarchy in its own territory insofar as they constitute a cohesive whole.

That will completely change the character of the German empire. Today, roughly 35 million Prussians confront only 22 million non-Prussians. Inclusion of the German Austrians will make Prussians and non-Prussians approximately equal in strength, especially after the Prussian Poles, presently three million strong, are deducted from the non-Prussians. Such a proportion would raise the danger of a strengthened opposition of the South against the North, a reinforcement of particularism, and a weakening of the unity of the German empire if it were to continue as a union of autonomous states. It would then be urgently necessary to complete the job neglected in 1870: to turn the federative state into a unitary one. The solution of the Polish question would thus be greatly facilitated because retention of the Prussian Poles in the current state federation serves the interests of a special Prussian state, not of the German people.

The Russian revolution, then, must impart a powerful impulse to proletarian movements in the rest of Europe and put the question of national unity once again on the agenda, not just in Austria and the Balkan countries but also in Germany itself in order to provide it with a definitive solution. Social Democracy would then have to prove itself as the advocate not only of a new social order but also of a new national and territorial order; the advocate not only of proletarian class interests but also of general national interests, towards which the other classes, which have grown conservative or fearful, will adopt either a passive or a directly hostile attitude.

Couldn't those struggles possibly result in the rule of the proletariat in Germany? That, however, would have repercussions on the whole of Europe. The political rule of the proletariat in Western Europe would offer to the proletariat of Eastern Europe the possibility of shortening the stages of its development and artificially introducing socialist arrangements by imitating the German example. Society as a whole cannot artificially leap over particular stages of development, but the backward development of some of its particular constituent parts can indeed be accelerated by the proximity of more advanced parts. They may even come to the forefront because they are not hindered by the ballast of traditions that the older nations have to drag along. The most brilliant example of that rule is America, which leaped over the stages of feudalism and absolutism and was spared the gruelling struggles against them as well as the burden of their ruins.

That *can* happen. But as we already said, we have gone beyond the field of discernible *necessity* and are at present considering only *possibilities*. History could also follow a completely different course.

*　*　*

After Russia, *Belgium* seems closest to the revolution at present. The industrial proletariat is exceptionally strong there, and the conservative peasantry rather weak.[36] … This social stratification is accompanied by political circumstances favourable to the revolution. Thanks to a franchise biased towards the propertied classes, the government is extremely reactionary, causing it to come into growing contradiction not only with the proletariat but also with the common interests of the nation. Wide circles of the people hate and despise the king. The army, thanks to a draft system that allows sending substitutes, is essentially recruited only among the propertyless classes; discontent is rife, and the troops are prone to mutinies. If a tense situation for the government

---

[36] [Here we have omitted the statistical data that Kautsky cites to compare Belgium with Germany in terms of occupational structure in the economy as a whole and in industry.]

were to coincide with a flare up of popular anger, it would be enough to reduce the area ruled by Leopold and his successor to the Congo.

Sure enough, a proletarian revolution limited to Belgium could not maintain itself for long. For purely economic reasons, that small area, with its seven million inhabitants, could not by itself establish a lasting socialist régime amid capitalist surroundings. Besides, it would also face more immediate political threats. A republican Belgium, ruled by the proletariat, would mean a steady revolutionary focus and a summons to proletarians of the other European countries to follow its example, which would be a source of constant ferment for lower classes of the people outside Belgium. The governments of Germany and France would have to rush to extinguish this fire, from which such threatening sparks would fly in the form of agrarian and industrial agitators to the flammable thatched roofs of neighbouring lands. But precisely the attempt to put out the revolutionary fire could lead to its generalised flare-up.

A people that defends its liberty is not so easily subjugated, as shown by the example of both South-African republics,[37] where hardly 400,000 whites, among whom there were at most 40,000 armed men, were able to offer victorious resistance to the English world empire for so long. The Belgian army, with its 150,000 men, would be reinforced by numerous enthusiastic volunteers from abroad – a task in which it would be mightily helped by the labour press. Each day of resistance would strengthen the ferment in the enemy camp and increase the danger of rebellion in its ranks.

But all that would hardly be enough to avert the crushing of the young republic, given the enormous superiority of the neighbouring powers, if another factor were not to come to its help: the antagonism between France and Germany, which in that case would serve the cause of liberty for the first time. Would France remain quiet if Germany defeated and occupied Belgium, or would a French army perhaps assume the role of Prussian gendarmes and march out hand in hand with the German army to strangle the Belgians? In both cases, the French government would be threatened with having to face an explosion of popular rage in which the most sublime as well as the most abject feelings – national hatred and international solidarity, petty-bourgeois obstinacy and proletarian revolutionary impetus – would unite with French élan to sweep away a régime that is treasonous to the people; and this would

---

[37] The Transvaal and the Orange Free State.

be relatively easy because in such circumstances the French army would hardly fight with enthusiasm for the government.

The government of the German empire would then declare war against France to defeat Belgium. That would not be a war like the one of 1870: a war to achieve a unity for which the nation had ardently longed for decades; a war against an impudent usurper, which with a few quick battles would carry away the popular masses in the general flush of victory. It would be a war in which nobody would be interested with the exception of a few privileged strata of adventurers because it would meet the most determined opposition from the only great class of the nation that still cherishes ideals. It would be a war destined solely to butcher a peaceful people who asked for nothing but to be left alone. It would be a war that, even if it ended in victory, would only be won after long, eventful and costly struggles because the armies of both camps are today equipped differently from 1870 and are animated by a spirit entirely different from that of [Charles Louis] Napoleon's praetorian guards.

It would be a war that could very well mean the beginning of the end.

Here the Polish question could also play a role, but again a different one from what Luśnia expects. For its own salvation, the revolutionary régime in Belgium and France would have to strive to provide material support to all revolutionary efforts abroad in order to split its opponents' forces and increase the excitement of the popular masses. Perhaps it would attempt to carry the revolution into Holland and Italy and to stir up unrest in Russia and Austria. Encouraging Polish aspirations would, among other things, be very suitable for this purpose. But the Polish aspirations would then be a means of weakening not only Russian but also Prussian reaction.

However, we have already advanced so far that if we want to analyse the possibilities of revolution we cannot limit ourselves to Europe. When comrade Wilshire argued in his criticism of my book that the United States is closer to revolution than Europe, he was possibly right. To be sure, I cannot agree with him when he declares that the centralisation of capital has already advanced so far that not only the working class but almost all the social classes see their saviour in socialism and will gladly welcome it.

Perhaps no other class needs socialism more than the small traders and artisans. Their prospects in capitalist society are much more dismal, for instance, than those of skilled wage-workers. In present society, they are headed for decline, and very often for decline into the lumpenproletariat. Yet for all that the small artisans and traders are often the fiercest opponents of Social Democracy. It is from these classes that its most fanatical enemies arise, as shown by the history of anti-Semitism. Socialism would save them, but socialism is the future – an unknown future – while present-day class interests force those strata to seek salvation in increased exploitation of the poorest of the poor. They are, therefore, even more hostile than the great capitalists to every advance of the workers, every law for their protection, and every organisation of the workers into trade and consumer unions.

The same is true of the small capitalists in America. They are oppressed by the great monopolies; they vent their indignation against them in the strongest words, as our anti-Semites do against capital; but when it comes to business, they seek to save themselves not through suppression of the monopolists but through increased exploitation of the workers. I do not expect the triumph of socialism in America to come from capitalists crossing over to the socialist camp – that dream of Bellamy[38] can today be safely laid to rest – but rather from the continuous sharpening of contradictions between capital and labour that the trusts must bring to the forefront not only for themselves but for the entire capitalist class. However much the nationalisation of trusts may be in the entire nation's interest, only the proletariat can actually bring it about; the struggle of other classes against them will only be a sham.

The monstrous growth of trusts, the crises and unemployment – all these factors, which in America already loom larger than in Europe, could very well have the effect of making the proletariat on the other side of the Atlantic Ocean seize political power earlier than we do; perhaps not with a clear socialist programme; perhaps, in conformity with Anglo-Saxon traditions, at first fighting only particular phenomena of capitalism such as unemployment or the trusts. But even in that case the proletarian régime would soon be driven to adopt measures that would result in socialist organisation of production.

Even if we succeed in imparting an understanding of socialist theory to the thoroughly 'practical' American workers, so that the proletarian régime would be consciously socialist from the outset – even in that case, an American revolution would have a physiognomy completely different from a European one.

---

[38] [Edward Bellamy, *Looking Backward: From 2000 to 1887*, was a famous American utopian novel, first published in 1888.]

Not only does political power appear completely different in the United States from the way it appears among us, but the social stratification is also different. It would therefore be going too far to describe the particular American conditions in detail: they would best be described by an American writer.

But whatever forms the social revolution might assume over there, it cannot leave Europe untouched. An American revolution must significantly strengthen the European proletariat and its drive to conquer political power. It would either lead to victory of the working class in Europe too, or if the attempt fails, to mass emigration and desolation of the old capitalist countries.

We must also keep an eye on that eventuality. The world is not so purposely organised as to lead always to the triumph of the revolution where it is essential for the interest of society. When we speak of the necessity of the proletariat's victory and of socialism following from it, we do not mean that victory is inevitable or even, as many of our critics think, that it will take place automatically and with fatalistic certainty even when the revolutionary class remains idle. Necessity must be understood here in the sense of the revolution being the only possibility of further development. Where the proletariat does not succeed in defeating its opponents, society will not be able to develop further; it must either stagnate or rot.

Examples of states that decayed because they needed a revolution and were not in a position to produce a revolutionary class are frequent in history. Even contemporary Europe displays such an example in Turkey. The fate of Europe will be like Turkey's if the proletariat fails to conquer political power. If, on the contrary, it were to triumph in America, all the elements of the proletariat and even the intelligentsia – those with any intelligence or energy – would flock over the ocean to the new freedom, and Europe would soon be in a position vis-à-vis America that would resemble, for instance, that occupied today by Southern Italy vis-à-vis Germany. It would cease to mean anything for social development and would be interesting only for its natural sights and its libraries and ruins as witnesses of former glory.

However, there is no reason for holding such dismal expectations in view of the pugnacity and fighting capacity of the European proletariat, which it combines with enthusiasm and readiness for sacrifice as well as prudence and self-possession. Even the English proletariat offers no cause for pessimism. It has already accomplished so much in the nineteenth century, and its lethargy is so recent by historical standards that one should certainly assume it is due to exceptional and temporary circumstances; that is, to the same exceptional position in the world market that also spoiled English capital and stunted its capacity to compete. Today, when it is evident to all that the exceptional position of England belongs to the past, the helplessness and passivity of English workers should disappear as well. In the struggle for liberal free trade, the English proletariat found itself in the same camp with the bourgeoisie; conversion of the bourgeoisie to protectionism must be followed by conversion of the proletarians to socialism.

One can see the multifarious problems that emerge when one begins to consider the possibilities of the coming revolution. Only one problem did not surface: the Polish question as Luśnia sees it. Considered in these terms, it is a problem of the past. But though our exposition has shown that the revolution can be conceived in many forms, and that many more possible forms are also conceivable because new and unexpected factors could and will probably appear, factors that no one today even considers, one thing is certain: the revolution of the future will not revert to forms and problems that already belong to the past.

Perhaps all this elaborate apparatus was too lengthy simply to come to this conclusion regarding the Polish question; the same result could have been reached more easily. But I also wanted to accomplish something else with these comments. I hope this discussion will clearly show the limits of political agitation in terms of accelerating the outbreak of revolution in Germany. In all the scenarii that I presented, and they seem to me the most probable ones, Germany remains barred from taking the revolutionary initiative and revolution is brought to it from the outside. How would these perspectives be altered, for instance, by a restriction of the franchise, by curtailment of the right of assembly, or by increased persecution of the socialist press in Germany? The German proletariat cannot, after all, be degraded to Russian conditions!

But the more closely German conditions resemble those in Russia, the more the situation of the German government will resemble that in Russia. The more the government comes into contradiction with general national interests, the more it must cripple economic life because free development of capitalism presupposes the freest initiative of individuals in society.

Development of capitalism will be all the more restrained, the more the individuals are constricted. Police oppression is incompatible with a thriving economy under developed capitalist conditions. A régime of protracted repression against Social Democracy would mean the economic decline of Germany, for the supporters of such a régime would be the most reactionary classes in economic terms: the Junkers and the anti-Semitic part of the petty bourgeoisie still organised in guilds together with that part of the peasantry that constitutes their following.

If one sows Russian conditions in Germany, one will reap financial bankruptcy, industrial stagnation, and corruption and disorganisation of the army and the bureaucracy, in short, all the weaknesses of the Russian government and, along with them, all the desperation of the Russian nation as well as the conditions making it probable that Russia will take the initiative in the coming revolution.

I do not expect, as I already said, that the next revolution will start in Germany. But if the facts give the lie to this expectation, the cause will surely be an aggressive régime of repression against Social Democracy.

I do not consider such a perspective to be likely because conditions in Germany are already too developed in a bourgeois sense. But I also do not believe that Social Democracy will be allowed to develop further in the present legal conditions. I expect an expanded edition of the zigzag course; a régime that will attempt to turn the working masses away from Social Democracy by means of great promises without having the power to realise them, a régime that embitters them all the more, the more they trust in it. Alternatively, the régime could improvise its way from case to case, aimlessly and spasmodically, carried away by fits of rage and violent measures, striking hard at particular individuals or bullying the entire proletariat, but ultimately only managing to provoke the workers' indignation without breaking their strength. But I do not expect a régime that will raise this ultimately suicidal policy into a lasting system of state terror, repressing every manifestation of proletarian energy.

But whatever way the ruling circles may choose – peaceful legality, Russian terrorism, or unstable vacillations between the two – they will not forestall the class struggle of the proletariat.

III. The political mass strike

1. *The armed insurrection*

Among the objections that Luśnia raised against me, one still remains to be mentioned, and that is the crucial point of his discussion that also gave the title to his article: the allegation that, without force of arms, the proletariat cannot conquer political power.

I remarked:

> We have no reason to assume that *armed insurrections* with barricade battles and similar warlike occurrences can play a decisive role even today. The reasons for this have been given so often that I have no need of dwelling on them further. Militarism can only be overthrown by rendering the military itself disaffected with the rulers, not through its being defeated by popular uprisings.[39]

Above all, Luśnia criticised the fact that I did not further develop reasons for this opinion. I was astonished that he still asked for the grounds of that view. If they are really unknown to him, he will find them most tersely summarised in Friedrich Engels's oft-quoted preface to Marx's *Class Struggles in France*.[40] Since that preface was written, no new points of view or new

---

[39] [Kautsky 1902–4, Vol. I, Part 3: The Social Revolution: Forms and Weapons of Social Revolution. In the English edition, which omits reference to 'armed insurrections', p. 88.]

[40] Engels 1895, pp. 506–24. [Kautsky's reference is misleading, because Engels's original text had been tampered with by his editors to avoid censorship. On 1 April, 1895, Engels wrote to Kautsky: 'To my astonishment I see in *Vorwärts!* today an extract from my "Introduction," printed without my prior knowledge and trimmed in such a fashion that I appear as a peaceful worshipper of legality at any price. So much the better that the whole thing is to appear now in the *Neue Zeit* so that this disgraceful impression will be wiped out. I shall give Liebknecht a good piece of my mind on that score and also, no matter who they are, to those who gave him the opportunity to misrepresent my opinion without even telling me a word about it.' Marx and Engels 1954, p. 568. However, the text was reprinted in *Die Neue Zeit* without the missing passages, and was printed in its entirety for the first time by David Ryazanov in 1930. On 3 April, 1895, Engels wrote to Paul Lafargue:
> Liebknecht just played me a nice trick. He has taken from my *Introduction* to Marx's articles on France of 1848–50 everything that could serve him to support the tactic of *peace at any price and of opposition to force and violence*, which it has pleased him for some time now to preach, especially at present when coercive laws are being prepared in Berlin. But I am preaching these tactics only for the *Germany of today*, and even then *with an important proviso.*

facts have emerged, and no serious attempt at refutation has been made that would induce us once again to investigate this question. I could do nothing here but plagiarise Engels.

Luśnia's own comments only serve to confirm Engels's point of view. He likewise has to concede that today an armed insurrection of the people against the military would be madness. If he thinks that the coming revolution will be fought with force of arms, he does not mean a struggle between the people and the military but between two fractions of the military, one of which will go over to the people's side. That is surely a scenario that could become real, but it would still only be a special form of the general postulate of the military becoming 'disaffected'. As long as that is not the case, it does not disprove the improbability of the military being 'defeated by popular uprisings'.

But do we have reasons to spend much time examining that special form? Reflections on future problems and the means of solving them are only significant if they are capable of influencing the praxis and theory of the present, i.e., if their results can affect the force and direction of our action, the success of our propaganda or the clarity of our thoughts. Since we have no intention of carrying out propaganda within the ranks of the army in order to incite them to insurrection – and nobody in the entire German Social Democracy thinks of doing that today – we have no need to debate the forms that such insubordination could and should assume.[41] On the other hand, it is certainly important even today, if not for our action then at least for our propaganda and theoretical conceptions, to state unambiguously that we expect nothing from an armed uprising of the people and that we will not allow ourselves to be provoked into it under any circumstances.

But there is another question that is no less important and is closely connected with that one. Though it seems impossible that the people could meet the weapons of the state with the force of arms, is the possibility also precluded that the proletariat could ever use force to ward off the brute force of its opponents? Should it surrender defencelessly in the case of a coup d'état? Does it dispose of no other political weapon than the ballot?

In France, Belgium, Italy, and Austria these tactics could not be followed in their entirety and in Germany may become inapplicable tomorrow. (Marx and Engels 1954, pp. 568–9.]

[41] [That situation changed shortly thereafter. See Liebknecht [1907] 1973.]

Politically, the fighting proletariat develops most satisfactorily under a constitution such as Germany's. It does not have the slightest reason for wanting to change it illegally and by force. But, precisely for that reason, it must be all the more prepared, the more its political power grows, for the overthrow of the existing constitution by its opponents, who will attempt to set up in its place a régime of violent repression of the proletariat and destroy its organisations – a régime of force that will categorically demand energetic self-defence.

It is impossible for such a régime to provoke an armed revolt of the people wherever the masses are led by Social Democracy. If it should finally call forth violent resistance from the proletariat, the working class could use only *one* forceful measure, which it often employs already in its economic struggles as the last means of forcing an issue: the *strike*.

If, because of its evident fruitlessness, this instrument proves at the outset as objectionable as the armed insurrection, that does not prove that the cause of the proletariat is hopeless. Even then we would have no need to despair for long. Today the proletariat so represents the future and even the present vital interests of the nation, that a government cannot repress it by force without confining and crippling the entire life of the nation – a condition that must sooner or later lead to its collapse in one of those crises from which no state is spared. To be sure, in that case the future of the proletariat would be insecure and more dependent on external events than on its own force, but victory would not be impossible.

But the confidence of the proletariat, its energy, self-assurance and the respect of its opponents, must grow considerably if it knows that it possesses a weapon by means of which it is able to checkmate the violence of its opponents using its own forces. And in this respect the discussion concerning the political strike – or the general strike as people still somewhat mistakenly call it – is of greater topical interest [than the discussion of armed insurrection].

2. *The different kinds of strikes*

However different the conclusions that individual participants in this debate may have reached so far, one thing has, in any event, been demonstrated clearly: the political strike is not a weapon that people can always employ at will as soon as the organisation of the proletariat is sufficiently developed. If it is to succeed at all, it can only be in special conditions.

But those conditions cannot be studied in the usual strikes undertaken for economic reasons because political and economic strikes are two entirely different things.

In economic strikes, the workers' strength derives, on the one hand, from the necessity of the reproduction process for the capitalist and, on the other hand, from utilising the competition between capitalists and eliminating the competition among workers.

The fixed capital of the manufacturers – buildings, machines and so on – also depreciates when it is not used. Sometimes, it is directly threatened with destruction during a stoppage of production, as with mines in the event of water infiltration when the pumps are idle. Sometimes the exchange-value of raw materials also declines by being stored too long, for instance, sugar beet in the refineries.

But these technical reasons, which make the interruption of activity involve a loss for the capitalist, are joined by other economic ones. The annual amount of profits depends not only on the degree of exploitation of the worker but also on the speed of the circulation of capital.

Let us assume that, out of a capital of 2 million marks, 400,000 correspond to wages, 1,600,000 to the constant capital during a turnover – and, for the sake of greater simplicity, let us set the fixed capital at zero. The rate of surplus-value amounts to 100 per cent, and its sum in each turnover is 400,000 marks. If the capital turns over once a year, it yields a profit of 400,000 marks. The rate of profit therefore amounts to 400,000/2,000,000 or 20 per cent. If the capital turns over twice a year, the sum of surplus-value, without increasing the exploitation of the workers, will reach 800,000 marks and the rate of profit will rise to 40 per cent. The rate of exploitation remained the same, but if the number of workers did not increase, their wages also doubled [like the rate of turnover] as a result, for instance, of more regular and productive employment of the workers, overtime, and the cancellation of holidays. The faster the turnover of capital, the higher the profit. However, a standstill in activity means a prolongation of capital's turnover period. Apart from the need for the fastest possible turnover of capital, a strike also exerts pressure on capitalists because they fear competition from their peers as well as the solidarity of their workers.

Almost all these factors work best on behalf of the workers in periods of prosperity. It is during those periods that capitalists seek more eagerly after workers, when the number of strike-breakers is lowest, when contributions to the strike fund flow most abundantly, when capital can turn over most quickly, when a disruption of the reproduction process lowers profits most obviously, and when it is often more profitable to concede a rise in wages than to interrupt production.

All these things are well known and are repeated only in order to illuminate the contradiction between political and economic strikes. The economic factors that contribute to the success of the workers are progressively less relevant in a mass strike the more it becomes a general strike. The general strike itself eliminates them. Suddenly the social reproduction process is completely interrupted; the manufacturer cannot dispose of his finished products or receive any raw materials. What interest could he have in getting the workers into the factory? He has no need to fear that his competitors will snatch the workers from under his nose; nor will his clients betray him since they cannot possibly find better service elsewhere. And the workers? Apart from unusually favourable circumstances, the workers of a single factory are at a disadvantage vis-à-vis the employer even if they are united. But if they do not succeed at the first attempt, if they are overcome after a tenacious siege, if they are rarely victorious, the workers of a factory can turn for support to their peers in the neighbouring plant; the workers of a locality to their peers in the entire state; the workers of one branch of production to all the proletariat of the country and even of the entire world. This support, with the exception of the last scenario, is impossible in the case of a general strike.

True, the idea of paralysing the entire economic life of capitalist society at once, thus making it no longer tenable, is very fascinating. But one must not forget that a mass strike, so long as it lasts, suspends not only capitalist production but also any sort of production whatever. And the workers are even more interested in the continuation of production than the capitalists because the latter are in possession not only of the means of production but also of all the large reserves of means of consumption. The capitalists can thus endure a general stoppage of production longer than the workers; in fact, they are in a position to starve them. A national mass strike whose duration would approach, for instance, that of the Crimmitschau strike,[42] is totally impossible.

---

[42] [A city of the German state of Saxony, on the Pleisse River, northwest of Zwickau. An industrial community since the eigtheenth century, with factories for

If it does not triumph during the first week, then the reserves of the workers and of the petty traders who provide them with credit would be exhausted. Then they can either submit or breach the existing legal order and provide themselves with food by violent means. However, they would then leave the terrain of the economic strike, the revolution of the poor with their arms crossed, and step into that of insurrection.

To be sure, even today there are strikes that cease to be purely economic and exert an indirect social and especially political pressure against a particular group of employers when direct economic pressure proves ineffective, so that the strike attains indirectly what it was unable to obtain directly. Such strikes occur particularly when some stratum of workers comes into conflict with the great monopolies. The position of the latter is too strong for the strike to upset them, but the strike causes so much harm to different levels of society, and the exceptional position of the monopolists creates for them so many enemies in bourgeois society, that the state or the community can force them through legislation to concede the demands of the strikers in order to prevent excessive damages to society.

The great strike of the Austrian coal miners in the winter of 1900 provided such an example. Economically, it was going to be lost. The coal barons could endure it calmly. But it produced so many disturbances in industry, and the super-profits that the coal mine owners pocket year in and year out are so enormous and arouse such bitterness that they have few friends even in bourgeois circles. In order to prevent a recurrence of the strike, the Austrian Imperial Assembly was finally willing to grant the nine-hour day, at least to the coal miners. It was one of the most remarkable results of the union of political and trade-union action. Each one, on its own, would have been unsuccessful. Members of the Social-Democratic fraction could have talked themselves hoarse in favour of shortening the working day in the coal mines, but without the strike they would have preached to deaf ears. The strike, in turn, would have ended to no avail without the intervention of the Social-Democratic members of the Assembly, who did not rest until the

----

cloth and knitted goods and spinning and weaving mills, it became a centre of the working-class movement in the nineteenth century. The strike of the Crimmitschau textile workers, from August 1903 to January 1904, had the effect of mobilising textile workers throughout Germany.]

government and the majority fulfilled, at least in some measure, the promises they had made at the time of the great coal emergency.

Many sympathy strikes and anarchist general strikes pursue similar aims. When a group of workers is not strong enough to deal with its employers, workers in other branches of production often cease work in order to make the stoppage of production more effective in the enterprises originally affected. That is the case, for instance, when transportation workers refuse to deliver goods produced by strike-breakers. However, the sympathy strike can go further and assume a more general, political character if it wants to cause inconveniences and losses to the whole of bourgeois society in order to force it to exert pressure on the recalcitrant group of employers.

These general strikes are often lumped together with the political mass strike, but they only have an outward resemblance because, in both cases, great masses of workers from different occupations lay down their tools. However, their aims are very different. Sympathy strikes that turn into mass strikes aim at incrementally increasing the economic pressure of the striking workers on a particular stratum of employers by putting pressure on bourgeois society and the bourgeois state. That pressure arises from the fact that the entire capitalist class has everything to win and nothing to lose from some concessions by particular employers. The political mass strike, on the contrary, exerts economic pressure on the employers in order to force the entire bourgeois society and the state to capitulate before the workers.

The political strike is therefore a strike of a totally unique kind, for whose analysis the experiences of other work stoppages are of little use. Apart from the Belgian and Dutch examples, we have no practical experiences at our disposal. But it is too dangerous an instrument for people to experiment with at random. We must attempt to come to definite conclusions about it even if the available data are insufficient. We will be greatly assisted in this task if we analyse the experience of the barricade struggles that the political strike is to replace.

3. *The power of organisation*

In the comparison between the political strike and the barricade struggle, one coincidence is noticeable above all: neither operates through the factor that is decisive in the field from which these forms of struggle developed. Just as the political strike has no prospect of being effective through the economic pressure it exerts, so the barricade fighters, even if they are successful, almost never prove tactically superior to their opponents. Trained troops are more than a match for a popular uprising not only because of their weapons but also through their *organisation*, which includes both their discipline and being directed according to a plan. The superiority of organised over unorganised masses is enormous even if their weapons are similar. When 10,000 Greek soldiers, whose later retreat was immortalised by Xenophon, were victorious in their struggle against half a million Asians, that was due not to their superior armaments (or if so, only to an insignificant degree) but rather to their tight organisation. It was also thanks to their organisation, rather than better weapons, that the *Landsknechts*[43] were able to cope with the rebellious peasants in 1525.

Superior organisation of the command apparatus constitutes the basis of any ruling power much more than its physical superiority. That is shown most clearly by the commanding position that the Catholic Church has reached and still maintains without, and even in opposition to, the power of weapons.

The more independent of society the state apparatus becomes, and the more absolute it is, the more jealously it strives to deprive its subjects of any possibility of developing a broad organisation independent of the state. But since social relations are always stronger than the state, it can only be successful when they do not work against its policy. Absolutism thrives where the mode of production isolates and disperses the population, making their organisation more difficult while at the same time favouring the creation of a vast state organism – for instance, in large agrarian states that appear in great plains because the peasant does not go beyond the village organisation. Where, on the contrary, the mode of production not only produces widespread states but also centralises the population and concentrates great masses with the same interests, and where a lively exchange of ideas occurs in a few points of decisive significance for national life, it is difficult to prevent their organisation. In that case, when formal and open organisations are forbidden the people build conspiratorial and secret ones, which are all the more energetic, even fanatical, the more the organisation involves a life-and-death issue for the

---

[43] [The *Landsknechts* were German mercenary pikemen and foot soldiers from the fifteenth to the late sixteenth century.]

classes in question. Political pressure and dissolution of all organisations by the state can actually, under certain circumstances, become a bond that holds together the oppressed classes more closely than any open organisation; a bond that raises to the highest degree the unity of their thought and will as well as their voluntary obedience to the authority of their own leaders in ways that the ruling classes cannot control.

The strongest form of organisation is the one based on voluntary and enthusiastic devotion. This is the form with which the Church achieved its most brilliant triumphs. Much less vigorous and resistant, given the same instruments of power, is a coercive organisation like the modern state, which becomes increasingly less vigorous the more it ceases to be an actual organisation of the ruling classes and becomes an organisation of elements who are paid (mainly badly) to serve them – and who are often forcefully pressed into their service so that the composition of the state apparatus will be increasingly less favourable to the ruling classes.

For instance, let us look at the army under general conscription. Most reliable for the ruling classes are conscripts from the country who come out of their villages unorganised, who are intellectually sluggish thanks to their traditional mode of production and their isolation, and who are still steeped in patriarchal views and stand in awe before any fatherly authority due to their peasant circumstances, especially the peasant right of succession. Least dependable for the ruling classes are the industrial proletarians who are organised by large-scale industry and city life, endowed with a feeling of independence and lively intellectual life and, through their early economic independence, are filled with contempt and even hostility toward all the traditional authorities. That is quite serious for the modern state power because the numbers of peasants both in society and in the army is declining rapidly.[44]

…But not only is the social composition of the *army* continually worsening for the ruling classes.

The mechanism of government is today also much more dependent on the wage-earning class. Economic and political development leads towards the nationalisation of more and more enterprises – first of all of the *transportation*

---

[44] [We omit here the statistical data that Kautsky cites to demonstrate his argument.]

system – on whose undisturbed functioning the whole of economic life increasingly depends. The more commodity production develops, the more each person produces not what he needs but what he doesn't need in order to exchange it, and the more the quantity of products grows that must be transported before they reach the hands of consumers. The division of labour tends in the same direction within each enterprise. The number of enterprises through which a product must pass, from its original form as raw materials until it is ready for use, increases continuously. Commerce and transportation are therefore the occupations that grow most rapidly. In Germany, from 1882 to 1895, the number of people employed in trade and transportation grew by 49 per cent, in industry by 29 per cent, while in agriculture it was only a trifling 0.23. The railway system grew by 53 per cent; the postal and telegraph system by 89 per cent.

But it was precisely in transportation that modern giant enterprises first developed and fell under the sway of high finance. Where the latter does not rule absolutely, the state soon attempts to take possession of those enterprises because of the great importance they have for the whole of national life and especially for development of its military forces. It is significant that France made as little progress with the nationalisation of railways as with the income taxes: despite the presence of socialists in the 'government bloc', high finance rules there absolutely.

But, whether the railway system is private or state property, its undisturbed functioning will increasingly become a life-and-death question for the modern state. The railway employees will, for that reason, be placed under an ever-stricter discipline, while at the same time more and more military forces will be trained to run the railway system. But, of all the major groups of wage-workers, the railway employees, next to workers in state-owned mines, are precisely the ones most immediately interested in bringing about establishment of a government dependent on the workers. They are the most sensitive to a government that is hostile to the proletariat.

On the other hand, a government will tend, all other circumstances being equal, to identify all the more with the capitalists, the larger the number of state enterprises and of workers exploited by them and the more direct the government's interest in capitalist profit.

The increasing nationalisations of enterprises are then, for the time being, not a means of peaceful growing over into socialism but rather a means of bringing into the government mechanism itself the modern class contradictions and class struggles and of making it more sensitive to them.

In the days of barricade struggles, the state did not yet depend so much on wage-workers in its enterprises and in the army, and it was therefore not so susceptible. But, even then, the success of barricade struggles depended more on their disorganising than on their tactical effects. Through the suddenness and universality of an outburst of popular rage, they confused and paralysed the government, while simultaneously creating for it a situation that required its greatest strength, cold-bloodedness and unity of purpose. Where barricade struggles did not manage to produce this effect, above all where the government was ready for them or even provoked them, the fighters inevitably succumbed. What a contrast there was in 1848 between the February days and the June days in Paris, and between the March and the October days in Vienna!

Given modern armaments, today it has become impossible to bring down a government, even the weakest and most foolish one, by means of armed resistance. Not only are the weapons of the military much more formidable than they were fifty years ago; the population is also much more defenceless. Today, one cannot mould the bullets for rifles, and even if the people did manage to break into an arsenal and provide themselves with weapons, these would be useless without the special ammunition.

The consciousness of technical military superiority makes it possible for any government that possesses the necessary ruthlessness to look forward calmly to a popular armed uprising – and a less ruthless government would not have to fear such an uprising because it would not have brought about the harsh antagonism with the popular masses that alone can produce a violent outbreak of utmost desperation. Today, it is not to be expected that a popular armed rising would have so powerful a moral impact as to unnerve and disarm the government.

What the barricade struggle no longer succeeds in doing should now be done through the political strike, *disorganising the government* while simultaneously making the utmost demands on its strength, self-possession and tenacity, forcing it either to retreat or resign. It would be a trial of strength between the state and proletarian organisation.[45] With a single blow, all production would

---

[45] That both the political strike and the barricade struggle operate by disorganising the government has been first shown, and in the most brilliant way, by Parvus in

be paralysed, the masses of the workers would be brought into the streets, the masses of the petty and great bourgeoisie would be driven into a state of frantic anxiety about their lives and property, and the entire armed power would be forced into a constant, exhausting activity because every proprietor in the country would crave for protection and the masses of striking workers would be everywhere and nowhere, avoiding any clash with the armed forces and gathering wherever they are not present. Each additional day of the strike would heighten the contradictions, extend the strike to those regions of the countryside wherever industry or large landed property are located, increase the number of vulnerable points, multiply the exertions of the troops, and sharpen the pains and passions of the strikers as well as the anxiety of the proprietors and the confusion of the government, which in one place will be carried away into the most horrible and senseless brutalities, while in another it will adopt the most cowardly subservience, all the while entreating all sides to put an end to the situation one way or the other while having no chance itself to come to grips with the passive resistance that would nowhere be tangible yet would paralyse it everywhere.

If the government is nonetheless strong enough to withstand the political strike without breaking down and being thrown into confusion; if it manages, in the general standstill of social life, to secure the undisturbed functioning of all parts of the state organism long enough to wear out the strength of the workers, until they are faced with the alternative of either crawling back under the yoke or attempting to attain through desperate deeds of violence what they were unable to achieve through the revolution of crossed arms, then the victory of the government is likely – to be sure, a victory that the government would have paid for dearly. All the horrors that the bourgeoisie expected from the victorious strike will be imposed upon the workers.

If, on the contrary, the strikers succeed in maintaining their cohesiveness and preserving their purposeful passivity long enough to disorganise the government at some points, then the proletariat is on the way to victory – whether because they managed to draw over to their side factors which the government needs, or because the government itself through *ordre, contreordre, désordre*[46] sowed confusion, spreading weakness and helplessness among its

---

Parvus 1896b, pp. 199–206, 261–6, which nobody who wants to study the question of the political strike should overlook. [Reprinted in Grunenberg (ed.) 1970, pp. 46–95.]

  [46] [Order, counter-order, disorder. In French in the original.]

followers. The propertied classes would then lose confidence in the ability of the government to protect them; they would increasingly fear that continuing resistance would bring ruin upon them; they would storm the government, give in, leave it in the lurch and reach an agreement with the rising powers in order to save what can still be saved. The government would feel the ground slip away under from under its feet, and state power would fall to the class that knew how to maintain longest its organisational unity in the crisis; the class whose composure and self-confidence most impressed the great, indifferent masses, and whose prudent use of force disarmed its opponents: that is, the proletariat educated by Social Democracy.

4. *The preconditions of the political strike*

For the proletariat to be able to reach victory through a political strike, it should first of all constitute a preponderant part of the population who are intelligent and organised enough to maintain discipline when organisation is formally dissolved. It should also be able to produce again and again from its midst new leaders, whom it should follow willingly if its customary leaders are arrested. It should not let itself be carried away by temptations and provocations into imprudent and hasty steps or into outbursts of anger or panic. Finally, it should not be distracted from its great goals by ancillary concerns. Industry must be highly developed, and the proletariat must go through a long school of political and trade-union struggles before it comes that far.

On the other hand, the government must exhibit certain distinguishing features for the strike to be able to unsettle it. The political strike is excluded beforehand in the case of a government elected by the people, one that does not lean upon external instruments of power that can be disorganised through a strike but rather upon the majority of the people. In Switzerland, for instance, the attempt to topple the government and conquer political power through a mass strike would be as hopeless as it would be superfluous. Because the political strike can triumph only through its disorganising effects on the government, not through its economic pressure on society, it can only be suitable in places where the government has attained a certain independence from the popular masses, as in the case of all the modern large states. But, in such states, the striking proletariat also has prospects of success only so long as it faces an outwardly strong and brutal but inwardly weak and headless government that no longer enjoys the trust of the propertied classes or even of the bureaucracy and the army. A strong and far-sighted government, which impresses all classes of the people, cannot be defeated by a political strike.

Luckily for the proletariat, modern development shows everywhere a tendency to weaken the government and make all classes discontented with it. That is no accident. As long as the state had great goals that were in the interest of the mass of the nation, its struggles easily produced great men behind whom stood cohesive and great parties. The case is totally different when, as at present, the state and the classes standing behind it have essentially attained all they wanted. There is no longer a great, common interest that could weld these classes together. Petty local and professional interests come to the foreground, and the parties of the propertied classes split more and more into small, short-sighted cliques. The governments are more and more coalition governments, whose tasks no longer consist in accomplishing a great programme but in reconciling elements that tend to pull apart. That is only possible by prompting each party to abandon its traditional programme, by increasing the legislative incapacity of the government, and by concentrating all its forces on some obvious measure – for instance, some custom duties or the police expulsion of a couple of priests and nuns – to the neglect of everything else.

Energetic and far-sighted men of action cannot thrive in such an atmosphere. It favours spineless flatterers, masters in the art of delaying and covering up, who are apparently ready to serve, by means of promises, the most contradictory tendencies, yet who in practice care only for the next day with no concern for the long-term consequences. They are slick diplomats, often intelligent, always charming, skilled in the art of alluring those they are dealing with but incapable of overcoming any great antagonism, of satisfying any great interest, or even of impressing their subordinates with their superiority. They are suitable helmsman for sunny days, but they break down in a storm, and their authority must wear out completely even before their own breakdown in view of the contradictory interests they serve – a contradiction that they seek not to overcome but only to conceal.

The more unexpectedly and suddenly the storm breaks out, the more helpless they will stand before it. Here we come to the second similarity between barricade battles and the political strike. We have seen that the fate of both depends on their moral effect, on the sudden disorganisation of the government. Because that was the decisive thing for barricade battles, and not the tactical overcoming of the army, they only had prospects of success where they broke out *unexpectedly* without giving the government time to make preparations. As a rule, that was the case only with *spontaneous* uprisings in which the people themselves mounted the barricades following a sudden inspiration, but the people were not always without organisation and leadership. In France these were provided to a large extent by secret societies. Where such secret organisations not only make use of the uprising but prepare it for a long time and stage it, they are not easily defeated. However, the police everywhere have their spies, and the government is usually warned in time of their intentions. Finally, the timing stipulated beforehand for the uprising does not always coincide with a strong oppositional agitation of the popular masses.

Something similar happens with the political strike if it is appropriate: it does not bring about victory through the economic pressure it exerts on the capitalists but through its paralysing and disconcerting effects on the mechanism of government. The more unexpected and spontaneous the strike, the sooner it will fulfill its aims. What holds good for any strike is also true of the political strike: the best part of its effect is lost when one announces it beforehand for a specific date. The only purpose of this announcement can be to use the strike as a threat. But such threats must wear out quickly, and when they are not followed by the most decided action they must produce discouragement and mistrust in the ranks of the workers.

The political strike thus has the greatest possibilities of success when it grows spontaneously out of a situation that produced the deepest agitation in the popular masses – such as a great wrong inflicted upon them, a coup d'état, or something similar – so that the masses are ready to risk everything and a watchword like the general strike [*Arbeitseinstellung*] can sweep away everything in its path. The suddenness, universality and force of the eruption can thus intimidate, bewilder and paralyse its opponents.

Nothing is more mistaken than thinking that the entire working class must first be organised in unions before the political strike can be started. This precondition would never be fulfilled and would only have some justification if the workers wanted to defeat their opponents through the economic pressure of a *protracted* strike. The general strike succeeds in paralysing enemies through its moral effects, and for this purpose it is not necessary to have a general *organisation* but rather a general *agitation* of the proletarian masses in the same direction – an agitation that would, to be sure, subside fruitlessly if it did not have behind it an organisation, or even a working class that went through the school of organisation, to lend the movement brains and backbone.

With the pertinent changes, what Marx wrote in 1852 about the armed insurrection can also be said about the political strike:

> Now, insurrection is an art quite as much as war or any other, and subject to certain rules of proceeding, which, when neglected, will produce the ruin of the party neglecting them....Firstly, never play with insurrection unless you are fully prepared to face the consequences of your play. Insurrection is a calculus with very indefinite magnitudes, the value of which may change every day; the forces opposed to you have all the advantage of organization, discipline, and habitual authority: unless you bring strong odds against them you are defeated and ruined. Secondly, once the road to insurrection has been taken, act with the greatest determination and on the offensive. The defensive is the death of every armed rising; it is lost before it measures itself with its enemies. Surprise your antagonists while their forces are scattering, prepare new successes, however small, but daily; keep up the moral ascendancy which the first successful rising has given to you; rally those vacillating elements to your side which always follow the strongest impulse, and which always look out for the safer side; force your enemies to a retreat before they can collect their strength against you; in the words of Danton, the greatest master of revolutionary policy yet known, *de l'audace, de l'audace, encore de l'audace!*[47]

Mutatis mutandis, that also holds true for the political strike. One does not play with it or pledge one's word to stage it at a definite date. When the time for it has come, when the working masses energetically demand it and the struggle against the government breaks out, the probabilities of victory will be all the greater the more quickly the decision to go on strike is executed without delay, without parleys, without interruption, before the opponents

---

[47] [Engels 1969, Chap. XVII: Insurrection (September 18, 1852). Kautsky and his contemporaries erroneously attributed the authorship of this book to Marx.]

have collected their instruments of power and drawn up their battle plan, and the less opportunity they are granted to come to their senses and catch their breath.

In that respect, the Belgian general strike of April 1902 showed us how it should not be made. First, the government was given an announcement regarding a life-and-death struggle at a fixed date; then, after it had been given time to collect and arm itself, to assemble troops and complete its preparations, the general strike was launched.

We have no intention of reproaching the Belgian comrades for those mistakes. Despite everything, they fought so magnificently and carried out such an orderly retreat that they made up for their errors as far as possible. And of course, it is much easier for spectators, especially after the event, to point out mistakes than for people engaged in action to avoid them. But the wish to spare any reproach to our Belgian comrades must not go as far as to conceal their errors, because in that case we run the risk of repeating them. We have no reason to blame the Belgian comrades, who have gone ahead into such thorny and unknown terrain, but we must learn from them to avoid entering upon the false path that led them away from the road to victory.

From the Belgian experiment we can see that it would be a fatal mistake for us in Germany to proclaim the political strike for a fixed date, for instance, in case of a restriction of the present franchise.

Another circumstance also weighs against this commitment. Here we can notice a further similarity between barricade struggles and the political strike.

Whatever the starting point of barricade struggles, they always dash forth to overthrow the existing government, not just to wring out some isolated concession. And that is completely natural. A barricade fight means risking one's life. And one runs into such risks only for the sake of a great goal. Only the consciousness of being able to shake off a yoke that has become unbearable could inspire in the masses the courage and the enthusiasm that they require to confront the armed forces.

But the latter can only be made to waver by the feeling that the ruling régime is about to collapse. As long as the soldier knows that he will have the same chiefs tomorrow, even if his revolt against them turns out well, he will shun any insubordination and the cruel punishment that would inescapably follow. He can only be made to waver by his awareness that going over to the side of the people or remaining passive in the struggle will help to bring down the government and thus transform insubordination from a crime into an act of the highest civic virtue.

Finally, the necessary disorientation in the government only appears when it perceives that any false step, whether in the form of weakness or ruthlessness, could cost it its very existence and not just a little more or less power or authority.

Similar considerations apply for the political strike. Here also great things are at stake. If not directly their lives, then the fighters risk their economic existence in an entirely different sense than in an ordinary strike, when behind the strikers of one branch of production in any single locality stands the entire working class with its intact organisations and resources. A defeat in a political mass strike, if it has been fought to the utmost, means a defeat for the entire working class, the destruction of all its economic and political organisations and the complete crippling of the proletariat's ability to fight for years to come.

At the last Vienna party congress, Victor Adler[48] argued that he sympathised with the general strike because the 'glorious retreat' of the Belgian comrades showed that 'it (the general strike) can be brought to an end in a sensible, cool-headed and clear manner'. From the context, Adler obviously meant by that expression not only the possibility of leading the general strike sensibly and cool-headedly to victory, but also the possibility of interrupting it without suffering a defeat when there are no prospects of victory. I would not count on the last possibility very strongly. A general who engages in battle with the expectation of being able to interrupt it at will if he realises that the enemy is stronger than expected can be very dangerous. Whoever begins a battle must be resolved to fight it out to a conclusion and must also count on the possibility of a defeat. In any great action that we undertake, only the beginning stands before us. How it will turn out in the end depends not only on us but also on our opponents.

The possibility of a defeat should not deter us from struggling. One would be a pathetic warrior if one were to engage in battle only when victory is

---

48 [Victor Adler (1852–1918) was a founder and leader of Austrian Social Democracy and a member of the International Socialist Bureau. He turned social chauvinist during World War I.]

certain. There can even be occasions when one must put up a fight when defeat is likely, because retreat without a struggle would mean complete moral bankruptcy.

But the more devastating the effects of an eventual defeat, the more one must beware of entering into a struggle unnecessarily and the greater must be the prize for the sake of which one takes up the struggle.

With a tottering, rotten régime, there is no need to prove that in the case both of a mass strike and of barricade battles the government loses its head all the more easily the greater the danger it faces, and only under such a régime can a mass political strike be declared. A resolute, centralised and energetic government, with roots in the popular masses, thrives in the face of danger. The method of overthrowing such a government has not yet been found.

But barricade struggles against the military have shown that the mechanism of government is thrown all the more easily into disarray the more the government is at risk. That also holds true for state employees. We have already pointed out that railway employees are even more interested in the installation of a proletarian régime than most other groups of workers. But they are precisely the ones who risk the most in a strike that does not end with their victory but leaves the government in place. Even a temporary victory can mean a defeat for them, as illustrated by the outcome of the Dutch strike, which led merely to the granting of some particular concessions and not to modification of the government system in a proletarian sense. In most countries the railway employees must weigh very carefully whether to join a political strike if it has no prospects of leading to establishment of a proletarian régime.

And the same rules that apply to the railway employees also hold true for other categories of workers upon whom the government depends for its functioning.

That is one reason why the last Belgian general strike failed. The railway employees, the soldiers and so on would have joined the strike much earlier if they had seen a prospect of successfully replacing the ultramontane government with an Anseele-Vandervelde[49] ministry.

---

[49] [Edward Anseele (1856–1938) was a leader of the Social-Democratic Belgian Workers Party (*Parti Ouvrier Belge*, P.O.B.) identified with the right wing of the Second International. Émile Vandervelde (1866–1938) was also a Belgian Social-Democratic leader. He joined the P.O.B. in 1886 and entered parliament in 1894. Vandervelde

The chances for the political mass strike are poor where Social Democracy is not strong enough and ready to take possession of the helm of state in case of victory.

If all the observations we have made here prove correct, then we must conclude that the political mass strike is a weapon that, under certain circumstances, can render excellent services, but the time to apply it successfully has not yet arrived. It is not a superior means with which to wring some concessions from the ruling classes or to preserve political liberties and rights that have already been won.

But the political mass strike can be the means for workers to seize power in a final, decisive struggle, when legal political means have been taken away from them, when they have little to lose politically and infinitely more to win, and when the strike breaks out in a favourable situation that finds the government either unprepared or in a dilemma. It is a truly revolutionary instrument and, as such, it is only suitable in revolutionary times. It should not be used to achieve some particular measures such as the franchise, the right of association or similar goals but in order to struggle for political power in its entirety.

If the political strike is not applicable in present conditions, it is, on the other hand, very doubtful whether it is an instrument whose application is necessary under all circumstances. We have seen that we cannot foresee the forms of coming struggles for political power: events abroad – and we include in that category a revolt in Belgium, a disastrous war in Russia, or a civil war in the United States – could have such repercussions for Germany as to lead to the conquest of political power by peaceful means without any catastrophes. On the other hand, the durability and strength of the political instruments of power at the disposal of the proletariat at this stage have not yet been put to the most extreme test. Ultimately, the future could have many surprises in store for us.

Nothing would be more precipitous than to commit ourselves to declare the political mass strike under certain conditions. But neither do we have the

------

played a leading role in the Second International, serving as the first president of the International Socialist Bureau. He also turned social-patriotic during the First World War and later served in many cabinets.]

slightest reason to do so at present. I concur completely with Adler when, in the speech already quoted, he said:

> I am not in favour of reassuring our enemies that they are safe from the general strike. We would in that case be fostering a dangerous illusion. We do not want to renounce the general strike. When, how and under what conditions we will use it, that has not yet been decided.

5. *The necessity of discussing the political strike*

If we can say almost nothing definite about a future application of the political strike, what is the purpose of discussing a method of struggle that we will perhaps not employ at all and that, when necessary, operates all the more energetically the more unexpectedly it is used? Doesn't that mean brooding over as yet non-existent issues and, on the other hand, disclosing our cards prematurely to our opponents?

To rack one's brains over the future would be pointless if our present actions did not help to shape the future and if our views of the future had no influence on our current activity. But where, on the contrary, such a reciprocal action exists, it is not only permissible but imperative to delve into the future. If employment of the political mass strike is not unconditionally necessary, it is even less unconditionally excluded. Precisely because, in order to be effective, it cannot be prepared beforehand for a fixed date by a small organisation, and because it must not be a putsch but a spontaneous outbreak of a profound, universal anger of the proletariat, we must discuss it openly. If the barricade struggles of 1848 began spontaneously, received the support of the people and were ultimately successful, that was only possible because many decades of practice with armed uprisings had familiarised the minds of the people with that method. Such schooling is today neither necessary nor desirable. Our present political rights enable us to discuss theoretically and in public the instruments of political struggle, which, before 1848, was impossible. By means of these discussions, we are able, to a certain extent, to supersede the necessity of learning from practice, and we would be fools if we did not avail ourselves of that opportunity. Contemporary forms of democracy do not render superfluous the great decisive struggles between classes for political power, as the revisionists think. But they do dispose of a large part of the costly and counter-productive attempts to provoke decisive battles prematurely, before the rebellious classes have the power and maturity to take possession of political power effectively and to employ it successfully. But, if we want to avoid making any experiments with the political strike, then we must develop its theory all the more and make the comrades realise that if, one day, the proletariat must use the weapon of the general strike, it will only be able to employ it appropriately if it has already attained a political grasp of it beforehand.

But public discussion of the political strike is not only an expedient replacement for the school of political experience; it could also exert a valuable influence on our political life.

Now, as in the past, Marx's saying remains true: *force* [*Gewalt*] is the midwife of any new society.[50] No ruling class abdicates voluntarily and nonchalantly. But that does not necessarily mean that *violence* [*Gewalttätigkeit*] must be the midwife of a new society. A rising class must have the necessary instruments of force at its disposal if it wants to dispossess the old ruling class, but it is not unconditionally necessary that it *employ* them. Under certain circumstances, *awareness* of the existence of such instruments can be enough to induce a declining class to come to an agreement peacefully with an opponent that has become overwhelming.

The more numerous and powerful the proletariat's instruments of force, and the more their existence is well known, the greater will be the probability of a peaceful transition from capitalism to socialism. To what extent that kind of social revolution is at all within reach does not depend on our peaceful protestations or on our renunciation of the 'ogre legend [*Fresslegende*]';[51] it does not depend on assurances or concessions that were either not seriously meant – and are therefore mere cant – or that can be construed as signs of weakness and will only strengthen the resolution of our opponents to refuse to grant any meaningful concession. Only through our instruments of power will we impose ourselves on our opponents and induce them to seek a peaceful contest

---

[50] ['Force is the midwife of every old society pregnant with a new one.' Marx, 1976, *Capital*, Vol. I, Part VII: Primitive Accumulation, Chap. 31: Genesis of the Industrial Capitalist, p. 916.]

[51] ['Bernstein…makes the Social-Democratic "ogre legend" – in other words, the socialist strivings of the working class – responsible for the desertion of the liberal bourgeoisie.' Luxemburg 1989, p. 72, Chapter VII: Co-operatives, Unions, Democracy.]

with us, which we also wish for if it is at all possible without endangering or delaying the emancipation of the proletariat. The old saying, 'If you want peace, prepare for war', applies here more than in any other case. If the first result of our discussions is the conclusion that we possess in the political strike a weapon that is surely doubled-edged and should only be employed in the most extreme situations – but also one that is dangerous and under certain conditions even lethal for our opponents – and the second conclusion is that the probability of eventually employing this weapon grows when all other weapons of political struggle have been taken away from us or blunted, then we have considerably improved our ability to preserve our political rights and prevent political catastrophes.

That also applies, finally, with regard to our own party. All the discussions of recent years sprang from a feeling in our ranks that with continuation of our present tactic and growth we are rapidly coming to a frontal confrontation with the ruling classes. If, in doing so, we dispose of no other political weapon than the one that has been granted to us by those classes themselves, namely, general suffrage, then our prospects would really be poor. It was then natural to look for a tactic that could postpone the decisive struggle for centuries, break it up into an endless series of meaningless mini-struggles or, in a Proudhon-like manner, circumvent the object of the struggle, political power. With all these attempts to avoid the enemy or even gain his approval, we run the risk of sacrificing, for the sake of the party's existence, what constitutes the foundation and the justification for that existence, thereby emasculating the party and leading to its gradual decomposition.

It is completely different when the proletariat is conscious of having at its disposal several means of power [*Machtmitteln*] that are independent of the good will of the ruling classes and that can give the proletariat the force with which to overcome its opponents even if they have recourse to the most brutal methods. In that case, the proletariat will calmly continue to advance along the road that it recognises as the correct one on which it has already advanced so far – without letting itself be provoked by agitators who would gladly drown the fighting proletariat in its own blood, but also without letting itself be intimidated by the warnings of those anxiously worried friends who desire its victory but abhor its struggle.

It seems to me that one of the most effective means of kindling in the proletariat an inspiring and resolute feeling of its own force, together with confidence in its victory, is to spread the consciousness of the ultimate feasibility and effectiveness of the political strike. It is for the sake of that invaluable effect, above all, that analysis of its feasibility and methods is today so necessary.

Chapter Six

'What Was Accomplished on the Ninth of January' (January 1905)

Parvus

Alexander Israel Helphand (Parvus) was one of the most controversial and visionary Marxists to participate in the Russian revolution of 1905.[1] His insight into Russian and world events came from his knowledge of Marx and his study of political economy, in which he earned a doctorate from a Swiss university in 1891. As early as 1895–6, he endorsed the tactic of the political mass strike,[2] initially as a means of proletarian self-defence and, by 1904, as a weapon of attack and a 'method of revolution' that presupposed thorough organisation of the workers in both the Social-Democratic party and trade unions.[3] Parvus was involved in most of the polemics as well as the intrigues of both German Social Democrats and Russian exiles. In the campaign against Bernstein's revisionism, he was one of the first to explain cyclical crises in terms of a modern theory of imperialism.[4] But Parvus enters the historiography of Russian Marxism primarily through the profound influence

---

[1] For a biography of Parvus see Zeman and Scharlau 1965.
[2] Parvus 1896b, pp. 199–206, 261–6, 304–11, 356–64, 389–95.
[3] Parvus 1904a.
[4] English versions of Parvus's articles against Bernstein can be found in Tudor and Tudor (eds.) 1988, pp. 174–204.

of his ideas on Leon Trotsky. In his biography of Trotsky, Isaac Deutscher says that, by 1904,

> Not only were Parvus's international ideas and revolutionary perspectives becoming part and parcel of Trotsky's thinking, but, also, some of Trotsky's views on Russian history, especially his conception of the Russian state, can be traced back to Parvus.[5]

Deutscher devoted an entire chapter to the 'intellectual partnership' between Parvus and Trotsky. In *My Life*, his autobiography, Trotsky wrote:

> Parvus was unquestionably one of the most important of the Marxists at the turn of the century. He used the Marxian methods skilfully, was possessed of wide vision, and kept a keen eye on everything of importance in world events. This, coupled with his fearless thinking and his virile, muscular style, made him a remarkable writer. His early studies brought me closer to the problems of the social revolution, and, for me, definitely transformed the conquest of power by the proletariat from an astronomical 'final' goal to a practical task for our own day.[6]

In February and March of 1904, Parvus published two articles in *Iskra* on the world economy and the Russian autocracy that influenced Trotsky's view both of imperialism and of the prospects for *permanent revolution*. The first article, 'Capitalism and War', began with a declaration that 'The Russo-Japanese war is the bloody dawn of impending great events'.[7] There followed a sweeping picture of geopolitics in which Europe was making feverish preparations for world war. Surveying the rise of militarism and imperialist barriers to trade, Parvus traced the expansion of capitalism around the globe and particularly into Asia. 'Each capitalist state,' he wrote, 'is an enormous and complex machine for squeezing labour out of the people and for the endless capitalist transformation of surrounding areas.' Capitalism produced a torrent of commodities that periodically surpassed the capacity of domestic markets and compelled a never-ending search for new peoples and territories to conquer. In the struggle over colonies, all the great states of

---

[5] Deutscher 1965, p. 105.
[6] L. Trotsky 1960, p. 167.
[7] *Iskra*, No. 59 (10 February, 1904).

Europe, together with America, Russia and Japan, were engaged in a titanic struggle extending into every corner of the globe.

Russia, alone among the imperialist powers, with its weakly developed economy, sought conquests for reasons other than the internal contradictions of the capitalist mode of production. Far from requiring outlets to foreign markets, Russian industry was incapable even of generating the revenues needed to support a modern army. The financial poverty of Russia was as boundless as its efforts to conquer other countries: 'The Russian government uses foreign gold to acquire foreign lands, and it seizes foreign lands in order once again to acquire gold for itself.'[8] Russia aspired to remain a great power, but its imperialist adventures were provoked mainly by domestic instability: 'The mindless quest of the Russian government for successes in foreign affairs is imperative in order to hide the empire's internal weakness.' With its poorly equipped peasant army, in February 1904 Russia blundered into the war with Japan, which Parvus declared would destroy 'the political equilibrium of the entire world'.

In a subsequent article on 'The Fall of the Autocracy',[9] Parvus related the war to impending revolution. The government hoped war would drown domestic opposition in a wave of 'military patriotism', but the final outcome would be cataclysmic defeat. A vigorous and youthful Japanese capitalism needed markets and resources on the Asian mainland, but Russia stood in the way of Japanese expansion. Russian forces depended upon supplies by way of the Trans-Siberian railway, but given the railway's limitations it was easier to reach New York than the besieged fortress at Port Arthur. In contrast, once Japan defeated the Russian fleet, Japanese forces were supplied and reinforced at will. The damage inflicted on Russia's credit was even more disastrous. Foreign bankers demanded a victory before extending new loans, but new loans were imperative merely to continue the war. With inevitable catastrophe in view, Parvus concluded:

---

[8] Foreign loans supported the government's budget deficits, and much of the budget went to the military. Russia needed to remain on the gold standard in order to sell government bonds in Europe and attract foreign capital for economic development.

[9] *Iskra*, No. 61 (5 March, 1904).

> The only way out of the disgraceful condition into which the Russian
> government has driven Russia is liquidation of the autocracy. Revolution
> alone can restore the national vitality of the country.

Most Social Democrats thought the war would at least compel the tsar
to introduce liberal reforms. Parvus went much further, believing the
outcome might well be 'a government of workers' democracy' headed by
Social Democrats. The tsarist state was a bureaucratic hybrid of European
absolutism and Asiatic despotism, and its successor might be just as unique –
a provisional workers' government in a country where industrial workers
were a small minority in a sea of peasants. To most contemporaries, this
suggestion seemed absurd – but not to Ryazanov[10] or Trotsky. Early in 1905,
Trotsky invited Parvus to elaborate his ideas in the article we have translated
here, which served as the preface to Trotsky's own pamphlet *Up to the Ninth
of January* (the next document translated in this volume).

In 'What Was Accomplished on Ninth January',[11] Parvus scorned Russian
liberals who entertained exaggerated notions of their own influence and
popular support. In Europe, liberalism had flourished in the context of urban
life and commerce, but Russian liberalism was an imported idea with shallow
roots. Historically, Russian urban life bore little resemblance to that in Europe;
the 'cities' were primarily administrative outposts of the autocracy, and the
commerce that bred modern capitalism was scarcely to be seen. The majority
of Russian cities were 'merely commercial bazaars for the surrounding gentry
and the peasantry'. When foreign pressures finally forced Russia to import
elements of capitalist modernity, an industrial proletariat emerged that
was concentrated in large factories. Whereas Russian liberalism was a head
without a body, the workers were a potentially powerful force in need only of
organisation and resolute leadership.

Parvus believed that, in the first stage of the Russian revolution, the opposing
forces of liberalism and socialism might find common ground, but overthrow
of the autocracy would initiate a prolonged political struggle in which they
would have to define their relations in terms of mutually conflicting goals.

---

[10] Ryazanov and Parvus were personal friends and political associates at the time.
They both came from Odessa and had studied there at the same school.
[11] Parvus completed this article on 18 (31) January 1905. It first appeared as a
foreword to N. Trotsky 1905b, pp. iii–xiv. It was also republished in Parvus 1907b,
pp. 134–43.

While liberals would attempt to co-opt working-class support for bourgeois constitutionalism, the most crucial obligation of Social Democrats would be to maintain the proletariat's organisational independence and commitment to a working-class programme. Social Democrats must make use of liberal support whenever possible, but they must also prepare for prolonged class struggle and even civil war, in which the historical experience of Europe might be dramatically abbreviated and the Russian proletariat might emerge as the vanguard of international socialist revolution. With an accompanying revolution in Europe, Russia, despite its historical backwardness, might even initiate the final goal of building a socialist society. Even apart from a European revolution, if the Russian working class temporarily took state power it would propel revolutionary change to the furthest limits compatible with private property and bourgeois democracy.

The greatest danger to the revolution was that liberals, upon discovering their own weakness, would compromise with tsarism in the interest of preserving 'order'. The inescapable conclusion was that workers alone could complete the revolutionary overthrow of absolutism. Social Democrats would then find themselves in power, or at least holding the majority in a provisional revolutionary government with an extraordinarily complex agenda: on the one hand, they would have to institutionalise the revolution and establish the constitutional freedoms needed for further organisation of trade unions and the workers' party; on the other hand, they must simultaneously begin to implement working-class demands that would inevitably intrude (as Kautsky argued in 'Revolutionary Questions') upon private property in the means of production. The outcome of this dilemma would depend partly upon the European revolution and partly upon the tenacity and skill of Social-Democratic leadership.

Parvus's vision was stunning in its audacity, but it also left profound questions unanswered: how far *would* a workers' government, once in power, be compelled by its own mission to move in the direction of socialism; and how far *could* it move before finally being overthrown by political reaction? At the beginning of 1905, few Russian Marxists regarded Parvus as anything more than a well-intentioned but seriously mistaken romantic. Most agreed that the only way to avoid repeating the failures of the 1848 revolutions in Europe was to *support* the liberals rather than *frightening* them. The most authoritative spokesman for this view was G.V. Plekhanov, the traditional leader and elder theorist of Russian Social Democracy. The novelty of Parvus's argument can be seen most clearly by comparing his views first with those of Plekhanov, speaking for the Mensheviks, and then with those of Lenin, speaking for the Bolsheviks.

In his criticism of the *Iskra* draft programme, Ryazanov had already made the argument for *permanent revolution*, to which Plekhanov had responded that 'The real question is how to achieve the triumph of a democratic republic'. In 1905, Plekhanov returned to the same theme in an essay 'On the Question of the Seizure of Power'.[12] He agreed that 'the dictatorship of the proletariat must be the first act of a socialist revolution', but, in Russia, the real issue was merely a '*bourgeois* revolution'. Although the proletariat would play the leading role, the revolution would go no further than creating the conditions needed to prepare for socialist revolution some time in the future.[13]

Responding to the question of how the proletariat could play the leading role but then refrain from seizing power, Plekhanov claimed that Marx had already provided the solution. When liberals betrayed the 1848 revolution, Marx expected the republican petty bourgeoisie to resume the struggle against feudal remnants and urged workers to support these efforts while maintaining organisational independence.[14] With working-class support, Marx expected the petty bourgeoisie to establish real bourgeois democracy. Plekhanov saw similar circumstances in Russia: the workers could not aim immediately for socialism, but they could 'dictate to the petty bourgeoisie such conditions as would significantly facilitate the future replacement of bourgeois-democratic supremacy with the rule of the proletariat'.[15] Of one thing Plekhanov was certain:

> the founder of scientific socialism…never even contemplated the idea
> that political representatives of the revolutionary proletariat might join
> with representatives of the petty bourgeoisie in establishing a new social
> order. Quite the contrary: after victory over the big bourgeoisie and the
> seizure of power by petty-bourgeois democrats, the workers, according
> to Marx's plan, would have to *come together as a strong opposition* party,

---

12 Plekhanov 1926b, pp. 203–11.
13 Plekhanov 1926b, pp. 203–4.
14 Plekhanov 1926b, pp. 205–6.
15 Plekhanov 1926b, pp. 207–8.

which, through criticism and agitation, would push the petty-bourgeois government forward....

This was what Marx meant by the term *permanent revolution*, and Plekhanov insisted that Russian Social Democrats must adopt precisely the same tactics.[16]

For Plekhanov, the lesson drawn from the experience of Marx and Engels was that the workers' party could never do more than criticise bourgeois liberals and republicans until the objective, subjective, and psychological conditions finally warranted direct struggle for the ultimate goal of socialism. When he made this argument, however, the object of his criticism was Lenin, not Parvus. By 1905, Plekhanov and Lenin had parted ways following the split between Bolsheviks and Mensheviks, and Lenin was now calling for a 'revolutionary-democratic dictatorship of the proletariat and the peasantry' and 'participation of the proletariat in the revolutionary government'.

In an essay on 'The Provisional Revolutionary Government', Lenin argued that 'Plekhanov's inference is entirely false'. When Marx and Engels set forth the tactics cited by Plekhanov, they expected the revolution to resume quickly after the defeats of 1848–9. Instead, Europe settled into political reaction. Reading from the same texts as Plekhanov, Lenin drew his own very different inference:

> If Marx and Engels had realised that the democratic system was bound to last for a fairly long time, they would have attached *all the more* importance to the *democratic* dictatorship of the proletariat and the peasantry with the object of consolidating the republic, of completely eradicating all survivals of absolutism, and of clearing the arena for the battle for socialism.[17]

The problem with Lenin's notion of a 'democratic dictatorship of the proletariat and peasantry' was obvious: in Russia, there was no revolutionary petty-bourgeois party with whom to co-operate. Lenin thought such a party must eventually emerge, but this was hardly a practical basis upon which to base political tactics. In effect, Lenin wanted the proletariat to pressure republicans from within 'the marble halls' of a provisional government that was really no more than a castle in the air.

---

[16] *Ibid.*
[17] Lenin 1905c, p. 472.

Within weeks of this exchange with Plekhanov, Lenin published another major essay, 'Two Tactics of Social-Democracy in the Democratic Revolution', and compounded the confusion by insisting that even a consistently democratic revolution in Russia 'will not weaken, but strengthen the rule of the bourgeoisie'; the most the proletariat could demand was 'realisation of all the immediate political and economic demands contained in our program (the minimum program)':

> Marxists are absolutely convinced of the bourgeois character of the Russian revolution. What does this mean? It means that the democratic reforms in the political system and the social and economic reforms, which have become a necessity for Russia, do not in themselves imply the undermining of capitalism, the undermining of bourgeois rule; on the contrary, they will, for the first time, really clear the ground for a wide and rapid, European and not Asiatic, development of capitalism; they will, for the first time, make it possible for the bourgeoisie to rule as a class.[18]

Lenin and Plekhanov agreed that the revolution would be limited to creating, at best, a régime of democratic capitalism; their chief difference concerned participation of the workers' party in a provisional government. Lenin thought the working class was '*decidedly interested* in the broadest, freest and most rapid development of capitalism', which would create the most suitable conditions for class struggle.[19] Yet, at the same time, he admitted that

> …our influence on the masses of the proletariat – the Social-Democratic influence – is as yet very, very inadequate; the revolutionary influence on the mass of the peasantry is quite insignificant; the proletarians, and especially the peasants, are still frightfully disunited, backward, and ignorant.[20]

---

[18] Lenin 1905k, p. 48.
[19] In Lenin 1905e, p. 292 Lenin wrote:
In this revolution, the revolutionary proletariat will participate with the utmost energy, sweeping aside the miserable tail–ism of some and the revolutionary phrases of others. It will bring class definiteness and consciousness into the dizzying whirlwind of events, and march on intrepidly and unswervingly, not fearing, but fervently desiring, the revolutionary–democratic dictatorship, fighting for the republic and for complete republican liberties, fighting for substantial economic reforms, in order to create for itself a truly large arena, an arena worthy of the twentieth century, in which to carry on the struggle for socialism.
[20] Lenin, 1905k, p. 57.

Notwithstanding this dismal outlook, he still insisted that 'the general democratic revolutionary movement *has already brought about the necessity* of an insurrection'.[21] Most readers would have found this argument curious: the 'frightfully, scattered, backward and ignorant' worker and peasant masses were, with Bolshevik leadership, to mount an *armed insurrection*, after which they would jointly create a revolutionary-democratic dictatorship – and they were to do so in conditions that would inevitably *strengthen the rule of the bourgeoisie*!

By comparison with Lenin's evident confusion, Plekhanov and Parvus at least put forth arguments that were coherent. Yet, when Lenin turned from Plekhanov (who he thought was lagging behind the revolution) to Parvus (who he believed was rushing ahead of it), he found himself on equally difficult terrain. While calling for armed insurrection, he dismissed Parvus's introduction to the 'windbag' Trotsky's pamphlet as 'bombastic' and totally unrealistic. When Parvus called upon Social Democrats to be 'more revolutionary than anyone else', Lenin replied that 'we will always be critical of such revolutionariness…and we will teach the need for a sober evaluation of the classes and shadings within the classes':

> Equally incorrect…are Parvus' statements that 'the revolutionary provisional government in Russia will be a government of working-class democracy', that 'if the Social-Democrats are at the head of the revolutionary movement of the Russian proletariat, this government will be a Social-Democratic government', that the Social-Democratic provisional government 'will be an integral government with a Social-Democratic majority'. This is *impossible*, unless we speak of fortuitous, transient episodes, and not of a revolutionary dictatorship that will be at all durable and capable of leaving its mark in history. This is impossible, because only a revolutionary dictatorship supported by the vast majority of the people can be at all durable (not absolutely, of course, but relatively). The Russian proletariat, however, is at present a minority of the population in Russia. It can become the great, overwhelming majority only if it combines with the mass of semi-proletarians, semi-proprietors, i.e., with the mass of the petty-bourgeois urban and rural poor. Such a composition of the social basis of the revolutionary-

---

[21] Lenin 1905k, pp. 72–3.

democratic dictatorship, possible and desirable: i.e. the possible and desirable revolutionary-democratic dictatorship will, of course, affect the composition of the revolutionary government and inevitably lead to the participation or even predominance within it of the most heterogeneous representatives of revolutionary democracy. It would be extremely harmful to entertain any illusions on this score.[22]

Throughout 1905, the debates between Mensheviks and Bolsheviks raged with increasing acrimony, convincing Parvus that fratricidal quarrels among Social Democrats were consuming more energy than real efforts to mobilise the masses and organise the workers. In the meantime, the tsarist government had made peace with Japan and issued reform proposals that portended some sort of elections. By mid-October, the St. Petersburg Soviet emerged and the capital city was paralysed by a political strike. While the Bolsheviks hesitated to join a Soviet not subject to party discipline, Trotsky and Parvus immediately supported the incipient workers' government. Together they edited a new newspaper, *Nachalo* [*The Beginning*], and used it to promote a strategy of permanent revolution, beginning with the mass strike for an eight-hour working day. *Nachalo* was to replace *Iskra*, whose editorial board had been torn apart by factional fighting. In the last issue of *Iskra*, Parvus summarised his impressions of the internal party struggle since Bloody Sunday.

> Organisational incompetence has brought us aimlessness in political thought and inability to give any decisive answer to the critical questions of the revolution. A victorious revolution is made by the class that leads it and controls state power....Since the revolution in Russia became a political fact, Russian Social Democracy has faced the task of seizing state power and making use of it in the interest of the working class – in accordance, naturally, with Russia's economic conditions. The Mensheviks have recoiled from this undertaking and become absorbed in discussions of whether it might be best, at the very time when the revolutionary army of the proletariat is on the upsurge, to surrender political power immediately and voluntarily to bourgeois democracy. This is the same timid thinking that, *mutatis mutandis*, led Bernstein to predict a 'colossal defeat' for German Social Democracy should it find itself in control of the state in the near future. Like Bernstein,

---

22 Lenin 1905e, p. 291.

they have used this idea as cover for a fatalistic understanding of the historical development that results from class relations.

If class relations were determined by the historical course of events in some simple and straightforward manner, then there would be no use in racking our brains: all we would have to do is calculate the moment for social revolution in the same way as astronomers plot the movement of a planet, and then we could sit back and observe. In reality, the relation between classes produces political struggle above all else. What is more, the final outcome of that struggle is determined by the development of class forces. The entire historical process, which embraces centuries, depends upon a multitude of secondary economic, political, and national cultural conditions, but above all it depends on the revolutionary energy and political consciousness of the struggling combatants – on their tactics and their skill in seizing the political moment.

Throughout the entire class struggle, state power plays an enormous role. With the aid of state power, a social class can maintain its supremacy even in spite of economic conditions. That is why in Western Europe capitalism has long stood in the way of the economic development of society. With the aid of state power, it is possible to accelerate the transition from capitalism to socialism in the same way as capitalism itself, simply by use of military force, has destroyed older economic forms and hastened the transition to capitalist production. Intermediate political forms are even more susceptible to change.

For decades, Russian autocracy has itself maintained power by use of force despite the economic and political development of the country. Without a social revolution in Western Europe, it is presently impossible in Russia to realise socialism. But the question of what *form* capitalist rule might take, how strong its state power might be, what kind of parliament might exist, how democratic the further development of our fatherland might be, and what role the proletariat will play – all these issues depend on the victory of the revolution, on how it develops, on the revolutionary energy of the workers, on the political decisiveness of Social Democracy, and on whether we succeed, even for a short time, in using state power in the interest of the toiling masses.

…Whatever the form of organisation, [what is required] above all else is *joint work* [between the rival factions of Russian Social Democrats]. In the course of its development, the movement will change and adopt the appropriate organisational form, yet people have been thinking the child must be made to fit the jacket. There is no iron straitjacket that can hold back growth of the workers' movement.

Whether the revolution develops on its own or is organised, whether we enter a provisional government or send democrats, above all Social Democracy must act as a *single, unified party*. Whatever the tactic might be, it is first necessary to create a political force in order to implement it. Apart from such a force, no theoretical discussions will serve any purpose. If there is such a force, then it will ultimately find its way to a proper tactic – the events will prevail over the ideas and plans of any chieftains.[23]

The principal theme of Parvus's writing in 1905 was the urgent necessity of organising the workers and preserving their tactical independence vis-à-vis all other parties and movements. Convinced that the tsarist régime had sounded its own death knell in the war with Japan, he and Trotsky joined in single-minded commitment to proletarian revolution. In the document that follows, Parvus makes the case for an exceptional revolutionary outcome based upon Russia's unique history and the resulting peculiarities in the alignment of class forces.

*　*　*

'What Was Accomplished on the Ninth of January'

The Bloody Sunday of Ninth January[24] begins a new era in Russia's historical destiny. Russia has entered the revolutionary period of its development. The old order is breaking apart, and a new political formation is rapidly taking shape. Only recently, the ideological propaganda of revolution forewarned of events and for that reason seemed to be utopian – now it is events that are revolutionising people's minds, and the determination of revolutionary tactics lags behind revolutionary developments. The revolution is driving political thought forward. In just a few revolutionary days, Russian public opinion has completed a more fundamental critique of governmental authority,

---

[23] Parvus 1907b, pp. 193–5.
[24] [22 January in the new style calendar.]

and has more clearly defined its attitude to forms of government, than one might expect during years of development – even if the country enjoyed a parliamentary order. The idea of reform from above has been thrown aside. Along with it, any faith in the popular mission of the autocracy has simultaneously vanished.

The revolution, making its imprint on all political tendencies and points of view, is generating a unifying ferment of opposition. Party differences are momentarily obscured by a common revolutionary task. At the same time, the revolution is driving the ideology of liberalism to its political limits. The liberal party now thinks of itself as being more radical than it can possibly be in reality; it is promising more and taking upon itself greater tasks than it could ever achieve with the help of those social strata upon whom it depends. The revolution is driving all opposition parties to the left and drawing them together in a common revolutionary idea.

A revolution clarifies the political change, but it also blurs the lines between political parties. This is an historical law that cannot fail to operate during our revolutionary epoch in Russia, where it finds particularly favourable conditions in certain unique aspects of the country's political development.

In Russia there has not been and never could be a clear delineation of political forces. To produce such a classification of society's political forces, and to counterpose them in terms of their particular economic interests, is one of the historic tasks of parliamentarism. With the ideological formula of popular government, parliamentarism draws every stratum of society into the struggle for political power. In the context of this struggle, which is legalised and regulated, the various classes determine their mutual political relations and take measure of each other's strength. But, in Russia, the different political tendencies – with the exception of proletarian class struggle and Social Democracy, of which more will be said later – have hitherto developed only in the ethereal realm of ideology; they have sought contact with the people, or with 'society', only in a very narrow sense of the word, that is, with the bourgeoisie. The undefined, formless, and fleeting masses are driven by political winds first in one direction and then another, easily dissolving and then reassembling. Parties adopt policies of the moment that can sharply contradict the requirements of their own political development, which are determined by the particular social strata upon which they are mainly based. The Russian *zemstvo*,[25] for example, which presently represents the main support of liberalism in Russia, is creating for parliamentary Russia an agrarian party with acutely conservative tendencies. Absolutism suppressed any political struggle of the agrarians against industrial capital with the result that it made enemies of both of them.

One of the effects of agrarian Russia's inability to give political expression to the struggle against advancing capitalism was a more intensive literary critique of industrial capitalism. Due to class divisions among the agrarians themselves and the influence of cultural developments in Western Europe, and in accordance with an immanent law that governs the development of all revolutionary criticism, this critique took on a democratic character. But because it did not lead to working-class socialism, which had already developed outside of Russia, it ultimately ended in a Tolstoyan doctrine. Failing to find cultural unity beyond capitalism, it ended up denying culture in general; that is to say, it raised its own idealistic fiasco to the level of an historical principle. In capricious and sometimes striking tones, mixing together an artistic reflection of life with the illusions of visionaries, and a vital urge for development with the romanticism of a bygone age, the ideas of this literary phantasmagoria became tangled up with political ideology and had the effect of further masking the underlying class motives of different political interests. This mixing of fiction with politics spread to all parties in the form of *narodnichestvo*.[26] With the exception of Social Democracy, it resulted in *belles lettres* taking precedence over radical tendencies.

Everyone knows that political radicalism in Western Europe depended mainly on the petty bourgeoisie; that is, on the artisans and generally on that part of the bourgeoisie that took part in industrial development but at the same time was not part of the class of capitalists. It must be remembered that the artisans of Western Europe created the cities. The cities flourished under their political leadership, and the master craftsmen put their stamp

---

[25] [The zemstvos were organs of rural self-government at the district and provincial levels. Although dominated by the nobility, many zemstvos maintained a professional staff and were active in building roads, providing basic schooling and health care, and in promoting agricultural improvement. Their authority and revenues, however, were limited, and they were viewed with suspicion by the central government bureaucracy.]

[26] [The narodniks were agrarian socialists who hoped Russia might bypass capitalism and reach socialism based upon the traditional village commune or *obshchina*.]

on several centuries of European culture. While it is true that the power of the craftsmen had long ago vanished by the time the parliamentary régime appeared, the existence of numerous cities remained a politically important fact, and within them only the emerging proletariat challenged the numerical predominance of the middle strata of society. As these social forces dissolved into the class contradictions of capitalism, democratic parties faced the task either of moving closer to the workers and becoming socialist, or else moving closer to the capitalist bourgeoisie and becoming reactionary. But, during the precapitalist period in Russia, the cities developed more along the lines of China than in accordance with the European pattern. They were administrative centres with a purely bureaucratic character and did not have the slightest political significance; in economic terms, they were merely commercial bazaars for the surrounding gentry and the peasantry. Their development had hardly progressed at all when it was interrupted by the capitalist process, which began to create large cities in its own pattern, that is, factory cities and centres of world commerce. The result is that, in Russia, we have a capitalist bourgeoisie but not the intermediate bourgeoisie from whom political democracy in Western Europe emerged and upon whom it depended. In Russia, as in the whole of Europe, the middle strata of today's capitalist bourgeoisie consist of the so-called liberal professions, that is, of doctors, lawyers, writers, etc., or those social strata that stand apart from the relations of production, and secondly, of the technical and commercial personnel of capitalist industry and trade and the corresponding branches of industry such as insurance companies, banks, and so forth. These diverse elements are incapable of producing their own class programme, with the result that their political sympathies and antipathies endlessly waver between the revolutionism of the proletariat and the conservatism of the capitalists. In Russia, moreover, there are also other déclassé elements, or the refuse of classes and strata from pre-reform Russia that have yet to be absorbed by the capitalist process of development.

It is in this urban population, which has never passed through the historical school of the West-European Middle Ages, and which has no firm economic connections, past traditions or ideal of the future, that political radicalism in Russia must find its support. That it should look elsewhere is no surprise. On the one side, it fixes upon the peasantry, and, in this context, the *belles lettres* character of Russian *narodnichestvo* finds its clearest expression, substituting a literary apotheosis of labour and need in place of a class-political programme. On the other side, political radicalism in Russia attempts to base itself upon the factory workers.

It is in these conditions that the Russian revolution is doing its work of drawing together and unifying the different anti-government tendencies. This drawing together of diverse elements constitutes the strength of the revolution before the upheaval occurs, but it also constitutes its weakness afterwards. Following the overthrow of the government, against which a common struggle was waged, the diverse and contradictory interests of the many political tendencies that coalesced in the revolution re-emerge, and the revolutionary army becomes disorganised and disintegrates into its mutually hostile parts. Until now, this has been the historical fate of all revolutions in class-divided society, and no other kind of political revolution is conceivable.

We all know that, in the revolutions of 1848, this internal struggle was already so intensive that it completely paralysed the political force of the revolution and cleared the way for reaction and counter-revolution, which in France ended in the bourgeoisie's bloody reprisals against the same workers alongside whom it had just waged the revolutionary struggle.

Following the overthrow of autocracy in Russia, the capitalist bourgeoisie will detach itself from the proletariat just as quickly as it did in Western Europe in 1848, but the revolutionary process will be much more protracted. This results from the complexity of political tasks that the revolution must fulfill. It is a question not simply of changing the political régime, but also of creating for the first time a state organisation that can embrace all the numerous aspects of life in a modern industrial country and replace the fiscal-police system into which the autocracy unilaterally evolved. In addition, there is the confusion of agrarian relations in Russia and, as we have already indicated, the formlessness and social incoherence of the non-proletarian political tendencies within the country.

In view of these objective conditions for the revolution's development in Russia, what are the tasks of the Social-Democratic party?

Beyond the overthrow of autocracy, which is just the *starting point* of the revolution, Social Democracy must keep in view the entire subsequent development.

It must not adapt its tactics to any single political moment, but must instead prepare for a long process of revolutionary development.

It must develop a political force that will be able not just to overthrow the autocracy, but also to take the lead in this revolutionary development.

The only such force is the proletariat, organised as a unique class.

Placing the proletariat at the centre and the head of the revolutionary movement of the whole people and the whole of society, Social Democracy must simultaneously prepare it for the civil war that will follow the overthrow of autocracy – for the time when it will be attacked by agrarian and bourgeois liberalism and betrayed by the political radicals and the democrats.

The working class must understand that the revolution and the collapse of autocracy are not the same thing, and that, in order to carry through the political revolution, it will be necessary to struggle first against the autocracy and then against the bourgeoisie.

Even more important than the proletariat's consciousness of its political uniqueness is the independence of its organisation and its real distinction from every other political tendency. We are told of the need to unify all the revolutionary forces in the country, but it is even more important that we take care not to divide and dissipate the proletariat's revolutionary energy.

It is imperative, therefore, that the proletariat have its own unique organisation and policy – not just in the interest of the class struggle, which continues before the revolution, during it, and even after it, but also in the interest of the revolutionary upheaval itself.

At the same time, this must not entail either the political isolation of the proletariat or indifference to the political struggle of the other parties.

It is imperative to grasp the political situation in all its complexity and to avoid simplifying things merely to find easy answers to tactical questions. It is an easy matter to say: 'Together with the liberals' – or 'Against the liberals!' Nothing could be simpler, but these would be extremely one-sided and therefore false responses to the issue. We must make use of all revolutionary and oppositional tendencies, yet, at the same time, we must know how to preserve our own political independence. In the case of a joint struggle with temporary allies, all of this can be summarised in terms of the following points:

1) Do not blur the organisational lines. March separately, but strike in unison.
2) Do not waver in our own political demands.
3) Do not hide differences of interest.

4) Keep watch of our allies in the same way as we watch our enemies.
5) Pay more attention to taking advantage of the situation created by the struggle than to the maintenance of an ally.

Above all else, this means organising the proletariat's revolutionary cadres as the force that must eliminate the political ballast in the way of revolution. In this category I include the influence of all those social strata and political parties that march in unison with the proletariat up to the overthrow of the autocracy but then, because of their manifest hostility, political indecision and lack of resolution, end up delaying, weakening and distorting the political revolution. We must drive forward all the various tendencies of political democracy and radicalism.

To drive the democrats forward means to criticise them. There are some queer minds, however, who think this means luring them with tender words, as one would attract a lap dog with sugar. The democrats are always ready to stop halfway – and, if we approve of them for the short stretch of road they have travelled, then they will stop.

To criticise them in words alone is not enough. Political pressure is needed, and this brings us back to the revolutionary party of the proletariat.

The class struggle of the Russian proletariat was clearly defined even under absolutism. The same condition that impeded the development of petty-bourgeois democracy also promoted proletarian class consciousness in Russia: that is, the weak development of the handicraft form of production. The proletariat found itself immediately concentrated in factories. It immediately faced economic domination in the most advanced form of a capitalist who stands apart from direct production; it also faced state power in its most concentrated form of autocracy, which relies exclusively upon military force. To all of this Social Democracy directly added the historical experience of the West.

The Russian proletariat has shown that it did not pass through these three forms of schooling for nothing. It has steadfastly pursued its own, independent revolutionary politics. It created the Russian revolution, it united around itself both the people and society, but it also avoided any dissolution of its own class interests in the general revolutionary movement, putting forth instead its own political programme of *workers' democracy*. In the interest of its class struggle, it demands political freedom, and along with civil rights it also demands labour legislation.

Our task now is to make the eight-hour day just as much a central postulate of the revolutionary uprising as the budgetary rights of parliament.

We must not only give a proletarian character to the political programme of the revolution; we must also avoid, under any circumstances, lagging behind the revolutionary course of events.

If we want to distinguish the revolutionary proletariat from all other political tendencies, then we must know how to stand at the head of the revolutionary movement and be more revolutionary than anyone else. If we lag behind revolutionary development, then the proletariat, precisely because of its revolutionary character, will not be embraced by our organisations and will dissolve into the spontaneous revolutionary process.

Our tactic must be revolutionary initiative.

The first act of the Great Russian Revolution is completed. It has placed the proletariat at the centre of politics and united around it all of society's liberal and democratic forces. This is a two-sided process; *the revolutionary consolidation of the proletariat* and its rallying of all the opposition forces in the country. If the government makes no concessions, this revolutionary process will progress steadily. The proletariat will become increasingly united and steeped in revolutionary consciousness. Our task is to translate this into revolutionary organisation. It is an open question whether society's liberal elements will follow this development or become frightened by the growing revolutionary strength of the proletariat. In all likelihood, they will waver first in one direction and then the other: in their fear of revolution, they will turn towards the government, but the government's reprisals will then turn them back towards the revolutionaries. The democratic elements will remain under the influence of the workers. But these elements, as we have already indicated, are especially weak in Russia. Ever-greater masses of peasants will be attracted into the movement, but their only capacity is to create greater political anarchy in the country. They will weaken the government as a result, but they are unable to constitute a coherent revolutionary army. This means that with the revolution's development a steadily increasing share of its political work will fall to the proletariat. At the same time, the proletariat will increase its own political self-awareness and grow in political energy.

The Russian proletariat has already become a revolutionary force that has accomplished far more than other peoples in times of revolutionary insurrection. It is no coincidence that the people have risen up in such great masses throughout the entire country. The peoples of Germany and France won their freedom with far fewer losses. The resistance of the Russian government is incomparably greater thanks to the military power at its disposal, but this resistance will serve merely to amplify the proletariat's revolutionary energy. When the Russian proletariat finally overthrows the autocracy, it will be an army steeled in revolutionary struggle, firm in its determination, and always prepared to use force to support its political demands.

In 1848, the French proletariat already succeeded in compelling the provisional government to include its representatives. Since the revolutionary government could not survive without support from the workers, it played out the comedy of state concern for their needs.

The Russian workers, having already imposed their proletarian demands on the political programme of the revolution, will be much stronger at the moment of upheaval and at least as forceful as French workers were in 1848 in expressing their class consciousness – they will certainly have their own people in the government. Then Social Democracy will face a dilemma: either to take upon itself responsibility for the provisional government or else to stand aside from the workers' movement. Whatever Social Democracy decides, the workers will regard this government as their own. Having created it through revolutionary struggle and become the main revolutionary force in the country, they will take even firmer control of the government than might be possible through election leaflets.

Only the workers can complete the revolutionary upheaval in Russia. A Russian provisional government will be a government of workers' democracy. If Social Democracy stands at the head of the revolutionary movement of the Russian proletariat, then this government will also be Social-Democratic. If it lags behind the proletariat in revolutionary initiative, then Social Democracy will be reduced to an insignificant sect.

A Social-Democratic provisional government will not be able to complete the socialist revolution in Russia, but the very process of liquidating the autocracy will give it favourable conditions for political work.

All of us who have fought in Western Europe against participation of individual Social-Democratic representatives in a bourgeois government have argued not that a Social-Democratic minister should be concerned solely with the social revolution, but that, by remaining in the minority in such a government, and lacking sufficient political support in the country at large, a minister will be able to accomplish *nothing at all* and will merely serve the capitalist government as a lightening rod to deflect our own criticism.

The case of a Social-Democratic provisional government will be altogether different. It will be an integral government with a Social-Democratic majority, created at the moment of revolution when government is unusually powerful. Behind it will stand a revolutionary army of workers, who will have just completed the political upheaval and, in the process, will have produced political energy without historical precedent. This government will deal at the outset with the political tasks that united the entire Russian people in revolutionary struggle. Obviously, a Social-Democratic government will be able to complete such work in a far more thoroughgoing way than any other government.

If the Russian government makes concessions in the future, this will, of course, do nothing to resolve political difficulties but will only confuse the situation even more. The process of Russia's political reconstruction will be protracted even in the case of a revolutionary development; it will obviously be more protracted if state power remains in the hands of a government that creates new obstacles to progressive development at each step of the way. Moreover, the process of setting up new political parties, which has been interrupted by the revolution, will resume with even greater intensity. But, so long as political parties are still emerging from the rosy mist of political ideology according to their own class interests, and so long as these parties have yet to reach a clear understanding of their political relations with each other and with the government, the country will be in a state of endless agitation. In these circumstances, the government itself will be moving first in one direction and then another, and it will be especially necessary to struggle continuously for the expansion of political rights and for the rights of parliament in particular. The result will be a prolonged period of political discord in which the ultimate and decisive factor, even if it is not continuously invoked, will be force: military force on the part of the government, and revolutionary force on the part of the people.

It follows that even in this event the proletariat will have an active political role. If it retains its political independence, it will be able to score significant political successes.

Already, the workers are being ardently courted from two different directions. The Russian government is promising expansion of labour legislation; the liberal and even semi-liberal press is filling its columns with articles dealing with the needs of the workers, with the workers' movement, and with socialism. One thing is clearly demonstrated in both cases, and that is how much the government and the bourgeoisie are seized by fear and by respect for the proletariat's revolutionary energy.

The tactic of Social Democracy in these conditions must be to revolutionise events – to widen political conflicts and endeavour to use them in order to overthrow the government and thereby create more room for revolutionary development.

Whatever the further course of political development, we must take care in every instance to distinguish ourselves from all other political tendencies. For the moment, the revolution is effacing political differences, and this makes it all the more important to determine how the political tactics of the parties developed prior to the historic Sunday of Ninth January. We know how weak and indecisive the liberals and democrats were in waging political struggle, limiting themselves to pressing the government to introduce reforms from above. They did not acknowledge any other possibility or see any other perspectives. And, when the government resolutely ignored their exhortations, pleas and pretensions, then, because they were out of touch with the people, they simply found themselves driven into a corner. They were powerless and turned out to be incapable of any opposition to the reactionary government. We also know how, in contrast, the political struggle of the Russian workers developed, how it continuously expanded and became suffused with ever-growing revolutionary energy.[27] Having made the revolution, the proletariat freed the liberals and democrats from a hopeless position – and now, accommodating themselves to the workers, they are discovering a new method of struggle as new resources are opening up. It was the revolutionary activity of the proletariat alone that caused the other social strata to become revolutionary.

The Russian proletariat has launched the revolution; its further development and success will depend upon the proletariat alone.

---

[27] See the essay by N. Trotsky, 'Up to the Ninth of January' (N. Trotsky 1905a), in his book *Our Revolution*, published by N. Glagolev (the next document in this volume).

Chapter Seven

Up to the Ninth of January[1] (1905)

Leon Trotsky

In the introduction to the previous document in this volume, Trotsky was quoted expressing his admiration for Parvus's 'fearless thinking and his virile, muscular style'. Trotsky's own style was radically different. Whereas Parvus wrote in a forthright and imposing manner – Trotsky spoke of him as a 'bulldog'[2] – Trotsky wrote like a swordsman: his pen was his sword, and his thrusts were fatal. In *The Prophet Armed*, Isaac Deutscher describes Trotsky's articles during the 1905 revolution as 'scholarly, rhetorical, and implacable'.[3] For Trotsky, the political pamphlet was a deadly art in which he excelled brilliantly.

The theme of *Up to the Ninth of January* is the political awakening of Russia in response to the Russo-Japanese war. Recounting the weakness of Russian liberalism, Trotsky translates the political strategy of permanent revolution into a narrative of betrayal and compromise that relentlessly points to the conclusion that neither liberals nor democrats could ever consistently oppose the autocracy. Only

---

[1] This article appeared in N. Trotsky 1905b, pp. 1–52. It was republished in L. Trotsky 1925, pp. 1–53. Trotsky originally wrote *Up to the Ninth of January* as several articles late in 1904. They were only published after 9 January 1905.
[2] L. Trotsky 1960, p. 167.
[3] Deutscher 1965, p. 121.

the proletariat, organised by the Social-Democratic party, was capable of imposing constitutional change, beginning with universal suffrage and a constituent assembly.

The conceptual background to Trotsky's essay was Parvus's account of the peculiarities of Russian history, particularly the role of the autocratic state in suppressing the political articulation of class contradictions.[4] The autocracy financed industrialisation with foreign loans and protective tariffs in the hope of providing a European type of conscript army to serve the semi-Asiatic state. The result was a concentrated industrial workforce that came face to face with state power in the absence of any strong, indigenous middle classes. When military defeats revealed the true hollowness of state power, there was a sudden surge of hope that the tsar would have to trade political concessions for popular support. Trotsky shared no such hope: he distrusted Russian liberals with the same passion as he despised Tsar Nicholas; all of them were prepared, should other options fail, to compromise at the workers' expense.

In the year preceding Trotsky's essay, the government had blundered from defeat to defeat in the war against Japan. According to Prince S.N. Trubetskoi, a professor of philosophy in Moscow, Russia was defending the whole of Europe against the 'yellow danger, the new hordes of Mongols armed with modern…technology'.[5] As the economy crumbled, liberal *zemstvos* initially assisted the government in the hope of political favour. In the summer of 1904 V.K. Plehve, Minister of the Interior and 'strongman' of the régime, was assassinated by a Socialist Revolutionary. The tsar replaced Plehve with Prince Svyatopolk-Mirsky, who promised a 'political spring' and partially dismantled censorship with the intention of maintaining support from *zemstvos* and city governments. The new tactic produced exactly the opposite effect, provoking the convening of a national Zemstvo Congress in November 1904 that in turn proposed constitutional reforms. Svyatopolk-Mirsky was inclined to support reforms, but the tsar denounced liberal and gentry critics as enemies of the state and ignited a series of political banquets across the country.

Trotsky recounts the events of 1904 and their implications for the tsar, the liberals, the democrats, and Social Democracy. To liberals and state

---

[4] Trotsky's most thorough account of the political implications of Russia's economic history occurs in his book L. Trotsky 1971a, pp. 3–56.

[5] Ascher 2004, p. 15.

bureaucrats, the thought of workers seizing the revolutionary initiative seemed absurd. Liberals and bureaucrats typically held the working class in contempt. Russian workers were treated as urban peasants, and industrial relations were modelled on those between the serf and the landlord. To organise trade unions was a criminal act – unless the police did the organising (as they often did in order to thwart independent unions); strikes were punishable with prison sentences; and the average workday was eleven and a half hours. The only class in worse circumstances was the peasantry. The crucial difference was that the horizons of peasant consciousness rarely reached beyond the village, whereas workers were already concentrated as a potential political force in their place of employment. This central fact opened the possibility for mass strikes that could cripple both the faltering government and the national economy (as Kautsky had projected in 'Revolutionary Questions').

Parvus, Trotsky's closest political comrade in 1905, had long been engaged in the dispute among German Social Democrats over the political use of mass strikes. Unlike Lenin, who distrusted the 'spontaneity' of trade unions, Parvus insisted that the mass strike was the workers' most powerful weapon in the struggle for the eight-hour day. Already distrustful of Lenin's penchant for a disciplined and tightly-knit party organisation, Trotsky found in Parvus's ideas the political formula for bringing down the autocracy. What Russian workers lacked in numbers, they more than compensated for by their strategic economic and political role. By promoting the mass strike as a political weapon, *Up to the Ninth of January* discounted the political agency of every class in Russia other than the industrial proletariat. If workers could avoid being co-opted by self-serving liberals and sham democrats, if they could build up their own organisations and simultaneously co-ordinate support from the countryside, Trotsky concluded that no force in the world – least of all the tsar's demoralised and defeated peasant army – could prevent a victorious Russian revolution.

Shortly before the appearance of Trotsky's essay, the year 1905 began in St. Petersburg with the Bloody Sunday of 22 (9) January and the shooting of more than four hundred petitioners on their way to the Winter Palace. Georgy Gapon, a populist priest with ties to the tsarist police, led the march and inadvertently triggered a general strike that paralysed the capital city. The next day, more than 160,000 workers stayed off their jobs in St. Petersburg and the strike quickly spread to most other cities in the country. On his way back to Russia from Europe, Trotsky stayed briefly with Parvus in Munich. Trotsky had been trying unsuccessfully to get his work published, and Parvus now took responsibility for seeing the work into print. Trotsky recounted the history and significance of his essay as follows:

> Beginning essentially with the well-known position of Plekhanov to the effect that the Russian revolutionary movement will triumph as a workers' movement or not at all,[6] in 1904, on the basis of the raging strike movement of 1903, I came to the conclusion that tsarism will be overthrown by a general strike, which will entail open revolutionary clashes that will develop and expand, resulting in dissolution of the army and, still better, in a part of it going over to the side of the insurrectionary masses. I gave this brochure to the foreign press of the Mensheviks, who at the time were divided over tactics and among whom an internal struggle was occurring.... The Mensheviks endlessly delayed publishing my brochure, and once the events of 9 January had occurred in Petrograd and fully confirmed the importance of the general strike, they then said my work was out of date. Comrade Parvus, who in those days took a genuinely international and revolutionary position, saw the proofs of my manuscript and concluded that if the revolution's prime mover is the working class, adopting the decisive methods of a general strike and an uprising, then the result, in the event of the revolution's victory, must be the transfer of power to the workers. In this connection Parvus wrote the preface to my brochure, and together we were determined to get it published. It appeared with the title *Up to the Ninth of January*....[7]

Trotsky's essay is here translated fully into English for the first time. An abbreviated version of the last section of the essay was translated in 1918 by M.J. Olgin.[8] We include the entire essay because it attaches names, intentions, hopes, disappointments and living identities to the historical actors that conventionally appeared as 'class forces' in debates over the party programme and revolutionary tactics. *Up to the Ninth of January* depicts Russian society in tumultuous movement at the same time as it reveals the movement of

---

[6] [Plekhanov thought the workers must lead the revolution, not that they would play any role in political power, which he expected to fall to the liberal bourgeoisie.]
[7] L. Trotsky 1925, p. 521.
[8] L. Trotsky 1918, ch. 2.

Trotsky's own thought in the direction of *Results and Prospects*, which a year later became his definitive statement on the theory of *permanent revolution*.

* * *

Up to the Ninth of January

War and the liberal opposition[9]

Let us review the events of the past three months.

The eminent *zemtsy*[10] gather in Petersburg, hold a meeting that is neither secret nor public, and work out their constitutional demands. The intelligentsia have numerous political banquets. Members of circuit courts sit alongside people who have returned from exile; members of the intelligentsia, sporting red carnations in their lapels, intermingle with state councillors; professors of state law sit solemnly beside workers who are under surveillance by the police.

---

[9] [The tsarist government expected war with Japan to relieve domestic tensions. From the outset of war in February 1904 until its end in September 1905, Russian naval and land forces suffered a series of defeats. On 9 January, 1905 (22 January by the new calendar), Bloody Sunday brought a massacre of peaceful demonstrators in the square of the Winter Palace in St. Petersburg. Strikes and unrest spread throughout the country. By August 1905 the government decreed election procedures for an advisory assembly, but the nation-wide uprising intensified in October and November, bringing formation of the St. Petersburg Soviet of Workers' Deputies. On 17 October (30 October new style) the tsar's Manifesto promised a constitution and an elected legislature (a national Duma). On 3 December, 1905 (16 December new style) Trotsky and other Soviet leaders were arrested. In Moscow, a new general strike was called, but military and police forces prevailed by the end of the year.]

[10] [*The Congress of Zemstvo Representatives* took place in St. Petersburg from 6–9 November, 1904 (19–22 November new style). The *zemstvos* were organs of rural self-government at the district and provincial levels. 'Zemtsy' was the Russian term for members of the zemstvo. Although dominated by the nobility, many *zemstvos* maintained a professional staff and were active in building roads, providing basic schooling and health care, and in promoting agricultural improvement. Their authority and revenues, however, were limited, and they were viewed with suspicion by the central government bureaucracy. Many zemstvo activists favoured liberal constitutional reforms, and their political campaign of 1904–5 figured prominently in the wave of social unrest that accompanied the Russo-Japanese war.]

Merchants of the Moscow Duma[11] proclaim their solidarity with the constitutional programme of the Zemstvo Congress,[12] and Moscow stockbrokers endorse the Duma merchants.

Barristers hold a demonstration in the street; in the press, political exiles agitate against exile; those who are under surveillance agitate against spies; a naval officer launches a public campaign against the entire Naval Department, and when he is thrown into prison the law society gets together to restore his *kortik*.[13]

What is improbable becomes real, what is impossible becomes probable.

The legal press reports on banquets, publishes resolutions, gives accounts of the demonstrations, even mentions in passing a 'well-known Russian saying',[14] and scolds generals and ministers – mainly, of course, those who are

---

[11] [The Moscow city Duma, or municipal government, resolved:
> To inform the highest authorities that in the opinion of the Moscow city Duma the following measures are urgently needed: to establish protection of the person against illegal arbitrariness, to put an end to the operation of extraordinary laws, to guarantee freedom of conscience and religion, freedom of speech and of the press, freedom of assembly and the right to form associations; to implement the aforementioned principles with the participation of the people's freely elected representatives in such manner as to make them permanent and inviolable; and to establish a proper relation between the activity of government and lawfully established control by society over the legality of administrative activity.

This declaration was the first of numerous similar ones made by city dumas throughout Russia.]

[12] [Unable to reach unanimous agreement on the question of a constitution, the *zemtsy* included two demands in a general resolution: one from the minority and another from the majority. The majority declared:
> In the interest of creating and maintaining a permanently vital and close relationship of unity between state power and society…it is unconditionally necessary that popular representatives regularly participate, through a special elected institution, in the exercise of legislative power, in establishing state accounts of revenues and expenditures, and in control over the legality of acts of by the administration.

The minority view said:
> In the interest of creating and maintaining a permanently vital and close relationship of unity between state power and society…it is unconditionally necessary that popular representatives regularly participate in the legislative process through a special elected institution.

In the concluding section of the resolution, both right and left *zemtsy* expressed hope 'that the state power will summon the freely elected representatives of the people'.]

[13] [A *kortik* was a double-edged dagger worn by naval officers in tsarist Russia as a mark of rank. The meaning of the passage is that the law society undertook to restore the officer's honour.]

[14] That is how the legal press referred at the time to the cry 'Down with autocracy!'

already deceased or retired. Journalists rush about, reminiscing about the past, sighing, hoping, and warning each other against inflated hopes; not knowing just how, they try to avoid servile language but fail to find the right words and end up being cautioned; they truly attempt to be radical, hoping to be summoned for something but not knowing what; they use caustic language – but only fleetingly, because they don't know what tomorrow will bring – and they hide their uncertainty behind clever phrases. Everyone is confused, and in the midst of all this confusion, each wants to make all the others think that he alone is not confused.

This wave is receding just now, but only to make way for another, even more powerful wave.

Let us take this moment to consider what has been said and done to date and then to answer the question: What next?

The immediate cause of the current situation is the war. It is dramatically accelerating the natural process of the autocracy's destruction, dragging the most indifferent social groups into the political arena and providing a powerful stimulus to the formation of political parties.

But to see things in their proper perspective we must step back a little from this 'springtime' of discord, return to the start of the war, and briefly review the policies adopted by various parties during this time of struggle on two fronts.

The war confronted society as a fact – the question was to make use of it.

The parties of tsarist reaction did everything possible in this regard. Although absolutism was totally compromised in terms of representing the nation's cultural development, in the favourable circumstances created by the war it could appear both to itself and to others as extremely powerful. The reactionary press adopted an aggressive tone and put forth slogans portraying the autocracy, the nation, the army and Russia as all united in the common interest of a speedy victory.

Novoe Vremya[15] endlessly repeated, and goes on repeating, that 'nothing expresses the unity of the nation more than its army. The army holds the

---

[15] [*Novoe Vremya* was a daily newspaper published since 1876 in St. Petersburg by A.S. Suvorin. Being essentially a semi-official voice, *Novoe Vremya* campaigned against revolutionary democracy, the working class, and the radical intelligentsia. During the revolution of 1905, it demanded decisive measures against revolutionaries and striking workers.]

nation's international honour in its hands. A defeat of the army is a defeat for the nation'.

The task of the reactionaries, therefore, was obvious: to turn the war into a national cause, to unite 'society' and 'the people' around the autocracy as the guardian of Russia's might and honour, and to surround tsarism with an atmosphere of loyalty and patriotic enthusiasm. The reactionaries did everything they could think of in pursuing this goal. They tried to ignite a sense of patriotic indignation and moral outrage, shamelessly exploiting the so-called treacherous attack against our navy by the Japanese. They portrayed the enemy as insidious, cowardly, greedy, insignificant, and inhuman. They played upon the fact that the enemy was yellow-faced and heathen, trying in this way to provoke an outpouring of patriotic pride together with disdain and hatred for the enemy.

But events did not live up to their expectations. The ill-fated Pacific fleet suffered losses and more losses. The reactionary press rationalised these misfortunes, explaining them in terms of fortuitous causes and promising revenge in the war on land. A number of land battles ensued, ending in monstrous losses and retreats by the invincible Kuropatkin,[16] the hero of so many caricatures in the European press. The reactionary press even tried to use the facts of defeat to provoke a sense of wounded national pride and a thirst for bloody revenge.

In the first period of the war, the reactionaries organised patriotic demonstrations by students and urban riff-raff; they covered the entire country with cheap popular posters that dramatically portrayed the superiority of the Russian army over the Japanese – a superiority that was evident, however, only to the patriotic poster painters.

When the numbers of the wounded began to grow, in the name of patriotism and humanitarianism the reactionaries called for support of the government-run Red Cross; as the superiority of the Japanese navy over our own became obvious, in the name of patriotism and the interests of state they urged society to make sacrifices on behalf of the navy.

---

16 [Kuropatkin, Aleksei Nikolaevich (1848–1925), 'was appointed Commander-in-Chief of His Majesty's Manchurian Army of Operations on 20 February 1904.... During his command, the Russian army suffered an unbroken series of defeats culminating in the Battle of Mukden, the largest land battle in history up until that time.' (http://www.russojapanesewar.com/kuro.html).]

In short, the reactionaries did everything conceivable and used every possible means to make the war serve the interests of tsarism – which means their own interests.

And how did the official opposition behave during this time of crisis? How did they use the instruments at their disposal, including the *zemstvos*, the *dumas* and the liberal press?

To be perfectly blunt, they behaved shamefully.

The *zemstvos* did not stop at humbly shouldering those burdens and costs of war for which they were legally responsible; no, they went even further and voluntarily helped the autocracy with their organisation to assist the wounded.

This criminal activity continues right up to the present day, and not a single voice among the liberals utters a word of protest.

'If your sense of patriotism leads you to get involved in the calamities of war, then help in providing food and warmth to those who are shivering from the cold, help in treating the sick and the wounded' – this was Mr. Struve's[17] advice as he sacrificed the last remnants of the opposition's political dignity and good sense – not to a 'sense of patriotism' but to patriotic hypocrisy. At a time when the reaction was promoting the bloody illusion of a popular cause, it is surely obvious that every honest opposition party should have recoiled from such shameful activity like the plague!

The government's Red Cross is a refuge for every embezzling official. But at the very moment when it is withering from a lack of funds, when the government is being squeezed in a financial vice, the *zemstvo* appears and volunteers both its oppositional authority and the people's money to assume part of the costs for the military adventure. Is it helping the wounded? Yes, it is helping them, but in doing so, it is also shouldering part of the government's

---

[17] [Pyotr Berngardovich Struve (1870–1944) participated actively in the struggle against the Narodniks at the beginning of the 1890's and in 1894 published *Critical Observations*, criticising *Narodnichestvo* from a Marxist point of view. In 1898 he was author of the manifesto of the Social-Democratic party, but by 1901 Struve became a critic of Marxism and Social Democracy. From 1902–15 he edited the illegal liberal journal *Osvobozhdenie*. Following the 1905 revolution, he joined the party of Constitutional Democrats (Cadets) and was elected to the second state Duma in 1907. He opposed the Bolshevik revolution in 1917 and briefly held a ministerial post in Wrangel's white-guard government before fleeing to Europe.]

financial burden and thus making it easier for it to continue waging the war and producing even more casualties.

And that is merely the beginning. The real task, surely, is to overthrow once and for all a system in which the senseless slaughter and mutilation of tens of thousands of people depends upon the political passions of a band of officials. The war made this task all the more urgent by revealing the total disgrace of tsarism's domestic and foreign policy – with its senseless, predatory, clumsy, wasteful, and bloody character.

The reactionaries attempted – quite expediently from the point of view of their own interests – to draw the material and moral support of the entire people into the whirlpool of military adventure. Where previously there were conflicting groups and classes – reaction and liberalism, the authorities and the people, the government and the opposition, strikes and repression – the reactionaries hoped to establish at a single stroke a kingdom of national-patriotic unity.

The opposition's task was to expose all the more forcefully, decisively, boldly and ruthlessly the real abyss between tsarism and the nation; it should have redoubled its efforts to drive tsarism, the true national enemy, straight over the edge of this abyss. Instead, the liberal *zemstvos*, with their own secret 'opposition' design (to take control of part of the war economy and thus to make the government dependent upon them!), harnessed themselves to the clanking chariot of war, picked up the corpses, and wiped away the bloody remains.

But they didn't limit themselves just to sacrifices in helping to organise the sanitation work. Immediately following the declaration of war, the same *zemstvos* and *dumas* that endlessly complain about their own inadequate resources turned around and suddenly devoted absurd amounts of money to the war effort and to strengthening the navy. The Kharkov *zemstvo* took a million roubles from its budget and put it directly at the tsar's disposal.

And even that was not the end of the story! It was not enough for the people of the *zemstvos* and *dumas* to join in the dirty work of a shameful slaughter and to take upon themselves – that is, to load upon the people – part of the expenses. They were not satisfied with tacit political connivance and acquiescent cover-up of the work of tsarism – no, they publicly declared to everyone their moral solidarity with those responsible for committing the greatest of crimes. In a whole series of loyal addresses the *zemstvos* and *dumas*, one after the other and without any exceptions, prostrated themselves at the feet of the 'majestic leader' who had just finished trampling on the Tver *zemstvo*[18] and was already preparing to crush several others. They declared their indignation in face of the insidious enemy, solemnly vowed their devotion to the throne, and promised to sacrifice their lives and their property – they knew, of course, that they would never have to do any such thing! – for the honour and glory of the tsar and of Russia. And behind the *zemstvos* and *dumas* trailed the professorial bodies in a disgraceful queue. One after the other they responded to the declaration of war with loyal pronouncements, using the formal rhetoric of seminars to express their political idiocy. This whole sequence of servile displays was crowned by the patriotic forgery of the Council of Bestuzhev courses, which declared not only its own patriotism but also that of students it never consulted.[19]

To add the final brush stroke to this hideous picture of cowardice, servility, lies, petty diplomacy and cynicism, it is enough to point out that the deputation from the Petersburg *zemstvo*,[20] which delivered a loyal address to Nicholas

---

[18] [At a session of the Tver zemstvo, late in December 1903 and early in 1904, one of its leaders raised the question of petitioning the government to allow all draft legislation affecting Tver province to be reviewed first at meetings of the Tver zemstvo. Interior Minister Plehve suspended the entire board of the Tver zemstvo.]

[19] ['Bestuzhev courses' refer to a prestigious higher education establishment for women that operated in pre-revolutionary Russia. In order to be admitted to it, women had to pass a difficult examination in Latin. A degree acquired here allowed women to teach in secondary schools. Women graduating from this institution were normally highly progressive intellectuals known as 'Bestuzhevki'.]

[20] [The editors of Trotsky's *Sochineniya* write:
In February 1904, Nicholas II received a deputation from the Petersburg provincial zemstvo in the Winter Palace.... The deputation delivered a patriotic declaration of loyalty including the following remarks:
> Your Majesty! An extraordinary meeting of the St. Petersburg provincial zemstvo, summoned in these remarkable times and deeply conscious of the indissoluble bonds and total unanimity between your loyal zemstvo and your Imperial Highness, declares its selfless devotion to you, its beloved ruler. Charged with safeguarding the material and cultural needs of the local population, and with representatives from all social strata working for the peaceful promotion of the people's welfare, the St. Petersburg provincial zemstvo declares its regret and indignation in face of the audacious enemy's presumptuous disruption of the peace that you so lovingly protected and unites as one man with the Father of our country. The greatness of Russia and its Monarch is unshakeable! May God bless the exploits of your Majesty's victorious armies and preserve your own precious strength and your health!

Nicholas replied to this address as follows:

II in the Winter Palace, included such 'luminaries' of liberalism as Messrs. Stasyulevich[21] and Arsenyev.[22]

Is it worth dwelling any longer on all these facts? Do they need any further commentary? No, merely to cite them is to deliver a stinging slap to the political face of the liberal opposition.

And what about the liberal press? This pitiful, mumbling, grovelling, lying, cringing, depraved and corrupting liberal press! With a secret, servile wish for tsarism's defeat in their heart, but with slogans of national pride on their lips, they threw themselves – every one of them – into the sordid torrent of chauvinism, struggling to avoid being outdone by the press of the reactionary thugs. *Russkoe Slovo* and *Russkie Vedomosti, Odesskie Novosti* and *Russkoe Bogatsvo, Peterburgskie Vedomosti* and *Kur'er, Rus'* and *Kievskii Otklik* – they all proved to be deserving of each other. The liberal Left took turns with the liberal Right in describing the perfidy of 'our enemy', his impotence and our strength, the peace-loving character of 'our Monarch', the inevitability of 'our victory', and the final completion of 'our mission' in the Far East – and they did it without for a moment believing their own words, all the while harbouring a secret, servile wish in their hearts for tsarism's defeat.

As early as October, when the tone of the press had significantly changed, Mr. I. Petrunkevich,[23] the ornament and pride of *zemstvo* liberalism, startled the reactionary press by telling readers of *Pravo* that

> whatever one's opinion of this war, every Russian knows that once it began,
> it must never end in a way that might harm the interests of state or the

---

I am very grateful to the St. Petersburg provincial zemstvo for its declaration of support. In these troubled times in which we live, I am deeply comforted by the unanimous expressions of patriotism coming to me from all the most far-flung regions of Russia. With God's help, and being profoundly convinced of our just cause, I firmly believe that the army and navy are doing everything expected of valiant Russian arms in defending the honour and glory of Russia.]

[21] [Mikhail Matveevich Stasyulevich (1826–1913) was liberal editor of *Vestnik Evropy* from 1866–1908.]

[22] [K.K. Arsenyev was a liberal publicist and prominent figure in the zemstvo movement of St. Petersburg province.]

[23] [Ivan Il'ich Petrunkevich was a leader of the zemstvo movement prior to 1905 and was exiled several times for his liberal activities. In June 1905 he was a member of a delegation that petitioned the tsar to summon a national assembly. Subsequently he became a leader of the Cadet party in the first State Duma.]

national interests of our country.... We cannot now propose peace to Japan. We must continue the war until Japan adopts terms that are acceptable to us with regard both to our national dignity and to the material interests of Russia.[24]

The 'best' and the 'most dignified' – they all disgraced themselves equally.

'... From the moment when the wave of chauvinism was first whipped up,' as *Nashi Dni* is now telling us – 'it not only met with no obstacles but was even supported by many leading figures, who apparently hoped that it would carry them to some idyllic shore.'

This was not accidental, a fortuitous mistake, or a misunderstanding. It was a tactic and a plan that expressed the entire spirit of our privileged opposition – compromise instead of struggling, and achieve a rapprochement at any cost. This explains the attempt to help absolutism to endure the emotional drama of such a rapprochement. Organise not for the struggle against tsarism, but in reality to serve it; not to defeat the government, but to seduce it; work to deserve its recognition and confidence, make it need us and, finally, buy it off with the people's money. This tactic is as old as Russian liberalism itself, and it has become neither wiser nor any more respectable with the passing years!

The Russian people will not forget that the liberals did only one thing at the most difficult moment: they tried to buy the confidence of the people's enemy with the people's own money.

From the very beginning of the war, the liberal opposition did everything possible to make a mess of things. But the revolutionary logic of events was unstoppable. The Port Arthur fleet was defeated. Admiral Makarov perished. Then the war turned into one of land battles. Yalu, Chengju, Tashichiao, Wafangkou, Liaoyang, the Shakhe River – all of these places are just different names for the same thing – the disgrace of the autocracy. The Japanese military smashed Russian absolutism not just on the seas and battlefields of East Asia, but also on the European bourses and even in Petersburg.

The position of the tsarist government became more difficult than ever. Demoralisation in its ranks made it impossible for it to be consistent or resolute in its domestic policy. Waverings to and fro, and attempts to reach

---

[24] See *Pravo*, No. 41.

agreements and compromise, became inevitable. The death of Plehve[25] provided the perfect impulse for a change of direction.

In Plehve's place came prince Svyatopolk-Mirsky.[26] He undertook to make peace with the liberal opposition and to achieve reconciliation with all who professed trust in the Russian people. That was stupid and insolent. Really! Is it up to a minister to trust the people? Isn't it the other way round? Isn't a minister supposed to win trust *from* the people?

The opposition should have acquainted prince Svyatopolk-Mirsky with this simple fact. Instead, it began to produce public declarations, telegrams, and articles expressing its rapturous gratitude. In the name of a hundred and fifty million people, it thanked the autocracy for declaring that it 'trusted' the people – who did not trust it.

A wave of hope, expectation, and gratitude surged through the liberal press. *Russkie Vedemosti* and *Rus'* joined forces to defend the prince against *Grazhdanin* and *Moskovskie Vedomosti*;[27] the district *zemstvos* expressed gratitude and hope; the cities expressed hope and gratitude – and now that the policy of trust has already turned full circle, the provincial *zemstvos*, one after the other, are belatedly sending the minister their own expressions of trust. That is how the opposition is prolonging the domestic turmoil and transforming a stupid political anecdote into the protracted political condition of a restless country.

And so, we come back to the same conclusion. The opposition, which had never before found itself in such a favourable position of being needed and fawned upon – an opposition that at the very mention of the government's trust rushed to declare its own trust in return – simultaneously deprived itself of the right to any trust whatever from the people.

---

25 [Vyacheslav Konstantinovich Plehve (1846–1904) was a proponent of repressive autocracy. As Minister of the Interior he supported police-controlled unions and Russian aggression in the Far East. He was assassinated in 1904 by a member of the Socialist-Revolutionary Party.]

26 [Petr Danilovich Svyatopolk-Mirsky (1857–1914) succeeded Plehve as Minister of the Interior and initiated a 'political spring', partially repealing censorship, returning prominent zemstvo activists from exile, and broadening the scope for zemstvo activities in the attempt to reach a reconciliation with Russian liberalism. He was dismissed from office following the Bloody Sunday of January 1905.]

27 [*Grazhdanin* and *Moskovskie Vedomosti* were two of the most reactionary newspapers of the time.]

By the same token, it also deprived itself of any claim to respect from the enemy. The government, in the personage of Svyatopolk, promised the *zemtsy* they would be able to convene legally – and then refused them permission to do so. The *zemtsy* did not protest, but instead convened illegally. They did everything possible to keep their congress a secret from the people. In other words, they did everything they could to deprive their congress of any political importance whatever.

At their meeting of 7–9 November, the *zemtsy* – representatives of provincial councils and generally prominent figures of local self-government – formulated their demands. On behalf of the *zemstvo* opposition, its most prominent representatives – although they were never formally empowered – announced their programme for the first time to the people.

The conscious elements among the people have good reason to scrutinise this programme very closely. What are the *zemtsy* demanding? What are they demanding for themselves, and what are they demanding for the people?

What are the *zemtsy* demanding?

1. The right to vote

The *zemtsy* want a constitution. They demand that the people participate in legislation through their representatives. Do they want a democratic constitution? Are they demanding that the whole people have equal rights to participate in legislation? In other words, do the *zemtsy* stand for universal, equal and direct suffrage, with secret ballots to guarantee a free and independent vote?

There is certainly more to a democratic programme than universal suffrage, and simply calling for universal suffrage does not make one a democrat: first, because, in certain conditions, this demand can be taken up by reactionary demagogues; and, second, because revolutionary democracy regards universal suffrage as more than just one of many separate demands – it is an integral part of a comprehensive programme. On the other hand, it is also an incontestable truth that without universal suffrage there can be no democracy.

So let us look at just how the *zemstvo* congress treated this cardinal democratic demand. We can read all the resolutions of the congress, point after point – and never find any mention of universal suffrage. That answers the question. We have to conclude that if the programme of the *zemstvo* people says nothing about universal suffrage, then the *zemstvo* opposition must not want universal suffrage.

Political mistrust is our right, but the entire history of the liberal opposition turns this right into a duty!

The *zemstvo* liberals are interested in their own influence and their own political reputation. They are interested in protecting themselves from being criticised and exposed by Social Democracy. They know that Social Democracy has demanded universal suffrage; they also know that Social Democracy is vigilant and suspicious in watching how all the other opposition parties respond to this demand.

That is why the *zemstvo* liberals, if they do support universal suffrage, must, in their own political interest, say so in bold letters when they publish their programme. They have not done so, and this can only mean that they do not want universal suffrage. One of the congress participants, the 'radical' Mr. Khizhnyakov,[28] a member of the Chernigov *zemstvo*, told a meeting of the Kiev literary-artistic society that the resolution of the *zemstvo* congress does not contradict the demand for universal suffrage.[29] But Mr. Khizhnyakov was engaging in empty scholasticism. He either forgot or did not know that besides formal logic there is also the logic of politics, in which silence sometimes means the same thing as denial. Mr. Khizhnyakov himself gave the best illustration of this when he signed the resolution of the Chernigov *zemstvo*, which demanded

---

[28] [V.V. Khizhnyakov was a left-liberal member of the Chernigov zemstvo, a participant at the all–Russia zemstvo congress, and later a member of the liberal *Osvobozhdenie* alliance.]

[29] [The editors of Trotsky 1925, p. 536) give this account:

At a meeting of the Kiev literary-artistic society in November 1904, following a report on 'the poetry of Ogarev,' Khizhnyakov,…who had just returned from Petersburg, gave a wide-ranging talk on the decisions of the zemstvo congress. Khizhnyakov dealt at length with the letter Milyukov had sent to the congress, with the congress resolutions, and so forth. His report was greeted with applause. But suddenly there was a voice of protest from the audience. Addressing Khizhnyakov, the speaker declared: 'You should never have disbanded before seeing your demands fulfilled. You forgot about the working class. You were silent on the main point – universal, direct, and secret voting. You were more concerned with idle chatter than with practical matters.…' This response was warmly approved by Social Democrats at the meeting. Vodovozov replied by urging Social Democrats to unite in common action, spoke of the impermissibility of a split, etc. The meeting divided into two groups: Social Democrats and representatives of the *zemstvos*.]

that the representatives of the *zemstvos* and the *dumas* be convened but not the representatives of the people. In all its endeavours, the congress never went any further than this. It simply hid the modest insignificance of its demands in a vague formulation.

Nevertheless, there is one point in the congress resolutions that appears to confirm not only that the *zemtsy* did not reject universal suffrage, but that they even spoke in favour of it. Point 7 says: 'The individual civil and political rights of all Russian citizens must be identical.'

Political rights surely include the right to participate in the country's political life, and that means, above all else, the right to vote. The *zemstvo* congress decided that this right must be equal for everyone.

Does this not prove that Vodovozov,[30] another 'radical' at the same meeting of the literary-artistic society, was correct in objecting when a Social Democrat condemned the *zemtsy* for their silence on universal voting? 'I protest absolutely – said Mr. Vodovozov – against the statement by the disgruntled speaker. Point 7 speaks of equal civil and political rights. If you were more knowledgeable in the science of statecraft, you would realise that this formula means universal, equal, direct and secret suffrage!'

Now, Mr. Vodovozov is, without question, very knowledgeable in the science of statecraft. The problem is that he seriously misuses his knowledge when all he does is confuse his audience.

There is surely no doubt that equality of political rights, if we take the term at all seriously, must mean the equal voting right of all citizens. But there is also no doubt that point 7 restricts this equality to male citizens and does not include women. So, does Mr. Vodovozov say that the *zemtsy* have women in mind? No, he says no such thing. Therefore, point 7 does not mean universal suffrage after all.

Nor does it mean direct elections. The citizens' right to vote may be equal, but it may also happen that the constitution only gives them the right to vote for a second group of representatives, who in turn vote for a third group, who will then be the 'people's representatives'. This kind of system is deadly for the people because it is far easier for the ruling classes to manipulate a small

---

[30] [V.V. Vodovozov (1864–1933) was editor of *Nasha Zhizn'* and wrote and lectured on questions of constitutional law and forms of voting.]

group of electors, who are detached from the people, than to manipulate the broad masses themselves.[31]

Moreover, equal suffrage, on its own, says precisely nothing about secret balloting. The fact is, however, that this technical side of the matter has enormous importance for all strata of the people who are dependent, in subordinate circumstances, and economically oppressed. This is especially true in Russia, with its centuries-old traditions of arbitrary rule and serfdom. Given our barbarian traditions, a system of open voting can indefinitely deprive universal suffrage of any significance whatever!

We have already said that the logic of point 7 does not extend beyond equal voting rights for men. But despite the instruction in statecraft coming from Mr. Vodovozov, the *zemtsy* hastened to point out that they also intended other limitations. Equal political rights would naturally apply not just to a future parliament, but also to the *zemstvos* and *dumas* themselves. However, Point 9 demands only 'that *zemstvo* representation not be organised in terms of particular social strata, but that all elements of the local population be drawn, so far as possible [sic!], into the self-government of the *zemstvos* and the cities'. This means we are to have equal political rights only 'so far as possible'. The *zemtsy* specifically object to a census based on social strata, but they make every allowance for the 'possibility' of one based on property. In any event, there is no doubt that any person who is not included in some kind of census based on permanent residency will be excluded from equal political rights, and that kind of census is necessarily directed against the proletariat.

Despite the assurances coming from opportunistic and politically hypocritical 'democrats', it therefore follows that Point 7 does not in fact imply either universal, or direct, or equal, or secret voting rights. In other words, it really means nothing at all. It is merely an exercise in political dissembling, intended to mislead simpletons and serve as a means of deception in the hands of opportunists who would corrupt political consciousness.

---

[31] This is why it is said that Mr. Witte, expecting to have his own 'turn', is preparing a draft constitution with two–stage elections. [Sergei Iulevich Witte (1849–1915) played a leading role in promoting Russian railway construction and early industrialisation. Beginning in 1892 he served as Minister of Finance for eleven years, putting Russia on the gold standard to facilitate capital imports. In 1905 Witte persuaded the tsar to issue the 'October Manifesto', which promised some measure of representative government. As Prime Minister, Witte suppressed the revolutionary movement in 1905–6, including the St. Petersburg Soviet. Once the autocracy had survived the crisis, Witte was obliged to leave public office.]

And even if equality of political rights were every bit as rich in meaning as suggested by Mr. Vodovozov's science of statecraft, we would still have to ask whether the *zemtsy* themselves understood their words to have exactly the same content as this 'science' implies. Of course, they did not. If they were really of a democratic mind, they would know perfectly well how to express their convictions in clear political form. We have to assume that one of the secretaries of the *zemstvo* congress, the Tambov radical Bryukhatov,[32] had good reason when he commented upon Point 7 in the democratic publication *Nasha Zhizn'* by saying that 'the people will acquire complete civil rights and all necessary [sic!] political rights'.[33] As to the question of just who is competent to distinguish unnecessary from necessary political rights, on this matter the radical *zemstvo* spokesman and the democratic press are maintaining deliberate silence.

People who make genuinely democratic demands always count on the masses and turn to them for support.

But the fact is that the masses know nothing of the deductions and sophistries of constitutional law. All they ask is that people speak to them clearly, call things by their proper names, and protect their interests with precisely formulated guarantees that will not be exposed to complaisant interpretations.

This is why we consider it our political duty to encourage the masses to distrust the Aesopian language that has become second nature to our liberals in the effort to conceal not only their political 'unreliability' but also their political ineptitude!

2. *The autocracy of the tsar or the absolute power of the people?*

What kind of political system does the liberal opposition think the people must participate in only 'so far as possible'? Not only do the *zemstvo* resolutions say nothing about a republic – even to confront the *zemstvo* opposition with the demand for a republic would be so preposterous as to make their ears ring! – they also say nothing about abolishing or limiting the autocracy, and they do not so much as mention the word 'constitution' in their manifesto.

---

[32] [L.D. Bryukhatov was a liberal leader of the zemstvo movement from Tambov.]
[33] *Nasha Zhizn'*, No. 2.

True, they do say it is necessary 'that popular representatives regularly participate…in the exercise of legislative power, in establishing state accounts of revenues and expenditures, in control over the legality of acts by the administration' – and therefore they must have in mind a constitution. They just avoid mentioning it. Is this something we should pause to consider?

We think it is. The European liberal press, which even-handedly hates the Russian revolution just as much as it sympathises with Russian *zemstvo* liberalism, speaks rapturously of this oh-so-tactful silence in the *zemstvo* declaration: the liberals knew perfectly well how to say what they wanted while at the same time avoiding any words that might prevent Svyatopolk from accepting the *zemstvo* decisions.

This is the explanation, the completely true explanation, of why the *zemstvo* programme says nothing either of a republic, which the *zemtsy* do not want, or of a 'constitution', which they do want. In formulating their demands, the *zemtsy* had in mind only the government, with whom they must make an agreement, and they completely ignored the people, to whom they might have appealed.

They worked out the details of a mercenary political compromise, not a set of directives for political agitation.

They did not depart for a single moment from their anti-revolutionary position – and this is perfectly obvious both from what they said and from what they did not say.

At the same time as the reactionary press affirms day in and day out how devoted the people are to the autocracy, and tirelessly repeats – look at *Moskovskie Vedomosti* – how the 'real' people of Russia not only have no wish for a constitution, but don't even understand this foreign word, the *zemstvo* liberals fear even to pronounce the word lest they make the people aware of its meaning. This fear of words only hides their fear of deeds, of struggle, of the masses, and of revolution.

I repeat: anyone who wants to be understood and supported by the masses must, above all else, express his demands clearly and precisely, calling everything by its proper name; a constitution must be called a constitution; a republic means a republic; and universal suffrage means universal suffrage.

Russian liberalism in general, and *zemstvo* liberalism in particular, has never deserted the monarchy and is not deserting it today.

Quite the contrary: it aims to demonstrate that liberalism itself will be the sole salvation of the monarchy.

Prince S. Trubetskoi writes in *Pravo* that

> The vital interests of the Crown and the people require that sovereignty not
> be usurped by a bureaucratic organisation, that the bureaucracy be bought
> under control and made responsible.... And this, in turn, is only possible
> with the help of an organisation that stands apart from the bureaucracy,
> that is, through a real drawing together of the people with the Crown in a
> living concentration of power....[34]

The *zemstvo* congress not only refused to disavow the principle of monarchy,
it even made it the basis of all its resolutions in the same sense as prince
Trubetskoi does when he formulates the 'idea' of the Crown as 'a living
concentration of power'.

The congress proposes popular representation not as the sole means by
which the people might take their own affairs into their own hands, but rather
as the means to unite the Sovereign Power with the people and to overcome
their current separation, which results from the bureaucratic structure (Points
3, 4, and 10). The absolute power of the people is not counterposed to the
autocracy of the tsar, only popular representation to the tsarist bureaucracy.
The 'living concentration of power' refers to the Crown, not to the people.

3. *Whose Constituent Assembly?*

This pathetic view, which attempts to reconcile tsarist autocracy with the
supremacy of the people, was most treacherously expressed in answer to
the question of just who would bring about state reconstruction – which the
resolutions of the *zemstvo* congress formulated with such sinister imprecision
as far as the people are concerned – and how it would be done.

In the eleventh and final point of its resolutions, the Conference (as the
zemstvo congress called itself) expressed its 'hope that the Sovereign Power
will summon the freely elected representatives of the people in order, with
their help, to lead the fatherland onto a new path of state development in
the spirit of establishing the principle of law and of reciprocity between the
state authority and the people'. This is the direction in which the opposition
wants to see the political renewal of Russia occur. The Sovereign Power is
to summon the people's representatives to help it. But, even in this decisive

---

[34] See *Pravo* No. 44, 1904.

point, the resolution still says nothing about who the people are. Moreover, we have not forgotten that in the 'Programme of Russian Constitutionalists', which *Osvobozhdenie*[35] described as its own programme, the role of people's representatives goes to the *zemstvo* and *duma* deputies, 'who essentially constitute the foundation of the future constitutional building'. 'As a matter of necessity', the 'Programme' continues,

> historical precedent must be followed in assigning this preparatory work to representatives from the existing institutions of social self-government.… This approach will be sounder and better than any "leap into the unknown", which would be the result of any attempt to hold *ad hoc* elections in present circumstances, where there would inevitably be pressure from the government and where the attitudes of social strata unaccustomed to political life would be difficult to anticipate.[36]

But, let us further suppose that the representatives of these qualified 'people' do assemble and begin the work of a Constituent Assembly. Who will have the decisive voice in this endeavour – the Crown, as the 'living concentration of power', or the popular representatives? This is the decisive question upon which everything else depends.

The Conference resolution says that the Sovereign Power will lead our fatherland in a new direction with the help of the people's representatives, who will be convened by the Sovereign Power itself. This means that the *Zemstvo* Conference assigns the constitutive authority to none other than the Crown. The very idea of a nation-wide Constituent Assembly, which would have the final word, is here completely abandoned. In establishing the 'principle of law', the Crown will enlist the 'help' of the people's representatives – but, if it finds itself in conflict with them, it will simply do without their help and send them packing by the same gates through which they were just invited.

This is the one and only constitutive power being envisaged, and the resolution of the *Zemstvo* Conference does not anticipate any other way of doing things. We must have absolutely no illusions on this account. Indeed,

---

[35] [*Osvobozhdenie* was a biweekly publication first appearing in June 1902 and edited by the former Marxist and Social Democrat P.B. Struve. In 1903 *Osvobozhdenie* became the organ of the 'Osvobozhdenie Union' and occasionally promoted universal suffrage, but at the height of the strike movement it condemned the 'extreme' role of Social Democrats. After 17 October, 1905, the publication ceased to appear.]

[36] *Osvobozhdenie*, No. 1.

answering the question this way means that the whole fate of a Russian constitution is left from the outset to the discretion of the Crown!

During a period of constitutive work, as in any other period, there can be only one 'Sovereign Power' – either the Crown or the Assembly. Either the Crown works with the help of the Assembly, or the Assembly works despite the opposition of the Crown. Either the people are sovereign or the Monarch is sovereign.

One might, of course, try to interpret the eleventh point of the *zemstvo* Conference's resolution to mean that the Crown and the representative assembly, as two independent and therefore equal forces, will work out a constitutional agreement. This is the most favourable assumption one could make concerning the *zemstvo* resolutions. But what would it mean? The Crown and the assembly would be independent of each other. Each side could respond to the other's suggestions with a 'yes' or a 'no'. But this would also imply that the two parties to the discussions might arrive at no agreement whatsoever.

In that case, who will get the last word? Where is there a third party? The assumption of two sides with equal authority leads to an absurdity: in the case of conflict between the Crown and the people – and such conflict is inevitable – there must be a third party to judge. When real life enters a legal blind alley, it never stays there for long. It always finds its own way out.

The only way out, in the final analysis, must be a revolutionary expression of popular sovereignty. Only the people can be the third judge in their own litigation with the Crown. Only a National Constituent Assembly – independent of the Crown and in possession of total power, having in its own hands both the keys and the master key of all rights and privileges, and having the right of final decision on all questions, including even the fate of the Russian monarchy – only that kind of sovereign Constituent Assembly will be able freely to create a new democratic law.

That is why honest and consistent democrats must tirelessly and relentlessly appeal not only over the criminal head of the monarchy, but also over the narrow minds of the representatives of the qualified people whom the monarchy invites to provide it with 'help' – why they must appeal tirelessly and relentlessly to the all-powerful will of the people, expressed in a Constituent Assembly through universal, direct and secret voting in which everyone has the same rights.

Does anyone need to be reminded that the *zemstvo* programme says not a single word about the agrarian or the labour question? It simply treats these questions as if they did not even exist in Russia.

The resolutions of the *zemstvo* Conference of 7, 8 and 9 November[37] represent the highest achievements of *zemstvo* liberalism. In subsequent meetings of provincial *zemstvos*, this liberalism retreated from its decisions in November.

Only the Vyatsk provincial *zemstvo* signed on to the entire programme of the *zemstvo* Conference.

The Yaroslav provincial *zemstvo* 'firmly believes' that Nicholas will 'be pleased to summon elected representatives to participate in a joint effort' – for the sake of 'reconciliation of the Tsar with his people' – 'in accordance with principles of "greater" [!] equality and personal immunity'. Of course, 'greater' equality for the Tsar's people – that is, greater than we have today – by no means rules out either civil or even political inequality.

The address of the Poltava *zemstvo* repeats the tenth point of the resolution, which discusses the 'proper participation of popular representatives in establishing the legislative power', but it devotes not a single word to 'political equality' and says absolutely nothing concerning the forms of 'popular representation'.

The Chernigov *zemstvo*

> most loyally requests His Majesty to hear the sincere and truthful voice of the Russian land by summoning the freely elected *zemstvo* representatives and commanding them [!] independently and on their own to draft a project of reforms…and to allow [!] this project to be presented directly to His Majesty.

In this case, the '*zemstvo* representatives' are clearly and openly called the representatives of 'the Russian land'. The Chernigov *zemstvo* requests that these representatives be given only a consultative voice, that is, only the right to draw up and present a project of reforms. And, what is more, the Chernigov *zemstvo* 'most loyally requests' that the representatives of the Russian land be commanded to be independent and to act on their own!

---

[37] [There is a misprint in the text, which speaks of December instead of November.]

The Bessarabia *zemstvo* asks the Minister of Internal Affairs to summon 'representatives from the provincial *zemstvos* and the most important cities of the Empire for a joint discussion' of the reforms being proposed.

The Kazan provincial *zemstvo* 'deeply believes that in the search for ways to implement the Autocratic Will, the *zemstvo* representatives, who have been freely elected for that purpose, will not be denied a voice'.

The Penzen *zemstvo* expresses its 'loyal and limitless gratitude' for the reforms anticipated by the tsar's decree and, for its part, promises 'ardent service…in a broad sphere of local improvements'.

Through the initiative of Mr. Arsenyev, who along with others signed the resolution of the *zemstvo* Conference, the Petersburg *zemstvo* proposes to raise a petition requesting that 'representatives of the *zemstvo* and municipal institutions be admitted to participate in discussing government measures and draft legislation'.

The Kostroma *zemstvo* petitions to have drafts that affect *zemstvo* life submitted for prior discussion by the *zemtsy* themselves.

Other *zemstvos* limit themselves either to faithful gratitude and delight concerning the tsar's decree or to an appeal addressed to prince Svyatopolk requesting that he 'preserve the spirit of the precious vow of trust'.

And that is how the opposition campaign of the *zemstvos* has ended for the time being.

'Democracy'

To this point, we have briefly considered the behaviour of the reaction and looked in more detail at that of the bourgeois-gentry opposition. Now we must pose another question: Where was democracy?

We are not speaking of the popular masses, of the *peasantry* and the petty bourgeoisie, who – the former in particular – *represent an enormous reservoir of potential revolutionary energy* but have thus far played too little of a conscious role in the country's political life. Instead, we have in mind the broad circles of the intelligentsia, who see it as their calling to formulate and articulate the country's political needs. We are thinking of representatives of the liberal professions, of doctors, lawyers, professors, journalists, and of the third element in the *zemstvos* and *dumas*, namely, statisticians, medical people, agronomists, teachers, and so on and so forth.

What did the intelligentsia democrats do?

Apart from the revolutionary students – who honestly protested against the war and who, despite Mr. Struve's shameful advice, raised the cry 'Long Live the Revolution!' instead of 'Long Live the Army!' – apart from them, the rest of the democrats simply languished in the knowledge of their own impotence.

They saw two alternatives: they could join up with the *zemtsy*, who they believed were a political force, but only at the expense of completely abandoning any democratic demands – or they could converge on a democratic programme at the cost of breaking away from the most 'influential' *zemstvo* opposition. The choice seemed to be either democratism without influence, or influence without democratism. Within the limits of their own political narrow mindedness, they did not see the third possibility: *to unite with the revolutionary masses*. This option offers strength; at the same time it not only makes way for but also requires development of a democratic programme.

The war found the democrats in a completely helpless situation. They did not dare come out against the 'patriotic' bacchanalia. Through the lips of Mr. Struve, they cried 'Long Live the Army!' and expressed their conviction that 'the army will do its duty'. They blessed the *zemstvos* for supporting the autocrat's adventure. They limited their opposition to the cry: 'Down with von Plehve!' They kept their democratism as their own hidden secret, along with their political dignity, their honour, and their conscience. They trailed along at the tail end of the liberals, who, in turn, plodded behind the reaction.

And the war continued. The autocracy suffered one blow after another. A black cloud of horror hung over the country. Among the people at large, elements of a spontaneous explosion accumulated. When the *zemstvos* did not take a single step forward, the democrats appeared to become more aware. Persistent voices began speaking in *Osvobozhdenie* of the need for an independent organisation based on a 'democratic platform'. Individuals spoke out against the war. This natural process was interrupted by the murder of Plehve and by the government's change of course, which then led to an unusual increase in the political activities of the *zemstvo* opposition. A happy outcome began to seem so possible, so close.

The *zemstvos* put forth the programme that we have already described – and the democrats rapturously and unanimously praised it to the skies.

When they found their democratic demands expressed in the *zemstvo* resolutions, they adopted them as their own.

Osvobozhdenie declared that

> although the *zemstvo* congress consisted exclusively of landowners, and
> mainly of the privileged gentry, nevertheless its resolutions were not only
> free of any class influence[38] but, to the contrary, abounded with a purely
> democratic spirit.[39]

The entire left wing of our liberal press just as solemnly acclaimed the democratic spirit of the *zemstvos*.

Responding to the November resolutions, *Nasha Zhizn'* proclaimed a complete merger of the *zemstvo*-liberal and democratic tendencies.

According to this newspaper, 'the long and horrible affliction of Russian life, the spiritual and cultural separation of the people from the intelligentsia…can only be overcome through the heroic project of constructing a democratic state'. The *zemtsy* understood this, resulting in their firm commitment to 'a common platform with the democratic intelligentsia. This is an historical event. It is the beginning of a social-political collaboration that can have enormous importance for the destiny of our country'.

Syn Otechestva,[40] which first appeared under the auspices of the Minister of trust but was cut down by him just as quickly, adopted the entire programme of the *zemstvo* congress. It began its brief existence by declaring that 'the remarkable characteristic of the historic moment in which we live is the radicalism of all political movements in the country'. The paper recommends to municipal representatives that they

> follow the same true and glorious path that the *zemstvo* people have already
> taken with such success, and repeat word for word and point by point
> everything that the representatives of *zemstvo* Russia have said and are
> saying so clearly, concisely, and convincingly, and with such dignity and
> forcefulness.

---

[38] In order, apparently, to underline clearly the absence of any 'class influence', the *zemtsy*, as we have already seen, uttered not a single word concerning the agrarian or labour question. What simplicity on the part of the *zemstvos*, what cynicism on the part of *Osvobozhdenie*!

[39] No. 61, p. 187.

[40] [*Syn Otechestva* appeared as a daily newspaper from 18 December, 1904, to 5 February, 1905. It reappeared in March 1905 and again briefly in December as *Nashi Dni*.]

In a word, the democrats summoned each and all to rally around the *zemstvo* banner. In their eyes, this banner was without stain or imperfection. So, we ask ourselves: Can the people really have any trust in such democrats?

Are we to give them a vote of confidence, regard their reservations as fortuitous, give a democratic interpretation to their beating about the bush, and proclaim that 'today there are no longer any disputes or differences of opinion such as existed in the recent past'[41] – are we to do all this for the sole reason that at a moment of upheaval, when they were being squeezed between pressure from below and 'permission' from above, the *zemtsy* scribbled on a sheet of paper their totally vague constitutional programme? Really! Is this what the tactics of democrats amount to?

Dear Sirs! These are the tactics of people who are betraying the democratic cause.

After 7 November 1904[42] there were many more decisive moments to come in the struggle for liberation – and the responsibility of the *zemstvo* opposition would extend far beyond merely outlining their constitutional resolutions with the unofficial protection of Svyatopolk-Mirsky.

Should we nourish any conviction that the *zemstvos* will rise to such occasions? If our history teaches us anything, and unless we believe in miraculous conversions, the answer must surely be: No! A policy of trusting in the democratism and oppositional steadfastness of the *zemstvos* is not our policy. What we must do today is rapidly assemble the forces that we will be able to put into the field against the all-Russian *zemstvo* at the decisive moment when they begin to trade in their counterfeit opposition for the real gold of political privileges.

But, instead of rallying forces around our own implacable slogans of democracy, we are supposed to sow confidence in the democratism of the liberal leadership and affirm to everyone, on both the right and the left, that the *zemstvos* are committed to the struggle for universal suffrage, that 'we had disagreements in the past, but today there are none'!

What's that? None?

---

[41] See the article by N. Karyshev in *Syn Otechestva*, No. 1.
[42] [The reference is to the zemstvo congress in November 1904.]

Does that mean that the *zemtsy*, led by Mr. Shipov[43] or Mr. I. Petrunkevich, have recognised that only the people can radically liquidate the autocratic economy and lay the foundations in Russian soil to support a democratic structure? Does it mean that the *zemtsy* have given up on the hope that the monarchy will make compromises? Does it mean that the *zemtsy* have abandoned their shameful co-operation with absolutism in its pursuit of military adventure? Does it mean that the *zemtsy* have recognised that revolution is the one and only road to freedom?

It is impossible for conscious elements among the people to have any confidence whatever in the anti-revolutionary, estates-based opposition; they will not for a single moment succumb to any illusions concerning the 'democratism' of democrats who are so confused and inconsistent that they have only one slogan – to unite with the anti-revolutionary and anti-democratic *zemstvo* opposition.

The classic example of democratic confusion, inconsistency and hesitation is the resolution put forth by a meeting of the Kiev intelligentsia for consideration by the *zemstvo* congress.

> ...The meeting considered the question of what the congress of representatives of the *zemstvo* boards must say regarding the necessary reforms. The meeting concluded that this congress, made up of people who have come together by their own initiative, has no right to regard itself as expressing the wishes of the people. Accordingly, the congress is obliged first and foremost to say to the government that it does not consider itself competent to submit a finished reform project, but instead recommends convening an assembly of the people's representatives, elected by universal [equal?], direct and secret balloting. That is the kind of constituent assembly that will, after reviewing the situation, have to propose [?] a reform project.

Isn't this forceful, decisive, and clear? But let us continue.

> If the government refuses to convene such an assembly, then the congress must adopt the minimum political demands that everyone accepts.... Some people suggested that such minimum demands must include freedom of the person, of conscience, of the press and of speech; freedom of assembly and

---

43 [Dmitry Nikolaevich Shipov was a leader of the zemstvo movement from the 1890s onwards and favoured reconciliation between the *zemstvos* and the government.]

public associations; and the demand for a legislative assembly consisting of the elected representatives of the *zemstvos* and the cities.... But others at the meeting, thinking such a legislative assembly would not comply with the principle of universal suffrage, expressed fear that a constitution based upon such principles would result in long postponement of the possibility of introducing universal suffrage. This part of the meeting considered it more appropriate for the congress of representatives to limit itself to the demand for freedom of the person, conscience, the press and speech, together with freedom of assembly and public associations.... The entire meeting subsequently agreed that it is necessary to restore the *Zemstvo* Statute of 1864.[44]

Thus spoke the 'democrats'.

A nation-wide constituent assembly must be demanded. If the government does not agree, then it will be enough to have a gentry-merchant council instead. Universal suffrage is to be requested, but it will be enough to have voting based on a census of rank and property. The resolution of the Kiev intelligentsia says essentially the following: if the autocracy wants to evade the demand for a constituent assembly of the entire people, all it has to do is respond by saying: I don't agree with this demand – and then we, in turn, will settle (oh, temporarily, of course!) for representation of the *zemstvos* and the *dumas*!

The Kiev meeting published its resolution and made no effort to keep it secret from prince Svyatopolk-Mirsky. Did the Kiev intelligentsia not realise that by so doing they were giving the government a very authoritative indication of how, without any real fuss or complications, it could simply file the demands for democracy in some archive? Nothing more was required than refusal to accept them. Can anyone doubt for a single moment that the government would immediately act upon this advice? In order not to follow the easy road being recommended to it, the autocracy would itself have to want universal suffrage. In other words, it would have to be more democratic than the authors of the resolution. And that, of course, is hardly likely.

In that case, what is the meaning of the entire first part of the declaration, which so clearly and categorically denies to the *zemstvos* any right to speak

---

[44] Recall that this statute withheld the right to vote from all people who owned fewer than 150 desyatins of land or whose gross income was less than 15,000 roubles!

in the name of the people, and which so decisively advances the demand for universal suffrage? The whole thing is nothing but empty democratic phrase-mongering, with the help of which the Kiev intelligentsia reconciled themselves to their real rejection of any democratic demands. But after betraying the political rights of the popular masses from the very outset, the Kiev 'democrats' put absolutely no price on this betrayal: as always, they had no answer to the question of what must happen if the autocracy, enticed by an easy victory over any democratic demands, simply refuses even to accept the minimal constitutional demands that the authors of the resolution considered necessary.

This resolution, which was adopted in Kiev, the centre of the left 'osvobozhdentsy', was by no means exceptional. The resolutions adopted by other democratic banquets differ from the one in Kiev only insofar as they do not even raise the question of what to do if the autocracy does not accept the democratic programme. They are no different at all from the *zemstvo* liberals, who thus far have never responded anywhere to the question: What is to be done if the autocracy rejects their programme of limited rights based on census qualifications?

Democracy and revolution

In the conditions of absolutism, genuine democracy can only be revolutionary democracy. In Russian political conditions, any party that insists on peaceful means as a matter of principle, and organises its activity in the expectation of an agreement rather than a revolution, cannot be a democratic party. This is perfectly clear and incontestable. Absolutism may enter into some agreement, or make one concession or another, but its goal in making these concessions will always be its own self-preservation, never its self-destruction. This fact predetermines the limits of any concessions and the democratic significance of any reforms.

The government may summon representatives of the people, or at least their more compliant elements, in the calculation that they can be transformed into a new basis of support for the tsarist throne. The democrats, if their name is anything more than a deception, will demand unlimited power for the people. They will counterpose the sovereign will of the people to the sovereignty of the monarch, and the collective 'I' of the people to the individual 'I' by the Grace of God.

But if democracy believes in its programme and counterposes the will of the people to that of the monarch, it must also understand that its task is to confront the force of the monarch with the force of the people. And that confrontation means revolution. Facing up to absolutism as it struggles for its own survival, democracy, if it believes in its own programme, can only be revolutionary democracy. Whoever understands this simple and incontestable conclusion will have no trouble in ripping away the false epaulets of democratism with which many liberal opportunists, who are corrupted to the bones, are increasingly adorning themselves.

Any deal between absolutism and the opposition can only be at the expense of democracy. From the point of view of absolutism, no other kind of deal would make any sense. When it confronts democrats who are true to themselves, absolutism has no alternative but a struggle to the end. And in that case, the same has to be said of the democrats.

This means that any democrats who turn their back on the revolution, or cling to the illusion of peacefully reforming Russia, are merely depleting their own forces and undermining their own future. This kind of democracy is a self-contradiction. Anti-revolutionary democracy cannot be democracy.

Osvobozhdenie, which today parades under the banner of democratism, assures us that

> thanks to the decisiveness and courage of the *zemtsy*, the option of peaceful constitutional reform is still open to the government. To be firm and resolute in choosing this road will be an elementary act of statecraft.[45]

The editor and publisher of the newspaper *Syn Otechestva* pathetically exclaims:

> As a son of my century, I reject the superstitions of past centuries and deeply believe that a new temple to the god of freedom, truth, and justice will be erected among us without any need for sacrifices and atonement....
>
> I deeply believe that...if not today, then tomorrow, we will hear the peaceful sound of the hammer cutting the first stone, and then hundreds of industrious masons will be summoned to Petersburg and will gather here to build the new temples.

---

45 *Osvobozhdenie* No. 60, p. 183.

That is how countless naïve 'sons of the fatherland' are thinking at the same time as they sincerely imagine themselves to be democrats. For them, revolution represents the 'superstition of past centuries'. In white aprons and pious conviction, they come to erect a temple to the so-called god of freedom, truth, and justice. They 'believe'. They believe it is possible to avoid redemptive sacrifices and keep their white aprons free from any stain. They believe 'in the possibility of peaceful transition to constructive work because people in the highest positions must ultimately become conscious of the inevitability of fundamental changes'.[46] These spineless Petrograd 'democrats' 'believe', and they will pathetically publish their belief until their propaganda enlightens those in the 'highest positions', who will then put an end to their idealistic chanting. And even then they will piously cling to their one political accomplishment – their faith in enlightened rulers. 'The road to peaceful constitutional reform – *Osvobozhdenie* assures us – is still open to the government. To be firm and resolute in choosing this road will be an elementary act of statecraft.'

Mr. Struve is trying to convince absolutism that constitutional reform is to its own – to absolutism's – political advantage. What conclusion can we draw from these words? There are only two possibilities.

One is that the 'peaceful constitutional reform' that Mr. Struve speaks of will require absolutism to forgo only part of its prerogative and thus stabilise its position by converting the liberal leaders into supporters of a semi-constitutional throne. The only peaceful reform that would be politically advantageous for the government would be one to protect an exposed absolutism, an absolutism discomforted by its own nakedness, by covering it up with a decorative 'legal order' and converting it into *Scheinkonstitutionalismus*, or illusory constitutionalism, which would be even more of a threat to democratic development than absolutism itself. That kind of a deal – the basis of which is being prepared by the spineless behaviour of the *zemstvos* – would certainly be in the interests of absolutism. However, such 'peaceful reform' could only be completed in one way, and that is through betraying the political interests of the people and the goal of democracy. Is this the outcome that Struve the 'democrat' is looking for?

---

[46] *Syn Otechestva* No. 9.

If the answer is 'No', then when Mr. Struve speaks of 'an elementary act of statecraft' he must simply be hoping to lure absolutism into a bad deal. He must be trying to 'charm' the enemy with talk; to convince the autocracy that rebirth and resurrection awaits it following baptism at the font of democracy; to persuade the government that there is nothing greater than its own self-sacrifice to the glory of democracy; to convince the wolf that it would be an act of elementary zoological wisdom to give the sorrowfully lowing democratic calves the gift of a *Habeas Corpus Act*. What a profound policy! What an ingenious strategic plan!

Either betray democracy in exchange for an imaginary constitutional deal, or use deceitful speeches to lure absolutism along the road to democracy.

What a futile, miserable, confused, insignificant plan! What a servile policy!

The fact is that our quasi-democrats are incapable of suggesting anything better so long as they cling to the spectre of peaceful constitutional reform and think of revolution as merely a superstition of past centuries.

If they can do no more, then they will be thrown aside by the further development of the revolution; they will be forced to renounce their democratic superstitions and join the tail-end of the *zemstvo* liberals in peaceful constitutional betrayal of the most elementary interests of the people.

Moskovskie Vedemosti summarises the issue clearly and concisely when it writes that 'among the population of Russia there is no political party that is strong enough to compel the government to undertake political reforms that would endanger its (the 'its' should refer to the government's, not Russia's) security and power'. This reactionary newspaper takes the question for what it is – a question of strength. This is exactly what the democratic press must do. It is time to stop seeing in absolutism a political negotiator whom we might enlighten, persuade, or, at worst, charm, *umlügen*, and entangle with lies. Absolutism cannot be convinced, but it can be destroyed. However, for that purpose, we need the logic of force, not the force of logic. Democracy must gather its forces, that is, mobilise the revolutionary rank and file. And this work requires that we destroy liberal superstitions about peaceful constitutional development and any reassuring prospects of governmental enlightenment.

Every democrat must recognise, as 'an elementary act of statecraft', that expressing hope for a democratic initiative on the part of absolutism –

whose sole interest is self-preservation – can only mean preserving belief in absolutism's future and surrounding it with an atmosphere of temporising, which really means stabilising its position and betraying the cause of freedom.

If we say these things clearly, we are also saying something more: there can be no agreement and no deals, just a solemn pronouncement of the people's will, namely, the revolution.

Russian democracy can only be revolutionary democracy – in any other case, it will not be democracy.

It can only be revolutionary because in our society and state there are no official organisations out of which the future democratic Russia might develop. In our country, we have the monarchy on one side, basing itself on the colossal network of a bureaucratic apparatus, and on the other side, the so-called organs of social self-government: the *zemstvos* and the *dumas*. The liberals would build the future Russia by starting with these two historical institutions. In their view, constitutional Russia must emerge as a legal product of a legal agreement between legally contracting parties: that is, between absolutism and the *duma* and *zemstvo* representatives. Their tactic is one of compromise. They want to carry over into the new Russia, or more accurately, the renewed Russia, the two legal traditions of Russian history: the monarchy and the *zemstvo*.

There are no national traditions upon which democracy can rely. Democratic Russia cannot simply be born by autocratic assent. Nor can it rely upon the *zemstvos*, for they are themselves not constructed on the basis of the democratic principle but on social estates and property. If democracy is true to itself, if it is really the party of popular supremacy, it cannot for a single moment acknowledge the *zemstvos* as having the right to speak in the name of Russia. Democracy must denounce, as a usurpation of popular sovereignty and a political masquerade, any attempt on the part of the *zemstvos* and *dumas* to enter an agreement with absolutism in the name of the people.

If neither absolutism nor the gentry *zemstvos* – then who? The people! But the people have no legal forms in which to express their sovereign will. They can only create them by taking the road of revolution. The appeal for a National Constituent Assembly is a decisive break with the entire official tradition of Russian history. By summoning the sovereign people onto the historical scene, democracy drives the wedge of revolution into Russian legal history.

We have no democratic traditions; we have to create them. This is possible only through revolution. A party of democracy can be nothing other than a party of revolution. This idea must penetrate social consciousness; it must permeate our political atmosphere; the very word 'democracy' must have revolution for its content, so that even touching it will burn the fingers of our liberal opportunists, who try to convince their friends and enemies alike that they became democrats the moment they began calling themselves democrats.

* * *

'Peaceful' co-operation with the *zemstvos*, or revolutionary cooperation with the masses? That is the question democracy must decide. We will force it to decide because we will continue to put the question to it not just abstractly, not simply in our literature, but in the most concrete way possible, in every living political action.

Of course, democracy wants an alliance with the masses and is drawn towards them. At the same time, however, it fears a break with its influential allies and dreams of playing the part of mediator between the *zemstvo* and the masses.

In a remarkably instructive article, *Nasha Zhizn'* puts forth the idea that for a 'painless' realisation of democratic reforms it is 'necessary for the intelligentsia immediately, without losing any precious time, to enter into close contact with the broad popular masses and to maintain continuous relations with them'. The article does not deny that a part of the intelligentsia has tried to do this in the past – but it did so 'by emphasising exclusively the class contradictions that exist between the popular masses and those strata of society that have provided, and will long continue to provide, the major part of the Russian intelligentsia'.[47] Today, we need a different kind of work. It is necessary to awaken in the 'people' themselves, amongst the peasantry in particular, the kind of person who will be 'a free citizen, aware of his rights and fearless in defending them'. This kind of work requires 'co-operation between the democratic intelligentsia and the elected representatives of the *zemstvos*'! In other words, the so-called democratic intelligentsia must awaken free citizens through 'friendly co-operation' with the *zemstvo* opposition rather

---

[47] *Nasha Zhizn'*, No. 28.

than 'emphasising exclusively' the class contradictions within the opposition. This means that the intelligentsia will not only deny itself the opportunity to be bold and decisive in raising the question of agrarian reforms – it will also deny itself any right to be revolutionary and democratic in posing the constitutional problem. There is an internal contradiction here: to awaken the masses, while dragging along at the tail end of the *zemstvos*, cannot be the way to create a worthy political role for democrats. In their political agitation, the democrats will inevitably end up telling lies – not the bold and partly unintentional lies of Jacobin demagogues, whose revolutionary self-sacrifice partly redeems them – but rather niggardly liberal lies, peering about with calculating eyes, fearfully avoiding difficult questions as if walking on tacks, speaking with a lisp and slurring words as if every 'yes' and every 'no' might set fire to their evasive language. A perfect example is the *Osvobozhdenie* proclamation on the war and a constitution, which we have already analysed in *Iskra*. This proclamation was written for the masses and tried to provoke their interest by speaking a language they would understand.

And what do the 'osvobozhdentsy' say in their proclamation to the people? They tell them that nobody benefits from the war, that the tsar didn't want it, that he loves peace, and that they know this for a fact. They add that the tsar was misled by wicked advisors who did not inform his Majesty of the people's true needs because 'some high dignitaries, rather than conscientiously managing state affairs, pay more selfish attention to their own pockets and the honours they receive, while other grandees are simply stupid'. In order to make things right, the people's representatives must be summoned. The tsar will then learn the truth from them, 'as in olden times when the Russian tsars lived in Moscow'. Then the sovereign, the ministers, and an assembly of the people's representatives will all govern together.

That is how the 'osvobozhdentsy' democrats are building a free Russia. They are taking both the tsar and the monarchy under their protection. In their constitution, they set aside a special place for the tsar. They will summon an assembly of the people's representatives – not to express the sovereign will of the people, but to help the Monarch. The 'Osvobozhdenie' party has yet to prevail in the struggle with the monarchy or even to enter this struggle. With the whole Russian people watching, they are simply kneeling down before His Majesty by the Grace of God.

That is what their liberalism amounts to!

The people's representatives are to be arranged about the throne, which exists by the hallowed right of historical tradition. But just what people will they represent? The people of the *zemstvos* and the *dumas*, who also enjoy the hallowed right of historical tradition? Will they represent the people 'without tradition', the people who have no privileges associated with social estate, property, or education? The proclamation gives no answer to this question. It bears in mind that the task of the 'liberationists' is not only to awaken a citizen in the man of the people, but also to remain on good terms with the privileged citizens from the *zemstvos*. Turning to the people with propaganda for a constitution, the 'osvobozhdentsy' say precisely nothing about universal suffrage.

That is what their democratism amounts to!

They don't dare say 'Down with the Crown!' because they lack the courage to confront a principle with a principle, monarchy with a republic. Even before the struggle for a new Russia begins, they stretch out their hand to seek an agreement with the crowned representative of the old Russia. Instead of appealing to a solemn declaration of the people's will in the future, they follow the example of the estates-based and consultative *Zemskie Sobory* of the past.[48] In a word: they appeal to the anti-revolutionary tradition of Russian history instead of creating a new historical tradition of Russian revolution.

That is what their political courage amounts to!

The result is that a Russian constitutional government is to consist of 'the sovereign (who needs him?), the ministers (who are they responsible to?) and an assembly of the people's representatives (what 'people' do they represent?).

State power is to be organised according to these principles, and then – here is the central point of the 'osvobozhdenie' *vademecum* – then all of the issues will resolve themselves, all the adversities and misfortunes of the Russian people will be removed as if by a sweep of the hand. In those countries where the people have succeeded in winning a constitution, according to the proclamation, they have 'everywhere created for themselves just law

---

[48] [*Zemsky Sobor* means 'assembly of the land'. The first Zemsky Sobor was summoned by Ivan the Terrible in the sixteenth century, and the last met in 1653. These were purely advisory assemblies drawn by separate elections from the Church authorities, the lords and landowners, and the free citizens of the towns.]

courts, equalised and reduced taxes, eliminated bribery, opened schools for their children, and enjoyed rapid prosperity.... And if the Russian people – so the 'osvobozhdentsy' write – demanded (how?) and received from the tsar (how?) a constitution (what type?), then they too would rid themselves of impoverishment, ruin, and every other kind of oppression, just as other peoples have done.... When Russia has a constitution, the people, through their representatives, will surely eliminate passports, establish excellent courts and public administration, sweep away arbitrary officials such as the land captains, govern themselves in local affairs through their own freely elected officials, open numerous schools so that everyone will be able to get a higher education, free themselves from every kind of ignorance and physical punishment (once they have received a 'higher education'?), and spend their lives in contentment. In a word, once there is a constitution – once the country is governed by a tsar (why not without a tsar?) together with an assembly of popular representatives – the people will be genuinely free to enjoy a good life.'

So write the 'democrats' who condemn 'emphasising exclusively class contradictions'!

Constitutional limits on the tsar's power will not only save us from the rod and the whip, but will also secure us against poverty, deprivation, economic oppression, and make it possible to have 'rapid prosperity' – that is the idea that they want to spread among the people. Just have a tsar together with a *Zemsky Sobor*, and then there will no longer be any issues of poverty, oppression, unemployment, prostitution, and ignorance. So say the 'osvobozhdentsy'. But to talk this way is clearly and shamelessly to mock the whole of social reality; to call what is black, white; what is bitter, sweet; and thus to close both one's own eyes and everyone else's to the entire historical experience of bourgeois Europe over the past hundred years. It means trampling on obvious facts and ignoring everything that any educated man might learn from a European newspaper; it means gambling entirely on the ignorance of the Russian popular masses, on the pitch-darkness of the police state, and yes – on a miserably low level of political morality within the ranks of one's own party. It means replacing enlightenment with distortions, agitation with lies, and political competition with underhanded speculation. It means confidently transforming their own party, which in ideological terms is supposed to represent 'the people', into a narrow clique that deliberately exploits the people's ignorance. We say these things as emphatically as we can, and it is imperative that we be heard not only by every revolutionary proletarian but also by every Russian 'democrat'.

Educated people wrote this proclamation, and they know perfectly well that nothing they are telling the people is actually true. They know that once the tsar accepts a *Zemsky Sobor*, Russia's social order will become bourgeois. They also know perfectly well that no constitution will save the small property owner from proletarianisation, provide work, or protect the worker against poverty and corruption. They know that higher education is not accessible to all, that it is the monopoly of the wealthy. They know all of this – they have read about it, they have seen it, and they have spoken and written about it themselves – they know it and they cannot help but know it. Do you, for example, Mr. Struve – you, who approve of this 'appeal that is simple in form but persuasive in content' – do you know all of this to be true or do you not? Tell us directly in *Osvobozhdenie*.[49] Yes, they know it all. However, above all else they know that the people to whom they appealing do not yet know these things. They are saying to the people things that are not true and that they do not believe themselves. They are lying to the people. They are deceiving the people.

Did they really think Social Democracy would let them get away with this for a moment, that it would not confront them with historical truth? Do they really fail to understand that this is the right and the duty of Social Democracy? Do they think Social Democracy will enter into some kind of comradely agreement with them to deceive the people?!

Even if Social Democracy were nothing more than a party of honest, resolute decisive, consistent and unwavering democrats, it would still have to step aside and take an independent stand. Even then it could not let its activity depend in the least on the action – or more accurately, the inaction – of a liberal opposition that lacks the courage to say what it stands for and does not have the slightest idea of how to attain something that it is afraid even to mention. Even then, it would not be able to give the slightest political credit to the kind of 'democracy' that has fought for democratic demands only in

---

[49] As long ago as last October, we invited Mr. Struve to respond directly to this question (in *Iskra*, No. 76). Inspired by moral idealism, the editor of *Osvobozhdenie* did not answer either directly or indirectly.

its dreams, while in reality it has played and continues to play the role of advocate, secretary, and errand boy for estates-based liberalism.

At a time when the opposition is really an anti-oppositional opposition that looks for compromise at any cost; when its devoted servant is anti-revolutionary and anti-democratic democracy; when the latter is allied with non-proletarian and anti-proletarian socialists[50] who, by uniting with anti-democratic democracy show the true value both of their own socialism and of their democratism – so long as this is the situation, Social Democracy alone is the party of honest, resolute, consistent, and unwavering democratism. And for precisely this reason it is secretly and sanctimoniously hated by all those 'democrats' who, by the very fact of its existence, find it difficult to liquidate the last remnants of the idea of 'duty to the people'.

*   *   *

Conscious Russian proletarians! The attitude of the united make-believe democrats to your party is one of hatred veiled by hypocrisy. This is something you must clearly understand.

Both *Osvobozhdenie* and *Revolyutsionnaya Rossiya*[51] condemn our in-transigence and our 'struggle on two fronts'. The liberal press is more and more frequently making similar charges against us. The democrats want us to become more subdued and conciliatory. In turn, they are magnanimously willing to reconcile with us – if only we abandon our obstinacy and begin to sing in unison with them – at the same time as they are singing the tune of the estates-based opposition.

Being wise with experience, *Osvobozhdenie* and *Revolyutsionnaya Rossiya* are modestly restrained in making this shameless demand. But the legal press of the 'democratic' bloc, emboldened by the fact that they face no immediate rebuff, are openly cynical when they insist that Social Democracy must clear out of the way.

'Besides the reactionaries – complains *Nasha Zhizn*'

> there are also other forces, unfortunately, even progressive forces, that still
>
> [!] talk about and primarily emphasise all kinds of contradictions rather

---

[50] [Trotsky is referring to the Socialist-Revolutionary party, which Plekhanov had called the party of *socialist-reactionaries*.]

[51] [*Revolyutsionnaya Rossiya* was the central organ of the Socialist-Revolutionary party.]

> than what we have 'in common' and the things that might eventually draw together all classes and strata. Nevertheless [this 'democratic' newspaper reassures us] in general terms the differences between classes and social strata are now disappearing in the powerful, living torrent that is sweeping over the Russian land and embracing everyone from the Moscow merchant to the *zemstvos* of Tambov, Saratov and elsewhere, together with the Petersburg official and the usual liberal intelligentsia.[52]

But as for you, the conscious proletarians, your party is the one guilty of posing demands that differ from those of the Moscow merchant, the Tambov nobleman, and the Petersburg official! The 'democratic' intelligentsia demands that you settle for what is 'common', for the things that unite all the classes and strata. What unifies people around these 'common' issues can only be the programme of the most backward part of the liberal opposition. The moment you want to rise beyond their political level, it turns out that you, just like the reactionaries and conservatives, are making demands that divide rather than unite. Conscious proletarians! 'Democracy' demands that you forsake your revolutionary democratism in the name of unity. 'Democracy' demands that you betray the cause of democratic revolution in the name of solidarity with the liberal opposition. The reason is clear: what distinguishes you so emphatically from all other 'classes and social strata' is precisely your unshakeable commitment to the cause of democratic revolution.

And your reply, comrades, is one of merciless indignation in face of these uncompromising supporters of opportunistic compromise – these 'democratic' stooges of the liberal and semi-liberal merchants, nobles, and bureaucrats.

You tell them: We proletarians do not demand that liberals repudiate their own class interests, adopt our viewpoint and struggle on behalf of our socialist programme – although we are prepared to say that if they do so, they will put an end once and for all to our policy of emphasising contradictions.

Nor do we blame the so-called democrats for not belonging to the party of revolutionary socialism – what we demand of them is simply that they be true to their own programme. They cannot refuse this demand and then blame us because we are unable to watch in silence while they hide behind the *zemstvo*

---

[52] *Nasha Zhizn'*, No. 37.

opposition and threaten our party, which is the sole representative of honest, resolute, and unwavering democratism!

Are we the ones who raise divisive issues rather than contributing to unity? Isn't the opposite the case? Isn't it you who are guilty of doing this?

We Social Democrats took up the revolutionary struggle in an epoch when there was a complete political lull. From the very beginning, we formulated our own revolutionary-democratic programme. We awakened the masses. We gathered our strength. We took to the streets. We filled the cities with the clamour of our struggle. We awakened the students, the democrats, the liberals. And, once these groups, whom we had aroused, began to work out their own slogans and tactics, they then turned to us with a demand that in straightforward, simple language amounts to this: 'Throw out and eliminate from your own revolutionary programme and your own revolutionary tactics everything that distinguishes you from us – abandon your demands that cannot be accepted by the Moscow merchant and the Tambov nobleman – in short, change the slogans that you adopted when we were still asleep in the swamp of political indifference, and abandon the tactics that made you strong and enabled you to accomplish the miracle of awakening us from our shameful political slumber.'

The *zemstvo* could not begin to move without setting in motion the intelligentsia, which fills its every pore, encircles its periphery, and is tied to it by bonds of blood and political interests. The *zemstvo* congress of 6–9 November[53] provoked the democratic intelligentsia to launch a whole series of banquets. Some banquets were radical, some not so radical; some speeches were bold, others not so bold; in one case they spoke of the people taking an active part in legislation, in another they demanded limits on the autocracy and even went so far as a nation-wide constituent assembly. But there was not a single banquet where a liberal from the *zemstvos* or some adherent of *Osvobozhdenie* stood up and said: 'Gentlemen! Soon the *zemtsy* will assemble (or they have already assembled) to demand a constitution. Next, in the local *zemstvos* and the *dumas* they will demand – if they demand anything – a constitution. Then the people from the *zemstvos* and the *dumas* will gather in banquets with the intelligentsia – just as we have gathered today – and they will again pass a resolution concerning the need for a constitution.

---

[53] [There is an error in the text, which refers to 6–8 November.]

The government will then respond with a more or less solemn manifesto in which – (and the speaker needn't be a prophet in order to foresee this) – the inviolable character of autocracy will be proclaimed. The *zemstvos* will be told to get back to their normal work, and any further mention of political banquets will be in reference to the corresponding criminal statutes. What then? How shall we react to such a declaration by the government? In other words, what, dear Sirs, should our tactic be in future?'

Upon hearing these plain-spoken words, everyone at the meeting would be embarrassed, the democratic children would look up to their *zemstvo* fathers in disbelief, the *zemstvo* fathers would raise their eyebrows in disapproval – and everyone would instantly sense that the speaker had been extremely indiscreet.

His indiscretion would be in telling a liberal banquet exactly how matters stand. But our speaker did not commit such an indiscretion, for in reality there never has been such a speaker. Not a single one of the *zemtsy*, nor a single member of their audience of 'osvobozhdentsy' democrats, ever asked aloud: What next?

Only proletarian socialists were capable of this kind of indiscretion.

They were in Kharkov, at a meeting of the Law Society, when the chairman proposed sending a telegram of greetings and gratitude to the ministry of springtime affairs.[54] One of them told the audience that the only spring the proletariat believes in, and the only spring that democracy can possibly believe in, is the one that will come with the revolution. They were also at the session of the Ekatorinodar *duma*, where a worker-speaker declared:

> The dying autocracy plans to set out bait for you…it intends to deceive you now just as it has always done in the past! – However,…it also senses that a new force has grown up in Russia, a force that from its first appearance has been an implacable and deadly enemy of tsarist despotism. That force is the organised proletariat. We – a handful of fighters from the great army of labour – invite you to join us. You and we represent opposing social classes, but we can still unite in our hatred for one and the same enemy – the autocratic system. We can be allies in our political struggle. But for that to happen, you must overcome your usual timidity, you must be brave

---

[54] [The reference is to Svyatopolk-Mirsky, Interior Minister and initiator of the 'political spring' that followed the assassination of Plehve.]

and publicly embrace our demand: Down with the autocracy! Long live the constituent assembly elected by the entire people! Long live universal, direct, equal and secret voting!

There were also proletarians at the banquet held by the Odessa intelligentsia. On that occasion, their speaker declared:

Citizens, if you have the courage to accept our democratic demands openly and without flinching, then we proletarian Social Democrats invite you to march side by side with us in the battle against tsarism. In this cruel struggle, we Social Democrats will defend the great principles of liberty, equality and fraternity to our last drop of blood.

Proletarian speakers never hesitated to pose the question openly – What is to be done? – for when they ask this direct question they also have a direct answer: We must fight, we must 'defend the great principles of liberty, equality and fraternity to our last drop of blood'!

As if to demonstrate that this is no mere phrase for the proletariat, the Baku strikers, those storm petrels of the approaching thunderstorm of the people, left on the ground tens of their dead and wounded who spilled their blood for the great principles of liberty, equality and fraternity![55]

This class, which teaches its sons how to fight and die, had its representatives at the liberal banquets, where they spoke admirably of heroic struggle and heroic death.

Did they have the right to be heard?

The liberal press has much to say about the gap between the intelligentsia and the people. The only oaths we ever hear from liberal orators are those sworn in the name of the people.

And suddenly they see before them the real people in the form of the proletariat – not as objects waiting to be enlightened, but as an independent, responsible, and demanding political figure.

And what happens?

'Get out of here!' cry the liberals, who had hoped that the high property qualification (the price of a liberal dinner ranges from two to four roubles) would bar the proletariat from crossing the divide that separates the 'intelligentsia' from the 'people'.

---

[55] [See note 60 below.]

Professor Gredeskul,[56] who could not find 'adequate words to express his indignation' when the workers distributed proclamations at the meeting of the Kharkov Law society, told everyone in the hall: 'if the people who did this were honourable and considerate, they would leave voluntarily'. But he doubted that they were honourable and considerate!

'This is a violation of the rules of hospitality!' exclaimed the chairman of the Rostov liberal banquet, who refused to read out a resolution submitted by workers who had been left standing in the cold to await a decision. 'Indeed, they are already in the street – complained the gentleman liberal – so they can assemble wherever they want.' He knew that the Rostov workers know perfectly well how to assemble – and they pay for their meeting place with blood, not with roubles.

The Odessa liberals greeted a speech from an Odessa proletarian with the same demand: 'Clear out of here! Out! Out! Out!' At every turn they interrupted him with the exclamation: 'Enough! Enough!'

These are the solemn circumstances in which the intelligentsia is reconciling with the people.

What rage must have filled the heart of the revolutionary worker, how the hot blood must have pounded in his head, how he must have clenched his fists when he stood as the herald of revolution before this educated society, intoxicated by its own self-love, in order to remind the liberals of their liberal obligations, in order to confront the democrats with their own democratic conscience, and when the only response to his first hesitant words – after all, Gentlemen, he is not accustomed to ceremonial dinners! – was that of liberals shouting from the bottom of their lungs: 'Down with him! Silence! Get rid of him!' – 'Citizens, in the name of the proletariat, who have gathered outside the building….' – 'Out! Out! Out! Be quiet! Get rid of him!'….

Anticipating the appearance of workers at *zemstvo* meetings, *Osvobozhdenie* is reprimanding them for their behaviour at Kharkov and Ekatorinodar and demanding that they observe the formal rules of order and the rights of the chair. In return, this 'democratic' organ is making its own promise:

---

[56] [Nikolai Andreevich Gredeskul (1864–1930) was professor and later Dean of the Kharkov Law School. He helped to found both the Osvobozhdenie Union and later the party of Constitutional Democrats (the Cadets). He was elected as a Cadet to the First State Duma in 1906.]

> We may expect that the *zemstvo* people will not be hostile or even inattentive to any declaration presented at *zemstvo* meetings so long as the rules and correct procedures are observed.[57]

Proletarians! Listen to that! They will not be hostile or even inattentive! You 'may expect' that if you conduct yourselves in a ceremonious manner, the gentlemen nobles of the *zemstvos* will not be hostile to your declarations – just listen to it – they won't even be inattentive!

I expect, comrades, that you will tell the polite representatives who are to intercede with the *zemstvo* nobles on your behalf, that you have no need to go begging for the liberals' attention, that you are not there to submit requests but to make demands and get answers – and when they respond with hostility or indifference to your demands on behalf of the people, it is your responsibility to expose them before the people. And you will fulfill this duty by going over the heads of the chairman and even of the whole meeting, regardless of all its rules of order!

When the German workers were still supporting the liberal bourgeoisie and did not yet have their own independent party, they turned to the liberal leaders in 1862 with two demands: first, that they include universal suffrage in their programme; and second, that they change the system of membership dues so that it would be easier for workers to join the liberal party organisation (the *Nationalverein*). The liberals were 'attentive' enough to these demands, but they were also extremely hostile: in response to the first demand, they flatly refused; and as far as the second was concerned, they explained that 'the workers can consider themselves natural-born members of the liberal party' – meaning? – meaning that they could stay exactly where they were, outside the threshold of the organisation.

Liberals believe that workers are born with a natural right to fight on the barricades and give their lives in the name of freedom – so long as their presence does not disturb the tranquillity of liberal organisations, meetings, and banquets!

Fortunately for itself and for the cause of freedom, our proletariat has no need to play the part of humble petitioners tapping on the windows of the

---

[57] *Osvobozhdenie*, No. 61.

liberal party. It has its own party, and the fate of its demands has nothing to do with being included in the programme of the bourgeois opposition.

But this does not mean that the Russian proletariat has no interest in what the liberals are saying in the *zemstvos* and *dumas*, which remain fenced off from the masses by the census of status and property, or in what goes on at the liberal banquets, which are fenced off by the four-rouble dinners.

Proletarians are going to liberal meetings and they will keep going: not as supplicants, not to beg for intercession, but to confront the liberals' spineless loquacity with the proletariat's own revolutionary action programme; they will go in order to summon to the revolution any democrats who have not yet fallen under the liberal spell. The gentlemen liberals will not be greeting petitioners with cries of 'Get out!' They will not be fencing themselves off from beggars by means of admission tickets. No! They are themselves the bankrupt debtors of the cause of freedom and democracy, and they faint at the prospect of determined bill collectors. They fear being exposed by the very people whom they love so dearly – at a great distance – and for whom they have such ardent sympathy when they die on the streets of Baku.

Proletarians will keep turning up at the meetings of 'society', and they will confront the liberals directly with the fateful question: What next?

The *zemtsy* have submitted their request for a constitution. It was not respectfully received. The Moscow *zemstvo* announced that it was upset and then terminated its session. The Chernigov and Smolensk *zemstvos* simply went home. The Simferopol *duma* adjourned its sitting without reviewing its budget. This kind of self-dissolution would be perfectly sensible if every *zemstvo* and every *duma* joined in after setting out a principled justification for their strike. But then the question would still remain in full force: What next?

The *zemstvo* resolutions 'expressed hope'.[58] The hope turned out to be utopian. In turn, the quasi-democrats of *Osvobozhdenie* have been expressing their 'hope' to the *zemtsy* for the past two years. The hope they placed in the *zemtsy* has been betrayed, just like the hope that the *zemtsy* placed in the autocracy.

What next? There is only one possible answer: an appeal to the masses, that is, to the revolution. But one can only go to the masses with a democratic

---

[58] [They hoped 'that the state power will summon the freely elected representatives of the people'. See note 12 above.]

programme. We have already tried to show that our democracy can only be revolutionary; now we must add that any adoption of revolutionary tactics is conceivable only if based on a democratic programme.

There is no way to resolve the question of political freedom apart from revolution. Even deaf-mutes and blind people must understand this after the recent period of government promises, *zemstvo* meetings, liberal banquets, and the tsar's decree.

The road to freedom is through revolution, and the road to revolution is through a democratic programme.

The proletariat must turn to the intelligentsia 'democrats' – we call them democrats with their future in mind, even though they are presently trudging along behind the *zemstvos* – with the same words that Uhland[59] once addressed to the Württemberg Landtag:

> Und könnt ihr nicht das Ziel erstreben,
> So tretet in das Volk zurück!...
>
> [If you cannot reach your goals,
> Go back to the people].

The proletariat and the revolution

The proletariat must issue the call to revolution, but, above all else, it must also move towards the revolution.

To move towards the revolution does not mean to equip oneself for an armed uprising on some specific day that is determined in advance. Unlike a demonstration, the day and hour of a revolution cannot be specified. The people have never made a revolution by command.

But the inevitability of an approaching catastrophe does enable us to determine the most favourable positions, to arm and inspire the masses with a revolutionary slogan, to deploy all our reserves simultaneously on the field,

---

59 [Johann Ludwig Uhland (1787–1862) was a German poet, literary historian and political figure. Following the revolution of 1848, Uhland was elected to the Frankfurt parliament as a left democrat who favoured the inclusion of Austria in a unified Germany. The editors of Trotsky's *Sochineniya* point out that Trotsky misquoted the first line, which should be: 'Und kann es nicht sein Ziel erstreben.']

to train them in military skills, to keep them constantly armed, and to sound the alarm all along the line at the appropriate moment.

Does this mean that we simply exercise our own forces without joining a decisive battle with the enemy's forces – does it mean just manoeuvres and not a revolution in the streets?

Yes, it does mean just manoeuvres. But they differ from military manoeuvres because, at any moment, and completely independently of our own will, they can erupt in a real clash that will decide the whole outcome of a campaign lasting many years. Not only can this happen; it must happen. It is guaranteed by the critical character of the political period in which we live and by its invisible accumulation of a mass of revolutionary material.

The exact moment when manoeuvres turn into a battle will depend on the numbers and revolutionary solidarity of the masses who have taken to the streets, on the thickening atmosphere of universal sympathy and support that these masses are breathing, and on the attitude of the troops that the government will send against the people.

These three elements of success must govern our preparatory work. The revolutionary proletarian masses are already at hand. Across the whole of Russia, we must be able to summon these masses into the streets and unite them with a single slogan.

There is hatred for tsarism in every stratum and class of society, which means there is also sympathy for the liberation struggle. *We must focus this sympathy on the proletariat as the only revolutionary force whose appearance at the head of the popular masses can secure the future of Russia.* Finally, the attitude of the army is less and less able to inspire the government with confidence. In recent years, there have been numerous alarming symptoms: the army is grumbling, discontented, and in a state of ferment. When the masses move decisively, we must do everything possible to ensure that the army does not see its own fate linked to that of the autocracy.

Let us begin with the latter two conditions, which will determine the course and outcome of the campaign.

The recent period has been that of Svyatopolk-Mirsky. It began with a trumpet call to an era of political renewal and ended with the whistling of the whip.[60]

---

[60] [The 'whistling of the whip' refers to a statement by the government on 12 December, 1904, announcing that 'all disturbances of peace and order and all anti-

Its final result has been to inspire unprecedented hatred for absolutism amongst all the conscious elements of society. The coming days will reap the fruit of all society's anxious hopes and all the government's unfulfilled promises. Political interests have become more defined. The dissatisfaction is more profound and 'principled'. Yesterday's vague ideas are today the focus of avid political analysis. Every manifestation of evil and arbitrariness rapidly leads to fundamental issues. No one is frightened off any longer by revolutionary slogans; on the contrary, the slogans echo back and forth a thousand times and are even becoming popular sayings. Like a sponge soaking up water, social consciousness is absorbing every negative word, every condemnation, every curse addressed to absolutism, which can no longer do a single thing with impunity. With every clumsy step, it is held to account. Its advances provoke derision; its threats arouse hatred. The enormous apparatus of the liberal press is every day publicising thousands of disturbing facts that irritate and inflame social consciousness.

These pent up feelings must be released. Thought endeavours to transform itself into deeds. But, at the same time as they are fuelling social excitement, the thousands of voices coming from the liberal press are also attempting to steer it into narrow channels. They are sowing superstitious respect for the omnipotence of 'public opinion', for sheer disorganised 'public opinion' that finds no satisfaction in action; they are discrediting *the revolutionary method of national emancipation* and promoting a hypnotic fascination with legality; they are focusing all the hopes and attention of the discontented strata on the *zemstvo* campaign – and in that way they are actually preparing a collapse of the social movement. The intensifying discontent, finding no outlet and discouraged by the inevitable failure of the legal *zemstvo* campaign, which depends upon an ethereal 'public opinion' with no traditions of revolutionary struggle nor any clear perspective on the future – this social discontent can erupt in a merciless paroxysm of terror while the democratic intelligentsia[61] remain sympathetic but passive in their weakness, and the liberals, suffocated

---

governmental gatherings will be prevented by all legal means at the disposal of the authorities'.]

[61] [There is an error in the text, which speaks of 'democratic masses' rather than the 'democratic intelligentsia'. The error was corrected in the Russian text of the next document in this volume, 'After Petersburg Uprising'.]

by their own platonic enthusiasm, provide no support but money.[62] This must not be allowed to happen. It is imperative that we catch hold of the declining wave of social excitement and turn the attention of the broad opposition forces to the colossal undertaking led by the proletariat – that is, to the nation-wide revolution.

The leading detachment must arouse every stratum of society, make its presence felt everywhere, and raise directly the questions of political struggle. It must sound the call, and reveal and unmask the hypocrites of democracy. It must knock together the heads of the democrats and the census liberals. It must awaken, appeal, unmask – and demand, time and again, an answer to the question: 'What next?' Never once retreating, it must compel the legal liberals to recognise their own impotence; it must detach any democratic elements from the liberals and turn them in the direction of the revolution. To complete this work means gathering up every thread of sympathy, from all the elements of the democratic opposition, and tying them to the revolutionary campaign of the proletariat.

Everything possible must be done to attract the attention and sympathy of the urban petty bourgeoisie for the actions of the proletariat. When the proletariat undertook mass actions in the past, for instance, in the general strikes of 1903,[63] almost no work of this kind was done, and this was one of the weakest aspects in our preparations. Newspaper correspondents noted that the most senseless rumours were circulating among the people concerning the strikers' intentions. People expected their apartments to be invaded; shopkeepers thought their shops would be looted; the Jews were afraid of pogroms. This must not be allowed to happen. *A political strike, if it takes the form of single combat between the urban proletariat on the one side, and the police and*

---

[62] [Trotsky is making a distinction between individual acts of terror, such as the assassination of Plehve, and revolutionary mass action. When he quoted this passage in 'After the Petersburg Uprising' he slightly amended it.]

[63] [The general strike of 1903 began in July in Baku, where strikers took control of the city for several days and organised talks with the oil industry. The strike ended when Cossacks arrived, but it then erupted in Tiflis, where workers took to the streets in sympathy with those in Baku. The strike then spread to Batum, Odessa, Kiev, Ekaterinoslav, and several other cities. The strike movement lasted for one and one a half months and ultimately involved as many as 200,000 workers. The central demands were for an eight-hour day, wage increases, and reductions in over-time work.]

the troops on the other, with the rest of the population remaining either hostile or even merely passive, would inevitably end with our crushing defeat.

The indifference of the people will have its greatest effect on the proletariat's own self-confidence, and then on the attitude of the troops. The behaviour of the authorities will be incomparably more resolute. The generals will remind the officers, and the officers will remind the soldiers, of Dragomirov's quip that 'Guns are made for shooting, and no one has the right to waste bullets.'[64]

This must not be allowed to happen. The party must surround its proletarian nucleus with a moral armour of sympathy from the entire population, and with the material armour that comes from non-proletarian auxiliary detachments. The more the population understands the meaning of a revolutionary strike, the more it will sympathise. The greater the sympathy, the more numerous will be the members even of 'society' who will join in. The greater their numbers, the more reluctant will the authorities be to resort to merciless bloodletting. After all, everyone knows that the blood of the revolutionary proletariat is worth less than the blood of members of the opposition who come from 'society'!

A successful political strike by the proletariat imperatively requires that it be transformed into a revolutionary popular demonstration.

The second important condition is the *attitude of the army*. There is obviously discontentment in the ranks and a vague feeling of sympathy for the 'rebels'. There is also no doubt that only a small part of this sympathy is directly due to our agitation among the troops. Most of it results from the practice of using the army in clashes with the protesting masses. All of the correspondents who have described battles between tsarist forces and the unarmed people emphasise that the great majority of soldiers resent the role of executioner. Only hopeless idiots and scoundrels shoot at living targets. The great mass of ordinary soldiers fire into the air. All one can say in that regard is that anything else would simply be unnatural. At the time of the general strike in Kiev, the Bessarabsky regiment was ordered to march on Podol. The regimental commander replied that he could not guarantee the mood of his troops. Then an order went out to the Kherson regiment, but there too not a

---

64 [Mikhail Ivanovich Dragomirov (1830–1905) was a highly decorated General and military writer. His writings on military tactics emphasised ruthless efficiency in the ranks and the primacy of offensive action through devastating short-range fire and bayonet charges.]

single half-company of troops would comply with the orders coming from their officers.

In that respect, Kiev was no exception.

Correspondents report that during the 1903 general strike in Odessa, soldiers frequently did not rise to the occasion. For example, in one case, they were posted to guard a doorway through which demonstrators had been driven, but they simply took it upon themselves to look the other way when those under arrest fled through adjoining doorways. As a result, between 100 and 150 people escaped. Workers were seen chatting peaceably with the soldiers, and there were cases where they disarmed them with no particular resistance.

That is how things stood in 1903. Then came the year of warfare. It is obviously impossible to say with any numerical precision how the past year has affected the consciousness of the army, but there is no doubt that its impact has been colossal. One of the main elements of military hypnosis is the faith energetically promoted among the soldiers that they are invincible, mighty, and superior to all the rest of the world. The war has killed that faith everywhere. Soldiers and sailors were sent to the East without any hope of victory. And when an army loses faith in its own invincibility, it is already halfway to losing faith in the invincibility of the social order it serves. The one leads to the other.

In the current war, tsarism has shown itself for what it really is. War is an event that focuses not just the public interest, but also the professional interest of the army. Our ships are slower; our guns have a more limited range; our soldiers are illiterate; our non-commissioned officers have neither compass nor map; our troops are barefooted, naked and hungry; our Red Cross steals; the commissariats steal – and the news and rumours of all this naturally penetrate the army and find eager listeners. Every such rumour acts like an acid that eats away at the corrosion of moral drill. Years of propaganda work during peacetime could never accomplish what is achieved by a single day of warfare. The result is that nothing remains but mechanical discipline; there is no longer any faith that things must, or even can, continue in the old way. The less faith there is in autocracy, the greater is the likelihood of faith in the enemies of autocracy.

We must make the most of this state of mind. We must explain to the soldiers the meaning of the mass working-class action being prepared by the

Party. We must fix this knowledge in their consciousness with a continuous stream of pamphlets. We must make every possible use of the one slogan that can unite the army with the revolutionary people: 'Down with the war!' We must do this so that the officers, on the decisive day, will not be able to trust the soldiers, and the soldiers will have the same distrust of their officers.

Everything else depends on the street, where the last remnants of the hypnosis induced by the barracks will dissolve in the revolutionary enthusiasm of the people.

Of course, it is easier to fire over people's heads than to refuse to fire altogether or to hand over one's rifle to the insurgent masses. That is a fact. But the difference is not so great as it may first appear to be. The same soldier who yesterday fired into the air will tomorrow hand over his rifle to a worker, provided he is confident that the people are not just being 'rebellious' but are able and determined to hold the bridges until they win recognition of their rights. That confidence can and will be instilled in the soldiers by the numbers and the enthusiasm of the crowds in the street, supported by the entire people, and by the news of simultaneous action throughout every region of Russia.

Therefore, *in order for the proletariat's political strike, once transformed into a demonstration by the entire people, to become the starting point for a victorious revolution, a sympathetic attitude must be widespread throughout the army.*

But the main factor determining a successful outcome will obviously be the revolutionary masses themselves.

During this period of war, the leading section of the masses, the conscious proletariat, has not yet openly shown the kind of determination that this historic moment requires. But to draw any kind of pessimistic conclusions from this fact would be to demonstrate one's own spinelessness and superficiality.

The war is a colossal burden on our social life. Like a terrible monster, breathing blood and fire, it has cast its shadow over the political horizon and seized the people in its steel claws, tearing them to pieces, covering them with wounds, and inflicting upon them such unbearable pain that at first they cannot even think about the cause of their suffering. As with every dreadful misfortune, the first result of war and its retinue of furies – crisis, unemployment, mobilisation, hunger and death – is a feeling of depression and despair, not of conscious protest. But the same popular masses, who only yesterday lay in a state of initial unconsciousness and had no influence on the revolutionary strata of society, today are forced by the mechanical blows of reality to face up to the war as the central fact of Russian life. Gasping for breath in the face of such horror, the entire people must now confront their affliction. Likewise, the revolutionary strata, who yesterday still ignored the passive masses and mounted their bracing and conscious protests either without regard or even in opposition to them, are today seized by the general atmosphere of depression and acute horror. Like a cloud of lead, this atmosphere has enveloped them and weighs on their consciousness. No voice of resolute protest has yet been raised in the midst of this spontaneous, almost physiological suffering. The revolutionary proletariat, not yet recovered from the cruel wounds inflicted during the July events of 1903, has not had the strength to stand up to the 'elements'.

But a year of warfare has not passed without consequences. The first effect of the war was to suppress all revolutionary initiative with the weight of the disaster, but it also focused the attention of the popular masses, who only yesterday lived out their lives spontaneously, on the common political misfortune that unites everyone. By its duration alone, if for no other reason, the war has inevitably created a need in the masses to comprehend this dreadful event and grasp its meaning. At its outset, the war suppressed the determined initiative of revolutionary thousands, but now it has awakened the political thought of hitherto unconscious millions.

The past year – every single day of it – has had its consequences. In the obscure depths of society, an imperceptible molecular process has been occurring irreversibly, like the flow of time, a process of accumulating discontent, bitterness, and revolutionary energy. The atmosphere that people are breathing in our streets today is no longer one of incomprehensible despair – no, it is now one of concentrated indignation that is searching for the ways and means of revolutionary action. Today, the leading strata of the people are already able – and they will be even more able tomorrow – to throw down a new challenge to tsarism. No longer are they meeting with indifference from the broad circles of the people as they did the day before yesterday; nor are they worrying that their protest will be washed away by a general wave of spontaneous grief, as might have happened only yesterday. Today, every purposeful action by the leading detachments of the working masses will win the support not only of our own revolutionary reserves, but also of thousands and hundreds of thousands of new revolutionary recruits – and this mobilisation, unlike the government's, will enjoy the general sympathy and active support of an enormous majority of the population.

The revolutionary proletariat will take to the streets with the vital sympathy of the popular masses and the active support of all the democratic elements of the population. It will confront a government that everyone hates, one that has failed in every undertaking, big or small; a government that has been defeated on the sea, defeated on land, humiliated, embarrassed, and lost faith in its own tomorrow; a government that both tramples and fawns upon people; that is both aggressive and in retreat, lying and caught in its lies, insolent and at the same time intimidated. We will face an army that has been demoralised by the whole course of the war; in which bravery, energy, enthusiasm, and heroism have been dissipated by governmental anarchy; a wavering army that has lost faith in the indestructibility of the order it serves and is now hearing the rumble of revolutionary voices; an army that is restive, grumbling, and in the past year has already broken free from disciplinary constraints on several occasions. These are the conditions in which the revolutionary proletariat will take to the streets. And we have to say that history could not possibly create better conditions for the final attack on absolutism. In its spontaneous wisdom, history has done everything it can – and now it waits for a response from the country's conscious revolutionary forces.

An enormous amount of revolutionary energy has accumulated. All we have to do is make certain that it does not disappear before bringing results, that it is not wasted on trifles, on separate strikes and confrontations that are disconnected and lack a unifying plan. We must make every effort to focus the discontent, the anger, the protests, the bitterness, and the hatred of the masses. We must give them expression in a single voice, a single militant summons to join together and unite, so that every component of this mass of people will know that they are not isolated, that people everywhere are rising up simultaneously with the same cry on their lips. If that kind of consciousness can be created, then the revolution will already be half won.

We must call all the revolutionary forces into simultaneous action. But how?

Above all else, we must clearly understand that the *main arena of revolutionary events will be the city*. Today no one will deny this. It is also perfectly clear that a demonstration can only grow into a popular revolution with the participation of the masses, that is, first and foremost, of the proletariat from the factories and workshops. The proletariat must take the lead in the streets in order to impart meaning to the actions of the revolutionary intelligentsia, especially the students and the urban petty bourgeoisie. In order for the working masses to move, there must also be points of assembly. The industrial proletariat already has such permanent points of concentration in the factories and the workshops, and it is here that things must begin. Every demonstration has shown that we will not succeed in gathering the working masses at some single, predetermined spot if we have to call them out from the residential districts where they live. But we will certainly succeed – and this has been proven by the experience of the Rostov strike, and especially by the disturbances in the south of the country during 1903 – in calling out a mass of people who are already pre-assembled in the factories and workshops. The point is not to gather up the workers one by one, or to summon them artificially at some hour determined in advance, but to begin where they naturally gather every single day. This conclusion necessarily results from all our past experience.

Our general plan of action must be to tear the workers away from their machines and lathes, lead them out of the factory gates and into the streets, send some to the next factory, announce the end of work there, attract new masses into the streets, and thus move from factory to factory and shop to shop, continuously growing in numbers and sweeping aside police barriers, attracting passers-by with speeches and appeals, absorbing new groups on the way, filling the streets, seizing control of the places suitable for popular meetings, fortifying ourselves in those places and using them for continuous revolutionary meetings with a constantly changing audience, bringing order to the comings and goings of the masses, raising their enthusiasm and explaining to them the goal and purpose of what is taking place – so that ultimately we will turn the city into an armed revolutionary camp.

I repeat: the starting point for all of this is determined by the composition of our main revolutionary contingents, and it must be the factories and workshops. This means that any serious street manifestations with the potential for decisive consequences must begin with a mass political strike.

Unlike a popular demonstration, it is always easier to launch a strike on a prescribed day for the simple reason that is easier to lead a pre-assembled mass of people than to gather them together.

It also goes without saying that a mass political strike – not a local strike, but an all-Russian strike – must have a shared political slogan. This does not mean that we should avoid putting forth the local and partial demands of particular groups of workers; quite the contrary, the more numerous are the needs and wants expressed in preliminary agitation, the more specialised will be the demands of separate groups of workers, and the greater will be the likelihood of the entire proletarian mass being drawn into the movement. All of our organisations must clearly understand this. Nevertheless, all these partial and specific demands must also be co-ordinated with the general strike and must be embraced by a single common and unifying political slogan. Obviously, that slogan is to end the war and convene a nation-wide Constituent Assembly.

The entire people must take up this demand – and that is precisely the task of the agitation that must precede an *all-Russian political strike.* We must use every possible occasion to popularise among the masses the idea of a National Constituent Assembly of the entire people. Without losing a single moment, we must set in motion all the technical resources and all the agitational forces of the Party. Through proclamations and speeches, study groups and mass meetings, we must popularise, explain, and intensify the demand for a Constituent Assembly. There must not be a single person left in the cities who does not know what to demand: a National Constituent Assembly.

Without losing a single day or a single opportunity, we must also extend this agitation *into the villages.* The countryside must know that its demand is likewise for a National Constituent Assembly. *The peasants* must be called upon to gather in their own meeting places on the day of the general strike and demand the convocation of a Constituent Assembly. Peasants who live nearby must be called into the cities to participate in the street activities of the revolutionary masses as they gather under the banner of the National Constituent Assembly.

Throughout the whole of Russia, students must also be summoned to coordinate their actions with the nation-wide demonstration in support of a Constituent Assembly. Every student or professional organisation, every society and every organ of self-government and the opposition press – they must all be forewarned by the workers that they are preparing an all-Russian political strike at some specific time in order to win the convocation of a

Constituent Assembly. The workers must demand of every corporation and every society that on the day appointed for the mass action they will all join together in the demand for a Constituent Assembly. Workers must insist that the opposition press popularise their demand and, on the eve of the appointed day, publish an appeal to the entire population to join up with the proletarian demonstration under the banner of a National Constituent Assembly of the whole people.

We must undertake the most intensive agitation among the troops so that at the moment of the strike every soldier who is sent to pacify the 'rebels' will know that before him stand the people, demanding the convocation of a National Constituent Assembly.

Chapter Eight

'After the Petersburg Uprising: What Next?' (Munich, 20 January [2 February] 1905)

Leon Trotsky

Leon Trotsky's essay 'After the Petersburg Uprising: What Next?'[1] celebrates the revolutionary implications of Bloody Sunday. Trotsky began writing this essay late in 1904, learned the details of Russian events mainly through the European press, and completed the work just eleven days after the tsar's troops fired on Father Gapon and the St. Petersburg workers. Trotsky writes of the treachery of Russian liberals and of the general strike as the ultimate weapon in toppling the autocracy. Contrary to Karl Kautsky's assessment in 'Revolutionary Questions', he also makes the case that armed struggle and the mass strike are inseparable elements of a permanent revolutionary process.

In 'Revolutionary Questions', Karl Kautsky had dismissed the possibility of successful insurrection on the grounds that mass enthusiasm could never match the technical superiority of modern weapons:

[1] This article first appeared in N. Trotsky, *Do Devyatavo Yanvarya* (Geneva: Tipografiya Partii Rue de la Coulouvrenière, 27, 1905), pp. 53–64. A slightly modified version was republished, including the retrospective commentary in the final section, in N. Trotsky 1906 and again in L. Trotsky 1925, pp. 54–67. Our translation comes from the *Sochineniya*. An abbreviated English translation of the article was published by Olgin in his 1918 collection, *Our Revolution*, with the title 'The Events in Petersburg'. Ours is the first complete English translation.

> Given modern armaments, today it has become impossible to bring down a government, even the weakest and most foolish one, by means of armed resistance.... The consciousness of technical military superiority makes it possible for any government that possesses the necessary ruthlessness to look forward calmly to a popular armed uprising....[2]

At best, Kautsky thought the political mass strike might serve as a peaceful substitute for armed struggle, but even then only in narrowly prescribed circumstances.

Trotsky makes precisely the opposite argument: a mass strike will necessarily lead to armed conflict when the government responds with orders to shoot down strikers. Kautsky reasoned that 'Militarism can only be overthrown by rendering the military itself disaffected with the rulers';[3] Trotsky declared that the order to shoot strikers must itself provoke revulsion among the troops and cause them to desert to the side of the people:

> Guns, rifles and munitions are excellent servants of order, but they have to be put into action. For that purpose, people are needed. And even though these people are called soldiers, they differ from guns because they feel and think, which means they are not reliable. They hesitate, they are infected by the indecision of their commanders, and the result is disarray and panic in the highest ranks of the bureaucracy.

In the confrontation on Bloody Sunday, the Guards regiments triumphed over the demonstrators, but Trotsky commented that 'Nicholas II had every right to say: "One more victory like that one, and I'll be without an army"'.

Trotsky writes as though he were reporting history even when he is anticipating it. He probes the hopes and fears of participants and weaves them into a drama that finally became reality in February 1917. Twenty-five years after this essay, he wrote his monumental *History of the Russian Revolution* in which two of the chapters – chapter VII, 'Five Days', and chapter VIII, 'Who Led the February Insurrection?' – appear like comprehensive reruns of the drama he originally projected in 'After the Petersburg Uprising: What Next?'.

---

[2] See above, p. 236.
[3] See above, p. 226.

Of course, not every reader was equally impressed by these early essays. Lenin thought Trotsky was recklessly exaggerating immediate revolutionary prospects. In particular, Lenin objected to Trotsky's narrow focus on the urban proletariat, emphasising that a truly 'great' revolution would also have to involve 'the mass of semi-proletarians, semi-proprietors…the mass of the petty-bourgeois urban and rural poor'. When Trotsky portrayed striking workers as the only significant actors, he was projecting the tactic of *permanent revolution* that he and Parvus hoped would culminate in a government of 'workers' democracy'. Lenin, thinking in terms of the 'revolutionary-democratic dictatorship of the proletariat and the peasantry', expected a far more protracted struggle with a more convoluted outcome.

For a brief period in 1905, Lenin was fascinated by 'Comrade Gapon', whom he regarded as the possible herald of a new populist movement that might attract the peasantry and emerge as a significant political ally. In a speech to the Bolsheviks' third congress in May 1905, Lenin recounted his negotiations with Gapon in mid-February. He reported that Gapon 'impressed me as being an enterprising and clever man, unquestionably devoted to the revolution, though unfortunately without a consistent revolutionary outlook'.[4] Although Gapon's scheme to unite all revolutionary forces in Russia under his own leadership failed, Lenin and the Bolsheviks kept open the possibility of alliances with other parties, including the Socialist Revolutionaries. In 'Social-Democracy and the Provisional Revolutionary Government', written just prior to the congress, Lenin specifically took Trotsky to task for his condescending treatment of Gapon. Lenin's comments seem petty and incongruous in retrospect, but they also reveal substantive differences concerning the possible composition of a revolutionary government. Lenin believed no revolutionary government could endure without the participation of the petty bourgeoisie and support from the masses of the rural poor:

> Such a composition of the social basis of the possible and desirable revolutionary-democratic dictatorship will, of course, affect the composition of the revolutionary government and inevitably lead to *the participation, or even predominance, within it of the most heterogeneous representatives of revolutionary democracy. It would be extremely harmful to entertain any illusions*

---

[4] Lenin 1905h, p. 416.

on this score. If that windbag Trotsky now writes (unfortunately, side by side with Parvus) that 'a Father Gapon could appear only once', that 'there is no room for a second Gapon', he does so simply because he is a windbag. If there were no room in Russia for a second Gapon, there would be no room for a truly 'great', consummated democratic revolution. To become great, to evoke 1789–93, not 1848–50, and to surpass those years, it must rouse the vast masses to active life, to heroic efforts, to 'fundamental historic creativeness'; it must raise them out of frightful ignorance, unparalleled oppression, incredible backwardness, and abysmal dullness. The revolution is already raising them and will raise them completely; the government itself is facilitating the process by its desperate resistance. But, of course, there can be no question of a mature political consciousness, of a Social-Democratic consciousness of these masses or their numerous 'native' popular leaders or even 'muzhik' [peasant] leaders. They cannot become Social-Democrats at once without first passing a number of revolutionary tests, not only because of their ignorance (revolution, we repeat, enlightens with marvellous speed), but because their class position is not proletarian, because the objective logic of historical development confronts them at the present time with the tasks, not of a socialist, but of a democratic revolution.[5]

Lenin's vision and timetable for the Russian revolution differed significantly from Trotsky's. Lenin had in mind vast expanses of the Russian countryside and the feudal 'remnants' that still oppressed the peasantry and stood in the way of rural class differentiation – all the conditions that necessitated the *agrarian* programme of Social Democracy and portended years of preparatory work before the working class could even think of a truly socialist programme. Trotsky believed the revolution was primarily a matter for the *cities*; the peasants, at most, might play a supportive role, but the decisive battles would inevitably be fought by industrial workers following the example of general strikes in the Caucasus, St. Petersburg and elsewhere. Whether Trotsky 'underestimated' the peasantry, as Stalinists repeated on thousands of occasions after Lenin's death, or Lenin 'overestimated' the peasantry, as others might well argue, the fundamental point remains that the expectations of the two men did differ substantially. What this reveals, more than anything

---

[5] Lenin 1905e, pp. 291–2. Italics added.

else, is Parvus's influence on Trotsky and the commitment he and Trotsky shared to the strategy of *permanent revolution*.

*   *   *

'After the Petersburg Uprising: What Next?'[6]

The facts speak with such triumphant eloquence – and words are so weak in comparison!

The masses have spoken. They lit the beacons of revolution first in the mountains of the Caucasus;[7] then, on the unforgettable day of 9 January, they clashed head on with tsarist Guards and Cossacks in the streets of Petersburg; in every industrial city, they filled the streets and public squares with the turmoil of their struggle.

This brochure was drafted before the Baku strike, and the material was collected prior to the Petersburg uprising. Much of what it has to say is already old news even though just a few days have past. We are not making changes, for otherwise it would never appear. Events follow events, and history works more rapidly than the printing press. Political literature, especially abroad, deals less with direct news than with retrospective summaries.

The brochure begins with a criticism of the liberal and democratic opposition and ends with the political necessity and historical inevitability of the mass insurrection. During the period when clamorous liberal banquets seemed to eclipse the politically silent masses, Social Democrats repeatedly declared that 'the revolutionary masses are a fact'. The clever liberals muttered sceptically, and the 'democrats', who had attached themselves to the liberals, were inflated with such unbearable haughtiness that they imagined themselves to be the architects of fate. Even some 'revolutionary heroes' could think of nothing better than to enter into a deal – behind the backs of the silent masses – with

---

[6] [The editors of Trotsky's *Collected Works* make this explanatory comment: 'The reference is to the 'Bloody Sunday' of 9 January. It is, of course, inappropriate to characterise this historic event as the 'Petersburg Uprising', for there was no uprising on 9 January, only a peaceful workers' demonstration. It appears that the term 'Petersburg Uprising' was taken from the foreign press, which exaggerated the events occurring in Petersburg and translated the shooting of peaceful demonstrators into an uprising. (See L. Trotsky 1925, p. 545.)]

[7] [The Baku oil workers waged a successful strike in December 1904, and revolutionary turmoil spread throughout the Caucasus by early 1905.]

these opportunists and sceptics. The ridiculous and insipid 'bloc' that met in Paris,[8] being responsible to no one and having absolutely no plan of action, was a product of this lack of faith in both the masses and the revolution. Social Democrats refused to join this 'bloc' because their faith in the revolution long pre-dated 9 January, 1905.

Social Democrats repeated on countless occasions that 'The revolutionary masses are a fact'. The wiseacres among the liberals contemptuously shrugged their shoulders. Of course, these gentlemen think of themselves as hard-headed realists only because, as everyone knows, they have no grasp of profound historical causes; the best they can do is play the role of servant to every ephemeral political fact. They consider themselves to be hard-headed politicians even though history treats their wisdom with contempt, tears their schoolboy notebooks to shreds, and with a single sweep erases all their schemes and then jeers magnificently at their profound predictions.

> The Russian people are still not a revolutionary force.
>
> The Russian worker is culturally backward, downtrodden (we have in mind particularly the Moscow and Petersburg workers), and is not yet ready for an organised social-political struggle.

That is what Struve wrote in his *Osvobozhdenie* on 7 January, 1905,[9] just two days before the uprising of the Petersburg proletariat that was put down by the Guards regiments.

'The Russian people are still not a revolutionary force.'

These words should be engraved on Mr. Struve's forehead. The problem is that his forehead already resembles a tombstone marking the burial of numerous other plans, slogans and ideas – socialist, liberal, 'patriotic', revolutionary, monarchist, democratic, and on it goes – all of which emphasise the need never to rush into things while always lagging hopelessly behind.

'The Russian people are still not a revolutionary force,' said Russian liberalism by way of *Osvobozhdenie*, having convinced itself over a three-month period that liberalism was itself the main actor on the political scene and that its programme and tactics are determining the whole fate of the country. But

---

[8] [Trotsky is referring to Gapon's trip to Europe in mid-February 1905, which Lenin discussed at the third Bolshevik congress. This section was obviously added to Trotsky's original manuscript.]

[9] The article appeared in no. 63 with the title 'The Vital Task of the Time'.

these words had hardly reached the intended readers when the telegraph wires carried to all the ends of the earth the great news of the beginning of the Russian popular revolution.

Yes, it has begun. We waited for it, and we never doubted it. For many long years, it was just a conclusion from our 'doctrine' that the nonentities of all political shades ridiculed. They have never believed in the revolutionary role of the proletariat – at the time they believed in the power of *zemstvo* petitions, in Witte, in 'blocs' that unite nonentities with nonentities, in Svyatopolk-Mirsky, or in a package of dynamite. There was no political prejudice that they would not believe in, yet they dismissed confidence in the proletariat as merely a prejudice.

But history does not consult with liberal oracles, and the revolutionary people need no licence from political eunuchs.

The revolution has come. At one stroke, it has leapt over tens of stages that society would have had to clamber up one by one in peacetime, pausing for breath along the way. It has destroyed the plans of countless politicians who dared to make their political calculations as if they were accountable to no one, that is, without considering the revolutionary people. Destroying tens of superstitions, it has demonstrated the power of a programme based on the revolutionary logic that governs the development of the masses. It is enough to look at one particular question, that of a republic. Until 9 January, the demand for a republic struck all the wise liberals as fantastic, doctrinaire and absurd. But it took only a single revolutionary day, a single grand 'encounter' between the tsar and the people, to prove that it was really the idea of a constitutional monarchy that had become fantastic, doctrinaire and absurd. Priest Gapon[10] confronted the real monarch with the idea of a monarch. But

---

[10] [Georgy Apollonovich Gapon (1870–1906). The editors of Trotsky's *Sochineniya* have the following to say of Gapon:

> G. Gapon was born in Poltava province in 1870 to a family of cossaks. He studied at the Poltava seminary, after which he served for a time as a zemstvo statistician. At the prompting of his wife, he took holy orders and soon entered the Petersburg religious academy and then was assigned to the Petersburg deportation prison. While still studying at the academy, he associated with workers and became close to the head of the Moscow secret police, Zubatov, and other high police officials, whom he served during all of his activities with workers' organisations. In the same year Gapon established in Petersburg the 'Assembly of Factory and Mill Workers', modelled after Zubatov's organisations, and became its chairman. At the beginning of 1904, Gapon organised a circle of workers in the printing trade, which ultimately

since he was supported by revolutionary proletarians, not by monarchist liberals, this limited 'uprising' quickly revealed its mutinous content in battles on the barricades and in the cry of 'Down with the Tsar'. The real monarch destroyed the idea of monarchy. Henceforth, the only political slogan that the masses will hear of is that of a democratic republic.

The revolution has come, and it has put an end to our political childhood. It has relegated to the archives our traditional liberalism, whose sole accomplishment was its faith that some auspicious change of personnel might occur in the government. This kind of liberalism flourished most luxuriantly during the stupid reign of Svyatopolk-Mirsky. Its most mature fruit was the tsar's edict of 12 December.[11] But the uprising of 9 January put an end to the

included 70 to 80 members. The circle opened a tea-room for discussions on Vasiliev island. Speaking of his contacts with the police, Gapon said they were necessary in order to fulfil the goals of the organisation. Dreaming of the creation of clubs to unite all workers throughout Russia, Gapon proposed to present political demands in the event of an economic crisis. During his talks, Gapon also developed some of the views that appeared in his subsequent petition. By December 1904, Gapon's Assembly of Factory and Mill Workers had district organisations throughout Petersburg. Despite the mistrust of conscious workers and warnings from Social-Democratic organisations, Gapon succeeded in attracting a large number of workers to his organisations. The strikes of early January 1905, and pressure from the working masses, obliged the Gapon society to assume leadership of the movement. In place of revolutionary struggle, Gapon turned the spontaneous movement of the masses towards a petition to the tsar. In the days immediately prior to 9 January, he personally delivered numerous inflammatory speeches at all the district meetings. He was wounded during the encounter at the Winter Palace but was rescued by his friends. With the help of Rutenberg, a Socialist-Revolutionary engineer, he fled abroad.

In Paris Gapon attempted to link up with revolutionary organisations and met a few times with Plekhanov, but he displayed a complete ignorance of political questions together with an ambitious desire for power. Subsequently, he lost contact with revolutionary organisations who quite justifiably suspected him of having links to the secret police.

After the October amnesty for political activists, Gapon returned to Russia and resumed his contacts with the secret police, being directed by them to resurrect his now defunct Assembly of Factory and Mill Workers. He received money and even planned to publish his own newspaper, but on 28 March, in a dacha...near Petersburg, he was killed by the same Rutenberg.]

[11] [Following the resolution of the zemstvo congress in November, Svyatopolk-Mirsky persuaded the tsar of the need for reform. Witte was assigned to draft a corresponding decree. The tsar crossed out any proposal for popular representation, but the decree did mention administrative reform, press freedom, and an extension of the people's rights. Following the decree, the government forbade any discussion of a constitution at public meetings.]

'spring',[12] replaced it with military dictatorship, and made General Trepov[13] Governor-General of Petersburg after the liberal opposition had just managed to push him out of the position of Chief of Police in Moscow.

The kind of liberalism that wanted nothing to do with revolution, spent its time whispering behind the scenes, ignored the masses, and counted solely on its own diplomatic genius, has now been swept aside. It is finished for the entire revolutionary period.

Now the left-wing liberals will turn to the people. In the coming period, they will try to take the masses in hand. The masses are a force. They have to be mastered. But they also happen to be a revolutionary force. They have to be instructed. That is the gist of the tactic adopted by the 'osvobozhdentsy'. *Our struggle for the revolution and our revolutionary preparations must also entail a merciless struggle against liberalism for influence over the masses and for the leading role of the proletariat in the revolution.* In this struggle, we shall have on our side the mighty force of the revolution's own logic!

The Russian revolution has come.

Of course, no one could foresee the forms taken by the uprising of 9 January. In a most unexpected way, history placed a revolutionary priest at the head of the working masses for a few days, and he left on events the impression of his personality, his views and his order. This form had the effect of hiding from many people the real content of events. But the inner significance of these events was exactly what Social Democracy had anticipated. The principal actor is the proletariat. It begins by launching a strike; it bands together, puts forth political demands, goes into the streets, wins the enthusiastic sympathy of the

---

[12] [After the murder of Plehve brought Svyatopolk-Mirsky to the Interior Ministry in 1904, A.S. Suvorin's *Novoe Vremya* spoke of a 'springtime' of reconciliation between the tsar and the people. Mirsky hoped to find a compromise between autocracy and limited public representation by relying mainly on the zemstvos. He initially invited the zemstvo representatives to assemble, but ultimately he withdrew permission and they met in private quarters and produced resolutions in support of a constitution. The result was a wave of banquets, petitions, protests and appeals that led to the tsar's edict, which made no mention of popular representation. Two days later the government forbade all discussion of the zemstvo resolutions and ordered an end to all public meetings. The political 'spring' ended with Bloody Sunday and the subsequent departure of Svyatopolk-Mirsky less than a week later.]

[13] [D.F. Trepov (1855–1906) was Moscow Police Chief from 1896–1905. In January 1905, he was appointed Governor-General of St. Petersburg. Trepov supported the police-unions started by Plehve. He tried to restrain the liberal press and closed down *Syn' Otechestva* and *Nasha Zhizn'*. During the general strike in October 1905, he made the famous declaration that 'cartridges have no regrets, and they don't fire blanks'.]

entire population, and then clashes with the troops. Georgy Gapon did not create the revolutionary energy of the Petersburg workers – he just revealed it. He found thousands of conscious workers and tens of thousands of people in a state of revolutionary excitement. He contributed a plan that united this entire mass on a single day. The masses set off to speak with the tsar. But in front of them were the Uhlany,[14] the Cossacks, and the Guards. Gapon's plan had not prepared the workers for this. What next? Wherever possible they seized weapons, erected barricades, and hurled dynamite. They ended up fighting even though they had come merely to petition. What this really means is that they did not come not to petition at all but to make demands.

The Petersburg proletariat displayed a political responsiveness and revolutionary energy that far exceeded the plan laid out for them by their heroic but purely accidental leader.

Georgy Gapon's plan contained a great deal of revolutionary romanticism. It collapsed on 9 January. But the revolutionary proletariat of Petersburg is a living reality, not some romantic idea. And this is true not just of Petersburg. A huge wave swept through the whole of Russia, and it has still not receded. All it took was a tremor for the proletarian districts to erupt in rivers of revolutionary lava.

The proletariat has risen. The impulse came from a chance event, the firing of two workers; from a fortuitous legal organisation, 'Russkoe Obshchestvo';[15] and from an accidental leader – the selfless priest. This was all it took for an insurrection, but it was not enough to secure victory.

To be victorious requires a revolutionary tactic, not some romantic scheme based on an illusory plan. Preparations have to be made for simultaneous action by the proletariat throughout the whole of Russia. This is the first condition. It is impossible any longer for local demonstrations to have any

---

[14] [A kind of light cavalry of Tartaric origin, first introduced into European armies in Poland. They were armed with lances, pistols, and sabres, and were employed chiefly as skirmishers.]

[15] [The reference is to the *Russkoe obshchestvo fabrichno-zavodskikh rabochikh* (The Russian Assembly of Factory and Mill Workers) founded by Gapon. By late 1904 the organisation had 7–8 thousand members in Petersburg. When 4 workers (Trotsky speaks of 2) were dismissed at the Putilov factory, Gapon's organisation, including representatives from the Socialist-Revolutionary party, resolved to defend them. The surrender of Port Arthur to the Japanese intensified the social unrest and contributed directly to Bloody Sunday.]

serious political significance. In the wake of the Petersburg insurrection, only an all-Russian uprising can follow. Scattered outbursts will only consume precious revolutionary energy without any results. Insofar as they break out spontaneously, as delayed echoes of the Petersburg insurrection, such outbursts must, of course, be energetically used to revolutionise the masses, to rally them, and to popularise among them the idea of *an all-Russian uprising as a task for the coming months*, perhaps even for the coming week. This thought, once it takes hold of the masses, will on the one hand concentrate their fighting strength and avoid partisan flare-ups; on the one hand, it will teach, through the experience of revolutionary outbursts, the need for revolutionary unity.

This is not the place to discuss the technique of a popular uprising. Questions of revolutionary technique can be posed and resolved only in practice, under the living pressure of the struggle and with the continuous involvement of all active members of the Party. But there can also be no doubt that *questions of the revolutionary-technical organisation of mass action are now assuming colossal importance*. Events are compelling the Party to turn its collective attention to these questions.

Here, we can only attempt to put questions of revolutionary technique in the proper political perspective.

What this involves, above all, is the question of taking up arms. The proletarians of Petersburg displayed enormous heroism, but the unarmed heroism of the crowd proved unable to withstand the armed idiocy of the barracks. This means that victory requires the revolutionary people to become the armed people. However, this response also contains an inner contradiction. Any conspiratorial 'arsenals' that may be at the disposal of a revolutionary organisation will not be sufficient to arm the people. If they are used to arm individuals who are directly associated with the organisation, that will be useful. But it is a long way from this to arming the masses; the two are as far apart as individual assassinations and revolution. Even if one or another group of workers seizes a weapons shop – and that, too, would be a good thing – it would be a far cry from what is needed to arm the people. The only abundant supplies of weapons are in the state arsenals, that is, at the disposal of our immediate enemy, and they are guarded by the very army against whom those weapons must be turned. To seize the weapons, it will first be necessary to overcome the resistance of the army. Yet that is exactly the reason why the weapons are needed in the first place. Nevertheless, this contradiction dissolves in the very process of a clash between the people and the army. If the revolutionary mass gains control over a part of the army, even just a small part, that will already be an enormous accomplishment. Afterwards, the further arming of the people and the 'demoralisation' of the army will proceed irresistibly as the one process reinforces the other. But how will the first victory be achieved over even a small section of the army?

As the soldiers file by on their way to the scene of 'military action', people will shower them from the windows with thousands of brief but fervent appeals; the troops will encounter passionate words from speakers on the barricades, who will take advantage of the slightest moment of indecision on the part of the military authorities; there will also be the powerful revolutionary propaganda of the crowd itself, whose enthusiasm will be transmitted to the soldiers through exclamations and appeals. Moreover, the soldiers have already been affected by the prevailing revolutionary attitude; they are irritated and exhausted, and they loathe their role of executioner. They tremble as they await the malicious command of their officer. The officer orders them to open fire – but then he himself gets shot down, maybe as a result of a previously agreed plan, maybe just in a moment of bitter resentment. Confusion breaks out among the troops. The people seize this moment to go among the ranks of the soldiers and convince them, face to face, to come over to the people's side. If the soldiers obey the officer's command and let loose a volley, the people respond by throwing dynamite at them from the house windows. The result, once again, will be disorder in the ranks, confusion among the soldiers, and an attempt by the revolutionaries – through appeals or by having the people mingle directly with the soldiers – to convince them to throw down their arms or bring them with them as they join up with the people. If this fails in one instance, there must be no hesitation in using the same means of fear and persuasion again, even with the same units of troops. Ultimately, the moral authority of military discipline, which restrains the soldiers from following their own thoughts and sympathies, will break down. Such a combination of moral and physical action, inevitably leading to a partial victory of the people, depends more on organised and purposeful street movements than on arming the masses in advance – and this, of course, is the main task of the revolutionary organisations. By winning over small units of the army, we will win control of larger units and eventually of the whole army, because victory over one part will give the people weapons. Universal conscription has created conditions in which there are always enough people in any crowd to take on the role of military instructors. In the hands of the people, the most modern weapons can serve the cause of revolution just as well as they have served the cause of reaction in the hands of a disciplined army. In the past few days, we have already seen that the tsar's canons, in the right hands, can scorch the Winter Palace with shrapnel.[16]

Not long ago an English journalist, Mr. Arnold White, wrote: 'If Louis XVI had possessed batteries of Maxim machine-guns, the French revolution would never have occurred.' What pretentious nonsense – to measure the historical prospect of revolution by the calibre of rifles and guns. As if rifles and guns controlled people, and not the reverse. Along with hundreds of other prejudices, the victorious Russian revolution will shatter this absurd and superstitious respect for Mauser rifles, which supposedly dictate the laws of history itself.

Both during the Great French Revolution and again in 1848, the army, as an army, was stronger than the people. The revolutionary masses triumphed not because of the superiority of their military organisation or military technology, but because they were able to infect the national atmosphere that the army breathed with the germs of rebellious ideas. Of course, it makes a difference for the to and fro of street battles whether the range of a gun is only a few hundred *sazhens*[17] or several *versts*,[18] whether it kills a single person or hits tens of people, but this is still only a secondary question of technology when compared to the fundamental question of revolution – the question of the soldiers' demoralisation. 'Whose side is the army on?' That is the question that decides everything, and it has nothing to do with what type of rifles or machine-guns may be used.

Whose side is the army on? On 9 January the workers of Petersburg put this question into 'action' on a colossal scale. They forced the Petersburg Guards to demonstrate their purpose and their role before the entire country. The demonstration turned out to be horrifyingly clear and profoundly instructive. The Guards were victorious, but Nicholas II had every right to say: 'One more victory like that one, and I'll be without an army.'

---

[16] During a parade on 6 January, 1905 [19 January new style], one of the cannons fired a live round instead of a blank.

[17] [One sazhen equals 2,134 meters.]

[18] [One verst equals 1.06 kilometre.]

The Petersburg regiments in general, and the Guards in particular, were specially selected and specially trained. But the provinces are another matter. The army there is incomparably more 'democratic', and a successful revolution does not depend on support from the entire army including the Guards regiments. Even less does it depend on the Petersburg regiments being the first to enter into revolutionary fraternisation with the people. In our country, Petersburg does not concentrate the political energy of the whole nation in the same way as Paris, Berlin or Vienna once did.[19] In recent days our provinces have been developing the kind of revolutionary work that would have been sufficient to finish the job in tens of other nations 50–100 years ago. They are still developing today – but separately, without coordination. The economic role of the proletariat, as the creator of the Russian revolution, gives to the provinces an importance that they did not and could not possess in Europe at the time of the petty-bourgeois revolutions of the XVIII and XIX century. A single example illustrates the point. The Siberian Union of our Party seemed only yesterday to be a haphazard organisation with little prospect of exercising any influence in the near future. But today, through the railway workers' strike, it has disrupted the country's communications with the theatre of military action and caused the entire governmental apparatus to shudder.

The South of the country is also an inexhaustible volcano of revolutionary lava. And what of Poland? The Caucasus? The North-Western territory? Finland? Even if we assume that through further skilfull recruitment and the effects of alcohol (an inevitable recipe during a time of revolution), the Petersburg regiments remain available for bloody acts of repression, the only result will be to turn the capital into a fortified camp in which gun batteries and canon will be trained on the gates of every factory. If, in a word, we assume that the 'plan' of Vladimir Romanov[20] is fully implemented, there is no doubt that Petersburg will still be surrounded on all sides by a fiery ring of revolution. How could anything or anybody help the Guards if in Moscow, or

---

[19] [The comparison being made is between Russia in 1905 and the revolutionary events of 1848 in Europe.]

[20] [Vladimir Romanov, the Tsar's uncle, hoped to prevent workers from entering the centre of the city by convincing the troops that there was a plan to destroy the Winter Palace and murder the tsar. Troops were posted on all the bridges and main streets, and Vladimir Romanov was in charge of all the preparations prior to Bloody Sunday.]

in the south of the country, there emerges a *Provisional Government whose first act will be a radical reorganisation of the army?* Will Vladimir send the Guards against the provinces? The Guards are too few in number to be up to the task. On the contrary, in past revolutions troops have always been drawn from the provinces to serve in the capital. If the Guards are sent against a Provisional Government, who will defend the Winter Palace against the Petersburg proletariat? The workers may be divided or tied down in one way or another, they may be bled white, but they can never be crushed or frightened off once and for all.

Arnold White decided that Louis XVI could have saved absolutism if he had only possessed long-range guns. Grand Duke Vladimir, who spent his time in Paris studying not only the whorehouses but also the administrative-military history of the Great Revolution, concluded that the old order would have been saved in France if Louis's government had crushed every sprout of revolution, without any wavering or hesitation, and if he had cured the people of Paris with a bold and widely organised blood-letting. On 9 January, our most august alcoholic showed exactly how this should be done. If the same experiment were sanctioned, systematised, and applied to the entire country, then the autocracy would be immortalised! What a simple recipe! Is it really possible that there was not a single scoundrel in the governments of Louis XVI, Friedrich Wilhelm IV[21] or Joseph II,[22] who might have insisted on the same plan that Vladimir Romanov has now learned from the experience of the French revolution? Of course, such saviours abounded. But revolutionary development is just as little determined by the will of such bloodthirsty cretins as it is by the diameter of a gun barrel. A dictator, carrying the salvation of the old regime on the end of his sword, inevitably becomes caught in the nooses strung up by the genius of the revolution. Guns, rifles and munitions are excellent servants of order, but they have to be put into action. For that purpose, people are needed. And even though these people are called soldiers, they differ from guns because they feel and think, which means they are not reliable. They hesitate, they are infected by the indecision of their commanders, and the result is disarray and panic in the highest ranks of the bureaucracy. A dictator enjoys no moral support; on the contrary, he runs into obstacles

---

[21] [King of Prussia from 1840–61.]
[22] [Holy Roman Emperor from 1765–90.]

every minute; around him forms a network of contradictory influences and recommendations; orders are given and then withdrawn; confusion grows; and the government's demoralisation spreads and deepens at the same time as it feeds the self-confidence of the people.

Along with the question of taking up arms, there is also the question of forms to be taken by the struggle in the streets. What is the role, or what could be the role, of barricades in our country? Most importantly: what was the role of barricades in old-style revolutions?

1. A barricade served as a point of concentration for the dispersed revolutionary masses.
2. A barricade imposed elements of organisation on the chaotic masses by posing a clear task: this is where they defend themselves against the troops.
3. A barricade impeded the movement of soldiers, brought them into contact with the people, and thus demoralised them.
4. A barricade served to protect the fighters.

In our day, barricades are much less important. At best, they retain some importance as a physical obstacle that brings the masses at one moment or another into contact with the soldiers. But they no longer have any real significance in terms of mobilisation or organisation. It is the strike that mobilises the working masses; they are organised first and foremost in the factories, and secondly by the revolutionary party. In the past, a fighter on the barricades was armed with living words addressed to the soldiers, and with a rifle as the ultimate argument. Today's revolutionary will more typically be armed with published appeals and, at least at the outset, with dynamite. Both of these are deployed more effectively from the windows of a second or third floor than from behind a barricade.

But enough of that. These are questions, as we have already said, that will have to be decided by revolutionary organisations on the spot. This work is, of course, only of secondary importance compared to political leadership of the masses, although it is also true that political leadership itself is impossible today without first doing this work. Technical organisation of the revolution in the coming period will be the axis on which the political leadership of the insurrectionary masses will turn.

What is required for such leadership? A few very simple things: freedom from organisational routine and the miserable traditions of a conspiratorial underground; a broad view of things; bold initiative; the ability to size up a situation; and bold initiative once again.

A revolutionary development gave us the Petersburg barricades on 9 January. That is our base line and starting point. But we must go beyond this stage in order to advance the revolution. We must use the political conclusions and revolutionary achievements of the Petersburg workers' insurrection to nourish our further work of agitation and organisation.

The Russian revolution, which has already begun, is approaching its culmination in a nation-wide uprising. To organise this uprising, which will determine the fate of the revolution in the near future, is the basic task of our Party.

No one will do this work except us. A Father Gapon could only appear once. To accomplish what he did, he needed the unique illusions that first created a role for him. But he could remain at the head of the masses only for a brief time. The revolutionary proletariat will always remember Priest Georgy Gapon. But he will be remembered as a solitary, almost legendary hero who opened the sluice-gates of revolutionary spontaneity. If a second such figure were now to appear, with the same energy, revolutionary enthusiasm and political illusions as Gapon, he would already be too late. What was great in Georgy Gapon would now only be ridiculous. *There is no room for a second Gapon; what is needed now is to replace fiery illusions with clear revolutionary consciousness*, with a precise plan of action and a flexible revolutionary organisation that can provide the masses with a slogan and lead them into the field of battle, an organisation that can take the offensive all along the line and carry things through to a victorious conclusion. Only Social Democracy can provide such an organisation. No one else will provide the masses with a revolutionary slogan, for no one, except our Party, is devoted entirely to the interests of the revolution. Apart from Social Democracy, no one is able to organise the activity of the masses because no one has the same ties to them as our Party does.

Our Party has made many mistakes and committed many sins that have bordered on the criminal. It has wavered, digressed, stopped short, and shown both indecision and stagnation. Sometimes it has even acted as a brake on the revolutionary movement.

But there is no revolutionary party other than Social Democracy!

Our organisations are imperfect. Our links with the masses are inadequate. Our technique is primitive.

But there is no organisation other than Social Democracy that is so bound up with the masses!

The proletariat is marching at the head of the revolution, and Social Democracy is leading the proletariat!

Comrades, let us do everything we can! Let us invest all our passion in our work. Let us not forget for a single moment the responsibility vested in our Party: responsibility both to the Russian revolution and to international socialism.

The proletariat of the entire world is watching us expectantly. The victorious Russian revolution is opening up vast prospects for humanity. Comrades, let us do our duty!

Let us close ranks comrades! Let us unite others and unite ourselves! Let us prepare both the masses and ourselves for the decisive days of the insurrection! Let us overlook nothing and devote every possible resource to the cause.

We are going forward with honour, with courage, and in unison, bound together by the indissoluble ties of unity and brotherhood in the revolution!

Postscript[23]

'Up to the Ninth of January'…appeared about two years ago in Geneva. The first part of the brochure gives an analysis of the programme and tactics of the opposition *zemtsy* and the democratic intelligentsia; much of what is said there now has the ring of truism. But our critique of the Cadet Duma is essentially based on the same principles as our critique of the first *zemstvo* meeting in Moscow. We must continue our exposures with the same persistence as the liberals show in repeating their mistakes. Even if the liberals are not persuaded and enlightened by our critique, it will teach others not to have any faith in them.

---

[23] [The editors of Trotsky's *Sochineniya* note that 'The closing section of this work came from Trotsky's foreword to his book *Nasha Revolyutsiya [Our Revolution]*, which was published in 1906.' Quite likely because of his differences with Lenin over the role of Gapon, Trotsky evidently relished the opportunity in his final remarks to affirm that his own initial appraisal, not Lenin's, had been essentially correct.]

Writing about the *zemstvo* congress and the November banquets of 1904, we said:

> The intensifying discontent, finding no outlet and discouraged by the inevitable failure of the legal zemstvo campaign, which depends upon an ethereal 'public opinion' with no traditions of revolutionary struggle nor any clear perspective on the future – this social discontent can erupt in a merciless paroxysm of terror while the entire democratic intelligentsia remain sympathetic but passive in their weakness, and the duplicitous liberals are suffocated by their own platonic enthusiasm.[24]

We argued that only the revolutionary proletariat could find a way out of this state of affairs. *Mutatis mutandis*, this same analysis and the same prognosis must be repeated with respect to the current moment.

The concluding section of the aforementioned brochure dealt with the tasks resulting from the January events in Petersburg. The reader will see for himself which parts of what we said then are now out of date. In passing, we only wish to say a few words concerning Georgy Gapon, one of the strangest of all historical figures to rise so unexpectedly on the crest of the January events.

Liberal society has long believed that the whole secret of 9 January lies in the personality of Gapon. They set him up in opposition to Social Democracy as a political leader who knows the secret of taking possession of the masses. They linked any new advance by the proletariat to the personality of Gapon. We do not share those expectations. We wrote:

> There is no room for a second Gapon; what is needed now is to replace fiery illusions with clear revolutionary consciousness, with a precise plan of action and a flexible revolutionary organisation.[25]

Exactly that kind of organisation appeared later in the Soviet of Workers' Deputies.

But even though we assigned to Gapon a completely secondary political role, there is still no doubt that we overestimated his personality. With his halo of priestly anger, and uttering priestly curses, he looked from a distance

---

[24] [See the previous document, pp. 323–4. Trotsky modified this comment slightly.]
[25] [See above, p. 349.]

like a figure of almost biblical style. It seemed that mighty revolutionary passions had awakened in the breast of the young priest of the Petersburg transit prison. And what happened? When the fires cooled, it became clear to everyone that Gapon was a complete political and moral non-entity.

His posturing before the socialists of Europe; his mercilessly 'revolutionary' writings from abroad, which were in fact both naïve and crude; his return to Russia; his conspiratorial dealings with the government, sustained by the coins of Count Witte; his pretentious and absurd conversations with contributors to conservative newspapers; his big mouth and his vainglory – all of these things, taken together, finally killed the image of Gapon that came with 9 January. We cannot help but recall the astute words of Victor Adler,[26] a leader of Austrian Social Democracy, who, upon receiving the first telegram concerning Gapon's arrival abroad, had this to say:

> What a pity.... It would have been better for his place in history if he had disappeared just as mysteriously as he first appeared. He would have left behind a beautiful romantic legend of a priest who opened the sluice-gates of the Russian revolution....

With a delicate irony that is so characteristic of this remarkable man, Adler concluded: 'There are some people who are better suited to be martyrs than party comrades...'.

---

[26] [Victor Adler (1852–1918) was one of the founders of the Austrian Social-Democratic Party and led the campaign for universal suffrage.]

Chapter Nine
'The Revolution in Russia'[1] (28 January, 1905)
Rosa Luxemburg

The disastrous defeat of Russia in the war against Japan, and particularly the surrender of Port Arthur, dealt a devastating blow to the tsarist régime. On 22 January 1905 (9 January by the Julian calendar, still in use in Russia at the time), some 140,000 proletarians, led by Father Gapon, marched in Petersburg to the Winter Palace in order to submit a petition to Tsar Nicholas II. They demanded election of a Constituent Assembly under universal, secret and equal suffrage as well as the following reforms:

I. *Measures to eliminate the ignorance of the Russian people and its lack of rights:*
   (1) Immediate freedom and return [from exile] for all those who have suffered for their political and religious convictions, for strike activity, and for peasant disorders.
   (2) Immediate proclamation of the freedom and inviolability of the person, freedom of speech and of the press, freedom of assembly, and freedom of conscience in matters of religion.
   (3) Universal and compulsory public education at state expense.

---

[1] Luxemburg 1905c, pp. 477–84.

(4) Accountability of government ministers to the people and a guarantee of lawful administration.

(5) Equality before the law for everyone without exception.

(6) Separation of the church from the state.

II. *Measures to eliminate the poverty of the people:*

(1) Abolition of indirect taxes and their replacement by a direct, progressive income tax.

(2) Abolition of redemption payments, provision of cheap credit, and gradual transfer of land to the people.

(3) Naval Ministry contracts must be filled in Russia, not abroad.

(4) Termination of the war according to the will of the people.

III. *Measures to eliminate the oppression of labour by capital:*

(1) Abolition of the office of factory inspector.

(2) Establishment in factories and plants of permanent commissions elected by the workers, which jointly with the administration are to investigate all complaints coming from individual workers. A worker cannot be fired except by a resolution of this commission.

(3) Freedom for producer-consumer cooperatives and for workers' trade unions – immediately.

(4) An eight-hour working day and regulation of overtime work.

(5) Freedom for the struggle of labour against capital – immediately.

(6) Wage regulation – immediately.

(7) Guaranteed participation of representatives of the working classes in drafting a law on state insurance for workers – immediately.[2]

The Tsar was not in Petersburg at the time but his uncle, Grand Duke Vladimir – the 'august alcoholic' to whom Trotsky referred in the previous document – gave orders to fire upon the demonstrators. Estimates of the number of victims vary,[3] but there appear to have been at least a thousand

---

[2] Kukushkin 1996, pp. 253–4.

[3] In 'The Beginning of the Revolution in Russia' Lenin spoke of 'thousands of killed and wounded', Lenin 1905i, p. 97. The historian Abraham Ascher reports that 'when the carnage ended some 130 people had been killed and 299 had been seriously wounded (Ascher 2004, p. 27). A Soviet historian, writing in 1930 (presumably with no reason to underestimate the number of victims) concluded that 'the 5,000 or more mentioned during the first days was obviously wrong, as also, most likely, was the

casualties, and the bloodbath immediately gave rise to a wave of protest strikes and peasant unrest that signalled the start of the 1905 revolution. In exile at the time in Geneva, Lenin wrote:

> The army defeated unarmed workers, women, and children. The army vanquished the enemy by shooting prostrate workers. 'We have taught them a good lesson!' the tsar's henchmen and their European flunkeys from among the conservative bourgeoisie say with consummate cynicism. Yes, it was a great lesson, one which the Russian proletariat will not forget. The most uneducated, backward sections of the working class, who naïvely trusted the tsar and sincerely wished to put peacefully before 'the tsar himself' the petition of a tormented people, were all taught a lesson by the troops led by the tsar or his uncle, the Grand Duke Vladimir.[4]

The lesson Lenin referred to was one in 'civil war' with the slogan 'Death or freedom'. While Lenin urged that Social Democrats must pursue their own 'independent path', he also reiterated the need for common action in bringing down the autocrat:

> We Social-Democrats can and must act independently of the bourgeois-democratic revolutionaries and guard the class independence of the proletariat. But we must go hand in hand with them during the uprising, when direct blows are being struck at tsarism, when resistance is offered the troops, when the bastilles of the accursed enemy of the entire Russian people are stormed.[5]

Rosa Luxemburg shared Lenin's revulsion at the slaughter, but her theoretical response was far closer to that of Parvus and Trotsky than to Lenin's hope for joint action with bourgeois-democratic revolutionaries. Like Parvus and Trotsky, she emphasised the impossibility of events in Russia following the same pattern as Europe had done. 'Formally' the revolution appeared to be a re-enactment of the events of 1848, but, in reality, it would be 'special and unique unto itself' as a result of Russia's exceptional history and class structure. In her short essay 'The Revolution in Russia' Luxemburg

------

government's figure of 429: 1,000 is apparently the approximately correct figure' (quoted by Schwarz 1967, p. 58).

[4] Lenin 1905i, p. 97.

[5] Lenin 1905i, p. 100.

sketches the relation of class forces in 1905, noting the absence in Russia of a revolutionary petty bourgeoisie and excoriating Russian liberalism for its 'pathological weakness and intrinsic cowardice'. The Russian revolution, she argued, was 'more purely proletarian than all those that preceded it'. Luxemburg was convinced that together with a simultaneous miners' strike in the Ruhr, 'Bloody Sunday' in St. Petersburg would herald a new upsurge of proletarian mass struggles both in Russia and in Western Europe.

*　　*　　*

'The Revolution in Russia'

> Bald richt' ich mich rasselnd in die Höh'
> Bald kehr' ich reisiger wieder![6]

The capitalist world and the international class struggle finally seem to be emerging from their stagnation, from the long phase of parliamentary guerrilla warfare, and to be ready once again to enter a period of elemental mass struggles. But, contrary to Marx's expectation, this time it is not the bold crowing of the Gallic cock that announces the next revolutionary dawn.[7] The quagmire of the parliamentary period turned out to be most dangerous precisely for France, which for the moment appears to have left to others the leadership of the international class struggle. The starting point of the new revolutionary wave has shifted from West to East. Now, two violent social struggles, two proletarian mass uprisings, have broken out almost simultaneously in Germany and in Russia. They have once more suddenly brought to the surface of modern society the elemental revolutionary forces

---

[6] ['Soon I will raise myself noisily on high, / soon I will reappear more gigantic than ever!' Ferdinand Freiligrath's farewell poem printed in the title page of the last number of Marx and Engels' Neue Rheinische Zeitung (19 May, 1849). Reprinted in Freiligrath's Neuere politische und soziale Gedichte, 1849–51. (http://gutenberg .spiegel.de/freiligr/gedichte/abschied.htm).]

[7] [In November 1848 Marx wrote in *Neue Rheinische Zeitung that 'European revolution* is taking a circular course. It started in Italy and assumed a European character in Paris; the first repercussion of the February revolution followed in Vienna; the repercussion of the Viennese revolution took place in Berlin. European counterrevolution struck its first blow in Italy, at Naples; it assumed a European character in Paris in June; the first repercussion of the June *counter-revolution* followed in Vienna; it comes to a close and discredits itself in Berlin. Marx 1848c, p. 15.]

at work in its bosom, and they have scattered like chaff in the wind all the illusions about continuing on the peaceful and 'lawful' course of development that sprang up so abundantly during the international period of calm. Who was it that 'wanted' the general strike in the Ruhr district,[8] and who 'called it forth'? If anything, in this case every force in the working class that was totally or partially class-conscious and organised – confessional [Christian] unions, free [Social-Democratic] trade unions, and Social Democracy – did everything possible to *prevent* the uprising rather than to provoke it. Had it been merely a larger strike and a wider fight for wages, like those that break out from time to time, perhaps it could have been thwarted, deferred, smashed. But it broke out with the elementary violence of a tempest because the whole character of the movement in the Ruhr region – due to the diversity of the factors underlying it and the imprecision of its most immediate causes, which taken together affected the whole existence of the mineworkers – was not that of a partial struggle against this or that particular phenomenon but actually of an uprising of wage slaves against *the rule of capital* as such and in its most naked form. All that remained to the conscious, organised part of the proletariat was a choice between standing at the head of the tidal wave or else being cast aside by it. For that reason, the general strike in the Ruhr region is a typical and instructive example of the role that will sooner or later fall to the lot of Social Democracy as a party in the impending proletarian uprisings; an example that shows the whole absurdity of smug literary disputes over whether we should 'make' the social revolution or discard those 'obsolete',

---

[8] [On 7 January, 1905, the workers of the Bruchstrasse mines in Langendreer went on strike to protest against the prolongation of the working time and the projected closure of pits. By 16 January some 100,000 workers from other mines joined the strike. Under pressure from the mineworkers, the leaders of the 'free' (i.e. Social-Democratic) trade unions, the Christian and Hirsch-Duncker mineworkers' unions and the Polish trade unions, which wanted the struggle to remain local, were forced to proclaim the strike official on 17 January. From then on about 215,000 mineworkers joined the struggle for the eight-hour workday, higher wages, pit security, and the abolition of disciplinary measures against political activity. On 9 February the leadership of the miners' unions, with their unemployment benefit funds running low and fearing that the government would send the army to the coal fields, called the strike off without achieving any results. The Ruhr miners' strike has been called 'the biggest strike in German history' up to that time by Reichard 1953, p. 139. For a contemporary Marxist analysis see Mehring 1905d, and Mehring 1905a. See also the documents in Stern (ed.) 1961, vol. 3, pp. 97–134.]

'uncivilised' methods of struggle and instead apply ourselves more diligently to the next parliamentary elections.

At this moment, *Petersburg* gives us the same historical lesson in another form. It is a peculiarity of great revolutionary events that however much they can be foreseen and expected as a whole and in their general outline, as soon as they come into being in all their complexity, in their concrete form, they always arise like a Sphinx, as a problem that must be observed, studied and understood in its most minute details. And it is perfectly clear that the present Russian Revolution can by no means be approached with phrases about 'melting ice sheets', 'endless steppes', 'silent, tearful, weary souls' and similar meaningless *belletristic* expressions in the spirit of bourgeois journalists, whose entire knowledge of Russia proceeds either from the most recent production of Gorky's *The Lower Depths* or else from a couple of Tolstoyan novels, and who glide over the social problems of both hemispheres with the same benevolent ignorance. On the other hand, it would obviously be a meagre increment to our political wisdom and historical instruction if, like Jaurès's *L'Humanité*, we were to consider the first and most important conclusion of the Petersburg revolution – an event that is truly shattering for Russian absolutism and inspirational for the world proletariat – to be that since the Petersburg bloodbath the last Romanov has become, so to speak, unfit for the salons of bourgeois diplomacy and should no longer be deemed worthy of an *alliance* by any 'constitutional monarch' or 'republican head of state'.

But above all it would be totally wrongheaded if the Social Democracy of Western Europe, with the vulgar misgivings of a Ben Akiba,[9] were to see in the Russian Revolution merely an historical aping of what Germany and France have already 'gone through' long ago. Contrary to Hegel, it can much more justifiably be said that history *never* repeats itself.[10] The Russian Revolution, which is *formally* just doing for Russia what the revolutions of February and

---

[9] [Akiba ben Joseph (Rabbi Akiva, c. 50–135 A.D.) was a Jewish Palestinian religious leader, one of the first Jewish scholars to compile systematically Hebrew oral laws, the *Mishnah*. Rabbi Akiba was active in the Bar Kokhba rebellion against Rome (132–135 A.D.). When the Romans declared they would build a pagan temple on the site of the destroyed Jewish Temple in Jerusalem, the Jews, led by Shimon Bar Kochva, rebelled. Rabbi Akiba at first proclaimed Bar Kochva to be the Messiah but later abandoned him. Following the failure of bar Kokhva's revolt, Rabbi Akiva was imprisoned and tortured to death.]

[10] [The reference is to Marx's comment in The Eighteenth Brumaire of Louis Napoleon: 'Hegel remarks somewhere that all great world-historic facts and personages

March [1848] accomplished for Western and Central Europe half a century ago, is yet at the same time – *precisely* because it is a very belated continuation of the European revolutions – totally special and unique unto itself.

Russia enters the world revolutionary stage as the most backward country in political terms. From the standpoint of *bourgeois* class development, it cannot bear any comparison with Germany before March 1848. For exactly that reason, and despite all the conventional opinions, the present Russian Revolution has the most pronounced proletarian class character of all revolutions to date. True, the immediate demands of the present uprising in Russia do not go beyond a bourgeois-democratic constitution; and the final result of the crisis, which perhaps – indeed, very probably – can last for years as a rapid succession of ebbs and flows, will possibly be nothing more than a miserable constitutional regime. All the same, the revolution that is condemned to give birth to this bourgeois bastard is more purely proletarian than all those that preceded it.

Above all, Russia totally lacks the social class that in all modern revolutions to date played the predominant and leading role. As an economic and political middle stratum between the bourgeoisie and the proletariat, that class served as the revolutionary *connecting link* between them. It gave to bourgeois class struggles their radical and democratic character through which the proletariat was won over by the call to arms of the bourgeoisie, thus creating the necessary material mechanism of the preceding revolutions. We are talking about the *petty bourgeoisie*, which was doubtless the living cement that in the European revolutions welded together the most diverse strata in a common action and which, in class struggles whose historical *content* made them movements of the *bourgeoisie*, functioned as creator and representative of the necessary fiction of the united 'people'. The same petty bourgeoisie was also the political, spiritual and intellectual *educator* of the proletariat. Precisely in the revolution of February [1848], in which the Parisian proletariat for the first time stepped forward as a class-conscious force and separated itself from the bourgeoisie, the influence of the petty bourgeoisie appeared most clearly.

---

appear, so to speak, twice. He forgot to add: the first time as tragedy, the second time as farce.' In Marx 1973b, p. 146.]

In Russia a petty bourgeoisie in the modern European sense is almost non-existent. There is a small-town bourgeoisie, but it is just the refuge of political reaction and spiritual barbarity.

To be sure, a wide stratum of the *intelligentsia*, the so-called liberal professions, plays a role in Russia more or less analogous to that of the petty bourgeoisie of the West-European states. For a long time, they have devoted themselves *en masse* to political education of the working people. But that intelligentsia is not, as it was previously in Germany and France, the ideological representative of certain classes such as the liberal bourgeoisie and the democratic petty bourgeoisie. In turn, the *bourgeoisie* as a class in Russia is the carrier not of liberalism but of reactionary conservatism, or what is really even worse, of purely reactionary passivity. Liberalism, for its part, has grown in the social witches' cauldron of Russia not out of a modern bourgeois and progressive tendency of industrial capitalism but rather out of the *agrarian aristocracy*, which was forced into opposition by the artificial nurturing of capitalism by the state, and liberalism was therefore unsympathetic to free trade. For that reason, Russian liberalism has neither the revolutionary force of a healthy modern class movement nor that natural affinity and those social points of contact with the working class that existed between the liberal industrial bourgeoisie and the industrial proletariat in the European countries. Hence the pathological weakness and intrinsic cowardice of Russian agrarian liberalism as well as its alienation from the urban industrial proletariat, which explains why liberalism was also excluded as a political leader and educator of the working class.

Therefore the work of enlightenment, education and organisation of the mass of the proletariat – which in all the other countries was carried out in pre-revolutionary epochs by bourgeois classes, parties and ideologists – remained in Russia the exclusive task of the intelligentsia; not, however, of the ideological-bourgeois intelligentsia, but rather of the revolutionary and *socialist* intelligentsia, the declassed intelligentsia, which functioned as an ideological substitute for *the working class*. All of the resulting class consciousness, political maturity and idealism, which the mass uprising of the Petersburg proletariat revealed, came into being exclusively on account of this decades-long and untiring mole work in the form of socialist – or, more exactly, Social-Democratic – agitation.

And the resulting extent of class consciousness, looked at more closely, is *enormous*. Admittedly, the first public appearance of the Petersburg working masses has also brought to the surface all sorts of dross, including illusions of the tsar's benevolence together with unknown, fortuitous leaders drawn from the past. As in all great revolutionary eruptions, the fiery lava first of all churns up assorted mud from the depths of the earth to the edges of the crater. But given all these contingencies of the moment and the remnants of a traditional world view, which, moreover, will be immediately cast off in the fire of the revolutionary situation, there clearly appears the powerful, healthy, rapidly growing germ of purely proletarian class consciousness as well as that plain heroic idealism – *without* the poses and *without* the theatrical bearings of the great *bourgeois* historical moments – that is a sure and typical symptom of all class movements of the modern, enlightened proletariat. Besides, as everyone acquainted to some extent with Russian conditions knows, contrary to the examples of the West-European proletariat, the proletariat in the Russian *provinces*, which are now about to be engulfed by the revolutionary wave – the proletarians of the South, of the West and of the Caucasus – are even more outstandingly class-conscious and better organised than the proletariat of the tsarist capitals.

True, the first mass uprising of the Petersburg working class was also, undoubtedly, a surprise for Russian Social Democracy itself, and the outward *leadership* of the grandiose political revolt apparently does not lie in the hands of Social Democracy. Consequently, some people have been inclined to say that events have 'outgrown' Russian Social Democracy. If one means by that expression that the elementary growth of the movement in its *extent* and *rapidity* has gone beyond the calculations of the agitators and beyond the available forces and means for their control and leadership, then the expression is, to a certain extent, applicable to the present moment in Russia. But woe betide the Social Democracy that is *not* able, in analogous historical circumstances, to conjure upon the social stage spirits that *in that sense* 'outgrow' it. In other words, that would prove that Social Democracy has not understood how to set in motion a real revolutionary *mass movement*, for revolutions that are called forth, organised and brought to a successful conclusion according to a plan – in short, 'made' revolutions – exist only in the florid fantasies of smug police spirits or of Prussian and Russian state attorneys.

But if one means by the revolution having 'outgrown' Social Democracy that the *direction* of the proletarian revolution, its *strength and* the *phenomenon* itself were a surprise for the politicians; if one means by this expression that in the revolution's stormy course its *goals* have gone far beyond expectations, then Social Democracy is today virtually the *only* factor in the public life of the tsarist kingdom that the Petersburg events have *not* 'outgrown' and that is intellectually in full control of the situation.

The sudden political mass uprising of the Petersburg proletariat was a bolt of lightning in a clear sky – not only for the brainless cretins of the ruling thieves' gang of tsarism, and not only for the narrow-minded and ignorant money bags who in Russia play the part of an industrial bourgeoisie: it was no less of a surprise for Russian liberals, for the gentlemen who gorged themselves *ad majorem libertatis gloriam* in the banquets in Kiev and Odessa and greeted proletarian speakers with loud cries of 'Fie!' and 'Out with you' – for Mr. Struve & Co., who, on the very *evening before* the Petersburg revolution actually regarded revolutionary action of the Russian proletariat as an 'abstract category' and believed that the safest way to bring down absolutism's walls of Jericho was through the whining and moaning of 'highly respected personalities'.

Finally, it was no less of a surprise for that loose, mobile layer of revolutionaries from the intelligentsia, who at one moment believed, like reeds shaken by the wind, in the saving deed of bombs and revolvers engraved with frightful words, at another moment in blind peasant riots, and finally – most typically – in nothing at all; who alternately shouted to the skies with delight and then grieved unto death; and who, like the drifting sands of the revolution, oscillated from terrorism to liberalism and back again and were incapable solely of having any firm faith in the independent class action of the Russian proletariat.

And it was only the rigid dogmatists of Russian Social Democracy, people like Plekhanov, Axelrod, Zasulich and their younger comrades – that unpleasant and stubborn society that in certain circles of the International enjoys the same honourable reputation of disagreeableness as the French *guesdistes*[11] –

---

[11] [Jules Guesde (1845–1922) opposed at the time any participation by socialists in bourgeois governments and called on workers to elect representatives sworn to 'conduct the class struggle in the halls of parliament'.]

who had, with the unshakeable calm and security that only a solid, scientific world view can bestow, *forecasted* the coming of the Petersburg uprising of 22 January decades ago and who, through their conscious agitation, *prepared* and *brought it about*.

It was precisely the Marxist 'dogma' that enabled Russian Social Democracy to foresee with almost mathematical certainty, despite the bizarre peculiarities of Russian social relations, the broad outlines of capitalist development already more than twenty years ago and to anticipate and realise its revolutionary consequences through methodical activity.

It was the Marxist 'dogma' that enabled Russian Social Democracy to discover the working class in the tsarist kingdom both as a political class and as the only future carrier first of all of the political emancipation of Russia and then of its own emancipation from the rule of capital.

That same Marxist 'dogma' made it possible for Russian Social Democracy to defend unflinchingly, against all and sundry, the independent class tasks and politics of the Russian proletariat at a time when even the *physical* existence of the working class in Russia had initially to be read between the lines from the tedious language of official industrial statistics, when Russian factories had first to be inventoried, and when almost every mathematical proletarian, so to speak, had first to be fought for through vehement polemics.

And the same was true when the wavering Russian intellectuals were again plagued by worries about Russian capitalism developing not 'in breadth' but 'in depth', i.e., worries to the effect that industry, furnished with ready-made foreign technique, employed *too few* proletarians so that perhaps the Russian working class would be numerically too weak for its tasks.

And it was true when the *cultural* existence of the Russian proletariat was first discovered for 'society' from the memorable publications about the influx of proletarians to the public reading rooms, much like the existence of new wild tribes in the American primeval forests.

It was also true later, when despite the existence of the working class and despite the great strikes people believed only in the political efficacy of student terror.

And it was true only the day before yesterday, when despite the enormous socialist movement in Russia, people abroad, with a truly doctrinaire conventionalism, actually believed first and foremost in the *liberal* movement of the tsarist kingdom.

It was also true yesterday, when in view of the [Russo-Japanese] War all hopes were actually placed again not on the class action of the Russian proletariat but on the action of the *Japanese*.

And it was true at the last moment, when time and again people believed not in the independent revolutionary policy of the Social-Democratic working class but at most in an amalgamation of all 'revolutionary' and 'oppositional' parties in Russia into a political pastry in which the proletarian policy was to be baked together as quickly a possible with all the others 'from the broadest point of view' and 'in light of the great moment'.

The 22 January has turned the word into flesh and shown the Russian proletariat in an independent political revolution before the entire world. It is the *Marxist* spirit that has fought the first great battle for Russian freedom in the streets of Petersburg, and it is that same spirit that, with the necessity of a natural law, will sooner or later be victorious.

Chapter Ten

'After the First Act' (4 February, 1905)
Rosa Luxemburg

In this short but historically significant article,[1] written just a week after the previous one in this collection, Rosa Luxemburg was the first to refer in the West-European socialist press to a 'revolutionary situation in permanence' in Russia.[2] As in her previous article, she discounts the significance both of Father Gapon and of Russia's '*liberal* heroes', instead attributing the spirit of the revolutionary outbreak to years of agitation on the part of Russian Social Democracy. Contrary to the views of Michał Luśnia – already criticised in this volume by Karl Kautsky in his essay on 'Revolutionary Questions' – Luxemburg also clearly rejoiced in the fact that the uprising had rapidly spread from St. Petersburg to several other major urban centres in Poland, Ukraine, and the Baltic region. Like Trotsky and Parvus, she expected the revolution to become permanent not merely in the sense of embracing all the peoples and regions of the tsar's empire, but also in terms of infusing a formally bourgeois event with the vital content of class-conscious proletarian struggle.

*   *   *

---

[1] Luxemburg 1905f, pp. 610–14.
[2] [See Schwarz 1967, pp. 246–54.]

'After the First Act'

A week ago we wrote about the Revolution in *Petersburg*.[3] Now it stretches over almost the entire empire. In all the large cities – in Moscow, Riga, Vilna, in Jelgava and Liepaja,[4] in Yekaterinoslav and Kiev, in Warsaw and Łódź – proletarians have responded to the Petersburg butchery with a mass strike (in Warsaw with a general strike in the literal sense of the word) and have energetically proven their class solidarity with the proletariat on the Neva.[5] To borrow Marx's words, as the 'thoroughness' of the action has grown, so too have the numbers of the masses involved.[6]

In Petersburg the uprising of the proletariat was spontaneous, and the signal for it was given by an accidental leader [Father Gapon] even when the goals, the programme and the *political character* of the uprising, as a sufficient number of reports have already confirmed, were directly determined by the intervention of *Social-Democratic* workers. In the rest of the empire, and especially in Poland, the authorship and leadership of the movement were from the outset in the hands of Social Democracy. To be sure, even here this did not mean that Social Democracy conjured up the mass strike of its own accord and at its own discretion. Rather, it had to adapt everywhere to the impulse of the workers, whose excitement sprang up with the very first rumours and reports of the Petersburg events, and who instinctively resorted to actions in solidarity. But it was Social Democracy that immediately gave

---

[3] [Luxemburg 1905c, pp. 477–84. See the previous document this anthology.]

[4] [Latvian cities (In German: Mitau und Libau).]

[5] [St. Petersburg is situated on the Gulf of Finland at the mouth of the Neva River.]

[6] [The reference is to the section on 'Spirit and Mass' in chapter VI of *The Holy Family* by Marx and Engels:

If the Revolution, which can exemplify all great historical 'actions', was a failure, it was so because the mass within whose living conditions it essentially came to a stop, was an *exclusive, limited* mass, not an all-embracing one. If the Revolution was a failure it was not because the mass was '*enthusiastic*' over it and '*interested*' in it, but because the most numerous part of the mass, the part distinct from the bourgeoisie, did not have its *real* interest in the principle of the Revolution, did not have a revolutionary principle of its own, but *only* an '*idea*', and hence only an object of momentary enthusiasm and only seeming *uplift*. Together with the thoroughness of the historical action, the size of the mass whose action it is will therefore increase. (Marx and Engels 1845, p. 82.)]

to the mass assault the necessary expression, political watchwords and clear direction.

Taken *as a whole*, the Russian Revolution likewise acquired in the very first days following the bloodbath of 22 January the marked character of a political class uprising of the proletariat. It is precisely the way the Petersburg events were echoed immediately in other industrial cities and regions of Russia that constitutes the best proof that what happened in Petersburg was not an isolated and blind act of revolt born of desperation, like the many bloody ones that have occurred from time to time among the Russian peasantry, but rather an expression of a uniform ferment and shared strivings that have animated industrial workers throughout the entire empire. Such a conscious and open act of solidarity – of *political* solidarity to boot – of the entire working class in the different cities and regions of Russia has never before occurred during the whole of the tsarist empire's existence. Not even May Day, whose ideals have a powerful effect in Russia, has ever been able to call forth anything approaching such a cohesive mass demonstration. It emerged suddenly as a result of the direct struggle, and it has proven for the first time that the working class in the tsarist empire is at present not merely an abstract concept or a mechanical aggregate of isolated proletarian groups with similar interests and parallel strivings, but an organic whole capable of united action, a *political class* with a common will and a common class consciousness. After the struggles of recent weeks, there are no longer to be found in the tsarist empire dispersed Russian workers in the North, South, and West, no longer separate Latvian, Jewish and Polish proletarians, with each group seething separately under the chains of the same slavery. There now stands opposed to tsarism *a single* closed proletarian phalanx that has proven, through enormous sacrifices in the struggle, that it has learned how to defeat utterly the ancient policy of *divide et impera* – the watchword of government wisdom for every despotism – and this phalanx has been cemented by bloodshed into *a single* revolutionary class much more effectively than through all the paper 'agreements' of secret party meetings.

That is the enduring importance of the last week of January, which is epoch-making in the history of the international proletariat and its struggle for emancipation. For the first time, the Russian proletariat has entered the political stage as an independent power; it received its historical baptism in blood during the butchery of 22 January just as the Parisian proletariat did in the butchery of June [1848], and it has joined the international family of the fighting proletariat as a new active member.

This immense fact did not exist for the bourgeois *literati*, who limited themselves to protesting immediately against the apprehended martyrdom of Maxim Gorky.[7] But, after all, that was to be expected. If, for the sake of amusement, one wishes to examine in their clearest form the grotesque reactions of the contemporary bourgeois 'intelligentsia' to the historical drama on the Neva, then one need only take the *Zukunft* of Mr. Harden, which is scintillating in all the colours of 'modern' decadent trash and, in emulation of Trepov's telegraph agencies, proves beyond all doubt that contemporary political conditions in Russia 'satisfy the needs of the Russian masses'. Mr. Harden rehabilitates before the world the 'poor' Petersburg workers as pious and naïve lambs of the tsar who were 'misled' by demagogues, and he declares that the march to their death by 2,000 proletarians struggling for freedom was child's play by comparison with the Decembrist revolt of 1825, in which '*even* officers of the Guards*'* had already proclaimed a republic. Normal bourgeois skulls have never comprehended the historical significance of proletarian struggles even at the best of times. The dwarf skulls of the decaying bourgeoisie are least of all qualified to do so.

But the revolt of the Russian proletariat is also a new phenomenon for international Social Democracy, and we must first assimilate it spiritually. No matter how dialectically we think, in our immediate state of consciousness we are all incorrigible metaphysicians who cling to the immutability of things. And though we are the party of social progress, even for us every salutary advance, which takes place imperceptibly and then suddenly arises before us as a finished result, is a surprise to which we must then adapt our conceptions. In the conception of many West-European Social Democrats the Russian proletarian still lives on as the *muzhik*, the peasant with long flaxen hair, foot wrappings and a stupid facial expression, who only yesterday arrived from the countryside as an exotic guest in the urban culture of the modern world. Almost no notice has been taken of the cultural and spiritual uplifting of the Russian proletariat first through capitalism and then through the Social-Democratic work of enlightenment, which has been accomplished

---

[7] [Maxim Gorky was arrested by the tsarist regime after the Petersburg demonstration of 22 January, 1905. He was released on bail on 27 January.]

in the oppressive conditions of absolutism and has transformed the *muzhik* of yesterday into the intelligent, inquisitive, idealistic, struggling, ambitious proletarian of today's great urban centres. And when one considers that actual Social-Democratic agitation in Russia has lasted scarcely fifteen years, and that the first attempt at a trade-unionist mass struggle in Petersburg dates from the year 1896, one must recognise that social progress has done its work of inner weakening at a truly *frantic* pace. All the dense fog and hovering fumes of stagnation have been dispersed and swept aside at once by the proletarian thunderstorm; and where only yesterday there seemed to loom a puzzling, ghost-like stronghold of rigid, centuries-old inertia, today there stands before us a country convulsed and thoroughly shaken by the most modern of tempests that casts the glare of a mighty fire over the entire bourgeois world.

The events in Petersburg have imparted to us a profound lesson of revolutionary optimism. Through a thousand obstacles, through all the feudal bastions and without the political and social conditions essential for modern life, the bronze law of capitalist development[8] triumphantly asserted itself in the birth, growth and class consciousness of the proletariat. And the volcanic eruption of the revolution has shown for the first time how quickly and thoroughly the young mole has done its job. How merrily it worked under the feet of Western-European bourgeois society! Wanting to measure the political maturity of the proletariat through statistics drawn from elections and union membership is like wanting to measure the Mont Blanc[9] with a tailor's tape. In the so-called normal times of everyday bourgeois life, we know almost nothing about how deeply our ideas have already sunk roots, how strong the proletariat is, or how inwardly rotten is the structure of the ruling society. All the vacillations and mistakes of opportunism can ultimately be attributed to a false estimation of the forces of the socialist movement and to a subjective illusion of *weakness*.

Vulgar narrow-mindedness, which only knows how to grasp the small change of so-called tangible material results, may inveigh against the 'miscarried revolution' and the ineffectual 'passing enthusiasm' of the

---

[8] [On the Capitoline hill in Rome there were bronze law tablets that one had to read by standing on a ladder, symbolising that they were sacred and inviolable.]

[9] [The Mont Blanc massif includes the highest glacier-covered peaks of the Alps.]

Petersburg uprising on the grounds that formally absolutism still exists, that the constituent assembly has not yet been summoned, and that the masses who are now on strike will perhaps appear to return to everyday routine tomorrow. But, in reality, the events of the last weeks have opened a breach in the fabric of Russian society that can no longer be closed. Tsarism has already received its inner death blow; and its further existence, be it long or short, can only be an agony. For the first time, it has stood face to face against that class of the people that is *appointed* to overthrow it. It has been proven before the whole world that tsarism no longer exists thanks to the passivity but, on the contrary, *against* the will of that stratum of the people whose will is politically decisive. The working class has for the first time openly fought as an organic whole and seized the political leadership of society against absolutism. Moreover, the ultimate weapon of brutal violence, with which absolutism has even today narrowly prevailed, was blunted by its employment. The civil war has demoralised and politically aroused the military in a way that decades of secret barracks agitation could never have done. Tsarism can hardly risk another military trial of strength with its own people.

And only now does the real task of Social Democracy *begin* in order to maintain the revolutionary situation in permanence. Its duty flows naturally from the inclination of politically short-sighted people to see failure and the end of the struggle where the beginning of the revolution is actually to be found. To counteract the pessimistic dejection of the working masses upon which the reaction speculates, to explain the intrinsic meaning and enormous results of the proletariat's first attack, to guard against the hangover that used to take possession of the masses in *bourgeois* revolutions as soon as the goal was not visibly attained at once, and that even tomorrow will undoubtedly seize Russia's *liberal* heroes – that is the vast work that first and foremost confronts Social Democracy. Contrary to what youthful braggarts may imagine, Social Democracy is not able artificially to create historical momentum or historical situations either in Russia or anywhere else in the world. But what Social Democracy can and must do is to make the most of the particular situation by making the workers conscious of its historical significance and its consequences, thus carrying the struggle over to a higher stage.

At the present moment in Russia the most pressing need is to assist the masses *after* the first struggles by enlightening, stimulating and encouraging them. And *this* task can be carried out neither by the Gapons, who usually flare up like meteors in the revolution and then disappear forever; nor by the liberals, who after every advance always fold up like a pocket knife; nor finally by all kinds of revolutionary adventurers who are ever ready to leap into a great attack. This task can *only* be fulfilled in Russia by Social Democracy, which rises above every particular moment of the struggle because it has a final aim that goes beyond all particular moments; which for that reason does not see the end of the world in the immediate success or failure of the moment; and for whom the working class is not a means to the end of achieving political freedom, but political freedom is rather a means to the end of emancipating the working class.

Chapter Eleven

'The Consequences of the Japanese Victory and Social Democracy' (July 1905)

Karl Kautsky

In this article by Karl Kautsky,[1] the expression 'revolution in permanence' was used for the second time in the West-European Marxist press to analyse the 1905 Russian Revolution[2] (following Rosa Luxemburg's February 1905 article 'After the First Act', the preceding document in this anthology). Kautsky's work appeared in four Russian editions, one of them in Lenin's journal *Proletarii*.[3]

'The Consequences of the Japanese Victory and Social Democracy' was originally published in three parts. The context for the second part, dealing with 'The Mood in German Social Democracy', was the debate in the German Social-Democratic Party (SPD) on the mass political strike, in which the revolutionary wing of the party for the first time clashed directly with the trade-unionist right wing grouped around the General Commission of Free Trade Unions of Germany (the Social-Democratic federation of trade unions).[4]

---

[1] Kautsky 1905f, pp. 460–8, 492–9, 529–37.
[2] See Schwarz 1967, pp. 246–7.
[3] Kautsky 1905h; Kautsky 1905k; Kautsky 1905a; Kautsky 1907d.
[4] The chairman of the General Commission for thirty years, from its establishment in 1890 until his death in 1920, was Carl Legien.

In October 1896, Eduard Bernstein had published the first of his series of articles 'Problems of Socialism' in the journal *Die Neue Zeit* revising Marxism. The articles were later collected in his book *The Preconditions of Socialism and the Tasks of Social Democracy*.[5] Two book-length 'orthodox' Marxist answers to Bernstein's revisionist arguments came in Rosa Luxemburg's *Social Reform and Revolution*[6] and Karl Kautsky's *Bernstein und das sozialdemokratische Programm: Eine Antikritik*.[7] Kautsky also sounded the alarm against the union leaders who were striving for independence from the Party under the slogan of 'neutrality' as far back as 1900 in the framework of the revisionist controversy.[8] In September 1903, the Dresden Congress of the SPD formally condemned 'theoretical' revisionism and endorsed revolutionary socialism.

The Russian Revolution of 1905 revived agitation within German Social Democracy in favour of the political mass strike. Alarmed by the militant mood in the ranks, the fifth congress of the Social-Democratic Free Trade Unions, held in May 1905 at Cologne, flatly rejected use of the mass strike and even forbade the 'propagation' (i.e. supportive propaganda or discussion) of this tactic. It also argued that the mass strike was defended by 'anarchists and persons without experience in economic struggles' and warned the organised workers 'to avoid being hindered from the everyday work of strengthening the workers' organisations by the adoption and promotion of such ideas'.[9] The General Commission's spokesman on this issue, Theodor Bömelburg (the president of the construction workers' union) attacked not only the SPD left wing but even Eduard Bernstein for advocating use of the mass strike to defend democratic rights. Bömelburg argued that in order to expand its organisations, what the labour movement needed above all was 'peace and quiet [*Ruhe*]'.[10]

A by-product of this controversy was the so-called '*Vorwärts* conflict'. When Kautsky criticised the Cologne resolution,[11] the central organ of the SPD, the *Vorwärts*, edited by Kurt Eisner, accused him of being a doctrinaire ideologue

---

5 Bernstein 1993.
6 Luxemburg 1900.
7 No English version is available, but a French one was issued in 1900 as Kautsky 1900. Available online at Gallica: ⟨http://gallica.bnf.fr/⟩.
8 Kautsky 1900, pp. 388–94, 429–33, 457–66, 492–7.
9 Luxemburg 1905a, pp. 580–86.
10 Referat Bömelburg 1905, pp. 115ff. Reprinted in Grunenberg (ed.) 1970, p. 353.
11 Kautsky 1905c, pp. 309–16.

who preached the neo-anarchist utopia of conquering political power through a political mass strike. In October 1905 Eisner and four other editors were dismissed, and a new left-wing editorial board took control of the *Vorwärts*.[12]

A month later, Kautsky argued that, at the precise moment when the bankruptcy of theoretical and political revisionism (ministerialism) had become evident,

> a new kind of revisionism arose, *trade-union revisionism*, which found its support in a part of the union bureaucracy. This revisionism preached, under the flag of neutrality, a disavowal of Social Democracy. It did not regard Social Democracy as the party of the working class, but as a party like any other – not as the party that *unites* the proletariat, but as one of the parties into which the proletariat is *divided*. Social Democracy was seen as a factor hindering the organisational union of the proletariat.[13]

At the Jena Congress of the SPD, convened in September 1905, August Bebel criticised the hostility of the trade-union leaders towards the political mass strike as dangerous 'pure-and-simple unionism [*Nurgewerkschaftlerei*]'.[14] Against the resolution of the Cologne trade-union congress, the Jena Congress adopted a resolution endorsing the use of the mass political strike in the fight for electoral and democratic rights, though, at the instance of Bebel, it was described as a defensive tactic against the expected assault of the bourgeoisie on the growing gains of the socialist movement.[15] But the union leaders rejected even this hypothetical use of the general strike, and therefore a secret conference was held on 16 February 1906, between the SPD executive and the General Commission, in which the party executive pledged itself 'to try to prevent a mass strike as much as possible'. If it should nevertheless break out, the party would assume the sole burden of leadership: the trade unions would not participate in it officially, and they agreed only 'not to stab it in the back'.

The agreement amounted to a practical annulment of the Jena congress resolution. In these circumstances, Kautsky wrote in August 1906 his major

---

[12] Salvadori 1979, pp. 96–7.
[13] Kautsky 1905g, pp. 313ff. Reprinted in Stern (ed.) 1961, vol. 4, pp. 765–6, emphasis in the original.
[14] SPD 1905, pp. 215ff. Reprinted in Grunenberg (ed.) 1970, p. 360.
[15] Kautsky 1905d, pp. 5–10. Rosa Luxemburg 1905g, pp. 595–604.

work on the relationship between the political party and the trade unions, where he argued against the political neutrality of the unions and demanded their subordination to the revolutionary leadership of the Party.[16] In his speech to the SPD congress in September 1906 at Mannheim, Kautsky compared the breach of discipline by the union functionaries (i.e. the rejection of the Jena resolution on the mass political strike by the Cologne trade union congress) with that of the French socialist members of parliament when Millerand became a minister of the bourgeois government headed by René Waldeck-Rousseau – a move that resulted in a split in French socialism and expulsion of eighteen deputies from the French socialist party. The resolution of the Mannheim Congress, again drafted by Bebel, explicitly recognised that the party executive could undertake no mass action without the approval of the unions, effectively giving them veto power over the SPD's policy.

While Kautsky and Luxemburg contended with theoretical and trade-union revisionists in Germany, Kautsky's assessment of Russia in the wake of Japan's victories provided crucial encouragement to Russian advocates of permanent revolution. During the same months when German unionists were rejecting the mass political strike, in Russia the number of new unions was rapidly growing and the strike movement was turning increasingly from economic to political demands, including abolition of the autocracy, conclusion of a peace with Japan, and fundamental changes to the country's economic system. Kautsky's support for permanent revolution lent authoritative weight and credibility to Russian Marxists such as Ryazanov, Parvus and Trotsky, who enthusiastically shared his hope that the Russian proletariat might assume international leadership in the revolutionary struggle. As Kautsky wrote,

> The Revolution in Permanence is…precisely what the workers of Russia need. It has already matured and grown enormously in strength, especially in Poland. Within a few years it could turn the Russian workers into an elite troop, perhaps into *the* élite troop of the international proletariat; a troop that will unite all the fire of youth with the experience of a praxis of world-historical struggles and the force of a dominant power in the state.

Kautsky believed, like Parvus, that the defeat of Russia by Japan was not merely revolutionising Russia but was also fundamentally transforming

---

[16] Kautsky 1906e, pp. 716–35, 749–54.

geopolitical relations. In a remarkably perceptive analysis, he anticipated a resurgence of anti-imperialist and nationalist sentiment throughout Asia, where Japanese arms had decisively punctured the illusion of Western military invincibility and set in motion new forces in China and India that would eventually shape the twentieth century.

Referring no fewer than seven times in this article to the 'Revolution in Permanence', Kautsky also repeated his conviction in the earlier article, 'Revolutionary Questions', that revolution in Russia could not fail 'to have repercussions on the rest of the European continent', beginning with Russia's 'state bankruptcy and the loss of many billions that European capital has lent to Russian absolutism in order to share in the fruits of the oppression and exploitation of the Russian people' – a premise that reappeared in Trotsky's account of the international dimension of permanent revolution in *Results and Prospects*. Kautsky's remarks on how Japan 'was able to leap over an important stage of development' by taking possession of 'the technique and knowledge of the highest stage of capitalism' likewise found a parallel in Trotsky's later formulation of 'uneven and combined development' and in his expectation that Russia might bypass the decadence of mature capitalism. In the historiography of Russian Marxism, Trotsky's work eventually became the defining treatise on permanent revolution, but the fact remains that Karl Kautsky had done much of the pioneering conceptual work in 'Revolutionary Questions' and in 'The Consequences of the Japanese Victory and Social Democracy'.

* * *

'The Consequences of the Japanese Victory and Social Democracy'

I. The revolution in Russia

Peace has not yet been made, and the peoples are still furiously attacking each other in Manchuria, yet Japan's victory must already be considered a fact. The only question that remains is how great the prize falling to Japan's lot will be – a very important question for the Japanese and especially for their ruling classes, but one of relatively minor importance for the international proletariat.

But whatever this prize for the Japanese victory turns out to be, its necessary consequences for the current stage of the emancipation struggle of the proletariat are too significant to be overestimated. Above all, the most immediate and striking consequence of this victory has been to shake Russian absolutism so deeply that it will be impossible for it to regain its balance. One can say that if a theory of *catastrophes* and collapses ever existed, here it would be celebrating its greatest triumph.[17] But the enthusiasm over this *collapse* must not lead one to forget that it would have been impossible without the untiring, slow and unnoticed work of *undermining* absolutism, which has proceeded for decades.

Nothing is less justified than separating imperceptible evolution from stormy revolution, or undermining from collapse. Both are inseparably linked together. Without undermining there is no collapse. One must not believe that the Japanese triumph alone caused the catastrophe of Russian absolutism. Many absolutist governments have suffered military disasters and have had to submit to ignominious peace conditions without having collapsed on that account. Only the army of the fighting proletariat, created by the protracted work of enlightenment and organisation, has made possible the transformation of this defeat into a catastrophe for absolutism.

But, if there is no collapse without undermining, there can also be no victory of the 'undermining' class without a collapse. Only in a violent trial of strength can it come to light how rotten the props of the ruling classes have become, how incapable they are of offering resistance to the force of the rising classes. The greatest trial of strength that a régime can undergo is a war. It is nonsense to see in war, especially given the technique of modern arms, a means of selecting the bravest individuals or even for cultivating lofty moral principles. But it certainly does constitute a powerful means for helping to clear away outdated social and state forms that are obstructing the free development of energetic and ascending classes. To that extent a war can be a means that serves social development, and the Russo-Japanese War ranks in the forefront among wars that have had such an effect.

What are the consequences of the war that will now ensue for Russia?

---

[17] [A reference to the Revisionist Controversy, in which Bernstein and his fellow revisionists accused the 'orthodox' Marxists of endorsing a theory of the collapse (*Zusammenbruchstheorie*) of capitalism.]

We must not fall into the illusions of bourgeois democrats, who, being blind to class contradictions, believe that the only thing an absolutist state needs is political freedom and that once it is achieved the revolution must be brought to a close. Political freedom has not yet been won, and the paths of the liberals and the Social Democrats are already separating. Comrade Luxemburg has rightly alluded in a recent issue of the *Sächsischen Arbeiterzeitung* to the open letter that the ex-Marxist Struve, nowadays a staunch liberal, addressed to Jaurès.[18] The distinguishing mark of this letter is the longing for a *strong régime* that will restore *order*. The greatest reproach that Struve has to make to the autocracy is to hint at the fact that it is no longer capable of restraining the popular masses, thus letting anarchy get the upper hand. This fear of 'anarchy', that is to say, of the rebellion of the lower classes of the people, is more and more becoming one of the most conspicuous characteristics of the Russian liberals. At the same time, in many cases, Russia's ostensible liberals and the socialists have as yet been so little separated – in other words, Russian liberals have so often felt themselves to be socialists – that this fear of anarchy has even found an echo in certain socialist circles.[19]

The liberals can wail for a strong régime and look forward to the growing chaos with fearful anxiety, but the revolutionary proletariat has every reason to greet it with the highest enthusiasm. That 'chaos' is nothing but the *Revolution in Permanence*. And in the current Russian conditions, revolution is the situation in which the proletariat can mature most rapidly, develop

---

[18] [Luxemburg 1905b, pp. 587–91.]

[19] Here and there that fear of anarchy has even influenced the Russian policy of the Vorwärts and elicited downright pessimistic remarks on the Russian Revolution. I have already had the opportunity of elucidating one such utterance (in the Vorwärts of February 10) in *Die Neue Zeit* (No. 21 of this year). A similar mood has recently reappeared in the reports of their correspondent in Petersburg (June 20), which overflow with 'pessimism' and 'exhaustion' and bewail' the 'chaos' 'where no trace can be found of order, law and purposeful activity … because when weariness prevails, people almost cease to hope, and without hope political thinking is dead'.

This totally incredible Jeremiad was published by the Vorwärts without a word of commentary – which was indeed unnecessary because it was immediately followed by a report on the assembly of the rebellious military officers; a report that must inspire in all real revolutionaries anything but pessimism, exhaustion and hopelessness.

Totally different and very refreshing was the impression left by a letter from Russia published by the Dortmunder Arbeiter Zeitung, which rejoiced: 'It is a pleasure to be alive.' The correspondent offered a gladdening picture of the untiring work of revolutionary struggle, organisation and enlightenment of the proletarian masses that is being currently accomplished by our comrades in Russia.

its intellectual, moral and economic forces most fully, stamp its mark most deeply on the state and society, and win from them the greatest concessions. Even if such a dominant position of the proletariat can only be temporary in a country as economically backward as Russia, it will produce enduring results that will be more extensive and profound the longer they last.

The events of the Great Revolution continue to have an effect on France to this day. If, despite the relative weakness of socialist organisations in France, the proletariat there exerts a greater power than in Germany with its three million socialist voters, that is due not at all to the ministerialist tactic [of Millerand and his revisionist supporters], and only to a very small extent to the democratic forms of the bourgeois republic, but mainly to the revolutionary instincts that continue to have an effect from the time of Jacobin rule to this day. Had things happened according to the will of liberals from time immemorial; had the revolution stopped at transforming the Estates-General into a National Assembly in order to make room for a régime of legal order; in short, had the revolution remained a 'nice' one according to bourgeois criteria, like the revolution extolled by Schiller in *Wilhelm Tell* or the one that exists in Norway to the satisfaction of all right-minded people; had the French Revolution not been 'defiled' by the 'reign of terror', then the lower classes of France would have remained totally immature and politically powerless, we would have experienced no 1848, and the emancipation struggle both of the French and of the international proletariat would have been retarded indefinitely.

The revolution in permanence is, then, precisely what the workers of Russia need. It has already matured and grown enormously in strength, especially in Poland. Within a few years it could turn the Russian workers into an élite troop, perhaps into *the* élite troop of the international proletariat; a troop that will unite all the fire of youth with the experience of a praxis of world-historical struggles and the force of a dominant power in the state.

We have every reason to expect that the Russian proletariat will arrive at the revolution in permanence or, to speak in bourgeois terms, at chaos and anarchy, rather than at the strong government for which Mr. Struve and his liberal friends are longing. Even among socialists there are some people depressed by the fact that Nicholas did not meet the revolution halfway with timely concessions, or that he was not forced to do so on 22 January [1905] by the Gapon movement. But precisely such a quick victory of the revolution would have paved the way for a strong government of liberalism. The continued existence of autocracy, on the other hand, means the beginning of the revolution in permanence. Nothing has more revolutionary effect, and nothing undermines more the foundations of all state power than the continuation of that wretched and brainless régime, which has the strength merely to cling to its positions but no longer the slightest power to rule or to steer the state ship on a definite course. The autocracy still has the strength to prevent a peace settlement, but no longer to lead a victorious war. It still has the strength to impede the establishment of a liberal government, but no longer to set limits to the spontaneous activity of the people. The autocracy itself is a source of anarchy insofar as in its desperation to hold its ground it unleashes civil wars, stirring up the lumpenproletariat in the cities and the Muslims in the Caucasus – its wildest and most unruly subjects. The autocracy hopes to defeat its opponents with these tools and does not realise that in that way it only incites the revolutionaries while at the same time driving even the most peaceful and docile citizens into the camp of its opponents. Those methods of the counter-revolution have always served only to make the revolution more determined and powerful and to bring progressively to the forefront the most ruthless among the revolutionaries. Without the revolt of the Vendée, which began in March 1793, the Mountain party would perhaps not have had the strength to overthrow the Gironde (June 1793), leading to the victory of the system of petty-bourgeois-proletarian terror.

The longer the autocracy succeeds in preventing the conclusion of an external peace and the establishment of a liberal government inside the country, the more profound must be its ultimate collapse and the more thorough must be the dissolution of all state power. And we can be certain that the tsar and his minions will mobilise everything in their power to whip the entire Russian people into the most ferocious revolution. That has become their historical mission, and everything indicates that they will accomplish it.

2. The revolutionary situation in Europe

The revolution in permanence in Russia cannot fail to have repercussions on the rest of the European continent.

Above all, it means state bankruptcy and the loss of many billions that European capital has lent to Russian absolutism in order to share in the fruits of the oppression and exploitation of the Russian people.

Sure enough, if a strong liberal government were established, one of its first concerns would be to pay faithfully the interest owing on the public debt; first of all because of the general capitalist class instinct, which makes profit and interest the holiest of holies and soiling them a mortal sin against the holy spirit; but also out of practical necessity because a strong government requires a strong army, whose reorganisation would be the first task of the new liberal régime. But that is impossible without new loans.

However, if that does not happen, if the autocracy succeeds in making a liberal régime impossible and the revolution permanent, the first consequence will be that no more taxes will be paid. Where would the resources then be found to redeem bond coupons? That is one of the reasons hindering the establishment of a strong liberal government, for its main task would be to collect taxes and impose new ones.

But it is not necessary for the dictatorship of the proletariat to come about in order to declare state bankruptcy. That is being accomplished by absolutism itself when it sees in such desperate measures a means to postpone for a while its own political bankruptcy. It is quite likely that the European capitalists will be punished together with their fellow sinners. Had they exerted their influence in a timely manner to compel the tsar to introduce a liberal régime, they could perhaps have prevented the revolution and saved their coupons. Through their unconditional support for the infamies and stupidities of the absolutist system they have fortunately prevented the establishment of the only governmental system that might have avoided state bankruptcy – a liberal government.

If bankruptcy does come, and as things stand today the odds are a hundred to one that it will indeed come, it is bound to be a crash such as the world has not yet seen; one that will make the Panama crash[20] look like child's play because the Panama crash concerned only France, particularly its petty bourgeoisie. A Russian crash will strike the entire capitalist class of Europe;

---

[20] [A reference to the bankruptcy of the Panama Company (*Compagnie du canal interocéanique*) headed by Ferdinand de Lesseps, the builder of the Suez Canal. The company collapsed in February 1889. Members of the government and of the two national chambers were charged with having taken bribes from the Panama Canal Company to withhold from the public the news that the Company was in serious debt. Approximately 1.5 billion francs were lost affecting 800,000 investors. The Panama affair was one of the major political crises of the Third Republic in France (1870–1914) and resulted in the fall of two cabinets.]

it will strike not only 'small savers' but also the great banks and, indirectly, industry as well – and where the banks and large-scale industry are closely linked, it will strike industry directly. The Panama crash involved something like a billion;[21] the Russian state debt is approximately fifteen times that sum. One has only to remember the commotion that the Panama crash caused in France, how it led that state to the brink of revolution, in order to form an idea of what must be the effects of a crash that will possibly multiply tenfold the devastations of the Panama crash and that will coincide with a savage civil war in Eastern Europe.

But the repercussions of the Russian Revolution on Western Europe will not stop there. The *state bankruptcy* will also be associated with the absence of Russian *grain exports*.

When the Russian peasant sells grain today, he does so not because he has a surplus but because he must pay *taxes*. He goes hungry, but he sells grain in order to meet the demands of the tax collector. As soon as the revolution in permanence abolishes fear of the tax officials, it will also remove the motive for selling grain. The peasant will use the impotence of the government during the revolution for once to eat his fill. Should the harvest be so abundant as to produce a surplus over his food requirements, he will surely employ it not in order to pay taxes but to buy industrial products. The grain surplus will thus go not to pay coupons abroad, but to pay wage-workers and employers in the Russian industrial districts.

If, then, a 'strong' liberal government is not established as soon as possible, a government that knows how to preserve 'order' and 'legality' among the peasantry, we must count on a sudden reduction of Russian grain exports in the coming years – perhaps even as soon as this autumn. What that will mean for the grain trade and for prices can be guessed from the fact that the share of the grain surplus provinces[22] of Russia in the grain exports of the country is from a quarter to a *third*, depending on the harvest (almost 10,000 million kilograms in 1903). Even the most favourable harvest in other export regions will not be in a position to cover a significant deficit in Russian grain exports. The consequence of this situation must be a strong rise in the price of grain, and something similar will happen to cattle prices.

---

[21] [It is not clear whether Kautsky meant a billion marks or a billion francs.]
[22] [Kautsky used the term *Staten*, which presumably refers to Russian *guberniyas*.]

That unintended rise in the cost of living will coincide in the German kingdom with the intentional, artificial rise brought about by the new protective tariff, which on its own is enough to impose an extremely heavy burden on the working classes. The new protective tariff must, however, lead to unbearable conditions if its consequences are intensified by a general rise in the cost of living in the world market and if it is implemented during a severe economic crisis.

For that reason, class antagonisms outside Russia must also sharpen to an unheard-of extent; and class struggles will be all the more violent, the more the simultaneous revolution in Russia heightens both the excitement of the lower classes and the nervousness of the ruling classes.

But the calamities will not stop there.

The military collapse of Russia has significantly shaken the European equilibrium and created the most difficult international problems. That situation more than ever demands a far-sighted, calm and purposeful foreign policy, but we can expect little from European governments in this respect. France and England are on the verge of the dissolution of their parliaments, which could bring many surprises. In Austria we have a senile Kaiser, who seems more and more to leave the reins of government in the hands of the heir to the throne, a firebrand of clericalism and personal rule. Perhaps that accounts for the struggle that the court in Vienna has just initiated against the political power of the Hungarian Junkers – a nobility even more obstinate, unruly and vigorous than the Prussian Junkers. That struggle could end as easily for the union between Hungary and Austria as the similar struggle over the union between Sweden and Norway,[23] but it will by no means occur in the same good-natured manner – and this at a time when revolution rages at the borders of Galicia and new turmoils are lurking in the Balkans.

But the German *Reich* has become the politically decisive power for the international politics of Central Europe, and it is precisely its foreign policy

---

[23] [Between 1814 and 1905 the kingdoms of Sweden and Norway were united under one monarch. Following growing dissatisfaction with the union, the Norwegian parliament unanimously declared its dissolution on 7 June, 1905. Though Sweden threatened war, a plebiscite on 13 August confirmed the parliamentary decision by a large majority. Negotiations led to agreement with Sweden and mutual demobilisation. Both parliaments revoked the Act of Union. The deposed king Oscar II of Sweden renounced his claim to the Norwegian throne and recognised Norway as an independent kingdom on 26 October, 1905.]

that has become more incomprehensible than ever. To be sure, the German government has no intention, for the sake of Morocco, of beginning a war against France without any cause; of igniting, for the sake of a trifle, a world war that must lead to the ruin of all parties concerned.[24] Such an intention would be madness or a crime. But it is precisely because the German government can relish no such intention that its foreign policy is so inexplicable – a whimsical policy of bolts from the blue that, without actually wanting war, leads its opponents to believe exactly the opposite, namely, that a war is being planned, thus engendering a state of nervous tension in which an accident can create a situation that will actually lead to war.

There has already been one instance where the Prussian government used a revolution in a neighbouring country to pursue a similar policy. When the great revolution broke out in France, Russia and Austria were at war with Turkey, and Prussia considered the moment opportune to weaken Austria and annex a new piece of Poland. The revolution in France had not yet lasted a year, and Friedrich Wilhelm II was already pushing for a war against Austria. Only the subservience of Austria, which accepted all of Prussia's demands, prevented it. But once the Polish question was raised, it now constituted a bone of contention between the three powers that by the time the revolution ended would create the Holly Alliance against France. At the beginning of the

---

[24] [Between March 1905 and May 1906 an international crisis over the colonial status of Morocco took place, known as the First Moroccan Crisis, or Tangier Crisis. It was brought about by the visit of Kaiser Wilhelm II to Tangier in Morocco on 31 March, 1905. The Kaiser made certain remarks in favour of Moroccan independence, meant as a challenge to French influence in Morocco. France had her influence in Morocco reaffirmed by Britain (by the Entente Cordiale) and Spain in 1904, a move that Germany saw as a blow to her interests and took diplomatic action to challenge. The speech turned the French public against Germany, and with British support the French foreign minister, Théophile Delcassé, took a defiant line. The crisis peaked in mid-June, when Delcassé was forced out of the ministry by the more conciliatory premier Maurice Rouvier. By July 1905, Germany was becoming isolated and the French agreed to a conference to solve the crisis. Both France and Germany continued to posture up to the conference, with Germany mobilising reserve army units in late December and France actually moving troops to the border in January 1906. The Algeciras Conference, lasting from 16 January to 7 April, 1906, was called to settle the dispute. Of the thirteen nations present, the German representatives found their only supporter was Austria-Hungary. France had firm support from Britain, Russia, Italy, Spain, and the U.S. The Germans eventually accepted an agreement in April that was signed on 31 May, 1906. France yielded certain domestic changes in Morocco but retained control of key areas. Continuing German dissatisfaction with the Moroccan situation led to a Second Moroccan Crisis in 1911 against a background of worsening international tensions that ultimately led to World War I (1914–1918).]

French Revolution, however, instead of joining together to proceed with full force against the common foe, they either did not fight at all (Russia) or only did so irresolutely (Prussia and Austria) because each of these powers feared being cheated or invaded by the others.

In that incomprehensible way, the monarchical diplomats of the time were ready, in their near-sighted avarice and stupidity, to tear each other to pieces at a moment's notice over the division of spoils when the very foundations of their rule were threatened.

But contemporary diplomacy is even more incomprehensible. Poland then had a totally different significance for Prussia than Morocco has today. Furthermore, in Prussia and Austria at the time there was no trace of a political opposition. Their governments were threatened above all from the outside, by the French revolutionary armies, not from within. The defeat of the Prussian and Austrian monarchies meant the triumph of the revolution in France, which resulted in formation of a revolutionary centre in the heart of Europe, but for a long time it still did not mean an immediate collapse of the absolutist system of government in other parts of the European continent. Since 1870, on the contrary, each inauspicious war means an internal revolution for a European state.

A Moroccan adventure is also not to be expected right now because the German government, for the time being, is able to overcome without considerable frictions the international difficulties that the collapse of Russia must inevitably have as a consequence.

Everything indicates that we face an epoch of the greatest intensification of contradictions between states and classes; an epoch in which the revolutionising of neighbouring countries can create, without any assistance from particular persons or parties, revolutionary situations in Western Europe itself.

3. The mood in German Social Democracy: a critical intermezzo

Already at this stage, the conditions described in the last article have influenced wide party circles and, above all, those who can see beyond the customary traditions and local boundaries of the 'fatherland'. That explains why interest in the idea of the political mass strike, which two years ago had a purely academic interest for our party, has grown exponentially.

Bömelburg[25] argued in Cologne that the more he considered the idea of the general strike, the more he became convinced that it is a question of the *revolution*: it can result in nothing but a revolution. That is not entirely true, as the examples of Belgium, Sweden, Holland and Italy show. The mass strike does not necessarily mean the revolution. It is a means of political pressure, of political force, which in different political situations and conditions can signify very different things. But one thing is true: in the *special political conditions* of Germany, a successful general strike is only conceivable in a revolutionary situation, and it would be hopeless, indeed ruinous, to attempt to employ it in a situation that cannot become a revolutionary one. For instance, it would be the greatest piece of folly to declare a general strike in Hamburg in defence of the local electoral law, to employ the mass strike – the ultimate and sharpest weapon of the proletariat, which demands its most complete devotion and its highest spirit of sacrifice – in a single city, merely in order to defend a quite miserable, local class suffrage law from further deterioration!

But even if the national electoral law were to be abolished, one should consider carefully whether to respond with the mass strike without more ado; that would depend entirely on the situation. If we consider it necessary to discuss the mass strike and to make the proletarian masses thoroughly familiar with its employment, it is because we also expect revolutionary situations in Germany that make the mass strike necessary as well as possible. To be sure, a deterioration of the electoral law for the Reichstag could contribute mightily to produce such a situation, and *to that extent* would be a provocation for a mass strike. But we also think it is no less necessary to discuss it precisely because it is not applicable everywhere and at all times, and its employment under the wrong circumstances could cause great harm.

We must reckon with the possibility that the situation in the most diverse countries outside Germany might turn out to be such as to make a mass strike both possible and necessary, and that this success might mislead us to attempt to apply it to Germany without further ado but in conditions that will preclude its success. People have already talked about its proclamation in Hamburg in order to defend the present franchise, as well as in Prussia and

---

[25] [Theodor Bömelburg was president of the construction workers' union and a forceful opponent of the mass political strike at the fifth congress of the Free Trade Unions, held in Cologne in May 1905.]

Saxony to overturn their class franchise. If we do not study the conditions and methods of the mass strike, we run the risk not only of not applying it where these conditions are favourable, but also of applying it where its application would be ruinous. Whoever despises theory and trusts in the superiority of practice over theoretical study must always pay dearly for his or her experience.

Nonetheless, our central organ, *Vorwärts*, continues by all means to forbid discussion of the mass strike in order to preserve harmony between the Party and the trade unions. It has said as much in its articles on the trade-union congress. When I criticised its odd standpoint in my introduction to the book by our comrade Roland-Holst on the general strike,[26] *Vorwärts* complained that I had wronged it and falsely represented its arguments. But it has failed to convince me of my mistake, and I see no reason to take back a single word of what I wrote there against *Vorwärts*.

Since then *Vorwärts* has aired the same views again in a detailed criticism of the book under consideration, using other arguments that appear to us no better than the previous ones.

Vorwärts has not even understood Roland-Holst's book. For instance, *Vorwärts* reproaches it with turning the political strike 'from an act of proletarian self-defence, whose application is possible and necessary only under very definite circumstances, into a *method of the class struggle*, into the true means for a proletarian victory'.

In Roland-Holst's book it is explicitly stated:

> It [Social Democracy] sees in the political mass strike not an antithesis, but a supplement to its hitherto existing means and methods; a supplement that is forced upon the working class in the course of and as a result of social evolution – including its own growth in strength and self-consciousness – as an historical product of the class struggles. Above all no contradiction separates the political mass strike from parliamentarism. Parliamentarism remains a very appropriate, perhaps indispensable means to educate the masses about the barbaric character of the present state, to awaken them from their dull indifference, to lead the proletarian emancipation struggle,

---

[26] [Roland-Holst 1905. Kautsky's introduction to this book was reprinted as an article under the title 'Ein Buch über den Generalstreik', Kautsky 1906c. The main passages appear in Stern (ed.) 1961, vol. 3, pp. 331–4.]

to wring reforms from the bourgeois parties, to drive them forward and to exploit their differences. It remains the only means to organise the entire proletariat against the entire ruling class and, irresistibly and inexorably, to lead it in the battlefield. The political mass strike, *which is only applicable in rare, definite historical situations*, cannot make parliamentarism superfluous, either totally or partially. It cannot under any circumstances replace it, as the extreme Left of the French and Italian parties argues – true, as a reaction to the parliamentary illusions of recent years. But it will in all probability be used as a means to make possible the parliamentary action of the proletariat, to defend and to broaden it, etc.

Those are the words of comrade Holst, whose book is by far the most important socialist publication of recent years on a tactical question that, in turn, is the most significant of all the tactical questions of our period. However, our central party organ criticises it without even understanding what it says.

This misunderstanding is the only thing *Vorwärts* is able to adduce in order to reject the method and conclusions of the book. Whatever it has to say on the subject beyond that consists of arguing that the entire discussion over the mass strike is superfluous. According to *Vorwärts*, there is a danger that

> ardent study and discussion of such questions will awaken in the imagination of the workers vague hopes that will divert their attention from important and more pressing tasks – not to mention the fact that abundant talk and threats about revolution are more suitable for strengthening reactionary efforts against Social Democracy than for strengthening the determination of the working masses [etc.].

Then: 'The leading principle of Social-Democratic tactics is and remains the revolutionising of minds.' And further: in exceptional circumstances 'all methods of self-defence are justified, not only the mass strike'. Moreover: 'In each land the situation is unique.' And finally: 'We would like fewer words and more vigorous action.'

The whole protracted litany, of which we can only give extracts here, reminds one of the sayings of Sancho Panza to Don Quixote; when he wanted to appear wise, he spouted a heap of proverbs that were beyond dispute but had nothing to do with the subject under discussion or could just as well have been applied to any other occasion.

There is, in fact, no great tactical question in the Party, not to speak of questions about the final aim, whose discussion one could not reject with such a concoction of commonplaces.

These wretched tirades are all that our central organ has hitherto deigned to contribute to the discussion on the mass strike. No wonder it finds the question uncomfortable. The incapacity of *Vorwärts* to serve in its present form as the leading organ of the Party in its internal questions has never appeared so clearly as in this connection. Naturally, by leading organ, one should not understand a bossing one, but rather one that, through the depth and weight of its arguments, through its knowledge and experience, is able to command universal respect and recognition.

Fortunately, in its aversion to 'the study and discussion of such questions', *Vorwärts* stands pretty much alone in the Party. As far as one can judge from the rest of the party press, apart from the editors of our central organ, there are only a few party comrades who share with it the rather Cossack notion that such 'study and discussion' will just inflame an unhealthy imagination among the workers and turn them away from useful activity. Almost the entire party press has shown more interest in and more understanding of the discussion on the mass strike than our central organ, so that *Vorwärts'* lack of understanding cannot be ascribed to the Party.

Besides the rapidly growing interest in and understanding of the political mass strike during the last two years, there is another remarkable phenomenon: the growing disdain for parliamentarism among the proletariat, which makes itself felt in all countries, including Germany. A symptom of that phenomenon seems to be our decline in votes during the by-elections for the Reichstag.

Many people like to attribute this decline to the Dresden party convention,[27] for instance Mr. Gerlach in his recent article 'The Social Democracy since Dresden', which appeared in the *Nation*. In a certain sense they are right, only in a way different from the one they mean and not because, as Mr. Gerlach writes, the manners there were 'so abusive, the struggle so purely

---

[27] [*Dresden Parteitag* – the Dresden Congress of the German Social-Democratic Party, held on 13–20 September, 1903. After discussing whether to co-operate with the Liberals in the Reichstag, the Dresden Congress denounced Bernstein's 'revisionist efforts...to supplant the policy of a conquest of power by overcoming our enemies with a policy of accommodation to the existing order' and rejected SPD participation in any capitalist government.]

personal'. If that were true, it would apply much less to the 'radicals' than to their opponents. But Mr. Gerlach himself does not stress that point, perhaps because the Dresden party convention disappointed wide circles.

> On June 16, [1903] [says Mr. Gerlach], the Social Democratic party seemed to be the most powerful socialist party in the world as well as the strongest party in Germany. 'The empire is ours, the world is ours!' proclaimed the *Vorwärts* in an ecstasy of triumphalism.

But what happened? Nothing. Everything remained as before. No new route was followed in Dresden. No doubt many people must have felt disappointed; and the more so, the greater the expectations they attached to the three-million-votes victory[28] – as if, as a result of it, the world laid open before us and we needed only to agree on how best to help ourselves to it. But these expectations were only the illusions of naïve souls, and they by no means held sway over the party. I must quote, as the example nearest to hand of more sober views, the words I wrote in *Die Neue Zeit* immediately after the great victory and even before the second ballot:

> If we consider all the contradictions and antagonisms within the government as well as within the ruling classes and parties, there can be no doubt that today, when our opponents more than ever need a united and consequential policy, one that sets major goals, the policy that they will actually follow will be more petty, contradictory and confused than ever before. We may hear big words and see great gestures of adopting a policy of reforms as well as of curtailing civil liberties and rights, but one does not get very far by means of resounding promises and threats. They will be followed by no actions and at most by spasmodic convulsions that can be very violent but will be overcome quickly. If concessions are made to the proletariat, their fulfilment will be so inferior to the promises that far from satisfying it even temporarily, they will rather embitter and infuriate it, just as threats and insults followed by no action can have no intimidating effect.

---

[28] [The Reichstag elections held on 16 June, 1903, resulted in significant gains for the SPD. It received 3.010.771 votes (23.3 per cent of the total) and 81 seats in parliament.]

Numerous other voices in our party expressed themselves similarly.

One can see that there is no reason to reproach the entire Social Democracy with triumphalism. Indeed, we recognised all the possible consequences that the three-million-votes victory could have even *before* the Dresden party convention.

But it is obvious that many of the 'triumphalists' expected more and became disappointed. Then our victory had the effect of whipping up our opponents, so that they charged against us more forcefully during the by-elections while the working masses did not react to this greater pressure with a greater counter-pressure and with increased enthusiasm.

That is surely not pleasant, but the Party could only be reproached for that outcome if it had the power to turn the three-million-votes victory into 'positive' results and neglected to do so. That was asserted by many critics.[29]

---

[29] *Vorwärts* also seems to endorse this view; more precisely, the majority of its editors – to whom alone what we have been saying on the *Vorwärts* in this article applies. Statements to this effect had already appeared when the leading article of *Vorwärts* about 'The Agenda of the Party Conference' appeared on July 6, in which the same tune is sung that Mr. Gerlach had formerly sung. The article points out that 'we (the editors) have insistently bemoaned the fact that the party conference was prevented by its own agenda from taking into account the great political opportunity opened by the imposing electoral victory of June 16'. By doing that the party had 'to a not insignificant degree given up the opportunity of immediately influencing the political life of Germany'.

This opinion would make absolutely no sense if *Vorwärts* were not of the opinion that another, more 'positive' arrangement of the agenda would have enabled us to draw practical results from the electoral victory, because it cannot be said that the Dresden party conference ignored the electoral victory in the Reichstag. Point 4 of the agenda reads: 'Tactic of the Party: Elections to the Reichstag, Vice-presidential Question, The Revisionist Endeavours'.

True, such tactical discussions do not suit *Vorwärts*. Its article has the tendency to shape the party conference like a propagandistic show along bourgeois lines; a show in which there is no discussion about the questions over which we disagree, but only concerning those questions about which we are in agreement, like the ten-hour working day, the struggle against militarism and the naval armaments race [*Marinismus*], etc.

The propagandistic handling of such questions is above all the task of the Reichstag fraction, which would be a superfluous adornment if it were not sufficient to handle that task. The party conference, on the other hand, should be the most powerful means for the *further development* of the party; it should decide all the controversial questions that are discussed in the party and over which there are divergent views. The spiritual advance of the party would be totally checked if it were not willing to discuss such questions from time to time, but on the other hand their endless discussion would lead to the disintegration of the party. The task of the party conference is both to ensure the free discussion of these questions and, after all the arguments have been exhausted, to determine what the majority of the party thinks about them, thus bringing the discussion to an end.

But just how could those 'positive' results have been won? By meeting the government halfway, by attempting to trade concessions? Such a wish, had it been entertained, would certainly have been nipped in the bud in Dresden, and rightly so.

If ever a situation was favourable to socialist ministerialism, it was the Dreyfus trial in France. It really required great clarity and strength of character to avoid that trap. Today, socialist ministerialism is also dead and buried in France. But, in Germany, there was from the outset not the slightest possibility of applying that policy; only political children and tomfools could have believed the opposite. In Germany, there can only be differences concerning the *tone* and the theoretical *foundation* of our opposition, but not concerning the *praxis*. In Germany, more than anywhere else, nothing can be expected from the government or from the majority in parliament. That is a fact that cannot be altered even by the three-million-votes victory.

On the contrary, the three-million-votes victory only gave it clearer expression. It has shown to the ruling classes the dangers that general and equal suffrage holds for them, but it was still not powerful enough to let the water reach their throats and force them to assume the no less imposing danger of directly abolishing the franchise. It was, however, a powerful motive to make the *product* of the general and equal suffrage, the *Reichstag*, even more impotent than it has been so far. Never were all the important subjects shifted to the Landtags [state parliaments] more than at present; never was the Reichstag treated with more contempt than at present – with the consent of its majority, including the Centre.

In that way an attempt is being made to undermine the general and equal suffrage, whose open abolition is still feared, by turning it into a corpse devoid of all life and significance.

To what extent a party conference also has the possibility of dealing with questions about which we are in agreement, i.e. to include them in the agenda for purely propagandistic purposes, depends on the extent and importance of the differences of opinion in our midst.

But precisely in the present revolutionary situation there is no question of greater importance for us than the mass strike. *Vorwärts* can consider it no more important than other controversial questions of the latest period, in which it only sees petty personal frictions, but the conference surely gave a more accurate expression to the feelings of the mass of our party comrades when it drafted its agenda.

The necessary reaction to this cunning policy is the growing indifference of the working masses towards the Reichstag and the Reichstag elections. They are increasingly doubtful about reaching anything substantial by that route. *Hence our electoral decline.*

But if someone were to infer from that growing impotence of the Reichstag the impotence of Social Democracy, and from our decline in votes at the by-elections a decline in the influence of our party on the people, he would be very much deceived. Luckily, we have another criterion to measure the extent of that influence besides the elections to the Reichstag – namely, *the circulation of our press.* No press carries its party character so decidedly on its masthead as the Social-Democratic press, and none has to wage a more difficult struggle against competition from the non-party press, for no press is and must be freer from unscrupulously speculating on the craving for sensation of the indifferent masses. Whoever reads a Social-Democratic publication evinces an interest in and sympathy for the ideology and tactics of Social Democracy. It is therefore remarkable that, despite the electoral decline in the by-elections, the number of readers of our party press is growing constantly and swiftly. The Dresden party convention did not bring about the slightest change in this respect.

The simultaneous growth of the trade-union organisations is also remarkable.

It clearly shows that in the current situation the working masses regard the press and the unions as more effective weapons for their emancipation struggle than the Reichstag elections. The bourgeois parties testify to their complete near-sightedness when they celebrate this development. The influence of Social Democracy on the working people does not shrink because of it. That would only be possible if the political interest of the proletariat had declined, or if another party had arisen next to Social Democracy that would be better able, or might appear to be better able, to look after proletarian interests than we are. Clearly that is not the case.

The indifference vis-à-vis the Reichstag elections will disappear the moment the Reichstag becomes the centre of a great political action. But if the Reichstag government and the Reichstag majority are able to prevent that, and if they continue to turn the Reichstag into an even greater nullity, that would only provide further impetus for the revolutionary mood that the Russian Revolution and its consequences must already have awakened in the German proletariat in any case.

The interest in politics and legislation will not be lessened but rather strengthened in that event, because the effects that the laws and the authorities have on economic life, and therefore on the proletarian movement, will then become more evident. But this political interest must turn all the more decidedly away from *electoral participation* the more ineffectual the elections are made to become; it will turn more and more to methods and actions that seem capable of influencing the legislative machinery *from outside* and of reorganising it in such a way as to turn it into a suitable tool for the proletarian emancipation struggle. Those who undermine the franchise or the significance of the Reichstag are, therefore, carrying grist to the mill of those who see in the mass strike a means to revive its atrophied power, a means to give new and greater powers to the Reichstag and to infuse it with the will and the strength to pass legislation truly favourable to the proletariat. The German proletariat will no more let itself be cheated out of the advantages of the general and equal suffrage than it will let itself be openly deprived of it.

4. East Asia and America

We will now turn from the nearest to the most far-off areas.

It is clear that the Japanese victory must have the greatest influence on Japan itself. Here, we can deal with that subject briefly because the war will not change the direction and nature of its development but only accelerate its tempo. Many important specific phenomena might result from it, but only a person with an intimate knowledge of the land and its people could judge them. In general, though, it can be said that the country will develop the capitalist mode of production in its own peculiar way even more than before. The distinguishing mark of Japan, and the root of its power, is that the country was able to leap over an important stage of development: the decadence of feudalism. Even if Japanese feudalism is in decline as a result of the development of the capitalist mode of production, it is still far from producing such rottenness as it did in Western Europe in the seventeenth and eighteenth centuries. With a people not yet enervated and corrupted by centuries of feudal decadence and primitive accumulation of capital, a people that stood at approximately the same level as the men of the Renaissance, Japan took possession of the technique and knowledge of the highest stage of capitalism. It combined the knightly energy and Spartan frugality of feudalism not only with all the strength of modern productive and military technology, but also with all the drive for expansion and all the revolutionary unrest of modern capitalism.[30]

This peculiar and perhaps most powerful of the different manifestations of capitalism in the twentieth century will receive through the present victory increased capital and a greatly expanded field of exploitation. If, as it is apparently the case, Russia is not in a position to pay war indemnities, the territory occupied by Japan will be all the greater, and the section of the Manchurian railroad – whose construction cost Russia approximately a billion marks – falling to its lot will be all the larger. And new capital sums will also flow into the new, rapidly growing great power through loans, which will be much more profitably employed than the countless billions pumped out of Europe by Russia.

But Japanese socialism must also develop alongside Japanese capitalism, and we must assume that it will show the same energy and drive for expansion as the entire Japanese nation, though, of course, in a totally different way and in fields far removed from those of the ruling classes. The peculiarities of its socialism will be commensurate with those of its capitalism; but, just as in the case of its capitalism, its socialism will take its tools from Europe and the United States. The more Japan becomes involved in world intercourse through its economic development, the more Japanese socialism will acquire an international character, despite all Japan's peculiarities.[31]

China will be influenced by this victory perhaps even more than Japan. There, it will bring about a complete revolution in the current situation and deliver the *coup de grâce* to the seclusion policy.

China is a land secluded from the rest of the world by nature. Its eastern border is an ocean, which, until recently, was used only to export to, but not to import from, the world market. Its coast, especially north of the Yangtze River, has few good deep-water harbours. To the south, the country is surrounded by almost impenetrable mountains and wildernesses. Its northern border is a scarcely populated area, while its western one consists of deserts that to a large extent protected China from the invasions and migrations of great masses of

---

[30] On this subject see the interesting observations of comrade Beer 1905, pp. 419ff.

[31] [On this subject see Katayama 1918.]

people. Even though they were repeatedly disturbed by predatory nomads, the people of China were generally able to dedicate themselves entirely to agriculture in the fertile river plains without a real warrior caste, a feudal aristocracy, coming into being and holding sway over the peasants in the long run. When such a social stratum appeared, it soon decayed due to the lack of military practice. The settled peasant is rendered pacific by his occupation. He refuses admittance to foreigners, whose presence generally frightens him. The peasant lacks the daring, the restlessness and the recklessness of the hunter, the nomadic shepherd and the sailor. Without proper training, he constitutes a bad soldier. But the peasants can only get that training, as well as an inspiring model in warfare, where a strong and active military nobility lives alongside them. That, however, was lacking in China. Its aristocracy is composed of aristocrats, not warriors.

Thus, when the Europeans reached the country from the sea, China, despite all its riches, was alarmed by their presence and saw its best defence in artificially maintaining the seclusion imposed upon it by nature. But, although the growing power of the Europeans was increasingly making a breach in the system, the Chinese authorities continued with their helpless and inadequate method of stubborn, passive resistance because they felt incapable of undertaking any active resistance. To be sure, they were forced by the continuous advance of the Europeans to borrow their weapons, but they lacked the military personnel without whom the best weapons are useless. China was the loser in every violent clash, which in turn strengthened the policy of passive resistance. But it was clear that this policy could not be successful in the long run because it only masked the weakness and lack of resistance in the country. Thus China appeared as an easy prey of the European powers; a victim whose life was only spared because the European powers were unable to reach an agreement about division of the booty.

This condition must now come to an end. Japan has delivered such a blow to Russia, the most dangerous enemy of China, that Russia's inclination to continue its policy of conquest in East Asia must recede for a long time. Moreover, Japan has proved that the Europeans are not invincible. It has also clearly shown that they can be overcome, not through isolation but by zealously adopting their best creations. If modern technique and modern science have until now penetrated only painstakingly in China, if they were only endured unwillingly and averted whenever possible, Japan's example will now serve as a model and the Japanese themselves will become the teachers not only in *science* and *technique*, which the Chinese can learn directly from the Europeans, but also and especially in *military affairs*. What China lacks, Japan has in abundance: a chivalric gentry that is excellently suited to lead in war as well as being both able and willing to drill the peaceful Chinese peasants in the murder trade.

As the *Independent Magazine* in America reports (quoted in the London *Social Democrat* of June 15, 1905), it is significant that of the 1,100 books that were printed in China during the last year – mostly translations from European languages to Chinese – no fewer than 120 dealt with military affairs.

But the strengthening of China will follow not only from that but also from the invigoration its national spirit has experienced as a result of the Japanese victory.

The hitherto existing mode of production in China – the preponderance of agriculture and of simple commodity production in the cities – is not favourable to the development of national thinking and a national feeling that would encompass the whole expanse of the nation. Each village is an organism in itself; the cities have only few connections with each other; the provinces constitute almost independent states. One should remember that the Chinese kingdom has as many inhabitants as the whole of Europe. The provinces are linked to the central power by little more than the payment of tribute. True, the central power rules absolutely, but it has few opportunities to interfere with the life of the people. Its most important economic function up to now was maintenance of the hydraulic engineering works, of the dams and canals that are indispensable for the continuation of agriculture in the flood plains, for protection against floods, for the irrigation of arable lands, and for the transportation of heavy loads. The construction and repair of those works exceeded the capacities of isolated communities.

There are few other affairs common to the entire kingdom. Even the wars that China conducted, or rather that were inflicted upon her, always affected only individual provinces and produced no profound effects beyond their boundaries.

Nevertheless, the germs of a national spirit have already begun to develop and have been strengthened mightily in the last years, when the danger of a partition of China by the Europeans assumed tangible forms – namely, when

Russia 'leased' Manchuria and Germany 'leased' Kiautschou [Jiaozhou].[32] The Hun campaign [*Hunnenfeldzug*] made a no less profound impression, but one entirely different from the one expected.[33] And the Japanese victory over the Russian intruders has finally excited the whole of China.

The economic relations guarantee that it will not be a passing enthusiasm. The construction of railways and telegraphs, as well as the upgrading of the postal traffic, until now carried on reluctantly and unwillingly, must assume a quick tempo under the impulse of Japan. That will bring all parts of the kingdom into intimate connection with each other and provide a solid economic foundation for a national consciousness and for a common interest in the affairs of the entire country.

The above-quoted *Independent Magazine* reports that a few years ago only 7 periodicals existed in China; today there are 157. The national postal system, which Sir Robert Hart organised recently, has 1,192 post offices. In 1903 it delivered 40 million postal packages, in 1904 already 72 million.

So the enormous area is being increasingly welded together into a united kingdom whose 400 million inhabitants will soon be sufficiently united and equipped to ward off any European attack and to expel any intruder. When that happens, any partition of China will be impossible.

Now Japan has the power to ensure that China remains unmolested until it strengthens to that extent. And it will also have the will to do so, because, at least for the foreseeable future, Japan's interests run parallel to China's. They have the same enemies and the same interest in not allowing any European power to gain a firm footing in China. Finally, due to its geographical position and its cultural kinship, Japan must increasingly play the central role in the work of China's economic and military reorganisation, the more so as

---

[32] [Jiaozhou Bay, on the southern coast of Shandong Peninsula, was a German colony from 1898 to 1914. See Kautsky 1898, pp. 14–26.]

[33] [In 1899 the anti-imperialist Boxer rebellion broke out in the North of China. On 27 July, 1900, Kaiser Wilhelm II took leave of the soldiers of the China expedition in Bremerhaven with a chauvinist diatribe, known as the 'Hun speech', in which he called upon them to repress the Chinese with the utmost brutality and to take no prisoners. The Boxer rebellion was finally crushed by the united armies of eight imperialist states under the leadership of a German General, Count von Aldersee. China was forced to pay extortionate war reparations and to grant territory for military bases to the intervention armies.]

European influences are excluded. Japan's industry will profit most from the 'Open Door' policy in China.[34]

The Japanese victory, therefore, probably saved not only Japan's industry but even China itself. It also made impossible any continuation of the expansionist policy by the capitalist nations of the white race. China was the last great area that seemed still open to division. If its partition has become impossible, then the entire world has already been divided up and no capitalist nation can expand by any means other than at the expense of its confrères. Accordingly, a new epoch in world history also begins in that respect.

Naturally, the sudden expansion of the area of exploitation for Japanese capitalism, and the improvement and enlargement of China's military power and communication system, cannot take place without widening the market for the whole of international capitalism. It is widely expected that the conclusion of the peace will bring a new era of prosperity, a new boom. But it seems that people should not set their expectations so high, especially in France and Germany.

To be sure, if it were possible to set up a powerful liberal régime in place of the permanent tumult now reigning in Russia, a régime capable of bringing order into the state finances without declaring bankruptcy, foreign industry would then be called upon quite extensively, and especially in order to refurnish the army and create a new navy. In that case the trusted supporters in distress, who have rendered so many favours to tsarism, would be considered in the first place [as suppliers]. But there can be no talk of such purchases at the moment, when the anarchy in Russia continues unabated.

From Japan and China, on the other hand, Germany and France have nothing to expect precisely because of the help they gave to Russia during the war. And Kiautschou remains a thorn in China's flesh that continues to incite it against Germany. Those little places in the sun [i.e. the 'concessions'] are the reason that German industry will make no inroads into East Asia until China is strong enough to show the door to the 'leaseholders' in its own territory.

---

[34] [On 6 September, 1899, US Secretary of State John Hay dispatched the first of his Open Door notes to Great Britain, Germany, France, Italy, Japan, and Russia – the powers that had partitioned China into 'spheres of influence' – asking them to declare formally that they would 'uphold Chinese territorial and administrative integrity' and guarantee equal trading rights for all nations. The American diplomatic move elicited no immediate response.]

The lion's share of the new prosperity will, in any case, fall to the lot of the United States, which through its geographical position as well as its clever policy has come closest to the East-Asian market. At the same time, however, a special aspect of the labour question will become particularly urgent for America, namely, Chinese immigration.

In each land the capitalist mode of production begins by expropriating through different methods a part of the agricultural population, thus creating a great army of the unemployed who are only slowly and never fully absorbed by the growing industry but who, until a strong capitalist industry comes into existence, constitute not only a reserve army of wage-workers but also a social stratum that can only choose between emigration and begging or stealing. People will have recourse to one or the other option according to the situation of the neighbouring countries and the extent of the traffic system.

America, with its still numerous uncultivated lands and its strong industry, is the Eldorado of all those elements. The surplus population of all nations prefers to emigrate there, and so do the Chinese. Their influx must inevitably grow, the more the railways penetrate into the Chinese interior and the more active becomes the shipping traffic between China and the United States.

The Australian and American workers, short-sighted and unprincipled 'pure and simple' trade unionists [*Nurgewerkschaftler*], have until now been able to protect themselves from the competition of low-wage workers of the yellow races by simply prohibiting their immigration. But this policy of exclusion must now come to an end. Japan, the new great power, will not patiently suffer its citizens being treated as belonging to a lower category than those of other countries; and China, too, does not seem to be willing much longer to put up with the exclusion of its sons. Sure enough, it cannot enforce their admission through the power of its cannons, but its market is so extensive that it is quite capable of exerting pressure in the sense of threatening its closure. It is very doubtful that the capitalists of the United States will be willing to harm their sales in China merely in order to keep low-wage elements away from their country.

In that way, the Chinese question can become an important object of dispute between American workers and capitalists and a cause of deepening contradictions between them. But the position of Social Democracy in America will at first surely not be made easier by that fact. American Social Democracy will find itself in a difficult dilemma between defending the interests of the

American wage-workers and those of international solidarity. It goes without saying that it has every right to thwart any immigration of *unfree* workers, whether indebted peons or contract workers. But it is just as clearly forbidden by the principle of international solidarity from preventing the workers of any nationality, when they are free men, from enjoying freedom of movement. However the struggles may develop, they will result in making American workers understand that any exclusionary policy is a futile defence and that their welfare lies in the progress of international socialism – which in this case means that the organisation and socialist education of the Japanese and Chinese in America as well as in East Asia must be recognised as one of the most important tasks of the American labour movement and must be promoted accordingly.

5. India and England

In addition to Japan and China, there is yet another enormous region that will be revolutionised by the Japanese victory, and perhaps even more than the Middle Kingdom – namely, India with its 300 million inhabitants.

Like China, India was also weak up to now due to the lack of a uniform national consciousness. The same mode of production as in China turned each Indian village community into a world unto itself that did not care about the rest of the world. But, whereas in China at least a common language, religion and literature are ties that bind the entire nation and considerably facilitate the rise of a uniform national feeling, that commonality is lacking in India. Much more easily accessible to foreign conquerors, from time to time it has seen mass invasions of alien peoples that have not always blended completely with the earlier inhabitants. In this manner, there has developed in the huge area, over the course of the millennia, a motley array of the most different peoples, languages, religions and castes that are not only alien to one another but often directly hostile. That is one of the strongest roots of the absolute régime that the English have established in India, which also rests upon the belief, confirmed by so many defeats in wars and rebellions, in the invincibility of European military strategy.

That belief was brought to an end by the brilliant military feat of Japan; by its victory over an enemy that the masters of India themselves feared so much that they made one concession after the other to it and let it reach the gates of their empire unopposed. Japan's military victories have not only boosted the self-confidence of the Asiatic peoples; they have also given rise to a sort of Asian national feeling that, if it has not completely superseded the old clan and tribal loyalties [*Stammesgefühle*], has caused them to recede to the point where a common action against the common enemy has been considerably facilitated.[35]

In recent days an article was published in our party press on 'The Awakening of Asia' that reports some very remarkable facts. It points out that people in India have begun to learn Japanese in high schools, that Indian students no longer go to England in order to study but to Japan, and that Japan is being held up as a model for all things in India. Similar events have been reported elsewhere. Among others, comrade Hyndman, who has an intimate knowledge of Indian affairs, has pointed out that under the influence of the Japanese victory, the self-assurance of the Indian population and its oppositional disposition against England have grown quickly. That oppositional mood can spread rapidly in India with its good communication system, its freedom of association and assembly, and its well-developed press; and just how easily the opposition can unite members of the most different nationalities against an unbearable oppression, even when freedom of the press and of assembly are lacking, is presently shown most convincingly by Russia.

The defeat of Russia can encourage growth of an Indian opposition to British rule in yet another way. As long as a strong, aggressive Russia lurked

---

[35] [In 1922 Karl Radek came to exactly the conclusions that Kautsky reached as early as 1905. In a commentary on the Versailles Treaty Radek wrote:

> When in 1905, Tsarist Russia was beaten by young Japanese Imperialism, an exultation caught hold of the various sections of the yellow race, who were regarded as a sort of human manure, but who desired to be regarded as a part of mankind. Their exultation sprang from the fact that the victory of military, semi-feudal and capitalist Japan over the Tsarist government was a victory of the yellow man over the white 'superman'. This victory was the starting point of the revolutionary movement in China, where, after the victory of the Japanese, a 300 million population said, 'I shall likewise be victorious.' It gave a new impetus to the revolutionary movement of India, where over 300 million people are striving for freedom. From that victory sprang the revolutionary surge, the waves of which are rolling forth and before they reach the shore, are increased and strengthened by the rising waves behind them. (See Radek, 1922 (Part 2), IV.)]

at India's borders, any energetic movement against the English régime ran the risk of furthering Russia's plans. No matter how oppressive the British administration could appear to be, it was still better than the Russian. The Indians would have leaped out of the frying pan into the fire if they had exchanged the British for the Russian yoke. Those considerations must have held back the most intelligent and far-sighted Indians from sponsoring a movement that could weaken England's position.

Today, after Russia's defeat, those fears have largely disappeared. To weaken England's hold on India no longer means to abet Russia's inroads there. There has already been one occasion when similar considerations cost England a colony. As long as the French possessed a large colonial empire in America close to the boundaries of the English colonies and threatening their independence with its advance, the English colonies abounded with the greatest loyalty to the motherland that protected them and whose suzerainty they preferred to the régime of soldiers, bureaucrats and Jesuits of French absolutism. But when France was defeated and had to renounce its colonial possession in the Paris peace treaty, a spirit of independence and rebelliousness against the motherland began to make itself felt immediately in the English colonies, which no longer needed its protection. It took only a few years for them to declare war on the mother country and to break away from it. The Paris peace was concluded in 1763, and already in 1773 there broke out in Boston the rebellion that began the War of Independence, which concluded ten years later, in 1783, with British recognition of the United States.

Naturally, it is not to be expected that in India the stimulating effects of the Japanese war will manifest themselves immediately in an independence movement, but they must strengthen and considerably intensify the opposition to the existing régime. That can have consequences of two kinds [on British policy in India]: either an attempt to crush the opposition by force, which must lend to the movement a more rebellious character than ever, or else an attempt to disarm it with concessions, by which means England can, to be sure, secure the possession of India for a long time, but only by renouncing the rich booty that it has been pulling out of the country year after year. The overall tendencies of English colonial policy and of English politics in general point to the latter method. But one must not forget that the Englishmen as a rule employ the method of concessions only where they have little to gain by using the opposite policy. It is the method of the calculating merchant. But no matter how much England may be ready to play that role, or to what extent it may be willing to bargain and accommodate the customers, it is pitiless, brutal and cruel wherever great profits are at stake. England has recently proved that in South Africa.[36]

But India is a matter of much greater consequence than South Africa. It is today the only great old-style colony.[37] The colonies of other countries are all very costly, and the other English colonies yield no significant income. But all of them, English and non-English, import capital rather than export it, whereas British India is a remnant from that period when colonies were means for the primitive accumulation of capital. They exported capital, or rather yielded riches through compulsory taxation that could be turned into capital and thus greatly increased the capital accumulation of the metropolis. Even today an enormous wealth flows yearly from India to Great Britain. In his book on India, Dadabhai Naoroji calculated it at 600 million marks.[38] In an article published in *Justice* on June 24, 1905, it was estimated at 700 million (more than 34 million pounds sterling) per year.

India has been plundered by England for centuries. At first only the treasure chambers of the great lords were emptied, and that much the country was able to bear. But the more they were emptied, the more the looting of the poor people through taxation came to the foreground; and this kind of plunder became more and more visible and ruinous. Its amount has *multiplied tenfold* in the last hundred years. That means a pauperisation of the popular masses and a crippling of the central branch of production, agriculture, to no less extent than in Russia. In both places, the spectre of famine is a permanent visitor, and overthrow of the system has become a question of life and death.

But it is a question of life and death not only for India but also, even if in another sense, for the ruling classes of England. One of the pillars of their

---

[36] [A reference to the Boer War of 1899–1902.]

[37] [On this subject see Kautsky 1975, Chapter V: Old Style Exploitation Colonies.]

[38] Naoroji 1901. [Dadabhai Naoroji (1825–1917), the son of a Parsee Priest, was born in Bombay. He was a Professor of Mathematics and Natural Philosophy at Elphinstone Institute. In 1886 Naoroji was elected President of the Indian National Congress. He then moved to England and joined the Liberal Party. In 1892 Naoroji became the first British Indian MP, and in 1895 he was appointed to the royal commission on Indian expenditure. Naoroji campaigned against the financial drain on India caused by British taxation and trade regulations. He then returned to India and was elected twice again as President of the Indian National Congress.]

economic power, England's undisputed industrial dominance, has already been broken, but there still remains another: the exploitation of India. And the more the former collapses, the more important becomes the latter. Lord Curzon, the Indian viceroy, justifiably declared in the *Times* (3 December 1898) that 'India is the pivot of our empire.... If the Empire loses any other part of its Dominions we can survive, but if we lose India the sun of our Empire will have set.'[39]

If the sun sets for the British Empire, the greatest in the world, then the entire economic system of Great Britain must experience a collapse from which socialism will offer the only way to a renewed prosperity.

But even a policy of concessions in India, which in order to prevent loss of the colony considerably reduces its exploitation and with it the sum of riches flowing to England – and England's prosperity (including that of a part of the English working class) depends on that flow of riches – even such a policy must increase unemployment and taxation in England, reduce state revenue from its present sources and sharpen class antagonisms.

True, for a quarter of a century we have been expecting again and again that the English working class would awaken to the fact that the exceptional position of England as the absolute industrial power in the world market has come to an end, and those expectations have proved to be deceptive. Until now, the capitalist class of England has only reflected the consequences of this fact in its growing hostility to any kind of proletarian organisation of struggle. But perhaps the rebellion of India will finally provide the impetus to awaken the dormant proletariat of England by shaking the second pillar of that exceptional position that resulted, at least for the short-sighted onlooker, in a sort of harmony of interests between the English capitalists and proletarians vis-à-vis foreign countries. Growing difficulties in India, economic crises, increased taxation, perhaps tariff burdens on the importation of foodstuffs, together with the Russian Revolution in Permanence, great political struggles in Germany and France, revolutions in Austria and Turkey, perhaps even international wars – if all that does not shake up the English workers, then they cannot be reckoned with at all in our coming liberation struggle; in that case the chosen people of 'pure and simple' unionism [*Nurgewerkschaftlerei*]

---

[39] [Elsewhere Curzon's statement is said to have been made in 1894.]

will only be ripe for socialism when the Japanese, Chinese, and Hindus are also ready for it (we will leave aside the Botocudos[40] for the time being).

But despite all the melancholy experiences, there are no reasons for coming to that kind of pessimistic conclusion. On the contrary, we must rather hope that the powerful convulsions that the Russo-Japanese War has brought into the political and social relations of the entire world will not disappear without leaving a trace in the British proletariat, and that they will be able to draw the three great conservative powers that formerly seemed inaccessible to the revolution – China, Russia and England – into the current of the great emancipation struggles of our time and in that way enormously accelerate their tempo.

Whatever forms those struggles may assume in practice, however unexpected their course may turn out to be and however much the conclusions that we have attempted to draw here from the available data may need to be modified, there is one thing that seems already now more than probable and can be regarded almost as certain: an era of revolutionary developments has begun. The age of slow, painful, almost imperceptible advances will give way to an epoch of revolutions, of sudden leaps forward, perhaps of occasional great defeats, but also – we must have such confidence in the cause of the proletariat – eventually of great victories. Therewith we will only reap what we and our predecessors have sown. Without the enlightening work of our great theoreticians and orators, without the untiring propagandistic and organisational routine work of our countless anonymous fighters, without all those efforts that have often appeared as the labour of Sisyphus – a labour whose modest outward results discouraged many people and so narrowed the vision of many others that any other form of progress no longer

---

[40] [The Botocudos, also known as the Aimorés or Aimborés, were a native Brazilian people. The original home of the tribe comprised most of the present province of Espírito Santo but the Botocudos were gradually expelled by white colonists westward beyond the Serra dos Aimorés into Minas Gerais. It was in the latter district that at the close of the 18th century they came into collision with the whites, who were attracted there by the diamond fields. During the frontier wars (1790–1820) every effort was made to extirpate them, since they were regarded by the Portuguese as no better than wild beasts. Smallpox was deliberately spread among them, poisoned food was scattered in the forests – and by such infamous means the coastal districts about Rio Doce and Belmonte were cleared. At the end of the nineteenth century many Botocudo tribes still existed, numbering between 13,000 and 14,000 individuals. Today only a few tribes remain, almost all of them in rural villages and Indian reservations.]

seemed possible to them – without all that assiduous preparatory work of decades, as well as the untiring revolutionary activity of capitalism, which undermines and uproots all the old relations – without all that, it would have been impossible today for small, far-off Japan to release such an amount of revolutionary energy all over the world.

But the fact that Japan was able to do that, that the victory of a remote East-Asian power was able to spur so powerfully the proletarian class struggle in Europe, also proves that the proletariat has become a world power and that nothing important can happen in the world any longer without accelerating the victorious advance of socialism.

Chapter Twelve

Introduction to *Ferdinand Lassalle's Speech to the Jury* (July 1905)

Leon Trotsky

The document translated here is Leon Trotsky's introduction to one of the most famous of Social-Democratic speeches – written but never delivered – by Ferdinand Lassalle.[1] In 1893, Eduard Bernstein's biography of Lassalle[2] portrayed a man of flamboyant character, enormous self-regard, and powerful intellect. While Lassalle was never fully a Marxist – he was much too influenced by Hegel in his view of the state, and by Ricardo in his acceptance of 'the iron law of wages' – he was nevertheless one of the heroic figures of the revolutions of 1848–9. In 1863, Lassalle founded the Allgemeiner Deutscher Arbeiterverein (General German Workers' Association), which in 1875 joined with the Social-Democratic Workers' Party, led by August Bebel and Wilhelm Liebknecht, to create the Socialist Workers' Party. In 1890, the Socialist Workers' Party became the Social-Democratic Party of Germany.

Lassalle's biography is the remarkable story of a man who in the course of a single lifetime became

---

[1] Lassalle 1905.

[2] Bernstein 1893. Bernstein's biography was a translation into English of his introduction to the complete German edition of Lassalle's *Speeches and Works*.

both revolutionary and reformer, at times a close associate of both Marx and Bismarck, a prodigious author, a playwright, and a hapless suitor who perished in 1864 in a duel over the affections of a young woman. Lassalle was also a self-taught lawyer. His adventures in the law courts began in 1846, when he met Countess Sophie Hatzfeld, who was seeking divorce from her husband. Lassalle undertook to rescue the Countess' fortune and waged numerous cases on her behalf until finally winning in 1854. But Lassalle's most memorable court encounter occurred in July 1849, when he faced charges of inciting armed resistance to the Prussian king and his officials. Bernstein gives this account of Lassalle's arrest and his 'speech' to the jury:

> Lassalle…was on the extreme Left of the Democratic party, whose organ was the *Neue Rheinische Zeitung* (the *New Rhenish Gazette*), edited by Karl Marx.…He frequently sent communications and correspondence to the *Neue Rheinische Zeitung*, and occasionally even appeared at the editorial office of the paper. Thus, gradually, a friendly personal relation came about between Lassalle and Marx.…
>
> Lassalle's attitude with regard to the inflowing tide of reaction in 1848 was identical with that of the editors of the *Neue Rheinische Zeitung*.…When, in November 1848, the Prussian Government disbanded the Berlin civic guard, proclaimed a state of siege in Berlin, and removed the seat of the National Assembly from Berlin to Brandenburg, a small provincial town, and when…the National Assembly [then] impeached the Prussian Ministry for high treason (*i.e.,* violation of the Constitution), and declared this ministry had forfeited the right of levying taxes, Lassalle, following the example of the *Neue Rheinische Zeitung*, called upon all citizens to organise and offer an armed resistance to the collection of taxes. Like the Committee of the Rhenish Democrats [which Marx supported], Lassalle was also indicted for inciting…armed resistance against the King's authority, and like them, too, he was acquitted by the jury. But the Reaction, growing more and more high-handed, brought a further charge against Lassalle of inciting…resistance against Government officials, with the object of getting him tried before the Correctional Police Court. And, in fact, this court – the Government undoubtedly knew its own judges – eventually did condemn Lassalle to six months' imprisonment.
>
> Lassalle's answer to the first of these charges has been published under the title *Assize Court Speech* [*Assisen-Rede*]. But, as a matter of fact, it was never

really spoken, and everything that has been said in the various biographies of the 'profound' impression it produced upon the jury and the public therefore belongs to the domain of fable. Even before the trial…Lassalle had sent the speech to the printers, and as some complete proofs had also been circulated beforehand, the court decided to exclude the public.…In spite of Lassalle's protest, and his declaration that the proofs had been circulated without his knowledge, and very probably at the instigation of…his enemies, the court decided to maintain its decision, and thereupon Lassalle declined to defend himself, but was none the less acquitted.

Whether spoken or not, the *Assize Court Speech*, in any case, is an interesting document for the study of Lassalle's political development. In it he takes almost the same standpoint as that taken three months earlier by Marx in his speech to the Cologne Jury.[3] A comparison of the two speeches demonstrates this as clearly as it demonstrates the difference of the natures of Marx and Lassalle. Marx refrains from all oratorical flourish; he goes straight to the point, in simple and terse language; sentence by sentence he develops incisively, and with ruthless logic, his own standpoint, and, without any peroration, ends with a summary of the political situation. Anyone would think that Marx's own personality was in no wise concerned, and that his only business was to deliver a political lecture to the jury. And, in fact, at the end of the trial, one of the jurors went to Marx to thank him, in the name of his colleagues, for the very instructive lecture he had given them! Lassalle's peroration, on the other hand, lasts almost from beginning to end; he exhausts himself in images – often very beautiful – and superlatives. It is all sentiment, and whether he refers to the cause he represented or to himself, he never speaks to the jury, but to the gallery, to an imaginary mass meeting, and after declaring a vengeance that should be 'as tremendous' as 'the insult offered the people,' he ended with a recitation from Schiller's Tell.[4]

Like Bernstein, Leon Trotsky obviously admired the grand rhetoric of Lassalle's *Speech to the Jury*. When Trotsky delivered his own speech to the tsar's court in September 1906, defending his role in the short-lived St. Petersburg Soviet, he clearly modelled himself after Ferdinand Lassalle.

---

[3] See the speech by Marx in Marx 1849d, pp. 227–47.

[4] Bernstein 1893, pp. 24–7. Marx's accounts in the *Neue Rheinische Zeitung* of Lassalle's imprisonment and trial are in the *Collected Works*, Vol. 8, pp. 344–6; 463–5; 474–6; Vol. 9, pp. 339–341; 372–6; 383–8.

But in the document translated here, Lassalle and the revolutions of 1848–9 served an immediate practical purpose. In the summer of 1905, Trotsky was intent upon demonstrating the striking, almost uncanny parallel between the betrayal of the European revolutions and the behaviour of Russian liberals and democrats in 1905. His account of the two historical events makes one the mirror image of the other.

In his criticism of the *Iskra* programme in 1903, Ryazanov had already pointed to the 'mistakes' of Marx and Engels in 1848–9, but Trotsky's command of the pen transformed Ryazanov's historical scholarship into living political drama. The theme of Trotsky's article is that the Russian bourgeoisie, like that of Germany in 1848, arrived too late to make its own revolution. As we have noted above, in their famous 'Address of the Central Committee to the Communist League', Marx and Engels concluded by March 1850 that German workers would have to make the revolution for themselves

> by taking up their independent political position as soon as possible, by not allowing themselves to be misled by the hypocritical phrases of the democratic petty bourgeoisie into doubting for one minute the necessity of an independently organized party of the proletariat. Their battle-cry must be: *The Permanent Revolution.*[5]

In this essay, Trotsky comes to the identical conclusion. In the historical drama that he recounts, the actors are German, Austrian or French, but they are also literary proxies for the class forces at work in Russia in 1905. Just as the liberals of 1848–9 preferred 'order' to emancipation, so Struve and his colleagues were reproaching Tsar Nicholas II for his failure to regain control of the country by concluding a compromise with the enlightened liberal opposition. Trotsky adds that neither intelligentsia democrats nor the Russian peasantry were capable of a consistent revolutionary role. The workers alone could decisively overthrow the old order, and they would have to do so first by arming the revolution and then by inspiring the workers of Western Europe to take up the struggle. From the very outset, Trotsky believed the victorious Russian revolution must assume an international character, 'making it the initiator of capitalism's worldwide liquidation, for which history has prepared all the objective preconditions'. With the power

---

[5] Marx and Engels 1850.

of historical analogy and his own mastery of the political pamphlet, Trotsky combines Marx's insight with Lassalle's passion to celebrate the prospect of permanent revolution both within Russia and throughout the capitalist world.

* * *

Introduction to *Ferdinand Lassalle's Speech to the Jury*

The 18th of March divided the old Prussia from the new. The people of Berlin won a decisive victory over royalist troops in a struggle on the barricades. Friedrich Wilhelm IV,[6] who swore that he would not allow a written sheet of paper, that is, a constitution, to come between him and Heaven,[7] was forced to give in to the people's demands: he withdrew his troops from Berlin, proclaimed all the 'freedoms', appointed the Rhine liberal Camphausen[8] to form a ministry, and had to summon the people's representatives to draft a constitution.

In this way, Prussian freedom emerged directly from the revolution. It was not won by some clever deal between the wise men of liberalism and the profiteers of reaction; it was won by the people in the streets. A written text was only needed to consolidate the victory of the popular uprising.

This work of 'consolidation' fell to the Prussian liberal bourgeoisie, who came to the forefront on the wave of revolution. Unorganised social forces and revolutionary 'spontaneity' were able to defeat absolutism and clear the way for creation of a new state, but they were not capable of building the new order on their own. This work inevitably fell into the hands of the liberal bourgeoisie, who, despite all their wavering[9] and hesitation to speak out, were the only class with political knowledge and political organisation.

---

[6] [Friedrich Wilhelm IV (1795–1861), King of Prussia.]

[7] ['Never will I permit a written sheet of paper to come between our God in heaven and this land…to rule us with its paragraphs and supplant the old, sacred loyalty.' <http://www.age-of-the-sage.org/history/1848/german_revolution.html>.]

[8] [For Marx's comments on Camphausen's role, see Marx 1849b, pp. 295–7) and elsewhere in *Neue Rheinische Zeitung*.]

[9] [Trotsky uses the word *kunktatorstvo* (in English, *cunctation*), alluding to Quintus Fabius Maximus Cunctator (The Delayer) 275–203 BC, who employed guerilla tactics to wear down Hannibal's forces in the Second Punic war. This is also the origin of the name of the British Fabian Society.]

The role they played in this context was determined by their entire social-historical position. Marx wrote in his *Neue Rheinische Zeitung*:

> The big landowners and capitalists became wealthier and more educated. With the development of bourgeois society in Prussia on the one hand – meaning the development of industry, trade, and agriculture – the former differences between estates lost their material basis. The aristocracy itself was largely bourgeoisified.…On the other hand, the absolutist state, which in the course of development lost its old social basis, became a restrictive fetter for the new bourgeois society with its changed mode of production and its changed requirements. *The bourgeoisie had to claim its share of political power, if only because of its material interests.*[10] Only the bourgeoisie itself could legally secure its commercial and industrial requirements. It had to wrest the administration of these, its 'most sacred interests', from the hands of an antiquated bureaucracy that was both ignorant and arrogant. The bourgeoisie had to demand control over state assets, which it claimed to have created. Having deprived the bureaucracy of the monopoly of so-called education, and conscious of the fact that it possessed a far superior knowledge of the real requirements of bourgeois society, the bourgeoisie also had the ambition to secure for itself a political status in keeping with its social status.…And so, the liberal opposition…was simply the bourgeoisie in opposition to a political form that was no longer appropriate to its interests and needs. But in order to oppose the Court, the bourgeoisie also had to court the people.[11]

However, to court the people and oppose the Court was not the same thing as openly leading the popular masses in relentless struggle against the old regime. This was something the German bourgeoisie could not do. It arrived too late with its slogans of emancipation. Standing face to face with a hostile proletariat, and corrupted to the marrow of its bones by the political experience of France, it was vigilant in ensuring that the popular movement not carry it too far and foreclose the possibility of doing a deal with the monarchy.

---

[10] [Trotsky's italics.]

[11] [Trotsky's source is *Itogi 48-vo goda* (Izd. 'Molot", 1905), p.6 et seq. See Marx 1848a, pp. 154–78.]

Without faith in itself and without faith in the people; grumbling at those above, frightened of those below; egoistical towards both and aware of its egoism; revolutionary with regard to the conservatives and conservative with regard to the revolutionaries; mistrusting its own slogans; using phrases instead of ideas; intimidated by the world storm and exploiting it for its own ends; displaying no energy anywhere, but resorting to plagiarism everywhere; vulgar because unoriginal, and original in its vulgarity; haggling over its own demands; without initiative, without faith in itself, without faith in the people, and without a world-historic mission; resembling an abominable dotard who finds himself condemned to lead and to mislead the first youthful impulses of a virile people so as to make them serve his own senile interests; *sans* eyes, *sans* ears, *sans* teeth, *sans* everything – this was the Prussian bourgeoisie that found itself at the helm of the Prussian state after the March revolution.[12]

Its class instinct told the bourgeoisie that the revolutionary method of completing its own historical task was rife with dangerous consequences. Its instincts were true. 'We lived through six centuries in the span of six years,' said Buassi d'Angla[13] in 1795. This was no mere phrase. Revolutions are the locomotives of history. In a brief period, they give the masses the political experience of centuries. In a few months, even days or hours, they tear from social relations the veil woven by politics, law, mysticism, and philosophy over a period of centuries. Society is revealed in all its nakedness as the organisation of class rule, in which all social institutions openly figure as levers in the hands of the ruling force, which, when threatened by revolution, openly proclaims its dictatorship, declares the territory of the state to be the battlefield, and imposes its own naked will in the form of martial law. Facing terrible danger, it has no time to hide its pretensions with the hypocrisy of law or the lies of mysticism. It mercilessly tears to pieces the legal webs, which it created itself, and reveals the bloody reactionary valour that it lacked in everyday life. For a time the *truth* prevails – the terrible, naked truth, with bloodstained brow, crusted wounds, and inflamed eyes.

---

[12] [Ibid.]
[13] [Buassi d'Angla (1756–1826) was one of the leaders of Thermidorian reaction in France and later a senator under Napoleon Bonaparte.]

Such an epoch is a school of political materialism. It translates all social norms into the language of force. It gives influence to those who rely upon force and are united, disciplined, and ready to take action. Its mighty tremors drive the masses onto the field of struggle and reveal to them the ruling classes – both those who are departing and those who are arriving. For exactly this reason, it is terrifying both for the class that is losing power[14] and for the one acquiring power.[15] Once they have entered upon this road, the masses develop their own logic and go much further than necessary from the viewpoint of the new bourgeois arrivals. Every day brings new slogans, each more radical than the previous one, and they spread as rapidly as blood circulates in the human body. If the bourgeoisie accepts revolution as the starting point of a new system, it will deprive itself of any opportunity to appeal to law and order in opposing the revolutionary encroachments of the masses. That is why a deal with reaction, at the expense of the people's rights, is a class imperative for the liberal bourgeoisie.

This applies equally to its position before, during, and after the revolution. The Prussian liberal bourgeoisie appealed not to the people against the king, but to the king against his bureaucracy. In essence, it hypocritically repeated the first naïve steps of the great French Revolution. Aulard says:

> Instead of holding the king responsible for the behaviour of his officials, the people declared that these officials were deceiving the king, that they were the true enemies of the king, that they were destroying and undermining his power to do good. The popular idea then was to free the king from these wicked officials in order that he might become better informed and use his power to benefit the nation in the struggle against the remnants of feudalism.[16]

---

[14] [The feudal aristocracy and absolutist rulers.]

[15] [The bourgeoisie.]

[16] Aulard 1902, p. 8. [Alphonse Aulard (1849–1928) was the first professional historian of the French Revolution. His works include several large collections of edited material, notably *Recueil des actes des comités de salut public* (16 vol., 1889–1904) and *La Société des Jacobins* (6 vol., 1889–97); his major studies are *Études et leçons sur la Révolution française* (9 vol., 1893–1924), *Histoire politique de la Révolution française* (1901; tr. *The French Revolution: A Political History*, 4 vol., 1910, repr. 1965), *Les Grands Orateurs de la Révolution: Mirabeau, Vergniaud, Danton, Robespierre* (1914), and *La Révolution française et le régime féodal* (1919).]

The Prussian liberal bourgeoisie pretended that between the king and freedom, which both of them, as friends, passionately longed for, stood the thorny hedge of the bureaucracy. It hoped, through this devilish cunning, to persuade the crown to push aside the noble bureaucracy and accept the bourgeoisie in its place. Feeling that it was not strong enough to defeat absolutism, the liberal bourgeoisie attempted to persuade the monarchy to make a bad deal. Of course, its stupid diplomacy did not deceive the monarchist government, which, like every ruling caste, had developed a refined instinct for self-preservation through centuries of exercising power. However, it did deceive the people, who had only just entered into political life. It impeded their spiritual emancipation and did everything possible to prevent a radical shake-up of ancient relations of patriarchy and servility. But when, despite all their efforts, it turned out that the fate of the country would still be decided in the streets, the bourgeoisie did everything it could to minimise such disorder and to give its offspring, Prussian freedom, a decent appearance.

Camphausen's liberal-bourgeois ministry, summoned to power by the king, worked out a theory saying that a constitution had to emerge from agreement[17] between the national assembly and the king. This meant that the national assembly forfeited in advance its sovereign, constitutive character and made the fate of a constitution dependent on the king's good will. The reason and the objective were perfectly clear.

To proclaim the sovereignty of the assembly (not in words alone, of course, as the all-German parliament did in Frankfurt),[18] would mean proposing to the king that he wait silently while his role was decided for him. But since, as Mr. Suvorin has aptly observed, there has never been a government so stupid as to hand over power voluntarily to a constituent assembly, it was obvious that once the chamber declared its own sovereignty, it would have to organise a swift response to reactionary forces by appealing to the nation and arming the people. In short, rather than liquidating the revolution, it

---

17 [*Vereinbarungstheorie.*]

18 [On 18 May, 1848, the Frankfurt parliament convened, following elections based on universal manhood suffrage, to promote German unification. Its deliberations were interrupted by war with Denmark and by conflicts between Austria and Prussia. By March 1849 it adopted a federal German constitution, excluding Austria. When Frederick William IV of Prussia refused to accept the crown of hereditary emperor from a popular assembly, the project collapsed.]

would have to do the opposite and develop it ever further. Meanwhile, the bourgeoisie assumed the burden of power precisely in order to put a hasty end to revolutionary anarchy.

The liberal bourgeoisie feared a 'leap into the unknown' and clung tenaciously to official historical traditions. Through a joint effort, the monarchy and the estates-based provincial councils[19] (the Landtags) would have to create a free Prussia without departing even for a moment from 'the terrain of law' – as if the day had never happened when the people of Berlin forced Friedrich Wilhelm IV, despite all legal norms, to doff his hat before the corpses of people who had fallen victim on 18 March.[20] Constitutional Prussia would have to arise not from the revolution, not through a provisional government like the February republic in France, but by legal means through a solemn manifesto. On 2 April, the United Landtag assembled in Berlin and accepted the law proposed by Camphausen's ministry – which had arisen on the bones of barricade fighters – providing for election of an assembly to reach agreement with the crown on the question of Prussia's state construction.[21] This assembly was to be formed through a system of *indirect* elections, meaning that voters would not choose their own deputies but, instead, only electors, who, in turn, would choose deputies. The reason for indirect elections was that the reactionaries, standing behind the liberal ministry, opposed direct elections that would make the fate of the monarchy directly dependent upon the same masses who were still seething on account of the battle on the barricades.[22] The March ministers, acting as pimps for the reactionaries in their relation to the liberals, had no difficulty in persuading the latter that two-stage voting was in their own interest. The liberal bourgeoisie dreaded the masses out of

---

[19] [Trotsky refers to them as *zemstvos* to make the analogy with Russia.]

[20] [Overwhelmed by the street fighting, Frederick William IV ordered his troops to their barracks and rode through Berlin to pay homage to the bodies of the victims.]

[21] [See 'The United Landtag of 1847 and 1848' <http://cscwww.cats.ohiou.edu/~Chastain/rz/united.htm>.

[22] ['...On March 30, leading military officers and officials of the old regime formed the court clique, or court party, which as a *ministère occulte* was expected to consolidate the power of the crown as a second government, or a counter-government against revolution and the bourgeois claim to power. The court clique was mainly based in the general adjutancy which was headed by the Adjutants General von Rauch and von Neumann, by General Leopold von Gerlach, the confidant of the king, by the House Minister Ludwig von Massow and, from autumn on, also by the Magdeburg Appellate Court President and conservative ideologue Ernst Ludwig von Gerlach.' <http://www.ohiou.edu/~Chastain/ac/courte.htm>.]

concern for its possessions and concluded for itself that the people were not 'mature' enough to express their will directly. The petty bourgeoisie proved sufficiently reactionary to support the slogan of two-stage elections, and the proletariat was too weak to win the right to direct elections in face of this entire coalition. It is true that the Berlin proletariat was far from apathetic regarding the electoral system. In April 1848 the prevailing slogans among the workers were '*Down with the electors!*' and '*Direct elections!*' But street protests were to no avail. The two-stage elections achieved their purpose: democrats remained a pitiful minority, and the representatives of anaemic liberalism triumphed along with masked reactionaries. The composition of the Prussian assembly included: 16 knights and nobles, 98 legal officials, 48 functionaries from the ministry of internal affairs, 28 city employees, 52 members of the clergy, 27 teachers, 31 merchants, 28 artisans, 68 peasants, 11 physicians, 3 writers, 4 officers, 1 travelling salesman, one craftsman, and 1 (just one!) worker.[23] Generally speaking, the Prussian assembly, once strained through the sieve of two-stage voting, turned out to be useful for nothing but preparing conditions for the complete triumph of reaction.

The national assembly opened on 22 May and constituted itself as a chamber of compromise in order to avoid any break with sacred 'legal continuity'; in other words, it scratched out 18 March, the real date of its birth, and eliminated it from official Prussian history, tracing its ancestry instead to the archaic United Landtag. In this way, even before the cock of counter-revolution could crow, the Berlin national assembly solemnly disavowed its origins in 'the streets'. But in so doing, the assembly also severed its ties with the masses and thus turned away from the only force upon which it could and must rely if it were to avoid becoming a simple 'private meeting', which would be able to produce resolutions but not to take the fate of the country into its own hands. The chamber began by making a fatal concession to counter-revolution, but the latter steadfastly refused to be satisfied with the concessions that liberalism, so magnanimous in its betrayal, was contemplating. The counter-revolution had its own objectives and its own methods – and it eagerly took advantage of every position that liberalism surrendered in order to launch new, more decisive attacks. Liberalism, in the trivial role of a deceived deceiver, only fulfilled its purpose when, after putting an end to revolutionary 'anarchy',

---

[23] *Ocherki po istorii Germanii v XIX v*, p. 331.

it fell into the bloody embrace of reaction. Using the same incantations, liberalism saved 'rational' freedom from democratic 'excesses' and at the same time summoned from police hell the dark spirits of a state of siege.

That is how history worked. While the crown, leaning upon the hilt of a sabre, step by step restored the pre-March order, the national assembly donned huge spectacles with tortoise-shell rims and occupied itself in polishing the paragraphs of a constitution with the precision of a diamond cutter. Within the confines of its professorial-shopkeeper narrow-mindedness, the chamber believed that its job was to circumscribe popular law within a mystical ring of sacramental paragraphs – and then the people's freedom, rational freedom, true freedom, 'freedom with order', would be secured forever. The shopkeepers of commerce and the shopkeepers of the faculties saw the people's struggle for power against the crown as a kind of civil litigation and hoped that the winner would be the one who demonstrated greater knowledge of the law codes and greater resourcefulness in litigation. They hoped to replace courage in combat and political initiative with the swindle of an attorney.

A good paragraph is, no doubt, a fine weapon against a poor paragraph, but the very best of paragraphs is useless against the very worst of bayonets. Indeed, there is nothing more helpless and insulting than the sort of unarmed freedom that cites its charter at the same time as it has a bayonet stuck in its chest.

The liberal ministry of Camphausen, having dreamed up the theory of constitutional reconciliation, *did not adopt so much as a single measure that could really consolidate the people's rights.*

The liberal ministry left in power the *entire personnel of the old bureaucracy* and all the ringleaders of the reactionary conspiracy.

It left defence of the people's rights to *pre-March courts* and even to *pre-March laws that dealt with political crimes.*

Finally, and most important of all, it left the army untouched, the *pre-March royalist* army, a powerful stronghold of reaction – and the army remained, as before, an organised and armed threat to the people's freedom. In these ways, thanks to the spinelessness of the liberal bourgeoisie, the crown retained the entire apparatus of its power and had only to wait for an appropriate moment to put it into operation.

What could the nation use to oppose the troops of reaction? A civil militia. The arming of citizens was a question of life and death in 1848, just as it had been in 1789. The new law, which the nation sent its representatives to create, needed armed protection because against it were still ranged the fully armed forces of the old law. Mirabeau, in the name of the national assembly, threw the following statement into the face of the king's messenger: 'We are gathered here by the will of the people and we shall yield only to bayonets.'[24] Although these were proud words, they expressed not only the national assembly's 'sovereign' right but also its weakness in face of royal bayonets. What would happen to the inalienable rights of man and the citizen if foreign regiments were to disperse the nation's representatives to their homes and to lock up the assembly's leaders in the Bastille?

But, at that point, Paris rises in defence of the assembly. It organises the insurgent Commune and a city militia of 48,000 citizens. The people burst into Les Invalides[25] and seize 28,000 muskets and 20 artillery pieces. They arm themselves and take the Bastille by storm. The provinces organise provisional government commissions and armed detachments of citizens. The new rights found their strength not in the debates of the national assembly, not in historic speeches, which flowed forth like liquid gold, but in the weapons that the French people seized for themselves.

The arming of Paris decides the revolution. The picture changes at once. In place of the assembly, surrounded by foreign troops and helpless before their bayonets and guns, we see an assembly with a menacing army at its disposal and conscious of its strength. 'Yesterday it spoke in a plaintive tone of insulted dignity and was moved by the kind of courage that is born of despair; today it speaks and acts like a sovereign authority.'[26]

Likewise, in 1848, a civil militia was one of the main slogans of the movement. Workers and democrats understood it to mean arming the people. The liberals and the bourgeoisie identified the citizen with a property owner. They needed a civil militia in order to protect their own interests, which they intended to transform into constitutional law. The crown encroached upon these interests, but they were also threatened by the proletariat. The militia's duty was to protect 'true' freedom both from police reaction and

---

[24] [Honoré-Gabriel Riqueti Mirabeau (1749–1791) was one of the leading figures of the National Assembly during the early stages of the French Revolution. The reference is to the Tennis Court Oath of 20 June 1789.]

[25] [A complex of buildings in Paris devoted to French military history.]

[26] Aulard 1902, p. 47.

from revolutionary anarchy. For that reason, several militias were formed by the 'good citizens', that is, by merchants, artisans, officials, students, artists and even students from the gymnasiums. These were the armed bourgeoisie, but they were not the armed people. It was already obvious that the bourgeoisie feared the armed proletariat more than the crown feared the armed bourgeoisie. It is very likely for this same reason that the bourgeoisie had more trust in the revolutionary courage of the proletariat than the crown had in the courage of the bourgeoisie. In Vienna during 1848, for example, the reactionary clique readily agreed to a militia because it hoped in that way first to put the bourgeoisie between itself and the revolution, and secondly, to deepen the division between the armed and sensible petty bourgeoisie on the one hand, and the unarmed insurrectionary proletariat on the other. In fact, it managed to do both.

Acting as an armed militia, the bourgeoisie fulfilled mainly police functions. It stood on guard for legality, and especially for property, and together with royalist forces it protected the arsenals from the proletariat, who had demanded weapons. The bourgeoisie's fear of the proletariat turned into panic after the bloody June days in Paris. Apart from the active opposition of the bourgeoisie, the proletariat was prevented from organising its own armed force by the backbreaking labour system. Work in the factories and shops, which belonged to the liberal bourgeoisie, consumed all their time, and the proletarian did not have a free moment for military training. For the proletariat, an eight-hour working day was a necessary precondition for playing any deliberate and conscious role in social reconstruction. But the consciousness of the German proletariat of 1848 was too underdeveloped, and it was too weak at the time of the revolution to raise and win its own fundamental demands: *an eight-hour working day and a people's militia.*

The bourgeois militia, which also included numerous officials as a result of suggestions from above, turned out to be a poor bulwark of 'freedom'. At the decisive moment, it displayed a cowardice equivalent to the rage with which it normally persecuted the unarmed proletariat.

That is how the liberal bourgeoisie entered upon its career in government, and it continued along the exact same path. Hansemann[27] followed

---

[27] [David Hansemann (1790–1864) was a wealthy financier and leading German liberal.]

Camphausen. Marx's organ, the *Neue Rheinische Zeitung*, displayed profound political insight when it exclaimed upon Camphausen's departure that 'He sowed reaction in the spirit of the bourgeoisie; he will reap it in the spirit of the autocracy and absolutism.'[28]

The only difference between the first and second ministries lay in the fact that the first was directly linked to the revolution, and this prevented it from following its 'hard' policy through to the end, whereas the second could build upon the treachery of its predecessor and be brave on that account. Hansemann, who invented the theory of reconciliation, held forth the prospect of a constitutional 'monarchy *on a broad democratic base*'. This is an international formula, not something uniquely Prussian. It has always been used willy-nilly by democrats, and it will continue to be used because it leaves open the possibility of turning either to the right or to the left. Its popularity is due to its inexpressible merits. It is as elusive as smoke, as pliant as a reed, and it stretches like rubber. Just what is 'a broad democratic base'? It can be everything: a single chamber, universal suffrage, and popular sovereignty. What is a 'broad democratic base'? It is equally nothing at all! Any census qualification will provide a 'broad democratic base' by comparison with a narrower one. Any two *elected* chambers are always more democratic than two chambers, one of which one is made up of officials and the hereditary nobility. What could be more convenient than the slogan of a 'broad democratic base' for the kind of political matchmakers who think the only thing needed to wed estates-based liberalism with consistent democracy is an appropriate turn of phrase? A broad democratic base! The phrase can be stretched, squeezed, cut to pieces and put together again; it can be flattened out and cut into a Jacobin cap; it can be woven into a rope to make a noose for democracy; it can be wrapped around words, straightened out again, dissolved into phraseology without leaving a trace, wiped out – and then rise anew. It is the ballast that can be thrown overboard in order to float upwards; it is also the life jacket that one can grab in order not to sink to the bottom. It is truly a remarkable thing! The same bourgeoisie that replaced patriarchal agreements, based upon conscience, with promissory notes and contracts, and that specifies every sum in writing and figures, prefers in politics a formula that promises everything to everyone and requires nothing of anyone. A broad democratic base! Ask

---

[28] [See Marx 1848d, p. 107.]

our own 'democratic' press what it means. They have given no answer from the time when they first appeared right up to the publication of these lines.

'A monarchy on a broad democratic base' – that is what Camphausen promised, and his successor, Hansemann, preserved continuity by giving the slogan a more definite formulation: 'a constitutional monarchy based on a two-chamber system with joint exercise of legislative power by both chambers and the crown'. The purpose of the liberal bourgeoisie's constitutional architecture was to take hold of the king but at the same time to leave him with sufficient strength to protect the bourgeoisie from the people. A monarchy based on two chambers was to solve precisely this task. The good-natured democrats, who believed in Camphausen's formula, had every right to stand agape, and that is just what they did.

Hansemann's ministry, or the 'ministry of action' as it called itself, was in fact the ministry of active bourgeois counter-revolution. It strengthened the police, finally converted the civil militia into a police organ, persecuted the press, and launched arrests; in a word, it suppressed 'anarchy', reinforced order, and thus systematically prepared the restoration of absolutism. The reaction, for its part was not sleeping. Alongside the apparent 'constitutional' ministry, it organised a secret court ministry that mobilised forces and took control of policy direction. Besides the customary police repression and use of military forces, which acted hand in hand with the bourgeois militia against the proletariat, the reactionary party elevated into a system the instigation of ignorant and depraved elements of the population against the proletariat and democracy. In the countryside, priests and feudal lords turned the peasants into fanatical opponents of the restless cities. In the cities, the reactionaries bribed tramps to murder democrats and turned out to be involved in organising pogroms against the Jews. In these ways, the reactionaries recruited partisan detachments of urban riff-raff and village idiots to support the regular military personnel. The scum of the street were transformed into sacred phalanges to protect the state, morals, and religion. Russian readers, who have passed through the schools of *Plehvovshchina* and *Trepovshchina*[29] need no explanation of these tactics. Of course, they could never have succeeded

---

[29] [The terrible times of Plehve and Trepov. Trotsky has in mind the brutal campaigns of the Black Hundreds in Russia and the government's periodical incitement of pogroms against Jews to divert public discontent.]

if the revolutionary movement, against which they were deployed, had not subsided through internal causes of its own.

On 11 September, the Hansemann ministry resigned. On the king's instructions, the elderly General Pfuel[30] assembled a new ministry. He made a show of respecting the constitution and behaving correctly towards the democrats.

At the same time, however, the reaction was making final preparations to overthrow the constitution and finally defeat democracy. General Wrangel,[31] having returned from Schleswig-Holstein, was appointed commander-in-chief of Brandenburg and moved 48,000 troops with 60 guns towards Berlin, all intended for use against the domestic enemy. The civil militia welcomed Wrangel to Berlin as a conqueror. His address, an insolent military challenge, was greeted with enthusiastic applause by the liberal cretins. The bourgeoisie impatiently made ready to clasp hands with reaction 'in the spirit of aristocracy and absolutism'.

The secret court ministry became more and more influential and finally succeeded in replacing Pfuel's ministry with that of Brandenburg,[32] which was openly absolutist. This operation, like all subsequent achievements of the counter-revolution, was prepared by a bloody clash between the bourgeois militia and the proletariat. The reaction saw that it had nothing to fear: the proletariat was revolutionary but unarmed, while the bourgeoisie was armed but reactionary. On 9 November, the new minister, General Brandenburg, appeared before the chamber and read to the 'sovereign' assembly a royal decree requiring it to adjourn immediately in order to reassemble on 27 November in Brandenburg rather than Berlin, since in Berlin the criminal crowd would supposedly prevent it from working with complete independence. The liberal chieftains did not have to be sages to understand what this meant, nor did they have to be revolutionary leftists to feel rising indignation. But the understanding came too late, and the indignation proved impotent.

---

[30] [Ernst von Pfuel (1779–1866) was a Prussian officer and Prime Minister from 21 September to 1 November 1848.]

[31] [Friedrich Heinrich Ernst Graf von Wrangel (1784–1877) was summoned to Berlin to suppress the riots. Wrangel proclaimed a state of siege and ejected the Liberal president and members of the Chamber.]

[32] [Friedrich Wilhelm Graf von Brandenburg (1792–1850), a militant counter-revolutionary, was Prime Minister of Prussia from 2 November 1848 to 6 November 1850.]

On 10 November the troops entered Berlin and expelled the assembly from its meeting place. On the 12th, Berlin came under a state of siege, the civil militia was disarmed, clubs and associations were dissolved, and democratic newspapers were shut down. The finely honed sabres of Wrangel took the place of any sacred foundations. That is how the counter-revolution armed itself. Instead of untangling the legal confusion, which resulted from a revolution that the bourgeoisie regarded as illegal, the counter-revolution simply trampled on the gains made by the people on 18 March. With Wrangel's sabre it slashed through the parchment of Habeas Corpus, and on the points of soldiers' bayonets it brought to Berlin its own law, the lawless law of a state of siege. The people's representatives, the bearers of national 'sovereignty', were dispersed to their homes with a rod, and the burghers of the civil militia were disarmed and sent back to the bosom of their families. The constitutional diamond cutters saw (and could hardly fail to see!) that they must resist. But to resist would pit force against force, the armed people against Wrangel's troops, which would mean appealing to the revolution. The national assembly, which through betrayal had freed itself from its illegal and revolutionary origins, was incapable of taking such an heroic step.

True, the civil militia refused to dissolve the assembly, and its commander even announced that the militia would defend the chamber in order 'to prevent a bloody conflict'. The workers also promised their support. They wrote to the assembly:

> The workers of Berlin are ready, arms in hand, to respond to your call if anyone dares to insult the rights of the people and its representatives. They place their hands and their blood at your disposal should any enemy attempt to betray you and the people's freedom.

The workers demanded weapons from the militia commanders, but they were refused. The proletariat, so shamefully betrayed by the bourgeoisie, manifested once more the profound political idealism that carries this class into the most dangerous situations whenever freedom is at stake, even the limited bourgeois freedom that the bourgeoisie itself had stolen from them. But the national assembly was unable even at this critical moment to rely upon the militia and the workers. It obviously needed to resist, but it feared the *activity* of the people. Hence it decided to *resist*, but only *passively*. It began its career by betraying 18 March, and it ended with the impotent protest of

'Passive resistance'! In its political destitution, the chamber was not satisfied merely to display its miserable helplessness; it had to give this helplessness a name, vote for it, and make it a law for the entire country. Passive resistance! – that is what the liberal bourgeoisie, who had so actively waged their own attacks on the proletariat, prescribed in response to the reaction's acts of violence against freedom.

On 16 November, 226 members of the chamber, meeting by stealth, decided on a tax strike as the supreme act of passive resistance. But the people, of course, who were asked to withhold payments to a royal government that was armed from head to foot, could not resist 'passively'. The tax collectors went about their work with armed protection. Tax collecting provoked disorders, followed by executions. In the provinces, democrats attempted to organise active resistance. The Rhine democratic committee, of which Marx was a member, issued a call to take up arms in defence of the chamber and its resolutions. Lassalle, in full agreement with the Rhine committee, tried to organise resistance in Düsseldorf and Neuss. He called for armed struggle against any collection of taxes. In his address to the Düsseldorf militia he wrote: 'Passive resistance is exhausted. We earnestly request that the national assembly issue a call to arms.' In Düsseldorf, he set up a commission to secure arms and posted public notices calling for contributions of money and arms for the struggle against the crown. He appealed to the Shenshtein peasants to rise up on signal, and he made the same appeal in his speech at Neuss: 'Once the signal for the insurrection comes from Düsseldorf, all must rise up to coincide with the expected uprising in Silesia.' All of this provided material for the charges levelled against Lassalle.

The parliamentary Pilates, after washing their hands in the water of 'passive resistance', left events to take their course. Naturally, none of this could produce a victory. The reaction took its revenge for 18 March, and democracy was mercilessly crushed. Lassalle's speech to the jury was a kind of swan song of Prussian democracy.

II.

Lassalle did not deliver his 'speech to the jury'.[33] When it was first published, he advised the reader that 'the royal judicial authorities were so arbitrary that they did not permit the accused to deliver this speech before the numerous members of the public who had gathered in the court room. Since the public were removed from the room, the accused announced that he considered it beneath his dignity to deliver the speech once openness had been eliminated by a single authoritative word. The accused declined to speak. Nevertheless, the jurors delivered a verdict of "not guilty".'[34]

However, the undelivered speech retains all of its importance. Legal in form, it is political in content. It is a courageous challenge to Prussian reaction, a restrained but still relentless condemnation of liberalism, and, as we said before, a fine swan song for revolutionary Prussian democracy.

In the movement of 1848, Lassalle belonged to the left-revolutionary wing of the bourgeois opposition. In terms of worldview, Lassalle describes himself

---

[33] [One biographer of Lassalle writes:

Lassalle had had his speech for the defence printed in April, and when the trial opened copies of this 'Assize Speech' were on sale at the doors of the court-house.

In Dresden, the Palatinate, and Baden, fresh revolts were in progress. The second act of the sanguinary comedy was beginning, and public feeling was heated to the boiling-point.

Two thousand Germans were repeating the sentences of the accused at the very time when the act of accusation against Lassalle was being read in court.

To every utterance of the prosecution, two thousand Germans knew Lassalle's answer before it had been spoken.

On May 4th, in a panic, the court decided to exclude the public.

Catastrophe seemed imminent!

Lassalle entered a protest: 'I regard the exclusion of the public from the court as an infamous betrayal of the laws.'

The protest was rejected.

Justice, like every assassin, dreaded publicity.

The court was cleared. (See Schirokauer 1932, p. 137.)]

[34] The procurator's office pursued Lassalle like a personal enemy. He was not only brought before a jury on the charge of calling for an uprising against the royal authority, but also before a court martial on the charge of calling for armed resistance against the officials and troops, although it was obvious that the second charge was already included in the first. The chairman excluded the public on the grounds that Lassalle's speech, part of which was published the day before, threatened social peace. Following vigorous but unsuccessful protests against this decision, the accused declined to speak. The jurors, whom Lassalle called upon not to fulfil their functions in view of the closed proceedings, refused to go that far, although they did return a verdict of 'not guilty'. Nevertheless, the court sentenced Lassalle to six months in prison.

in his speech as a supporter of a social-democratic republic. He ranked far above bourgeois democracy, but by siding with the latter, he, like Marx and Engels, only followed his immediate political duty. In backward Germany, there was still no *independent* political movement of the workers. In these conditions, participation in the revolutionary events, which had developed unexpectedly, could only mean, for a socialist like Lassalle, joint action with the radical bourgeoisie. It is in this sense that one must interpret everything that Lassalle says in his speech about 'unity', which might otherwise bring quiet joy to many innocent souls. At that critical moment, Lassalle would have been justified in creating division within the democratic movement only if he could have relied upon some other force, standing apart from the democrats, and if his struggle against the latter could have strengthened this new militant force. But Lassalle saw that this was *not yet* the case. The time for open and relentless struggle against the supposed bourgeois democrats for influence over the masses came later, and the *Assisen-Rede*[35] (the speech to the jury) is thus a testament from Lassalle, as a member of a democratic club, to the Lassalle who founded the German General Workers' Union.[36]

Confronting royal Prussian justice, which was defending November's victorious violence by the reactionaries against the people's representatives, in his *Assisen-Rede* Lassalle shows the greatest political restraint in judging the defeated popular representatives. Where possible, he mentions the indecision, inertia, obsequiousness, and servility of the liberal opposition in order all the more emphatically to highlight the oppressive tactics of the government. There is only one place where Lassalle – in the interest not merely of his own defence but also of freedom – directs the full weight of his anger against the former chamber, and this concerns the question of 'passive resistance'. He says:

> Gentlemen, on the matter of passive resistance we must even agree with our enemies that the national assembly's passive resistance was, whatever the circumstances, a crime. One or the other! Either the crown was within its rights acting as it did – in which case the national assembly, having

---

[35] [The Assize Court speech.]

[36] [Lassalle founded the *Allgemeiner Deutscher Arbeiterverein* in May 1863 and was its first president. In 1875 Lassalle's union joined with Marx's supporters, August Bebel and Wilhelm Liebknecht, to form the Socialist Workers' Party, later the Social Democratic Party of Germany (SPD).]

opposed the legal rights of the crown and brought strife to the country, was nothing but a gang of mutineers and rebels. Or else the actions of the crown constituted illegal violence, in which case it was necessary to defend popular freedom *actively*, with *blood* and *lives*, and the national assembly was obligated to summon the country openly to arms! In that event, this remarkable discovery of passive resistance was a cowardly betrayal of the people and a base abandonment of the assembly's duty to defend the people's rights....

…Passive resistance, gentlemen, is self-contradictory; it is a resistance that will tolerate anything; it is a non-resisting resistance; it is resistance that is no resistance at all....

Passive resistance is a *malevolent inner will* that finds no issue in action. The crown confiscated the people's freedom and, in defence of the people, the national assembly declared its *inner vexation.*

Fourteen years later, when conflict between the crown and the people's representatives flares anew, Lassalle returns to his criticism of passive resistance. In November 1862, he shows in his essay 'What Next?' that the tactic of passive resistance cannot be applied in Prussia, where a paper constitution only covers up absolutism: either it will not be *resistance*, or else it will not be passive. As a method of struggle against the government or even merely as a threat, refusal to pay taxes might work in England, where there *really* is constitutional rule, where organised force is in the hands of the people, and where it is possible at any moment to use the whole constitutional apparatus, already won and already existing, against any anti-constitutional encroachments by the crown. But, in Prussia, with its pretence of a constitutional system, a tax strike cannot legally be carried out by measures of passive resistance. Either the refusal to pay taxes will amount to nothing, as in November 1848, or else it will overstep the bounds of legality in the direction of popular insurrection.

In order to explain this better, Lassalle compares the consequences of a refusal to pay taxes in Prussia and England. Let us assume, he says, that the assembly has rejected some tax, but the government has decided to collect it by force. The English tax collector comes to me for the money. I resist and turn him out of my house. I am taken to court, but the court finds me innocent and even praises me for resisting a clear violation of the law. Then the tax collector comes again, this time accompanied by soldiers. Once again, I resist, together with my friends and neighbours. The soldiers open fire, wounding and killing some of them. I take them to court, and they cite the order from their superiors. But since an order from above cannot justify criminal behaviour in England, the soldiers are convicted of murder and sentenced to death. Now assume that I and my friends, in response to the shooting by the soldiers, began to shoot back and wounded and killed some of them. I am taken to court. As in the first case, the court finds me innocent because I was only defending myself against violence. Since every Englishman knows in advance the whole course and outcome of the conflict, suppose they all quietly and confidently refuse to pay taxes. The government will then be defeated. It cannot employ the army against the people. The English army is too small; its upkeep, and therefore any increase in its numbers, depend entirely upon the good will of Parliament.

Describing the constitutional advantages of the English military system, Lassalle naturally understood very well that this system is still far from a democratic programme, which demands complete dissolution of the standing army and its replacement by a militia, that is, by the armed people.

Now let us look into the matter further. Facing resistance from the courts and lacking support from the army, the English government will not even be able to rely on the bureaucracy in its struggle against the people. Officials are zealous, unwavering and energetic when they are convinced that the government will win. But, in England, if they want to retain their position and their salary, they have no alternative but to support the people in the case of conflict between the crown and the chamber. This means the local mayor is left to collect the taxes himself, facing gunfire and imprisonment, at best with the help of 'a gang of scoundrels who have nothing to lose'. This is obviously a hopeless undertaking. The result is that, in England, it takes a single decree from the chamber concerning refusal to pay taxes, and the government concedes.

In Prussia, things are entirely different. The government here, ignoring the decision of the chamber, will take the most energetic measures to collect the taxes. If I happen to be a good tax collector yet oppose the authorities, the Prussian courts will straight away imprison me. The soldiers come, they shoot, and they kill. They are not charged, for they acted upon the orders of their superiors. If I should shoot at them and kill someone, I will be sentenced to death. In Prussia, the royal government controls the army, the courts, and the bureaucracy and can turn them on the people at any time.

In these circumstances, a refusal to pay taxes, on its own, has no chance whatever of succeeding.

Thus Lassalle concludes that refusal to pay taxes is a realistic tactic only in the hands of a people that *already* has all the real means of organised force on its side, a people that has already taken the fortress. In the hands of a people that has merely a written constitution, not to mention one with no constitution at all, this tactic has no force whatever: '*For a people that has yet to take the fortress, refusal to pay taxes would only make sense as a means of provoking a general uprising.*' [37]

The Prussian people could only have allowed itself the luxury of passive resistance in November 1848 if in March of the same year it had organisationally secured the fruits of its revolutionary victory.

It should have speedily dissolved the standing army, which was organised and trained by the reaction. It should have created a militia – not cadres of the armed bourgeoisie, but a genuine people's militia. It should have reconstructed the entire bureaucratic apparatus, including the police, organising officialdom on an electoral basis and making it answerable to the courts. It should have made the courts subject to election and independent of the administration. Without the army, court and bureaucracy, there is neither power nor sovereignty. Supreme power will belong to the people in fact, not in words, only if the courts and the bureaucracy are responsible to them and if the army is the people themselves. The victorious March revolution should have disarmed the reaction and armed itself; if this had been done, General Wrangel would have been deprived of any physical means of overturning such a fine constitution with his boots. But these things were not done.

Following the people's decisive victory in the streets of Berlin, the liberal bourgeoisie left the crown with soldiers, with Wrangel, cannons, sabres, the local councils, police officers, the courts, and the procurators.

---

[37] [The discussion here of passive resistance is especially ironic. In mid-December 1905, Parvus, on behalf of the St. Petersburg Soviet, issued a declaration calling for a tax strike and withdrawal of bank deposits with the aim of destroying both the banking system and the tsarist government's finances. In the completely different circumstances of July 1906, when the tsar dissolved the first Russian Duma, the Cadets issued their 'Vyborg Manifesto' and likewise called for a tax strike and refusal to serve in the military. The Cadet action was an exercise in futility. Armed insurrection was inconceivable by the time of their declaration, and they proved as impotent as the Prussian representatives described in Trotsky's essay.]

It armed itself only with *passive resistance*. It expected to benefit from this modesty, and thus to achieve the most stable, the most alluring, the most rational freedom – the freedom prescribed in the *Manifesto*.[38] Alas, instead of 'rational' freedom they were 'prescribed' a state of siege!

Every political party can make mistakes. But there are 'youthful mistakes' and the sins of old dogs. The mistakes of the liberal bourgeoisie in the critical hours of 1848 belong entirely to the latter category. Instead of learning from experience, they were corrupted by it. For them, politics was simply a school of hypocrisy.

In July of this very year, one of the leaders of Hungarian national politics, Count Aponyi, described the Austrian government in a speech to a peasant meeting. A cry rose from the crowd: 'We are already whetting our scythes!' The Count objected: 'Scythes can achieve nothing against Manlikher rifles. We have a tried and proven weapon – *the law statutes*! They are stronger than we are and stronger than *Manlikher rifles*.'

The orator was quite likely delighted with his own wit, which allowed him to set aside the peasant scythe with such dignity. But if the Hungarian Count had learned even a little from the lessons of the past, he would probably have had less respect for a constitutional paragraph and more for the peasant's scythe. The Hungarian national opposition has always had enormous respect for paragraphs. But this did nothing to save them from Manlikher rifles or even from the flint-lock weapons of 1848. The leaders of the national movement vowed at that time to take their stand on the constitution granted to Hungary by King Ferdinand.[39] And they were right. The paragraphs did support them.

---

[38] [The *Communist Manifesto*. The first printing was at the end of February, 1848.]

[39] [In March 1848, revolution erupted in Vienna, followed by unrest in Hungary. The Buda fortress was stormed, prisoners were released, and on 16 March the Diet's lower house demanded a national government responsible to elected representatives. On 22 March a new national government took power with Count Louis Batthyany as chairman, Kossuth as minister of finance, and Szechenyi as minister of public works. Under duress, the Diet's upper house approved a sweeping reform package, signed by Emperor Ferdinand of Austria (separately crowned King of Hungary in 1830). These April Laws created independent Hungarian ministries of defence and finance, and the new government claimed the right to issue currency through its own central bank. Feudal and guild privileges were abolished, freedom of press and assembly proclaimed, and a Hungarian national guard was established (http://www.countrydata.com/cgi-bin/query/r-5767.html).]

But ranged against them were Ban Jellacic with Croatian troops,[40] the army of Windischgrätz,[41] and 140,000 soldiers of Nicholas I.[42] Kossuth,[43] who tried to take a stand on the 'basis of law', was all the same accused of treason. The courageous Hungarian General Aulich[44] even proclaimed his fidelity to the constitution before the courts and the chambers. There is no doubt that the paragraphs supported him. But his enemies had guns and the gallows on their side, and Aulich was hanged along with numerous others. No paragraph saved a single victim from the bloody grasp of the Austrian counter-revolution.

Fortunately for their cause, the Hungarians had strong forces and courageous generals, not just loyalty. Kossuth travelled about the country calling upon the peasants to 'whet their scythes' and join the ranks.

'Legal resistance' was mounted through *armed force*. And since *force* alone gave the Hungarians an advantage, their leaders quickly abandoned loyalty and declared Hungary to be an independent state.

The combined forces of reaction crushed the Hungarian insurrection, leaving Hungarians to try to salvage in parts what the revolution had won and the reaction had taken back from them. Today the struggle of Hungarians

---

[40] [The April Laws made no separate provisions for the Kingdom of Croatia or other national minorities. Josip Jellacic became governor of Croatia on 22 March and severed relations with the Hungarian government a month later. By summer, the Austrians ordered the Hungarian diet to dissolve. In September Jellacic led an army of 45,000 into Hungary. A committee of national defence under Kossuth took control, established a Hungarian army, and issued paper money to fund it. On 30 October, 1848, imperial troops entered Vienna and suppressed a workers' uprising, effectively ending the revolution everywhere in the empire except Hungary, where Kossuth's army had overcome Jellacic's forces. In December Ferdinand abdicated in favour of Franz Joseph (1848–1916), who had given no pledge to respect the April Laws. The Magyars refused to recognise him as their king because he was never crowned. The imperial army captured Pest early in 1849, but the revolutionary government remained entrenched in Debrecen. In April a 'rump' Diet deposed the Habsburg Dynasty in Hungary, proclaimed Hungary a republic, and named Kossuth governor with dictatorial powers. After the declaration, Austrian reinforcements were transferred to Hungary, and in June, at Franz Joseph's request, Russian troops attacked from the east. The Hungarian army surrendered on 13 August, Kossuth escaped to the Ottoman Empire, and a period of harsh repression followed. (http://www.countrydata.com/cgi-bin/query/r-5767.html).]

[41] [Alfred Windischgratz (1787–1862) was an Austrian field Marshal and a notorious reactionary whose troops occupied Budapest in January 1849.]

[42] [Nicholas I (1796–1855), Tsar of Russia.]

[43] [Lajos Kossuth (1802–1894) led the struggle for Hungarian independence in 1848–49).]

[44] [Lajos Aulich (1792–1849) was Hungarian Minister of War during the 1848 struggle for independence. Aulich was subsequently executed.]

is again staying within constitutional limits. The people are beginning to sharpen their scythes, but bourgeois leaders such as Count Aponyi, who are incapable either of forgetting or of learning anything, are again playing the same role, which means they are preventing the movement from rising beyond its own limitations.

Are not Messrs. Struve, Milyukov, Petrunkevich and Rodichev playing the identical role in our revolution?[45] Historical experience teaches the liberal bourgeoisie nothing; it merely corrupts them. But let us return to the speech. For us Russians, it is interesting not simply for the warning it gives but also as a remarkable human document. In his later years, Lassalle never enjoyed hiding – nor did he know how to hide – his own '*I*', and it is no surprise that in this speech of a 24-year old youth he revealed himself completely, with all his strengths and all his weaknesses.

Both in his speeches and in the political movement in general, Lassalle provides *a classic example of revolutionary action*. While Marx sees his first task and duty in *explaining* events and all their obscure causes, Lassalle endeavours above all to disclose the vital force that permits one to drive events forward in the present. He was concerned in his studies not with advancing science, which he actually worshipped, nor with the workers' movement as a whole, of which he was the servant – he was always interested in a particular political action. As he later wrote to Engels, 'I would willingly leave unrecorded everything that I *know*, if that would mean I could instead accomplish even a part of what I *know how*.' If we can say that Marx embodied the *consciousness* of the workers' movement, Lassalle was its intense *will*.

This difference between two psychological types is remarkably evident in the speeches that Marx and Lassalle made in their own defence against completely identical charges.[46] In his speech to the Cologne court, Marx generally takes the same viewpoint as Lassalle would take a few months later in his undelivered address. But unlike Lassalle, Marx does not lower himself to the extent of entering a contest with his opponent. For him, there essentially are no opponents. He regards them as 'organs of a class'. Their speeches are an official echo of the ruling interests. They accuse him of violating some paragraph or other! But what do these statutes mean when he has before him

---

⁴⁵ [See L. Trotsky 1905.]
⁴⁶ [For Marx's speech, see Marx 1849a, pp. 304–22.]

world social-revolutionary perspectives? A violation of laws and a threat to society's foundations? These are the fabrications of jurists! Society does not rest on laws, and it cannot be threatened by their violation. On the contrary, the laws depend upon society. For Marx, the Prussian constitutional conflicts from March through November were mere manifestations of the struggle of social forces and class interests. Marx does not deliver a defensive speech to the court: instead, he helps his listeners – who happen to be the jury – to comprehend the whole political state of affairs.

Lassalle also knows – after all, he was under Marx's ideological influence, even though he was not his 'student' in the same sense, for example, as Liebknecht[47] – Lassalle knows that the legal point of view concerns only the surface of social development. He knows that the law is merely a reflection of society's spirit and its needs projected on a screen of law. But he says in advance that in his speech in his own defence he will descend from these heights and take his stand on law and the existing constitution in order to make his arguments more understandable and conclusive for his opponent.

Marx demonstrates to his court audience that his enemies are the representatives of an obsolete social formation. Lassalle grapples with his opponents in front of his listeners. With a single generalisation, Marx cuts the ground from under his opponents and destroys them. Lassalle attacks and, before delivering a final, solemn, deadly blow, he strikes at all his opponent's undefended positions. In order to prolong the sparkling triumph of his thought, his festival of combat, he gives his enemy arguments from his own surplus; he makes him wiser, more insightful, more consistent than he naturally is; he gives him weapons from his own arsenal – and then, taking pride in the regal generosity of his own wondrous thought, and convinced of victory in advance, he resolutely attacks his enemy, toys in the sun with swords and armour, powerfully crosses weapons, drives the opponent from all of his positions, and compels him to crawl in the dust and writhe under the heel of the victor.

His 'Speech to the Jury' is a living example of a Lassallean offensive. Through one page after the other, he wages his menacing attack with inexhaustible energy. He leads you from argument to argument with an iron hand, he

---

[47] [Wilhelm Liebknecht (1826–1900) was a close associate of Marx and eventual co-founder, with August Bebel, of the German Social-Democratic Party.]

leaves you with no room to retreat, he does not allow you to rest, and at times you want to exclaim: 'To hold his hand is like gripping a stone!' Finally, when you reach the conclusion, you are enthusiastically proud of the author as you look back on the road that you and he have travelled together.

It is true that every speech has its imperfections – both external and internal: the argumentation might be excessive and thus in some places less convincing, the subtle juridical dialectic at times threatens to become sophistry, and pathos sometimes becomes rhetoric – but these are mere scratches on the walls of a splendid building, built from the noble metal of logic and inspired by gothic towers of angry pathos.

III.

Following 1848, bourgeois democracy no longer plays any role in Prussia. It reappears in the 1850s, impotently flounders, and bows in repentance at the feet of Bismarck. Its short and miserable fate is directly tied to the short and miserable fate of the entire German revolution.

By comparison with the Great French Revolution, the German one took place on a miniature scale. On the one hand, it came too early; on the other, it came too late. The kind of gigantic effort that bourgeois society needs in order to settle accounts radically with the gentlemen of the past can *only* be achieved through the powerful *unanimity of an entire nation* that has risen against feudal despotism, or else through a mighty *development of class struggle* within the nation that is emancipating itself. In the first case, which we saw in 1789–93, the nation's energy condensed into terrifying opposition to the old order and spent itself completely in the struggle against reaction. In the second case, which has not yet happened in history but faces us today as a possibility, the real energy needed to win victory over history's dark forces is generated within a bourgeois nation through 'internecine' class struggle. Severe internal frictions consume vast energy, deprive the bourgeoisie of any chance to play the leading role, and propel its antagonists forward, giving them the experience of decades in the span of a few months, bringing them to the forefront and entrusting to them the tightly drawn reins of government. Being decisive and confident, they impart to events a grandiose scale.

Either the nation gathers tightly together, like a lion about to leap, or else it finally breaks apart in the process of struggle in order to free up its best elements to complete the tasks that the nation as a whole cannot accomplish. These are, of course, two polar types, two pure forms of possibility that can be separated only in logic.

The middle way, in this case as in so many others, is the worst of all, and it was the middle way that occurred in 1848.

In the heroic period of French history, we see a bourgeoisie that is enlightened and active. It has yet to understand the contradictions inherent in its own position, to which history has summoned it to lead the struggle for a new order of things – not merely against the obsolete institutions of France, but against all the reactionary forces of the whole of Europe. The bourgeoisie consistently knows, and all of its different fractions know, that it is the nation's leader, that it is drawing the masses into the struggle, giving them slogans, and dictating their tactics for the fight. Democracy is the political ideology that binds the nation together. The people – the petty bourgeoisie, peasants, and workers – send members of the bourgeoisie to be their deputies, and the mandates they give them are written in the language of a bourgeoisie that is becoming conscious of its messianic role. Although class antagonisms may break out during the revolution itself, the powerful inertia of revolutionary struggle casts aside the most stagnant bourgeois elements. Every stratum makes its departure only after it has passed on its energy to those that follow. The nation as a whole continues in these circumstances to fight for its objectives with increasingly forceful and decisive means. The nation is on the move, and by the time the upper elements of the wealthy bourgeoisie break away from the main body to ally with Louis XVI, the nation's democratic demands have already turned *against* this bourgeoisie and are focusing on universal suffrage and a republic, which are the logically inevitable forms of democracy.

The Great French Revolution is a truly national revolution. Indeed, it is more than that. What we see here within national limits is the classical expression of a world struggle on the part of the bourgeois system for supremacy, power, and undivided triumph.

By 1848, the bourgeoisie was already incapable of playing such a role. It neither wished nor had the courage to take responsibility for liquidating a social order that had become an obstacle to its own supremacy. We already know *why*. Its task – and it was clearly aware of this task – was to incorporate into the old order the necessary guarantees; not guarantees of its own political rule, but merely of co-rule with the forces of the past. It was wise in its restraint because of the experience of the French bourgeoisie, corrupted by its own betrayals, and frightened by its own failures. Not only did it fail to lead the masses in storming the old order, it even bent its back to support the old order and repel the masses that were pushing the bourgeoisie forward.

The French bourgeoisie knew how to make its revolution great. Its consciousness was the consciousness of society, and nothing could be embodied in institutions without first being conceived in its consciousness as a goal and a task of political creation. It frequently took up a theatrical pose in order to hide from itself the limitations of its own bourgeois world – but it still moved forward.

From the very outset, the German bourgeoisie, rather than 'making' the revolution, distanced itself from it. Its consciousness rebelled against the objective conditions of its own supremacy. The revolution, which could not be made by it, had to be made against it. It saw democratic institutions not as the goal of its struggle but rather as a threat to its wellbeing.

What was needed in 1848 was a class able to bypass the bourgeoisie and lead events without them, a class that was prepared not only to drive them forward with the force of its own movement, but also to throw their dead political carcass out of the way at the decisive moment.

Neither the petty bourgeoisie nor the peasants could do this.

The petty bourgeoisie was hostile both to the past and to the future. Still entangled in medieval relations, yet already unable to compete against 'free' industry; still imposing its imprint upon the city, but already losing its influence to the middle and big bourgeoisie; burdened with its own prejudices, stunned by the thunder of events, exploiting and exploited at the same time, avaricious yet impotent in its greed, the provincial petty bourgeoisie had no capacity to lead world events.

The peasantry was even less capable of any independent political initiative. Enslaved over the course of centuries, impoverished, embittered, and uniting in itself all the elements of both the old and the new forms of exploitation, the peasantry represented a bountiful source of chaotic revolutionary energy at a certain moment. But being scattered, dispersed, and shut out of the cities, the nerve centres of politics and culture; being dull, confined within their local horizons, and indifferent to everything that concerned the cities, the peasantry could not have any leading significance. It was pacified the moment the burden of feudal obligations was lifted from its shoulders; and it repaid the city, which had struggled for its rights, with dark ingratitude. The emancipated peasants became fanatics of 'order'.

The intelligentsia democrats, with no class strength, first plodded along behind their older sisters as the tail end of the liberal bourgeoisie and then fell behind it at critical moments in order to demonstrate their own weakness. They found themselves confused within contradictions that had not yet matured, and they carried their confusion with them everywhere they went.

The proletariat was too weak, being deprived of organisation, experience, and knowledge. Capitalist development had progressed sufficiently to require elimination of the old feudal relations, but not far enough to bring forth the working class, the product of new relations of production, as the decisive political force. The antagonism between the proletariat and the bourgeoisie, even within the national confines of Germany, had gone too far to permit the bourgeoisie to come out fearlessly in the role of national *hegemon*, but not yet far enough to permit the proletariat to take on this role itself. True, the internal tensions of the revolution prepared the proletariat for political independence, but then they grew weaker and lost the capacity for united action, spent their energies without result, and thus caused the revolution, after its first successes, to languish and mark time in order later, under the blows of reaction, to retreat.

Austria provided an especially clear and tragic example of such incomplete and unfinished political relations during a revolutionary period.

In 1848 the Viennese *proletariat* demonstrated amazing heroism and inexhaustible energy. Time and again, it went into the fire, moved only by vague class instinct, lacking any general understanding of the struggle's goals, feeling its way from one slogan to another. In a surprising manner, leadership of the proletariat fell to the *students*, the only active *democratic group*, whose activity won them considerable influence over the masses and thus over events as well. There is no doubt that the students were able to fight courageously on the barricades and knew how to fraternise honestly with the workers, but they were unable to give the revolution direction and entrusted it instead to their 'dictatorship' of the streets.

And what happened? When all of working Vienna, in response to a summons from the students, stood up on 26 May in order to fight against disarming the students (the Academic Legion); when the population of the capital, after covering the entire city with barricades, showed surprising strength and took control of the city; when all of Austria stood behind armed Vienna; when the monarchy was in flight and had ceased to be of any importance; when, under popular pressure, the last troops had been driven from the capital; when governmental power in Austria was an estate looking for an heir – there was simply no political force to take over.

The liberal bourgeoisie deliberately had no wish to make use of power won by means of theft. All it could do was dream of the emperor's return from Tyrol, where he had fled from orphaned Vienna.

The workers were courageous enough to break the reaction, but they were neither sufficiently organised nor sufficiently conscious to inherit what it left behind. There was a powerful workers' movement, but no developed proletarian class struggle with its own defined political objectives. Unable to take the helm, the workers were powerless at this historic moment to complete the heroic deed or to drive forward bourgeois democracy, which, as it so often does, went into hiding at the most decisive moment. In order to compel this absentee to fulfil its duty, the proletariat would have had to possess at least the same strength and maturity that would have enabled it to organise its own provisional workers' government.

Generally speaking, what emerged was a state of affairs that one contemporary described perfectly when he said: 'A republic was in fact established in Vienna, but unfortunately no one saw it…'. The republic that no one noticed eventually vanished from the scene and gave way to the Habsburgs. Once lost, a particular conjuncture of events does not return a second time.

From the experience of the Hungarian and German revolutions, Lassalle concluded that henceforth a revolution could only be supported by the class struggle of the proletariat.

In his letter to Marx on 24 October, 1849, Lassalle writes:

> Hungary has a better chance than any other country to conclude the struggle successfully. Among other reasons, this is because the parties there are not yet clearly divided by the same sharp antagonisms as in Western Europe, and the revolution has been greatly facilitated in the form of a national struggle for independence. Nevertheless, Hungary was conquered precisely through betrayal by the *national* party.
>
> From this [Lassalle continues, referring to the history of Germany in 1848 and 1849] the firm lesson I draw is that no struggle can be successful in

> Europe unless it declares itself to be purely socialist from the very beginning;
> no further struggle can succeed if it is outwardly waged under the banner
> of national rebirth and bourgeois republicanism, with social questions
> obscured and relegated to the background....[48]

We shall not take time to criticise these firm convictions. They are certainly correct in one respect; and that is that, already in the mid-nineteenth century, the national task of political emancipation could not be completed through the unanimous and coordinated pressure of the entire nation. Only the independent tactics of the proletariat, which derives strength for the fight exclusively from its own class position, could have ensured the revolution's victory.

More than half a century has now passed, and Russia has entered the arena of bourgeois revolution. It is *now* even less possible than in 1848 to expect initiative and decisiveness from the bourgeoisie. On the one hand, the obstacles are much more colossal; on the other, the social and political differentiation of the nation has progressed much further. A tacit conspiracy of the national and world bourgeoisie creates terrible obstacles in the way of a rigorous process of emancipation, attempting to block it from advancing beyond an agreement between the propertied classes and representatives of the old order aimed at suppressing the popular masses. In these conditions, a democratic tactic can actually be developed only in the struggle against the liberal bourgeoisie. On this point, we must be absolutely clear. What is needed is not some fictitious 'unity' of the nation against its enemies, but profound development of the class struggle within the nation.

Intelligentsia democrats, neither wishing nor able to understand that the enormous work cannot be completed except through the great force of class struggle, will merely impede the movement by their helpless confusion and inhibition, and by offending people's ears with their incantations for unity, which are reactionary, impotent, and sentimental all at the same time. Despising the 'principle' of class struggle (because this *principle* is for them the expression of a hostile *fact*), they will try to steer the course of history in accordance with their own supra-class principles, and they will do so with the same success as Dickens's heroine, who tried to stem the tides of

---

[48] *Pis'ma F. Lassalya*, St. Petersburg, 1905, p. 7.

the ocean with a broom. The democrats will think they are capable of giving true guidance to both 'the people' and 'society', when their own behaviour is about as clearly defined as clouds driven by the wind. The moment there are powerful explosions from below, they will experience a wave of democratic sentiment, open the windows of their editorial offices halfway to catch hold of slogans from the streets, and then swear loyalty to them in their newspapers and at their banquets. At times of calm, they will turn their expectant gaze to the right, where the wealthy opposition is busily at work, and impress themselves with the great moderation of their demands and the measured steps of their movement. Full of anxiety and dread, they will run from right to left and then from left to right, chasing after their flickering flame of hope; in the finest and most democratic spirit, they will interpret for the plebs the intentionally vague slogans of the estates-based opposition, and then they will try to persuade and charm the latter to understand its own slogans in the same fine democratic spirit. When their efforts break apart on the hard facts of class egoism, for the hundredth time they will begin to tear themselves to pieces with democratic doubts. Universal, equal, direct, and secret voting? Is this really where the truth lies? Would it not be better to compromise somehow in the interest of unity? Then they will begin to omit first one thing and then another, all in the fantastic hope of finding a formula that will unite and reconcile everyone. A single chamber? No, say the estates-based opposition, we insist on two, and with no concessions. Then they begin to think this is a question yet to be 'decided'; they leave it 'open' (see *Syn Otechestva*) and claim it is possible to speak with supporters of both views, or, more accurately, that the issue is really just an unresolved question of constitutional mechanics and has nothing to do with a severe clash of class interests. Oh, these hesitant bourgeois democrats! They are afraid to merge with the estates-based opposition lest they become detached from the masses (to whom they have never been attached in the first place!), and they fear connecting up with the proletariat lest they break their ties with the estates-based opposition (over whom they have no influence!).

There is no doubt that the class struggle of the proletariat can drive even the bourgeoisie forward, but this is *only* possible through class struggle. On the other hand, there is equally no doubt that the proletariat, compelling the bourgeoisie to overcome its stagnation, will still find it to be a direct obstacle and will clash with it at a certain moment *even in the most normal course of events*. A class that is *able* to overcome this obstacle *must do so* and thereby take upon itself the role of *hegemon* if the country is ever to experience radical democratic rebirth. This means the supremacy of the 'fourth estate'. It goes without saying that the proletariat is fulfilling its mission by relying, just as the bourgeoisie once did, on the peasantry and the petty bourgeoisie. It is leading the countryside, drawing it into the movement, and interesting it in the success of its plans. But it alone inevitably remains the leader. This is not a 'dictatorship of the proletariat and peasantry'[49] – it is the dictatorship of the proletariat supported by the peasantry. And its work, of course, extends beyond the limits of the state. The very logic of its position will quickly propel it outwards into the international arena.

More than fifty years have passed since 1848. It has been a half century of capitalism's uninterrupted conquests throughout the entire world, a half century of the 'organic' process of mutual adaptation between the forces of bourgeois reaction and those of feudal reaction, a half century in which the bourgeoisie has revealed its rabid thirst for domination and its willingness just as rabidly to fight for it!

Like the imaginary engineer in search of the *perpetuum mobile*, who encounters one obstacle after another and piles up mechanism after mechanism to overcome them, the bourgeoisie modifies and reconstructs its apparatus of domination, avoiding any 'extra-legal' confrontations with hostile forces. But just as the self-taught engineer eventually runs into a final, insuperable obstacle – the law of the conservation of energy – so the bourgeoisie must run into a final inexorable barrier: the class antagonism that inevitably brings conflict.

Imposing its own type of economy and its own relations on all countries, capitalism has transformed the entire world into a single economic and political organism. And just as modern credit binds thousands of enterprises together by an invisible thread and imparts astounding mobility to capital, eliminating numerous small and partial crises while at the same time making general economic crises incomparably more serious, so the entire economic and political functioning of capitalism, with its world trade, its system of monstrous state debts and international political alliances, which are drawing all the reactionary forces into a single worldwide joint-stock company,

---

[49] [Lenin's formulation.]

has not only resisted all partial political crises but has also prepared the conditions for a social crisis of unprecedented dimensions. Internalising all the pathological processes, circumventing all the difficulties, brushing aside all the profound questions of domestic and international politics, and hiding all the contradictions, the bourgeoisie has postponed the denouement while simultaneously preparing a radical, worldwide liquidation of its supremacy. It has avidly clung to every reactionary force without questioning its origins. Its friends range from pope to sultan and beyond. The only reason it has not extended its bonds of 'friendship' to the Chinese Emperor is that he is not a force: it was more profitable for the bourgeoisie to plunder his possessions than to support him through the work of a worldwide gendarme and then have to pay his expenses from its own chests. In this way, the world bourgeoisie has made the stability of its state system deeply dependent upon the stability of pre-bourgeois bulwarks of reaction.

From the very outset, this fact gives currently unfolding events an international character and opens up majestic prospects. Political emancipation, led by the Russian working class, is raising the latter to heights that are historically unprecedented, providing it with colossal means and resources, and making it the initiator of capitalism's worldwide liquidation, for which history has prepared all the objective preconditions.

This small planet on which we live will only complete this task once. How fortunate is the generation that will shoulder this responsibility!

Chapter Thirteen

'Social Democracy and Revolution' (25 November [12 November] 1905)
Leon Trotsky

In 1929, Leon Trotsky published *The Permanent Revolution* in response to Stalinist attacks on his book *Results and Prospects*, written in 1906. According to Stalinist propaganda of the 1920s, Lenin condemned Trotsky's theory of permanent revolution at the time of the 1905 revolution for 'under-estimating' the peasantry. In this volume, we have pointed out in several places that Trotsky did indeed reject Lenin's slogan of 'the democratic dictatorship of the proletariat and the peasantry' on the grounds that the peasants would be unable to produce a coherent political party to serve as a reliable ally of Social Democracy. In terms of the historical evidence, Trotsky showed greater foresight on this matter than Lenin. After the Bolsheviks signed the Brest-Litovsk Treaty in 1918, only a handful of Left SRs continued to support the revolutionary government, and, in August 1918, it was a Socialist Revolutionary, Fanya Kaplan, who attempted to assassinate Lenin.

The debate over *permanent revolution* only resurfaced after Lenin's death in 1924 because Stalin wrapped his claim to succession in the slogan of 'Socialism in One Country'. Trotsky was said to lack confidence in the revolution's long-run survival because a) he had *always* premised success on an international revolution, and b) he was *still* under-estimating the need for support from the peasantry, whom he allegedly proposed to tax excessively in order to finance industrialisation. Countless volumes have been written on the debate over socialism in one country, and this is not the place to review them.[1] In the fourth chapter of *Permanent Revolution*, Trotsky summarised the position he had taken in 1905 by quoting the final lines of the article we have translated here:

> The complete victory of the revolution signifies the victory of the proletariat. The latter, in turn, means further uninterrupted revolution. The proletariat is accomplishing the basic tasks of democracy, and at some moment the very logic of its struggle to consolidate its political rule places before it purely socialist problems. Revolutionary continuity [*nepreryvnost'*] is being established between the minimum and the maximum programme. It is not a question of a single 'blow', a day, or a month, but of an entire historical epoch. It would be absurd to try to fix its duration in advance.

'This one reference,' Trotsky declared in 1929, 'in a way exhausts the subject...'.[2] To settle the point, he added that in November 1905 the Bolshevik newspaper *Novaya Zhizn'*, edited by Lenin himself, dismissed any significant differences between the two men:

> This gratuitous assumption is of course sheer nonsense. Comrade Trotsky said that the proletarian revolution can, without halting at the first stage, continue on its road, elbowing the exploiters aside; Lenin, on the other hand, pointed out that the political revolution is only the first step. The publicist of *Nasha Zhizn* [a liberal newspaper] would like to see a contradiction here.... The whole misunderstanding comes, first, from the fear with which the name alone of the social revolution fills *Nasha Zhizn*; secondly, out of the desire of...[*Nasha* Zhizn'] to discover some sort of sharp and piquant difference of opinion among the Social Democrats; and thirdly, in the figure

---

[1] Insofar as the dispute involved something more than propaganda and personal vendettas among Lenin's potential successors, the salient issue for Trotsky really concerned economic policy in general, and industrialisation strategy in particular. This argument was first made in 1973 by one of the editors of this volume. See Day 1973.

[2] L. Trotsky 1962, p. 86.

> of speech used by Comrade Trotsky: 'at a single blow.' In No. 10 of *Nachalo*,
> Comrade Trotsky explains his idea quite unambiguously....[3]

Lenin obviously believed in November 1905 that his theoretical differences with Trotsky were of little immediate or practical significance. In fact, in 'Social-Democracy's Attitude Towards the Peasant Movement', published in another Bolshevik newspaper (*Proletarii*) in mid-September 1905, Lenin also wrote of the need for *uninterrupted revolution*:

> from the democratic revolution we shall at once, and precisely in accordance with the measure of our strength, the strength of the class-conscious and organised proletariat, begin to pass to the socialist revolution. We stand for *uninterrupted revolution*. We shall not stop half-way.[4]

In the 1920s, however, Stalinists insisted that there was a fundamental difference between the words 'uninterrupted' and 'permanent'. Bertram Wolfe, a respected historian and author of *Three Who Made A Revolution*, magnified the claim by declaring that Stalinist editors actually forged translations of Lenin's article 'Social-Democracy's Attitude Towards the Peasant Movement'. Wolfe wrote that Lenin had actually used the very same words as Trotsky; in other words, Lenin's statement was: 'We stand for *permanent* revolution. We shall not stop half-way.'[5] Wolfe added that this was 'Much as if some translator of Einstein would try to conceal his relation to Newton by substituting for the technical term "force of gravity" the words "force of heaviness"'.

How is sense to be made of this? The answer is simply that, in Russian, the words 'permanent revolution [*permanentnaya revolyutsiya*]' and 'uninterrupted revolution [*nepreryvnaya revolyutsiya*]' are semantic equivalents and completely interchangeable. The single difference is that *nepreryvnaya* is a more authentically Russian word, the word that native speakers would typically use in everyday speech. The most compelling evidence of this equivalence is the fact that Trotsky himself, as editor of the newspaper *Nachalo*, translated the title of the next article in this volume, by Franz Mehring, in exactly this

---

[3] L. Trotsky 1962, pp. 85–6. The article referred to is the one translated here from *Nachalo* No. 10, 25 [12] November, 1905.

[4] Lenin 1905f, pp. 236–7.

[5] Wolfe 1966, p. 336. Wolfe was mistaken in this assertion: in *Proletarii* No 16, on 14 (1) September 1905, Lenin did use the term 'uninterrupted revolution', not 'permanent' revolution as Wolfe claimed.

way. Mehring's original title in German was 'Die Revolution in Permanenz', which *Nachalo* translated as 'Nepreryvnaya revolyutsiya'. Near the end of the article translated here, Trotsky likewise expressed the concept of permanent revolution by using the words 'nepreryvnaya revolyutsiya'. In his foreword to Marx's essay on the Paris Commune, he again spoke of 'a revolution *in Permanenz*, or an *uninterrupted* revolution'.[6]

That this use of words was no quirk on Trotsky's part can further be seen in the fact that Ryazanov, writing at about the same time, declared in 'The Next Questions of our Movement' that 'Our motto must be the revolution *in Permanenz* (uninterrupted revolution) – not "order" in place of revolution, but revolution in place of order.'[7] Parvus, in another essay published late in 1905, followed the exact same practice, referring to political tactics 'from the point of view of an organisation of the social-revolutionary army of the proletariat that would make the revolution uninterrupted (permanent)'.[8]

There would be no need to clarify this terminology in such detail were it not for the fact that a vast literature has made a shibboleth out of the word 'uninterrupted' as distinct from 'permanent', as if they implied a basic difference of political tactics and prognoses. The salient question did not concern words: it involved the issue of whether the revolution would come to a halt once bourgeois liberals took power (as Plekhanov and his supporters expected), in which case the proletarian party should reconcile itself merely to a supportive role, or whether, instead, to follow the tactics of permanent revolution outlined by Marx in the 1850 'Address of the Central Committee to the Communist League'.[9] This is the question addressed by Trotsky in 'Social Democracy and Revolution'; and this question alone, as he said in 1929, effectively 'exhausts the subject'.[10]

*　*　*

---

[6] See below, p. 501.
[7] See below, p. 474.
[8] Parvus 1905b, p. 18.
[9] Marx and Engels 1850.
[10] L. Trotsky 1969, p. 210.

'Social Democracy and Revolution'

Russian Social Democracy is presently at the centre of society's attention, and with good reason. Liberalism sees in our activities a threat to 'freedom' and 'order'. The reaction sees a threat to its own existence. They are both correct. Yesterday we were merely underground circles. The police, it is true, paid a great deal more attention to us than we would have liked, but the work of the police was aimed essentially at eliminating underground 'conspirators'. The democratic intelligentsia, who did not believe in the proletariat's revolutionary future, fought against us only because they saw a hostile ideology. Today things have changed dramatically. Social Democracy has matured and is leading the proletariat, which stands at the centre of revolutionary events. This means that Social Democracy is the focus of hostile attention from the entire press, whether reactionary, conservative or liberal.

Just yesterday, we were being accused from all sides of applying a European doctrine and European tactics to unique Russian circumstances. Today hundreds of voices are claiming that we are not worthy of our honourable name because our tactics have nothing in common with those of European Social Democracy.

Mr. Struve, who is regarded as an authority on such questions in bourgeois circles because he is a deserter from the Marxist camp, is categorically declaring that Russian Social Democracy is simply 'a blend of anarchism and Jacobinism'.

Citing Mr. Struve, *Novoe Vremya*, which currently sides with him on all the basic political questions, is confidently declaring that Social Democracy, 'in its genuine German form, is not only tolerable, but is possibly the most respectable of all the German parties'. According to this newspaper, even in Russia there is such a group of 'honest and peaceable Social Democrats', but they are being brushed aside by a group of anarchists 'who have dressed themselves up in respectable German clothes'.

Some mysterious 'Marxists', who have hitched a ride on the carriage of *Nasha Zhizn'*, the Cadet newspaper, are joining the general chorus and accusing us of Social-Revolutionary adventurism. This bourgeois newspaper believes that the entire doctrine of 'evolutionary' Marxism stands in opposition to our attempt 'to put an end both to autocracy and to capitalism at a single blow'. In the opinion of *Nasha Zhizn'*, Social Democrats could be playing an enormous role. 'The proletariat has placed its confidence in them and is willing to put its fate in their hands.' The intelligentsia sympathises with Social-Democratic ideals. The democratic bourgeoisie would follow the intelligentsia. Social Democracy could stand at their head and lead the nation to victory. But that would require a tactic of 'concentrating' all democratic forces, as in the case of German Social Democracy. Instead, Russian Social Democracy is isolating the proletariat and making it stand alone, thereby digging the grave of democracy.

There is nothing surprising for us in the fact that the nationalistic *Novoe Vremya* is indignant over our departure from the 'respectable' German pattern. Feeble-minded reaction has never done more than contrast the 'anarchic' socialists of its own country with the 'patriotic' socialists of other countries. Whenever the government of a bourgeois republic has to resort to repression of anti-militarist agitation by socialists, it invariably justifies itself by referring to the 'patriotic' socialists of Germany, who are devoted to their fatherland.

Although Prince Bülow[11] prevents Jaurès[12] from visiting Berlin for the purpose of agitation, he nevertheless considers it his duty as a wise chancellor to compare Bebel and other Social Democrats, who 'take no responsibility for their fatherland', to French socialists of the most 'stately' type such as Jaurès. Why would it surprise us if a reptile who has served the tsarist government for decades by preventing a single word of European Social Democracy from crossing the border, now, in order to destroy our party, compares our Jacobinism to the wisdom and political piety of our European comrades? Why would it surprise us if the entire reactionary press simultaneously sympathises with the penitent psalms of Mr. Gapon, who, with the self-confidence of an ignoramus accuses us of transplanting European theories into the foreign and unique soil of Russia while at the same time applauding the liberal-prosecutorial speeches of Struve concerning our anarchistic renunciation of the European pattern?

It is perfectly understandable that Mr. Struve, having lost all sense of decency in his quest for an honourable official position, openly anticipates the repression of Social Democracy – or that the Petersburg prosecutor only

---

[11] [Prince Bernhard von Bülow (1849–1929) was German imperial chancellor and Prussian prime minister from 1900–1909.]

[12] [Jean Jaurès (1859–1914) was French socialist leader and member of the Chamber of Deputies.]

expresses official thinking when he respectfully cites his future boss in his speech of accusation in the matter of a 'militant organisation'.

For that reason, we will ignore the foul sorties of reaction and concentrate only on the bewilderment expressed by the 'evolutionary' Marxists of *Nasha Zhizn'*.

The final goal of German Social Democracy is seizure of state power by the proletariat. That is our goal. The path taken by our fraternal party in Germany is development of the class consciousness of the working masses and their unification as a single social-revolutionary force. That is our path. As the party of the proletariat, which is fighting for class dictatorship, we neither resemble nor have anything in common with any of the bourgeois parties either on the Right or on their far Left – but at the same time we are of the same flesh and blood as international Social Democracy. Nevertheless, our tactics differ from those of German Social Democracy during a period of reaction. For forty years, the proletarian party in Germany has been developing in an epoch of intensive bourgeois reaction, which is different from a period of revolution. In 1871, the proletarian commune of Paris was crushed; the red flag was torn up by bourgeois vandals; the Prussian helmet, a symbol of blind and conceited militarism, prevailed everywhere; and the Third Republic in France, covered with the blood of the communards and humiliated by Prussia, entered into an alliance with tsarist Russia. The bourgeoisie, with the Great Revolution in its past, undertook to preserve Asiatic absolutism, in which it quite correctly saw an appropriate figure to play the role of gendarme of world reaction. Capitalism achieved its 'peaceful' conquest on the bones of its countless victims; bourgeois democracy no longer worried about its own existence; revolutionary traditions, which prematurely died in 1848, were betrayed and forgotten – and the fumes of capitalist oppression and bourgeois chauvinism hung like dense clouds in the political atmosphere of Europe.

It was in this suffocating and impenetrable atmosphere of reaction that German Social Democracy emerged and developed. Lacking both previous experience of the politically organised class struggle of the proletariat and direct revolutionary traditions, it advanced with amazing persistence and constructed, stone by stone, the superb edifice of party democracy that is now such a source of pride to international socialism.

The Russian proletariat has taken each political step 'outside the law'. In the political school that it has experienced, the fetishism of 'legality' was the last thing to command its devotion.

Indeed, the autocracy stood before the proletariat as the embodiment of a stupid and openly oppressive state, directly convincing the proletariat that codified 'laws' are nothing but fetters that the ruling powers forcibly impose in the interest of their own domination. Revolutionary methods of struggle demonstrated to the proletariat all the advantages of a direct, 'extra-legal' and revolutionary test of strength.

While the Social Democracy of red, proletarian Saxony vainly protested year after year, within the constraints of parliamentary tactics, against the three-class system of elections, the proletariat of 'peasant' Russia, with a single revolutionary blow, threw the fundamental law concerning the State Duma onto the rubbish heap. Thanks to the revolutionary character of the times, the Russian proletariat is quite possibly closer to realising an eight-hour working day than the proletariat of England with all its powerful trade unions.

The workers have mastered the revolutionary method, and they will not voluntarily give it up. Social Democracy has transformed the fundamental demand of the working class into a slogan of the revolution and thereby enriched the revolution with all the class energy of the proletariat.

In these circumstances, what can the tactic of 'concentrating' the democratic forces mean? Either the proletariat must abandon its class demands, or – and this means essentially the same thing – it must repudiate its independent tactics. If democratic 'concentration' is more than simply a turn of phrase, what it means is adapting proletarian tactics to the behaviour of bourgeois democracy. But this would throw us back by half a century.

In the Prussian and Austrian revolutions there was a political 'concentration' in the spirit proposed by democrats from *Nasha Zhizn'*. Defying the logic of class struggle, revolutionary democracy attempted to unite the proletariat and the bourgeoisie. In the name of unity, Lassalle called upon the workers to renounce republican demands. But democracy, having attempted to unite the divided nation with a democratic ideology, proved unable either to drag the liberal bourgeoisie forward or to prohibit the class instinct of the proletariat. Amorphous class tensions weakened the tactic of 'concentration'; at the same time, the proletariat's political dependence deprived it of the possibility of using its class strength for independently organising the revolution. The heroic proletariat of Vienna defeated the monarchy in open battle. But the bourgeoisie had no desire for the republican fruits of this victory or to shoulder the cause of democracy, and the proletariat, on its own, was not sufficiently prepared to pluck the fruits for itself.

The class dismemberment of a bourgeois nation has gone much further in our country than in Prussia and Austria in 1848. Our liberal bourgeoisie turned out to be counter-revolutionary even before the revolution reached its culmination. At every critical moment, our intelligentsia democrats displayed their impotence. The peasantry as a whole represents spontaneous insurrection – but it can be put into service of the revolution only by a force that will take state power into its own hands.

That leaves the proletariat.

The terrible resistance of absolutism is still further strengthening our revolutionary development, which is more systematic than ever before in history. Overcoming the mighty resistance of the autocratic state and the conscious inactivity of the bourgeoisie, the working class of Russia has developed into an organised fighting force without precedent. There is no stage of the bourgeois revolution at which this fighting force, driven forward by the steel logic of class interests, could be appeased. Uninterrupted revolution[13] is becoming the law of self-preservation for the proletariat.

The vanguard position of the working class in the revolutionary struggle; the direct link it is establishing with the revolutionary countryside; the skill with which it is subordinating the army to itself – all of these factors are inevitably driving it to power. The complete victory of the revolution signifies the victory of the proletariat.

The latter, in turn, means further uninterrupted revolution. The proletariat is accomplishing the basic tasks of democracy, and at some moment the very logic of its struggle to consolidate its political rule places before it purely socialist problems. Revolutionary continuity is being established between the minimum and the maximum programme. It is not a question of a single 'blow', a day, or a month, but of an entire historical epoch. It would be absurd to try to fix its duration in advance.

---

[13] [*nepreryvnaya revolyutsiya*].

Chapter Fourteen
'The Revolution in Permanence'
(1 November 1905)
Franz Mehring

In 1899, at the height of the revisionist controversy, Franz Mehring defended the theory of permanent revolution against Bernstein's attacks in the pages of *Die Neue Zeit*.[1] Against Bernstein's accusation that Marx and Engels had pursued a 'Blanquist' (i.e. putschist) tactic during the revolutionary years 1848–9, Mehring pointed out that they had never

> over-estimated the 'creative power of revolutionary violence for the socialist transformation of modern society'. For them, the important thing was to seize as many positions as possible from the counter-revolutionary powers; in that sense they opposed the cowardly Philistine clamour for the 'closing of the revolution' and demanded instead the 'revolution in permanence'.[2]

Mehring went on to defend the March 1850 circular[3] (where Marx and Engels first formulated the theory of permanent revolution) against Bernstein's criticisms:

---

[1] Mehring 1899, pp. 147–54, 208–15, 239–47.
[2] Mehring 1899, pp. 244.
[3] Marx and Engels 1850.

In March 1850 they issued a circular to the League of Communists that inspires special anger in Bernstein, because in it 'the Blanquist spirit manifests itself more sharply and unrestrainedly' than anywhere else. Bernstein closes a long condemnation of this circular with the indignant sentence: 'All economic understanding vanishes before this programme; no newly arrived salon revolutionary could have drawn up a more illusory one.' In order to appreciate this circular correctly, one must picture for oneself the whole historical context in which it originated. When the German revolution broke out in March 1848, Marx and Engels believed that it would run its course through decades-long struggles, like the English Revolution of the seventeenth and the French Revolution of the eighteenth century. But very quickly it became evident that the German bourgeoisie differed from the English and French bourgeoisie in a very essential respect, namely, in the fact that out of fear of the incomparably more highly developed working class of the nineteenth century, it was ready to accept the 'closure of the revolution' at any moment, even at the price of the most ignominious concessions to absolutism and feudalism. From this followed a change of tactics on the part of the working class, and already in April 1849 Marx and his close followers retired from the democratic district committees in Köln because they saw the necessity for a close union of the workers' associations against the weaknesses and treacheries of the bourgeoisie. At the same time they decided to attend the workers' congress planned for June 1849, which had been convoked in Leipzig by the workers' movement east of the Elbe, to whom the *Neue Rheinische Zeitung* had not paid much attention until then. Subsequently, the miserable cowardice of the German bourgeoisie became even more evident, and so the circular of March 1850 [the 'Address of the Central Committee to the Communist League'] gave precise instructions, in the event of an imminent new outbreak of the revolution, for the Communists everywhere to mobilise the workers in order to make the revolution 'permanent'. Since Marx and Engels proceeded from the assumption that the revolution would be accomplished through thirty or fifty years of class and national struggles, the basic principles of revolutionary proletarian policy were indicated there in a perfectly correct way – even if no newly arrived Blanquist or 'newly arrived salon revolutionary' could have drawn up the policy so clearly and precisely.[4]

---

[4] Mehring 1899, pp. 244–5.

In the article translated here,[5] Mehring addressed the Russian revolution in the same terms as Trotsky. Mehring's article was first published in German in *Die Neue Zeit* and then translated into Russian by Trotsky and Parvus in their newspaper *Nachalo* (No. 10, 25 November 1905), together with Trotsky's 'Social Democracy and Revolution' (the preceding article in this anthology). Translating Mehring's original title, 'Die Revolution in Permanenz', into 'Nepreryvnaya Revolyutsiya' or 'Uninterrupted Revolution', Parvus and Trotsky explained in a footnote that

> on questions concerning the Russian revolution, this outstanding historian and publicist of German Social Democracy adopts our view, which sycophants and philistines are trying to depict as anarchism and Jacobinism.

*   *   *

'The Revolution in Permanence'

Fortunate are those who have lived to witness this glorious year, the year of the Russian revolution, which in the history books will be no less epoch-making than the French Revolution of the year 1789. All the revolutions of the nineteenth century were only descendants of the French Revolution; legitimate descendants to be sure, but also weaker – and that is true even of the European movement of the year 1848. However powerful [the 1848 revolution] was, and however far its indirect results extended, it only spread the consequences of the year 1789 over the European continent, and its wave retreated before the wall of the Russian borders.

What distinguishes the great Russian revolution from the great French Revolution is its leadership by the class-conscious proletariat. The Bastille was also stormed by the workers of the *faubourg* St. Antoine; and the victory at the barricades of 18 March 1848, was won by the Berlin workers against the Prussian guards. But the heroes of these revolutions were at the same time the victims; the very day after the victory, the bourgeoisie snatched the prize away from them. And that is why the revolutions modelled on 1789 eventually died out. The counter-revolution had such an easy job in the years

---

[5] Mehring 1905b, pp. 84–8. The translation given here is from the original German and has been checked against the translation that appeared in the Russian newspaper *Nachalo*, edited by Trotsky and Parvus.

1848 and 1849 because the workers had become tired of pulling the chestnuts out of the fire only to be betrayed by those who ate them up, and because their class consciousness was not developed enough for them to find their way between feudal power and bourgeois treachery.

What was the weakness of the European Revolution of 1848 is the strength of the Russian revolution of 1905. Its moving force is a proletariat that has understood the 'Revolution in Permanence'[6] that the *Neue Rheinische Zeitung* formerly preached in the wilderness. While their blood flows in streams under the guns and sabres of the tsar's executioners, the Russian workers are holding fast to their demands with tenacious strength; and with the powerful weapon of the political mass strike they have shaken the tsarist power to its foundations. In the newest manifesto of the tsar, Asiatic despotism abdicates forever; by promising a constitution it has crossed the Rubicon from which there is no return.[7]

It is the first great success of the Russian proletariat, greater than any other ever won by the proletariat of another country in a revolutionary movement. The assailants of the Bastille and the fighters at the Berlin barricades were also capable of a heroic uprising, but not of that untiring and stubborn struggle that the Russian workers have unflinchingly carried on despite all the momentary failures. But this first success now sets before them a new and incomparably greater task: the task of preserving the old readiness to fight even after the victory. It is a recurrent experience in military history that after a brilliant victory it is difficult to bring even the bravest troops under fire again in order to consolidate their victory by pursuing the enemy. And that is all the more difficult, the more splendid the victory. The need for a restoring period of calm after experiencing extreme tension is deeply rooted in human nature, and the bourgeoisie has always speculated upon this fact with the greatest success whenever the proletariat had shaken down for it the fruits from the trees of the revolution.

---

[6] [As noted, Mehring's expression appears in the Russian text as 'Uninterrupted [*Nepreryvnaya*] Revolution'.]

[7] [In August 1905 the tsar accepted proposals for reform submitted by a committee headed by Alexander Bulygin, who had replaced Svyatopolk-Mirsky as Interior Minister. Known as the 'Bulygin Constitution', these proposals provided for an elected State Duma with consultative functions, leaving the tsar with the ability to pass legislation with the support of an upper chamber, the State Council, composed of dignitaries whom the tsar would himself appoint.]

One bourgeois newspaper has quite justifiably commented that the tsar's manifesto is vividly reminiscent of the promises made by Friedrich Wilhelm IV once the revolution smashed his authoritarian insolence. In fact, they are almost the same promises: inviolability of the person, freedom of conscience and of speech, popular representation with a wide franchise and with decisive participation in legislation. Then, as is the case now, the bourgeois opposition knew, and still knows very well, that when a defeated despot is forced to make such concessions he cannot be trusted at his word but must offer real guarantees that an autocracy compelled by force to humiliate itself so dramatically will never again be able to raise its head with tyrannical strength. But it is in the interest of the bourgeoisie to belittle the achievements of the revolution in order to disarm the proletariat; to present it as a *Fata Morgana*[8] that can only come true with the greatest prudence; to warn the proletariat against any bold crow that could, so to speak, scare away the nocturnal ghosts. Thus, after every revolutionary victory, the bourgeoisie raises the cry for 'peace at any price', ostensibly in the interests of the working class but in fact out of the cold-blooded, cunning calculations of the bourgeoisie itself.

This is the most dangerous hour of the revolution, but fatal as it has often been to the proletariat until now, this time the Russian working class has passed the test brilliantly by responding resolutely to the tsar's manifesto: the revolution in permanence[9] is continuing. It is a great honour to our Russian brothers when bourgeois newspapers report today from Petersburg that

> Under the influence of the socialists, public opinion has become significantly more ill-disposed than was previously expected. At present the excellent organisation of the socialists has the upper hand over the bourgeois elements.

The Russian workers have no intention of disarming. The victors of today do not want to be swindled tomorrow, and it is precisely in this respect that we see the world-historical progress that the Russian revolution has made over all its predecessors.

Of course, the saying that miracles do not happen tomorrow also applies to the Russian workers. It is not in their power to skip the stages of historical

---

[8] [An illusion.]
[9] [Here the Russian version of Mehring's text again speaks of 'the uninterrupted revolution'.]

development and instantly to create a socialist community out of the despotic tsarist state. But they can shorten and smooth the road of their struggle for complete emancipation, provided they do not sacrifice their hard-won revolutionary power to the deceptive mirages of the bourgeoisie but keep asserting it in order to accelerate the historical, that is to say, the revolutionary development. In months or weeks they can now obtain what would take them decades of laborious effort if, after victory, they abandoned the field to the bourgeoisie. They cannot write the dictatorship of the proletariat into the new Russian constitution; but they can insert into it universal suffrage, freedom of organisation, the legally regulated working day, and unrestricted freedom of the press and speech; and they can also extract from the bourgeoisie guarantees for all these demands as firm as those that the bourgeoisie will extract from the tsar for its own needs. But the workers can do all this only if they do not for an instant lay down their weapons and if they do not permit the bourgeoisie to advance even a single step without themselves taking a step forward.

It is precisely by means of the revolution in permanence[10] that the Russian working class must reply – and judging by the news to date, has already replied – to the bourgeois cry for 'peace at any price'. It is false to say that this can infuse new vitality into the just defeated despotism. A historian of the great French Revolution – Tocqueville if I am not mistaken – quite rightly said that a crumbling regime is never weaker than when it begins to reform. And that is even truer of the decaying autocracy in Russia than of the decaying monarchy in France, because its entire governmental machinery is rotten to the core. As soon as the state machinery gives up the pretence of strength that it has laboriously maintained until now, it is defenceless against any strong blow. In reality, it is the autocracy that needs 'peace at any price' if it is to be rebuilt on new foundations. That is the treacherous meaning of this slogan, which one must hope has now lost forever its ominous role.

The Russian workers have thus become the leading fighters of the European proletariat. They have had the good fortune – not shared by any proletariat of the West-European nations – of beginning the revolution with accumulated experiences, with a clear, deep and broad theory, but they have also understood how to turn that good fortune to their advantage. Decades of

---

[10] [Here the Russian text again refers to 'uninterrupted revolution'.]

struggle and the sacrifices of countless victims have turned the theory of the proletarian revolution for them into flesh and blood, and what they received, they are now amply returning. They have disgraced the faint-hearted, for they have proved that what many considered impossible was indeed possible. The European workers now know that they have outlived the methods of struggle of the old revolutions only in order to add new and more effective ones to the history of their emancipation struggle. Sparks from the bonfire of the Russian revolution have fallen on the working class of all the European countries, and in Austria bright flames are already breaking out.

Last but not least, the German workers are also taking part in the struggle led by their Russian brothers. The Prusso-German tributary state is so tightly entangled with the fate of tsarism that the downfall of Russian absolutism will have the most profound effects on the kingdom of the Junkers to the east of the Elbe. The powerful economic upheavals resulting from the Russian Revolution may also have an unsettling effect on the clique of usurers in the grain trade, if only for a brief time and without any disastrous consequences, compelling them to become even more tight-fisted. But over the longer term, the Russian revolution can no more be confined within Russian borders than the French Revolution could be confined within the borders of France, and nobody knows that better than the ruling classes in Germany.

We can be certain that they are following the development of the Russian revolution with the closest attention and that they will await the moment to attempt to deal it a crushing blow when they think they have the greatest prospects of success.

The German working class must be equally aware that that the cause of its Russian brothers is also its own.

Chapter Fifteen

The Next Questions of our Movement (September 1905)

N. [David] Ryazanov

The exact date when this document was published is not clear from the text.[1] Since Ryazanov opens with the statement that 'Peace has been concluded,' it was apparently published shortly after the Treaty of Portsmouth, signed in New Hampshire on 5 September 1905. Ryazanov's major concern was that the tsarist government, having made peace with its external enemy, would now have a free hand to settle accounts with its only real domestic enemy, the revolutionary workers. Defending the strategy of permanent revolution, Ryazanov avoided naming Plekhanov and Lenin for the sake of preserving an appearance of Social-Democratic unity, but he tacitly criticised them both: Plekhanov for assuming that Russian liberals would somehow marginalise the tsar once an 'elected' state Duma was in place; and Lenin for advocating an armed insurrection on the assumption of support from the 'people' at large. Ryazanov argued that only the revolutionary workers were capable of waging a consistent

---

[1] Ryazanov 1905.

struggle, and success would depend above all on overcoming fratricidal divisions within Social Democracy between the Menshevik and Bolshevik factions.

The government's hope of regaining control over internal affairs depended either upon silencing all opposition – which was now impossible – or else upon reaching some sort of accord with liberals and democrats. In February 1905, the tsar had assigned Alexander Bulygin, Svyatopolk-Mirsky's replacement as Interior Minister, to head a commission to draft proposals for some sort of legislative assembly. Bulygin's report in August recommended a purely consultative Duma with a highly restricted suffrage and elections in three or four stages, with workers almost completely disenfranchised. Even liberals dismissed this archaic project, but the government did succeed in dividing its opponents as they debated whether or not to participate in any forthcoming elections.

Among Social Democrats, Plekhanov accused Lenin of driving the bourgeoisie to the right, while Lenin demanded a boycott of elections and preparation for an armed uprising. With reference to Plekhanov, Ryazanov repeated his warning that tsarism was far more than an obsolescent remnant of the past.[2] Tsarism had survived previous crises, and the history of Europe since the 1848 revolutions demonstrated that absolutist régimes were perfectly capable of co-habiting with *ersatz* democratic institutions through reconciliation with a bourgeoisie that feared the proletariat more than a monarch. Ridiculing the Bulygin proposals as a modified version of a 'sheep's parliament', Ryazanov had one answer to the debate over the appropriate attitude for Social Democrats:

> To boycott or not to boycott the State Duma, to take part in the elections or not to take part – these questions do not even exist for the proletariat. The State Duma must be destroyed. To recognise it, to try to use it as a tribune or to reform it – these are not just stupid and senseless ideas. To pursue them would be a political crime by which the proletariat would repudiate any independent policy. We will exert the most rational *pressure* on the State Duma when we adopt the goal of *crushing* it as rapidly as possible.

---

[2] See in this volume N. [David] Ryazanov, 'The Draft Programme of *Iskra* and the Tasks of Russian Social Democrats' and G.V. Plekhanov's reply, '"Orthodox" Pedantry'.

An *independent* proletarian policy was one rooted in the fundamental economics of class struggle, not in superficial *political* strategies or electoral accommodations. As a proponent of *permanent revolution*, Ryazanov saw the general strike as the proletariat's ultimate weapon, serving simultaneously both to *organise* the workers and to provide leadership for other dissident elements of the population. While criticising Plekhanov for anticipating some form of accommodation with liberalism, Ryazanov also took Lenin to task for the opposite error of thinking that somehow the entire 'people' could be mobilised for a decisive armed confrontation with the autocracy:

> …before everything else, there is something supremely important that our revolutionary strategists and tacticians too often forget – and that is that before we can create an organisation of 'the people', it is above all imperative that we unite ourselves and create a stable organisation of the proletariat.

Ryazanov saw only one tactic for dealing with tsarist absolutism: 'Go for its throat and put a knee to its chest!' in the hope that 'governmental power might fall into the hands of the proletariat'. The issue, he declared, 'will not be *participation* in a provisional government, but rather seizure of power by the working class and conversion of the "bourgeois" revolution into a direct prologue for the social revolution'. The outcome of revolution in Russia would be decided internally by the class struggle of the Russian proletariat, and externally by one of two events: either the international bourgeoisie would lend renewed financial support to the tsar, or alternatively the proletarian revolution would spread to Western Europe. In the meantime, the slogan of revolutionary Social Democrats must be 'the revolution *in Permanenz* (uninterrupted revolution)', which required

> *relentless criticism of all the constitutional projects of our liberals and bourgeois democrats, unmasking the class background of all programmes on behalf of 'the entire people' and destroying all illusions of some community of political goals on the part of all classes of the population, particularly of the bourgeoisie and the proletariat.*

*   *   *

The Next Questions of our Movement

Peace has been concluded. And no matter how hard our officials, aided by the venal West-European press, try to exalt the Russian government's 'diplomatic victory', the facts speak too eloquently. Russia has never before concluded such a disgraceful peace, and tsarist absolutism has never before sustained a more shameful defeat. All that remains of 'supremacy in the Far East' is the miserable consolation that 'Russia is still a great power'. Hundreds of thousands of human lives were lost in the fields of Manchuria and on the waves of the Great Ocean, and hundreds, even thousands of millions of roubles were squeezed out of the toiling masses – and Russia has had to pay all this for an adventure by a small clique of crowned and uncrowned capitalist predators.

While the international financial barons were indifferent to stock-market bulletins concerning the defeats of the Russian army and navy, reacting with an almost imperceptible decline in the price of Russian state securities; and while they and the Russian plutocrats often thought this implied rising 'hopes for the conclusion of peace', after 9 January the financial barons anxiously followed growth of the proletariat's revolutionary movement and responded to each new outburst with a sharp decline in the price of Russian industrial securities. It seemed that Russian absolutism, this last remaining pillar of 'order and property', might not withstand the combined pressure of its 'internal' and 'external' enemies. Further delay became inadmissible, and it was only thanks to intervention by the 'honest broker' Roosevelt, acting on instructions from the magnates of the international bankocracy – the Seligmans, Mendelsohns and Bleichroeders – that Russia escaped paying billions in reparations. Still, the tsarist government acceded to Japanese 'requests' and surrendered not just the districts it had occupied in China but also half of Sakhalin, part of the 'age-old Russian land'.[3]

---

[3] [On 5 September, 1905, the Treaty of Portsmouth formally ended the Russo-Japanese War. President Theodore Roosevelt brokered the treaty with the intention of requiring Japan to follow an 'Open Door' policy in Manchuria and to accede to American freedom of action in the Philippines. Russia recognised Japan's 'paramount political, military, and economic interests' in Korea and agreed to put Manchuria under Chinese sovereignty. Russia surrendered the south Manchurian railway to Japan, together with Port Arthur and the southern part of Sakhalin Island. For his mediation in the Russo-Japanese War, Roosevelt – one of the founding fathers of American imperialism, who in his memoirs declared that he 'took Panama' from

But politically bankrupted Russian absolutism, although covered in shame and inundated with the blood of its 'subjects', still managed to remain upright on its 'feet of clay'. Saved from its 'external enemy', it can now breathe more easily and is all the more furiously attacking its 'internal enemy'. Its strength is still far from exhausted, especially when it can draw that strength from two sources – one within Russia itself, the other in international political relations.

Russian absolutism is by no means merely 'a relic of pre-capitalist formations' or simply 'the most powerful and vile remnant of serfdom'.

In historical terms, our autocracy really is rooted in the past, but that is equally true of many other aspects of social life. Unlike other 'remnants', however, it is more than just a *vestige* or a fragment of the past that happens to be preserved.

Created by the ruling classes to protect domestic exploitation against invasion by external enemies, it was always a weapon in the hands of one social class or another. Russian history knows of no autocracy that somehow stood *above classes*, oppressed the *entire* population *equally*, or was equally resented by *all* classes. The social-economic structure changed, the array of class interests changed within the ruling classes, and so did the character of our autocracy. Following a more or less prolonged crisis, which tore up some of its roots in the *past*, it sank new roots in fresh soil and, after surviving a period of 'political instability' or 'great reforms', it adjusted to *current* conditions and continued as before to play the role of a vampire, draining the vitality of the toiling masses for the benefit of one or another group of privileged leeches from the ranks of the ruling classes.

Today Russian absolutism is living through a similar crisis. Historical legends of the time when it was an instrument solely in the hands of the nobility are gradually being stifled by the rapid and forceful growth of capitalism. The old absolutism is still trying to preserve a balance between agriculture and the industrial bourgeoisie, but development of capitalism is creating growing contradictions between these two sources of support and leading it towards destruction despite all its efforts to adjust to the changed

---

Colombia, and whose infamous corollary to the Monroe Doctrine is known as 'Big Stick Diplomacy' because he argued that US foreign relations towards Latin American should be ruled by the African proverb, 'Speak softly and carry a big stick' – was awarded the Nobel Peace Prize in 1906.]

class structure. Perishing in one form, however, the autocracy might, as in the past, re-emerge in another.

Our absolutism is still far from isolated and continues to be solidly based in the 'present'. It is supported by all the large-scale feudal landowners, with the great princes at their head; by our upper clergy, with all their monasteries; by the entire financial bourgeoisie; by the black-hundred[4] elements of the commercial-industrial bourgeoisie; and by the entire reactionary petty bourgeoisie. Moreover, the political indifference of the peasants continues, and they have yet to finally abandon their faith in the 'tsar-father'. Of course, it is also true that today 'capital is rebelling'; the 'enlightened' nobility are playing at opposition after tasting fruit from the capitalist tree of knowledge of good and evil; and bourgeois ideologues, members of the various 'liberal professions' are sulking – but all of this is merely a 'debate among Slavs', a debate between the different fractions of the economically ruling classes over how best to ensure the 'order and calm' that has been disrupted by the restive proletariat, and how to create a 'strong government' that might deal with 'sedition'. The only question of any interest to the 'seditious' proletariat is just who among this worthy company represents the 'lesser evil'. As allies in the struggle against autocracy, even the most 'left' among them are completely untrustworthy and will readily sell out the interests of the toiling masses in exchange for 'a mess of pottage' in the form of trivial reforms.

But the autocracy draws its strength not only from its 'original' sources. It is also strongly supported by the entire golden international,[5] and its financial credit is yet to be undermined.

As in the past, it remains today a most trustworthy support for every reactionary undertaking. Its prestige as a great military power has declined, but its reputation as the European 'gendarme' remains intact. The war with Japan would have ended much more shamefully had it not been for continuous support from international capital. And we can say with certainty that this support will not only continue in the near future but will even increase,

---

⁴ [The Black Hundreds were bands of counter-revolutionaries and anti-Semites, including the League of the Archangel Michael, the League of the Russian People, the Council of the United Nobility and other organisations. They were frequently responsible for pogroms and for terrorist acts against revolutionaries.]

⁵ [The international bankers.]

despite the fundamental change that has occurred in the international political position.

Renewal of the alliance between Japan and England, with the goal of preserving the status quo throughout *all* of Asia – that is, not just in the Far East but also in Central Asia – will for a long time, and perhaps forever, make it impossible for Russian absolutism to carry on fulfilling its 'historical mission' in the Far East. Like it or not, the centre of gravity in Russian foreign policy again has to shift to Europe and the Near West. Whether Russia will move in this area hand in hand with Germany, which has long ago sunk deep roots in Asia Minor and the Balkan peninsula and might seek to supplement the alliance in domestic policy with a similarly close alliance in foreign policy; whether there will be a new 'holy alliance' between Russia, Germany and Turkey, or perhaps a new rapprochement with France – whatever may happen, in its struggle against the 'internal enemy' Russian absolutism can count on the most active support from European reaction and friendly neutrality from the liberal bourgeoisie.

Of course, the end of the war by no means implies an end to the misadventures of Russian absolutism. The revolutionary movement continues: it is growing both in central Russia and in the outlying areas; it is gaining strength in Poland, in Finland, in the Baltic territory and in the Caucasus. In relation to the powerful movement of the workers, military forces are just as hopeless as the reinforced secret police. We have no need to fear, therefore, that the revolutionary movement will die down again as it did in the eighties.

Now the country faces a new calamity of dreadful hunger as the mutilated and wounded soldiers will soon begin returning from the fields of Manchuria, representing a living chronicle of crimes committed by the autocratic régime. At the same time, financial oppression continues its destructive work. All of this creates a continuous source of agitation and reinforces even more the hatred of the toiling masses for the existing régime.

The new State Duma, this modified and appended version of a 'sheep's parliament', creates an equally explosive source of agitation. Having excluded almost the entire population from the elections, absolutism is clearly underlining its class character. The State Duma will not serve it even as a 'fig leaf'. It provides a living example for demonstrating to the toiling masses that they can expect nothing from the existing political régime, that for as long as the autocracy exists nothing but 'paper' reforms are possible, no matter how much they cost, and that there is no hope for the working class to escape from this hell except through revolution.

We shall leave it to the revolutionary democrats to amuse themselves with illusions: 'Democrats are defenders of *the people's rights*, and their interests are the people's interests. Hence, on the eve of the struggle, they see no point in analysing the interests and positions of different classes or of carefully weighing their own resources. Indeed, all they have to do is give the signal – and then *the people*, with all their inexhaustible might, will throw themselves upon the oppressors.' Our autocracy *has survived* more than one revolutionary movement, and it *will survive* still more if we ever forget that it is an organ of class rule against which only the proletariat can fight, because it is the one class whose very position makes it an implacable enemy.

The better the organisation of the Russian proletariat, the more conscious its revolutionary movement becomes, and the more solidarity there is in the revolutionary activity of the different sections of the Russian proletariat, the more successful will this struggle be.[6]

*   *   *

The debate that has recently erupted concerning a *provisional government* and participation in it by Social Democrats, is, in our opinion, not merely a fortuitous episode involving literary polemics between two factions. Quite the opposite: it is a delayed consequence of 'politicism'[7] and a logical conclusion drawn from a simplified understanding of Social Democracy, which, along with the author of *What Is to Be Done?*, sees the main task in 'the preparation, planning and enactment of an uprising by the entire people'.[8]

So long as Russian Social Democracy is completely disorganised, this is a purely academic question. It can only assume practical importance when Russian Social Democracy joins together in a single united party, when it becomes the main conscious factor in a revolution that is occurring before our eyes. The hotter are the flames in the hearth of revolutionary protest,

---

6 [Ryazanov 1905, pp. 3–7.]

7 [Ryazanov uses this phrase as the counterpart of 'economism', or concentration upon the economic struggle. Lenin accused Ryazanov and others of 'economism' at the expense of political organisation. 'Politicism' refers to a one-sided emphasis upon political tactics, forgetting the strike movement and the economic basis of the proletarian class struggle.]

8 [See Lenin 1905a and Lenin 1906a.]

making the proletariat the most revolutionary class of present-day Russia; the greater is the solidarity of Russian Social Democracy; the more extensive is the revolutionary movement it leads; and the more the toilers and the exploited regard it as the most committed defender of their interests – the more likely it is that in the course of the revolution itself conditions will emerge in which governmental power might fall into the hands of the proletariat.

Whatever the circumstances, Social Democracy must not endeavour to *participate* in a provisional government made up of bourgeois elements. In order to remain the party of the most extreme opposition, it must put forward 'the question of property, as the basic question of the entire movement'. Accepting no responsibility for the acts of a provisional government, it must, at the same time, drive it forward along lines of extreme social reforms to the benefit of the working class and the deprived peasantry. In concentrating all its efforts on completing *its own* tasks, it simultaneously approaches the moment when the issue will not be *participation* in a provisional government, but rather the seizure of power by the working class and conversion of the 'bourgeois' revolution into a direct prologue for the social revolution.

It is important to *win* power, but it is incomparably more important to *hold on* to it. And in this respect the international political and economic position will be decisive. In Western Europe, reaction has prevailed for many years with the support of the entire bourgeoisie. Should it become even stronger, should world industry recover in the near future from its latest crisis and enter a new era of industrial prosperity – and the symptoms of such a turn of events are becoming all the more clear and numerous – then the Russian revolution, remaining isolated, might take on a protracted character and, given the well-known habits of the Russian bourgeoisie, temporarily lead to 'Asiatic' despotism being transformed into European absolutism concealed merely by some forms of constitutional order. This means that rather than making the question of a *provisional government* into an issue of disagreement justifying an organisational split, our party literature would serve a much more useful purpose by giving a great deal more space to *studying the pace of development of the world economy and world politics, the financial policy and diplomacy of the Russian autocracy, and so forth.*

It is only by clarifying for ourselves the causes and pace of a fundamental upheaval in international economic and political relations, to which *the Russo-Japanese War* made a contribution only from the sidelines, that we will be in a position to resolve, in a more or less certain manner, the question of the *possible forms of the Russian revolution*. Things might lead to the 'granting' of some kind of 'truncated' constitution through a homeopathic expansion of the authority of the State Duma and the number of voters; there might be an announcement of a national constituent assembly, summoned by the victorious monarchy to reach 'agreement with the people'; or a constituent assembly might be called by a provisional government – but the answer to all of these questions will depend on the scope of the revolution and how far it spreads internationally.

Whatever the conditions of our future revolutionary work, and whatever our tactics during an election campaign, the necessary condition for success is unification of our party. We must also never forget that the main arena of our activity is not parliament but the street, that our main forces must be spent not in 'positive' parliamentary work but in 'negative' work among the toiling masses, that our work in parliament will be even more practical the more 'impractical' are our efforts beyond its walls. If Social Democrats should find themselves participating, they will be there only to convey from without the pressure that the party, with the support of the working masses, will be exerting on parliament. Our main task is to prevent the revolutionary tempest from cooling, to drive the revolution forward, and to lead it to extreme conclusions.

Our motto must be the revolution *in Permanenz* (uninterrupted revolution) – not 'order' in place of revolution, but revolution in place of order. The more revolutionary are the demands put forth by Social Democracy, the more forcefully it intrudes *in fact* upon all the sacred and inviolable rights, the more the people *in fact* seize all their rights and freedoms during the revolutionary period, and the more numerous the circle of people with an interest in the revolution's accomplishments – the deeper will be the divide between the past and the future, and the more favourable will conditions be for the further development of Social Democracy.

Institutions that guarantee complete democratisation of the entire political system, including civil and criminal law, justice, military law and the entire state economy, and the conditions needed to satisfy universal labour and social legislation – all of these issues must be thoroughly studied in party literature in order to provide our comrades with material for agitation during an election period and to give them the weapons they need in the struggle against all the bourgeois parties.

The stronger the movement of the working class becomes, and the more the revolutionary movement begins to threaten the 'foundations' of the entire social system, the more zealously will the liberals strive to preserve these foundations. Knowing that 'a moderate party with a clever tactic can profit from intensifying struggle between extreme social elements', they are manoeuvring between the Scylla of despotism and the Charybdis of revolution. Anticipating the blessed time when they will become 'the cretins of parliamentarism', they have already become cretinous proponents of 'parleying a truce' with absolutism. Beginning with the conviction that Russia now 'needs a strong, a terribly strong government', they dream in every quarter of rewarding their fatherland with a 'mongrel constitution' that would combine a 'strong power' with a few concessions to the toiling masses. In all its political activities, our bourgeois democracy demonstrates that its political demands differ from those of the worker not just by degree but also in principle. Bound to the interests of 'working' property owners, it seeks democratisation of the bourgeois system, but only with the goal of concealing and masking the class antagonism at its foundation. It parades the extreme nature of its political demands and, at the same time, willingly merges with liberalism whenever the latter's constitutional projects curtail the rights of the working class. It is perfectly clear, therefore, that one of the most imperative political requirements of the present moment, and one of the most vital tasks of party literature, is *relentless criticism of all the constitutional projects of our liberals and bourgeois democrats, unmasking the class background of all programmes on behalf of 'the entire people' and destroying all illusions of some community of political goals on the part of all classes of the population, particularly of the bourgeoisie and the proletariat.*[9]

*   *   *

The polemics over a provisional government hardly flared up in the pages of our two central organs when a new, even more bitter argument arose concerning relations to the State Duma. In this way, a question that otherwise might be debated quite freely within a single organisation is simply providing another occasion to intensify and deepen the split in the party. Both sides, following their usual methods, are looking for some new tactical 'incantation', as if Social Democracy does not have enough tried and proven 'slogans' in its arsenal, as if its tactics in this case are not dictated by the perfectly obvious and clear interests of the proletariat.

---

[9] [Ryazanov 1905, pp. 38–42.]

To boycott or not to boycott the State Duma, to take part in the elections or not to take part – these questions do not even exist for the proletariat. The State Duma must be destroyed. To recognise it, to try to use it as a tribune or to reform it – these are not just stupid and senseless ideas. To pursue them would be a political crime by which the proletariat would repudiate any independent policy. We will exert the most rational *pressure* on the State Duma when we adopt the goal of *crushing* it as rapidly as possible.

…The worst outcome would be…gradual conversion of the State Duma into a representative institution, repeating in some manner the evolution of a 'strengthened state council' in Austria, which required nearly forty years.

Hence, we say: Down with the State Duma! But this certainly does not mean that we just 'fold our hands'. If the State Duma is nothing but a new addition to the cattle shed of the old state, if it is more difficult even for a true liberal to pass through it than for a camel to pass through the eye of a needle, then the very statute on the State Duma and the very fact of its existence provide Social Democracy with the opportunity for widespread agitation throughout the entire 'election period'.

How to do this will depend on circumstances of time and place. While resisting any provocation by the local authorities, and avoiding any unnecessary and useless confrontations with the police and troops, Social Democracy must also make use of every 'snag' that the 'election statute' provides.

While not adopting the utopian goal of organising the 'revolutionary self-government of the people', and rejecting the equally utopian preparation of a general 'armed uprising by the people',[10] Social Democrats must make use of 'pre-election agitation' to organise the working masses, to increase our influence on all the 'toilers and the oppressed', and to popularise our programme, which will then acquire enormous educational and organisational significance. Consciousness of *class* interests is the binding cement of the *class* organisation of the proletariat, which alone creates and strengthens the *class* bonds that unite the workers into a single cohesive and indivisible whole. By developing class consciousness among the working masses, the *programme* simultaneously gives them a banner around which to rally in order to repel their enemies – and especially their 'friends'.

---

[10] [These were Lenin's phrases in Lenin 1905j.]

With the growth of our agitation, the revolutionary movement will become all the more intensive and uninterrupted, and the shocks affecting the whole of social-political life will become all the more acute and severe. A whole series of mass political strikes, alternating and moving from one place to another, would keep the entire country in a state of tension and, in favourable conditions, could culminate in an all-Russian strike. Only then will a 'position' emerge in which 'all roads for retreat are closed', which will make the abolition of absolutism a question of life and death for the ruling classes.

'We all know our old absolutism quite well enough. Hence, away with all compromises! Away with all indecision! Go for its throat and put a knee to its chest!'[11]

But before everything else, there is something supremely important that our revolutionary strategists and tacticians too often forget – and that is that before we can create an organisation of 'the people', it is above all imperative that we unite ourselves and create a stable organisation of the proletariat.[12]

---

[11] [Here Ryazanov is referring to a comment by Lassalle in a speech 'On the Essence of the Constitution' delivered before the parliamentary elections in Prussia in 1862. See Bernstein 1893, p. 115.]

[12] [Ryazanov is criticising Lenin for emphasising the revolutionary role of 'the people' as distinct from the workers. Numerous such comments occur in Lenin's 'The Revolutionary Army and the Revolutionary Government' (Lenin 1905j), some examples of which follow:

1) 'The revolutionary government must rouse the "people" and *organise* its revolutionary activity.'

2) 'In every attempt to establish a provisional revolutionary government it is important to advance precisely the basic demands in order to show to the whole of the people, even to the most unenlightened masses, in brief formulation, in sharp and clear outline, the aims of this government and its tasks that are of significance to the entire people.'

4) 'The task of establishing a revolutionary government is as new, as difficult, and as complicated as the task of the military organisation of the revolutionary forces. But this task, too, can and must be fulfilled by the people.'

5) 'We must know how to appeal to the people – in the true sense of the word – not only with a general call to struggle (this suffices in the period preceding the formation of the revolutionary government), but with a direct call for the immediate implementation of the most essential democratic reforms, for their independent realisation without delay.'

6) 'The revolutionary government is needed for the political leadership of the masses, at first in that part of the country which has been wrested from tsarism by the revolutionary army, and later in the country at large. The revolutionary government is needed for the immediate launching of the political reforms, for the sake of which the revolution is being made – the establishment of a revolutionary self-government of the people, the convocation of a truly popular and truly Constituent Assembly, and the introduction of "liberties" without which there can be no true expression

And it is already obvious that this is impossible without calling a constituent congress.[13] This is the only way to put an end to the internecine warfare that is bringing Russian Social Democracy to ruin. It is the only way to restore and extend its influence on the working masses, an influence that was won through decades of stubborn propaganda and agitation and through the suffering and sacrifices of countless fighters drawn both from the 'intelligentsia' and from the workers. It is the only possible way to attract once more into our ranks the working masses, who are currently regarding our dissension with sorrowful dismay and frequent anger.

By facilitating the speediest possible convening of a *constituent congress*, which will put an end to the split in our party and really create a single, united Social-Democratic workers' party, we will advance the day when a *constituent assembly*, called on the basis of universal, equal, direct and secret voting, will eliminate Russian absolutism, and the Russian proletariat, together with the proletariat of all countries, will destroy both class society and class rule!

---

of the people's will. The revolutionary government is necessary for the political unification and the political organisation of the insurgent section of the people, which has actually and finally broken away from the autocracy. Of course, that political organisation can only be provisional, just as the revolutionary government, which has taken power in the name of the people in order to enforce the will of the people and to act through the instrumentality of the people, can only be provisional. But this work of organisation must start *immediately*, and it must be indissolubly combined with every successful step of the uprising; for political consolidation and political leadership cannot be delayed for a single moment. Immediate political leadership of the insurgent people is no less essential for the complete victory of the people over tsarism than the military leadership of its forces.']

[13] [A congress to reunite Russian Social Democrats.]

Chapter Sixteen
'Our Tasks' (13 November 1905)
Parvus

This article appeared in the first edition of the Menshevik newspaper *Nachalo*, edited by Parvus and Trotsky, on 13 November 1905. It was republished in Parvus's book *Rossiya i revolyutsiya* in 1907. It was also translated into German for anonymous publication in the journal *Die Neue Zeit*, 1906, Vol. 24, No. 1, pp. 151–8, under the title 'The Tasks of Social Democracy in Russia: Programmatic Article from the First Number of the Russian Social-Democratic Daily *Nachalo* [*The Beginning*]'. The editors of *Die Neue Zeit* added this prefatory note:

> Although this translation has reached us somewhat late, the article seems to us to be of topical interest even today. *Nachalo*, as is well known, was the Petersburg organ of a fraction of our Russian sister party [the Mensheviks], which was earlier grouped around *Iskra*. The organ of the other fraction [the Bolsheviks] was *Novaya Zhizn'*. In the meantime, both were suppressed and then reappeared as *Severnyi Golos* [*The Voice of the North*], the common organ of both tendencies, which, however, soon suffered the same fate as its predecessors. Nonetheless, we hope that the union of both tendencies, which was brought about by the prohibition of the

magazines, will not be a passing one, but will lead to a general and lasting union, and that the ravings of reaction today in Russia will produce the same results as in Germany thirty years ago: the close amalgamation of all the Social-Democratic elements in a united organisation.

There is no doubt that Parvus sincerely shared this hope for party unity and, like Ryazanov, considered it vital to the success of the Russian revolution. While Ryazanov insisted that the Duma must be destroyed, however, Parvus was becoming more circumspect. By the closing months of 1905, neither party unity nor the revolution's triumph seemed quite so imminent as in the days immediately following Bloody Sunday. Although the autocratic régime was gravely shaken by military defeat, peace had been declared at the beginning of September and new political forces were rapidly consolidating at the same time as factional divisions deepened within Social Democracy. This article was written after the St. Petersburg Soviet, in which Trotsky and Parvus were key figures, had been forced to call off a general strike in the capital. Liberals had opposed the strike, and employers had responded to the demand for an eight-hour day with a lockout that affected as many as one hundred thousand workers.

In 'What Was Accomplished on Ninth of January', Parvus had entered Russian revolutionary history as the visionary who inspired Trotsky's interpretation of permanent revolution.[1] However, even then he cautioned that overthrow of the autocracy would be only 'the *starting point*', beyond which lay 'a long process of revolutionary development'. A successful outcome presupposed an independent and unified workers' organisation, which would 'take care not to divide and dissipate the proletariat's revolutionary energy' and, at the same time, would avoid 'either the political isolation of the proletariat or indifference to the political struggle of the other parties'.

Parvus thought the latter observation applied particularly to Russian liberals. 'It is an easy matter,' he wrote in January, 'to say: "Together with the liberals" – or "Against the liberals!" Nothing could be simpler, but these would be extremely one-sided and therefore false responses…'. The real issue was to 'make use of all revolutionary and oppositional tendencies' by adopting a tactic

---

[1] L. Trotsky 1960, p. 167. Trotsky wrote that it was Parvus who, 'for me, definitely transformed the conquest of power by the proletariat from an astronomical "final goal" to a practical task for our own day'.

of marching separately but striking in unison. 'Revolutionary consolidation' required 'revolutionary organisation' – the *mass* organisation of workers – but it was also imperative 'to struggle continuously for the expansion of political rights and for the rights of parliament in particular'.[2]

By the time 'Our Tasks' was published, the Tsar had issued a manifesto promising civil liberties and an elected Duma. The founding congress of the Constitutional Democrats (Cadets) was in session when the manifesto appeared; the Octobrist party was already emerging to represent the right wing of the liberal movement; reactionary groups were proliferating; and the Socialist-Revolutionaries were becoming a mass party fuelled by spontaneous peasant revolts. Parvus thought that Social Democrats were compelled to determine an appropriate response to the changing circumstances.

For Lenin and the Bolsheviks, the answer seemed perfectly clear and straightforward. The workers' party must organise an 'active boycott' of any elections and prepare an armed insurrection leading to the 'democratic dictatorship of the proletariat and the peasantry'.[3] Lenin explained that the tactic of 'active boycott' by no means meant 'passive abstention': 'an active boycott should imply increasing agitation tenfold, organising meetings everywhere, taking advantage of election meetings, even if we have to force our way into them, holding demonstrations, political strikes, and so forth.'[4] An active boycott meant provoking confrontations with the police and the military with a view to inciting the insurrection.

Parvus replied that 'If we interfere with these meetings, if we disrupt them, we shall merely be rendering a service to the government' by creating an excuse for martial law. Instead, he looked to the experience of German Social Democracy and urged that the various parties should come to an agreement

---

[2] In this volume, see p. 271.

[3] In 'Friends Meet', published on 13 (26) September, Lenin wrote:

Only an uprising holds out the possibility that the Duma farce will not be the end of the Russian revolution, but the beginning of a complete democratic upheaval, which will kindle the fire of proletarian revolutions all over the world. Only an uprising can guarantee that our 'United Landtag' will become the prelude to a constituent assembly of a non-Frankfurt type, that the revolution will not end in a mere March 18 (1848), that we shall not only have a July 14 (1789) but also an August 10 (1792). (Lenin 1905b, p. 261).

[4] Lenin 1905d.

to safeguard electoral procedures from reactionary intervention 'just as agreements are made between the various parties in a parliament'.[5]

> Each party should organise its own election committee for the conduct of the election campaign throughout the country. The parties should agree among themselves about practical measures for extending freedom of speech, of assembly, and so forth, during the elections. They should bind themselves together by joint political responsibility so that if an official representative of any political party is prosecuted…by the police or condemned in court, the representatives of all the other parties should declare their solidarity with him and all together organise a popular protest and, if possible, a popular uprising in his defence.[6]

Lenin reacted with bitter invective. Parvus, he exclaimed, had been duped into adopting the tactics of 'parliamentary cretinism'. Only 'clowning intellectuals' could propose such 'playing at parliamentarism'. This 'bourgeois' reasoning was merely 'so much empty and sentimental phrase-mongering'. The 'esteemed heroes' of parliamentary agreement – including both Plekhanov and now Parvus – thought they were 'supermen' who could ignore party resolutions. In fact they were expressing *all the shortcoming of the turncoat*. In the Bolshevik publication *Proletarii*, Lenin wrote that Parvus was a 'confused', 'stupid' and 'ignorant' political infant with whom he declared a rupture of all political relations: 'Good riddance to you, my dear Parvus!…our ways have parted.'[7]

Parvus answered in a little-known article entitled 'What Are Our Disagreements?'.[8] It was Lenin, he claimed, who was posturing – as a super-revolutionary – but now it was time to explain to him some changing political facts. To begin with, the manifesto announcing plans for a State Duma was a fact. It was also a fact that no one could be certain of overthrowing the autocracy before the Duma assembled. In the meantime, the only prudent tactic was to use the elections to make active propaganda rather than continuing the ritual of calling for immediate armed insurrection. Lenin's problem was that he was

---

[5] Ibid. p. 274 (quoted by Lenin).
[6] Ibid. p. 275. In 1893 Parvus had also supported Bernstein's call to participate in Prussian elections despite the restricted suffrage.
[7] Ibid. pp. 276–7.
[8] Parvus 1905b.

seeing 'double': between 'revolutionism' and parliamentarism' all he could discern was a 'metaphysical' divide with no dialectical space for real 'political struggle'.[9] Proponents of 'exclusive revolutionism' could not see beyond

> absolute contradictions: Yea is yea; nay is nay; whatsoever is more than these cometh of evil. This is why, for Lenin, a 'parliamentary tactic' and a 'revolutionary tactic' are mutually exclusive. He does not understand how a parliamentary tactic can be used in order to revolutionise the working masses.[10]

Parvus worried that the Bolsheviks' demand for an 'active boycott' would simply isolate Social Democrats and effectively exclude the proletariat from real 'political life'.[11] When German Social Democrats could not elect their own candidates, they voted for liberals as the 'lesser evil'. Russian liberals were now demanding universal suffrage, and they should be held to their commitment not only by criticism but also by support. In exchange, they should be obliged to support Social Democrats where liberals could not be elected. 'We condemn liberalism,' Parvus objected, 'for not supporting us adequately in our struggle against absolutism – so how can we refuse them support when they actually wage this struggle?'[12] Claiming that Lenin saw revolution as 'an affair of the moment' – a passing moment that 'might be lost' – Parvus spoke of 'an irreversible historical process'. He continued:

> He [Lenin] thinks that a revolutionary uprising is what creates the revolution; but I suggest that the revolution is what makes an uprising victorious. He looks about for allies to support a revolutionary uprising because he does not believe in the revolutionary energy of the proletariat, whereas I lead the workers into the political struggle and into political relations with other parties in order to manifest their revolutionary energy.
>
> Lenin divides tactics into two stages – the revolutionary and the parliamentary, whereas for me a revolutionary tactic arises from the class struggle of the proletariat at all times and in all circumstances, including parliamentarism, which itself has to be transformed into class struggle.

---

[9] Parvus 1905b, p. 4.
[10] Parvus 1905b, p. 14.
[11] Parvus 1905b, pp. 6–7; cf. p. 9.
[12] Parvus 1905b, p. 5.

Lenin thinks of tactics from the point of view of overthrowing the autocracy and the direct victory of the revolution, whereas I regard the matter from the point of view of organising the proletariat's social-revolutionary army, which will make the revolution uninterrupted (permanent).

Not only the State Duma, as it is presently being convened, but even the most developed capitalist parliament would not for many years be capable of dealing with the confusion of social and national relations and the resulting political struggle that is the consequence of Russia's social development and the retarding yoke of absolutism. There will be agitation and uprisings together with heated and complex parliamentary struggle – and in all of this the proletariat will play a more prominent role, and will use political development all the more to serve its own interests, the sooner, the more consciously, the more diversely and the more decisively it takes part in all forms and manifestations of the country's political life, subordinating them all to its final goal – the conquest of political power.[13]

Lenin thought revolutionary tactics were limited to overthrowing the autocracy by armed force; Parvus reminded him that, barely three years earlier, when liberals were of no political significance, it was Lenin himself who had insisted upon supporting them with Social-Democratic organisation and publications.[14] Now Lenin had adopted a new 'political scheme' – springing like Minerva from the forehead of Jupiter – and was once again ignoring political reality. 'At the basis of his revolutionary ardour,' Parvus wrote, 'is *lack of revolutionary confidence.*'[15]

Lenin's fixation on armed insurrection was a variation of arguments he had first made in *What Is to Be Done?* Flailing so-called 'economists', condemning trade unions as spontaneously opportunistic, and insisting upon centralised control of the entire workers' movement, Lenin was consistent only in his mistrust of workers and his commitment to the worst aspect of the Russian revolutionary tradition: the narrow-mindedness and manipulative proclivities of 'revolutionary circles of the intelligentsia'. Unlike Social Democrats

---

[13] Parvus 1905b, pp. 18–19.
[14] Parvus 1905b, p. 11. See also Lenin 1905d.
[15] Parvus 1905b, p. 15.

in Germany, Lenin intended to subordinate the masses to 'a handful of ideologues'.[16] The revolution had to respond to changing circumstances, but

> In front of this grand historical process there stands a little man with a menacing grimace and a revolutionary hand outstretched, fussing and bustling to ward off the disappearance of socialism and the revolution!

Parvus recalled an article he had published in December 1903 in the German party press. Although he did not mention Lenin, he sympathised at that time with Ryazanov's criticism of the *Iskra* programme[17] and the object of his concern was perfectly apparent:

> We know that it is not within our power to determine events. Our entire task consists of keeping the proletariat prepared so that it can drive political development forward when events do occur. It follows that for Social Democracy in Russia, there is one requirement that takes precedence over all others – *organisation*. But organisation does not mean throwing a rope around the masses in order to keep them together.... Whoever suggests that the whole purpose is to collect every thread into a single hand at some single point, whether it is Petersburg or Geneva, in order to give commands to the workers, is really succumbing to the absurd notion that Social Democracy can tyrannise the masses to a greater degree even than Russian absolutism. Above all else, Russian workers must learn how to unite and go forth as a single political force with a conscious will. Whoever tries merely to create an organisation of agitators, ignoring organisation of the masses, really believes that he can make use of the workers as material for the revolution in the same way as they provide cannon fodder for the army.... At all times and in every circumstance, our hope and support must focus on the social-revolutionary character of the working class.[18]

Whereas Lenin saw election meetings as liberal gatherings to be broken up by force in order to incite a police response, Parvus saw in the same meetings an opportunity to organise the working class in real political engagements. Lenin, he claimed, saw organisation as nothing more than a fixed plan laid down by a leader, who would blow his own horn and expect to bring down

---

[16] Parvus 1905b, p. 23.
[17] Parvus 1905b, pp. 20–1.
[18] Parvus 1905b, pp. 24–5.

both the towers of absolutism and the walls of capitalist Jericho. As a result,
Lenin

> sees his main task not in using every possible means to lead the proletariat
> into political struggle but rather in preventing the political struggle…from
> becoming opportunistic.…That is why he tries to suppress and smother
> everything that cannot be compressed into his own narrow template for the
> party; that is why he declares that all who do not share his political ideas are
> traitors to the revolution. It is also why he has been doing destructive work
> in the party for the past two years. He aims for revolutionary dictatorship,
> but he has shown himself to be completely incapable of uniting and
> leading the revolutionary forces. He wants to organise the revolution with
> propaganda, but he is provoking internecine warfare within the party and
> disorganising it all the more.…An organisation that is detached from the
> working masses and suspended above the working masses is…not Social-
> Democratic.…There is nothing worse than a tactic that disorganises and
> demoralises a fighting army through internal discord.[19]

At the end of 'What Are Our Disagreements?', Parvus declared that he had
no interest in debating further with Lenin but had been compelled to respond
to personal attacks and provocations. He summarised by comparing the
sweep of revolutionary transformation with the pettiness of an intellectual's
conspiracy. The essential point was that the workers must not only overthrow
the capitalists but also acquire the knowledge and skills to replace them.
Socialism must transform the whole of social life, eliminate wage-labour,
reconstruct the entire process of production, transform family and human
relations in general, and create the opportunity for unprecedented cultural
advance. This 'grandiose historical process' would be long and difficult, and
it would never succeed unless Russian comrades transcended their own
limitations by recognising that it was not *their* job to free the workers – that
was inescapably the task of *the workers themselves*.[20]

The Russian proletariat did not lack revolutionary energy; what it lacked
was *consciousness* and the enlightenment that springs from active political life:
'To a mind that is made despondent by slavery, there is much that seems

---

[19] Parvus 1905b, pp. 25–6.
[20] Parvus 1905b, p. 27.

impossible and there are many decisions that cannot be made, whereas others make such decisions freely and regard doing so as their natural right.' To date, the workers had been carrying the revolution on their own shoulders, enabling every other stratum of society to speak out loudly and freely for the first time, but the workers themselves had still said virtually nothing. In place of factional fighting, he urged Bolsheviks and Mensheviks alike to strive for the workers' enlightenment:

> Make them speak out. Make them write. Awaken their thoughts. Awaken their initiative in the economic and political struggle and in every other form of social life. Open up before them every small detail of political life, for there is much that they cannot see due to lack of knowledge. It is much better to commit a tactical error while expanding the political activity of the workers than to restrict their political activity out of fear of a tactical error. The main thing is to conceal nothing from them … for in that case you build your plan not on the basis of their political understanding but rather on the people's ignorance. Teach the workers to create organisations and manage them themselves. Do all of this in order that they will be able to manage on their own, even without you. To the extent that you succeed, you will then make the workers into a conscious political force. By virtue of their class position, they will also be a social-revolutionary force that will block the road to any betrayal of the revolution by the bourgeoisie and will not permit the revolution to die out. This force will open up new opportunities and a new basis for the organisation of revolutionary uprisings.[21]

'What Are Our Disagreements?' provided the political context for 'Our Tasks', which appeared at approximately the same time. As in his earlier work, 'What Was Accomplished on the Ninth of January', in 'Our Tasks' Parvus portrayed a multiplicity of class relations in varying stages of maturity, all the result of Russia's late capitalist development. In Western Europe, more than a century of revolutionary struggle had clearly defined class positions and ranged the proletariat directly against the bourgeoisie so that a final settling of accounts could come at any time. In Russia, however, this work of clarification was at a much earlier stage. Russian history had created an 'unusual tangle of class relations', requiring various contenders to measure

---

[21] Parvus 1905b, p. 28.

their strength in conditions where the old state was coming apart but nothing new had replaced it. The task of Social Democrats was to build trade unions and a political party that would have the strength to transform a bourgeois revolution into a régime of *workers' democracy*, which would institutionalise freedoms and create the conditions in which organised workers could drive capitalism and liberalism beyond their own limits. *Permanent* revolution was a process, not an event, and its final outcome would depend on class consciousness and a unified Social-Democratic organisation.

* * *

'Our Tasks'

Political revolution is the foundation of the programme of Social Democrats in all countries – the proletarian revolution that will complete the cycle of revolutions that began with the Great French Revolution.

To break up the old estates-based society, the bourgeoisie had to set the nation against the estates and rely upon support from the people. But from the first moment of the common struggle, when liberty, equality, and fraternity were declared, it turned out that the nation was not united. Although differences between estates were eliminated, class differences became clear and determined the further course of the revolution. Having overthrown absolutism, the bourgeoisie was divided by its own internal contradictions and was unable to create a stable state power. Amidst the general political chaos, the rudder of state passed from one hand to another and from one social stratum to another. The political system changed like the light of a kaleidoscope, but under pressure from the petty bourgeoisie and the workers it became ever more radical in moving towards political democracy. Because of its indeterminate class character and resulting lack of coordination, the petty bourgeoisie was unable to govern the country. It proved helpless, and in its helplessness it became a perpetually resentful and agitated element of political demoralisation within the bourgeois parties while at the same time fomenting revolutionary excitement among the popular masses. With the help of workers and handicraftsmen, the petty bourgeoisie assumed power, but, since it was unable to provide an economic programme that would create a bond with the workers, in order to maintain its power it was compelled to bring out the guillotine, only later to become its victim. The proletariat, in turn, could not help but see that political equality would never free it from the oppression of the factory owners and masters. It struggled against bourgeois domination and drove the revolution forward, vaguely hoping that a state system would eventually emerge that would free it from economic subservience. But it was only at the end of the revolution, under determined class pressure from the proletarian opposition, that the conspiracy of Babeuf brought forth a socialist programme.

Passing swiftly through these changing phases, the Great French Revolution completed the entire development that has since become typical for Western Europe and for all bourgeois countries: the ascendancy of the capitalist class, the democratic opposition of the petty bourgeoisie, and the social-revolutionary opposition of the working class in anticipation of the dictatorship of the proletariat. These forms of development were repeated during the revolution of 1848, but because class relations were more defined by that time and more clearly expressed in political programmes, the transition occurred much more rapidly and ended in open struggle between the first and the last, that is, between the capitalist class and the proletariat. At the time of the Commune in 1871, the intermediate phase passed almost without notice. The proletariat found itself in power from the outset and had to defend its position against the bourgeoisie. In the form of a long drawn-out process, these phases of development have occurred throughout the whole parliamentary history of Europe. The process has yet to reach completion anywhere, but its beginning and end points are now clearly confronting each other in Western Europe.

The capitalist class of Western Europe long ago betrayed the revolution and is now looking to support itself through strengthening governmental power. On the other side the proletariat, united in the Social-Democratic party, sees the starting point of its struggle in overthrowing the political supremacy of the bourgeoisie and seizing state power. In this connection, however, Social Democracy has set out a number of legislative demands that can be achieved without destroying the capitalist order. The goal of its programme is to democratise the state and free the workers from the most oppressive forms, methods and consequences of exploitation, so that they might win more promising conditions for political struggle and thus intensify their social-revolutionary energy.

Following a revolutionary overthrow of the state system, the bourgeoisie has never succeeded, anywhere or at any time, in rapidly and smoothly establishing its own 'order'. This has always and everywhere been preceded by a more or less prolonged period of political turmoil and cruel class struggle.

The same thing is happening in the revolution that we are now experiencing.

The revolution in Russia was delayed. It was held back by European capital, which for many years supplied the autocracy with weapons and cash, fortifying it in the interest of European capital's own profits and supremacy. While our proponents of Russia's distinctive character looked for the basis of autocracy in the Russian soul of the orthodox peasant, the autocracy had long been sinking its roots into the cash boxes of Rothschild, Mendelssohn, the Crédit Lyonnais, etc. However, that same European capital transformed the entire social and cultural condition of Russia, created the revolutionary proletariat, and ultimately drove the government into a war that destroyed its military power and shook the state to its foundations.

Presently, we are living through a time of political anarchy. The old bonds of the state have broken apart, and nothing new has replaced them. The new can only emerge when all classes have measured their strength in the struggle for political power.

The delay of revolution in Russia is due to the unusual tangle of class relations that the revolution must take into account. Moreover, the revolution is also happening in new international circumstances. The European *bourse* is strongly represented within the capitalist class and is independent of the Russian state. Rather than being subordinated to the state, the *bourse* endeavours to subordinate the state to itself. Yesterday it speculated on the rising stock of the autocracy; today it speculates on its decline. From its own point of view, the fate of the Russian state matters no more than that of the Ethiopians in Abyssinia. It does fear, however, for its capital, and if it had its own way it would be willing to send Prussian or Austrian troops to Russia in order to restore order and guarantee against any default in interest payments on its loans. Associated with the money market is a group of foreign capitalists who have, in one form or another, invested large sums in Russian commercial and industrial enterprises. This means that Russian plutocrats and banks are connected by credit ties with the financial institutions of Europe. Behind all of them stands world capital, which is impatient to plunder the wealth of Russia and enslave its people.

At the same time, the 'national' capital of Russia is engaged in every form and variety of capitalist predation: this includes the 'enlightened' factory owner of the English type; the mill owner who gets rich on state orders; the trader with a far-flung sales organisation; the supplier, whose entire commercial technique consists of bribery; the old-testament merchant, who more closely resembles a Chinese than a European trader; and all those engaged in numerous varieties of primitive accumulation – from the money-lender and the well-to-do peasant, who fleece the people, to the shopkeeper who gets rich by selling spoiled fish.

Relations in agriculture are just as complex, including the aristocrat with enormous landed estates that he visits only to go hunting; the gentry-merchant who has connections with the grain exchanges in Berlin and London; the Prussian type of gentry-industrialist, who depends upon industrial activities such as brick works, distilleries or sugar mills as a side-line to agriculture; the gentry-farmer, engaged in modern agriculture; the merchant-landowner, looking principally for a rapid turnover of capital, as in the case of ruined gentry-landlords; peasant-traders in the vicinity of large cities; millions of peasants who are semi-serfs; millions of impoverished peasants and peasant-proletarians; and vast expanses of land owned by principalities, the treasury, the church or monasteries.

There are millions of poverty-stricken and vagrant people in the country. There is a very poor stratum of handicraftsmen. And then there are the extremely numerous members of the intelligentsia. Finally, there is the factory proletariat, forged into a single class not by the pitiful mills and factories of eighteenth century France, but by modern large-scale industry, while, at the same time, large numbers of factory workers still have not severed their connection with the land. Each of these groups has its own special needs, its own demands, and its own political character. And all of these diverse needs, demands, and economic and political elements of the revolution are colliding with one other in the general whirlpool of political struggle.

It was no decree of ours that started the revolution, nor is it for us to decree its end. The essence of the matter is not whether we regard the revolutionary struggle as desirable or undesirable. Revolutionary struggle is not the same as revolutionary insurrection. The insurrection did not create the revolution; rather the revolution created the insurrection as its natural and decisive, although by no means its sole, mode of struggle. The revolution is an historical process of the most intensive political struggle, and it assumes all possible forms and variations: it is a desperate struggle between different social classes, strata, and groups for state power. To arrive at a final historical outcome of this maelstrom of social forces, given the tangle and confusion of class relations that we have described in present-day Russia, involves a long and agonising process that is replete with shocks and sudden transitions.

We must reckon, therefore, not with any single moment, but with a long, drawn-out development, and we must determine our tactics with this perspective in mind.

Our first and most fundamental task is to clarify for the proletariat its class position and historical role, thereby facilitating its separation from other classes, a process that is occurring due to objective conditions. This is a question of forming a Social-Democratic workers' party. In this connection, we must merge the old conspiratorial organisation with a new mass organisation. Propaganda to this end, together with agitation based upon the facts of political struggle, is our most immediate objective.

Along with the political organisation of the proletariat, we must also develop its professional organisations. The trade unions constitute the closest possible bond between workers. By organising their direct struggle against capitalist exploitation, they promote class awareness. It is true that, at a certain stage of development, they pass through a period of opportunism, or adaptation to the capitalist state system, but this danger is still remote as far as the workers' organisations in Russia are concerned, and it is absolutely non-existent at a time of revolution, when the struggle for state power is at the centre of political life. In the case of Russia, it may be possible to avoid such a danger entirely thanks to the experience of Western Europe and, more importantly, because the class struggle has intensified throughout the entire world and has led even the English trade unions to organise an independent workers' party.

Organisation of the proletariat is the basis of all our further activity. In this regard, the upsurge of social interest and energy, created by the revolution, opens up vast opportunities for us. What would have required years at another time can be accomplished today in months or even weeks. The entire working class of the factories and plants must join the Social-Democratic party. Also, we now have greater access than ever before to the agricultural proletariat. Our task is to cover the entire country with political clubs and workers' professional organisations. We must also promote development of a workers' press with every possible means.

The widest and most energetic use of political rights is the best possible guarantee against any return to the previous condition of arbitrary rule. And since peaceful parliamentary development in Western Europe has enabled the class organisation of the proletariat to become a revolutionary force that is leading inevitably to a political catastrophe, there can be no doubt that the proletariat's class organisation in Russia, during a time of revolution, will both fortify revolutionary energy and increase the political possibilities for the revolution.

The direct revolutionary goal of the Russian proletariat is to achieve the kind of state system in which the demands of workers' democracy will be realised. Workers' democracy includes all of the most extreme demands of bourgeois democracy, but it imparts to some of them a special character and also includes new demands that are strictly proletarian. For instance, the freedoms of assembly and association, from a general democratic point of view, are only variations of freedom of thought and speech, but for the workers they are fundamental guarantees for their class struggle. Hence the workers formulate this part of a democratic programme by taking particular care to include in freedom of organisation the right to strike. The proletariat also adds to the democratic programme the demand for labour legislation, especially for a normal eight-hour working day. Along with political guarantees of civil rights, the proletariat demands for itself economic guarantees of the opportunity to make use of them, that is, the right to time off from work.

In this way, the revolution in Russia creates a special connection between the minimum programme of Social Democracy and its final goal. This does not imply the dictatorship of the proletariat, whose task is a fundamental change of production relations in the country, yet it already goes beyond bourgeois democracy. We are not yet ready in Russia to assume the task of converting the bourgeois revolution into a socialist revolution, but we are even less ready to subordinate ourselves to a bourgeois revolution. Not only would this contradict the first premises of our entire programme, but the class struggle of the proletariat also drives us forward. Our task is to expand the limits of the bourgeois revolution by including within it the interests of the proletariat and by creating, within the bourgeois constitution itself, the greatest possible opportunities for social-revolutionary upheaval.

Even now, the government has made greater concessions than would have been needed in order to satisfy the liberal parties before the revolution, and there is no doubt that it will have to go still further. It was the stubbornness of reaction that created the revolution and made every political question more decisive. But this refers only to appearances on the surface of events. Whatever the form of transition to a parliamentary order, the social forces responsible for the revolution would have manifested themselves and driven it beyond any remaining limitations. The government was quite justifiably afraid of revolution, and this fear prevented it from undertaking any reforms. The stubbornness of the government merely determined its own fate, but the revolutionary course of events is determined by the chaotic social relations that have been created in Russia by historical circumstances.

Fearing the growing political power of the proletariat, the bourgeoisie is becoming reactionary. But its own class relations lead to a struggle for power in its midst and struggle against the government. This means it will waver back and forth between revolutionary excitement and reactionary embitterment. A politics of vacillation is merely a politics of impotence. The class that the revolution prepares for political supremacy turns out, during the revolution itself, to be the one least capable of controlling events. This will work to the political advantage of the organised proletariat, which from the very beginning of the revolution has become its leading force as a result of its class ties and revolutionary energy.

We will drive the bourgeoisie onwards. It is frightened by every step it takes in democratising the state because it benefits the proletariat. This is exactly the reason why it is in the proletariat's interest to support the bourgeoisie in the liberal opposition. We have no fear of liberalism's successes; on the contrary, they are the conditions for our own further successes. Then, whenever liberalism retreats, we will pursue it in every way possible. In every circumstance and at every opportunity, we will mercilessly criticise the class character of the bourgeois parties, whether they be liberal or democratic.

The victory of the revolution also brings the peasantry onto the political scene. The peasants assisted the revolution by amplifying political anarchy, but they were not capable of focusing their political struggle. They are now imposing on the struggle of parties all the confusion of their own economic demands and frustrations.

The capitalist system is incapable of resolving the peasant question, with the result that peasant involvement will complicate and prolong the revolution and prevent any stabilisation of bourgeois order.

Social Democracy bases itself on the proletariat not merely because it is exclusively a workers' party, but also because it sees in the proletariat the sole force that is capable of reconstituting production relations in a way that will free the entire population of toilers from exploitation. Insofar as the workers and the peasantry are subjected to exploitation, either directly or indirectly, it immediately defends their interests. But in the interest of the workers and the peasantry itself, Social Democracy also opposes any return to obsolete kinds of economic relations that impede the development of production. Our task is to express and broaden the economic demands of the peasantry while leading it towards socialist transformation.

In this connection, we simultaneously reveal all the forms of class struggle based upon agrarian relations and endeavour to merge with the workers of the factories and cities those strata of the agricultural proletariat and small-holding peasants whose position is close to that of the workers.

The revolutionary period has also bequeathed to us the socialist intelligentsia. Our task is to take the enormous intellectual and revolutionary energy that has accumulated in its midst and to employ it within the ranks of the Social-Democratic workers' party to extend the political and cultural tasks of the revolution and thus delay as long as possible the inevitable final result of the bourgeois intelligentsia going over to the vital ideals and commitments of the bourgeoisie.

The political confusion of the Russian revolution is also intensified by the struggle between the nationalities, which the autocracy has kept in a state of mutual hostility through use of discriminatory laws and a policy of national oppression. The national question has been resolved through democratic-republican practice in Switzerland and in the United States of America. We must achieve the same kind of free community of nations in Russia. Our task is to remove all obstacles in the way of independent political and cultural development on the part of all the individual nationalities. At the same time, it is equally important for us to separate the proletariat of each nationality in Russia from all the other classes and to unite them in a common social-revolutionary army. The result will be a closely knit all-Russian bond – not in opposition to the will of individual nationalities, but simply because of the internal class contradictions that inevitably dissolve national consciousness within the capitalist system. We shall unite all the nationalities not through use of state power, but rather in the struggle against the capitalist state.

The Russian autocracy has been supported by West-European capital. The Russian revolution will find its support in the West-European proletariat. If we presently have no fear of military intervention by Germany or Austria, that is exclusively due to West-European Social Democracy. Any attempt to put down the Russian revolution through use of outside military force will certainly provoke the proletarian revolution in the countries involved. As the social-revolutionary army of the proletariat is organised in Russia, it will expand and deepen its ties with Social Democracy throughout the entire world. The transition from struggle against autocracy to struggle for a workers' democracy will create a community of immediate political struggle. The struggle for an eight-hour day will immediately bring the Russian proletariat into step with the proletariat of the entire world. The successes of the revolution in Russia have thoroughly frightened the governments of Western Europe and significantly inspired the revolutionary energy of West-European Social Democracy. What we have accomplished in Russia still lags far behind what has been accomplished by the peoples of the West, but the very possibility of revolution has evoked a mighty response in the extremely tense political atmosphere of Western Europe. The Russian proletariat's further revolutionary successes on the road to achieving a workers' democracy will also be successes for the proletariat of the whole world and may provide a powerful impulse for decisive struggle between the social-revolutionary organisations of the proletariat and the state authorities of Western Europe. By that time, the Social-Democratic organisations of the Russian proletariat will have become steadily stronger, embracing the entire working masses, developing and raising their political consciousness, and strengthening their revolutionary conviction. Then we shall face the task of extending our revolutionary programme beyond the limits of workers' democracy.

The Russian revolution is still at the beginning of its development, but in the process it will inspire peoples everywhere and shake the entire capitalist world to its very foundations.

Long live the Russian revolution!

Long live socialism!

Chapter Seventeen

Foreword to Karl Marx, *Parizhskaya Kommuna* (December 1905)

Leon Trotsky

Leon Trotsky's foreword to Marx's account of the Paris Commune[1] marks an important break with the naïve economic determinism that often characterised Second-International Marxism. In this article, even more than in his previous writings on permanent revolution, Trotsky emphasised the *interaction* between economic conditions and *revolutionary consciousness*. In 1871, he noted, the workers of Paris did not seize power because economic circumstances suddenly 'matured' at some particular moment; on the contrary, it was *the logic of class struggle* that dictated a revolutionary course of events. The French bourgeoisie betrayed the nation because it feared arming the proletariat more than it feared the armies of Bismarck:

---

[1] St. Petersburg (Knigoizdatel'stvo Molot', 1906). See Marx 1871. [Of special significance is Engels's concluding paragraph to his 1891 Introduction on the 20th Anniversary of the Paris Commune: 'Of late, the Social-Democratic philistine has once more been filled with wholesome terror at the words: Dictatorship of the Proletariat. Well and good, gentlemen, do you want to know what this dictatorship looks like? Look at the Paris Commune. That was the Dictatorship of the Proletariat.' Frederick Engels, London, on the 20th anniversary of the Paris Commune, 18 March, 1891 (CW, Vol. 27: 179–191, p. 191)].

> The proletariat saw that the hour had come when it must save the country and become master of its own destiny. It could not avoid seizing power; it was compelled to do so by a series of political events. Power took it by surprise.

In Russia, likewise, the precipitating condition for proletarian revolution was social paralysis, symbolised by the co-existence of soviets with the autocracy, from which the only escape was through a workers' government. 'The bourgeoisie,' Trotsky wrote, 'is incapable of leading the people to win a parliamentary order through the *overthrow* of absolutism. And the people, in the form of the proletariat, are preventing the bourgeoisie from achieving constitutional guarantees through any *agreement* with absolutism.' In this impasse, the proletariat, as 'the *sole* force leading the revolution and the *principal* fighter on its behalf', must follow the example of the Communards by seizing power and taking responsibility for itself and the country.

Russian liberals (together with many Social Democrats) understood Marxism to say that 'Capitalism must "exhaust itself" before the proletariat can take state power into its own hands'. Trotsky replied that this mechanistic understanding ignored completely the dynamic of class struggle. Critics of permanent revolution had

> ... only managed to memorise a few isolated elements of the Marxist theory of capitalist development, but they have remained primitive bourgeois barbarians in everything that concerns class struggle and its objective logic. When they appeal to 'objective social development' in response to the idea of uninterrupted revolution, which for us is a conclusion following from *social-political relations*, they forget that this same development includes not merely economic evolution, which they so superficially understand, but also *the revolutionary logic of class relations*, which they cannot bring themselves even to consider.[2]

Given Russia's peculiar combination of capitalist and precapitalist elements,[3] the decisive factor in class relations was the relative weakness of the bourgeoisie

---

[2] [Italics added.]

[3] [Trotsky later interpreted this combination in terms of the laws of uneven and combined development. For a full statement, see L. Trotsky 1987, Chap. 2; also L. Trotsky 1977, Vol. 1: The Overthrow of Tzarism, Chap. 1: Peculiarities of Russia's Development.]

in confronting the semi-feudal autocracy. In these circumstances, the 'logic of class relations' superseded the constraints of economic backwardness:

> *In an economically backward country, the proletariat can come to power sooner than in a country of the most advanced capitalism....* Any thought of some kind of automatic dependence of the proletarian dictatorship upon the technical means and forces of a country is nothing but a prejudice of 'economic' materialism simplified to the extreme. That kind of thinking has nothing in common with Marxism.[4]

Trotsky acknowledged the obvious: socialism could never be implemented by 'a few decrees'. However, he added that

> The state is...the greatest means of organising, disorganising, and reorganising social relations. Depending upon whose hands control it, it can be either a lever for profound transformation or an instrument of organised stagnation.

Just as tsarist institutions impeded economic progress, so a workers' state would accelerate it in new directions.

In 'Revolutionary Questions', Karl Kautsky had already argued that

> wherever the proletariat has conquered political power, socialist production follows as a natural necessity....[The proletariat's] class interests and economic necessity force it to adopt measures that lead to socialist production. The *conquest of political power* – that is the alpha and the omega....[5]

Following the same logic, Trotsky wrote that with the capture of state power, a workers' government in Russia would implement the eight-hour day and progressive taxation. When the bourgeoisie responded by locking workers out of the factories, the government would be compelled to begin organising production on a collective basis. The countryside would support such measures, for the workers would also recognise revolutionary land redistribution and *'stand before the peasantry as the class that emancipates it'*. In international terms, the Russian proletariat must

---

[4] [Italics added. See also L. Trotsky 1960, pp. 194–200.]
[5] See above, p. 199.

> do everything that circumstances permit to link the fate of its national cause
> immediately and directly to the cause of world socialism. We are called upon
> to do so not merely by the common international principles of proletarian
> politics, but also by the powerful voice of class self-preservation, which
> compels us to move in this direction.

Trotsky had begun the year 1905 by taunting Russian liberals with the question, 'What next?'. In this essay, he gave his own conclusion in a way that directly anticipated *Results and Prospects*, his definitive statement on *permanent revolution*.[6]

* * *

Thirty-Five Years, 1871–1906

> ...the proletarians, witnessing the defeat and betrayal by the ruling classes,
> realised that the time had come when they must save the country themselves
> and take control of social affairs into their own hands....They understood
> that this obligation had fallen to them, and that they had the indisputable
> right to become the masters of their own fate and to take governmental
> power into their own hands. (Proclamation of the Central Committee of the
> National Guard, Paris, 18 March, 1871)

The Russian reader can learn the history of the Paris Commune of 1871 from the book by Lissagaray,[7] which, if I am not mistaken, will soon appear in several editions. The reader can familiarise himself with the philosophical side of that history by studying the timeless pamphlet by Marx and its very valuable introduction by Engels. As far as we are aware, Marxist literature over the next 35 years added nothing essential to what Marx already said about the Commune. As for non-Marxist literature, there is nothing worth mentioning: by its very nature, it is unable to say anything on this

---

[6] For Trotsky's later assessment of the Paris Commune in light of the Russian Revolutions of 1917, see his L. Trotsky 1917, and L. Trotsky 1921. Both articles were reprinted in L. Trotsky 1955.

[7] [Prosper Olivier Lissagaray (1838–1901) was a French journalist and revolutionary at the time of the Paris Commune, also author of *History of the Paris Commune of 1871*, translated into Russian in 1906. In 1886 it was translated to English by Leonor Marx. It was reissued in London by New Park Publications in 1976.]

subject. Until the recent translations appeared, all that was available in the Russian language were slovenly expositions provided by toothless gossips of international reaction and flavoured with the philosophical and moral judgments of the policeman Mymretsov.[8]

The conditions of police censorship have been one factor preventing us from learning about the Commune. Another has been the very character of the ideologies prevailing amongst our progressive circles – the ideologies of liberals, liberal-narodniks, and narodnik-socialists – which were completely hostile to the kind of relations, interests, and passions expressed in this unforgettable episode of proletarian struggle.

But, while it seemed only a few years ago that we were further from the traditions of the Paris Commune than any of the European nations, now we are in the first phase of our own revolution, which the struggle of the proletariat is making into a revolution *in Permanenz*, or an *uninterrupted* revolution, and we are relying more directly than any of the European nations on the testament of the Commune of 1871.

Today the history of the Commune is for us not merely a great dramatic moment in the worldwide struggle for emancipation, not merely an illustration of some kind of tactical approach, but rather a direct and immediate lesson for the here and now.

1. The state and the struggle for power

A revolution is an open contest of social forces in the struggle for power. The popular masses rise up, driven by vital elementary motives and interests, and frequently have no awareness of the movement's goals or the paths it will take: one party inscribes 'right and justice' on its banner, another 'order'; the 'heroes' of the revolution are either impelled by a sense of 'duty' or carried away by ambition; the army's behaviour is determined by unquestioning discipline, by a fear that consumes discipline, or else by revolutionary insight that overcomes both discipline and fear. Enthusiasm, self-interest, habit, bold flights of thought, superstition and self-sacrifice – thousands of different

---

[8] [In G.I. Uspensky's *Budka (The Sentry Box)*, Mymretsov was a boorish policeman from small-town Russia. According to Lenin in *The Right of Nations to Self-Determination*, Mymretsov's motto was 'grab 'em and hold 'em', Lenin 1920, p. 421).

feelings, ideas, attitudes, talents, and passions are swept into and swallowed up by a mighty whirlpool in which they either perish or rise to new heights. But the objective meaning of revolution is the struggle for state power for the purpose of reconstructing antiquated social relations.

The state is no end in itself. It is only a working machine in the hands of the ruling social forces. Like any machine, the state has its motive power, its mechanisms of transmission, and its working parts. The motive power is class interest; its mechanisms are agitation, the press, the propaganda of churches and schools, parties, street meetings, petitions, and uprisings. The transmission mechanism is the legislative organisation of caste, dynastic, estate, or class interest according to the will of God (in absolutism) or of the nation (in parliamentarism). Finally, the executive mechanism is the administration together with the police, courts and prisons, and the army.

The state is no end in itself. It is, however, the greatest means of organising, disorganising, and re-organising social relations. Depending upon whose hands control it, it can be either a lever for profound transformation or an instrument of organised stagnation.

Every political party worthy of the name endeavours to control governmental power in order to make the state serve that class whose interests it expresses. Democracy, as the party of the proletariat, naturally seeks the political supremacy of the working class.

The proletariat grows and becomes strong together with the growth of capitalism. In this sense, growth of capitalism is also the development of the proletariat in the direction of its own dictatorship. However, the day and the hour when power will pass into the hands of the working class do not directly depend upon the level of the productive forces, but rather upon the relations of class struggle, the international situation, and finally, upon a number of subjective factors that include tradition, initiative, and readiness for the fight.

In an economically backward country, the proletariat can come to power sooner than in a country of the most advanced capitalism. In 1871, they deliberately took 'control of social affairs into their own hands' (see the epigraph) in petty-bourgeois Paris. True, this was the situation only for two months, but this has not happened for even a single hour in the major capitalist centres of England or the United States. Any thought of some kind of automatic dependence of the proletarian dictatorship upon the technical means and forces of a country is nothing but a prejudice of 'economic' materialism simplified to the extreme. That kind of thinking has nothing in common with Marxism.

The Parisian workers took power into their own hands not because the relations of production matured for the dictatorship of the proletariat on 26 March, and not even because it seemed to them on that day that these relations had 'matured', but because they were compelled to do so by the bourgeoisie's betrayal of national defence. Marx illustrates this. It was only possible to defend Paris and the rest of France by arming the proletariat. But the revolutionary proletariat was a threat to the bourgeoisie, and an armed proletariat was an armed threat. The government of Thiers,[9] having no interest in rallying labouring France against the hordes of Bismarck's soldiers who had surrounded Paris, but undertaking instead to rally France's reactionary hordes against proletarian Paris, moved to Versailles to carry on its intrigues and left the capital in the hands of the workers, who wanted freedom for their country and prosperity for themselves and its people. The proletariat saw that the hour had come when it must save the country and become master of its own destiny. It could not avoid seizing power; it was compelled to do so by a series of political events. Power took it by surprise. Nevertheless, once it had power, it was as if its own class law of gravity directed it – despite one deviation or another – along the proper road. Its class position, as Marx and Engels explain, compelled it above all to take expedient action in reforming the apparatus of state power and prompted it to adopt appropriate policies for the economy. If the Commune was smashed, it was certainly not because of some inadequacy in development of the productive forces. Instead, it was due to a whole series of political causes: the blockade of Paris and its separation from the provinces, the extremely unfavourable international conditions, its own errors, and so forth.

---

[9] [Louis-Adolphe Thiers (1797–1877), originally favoured war with Prussia but subsequently, as President of the Republic, used French troops in cooperation with the Germans to crush the Commune.]

2. The republic and the dictatorship of the proletariat

The Paris Commune of 1871 was not, of course, a socialist commune; its régime was not even one of a consistently developed socialist revolution. The 'Commune' was only the prologue. It established the dictatorship of the proletariat, which was the necessary precondition of socialist revolution. Paris moved to the régime of proletarian dictatorship not by proclaiming a republic, but by virtue of the fact that 72 of its 90 representatives came from the workers and that it was under the protection of the proletarian guard. It would be more accurate to say that the republic itself was but a natural and inevitable expression of the fact that a 'workers' government' was established.

Alexandre Millerand,[10] who played the part of 'socialist' hostage in the bourgeois cabinet of the late Waldeck-Rousseau, serving alongside the former butcher of the Commune, General Gallifet[11] – this one-time socialist, Millerand, stated his political motto as follows: 'A republic is the political formula of socialism, and socialism is the economic content of a republic.' We must say, however, that this 'political formula' has been deprived of all 'socialist content'. Today's republics, while formally democratic organisations and expressions of the people's will, remain essentially a state 'formula' for the dictatorship of the propertied classes. After Norway separated from Sweden and became a republic, it might easily have preserved the status in which it found itself after separation; that is, it might have retained a republic without in any way making it into a 'political form of socialism'. Had it done so, we can be certain that not so much as a single hair would have fallen from the head of burgomaster Stockman[12] or the other 'pillars of society'. But Norway preferred to find itself a king – certainly there was a vast reserve army of august candidates – and thus it 'crowned' its independent and temporarily republican structure.

---

[10] [Alexandre Millerand (1859–1943) was elected as a socialist deputy in 1885. He joined René Waldeck-Rousseau's government in 1899 as Minister of Commerce.]

[11] [Gaston-Alexandre-Auguste Gallifet (1830–1909) savagely repressed the Commune in 1871.]

[12] [In Henrik Ibsen's play, *An Enemy of the People,* burgomaster Stockman declares his brother, a doctor, to be an enemy of the people for discovering that the baths are contaminated and then making the news public. The burgomaster prefers the contamination to the costs that repairs would entail.]

A certain Mr. Grimm, apparently a professor, a liberal writer and, besides all that, a collaborator of *Polyarnaya Zvezda*, recently explained to us 'doctrinaire book enthusiasts' that a 'democratic republic' is neither a 'cure-all' nor an 'absolutely perfect form of political organisation'. If Mr. Grimm were even remotely familiar with the doctrinaires upon whom our 'book enthusiasm' is based, he would know that Social Democrats have no illusions whatever about a democratic republic being a 'cure-all'. One need look no further than to Engels, who in his preface to *The Civil War* explicitly said the following:

> ...people think they have taken quite an extraordinary bold step forward when they have rid themselves of belief in hereditary monarchy and swear by the democratic republic. In reality, however, the state is nothing but a machine for the oppression of one class by another, and indeed in the democratic republic no less than in the monarchy....[13]

But, while Mr. Grimm puts forth the cheap little idea that the real issue is 'a proper arrangement of the various organs of state power', in which a monarchy is equally as suitable as a republic, international socialism believes that a republic is the only possible form of social emancipation – provided that the proletariat seizes it from the hands of the bourgeoisie and converts it from 'a machine for the oppression of one class by another' into an instrument for the social emancipation of humanity.

3. Economic development and the dictatorship of the proletariat

When the socialist press formulated the idea of *uninterrupted revolution*, linking the liquidation of absolutism and civil serfdom with socialist revolution through a series of intensifying social conflicts, uprisings by new sections of the masses, and continuous attacks by the proletariat upon the political and economic privileges of the ruling classes, our 'progressive' press unanimously raised a malicious howl of indignation. Oh, they can endure a great deal, but this was too much. A revolution, they exclaimed, cannot be 'legalised'! The use of extraordinary means is only permissible in extraordinary circumstances. The objective of the emancipation movement is not to perpetuate the revolution, but to steer it as speedily as possible into

---

[13] [Engels 1891, p. 190.]

legal channels. And so they continued, on and on. This is the position taken by the majority of so-called 'constitutional democrats'. The publicists of this party, including Messrs. Struve, Hessen, and Milyukov,[14] who so tirelessly compromise themselves in all their plans, predictions and warnings, rose up long ago against revolution in the name of 'rights' already won. Before the October strike, they tried to steer the revolution (by their wailing!) in the direction of the Bulygin Duma,[15] arguing that every *direct* struggle against the latter played into the hands of reaction. Following the manifesto of 17 October, they finally decided to license the revolution retrospectively for 3½ months (from 6 August to 17 October), magnanimously adopted the October strike, and gave it the title of being 'glorious'. But to make certain that no one get the impression they had learned anything, with shocking resourcefulness they also demanded that the revolution fit into the Procrustean bed of the Witte constitution,[16] declaring that any further direct struggle against the latter also played into the hands of reaction. It is no wonder that these gentlemen, after giving the revolution a three-month *post facto respite*, subsequently gnashed their teeth in opposition to any idea of a *permanent* revolution.[17] Only fully stabilised constitutionalism, with rare elections and, if possible, extraordinary laws against Social Democracy (against which the liberals would conditionally protest), and with sleepy opposition interpellations combined with vital backroom deals – only this condition of 'law', provided it was based on continuous exploitation of the popular masses and was constitutionally bridled with the help of the monarchy, two houses, and the imperial army – could adequately reward these politicians for all the wrongs they had suffered, and ultimately create the conditions in which they

---

[14] [I.V. Hessen and P.N. Milyukov edited the daily newspaper *Rech'*, which from March 1906 served as the central publication of the party of Constitutional Democrats (the Cadets). Struve was a close collaborator.]

[15] [In February 1905, A.G. Bulygin, who replaced Svyatopolk-Mirsky as Interior Minister, was ordered by the tsar to draft a plan for a limited consultative assembly in which most classes of the population would not be represented. The proposal was abandoned after the strikes in October, which led the tsar to issue a manifesto promising a more representative body.]

[16] [Witte was the moving force behind the tsar's October Manifesto. In Greek mythology, Procrustes was a bandit who compelled his victims to fit into an iron bed. He stretched those who were too short and amputated the legs of those were too tall. In either case, the victims died.]

[17] [Here Trotsky speaks of *бессрочная революция*, a revolution with no time limits.]

could play a 'state' role. But events have mocked these chieftains, mercilessly revealed their blindness and their impotence, and long ago freed us from any need to solicit their permission for the revolution's continuation.

The less corrupted members of that same democracy do not risk coming out against the revolution from the point of view of the existing constitutional 'accomplishments': even they think that this parliamentary cretinism, which has actually forestalled the emergence of parliamentarism, is not an effective weapon for struggle against the revolutionary proletariat. They choose a different course: they take their stand not on law, but on what they regard as facts, on historical 'possibilities' and political 'realism' – and finally…finally, even on 'Marxism' itself. Why not? As Antonio, the pious bourgeois of Venice, succinctly said:

> Mark you this, [Bassanio],
> The devil can cite Scripture for his purpose.[18]

These gentlemen, often former 'Marxists' who now have the precious freedom of spirit that comes only from the absence of any coherent worldview, all have the same inclination to abandon Marxism's revolutionary conclusions under the cover of 'criticism' and at the same time to use Marxism itself against the revolutionary tactics of Social Democracy. They all resolutely accuse us of slavishly sticking with outmoded doctrines and of fundamentally betraying Marxism's evolutionary theory.

An uninterrupted revolution? A socialist revolution? But doesn't Marxism teach that no social order ever gives way to a new society without first fully realising its own potential and developing its own tendencies to the *maximum*?[19] Has Russian capitalism really exhausted itself? Or do Social Democrats think, like subjectivists, that it is possible to overcome capitalism ideologically? And so on, and so forth. The most obdurate liberals, those who think even the constitutional democrats are too immoderate, at times adopt this kind of argument from former 'Marxists' who want to cite the conclusions of holy 'Scripture'. Thus Mr. Alexander Kaufman quite seriously exclaimed, in *Polyarnaya Zvezda*, that

---

[18] [The remark is from Shakespeare's *Merchant of Venice* (Act I, Scene III).]
[19] [See Marx 1859, pp. 19–23.]

> Many of us who believe in the final triumph of the socialist ideal share the view of Rodbertus[20] that modern man [who?] is not yet sufficiently mature for the 'Promised Land of socialism', and together with Marx we are convinced that socialisation of the means of production can only result from gradual development of the productive forces of the people and the country.[21]

This Mr. Kaufman, who for his own purposes swears simultaneously by Rodbertus and Marx, the Pope and Luther, is a living example of the malicious ignorance that liberal critics flaunt at every turn when dealing with questions of socialism.

Capitalism must 'exhaust itself' before the proletariat can take state power into its own hands. What does that mean? To develop the productive forces to the maximum? To maximise the concentration of production? But in that case, just what is the maximum? How is it objectively ascertained?

Economic development in recent decades has shown that capitalism not only concentrates the main branches of industry in a few hands, but also surrounds giant economic organisms with parasitic offshoots in the form of small industrial and commercial enterprises. In agriculture, capitalism sometimes completely kills off small-scale production, transforming the peasant into a landless labourer, an industrial worker, a street trader or a tramp; in other cases it preserves the peasant farm while seizing it in its own iron grip; and in still other cases it creates petty and minuscule farms while enslaving peasant workers in the service of large landowners. What is clear from the enormous mass of interwoven events and facts that characterise capitalist development is that the values created by large enterprises, which prevail in the main branches of social labour, continuously grow by comparison with the values created in small enterprises, and this increasingly facilitates socialisation of the main branches of the economy. But just what, in the opinion of our critics, must the percentage relation be between these two sections of social production before we can say that capitalism has exhausted its potential and that the proletariat has the right to decide the hour has come to reach out and pluck the ripened fruit?

---

[20] [Karl Johann Rodbertus (1805–75) was a German economist and social reformer who considered a socialist republic to be possible but also hoped that a German emperor might emerge as a social emperor.]

[21] No. 2, p. 132.

Our party has no illusions about seizing power and then producing socialism from the womb of its own socialist will; in socialist construction, it can and must rely only upon the objective economic development that we must assume will continue when the proletariat is in power. But the point is – *and this is an extremely important part of the question* – that, in the first place, economic development has already made socialism an objectively advantageous system, and secondly, that this economic development does not in the least involve some objective points that must first be passed before it becomes possible for the state to begin a planned intervention in spontaneous evolution with the goal of replacing the private economy with a social economy.

It is true, beyond any doubt, that the higher is the form of capitalist development that compels the proletariat to take power, the easier it will be to manage its socialist tasks, the more directly it will be able to turn to the organisation of a social economy, and the shorter – *ceteris paribus*[22] – will be the period of social revolution. But the fact is – *and this is another important part of the question* – that choice of the moment when it might seize state power by no means depends on the proletariat. Developing on the basis of capitalist evolution, class struggle is the kind of *objective* process that has its own irreversible internal tendencies, just like economic evolution.

Unfortunately, the logic of class struggle is merely an empty phrase for all bourgeois politicians, including those who flirt with theoretical Marxism in order to struggle even more 'independently' against its political expression in Social Democracy. Every argument that begins with the relations of class struggle grates on their consciousness like cut glass. They have only managed to memorise a few isolated elements of the Marxist theory of capitalist development, but they have remained primitive bourgeois barbarians in everything that concerns class struggle and its objective logic. When they appeal to 'objective social development' in response to the idea of uninterrupted revolution, which, for us, is a conclusion following from social-political relations, they forget that this same development includes not merely economic evolution, which they so superficially understand, but also the revolutionary logic of class relations, which they cannot bring themselves even to consider.

---

[22] [Other things being equal.]

Social Democracy aspires to be, and must be, a conscious expression of objective development. But, once the moment arrives when the objective development of class struggle confronts the proletariat, at a certain stage of the revolution, with the alternative of taking upon itself the rights and duties of state power or else surrendering its class position, Social Democracy makes the conquest of state power its *immediate* objective. In doing so, it does not in the least ignore the deeper processes of objective development, including the processes of growth and concentration of production. But it does say that, once the logic of class struggle, which, in the final analysis, depends on the course of economic development, drives the proletariat to establish its dictatorship even before the bourgeoisie has 'exhausted' its economic mission (it has hardly even begun its political mission), this can only mean that history has imposed upon the proletariat tasks of colossal difficulty. It may happen that the proletariat will become exhausted in the struggle and even collapse under this weight – that is a possibility. Nevertheless, it cannot evade these tasks without risking class demoralisation and descent of the entire country into barbarism.

4. Revolution, the bourgeoisie, and the proletariat

A revolution is not some whirligig that can be made to spin with a whip. Nor is it an obedient Red Sea that liberals, like Moses, can part by crying out or waving a staff. When we speak of uninterrupted revolution, it is not because we are reluctant to lead the workers' movement in 'lawful' channels. (Whose law? That of the autocrat, of Mr. Witte, of Mr. Durnovo,[23] or the legal schemes of Mr. Struve? Just whose law?) We begin with our analysis of class relations in the unfolding revolutionary struggle. We have made this analysis tens of times. We have looked at the question from every perspective, and every time the facts have justified our political analysis. Bourgeois politicians and publicists have grumbled against us, but they have never attempted any real response.

In the past year, the revolution has demonstrated colossal energy and endurance. Nevertheless, it has yet to create even a single state institution as

---

[23] [Pyotr Nikolaevich Durnovo (1845–1915) was security chief under Tsar Nicholas II and responsible for suppressing the revolution.]

a real support and 'guarantee' of 'freedom'. The Duma of 6 August is dead. The Duma of 17 October–11 December is doomed.[24] The liberals, who are always impatiently waiting for the revolutionary mountain ultimately to give birth to their mouse, are horrified by the revolution's 'futility'. Meanwhile, the revolution has every right to be proud of this 'futility', which is merely the external expression of its inner strength. Every time absolutism attempts to reach agreement with the confused representatives of the propertied classes and, counting upon their support, begins to draft the outline of a constitution, there is a new revolutionary swell, far more powerful than all the previous ones, that washes away the plans and throws off or sweeps away the bureaucratic and liberal draftsmen.

The bourgeoisie is incapable of leading the people to win a parliamentary order through the *overthrow* of absolutism. And the people, in the form of the proletariat, are preventing the bourgeoisie from achieving constitutional guarantees through any *agreement* with absolutism. Bourgeois democrats cannot lead the proletariat because the proletariat is too mature to follow them and wants to take the lead itself. And the democrats have turned out to be even more impotent than the liberals. They are cut off from the people just as liberalism is, but they do not have the social advantages of the bourgeoisie. They are simply a nullity.

The proletariat is the *sole* force leading the revolution and the *principal* fighter on its behalf. The proletariat seizes the entire field and is never satisfied, nor will it ever be satisfied, by any concession; through every respite or temporary retreat, it will lead the revolution to the victory in which it will take power.

There is no need for us to recount the facts of the past year. The reader can refer to the Social-Democratic literature of the period.[25]

---

[24] [On 6 August (19 August new style) the tsar issued a manifesto concerning convocation of a consultative Duma. Through the appointed State Council, however, the tsar would have been able to pass legislation despite the opinion of the Duma. On 17 October (30 October), the tsar issued a new manifesto promising that no law would take effect without the Duma's approval. The document is available at (http://artsci .shu.edu/reesp/documents/october%20manifesto.htm).]

[25] See our brochure *Up to the Ninth of January* and especially the foreword to it by comrade Parvus [in this volume, see the essay by Parvus entitled 'What Was Accomplished on the Ninth of January']. In addition, we refer the reader to certain articles in *Nachalo* and our foreword to Lassalle's *Speech to the Jury* [also included in this volume]. This foreword, written in July 1905, has had a complex history and is only now appearing in the press.

Here, we need only give one illustration of the impotence of the bourgeoisie in the struggle for a parliamentary order.

Popular representation, the price of a deal between the bourgeoisie and the monarchy and the issue that such deals always involve, is killed by the revolution every time it is about to emerge. The other historical institution of bourgeois revolutions, a civil militia, has been killed in embryo, indeed, even at the moment of conception.

A militia (or national guard) was the first slogan and the first achievement of all revolutions – in 1789 and 1848 in Paris, in all the Italian states, in Vienna, and in Berlin. In 1848 the national guard (the arming of property owners and the 'educated' classes) was the slogan of the entire bourgeois opposition, even the most moderate elements. Its purpose was not only to safeguard freedoms extracted, or merely about to be 'conferred', against being overturned from above, but also to protect bourgeois property from encroachments by the proletariat. Thus, the demand for a militia has always been an adamant class demand of the bourgeoisie. A liberal English historian of Italy's unification says:

> The Italians understood very well that the arming of a civil militia would make the continued existence of despotism impossible. Moreover, for the possessing classes this was a guarantee against the possibility of anarchy and all the disorders hidden below.[26]

The ruling reactionaries, not possessing sufficient military forces at the centres of activity, armed the bourgeoisie in order to deal with 'anarchy', that is, with the revolutionary masses. Absolutism first left it to the burghers to suppress and pacify the workers, and then it disarmed and pacified the burghers in turn.

With us, the slogan of a militia has no credit whatever amongst the bourgeois parties. The liberals must surely understand the importance of arms; absolutism has taught them a few object lessons in this regard. But they also understand the complete impossibility of creating a militia in our country without the proletariat or in opposition to the proletariat. Russian workers bear no resemblance to the workers of 1848, who filled their pockets with

---

[26] King 1901, p. 220.

stones or took up crowbars while the shopkeepers, students, and barristers shouldered royal muskets and had sabres at their sides.

To arm the revolution, in our case, means above all to arm the workers. Knowing and fearing this fact, the liberals reject a militia. On this issue, they surrender to absolutism without a fight – just as the bourgeoisie of Thiers surrendered Paris and France to Bismarck rather than arming the workers.

In a collection entitled *The Constitutional State*, a manifesto of the liberal-democratic coalition, Mr. Dzhivelegov, discussing the possibility of revolution, quite rightly says that 'Society itself, at the necessary moment, must be prepared to stand up in defence of its Constitution'. But since the obvious conclusion that follows is the demand for arming the people, this liberal philosopher thinks it 'necessary to add' that 'it is not at all necessary for everyone to bear arms' in order to prevent coups.[27] It is only necessary that society itself be prepared to resist – just how remains to be told. If there is any conclusion to draw from this subterfuge, it can only be that, in the hearts of our democrats, fear of the armed proletariat is greater than fear of the autocrat's troops.

It follows that the task of arming the revolution falls entirely upon the proletariat. A civil militia, which was the class demand of the bourgeoisie in 1848, is in Russia from the very outset a demand for arming the people and above all the proletariat. The entire fate of the Russian revolution is summarised in this question.

5. The proletariat and the peasantry

The first tasks that the proletariat will face immediately upon seizing power will be political ones: to fortify its position, to arm the revolution, to disarm the reaction, to extend the base of the revolution, and to rebuild the state. In completing these tasks, particularly the last one, Russian workers will not forget the experience of the Paris Commune. Abolition of the standing army and police, arming of the people, elimination of the bureaucratic mandarinate, introduction of elections for all public servants, equalisation of their salaries, and separation of the church from the state – these are the measures that must be implemented first, following the example of the Commune.

---

[27] *The Constitutional State: A Collection of Articles*, 1st edition, p. 49.

But the proletariat will not be able to stabilise its power without expanding the base of the revolution itself.

Many strata of the toiling masses, especially in the countryside, will be drawn into the revolution for the first time and become politically organised only after the vanguard of the revolution, the urban proletariat, has already seized the helm of state. Revolutionary agitation and organisation will proceed with the assistance of state resources. Ultimately, the legislative power will itself become a powerful instrument for revolutionising the popular masses.

In these circumstances, the character of our social-historical relations will be such as to place on the proletariat's shoulders all the burdens of the bourgeois revolution and will not only create for the workers' government enormous difficulties, but will also give it an invaluable advantage in terms of relations between the proletariat and the peasantry.

In the revolutions of 1789–93 and 1848, power first passed from absolutism to moderate elements of the bourgeoisie, which, in turn, emancipated the peasantry (just *how* is another question) before revolutionary democracy took power or was even prepared to take power into its own hands. The emancipated peasantry lost all interest in the political ventures of the 'townspeople', that is, in further development of the revolution, and became a solid foundation in support of 'order', thus delivering up the revolution's head to a caesarist or absolutist reaction.

The Russian revolution, as we have already said, does not allow for establishment of any kind of bourgeois-constitutional order that might resolve even the most elementary tasks of democracy. As for reformer-bureaucrats such as Witte, all of their enlightened efforts will go to ruin in the struggle for their own survival. As a result, the fate of the peasantry's most basic revolutionary interests – even those of the peasantry *as a whole*, as an *estate* – are tied to the fate of the entire revolution, which means they are tied to the fate of the proletariat.

The proletariat in power will stand before the peasantry as the class that emancipates it.

As in the case of the Commune, it will be entirely justified in saying to the peasantry: 'Our victory is your victory!'

The supremacy of the proletariat will mean not only democratic equality, free self-government, transfer of the entire tax burden to the propertied classes, dissolution of the standing army and its replacement by the armed people, and the elimination of obligatory requisitions by the church, but also recognition of all the revolutionary land redistributions (seizures) undertaken by the peasantry. The proletariat will make these changes the starting point for further state measures in agriculture. In these conditions, the Russian peasantry will be at least as interested, from the very beginning and during the most difficult initial period, in supporting the proletarian régime (workers' democracy), as the French peasantry was in supporting the military régime of Napoleon Bonaparte, which used its bayonets to guarantee to the new property owners the security of their land holdings. This means that the people's government, convened under the leadership of the proletariat and enjoying the support of the peasantry, will be nothing other than the democratic form for the supremacy of workers' democracy.

Could it happen that the peasantry itself will push the proletariat aside and take its place?

This is impossible. The whole experience of history protests against this assumption and demonstrates that the peasantry is completely incapable of an *independent* political role.[28]

The history of capitalism is the history of the countryside's subordination to the city. In its own time, the industrial development of European cities rendered impossible the continuation of feudal relations in the sphere of

---

[28] Does not the emergence and development of the 'Peasant Union' contradict these and subsequent arguments? Not at all. What is the 'Peasant Union'? It is an association of certain elements of radical democracy, who are looking for mass support, with the most conscious elements of the peasantry – evidently *not* the lower strata – in the name of democratic revolution and agrarian reform. However quickly the 'Peasant Union' has grown, there is no doubt that it is extremely far from becoming a political organisation of the peasant masses. All other considerations aside, the revolution is advancing at such a tempo that there is no possibility of expecting that the 'Peasant Union' will be able, at the moment of the final overthrow of absolutism and the transfer of power into revolutionary hands, to become a serious competitor of the organised proletariat. Moreover, we must not forget that the main revolutionary battles are occurring in the cities, and this fact alone relegates the 'Peasant Union' to the role of a subordinate fighting detachment, which in turn determines its place on the scale of political forces.

As for the agrarian programme of the 'Peasant Union' ('equalisation of land tenure'), which is its main reason for existence, the following must be said: the wider and deeper the agrarian movement becomes, the more quickly will it arrive at confiscations and reallotments, which means that the 'Peasant Union' will itself dissolve all the more quickly as the result of a thousand contradictions involving class, localities, everyday life, and technique. Its members will exercise their share of influence in *peasant committees*, as local organs of the agrarian revolution, but it goes without saying that the peasant committees, as *economic-administrative* institutions, will not alter the *political* dependence of the countryside on the city, which is one of the fundamental characteristics of modern society.

agricultural production. But the countryside itself never produced the kind of class that was able to manage the revolutionary task of abolishing feudalism. The same city that subordinated agriculture to capital also brought forth the revolutionary forces that took political hegemony over the countryside and extended to it the revolution in state and property relations. With further development, the countryside ultimately fell into economic servitude to capital, and the peasantry into political servitude to the capitalist parties. They re-established feudalism in parliamentary politics by converting the peasantry into their own political *demesne* for vote-hunting purposes. The modern bourgeois state, by means of taxation and militarism, drives the peasant into the clutches of usurer capital; and by means of state priests, state schools, and the corruption of barrack life, it makes him a victim of usurer politics.

The Russian bourgeoisie will surrender all of its revolutionary positions to the proletariat. It will also have to surrender hegemony over the peasantry. In the situation that will be created by transfer of power to the proletariat, the peasantry will have no option but to ally with the régime of workers' democracy, even if it does so with no more conscious commitment than it usually shows when associating itself with the bourgeois régime! But while every bourgeois party, after winning the peasants' votes, rushes to use power in order to fleece the peasantry, deceive it, and betray all its expectations and all the promises made to it, and then, if worst comes to worst, gives way to another capitalist party, the proletariat, relying upon the peasantry, will put in motion all possible forces to raise the cultural level of the countryside and to develop the peasantry's political consciousness.

Marx says that the prejudices of the French peasant

> could not withstand the Commune's appeal to the vital interests and essential needs of the peasants. The landlords understood very well (and feared most of all) that if Communal Paris were to communicate freely with the provinces, then within three months or so a general peasant insurrection would break out. That is why they rushed so frantically to surround Paris with a police blockade in order to stop the spread of infection....[29]

---

[29] [See Marx 1871.]

How we regard the idea of a 'dictatorship of the proletariat and peasantry' will be clear from all that we have said thus far.[30] The essential point is not whether we consider it admissible in principle, whether we 'want' or 'do not want' such a form of political co-operation. We consider it incapable of being realised, at least in any direct and immediate sense.

Indeed, such a coalition presupposes either that one of the existing bourgeois parties seizes control of the peasantry, or else that the peasantry creates its own powerful and independent party. Both outcomes, as we have tried to demonstrate, are impossible.

Nevertheless, the dictatorship of the proletariat will undoubtedly represent all the progressive and real interests of the peasantry – and not just of the peasantry, but also of the petty bourgeoisie and the intelligentsia. 'The Commune,' Marx says, 'served as the true representative of all the healthy elements of French society; for that reason, it was a genuine *national government.*'[31]

But it remained the *dictatorship of the proletariat.*

6. The methods and goals of the dictatorship of the proletariat

The dictatorship of the proletariat does not at all mean the dictatorship of a revolutionary organisation *over* the proletariat and, through it, over the whole of society. This is demonstrated best in the experience of the Paris Commune.

The Vienna revolution in March 1848 delivered power to the students, the only part of bourgeois society that was still capable of decisive revolutionary politics. The proletariat, being unorganised and lacking both political experience and its own independent leadership, followed the students. At every critical moment, the workers invariably offered 'the gentlemen who work with their heads' the assistance of those 'who work with their hands'. The students first called upon the workers, but then they themselves blocked their way from the suburbs. At times, using the force of their own political authority and relying on the arms of the Academic Legion, they barred the workers from putting forth their own independent demands. This was a

---

[30] [This was Lenin's term in the summer of 1905. See Lenin 1905k and 1905l.]
[31] [See Marx 1871.]

classic and obvious form of benevolent revolutionary dictatorship *over* the proletariat.

In the Paris Commune, everything depended on the independent political activity of the workers. The Central Committee of the National Guard advised the Commune's proletarian voters to remember that the only people who would serve them well were those selected from the workers themselves. The Central Committee wrote: 'Avoid those with property, because it is an extremely rare event when a well-to-do man regards the worker as his brother.' The Commune was a business-like proletarian board, the National Guard was its army, and the officials were its responsible servants. That was the dictatorship of the proletariat.

The Russian working class of 1906 bears absolutely no resemblance to that of Vienna in 1848. The best evidence is the fact that Soviets of Workers' Deputies are springing up throughout Russia. These are not conspiratorial organisations that were prepared in advance and seized power over the proletarian masses at the moment when the excitement broke out. No, these organs were deliberately created by the masses themselves to coordinate their revolutionary struggle. And these Soviets, elected by the masses and responsible to them as unconditionally democratic institutions, are pursuing the most resolute class policy in the spirit of revolutionary socialism. This is still far from having a provisional government, and they might ultimately amount to nothing – but we certainly see here the future organs of local support for a provisional government. The entire activity of the workers' Soviets clearly demonstrates that the politics of the Russian proletariat in power will be a new and colossal step forward by comparison with the Commune of 1871.

The Parisian workers, says Marx, demanded no miracles from the Commune. Nor can we expect all kinds of miracles from the dictatorship of the proletariat today. State power is not omnipotent. It would be foolish to think that all the proletariat must do is acquire power and then issue a few decrees to replace capitalism with socialism. The economic system is not a product of state activity. All the proletariat can do is apply all its energy in using state power to ease and shorten the road of economic evolution in the direction of collectivism.

The proletariat will begin with those reforms that are included in its so-called minimum programme, and then, by the very logic of its position, it will be compelled to move directly towards collectivist practices.

Introduction of the eight-hour working day and a steeply progressive income tax will be comparatively easy, although, here too, the central point is not issuing the 'act' but rather organising its practical implementation. But the chief difficulty – and here we have the transition to collectivism! – will be in having the state organise production in those factories and plants that will be shut down by their owners in response to publication of these acts.

To issue and put into practise a law abolishing the right of inheritance will likewise be a comparatively simple matter. Small legacies in the form of money-capital are also not a problem for the proletariat and do not impose any burden on its economy. But to become the inheritor of landed and industrial capital means the workers' state must take it upon itself to organise the economy for public purposes.

The same will be true, on an even greater scale, in the matter of expropriation – with or without compensation. Expropriation with compensation is politically advantageous but creates a financial burden, whereas expropriation without compensation is financially advantageous but politically difficult. But these and other such difficulties will still be secondary compared to those involved in management and organisation.

I repeat: the government of the proletariat does not mean a government of miracles.

Socialisation of production will begin with those branches that pose the least difficulty. In the first period, socialised production will be like oases, connected with private economic enterprises by the laws of commodity circulation. The wider the field of socialised production becomes, the more evident will its advantages be, the more secure will the new political régime feel itself to be, and the bolder will the ensuing economic measures of the proletariat become. In taking these measures, it can and will rely not merely upon the national productive forces, but also upon international technology, just as it relies in its revolutionary politics not merely upon the immediate facts of national class relations but also upon the entire historical experience of the international proletariat.

Furthermore, having taken power through revolution, the Russian proletariat will do everything that circumstances permit to link the fate of its national cause immediately and directly to the cause of world socialism.[32] We are called upon to do so not merely by the common international principles of proletarian politics, but also by the powerful voice of class self-preservation, which compels us to move in this direction.

The Russian proletariat will not be driven back, but it will only be able to carry its great cause through to the end if it succeeds in expanding the limits of our great revolution and in making it the prologue for the world victory of Labour.

---

[32] We commented in general terms on the revolution's international perspectives in the previously mentioned foreword to the speech by Lassalle [note 25 above and Chapter 12 in this volume].

Chapter Eighteen

'The Russian Revolution' (20 December 1905)

Rosa Luxemburg

Almost all the writings of Rosa Luxemburg between February 1905 (when 'After the First Act' was published) and December 1905 elaborated the idea that the Russian revolution was not purely bourgeois but a *sui generis* historical phenomenon combining bourgeois and proletarian features. For instance, in April 1905, she wrote in her Polish journal:

> The present revolution in our country as well as in the rest of the tsarist kingdom has a dual character. In its immediate objectives, it is a *bourgeois* revolution. Its aim is the introduction of political freedom in the tsarist state, the republic and the parliamentary order that, with the dominion of capital over wage-labour, is nothing but an advanced form of the bourgeois state, a form of the class rule of the bourgeoisie over the proletariat. But, in Russia and Poland, this bourgeois revolution was not carried out by the bourgeoisie, as was previously the case in Germany and France, but by the working class – moreover, by a working class that is to a high degree conscious of its class interests; a working class that has not conquered political freedom for the bourgeoisie but, on the contrary, with the objective of facilitating its own struggle against

> the bourgeoisie with the aim of accelerating the triumph of socialism. For
> that reason, the present revolution is at the same time a *workers'* revolution.
> Therefore, the struggle against absolutism in this revolution must go hand
> in hand with the struggle against capital, against exploitation.[1]

The most finished expression of this idea of a dual revolution is perhaps the current article,[2] which was first published in German in a Festschrift entitled *1649–1789–1905* (see the introduction to Kautsky's article 'Old and New Revolution', the next document in this anthology). A Polish version was published simultaneously in *Trybuna Ludowa*, Nr. 4, 20 December, 1905. A German translation from that version, virtually identical with the one found in Luxemburg's *Gesammelte Werke* and carrying the title 'Die Revolution in Rußland', also appears in the German edition of her Polish writings.[3]

The documents in this collection have shown that the concept of permanent revolution was typically set forth from two perspectives; one emphasised the exceptional historical and social-class relations within Russia due to its delayed economic development; another assessed Russian revolutionary prospects in terms of the international context, with particular stress on the role of foreign capital and the connections between revolution in Russia and impending socialist revolution throughout Europe. This article by Luxemburg is distinguished by a brief but compelling Marxist analysis of how the Russian revolution was related to European history following the French Revolution of 1789. Luxemburg's theme is that a *dual* revolution in Russia would simultaneously *complete* the series of bourgeois revolutions inaugurated in 1789 and *begin* a new round of proletarian revolutions leading to socialism's international triumph. Just as the Great French Revolution affected the entire political history of the nineteenth century, she expected the Russian revolution would have a similar influence on the twentieth century. By conceiving the dual character of permanent revolution in terms of completing one historical project and launching another, Luxemburg provided a persuasive explanation of Russian events in terms of a coherent Marxist account of Russia's peculiar relation to European history.

*　*　*

---

[1] Luxemburg 1905e, p. 556.
[2] Luxemburg 1905d, pp. 5–10.
[3] Luxemburg 1905c, pp. 291–7.

'The Russian Revolution'

The present revolution in Russia is formally the last offshoot of the Great French Revolution of a hundred years ago. The entire past century actually only accomplished the task set for it by that great historical upheaval, namely, establishment of the class rule of the modern bourgeoisie and of capitalism in all countries. In the first act of this century-long, drawn-out crisis, the actual revolution uprooted medieval feudal society, shook it to its foundations, turned everything upside down, first carved out the modern classes in a rough and crude way, clarified to some extent their social and political aspirations and programmes, and finally suppressed feudalism all over Europe through the Napoleonic Wars. In the following stages, the class division of modern bourgeois society, initiated by the Great Revolution, was continued in and through the class struggle. During the Restoration period [in France] after 1815, high finance came into power and was overthrown by the revolution of July [1830]. In the July revolution, the great industrial bourgeoisie succeeded in seizing power and was overthrown by the revolution of February [1848]. The February revolution finally led to the rule of the broad mass of the middle and small bourgeoisie. In the shape of the contemporary [French] Third Republic, modern bourgeois class domination reached its most highly developed and final form. But, meanwhile, in all these internal struggles of the bourgeoisie there also developed a new division: that between the whole of bourgeois society and the modern working class. The formation and ripening of these new class contradictions runs parallel with the *bourgeois* class struggle throughout the entire history of the [nineteenth] century. Already the first general convulsions of the Great [French] Revolution pulled to the surface of bourgeois society all its elements and internal contradictions – including the proletariat and its social ideal: communism. The short rule of the party of the Mountain,[4] which marked the high point of the Revolution, was the first historical appearance of the modern proletariat. Yet it did not step forward

---

4 [The party of the Mountain [*Montagne*] constituted the radical left wing of the National Convention during the Great French Revolution. It ruled from July 1793 to July 1794 in the form of the revolutionary democratic dictatorship of the Jacobin party, whose most famous leaders were Maximilien Robespierre, Georges-Jacques Danton, and Jean-Paul Marat. On 27 July 1794, (9 Thermidor Year II according to the French Republican Calendar) Robespierre and Saint-Just were arrested and guillotined the following day, marking the beginning of the Thermidorian reaction.]

independently but still remained in the fold of the petty bourgeoisie and at first constituted, together with it, 'the people', whose opposition to bourgeois society assumed the misleading form of an opposition between the 'popular republic' and the constitutional monarchy. In the February Revolution, in the frightful June battle [of 1848], the proletariat also finally separated itself completely as a class from the petty bourgeoisie and, for the first time, recognised that, in bourgeois society, it is totally isolated, left completely to its own resources, and in mortal enmity with that society. Thus was first formed in France the modern bourgeois society, which completed the work begun by the Great French Revolution.

If these main acts in the dramatic history of capitalist society had *France* as their stage, it was nevertheless the history of Germany, of Austria, of Italy – of all the modern countries of the entire capitalist world – that was acted out there at the same time. Nothing is more foolish and absurd than wanting to regard modern revolutions as national incidents, as events that display all their force only within the borders of the state in question and exert only a more or less weak influence on the 'neighbouring states' according to their 'internal situation'. Bourgeois society, capitalism, is an international, *world* form of human society. There are not as many bourgeois societies, as many capitalisms, as there are modern states or nations, but only *one* international bourgeois society, only *one* capitalism, and the apparently isolated, independent existence of particular states within their state frontiers, alongside the single and inseparable world economy, is only one of the contradictions of capitalism. That is why all the modern revolutions are also at bottom *international* revolutions. They are also one and the same violent bourgeois revolution, which took place in different acts over the whole of Europe between 1789 and 1848 and established modern bourgeois class rule *on an international basis*.

The Russian empire apparently constituted an exception to this world revolution. Here, medieval absolutism seemed to want to preserve itself, despite all the upheavals in the rest of capitalist Europe, as an indestructible survival of the precapitalist period. Now absolutism, already shattered by the revolution, is also in a sorry state in Russia. What we are now witnessing are no longer struggles of the revolution against a ruling absolutist system but, on the contrary, struggles of the formal remains of absolutism against a modern political freedom that has already become a living fact, as well as struggles between the classes and parties over the limits of this freedom and their institutionalisation in a constitution.

As we said, the Russian revolution is formally the last offshoot of the period of *bourgeois* revolutions in Europe. Its immediate outward task is the creation of a modern capitalist society with open bourgeois class rule. But – and here it becomes evident that even Russia, which had apparently remained motionless and secluded throughout the entire [nineteenth] century, has actually taken part in the general upheaval of Europe – this formally bourgeois revolution will no longer be accomplished in Russia by the bourgeoisie but by the working class. Moreover, the working class is no longer an appendage of the petty bourgeoisie, as in all previous revolutions, but appears as an independent class with full consciousness of its special class interests and tasks; that is to say, as a working class led by Social Democracy. To that extent, the present revolution follows directly from the Parisian June battles of the year 1848 and, from the outset, carries to its logical conclusion, for the first time, the separation between the proletariat and the whole of bourgeois society. At the same time, the Russian proletariat in its revolutionary action availed itself of the entire historical experience and class consciousness accumulated by the international proletariat since that first lesson in June 1848, including the later parliamentary period in France, Germany and elsewhere.

Thus, the present Russian revolution is a much more contradictory phenomenon than all previous revolutions. The political forms of modern bourgeois class rule were here won through the fight not of the bourgeoisie, but of the working class against the bourgeoisie. But the working class, although – or rather because – it appeared for the first time as an independent class-conscious element, did so without the utopian-socialist illusions that it shared with the petty bourgeoisie in the previous bourgeois revolutions. The proletariat in Russia does not set for itself the task of realising socialism today, but of first creating the bourgeois preconditions for the realisation of socialism. But the fact that this bourgeois society results from the work of a class-conscious proletariat also imparts to it an absolutely peculiar character. True, the working class in Russia does not see its immediate task in realising socialism, but even less does it set for itself the task of securing the inviolable and untroubled dominion of capitalist class rule, such as resulted from the bourgeois revolutions of previous centuries in the West.

Instead, the proletariat in Russia leads the struggle against both absolutism and capitalism simultaneously and in a single action. It wants only the forms of bourgeois democracy – but it wants them *for itself*, for the purpose of proletarian class struggles. It wants the *eight-hour working day*, the popular militia, the republic – clear demands that are intended for bourgeois, not for socialist society. But these demands at the same time push so hard on the outer *limits* of capital's rule that they appear likewise as forms of transition to a proletarian dictatorship. The proletariat in Russia is struggling for realisation of the most elementary *bourgeois* constitutional rights: the right of assembly and association, freedom of organisation, freedom of the press. But, already now, in the storm of the revolution, it has used these bourgeois freedoms for the creation of such powerful economic and political class organisations of the proletariat – trade unions and Social Democracy – that, in the course of the revolution, the class that is formally called upon to rule, the bourgeoisie, emerges with unprecedented weakness while the formally ruled class, the proletariat, will win unprecedented predominance.

Thus, *in its content*, the present revolution in Russia goes far beyond previous revolutions, and, in its methods, it cannot simply follow either the old bourgeois revolutions or the previous – parliamentary – struggles of the modern proletariat. It has created a new method of struggle, which accords both with its proletarian character and with the combination of the struggle for democracy and the struggle against capital – namely, the revolutionary mass strike. In terms of content and methods, it is therefore a completely new type of revolution. Being formally bourgeois-democratic, but essentially proletarian-socialist, it is, in both content and method, *a transitional form* from the bourgeois revolutions of the past to the proletarian revolutions of the future, which will directly involve the dictatorship of the proletariat and the realisation of socialism.

It is so not only logically, as a specific type of revolution, but also *historically*, as the starting point for certain social class and power relations. The society that will arise from such a peculiar revolution in Russia cannot resemble those that resulted from the previous revolutions in the West after 1848. The power, the organisation, and the class consciousness of the proletariat in Russia will be so highly developed after the revolution that they will go beyond the framework of a 'normal' bourgeois society at every turn. Along with the simultaneous weakness and cowardice of a bourgeoisie that senses its impending doom and is without any political or revolutionary past, the result will be a combination of forces that will continually upset the equilibrium of bourgeois class rule. It will also open up a new phase in the history of bourgeois society in which, given the lack of a stable equilibrium, class relations will experience continual upheavals; this phase, with greater or smaller pauses and with more less vehemence, cannot have any other outcome but the social revolution – the dictatorship of the proletariat.

All this refers first of all to Russia. But just as the fate of Russia and of the whole of Europe during the French revolutions was decided by battles in the districts of Paris, so the fate not only of Russian society but of the entire capitalist world will now be decided in the streets of Petersburg, Moscow and Warsaw. The revolution in Russia and the peculiar social formation that will result from it are also bound to shift the class relations in Germany and everywhere else in one fell swoop. The Russian revolution has closed a period of nearly sixty years of peaceful, parliamentary rule of the bourgeoisie. With the Russian revolution, we are already entering the transitional period from capitalist to socialist society. How *long* that transitional period may last is of interest only to political fortune-tellers. For the international class-conscious proletariat, all that matters is firm and clear insight concerning the proximity of this cathartic period and the necessity of developing in tenacity, clarity and heroism during the coming storms – and of doing so with the same speed as the Russian proletariat is now demonstrating, daily and hourly, before our very eyes.

Chapter Nineteen

'Old and New Revolution' (December 1905)

Karl Kautsky

This article[1] first appeared in German in the *Festschrift 1649–1789–1905*, published in commemoration of the first anniversary of 'Bloody Sunday'.[2] The *Festschrift* includes the song Ich war, ich bin, ich werde sein ('I Was, I Am, I Shall Be') by Ernst Preczang, letters from a political exile in Siberia, excerpts from Marx's *The Eighteenth Brumaire of Louis Napoleon* and from Kautsky's *Die Klassengegensätze von 1789*, and four articles comparing the Russian Revolution of 1905 with the French Revolution of 1789 and the Puritan Revolution of 1649 in England. The articles are Kautsky's 'Alte und neue Revolution' ['Old and New Revolution'], Hugo Schulz's 'Schicksalsmomente der englischen Revolution' ['Decisive Moments of the English Revolution'], Franz Mehring's 'Die französische Revolution' ['The French Revolution'], and Rosa Luxemburg's 'Die russische Revolution' ['The Russian Revolution'].

Rosa Luxemburg's article and Kautsky's 'The *Sans-Culottes* of the French Revolution' (a chapter from his 1886 booklet on the French Revolution)

---

[1] Karl Kautsky 1905b, pp. 3–5. (Although the *Festschrift* was to mark the anniversary of Bloody Sunday in January 1905, it appears to have been published in December 1905, the date we have provisionally used here.)

[2] The *Festschrift* is referred to as *Gedenkschrift zum ersten Jahrestag des Beginns der russischen Revolution von 1905* in Stern (ed.) 1961, vol. 5, pp. 1252–9.

are included in this anthology. Mehring's article on the French Revolution was not reproduced in the two editions of his collected writings. Hugo Schulz (1870–1933), who in the *Festschrift* wrote about the English Revolution of the seventeenth century, was an Austrian Social-Democratic journalist and military writer. His main work was the two-volume book *Blut und Eisen: Krieg und Kriegertum in alter und neuer Zeit* [*Blood and Iron: War and Warfare in Ancient and Modern Times*], published in 1906.[3] After the outbreak of the First World War, Schulz was mentioned as a social-patriot in Rosa Luxemburg's *Junius Broschure*.[4] Kautsky's article was published separately in Russian, French and Italian periodicals.[5] An English version appeared in 1906 in the *International Socialist Review*, the theoretical organ of the left wing of the Socialist Party of America, under the title 'Revolutions, Past and Present'.[6] A Russian version of the entire *Festschrift* was published the same year.[7]

In 'Old and New Revolution', Kautsky pursues a theme similar to Rosa Luxemburg's in 'The Russian Revolution'. Speaking of a 'dual' revolution, Luxemburg conceived the Russian Revolution as *formally* 'the last offshoot of the Great French Revolution of a century ago', meaning its 'immediate outward task is the creation of a modern capitalist society with open bourgeois class rule'. But in terms of *content* and *method*, the Russian Revolution represented '*a transitional form* from the bourgeois revolutions of the past to the proletarian revolutions of the future, which will directly involve the dictatorship of the proletariat and the realisation of socialism'.

In the document translated here, Kautsky made much the same argument: in terms of its violence and scope, the Russian Revolution could be compared to those in England in 1648–9 and France in 1789, but, beyond superficial resemblances lay fundamental differences that distinguished events in Russia as an entirely *new* type of revolution. In the first place, the proletariat was now the principal driving force, not the petty bourgeoisie; second, the peasantry – as in France but not in England – would demand redistribution of the landed estates and would subsequently defend the revolution against any attempt to

---

[3] Schulz 1906. See the review of this work by Mehring 1907, pp. 374–6.
[4] Luxemburg 1915, Chap. VII (the note does not appear in the English editions of the *Junius Pamphlet*).
[5] Kautsky 1905i; Kautsky 1906b.
[6] Kautsky 1906f.
[7] Kautsky (ed.) 1906.

restore the landed gentry; and finally, given the interdependencies of modern capitalism, the Russian Revolution would necessarily awaken revolutionary struggles throughout the rest of Europe. The English Revolution was 'a purely local event'; the French Revolution, while it convulsed all of Europe, nevertheless ended in Napoleon's military regime; but the Russian Revolution promised 'to inaugurate…an era of European revolutions that will end with *the dictatorship of the proletariat*, paving the way for the establishment of a *socialist society*'.

*　　*　　*

'Old and New Revolution'

What many, even within our own ranks, may have doubted a year ago, is today plainly evident: Russia is now in the midst of a revolution that in terms of its violence and significance may well be compared with the two greatest revolutions that history has yet known, the English Revolution of the seventeenth and the French of the eighteenth century.

It is easy to draw comparisons between them, and their superficial resemblances are striking. Each of these revolutions was directed at absolutism, against which the mass of the nation arose because its yoke had become unbearable – because it had brought misery, despair and shame upon the country.

But the resemblance does not go much further. We meet with fundamental differences the moment we penetrate beneath the political surface and investigate the class antagonisms that furnish the effective driving force of the movement.

There we find, first of all, as the great difference between earlier revolutions and the present one, that in the latter, for the first time in the history of the world, the industrial proletariat rises triumphantly as the dominant, independent directing force. The rising of the Paris Commune in 1871 was but the revolt of a single city and was suppressed within a few weeks. Now, we see a revolution extending from the Arctic Ocean to the Black Sea and from the Baltic to the Pacific, one that has already continued for a year and in which the proletariat grows ever mightier in terms of power and self-consciousness.

To be sure, we do not yet have complete power, the dictatorship of the proletariat; we do not yet have the socialist revolution, but only its beginnings.

The proletariat of Russia is only breaking its chains in order to free its hands for the class struggle against capital; it does not yet feel itself strong enough to attempt the expropriation of capital. But the fact that the watchword of a proletarian class struggle has been raised is a tremendous advance from the socialist standpoint, as contrasted with the revolutions of 1648 and 1789.

In each of these revolutions, the class that was finally victorious was the capitalist class. But, politically as well as economically, this class lives by exploiting the strength of others. It has never made a revolution, it just exploited them. It has always left the making of the revolution, the fighting and its perils, to the popular masses. But during the seventeenth and eighteenth centuries, the real driving force within these masses was not the proletariat but the *petty bourgeoisie*; the proletarians were always just its unconscious followers. It was the bold and self-conscious petty bourgeoisie of the metropolitan cities, of London and Paris, that dared to take up the leadership in the battle against absolutism and succeeded in overthrowing it.

In Russia, the petty bourgeoisie has never been bold or self-conscious, at least not during recent centuries when there has been tsarism. The Russian petty bourgeoisie has been recruited almost exclusively from uprooted peasants, who, but a few decades ago, were still serfs. Besides, there is no great city dominating the whole Russian kingdom. Moreover, even in France and England, the capital cities have today lost their absolute domination, which they must now share with the industrial centres; even in Western Europe, the petty bourgeoisie has ceased to be revolutionary and has instead become a pillar of reaction and governmental power.

It is no wonder, therefore, that the petty bourgeoisie of Russia, together with the lumpenproletariat, have from the beginning joined the counter-revolutionary elements, placing themselves at the disposal of the police for suppression of the revolution. But, since this petty bourgeoisie has no programme, no political goal, it can be driven into the battle against the revolution only by the promise of private gain or the stimulus of personal revenge. But there is no booty to be gained by fighting the propertyless proletariat and, where it is armed, its repressors can only expects wounds and death. Consequently, the reactionary petty bourgeoisie, as soon as it no longer has any political ideal, becomes as cowardly as it is brutal; it vents its rage only on the weakest members of society. As an exploiter, it prefers women and children; in the present battle against the revolution it attacks only Jews and isolated students and not the sturdy workers. So the Russian counter-revolution soon became just an orgy of plunder, murder and arson. Therefore, the revolutionary proletariat, in its battle against reaction, has already proved to be a politically indispensable element for social progress, just as it has long been the most significant element economically. On the other hand, the petty bourgeoisie, so far as it does not join the proletariat, has shown itself to be a political factor capable only of producing harm and social destruction, just as economically it has today for the most part become little more than a parasite on the social body that can prolong its own existence only at the expense of society.

In previous revolutions, the peasantry ranked next to the petty bourgeoisie as the most important revolutionary element. To be sure, the Peasants' War showed that, even in the Reformation period, the peasantry was capable only of shaking the state but not of establishing a new independent political domination.[8] The peasantry can no longer be regarded as an independent party, a special political army, but only as *auxiliary troops* of some other army or political party. Nevertheless, it is by no means insignificant, for depending upon whether it throws its strength to one side or the other it may determine defeat or victory. The peasants sealed the downfall of the revolution in France in 1848 as well as its triumph in 1789 and the years that followed.

The role played by the peasantry in the Great French Revolution, however, was completely different from its part in the English Revolution. In France, the landed possessions of the nobility and clergy had maintained a feudal form; they lived from the exploitation of the serf-like peasantry, whom they had degraded to an inconceivable degree of misery and to whom they rendered no reciprocal service since they had become attachés of the court. The destruction of these landed possessions was one of the imperative tasks of the revolution and was the bond that secured the firm allegiance of the peasants.

In England, the old feudal nobility was destroyed during the War of the Roses and was replaced by a new nobility who understood quite well the needs of capitalism. The Reformation had plundered the churches for the benefit of this nobility. The old feudal economy had completely disappeared by the seventeenth century. What peasants remained were free masters of their own

---

[8] [See Engels 1850b, pp. 397–482.]

ground. The great landed possessions were not operated by the compulsory service of feudal peasants but through capitalist tenants who employed wage-workers. Very few of the landed nobility had become attached to the court. The majority remained on their property throughout the year and served as justices or in the local governments.

As a consequence, the English Revolution showed no tendency toward a general overthrow of landed property. To be sure, there were plenty of instances of property confiscation, but always as *political* and not as *social* measures. However covetous the peasants and tenants might have been of the great estates, no necessity compelled their dismemberment, while fear of the numerous agricultural wage-workers effectively frightened their owners from beginning a process that might easily have proved dangerous to themselves. The great English landed aristocracy did not simply survive the revolution; they reached a compromise with the bourgeoisie, which had also grown tired of the domination of the petty bourgeoisie, and they thereby so fortified its rule that today there is no landed aristocracy, not even that of the German provinces east of the Elbe or of Hungary, that sits as firmly in the saddle as the English one.

Things will develop very differently in Russia, where the condition of the peasantry is practically identical in all its details to that of the French peasants before the Revolution. Here, the result of the two revolutions will be the same, to the extent that we may expect the disappearance of today's great landed estates throughout the whole Russian kingdom and their transformation into peasant possessions. Next to tsarism, it is the large landed estates that will pay the bill of the revolution.

It is impossible to foresee what kind of agricultural mode of production will develop upon the new foundations, but one thing is certain: in this regard, the Russian and the French revolutions will also be alike, in that the breaking up of the great private landed estates will constitute a tie that will bind the peasants indissolubly to the revolution. We do not yet know what battle of races the new revolution may conceal within its bosom, and it is easily possible that differences may arise between the peasants and the urban proletariat, but the former will fight tooth and nail to defend the revolution against anyone seeking to re-establish the old aristocratic landed regime, even by foreign intervention. This brings us to the third factor to be considered in this comparison between the three revolutions: the foreign conditions that they create.

During the seventeenth century, international intercourse was still so limited that the English Revolution remained a purely local event that found no echo in the remainder of Europe. It was not foreign wars but the long drawn-out civil war arising from the great power of resistance of the landed nobility that created the revolutionary military domination and finally led to the dictatorship of a victorious general, Cromwell.

The end of the eighteenth century already found a more developed intercourse between the European nations, and the French Revolution convulsed all Europe; but its liberating efforts found only a weak echo. The convulsion was a result of the war that the united monarchs of Europe waged against the one republic; a war that in France led to the rise of a military régime and the empire of a victorious general, Napoleon.

Now, at the beginning of the twentieth century, international relations have become so close that the beginning of the revolution in Russia was enough to awaken an enthusiastic response in the proletariat of the whole world, to quicken the tempo of the class struggle, and to shake the neighbouring empire of Austria to its foundations.

As a consequence, any *coalition* of European powers against the revolution, such as took place in 1793, is inconceivable. [Austria is at the present moment absolutely incapable of any strong external action. In France, in spite of everything, the proletariat will be strong enough vis-à-vis the republican government to prevent any interference on behalf of tsarism if it ever were insane enough to think of such a thing.[9]] There is no fear of a coalition against the revolution; there is only a *single power* that could conceive the idea of intervening in Russia – the *German Empire*. But even the rulers of the German Empire will think carefully before they embark on a war that will not be a national war but will be looked upon as a dynastic war and will be as unpopular, as hated, as that which Russia led against Japan, and which may easily have for the German government internal consequences similar to those that the Russo-Japanese War had for Russia. Whatever may happen, there is no occasion to expect an era of long world wars such as the French Revolution ushered in; accordingly we need not fear that the Russian revolution will, like the former, end in a military dictatorship or some sort of

---

[9] [These two sentences are lacking in the German original, but they appear in the French and American editions of the article.]

'Holy Alliance'. What it promises to inaugurate is rather an era of European revolutions that will end with the *dictatorship of the proletariat* paving the way for the establishment of a *socialist society*.

Chapter Twenty

'The *Sans-Culottes* of the French Revolution' (1889, reprinted December 1905)

Karl Kautsky

This article[1] was first published in German, together with Kautsky's 'Old and New Revolution' and Rosa Luxemburg's 'The Russian Revolution', in the *Festschrift 1649–1789–1905*. It was actually a chapter from Kautsky's 1889 booklet on the French Revolution, *Class Antagonisms in 1789: On the Hundredth Anniversary of the Great Revolution*, which in turn was first published as a series of articles in *Die Neue Zeit*.[2] The book was never translated into English, but a French version appeared in 1901 and was reprinted in 1999.[3] Even more important is the fact that four Russian editions were issued before and during the 1905 Revolution.[4]

Kautsky described the policy of the *sans-culottes* in 1793–4 as one of 'Revolution in Permanenz'.

---

[1] Karl Kautsky, 'Die Sansculotten der französischen Revolution' (Aus: Kautsky 1889b) in *Festschrift '1649–1789–1905* (Berlin: Buchhandlung Vorwärts, 1905), pp. 11–12.

[2] Kautsky 1889b, pp. 49–53. Separat-Abdruck aus der *Neuen Zeit*, 1889, Vol. 7, pp. 1–9, 49–56, 97–108, 145–57. A second edition appeared in 1908: *Die Klassengegensätze im Zeitalter der Französischen Revolution: Neue Ausgabe der Klassengegensätze von 1789*, 2. Auflage (Stuttgart: Dietz, 1908). In a letter from London dated 20 February 1889, Engels wrote some critical remarks on this work. See Frederick Engels to Karl Kautsky, 20 February 1889. In Marx and Engels 1954, pp. 481–6.

[3] Kautsky 1901, pp. 79–87.

[4] St. Petersburg, 1902 (translated by G.F. L'vovich), Kiev, 1902 (translated by I.S. Bisk, Rostov, 1903), and (Rostov: Donskaya Rech', 1905).

Kautsky's use of the theory of permanent revolution to analyse the French Revolution was probably due to the influence of two items published by Engels in 1884–5. On the occasion of the first anniversary of Marx's death, Engels published in the *Sozialdemokrat*, Nr. 11 (13 March 1884) the article 'Marx and the *Neue Rheinische Zeitung* (1848-49)', where he declared that, like Marat in 1793, Marx and he 'did not want the revolution [of March 1848] declared complete, but lasting [*nicht für abgeschlossen, sondern in Permanenz erklärt wissen*]'.[5] This is the conventional English rendering of this passage, but it is misleading in that the word 'lasting' omits the conceptual significance of 'in Permanenz'. In 1885, Engels also republished the March 1850 'Address of the Central Committee of the Communist League'. We include Kautsky's essay here for the same reason that it was repeatedly published in Russia during the 1905 revolution: by recounting the fate of the *sans-culottes*, Kautsky's work served to caution Russian Social Democrats once more against compromising with the bourgeoisie – a conviction that he expressed all the more emphatically in November 1906 in his response to Plekhanov's query concerning the driving forces of the Russian revolution.

* * *

'The *Sans-Culottes* of the French Revolution'

Below the mass of labourers and petty bourgeois lived a large and growing lumpenproletariat, which streamed to the cities, above all to Paris, in order to find honest or dishonest occupations. The beggars constituted five per cent of the population: in 1777 there were an estimated 1,200,000. In Paris, they amounted to one sixth of the population, or 120,000.

A large section of this lumpenproletariat was not yet completely corrupted and was still able to experience a moral upsurge as soon as a glimmer of hope appeared. They enthusiastically joined the revolutionary movement that promised to end their sufferings. As heterogeneous as this assemblage was, it was to a certain extent united: it was really a revolutionary mass. Their common bond was an intense hatred not only of the privileged, the guild

---

[5] Engels 1884a.

masters, the priests, the aristocrats, but also of the bourgeoisie, which partly exploited them as tax collectors, grain speculators, usurers, entrepreneurs, etc., and partly faced them as competitors, and in all cases always wronged them. But, despite that hatred and the intensity with which it was sometimes expressed, these revolutionary elements were not socialists. The proletariat, as a class conscious of its own separate interests, did not yet exist before the revolution. It still lived totally within the circle of ideas of the petty bourgeoisie, whose goals and demands did not go beyond the boundaries of commodity production.

It would be totally false to identify those elements with the modern wage-workers of large-scale industry and to assume that they had the same political orientation; this would mean forming an entirely false conception not only about the 'sans-culottes',[6] as they were called, but also about the revolution, on whose character they exerted such a powerful influence.

The bourgeoisie did not constitute in any sense a homogeneous revolutionary mass. Some fractions were directly interested, due to momentary advantages, in the preservation of the privileged estates; others regarded the revolution with mistrust and aloofness; while others, who sympathised with it, lacked courage and force. The revolutionary section of the bourgeoisie alone could not have withstood the blows of its adversaries, above all the court, which could count unconditionally on a part of the army (on the French regiments recruited from the reactionary provinces, and on the regiments from Switzerland and Germany), and which, moreover, had allies abroad and incited the civil war at home. In order to resist the counter-revolution, people other than the bourgeoisie were necessary; people who had nothing to lose from a social storm, who did not have to defer to a rich clientele, and who could contribute to the struggle the force of their arms. Above all, great masses were necessary. Among the peasants, the petty bourgeois and the proletarians, the revolutionary fraction of the bourgeoisie found the support without which it would have been defeated.

---

[6] 'Sans-culottes' means 'without knee breeches', which were then part of the dress of the dominant estates. The popular strata from which the *sans-culottes* were recruited wore instead trousers [*pantalons*] as we do today.

The centres of the revolution were the neighbourhoods of Paris, immediately close to the seat of government, where the policy of the privileged estates themselves had concentrated the most energetic and determined elements of the country, the people who had nothing to lose and everything to win.

It was they who protected the National Assembly from the attacks of the court; it was they who on 14 July, 1789, by storming the Bastille – whose canons threatened the revolutionary neighbourhood of Saint-Antoine – nipped in the bud a counter-revolutionary attempt by the court and gave the signal for the general revolt of the peasants. It was also they who, by capturing the king and bringing him to Paris under their guard (5–6 October 1789), prevented the second attempt by the court to crush the Revolution with the help of a loyal part of the army.

But soon the *sans-culottes*, after having been allies of the bourgeoisie, became its masters. Their authority, their power, their maturity, their self-assurance grew with every blow directed against the revolution, which only their opportune and vigorous intervention was able to ward off. The more dangerous the situation became for the Revolution, the more indispensable became the revolutionary neighbourhoods and the more exclusive their domination. The revolution reached its zenith when the coalition of European monarchies marched on France while counter-revolutionary uprisings broke out simultaneously in several provinces and the army leaders sometimes conspired with the enemy. The Revolution was then saved neither by the Legislative Assembly nor by the Convention, but by the *sans-culottes*. They seized control of the Jacobin Club,[7] an organisation whose centre was Paris with branches all over France. They seized control of the Paris Commune, gaining absolute mastery over the huge instruments of power of that city. And, through the Jacobin Club and the Commune (and, where that was not enough, by insurrection), they dominated the Convention, the government and the entire country. In the midst of the war, in a desperate situation, surrounded by perils from all sides, threatened with extermination, they applied the most pitiless martial law, employing the most extreme means to avert the danger and drowning in the blood of the suspects not only every resistance and every betrayal, but also any possibility of resistance and betrayal. But terrorism was

---

[7] ['Club' was the eighteenth-century equivalent of the contemporary word 'party'.]

more than a weapon of war to unnerve and intimidate the stealthy internal enemy; it also served to inspire confidence in the defenders of the revolution to continue their struggle against external enemies.

The war enabled the *sans-culottes* to seize power. But they wanted to wage war in order to create a state and a society according to their wishes. Feudal exploitation had been defeated, but not capitalist exploitation, which had already developed under the régime of the privileged. And it was precisely the removal of the feudal barriers that had paved the way for the capitalist mode of production, for capitalist exploitation, to develop quickly. To suppress or at least to check the different kinds of capitalist exploitation, particularly in commerce, speculation and usury, soon seemed to the *sans-culottes* as important as fighting those who wanted to restore feudal exploitation. But to do away with the foundations of capitalism was then impossible, because the conditions for the transition to a new, superior mode of production did not yet exist.

As a result, the *sans-culottes* found themselves in a hopeless situation. The circumstances had placed political power in their hands but also denied them the possibility of creating lasting institutions to serve their own interests. With the instruments of power of the whole of France at their disposal, they could not – and could only irresolutely even attempt to – put an end to the misery produced by rapidly developing capitalism and multiplied by the war. They had to fight against it by violently interfering in economic life: through requisitions, by fixing maximum prices for the necessities of life, by sending to the guillotine the exploiters, the speculators, the stock-market gamblers, the corn usurers and the fraudulent government contractors, but without getting any closer to their goals. Capitalist exploitation was like a hydra: the more heads were stricken off, the more they grew again. In order to combat it, the *sans-culottes* had to adopt ever more extreme measures; they had to declare the revolution in permanence and intensify all the more the terrorism that the war conditions had rendered necessary, the more their struggle against capitalist exploitation placed them in opposition to the needs of the mode of production and to the interests of other classes.

But when victories of the French armies over the internal and external enemies consolidated the situation of the Republic, the terror ceased to be a necessity for preserving the Revolution. It became more and more intolerable as an obstacle to economic prosperity. The adversaries of the *sans-culottes* grew quickly, while the *sans-culottes* themselves, already decimated by their perpetual internal struggles, just as quickly lost their strength through desertions and demoralisation.

Their fall, which began with the overthrow of Robespierre (on 9 Thermidor, or 27 July 1794), has been called the shipwreck of the Revolution. As if an historical event, a fact resulting from circumstances, could be 'shipwrecked'! An enterprise projected by individuals, a putsch or an uprising, can fail, but not a development culminating in a revolution. A revolution that fails is not a revolution. A ship can be wrecked in a storm, and parties can be shipwrecked in a revolution, but the revolution should not be identified with those parties, and the aims of the two should not be confused.

The Jacobins and the neighbourhoods of Paris failed because the circumstances did not allow a petty-bourgeois or proletarian revolution, and because their policy was incompatible with a capitalist revolution. However, their work was not in vain. They saved the bourgeois revolution and destroyed the feudal régime in a way never before witnessed anywhere else. They prepared the terrain on which, in the period of just a few years under the Directory and during the Napoleonic era, a new form of production and a new society sprung up with marvellous rapidity. It is a colossal irony that the bitterest enemies of the capitalists involuntarily accomplished for them what they were unable to accomplish by themselves.

But the struggle of the revolutionary petty bourgeois and proletarians of France, especially of Paris, even if it eventually ended in defeat, was not fruitless for them either. The enormous force that they unleashed, the gigantic historical role they played, gave them a self-confidence and a degree of political maturity that they never lost and that still live on today.

Chapter Twenty-One

'The Role of the Bourgeoisie and the Proletariat in the Russian Revolution', Speech to the Fifth (London) Congress of the Russian Social-Democratic Labour Party (25 May 1907)

Rosa Luxemburg

The Fifth Congress of the RSDLP met in London from 13–27 May, 1907. The most contentious issues concerned the role of Social-Democratic representatives in the Duma and the related question of attitudes towards the bourgeois parties. Rosa Luxemburg's contributions came in greetings she conveyed from the German Party and in her subsequent formal report, which is translated here.[1] Leon Trotsky also attended the congress and in a brief fifteen-minute address denounced the Menshevik view that 'the Cadets are the symbol of bourgeois democracy, and bourgeois democracy is the natural claimant to revolutionary power'.[2] On all points of principle Trotsky agreed with Luxemburg:

---

[1] This speech is translated from RSDRP 1907b, pp. 383–92 (and pp. 432–7 for the Concluding Remarks).

[2] Trotsky condemned the Mensheviks in the context of a familiar summary of Russia's historical peculiarities and the relative weakness of other parties compared to the proletariat. With the exception of short introductory comments, his speech is available as an Annex (Chapter 23) to L. Trotsky 1971a, 290–9.

I am pleased to say that the point of view presented here by comrade Luxemburg on behalf of the Polish delegation is very close to the one that I have defended and continue to defend. Any possible differences between us are more a matter of individual nuances than of political direction. Our thinking moves on one and the same track of materialistic analysis.[3]

Prior to the Congress, three draft resolutions had been submitted concerning Social Democracy's relation to the bourgeois parties: one from the Bolsheviks, another from the Mensheviks, and a third from Luxemburg and the Polish delegates. The Bolshevik draft was written by Lenin and defined the class character of non-proletarian parties, beginning with the Black Hundreds of 'feudal-minded landowners' and ending with 'the Narodnik or Trudovik parties', who came 'more or less close to expressing the interests and the viewpoint of the broad masses of the peasantry and urban petty bourgeoisie'.[4] While the proletariat must lead 'the bourgeois-democratic revolution', Lenin urged every effort to free the peasant parties from liberal influences in order

---

[3] RSDRP 1907b, p. 397. Two years after the congress, in 'The Aim of the Proletarian Struggle in Our Revolution' Lenin was still complaining that 'Trotsky's major mistake is that he ignores the bourgeois character of the revolution and has no clear conception of the transition from this revolution to the socialist revolution'. Lenin 1909b, p. 371).

[4] Lenin 1907f. Lenin claimed that 'The Cadets stand for the preservation of landlordism and for a civilised, European, but *landlord* bourgeois evolution of agriculture. The Trudoviks (and the Social-Democratic workers' deputies), i.e., the representatives of the peasantry and the representatives of the proletariat, advocate a *peasant* bourgeois evolution of agriculture.' Lenin 1907e, p. 247). In 1909 Lenin remained convinced that an organised peasant party was both inevitable and imperative if the bourgeois-democratic revolution was to be completed:

> The history of the Russian revolution shows that the very first wave of the upsurge, at the end of 1905, at once stimulated the peasantry to form a political organisation (the All-Russian Peasant Union) which was undoubtedly the embryo of a distinct peasant party. Both in the First and Second Dumas – in spite of the fact that the counter-revolution had wiped out the first contingents of advanced peasants – the peasantry, now for the first time acting on a nation–wide scale in the Russian general elections, immediately laid the foundations of the Trudovik group, which was undoubtedly the embryo of a distinct peasant party. In these embryos and rudiments there was much that was unstable, vague and vacillating: that is beyond doubt. But if political groups like this could spring up at the beginning of the revolution, there cannot be the slightest doubt that a revolution carried to such a 'conclusion', or rather, to such a high stage of development as a revolutionary dictatorship, will produce a more definitely constituted and stronger revolutionary peasant party. To think otherwise would be like supposing that some vital organs of an adult can retain the size, shape and development of infancy. (Lenin 1909b, p. 374.)

that they might enter into 'joint action' with Social Democrats,[5] culminating in a 'revolutionary-democratic dictatorship of the proletariat and the peasantry'.

Lenin thought 'the aims of the revolution that is now taking place in Russia do not exceed the bounds of bourgeois society' and 'this should be absolutely beyond doubt to any Marxist'. The revolutionary-democratic dictatorship would consummate the bourgeois revolution by expropriating the large landed estates, nationalising the land, abolishing ground rent as an obstacle to capital accumulation and allowing for agricultural development in 'the American way' of small-scale private holdings rather than 'Junker-type, capitalist farms'.[6] The struggle for land was forcing 'enormous masses of the peasantry into the democratic revolution' and would inevitably throw up peasant parties to represent them. The Trudoviks were 'not fully consistent democrats', but when they and the Socialist-Revolutionaries vacillated between liberals and the proletariat, the proper tactic for Social Democrats was to 'expose and castigate their petty-bourgeois inconsistency' and to demonstrate that '*only the workers' party is the genuinely reliable and thoroughly faithful defender of the interests... of the entire peasant masses, who are fighting against feudal exploitation*'.

The draft submitted by the Mensheviks (signed by Axelrod, Martynov, Dan and Kostrov) also identified the proletariat as the 'main motive force' of the revolution, but it specified that the goal was neither socialism nor a revolutionary dictatorship, only 'a democratic republic as the best condition of struggle'. To the Mensheviks, a democratic republic meant a parliamentary republic with liberals as the principal beneficiaries. Anticipating that the struggle would be 'prolonged', the Menshevik authors spoke of supporting 'oppositional and revolutionary steps' by other parties, but it was clearly the liberals they had in mind. Since Russia's particular historical circumstances were impeding development of a bourgeois-democratic movement, they

---

[5] Lenin 1907b, p. 138.

[6] Lenin followed Marx in believing that in America, as long as the colonisation process continued, the land was either distributed free of charge (for homesteads, etc.) or for merely nominal prices, and that this constituted the peculiarity of 'the American path of bourgeois development' and explained the rapid growth of the American economy. In 'The American Worker', the final document in this anthology, Karl Kautsky drew this comparison succinctly and convincingly. Kautsky's argument evidently was the source of Lenin's thinking on this matter.

cautioned against the ruinous consequences of 'agrarian utopias and the superficial revolutionism of the Narodniks' and instead urged *ad hoc* agreements with liberal and democratic parties.[7]

The third draft, submitted by the Poles and later withdrawn in favour of Lenin's, declared that bourgeois liberalism was clearly counter-revolutionary and that Social Democracy must never sacrifice its own tasks 'with the goal of creating united oppositional actions with any other political parties whatever'. However, this draft, like Lenin's, did countenance short-term tactical co-operation with Trudoviks, Narodniks and Socialist Revolutionaries to realise '*the democratic tasks of the liberation movement*' before pressing on in the direction of socialist tasks.

In her speech conveying greetings from Germany, Luxemburg began by congratulating the Russians, saying their efforts had inspired 'a great awakening of spirit in Social-Democratic ranks'.[8] German workers were fixing their gaze 'on the struggle of their Russian brothers as…the vanguard of the international working class'.[9] She dismissed any hope for revolutionary liberalism and pointed out that, even in Germany, liberals were betraying bourgeois democracy, in part out of fears issuing from events in Russia. The Russian revolution 'was one of the factors that united and rallied all layers of bourgeois society' in the January 1907 elections, the so-called 'Hottentot Elections', when a wave of imperialist chauvinism resulted in the SPD losing nearly half of its seats in the Reichstag.[10] In both countries, the liberals had become allies of reaction:

> Bourgeois liberalism and democracy definitively and irrevocably took their stand on the side of reaction in the struggle against the revolutionary proletariat. It is precisely the treason of liberalism, above all, which delivered

---

[7] 'RSDRP 1907a, pp. 644–5.
[8] Luxemburg 1907a, p. 201.
[9] *ibid.*, p. 204.
[10] In her *Junius Pamphlet* of 1915 Luxemburg had this to say of the 1907 elections: The Reichstag election of 1907, the so-called Hottentot Elections, found the whole of Germany in a paroxysm of imperialistic enthusiasm, firmly united under one flag, that of the Germany of von Buelow, the Germany that felt itself ordained to play the role of the hammer in the world. These elections, with their spiritual pogrom atmosphere, were a prelude to the Germany of August 4, a challenge not only to the German working class, but to other capitalist nations as well, a challenge directed to no one in particular, a mailed fist shaken in the face of the entire world…' (Waters (ed.) 1970, p. 285)

us directly into the hands of the Junker reaction in the last elections. And, although presently the liberals in the Reichstag increased their representation, they nevertheless are nothing but the liberal cover-up for the pathetic toadies of reaction.[11]

German experience demonstrated that, even in advanced capitalist countries, bourgeois freedoms 'are not seriously guaranteed and are subject to constant attack'.[12] Whereas Mensheviks believed Russia's special circumstances warranted compromises and collaboration with liberalism in order to overthrow the autocracy, Luxemburg came to exactly the opposite conclusion. Russia may be special, but only in the sense that here Marxism had to be applied not in a period of 'quiet' parliamentary life but for the first time in 'a stormy revolutionary period':

> The only experience that scientific socialism had previously in practical politics during a revolutionary period was the activity of Marx himself in the 1848 revolution. The course…of the 1848 revolution, however, cannot be a model for the present revolution in Russia. From it we can only learn how not to act in a revolution.[13]

In 1848, Marx had taken a position on the extreme left of bourgeois democracy such as the Mensheviks were now contemplating. The difference was that Marx supported liberalism with 'whips and kicks' and 'considered it an inexcusable mistake that the proletariat allowed, after its first short-lived victory of 18 March, the formation of a responsible bourgeois ministry of Camphausen-Hansemann'. Marx understood the impotence of the Frankfurt National Assembly, the German counterpart of the Russian 'Duma', and by late 1849 he abandoned the position of 'extreme bourgeois democracy' in favour of 'pure class-struggle politics'. The conclusion was obvious: Russian comrades had to begin 'not where Marx began, but where Marx ended in 1849, with a clearly expressed, independent proletarian class policy'.[14]

In her subsequent report on attitudes towards the bourgeois parties, Luxemburg again criticised the Mensheviks, Plekhanov in particular, for harbouring fantasies concerning the liberals' commitment to revolution.

---

[11] Luxemburg 1907a, p. 202.
[12] Luxemburg 1907a, p. 203.
[13] Luxemburg 1907a, pp. 204–5.
[14] Luxemburg 1907a, pp. 205–6.

Revolutionary liberalism was 'an invention and a phantom', nothing more. To postpone the proletarian class struggle until stable parliamentary institutions were in place would mean postponing it indefinitely. At the same time, though, she also criticised the Bolsheviks for over-estimating 'the so-called armed uprising'. 'Conspiratorial speculation and crude revolutionary adventurism' were the political counterparts of Menshevik vacillation and no substitute for mass action. Bolshevik rigidity was 'the form taken by Social-Democratic tactics on the one side, when the other side represents the formlessness of jelly that creeps in every direction under the pressure of events'.

On the question of the peasantry, Luxemburg disputed both Menshevik and Bolshevik positions. Contrary to the Mensheviks, she believed the peasants were playing an objectively revolutionary role by demanding a settlement of the land question that was ultimately inconceivable without a socialist revolution. Like Trotsky, however, she also doubted Lenin's belief that the peasants could produce a political party capable of joint action with Social Democracy in some sort of 'left bloc'. The peasants could mount a *jacquerie*, but 'peasant movements are completely unable to play any independent role and are subordinated in every historical context to the leadership of other classes that are more energetic and more clearly defined'.

If liberals were treacherous and peasants were incapable of independent organisation, it followed that the only trustworthy allies of Russian workers were workers in other countries. The final outcome of the revolution depended upon the international context. While Trotsky had claimed in *Results and Prospects* that victory in Russia would inevitably spread through Poland and Austria to Germany,[15] Luxemburg was more circumspect. Russian workers must 'strive to win political power in order to realise the tasks of the present revolution'. But should they succeed on their own, they would quite likely also find themselves 'in situations that are extremely complex and rife with difficulties', including the prospect of 'a major temporary defeat'.

In *Results and Prospects*, Trotsky had warned that 'Left to its own resources, the working class of Russia will inevitably be crushed by the counter-revolution the moment the peasantry turns its back on it.'[16] Luxemburg shared Trotsky's apprehension. She added, however, that temporary defeats 'are inevitable historical steps that are leading to the final victory of socialism'. In view of her

---

[15] L. Trotsky 1969, Ch. IX, 'Europe and Revolution': pp. 107–115.
[16] Ibid., p. 115.

own fate twelve years later at the hands of German reactionaries, there was prophetic irony in her conclusion: while there could never be any guarantee of victory, 'it is a poor leader and a pitiful army that goes into battle only when it knows in advance that victory is in its pocket'.

* * *

'The Role of the Bourgeoisie and the Proletariat in the Russian Revolution'

I and the representatives of the Polish delegation are interested in the present question not from the viewpoint of internecine fractional struggle but from that of the principles of international proletarian tactics. The position of the right wing of our Party with regard to the bourgeois parties is a perfectly consistent construction based upon a certain view of the historical role of the bourgeoisie and the proletariat in our revolution. Underlying this view is a certain scheme that is precisely and clearly formulated by one of the deeply respected veterans and most profound theoreticians of Russian Social Democracy. In his 'Letters on Tactics and Tactlessness', Comrade Plekhanov says:

> The creators of the *Communist Manifesto* wrote 58 years ago: 'The bourgeoisie, historically, has played a most revolutionary part....The bourgeoisie cannot exist without constantly revolutionising the instruments of production and their organisation together with all social relations'.

And, further, concerning the political mission of the bourgeoisie:

> The bourgeoisie finds itself involved in a constant battle first with the aristocracy, and later with those strata of its own class whose interests contradict the development of large-scale industry....In each of these cases the bourgeoisie is compelled to appeal to the proletariat, to ask for its help, and thus to drag it into the political arena. The bourgeoisie therefore supplies the proletariat with its own political education, in other words, it furnishes it with weapons for fighting the bourgeoisie itself.[17]

---

[17] [Luxemburg is citing 'Letter 5' in a collection published by Plekhanov in 1906 with the title *Letters on Tactics and Tactlessness* (in Plekhanov 1926a, pp. 134–5). Plekhanov was fond of quoting this part of the *Manifesto* as early as 1883 in his famous work *Our Differences*. See Plekhanov 1884, p. 187).]

In the opinion of one wing of our Party, it is this view of the bourgeoisie that must determine the entire tactics of the Russian proletariat in the current revolution. The bourgeoisie is a revolutionary class that is attracting the popular masses into the struggle against the old order; the bourgeoisie is the natural vanguard and tutor of the proletariat. In present-day Russia, therefore, only malicious reactionaries or hopeless Don Quixotes could 'hinder the bourgeoisie' in achieving political power, meaning that attacks on Russian liberalism must be put aside until the Cadets are in power, that we must not put a spoke in the wheel of the bourgeois revolution, that any tactic of the proletariat that might weaken or frighten the liberals is supremely tactless, and that every attempt to isolate the proletariat from the liberal bourgeoisie renders a direct service to reaction. This is certainly a complete and coherent set of views, but it also urgently requires examination with regard both to historical facts and to the fundamentals of proletarian tactics.

'58 years ago Marx and Engels wrote in *The Communist Manifesto...*'. Unfortunately, I am not familiar with all the works of our respected theoretician and creator of Russian Marxism, but I am not aware of a single one of his writings in which he fails to impress upon Russian Social Democrats the fact that only metaphysicians speak in terms of the formula that 'Yea is yea; nay is nay; whatsoever is more than these cometh of evil';[18] the dialectical thinking that characterises historical materialism requires that one assess phenomena not in a frozen state but in their movement. A reference to the way Marx and Engels characterised the role of the bourgeoisie fifty-eight years ago, when applied to present-day reality, is a startling example of metaphysical thinking and amounts to converting the living, historical views of the creators of the *Manifesto* into frozen dogma. One has merely to look at the features and relations of political parties, especially at the condition of liberalism in Germany, France, Italy and England – in the whole of Western Europe – in order to understand that the bourgeoisie has long ago ceased to play the political-revolutionary role that it once did. Today, its universal turn to reaction and a policy of tariff protection, its worship of militarism and its bargain everywhere with agrarian conservatives, all show that the fifty-eight

---

[18] [Plekhanov used this aphorism in his criticism of Ryazanov as a 'metaphysician' (see above, p. 145) and also of Struve in 'A Critique of our Critics' (1901), in Plekhanov), p. 587 *et seq.*]

years that have passed since the *Communist Manifesto* have had important consequences. And doesn't the brief history of our own Russian liberalism likewise show just how inapplicable is a scheme taken from the words of the *Manifesto?*

Let us recall what Russian liberalism was just five years ago. At that time, it was doubtful whether there even existed in Russia this 'tutor of the proletariat' that must not be 'hindered in achieving power'. Up to 1900, Russian liberalism endured and passively suffered every oppression by absolutism and every manifestation of despotism. It was only after the Russian proletariat, educated through long years of effort by Social Democracy and shaken by the Japanese war, entered the public arena through the grandiose strikes in the south of Russia and through mass demonstrations, that Russian liberalism also decided to take its first timid step. Thus began the notorious saga of *zemstvo* congresses, professorial petitions and lawyers' banquets. Intoxicated by its own eloquence and by a freedom it had not expected, Russian liberalism was ready to believe in its own strength. But how did this saga end? We all remember that remarkable moment when, in November–December 1904, the 'liberal spring' suddenly came to a halt and absolutism, having recovered, at once and unceremoniously shut liberalism's mouth by simply ordering it to be silent. We all saw how liberalism, with a single kick and a crack of the whip by absolutism, instantly tumbled from the heights of its imaginary might into the abyss of desperate impotence. Liberalism had precisely no response whatever to a blow from a Cossack's whip; it shrivelled up, kept silent, and saw with its own eyes its total insignificance. And the liberation movement in Russia then hesitated for several weeks until the 9 January brought the St. Petersburg proletariat into the street and demonstrated just who is called upon in the present revolution to be the vanguard and 'tutor'. In place of the corpse of bourgeois liberalism there appeared a living force. [*Applause.*]

Russian liberalism raised its head for a second time when the pressure of the popular masses compelled absolutism to create the first Duma. Once again, the liberals thought they were in the saddle, and once again they believed that they were the chieftains of the emancipation movement, that lawyers' speeches could accomplish something, and that they were a real force. Then came the dispersal of the Duma, and, for a second time, liberalism flew headlong into the abyss of impotence and insignificance. The sole response that they were capable of mounting on their own to the attack by reaction was the notorious Vyborg proclamation,[19] that classic document of 'passive resistance', the same passive resistance that Marx wrote about in 1848 in the *Neue Rheinische Zeitung* when he said it amounted to the opposition of a calf to the butcher who wants to slaughter it.[20] [*Applause.*]

At this point, liberalism completely abandoned any illusion of its own strength and its leading role in the present revolution. To be precise, in the first Duma it overcame the illusion that it could bring down the walls of the absolutist Jericho with the trumpets of eloquent speech-making by lawyers and parliamentarians; and, when the Duma was dispersed, it overcame the illusion that the proletariat is summoned merely to play the role of frightening absolutism, that it could be kept off stage by the liberals until needed and then called out by the wave of a kerchief in order to frighten absolutism and strengthen the liberals' own position. The liberals had to be convinced that the Russian proletariat is not a mannequin in their hands, that it has no wish to be cannon fodder, to be on hand always to serve the bourgeoisie, that it is, on the contrary, a force that follows its own line in this revolution and that in its actions it obeys laws and a logic of its own in a way that is independent of the liberal movement.

Since then, the liberals have moved decisively in reverse, and now we are witnessing their shameful retreat in the second Duma, in the Duma of Golovin[21] and Struve, the Duma that is voting for a budget and conscription, for the bayonets with which the Duma will tomorrow be dispersed. That is how this bourgeoisie looks, this bourgeoisie that we are urged to regard as a revolutionary class, that we must not 'hinder' from achieving power, and that is called upon to 'educate' the proletariat! It turns out that a rigid scheme is completely inapplicable to present-day Russia. It turns out that revolutionary liberalism, which is supposed to be struggling for power, to which we are to adapt the policy of the proletariat, and for whose benefit we are readily to

---

[19] [When the tsar dissolved the first Duma in July 1906, the Cadets responded with a futile call for passive resistance and civil disobedience in which citizens were to withhold taxes and refuse to serve in the army.]

[20] [The reference is to Marx 1848b. Marx wrote: '*Passive* resistance must have *active resistance* as its basis. *Otherwise it will resemble the vain struggle of a calf against its slaughterer.*' CW, Vol. 8, pp. 37–8).]

[21] [Fyodor Golovin (1867–1937) was Chairman of the Second Duma from February to June 1907.]

curtail the demands of the proletariat – this revolutionary Russian liberalism does not exist in reality, only in the imagination. It is an invention and a phantom. [*Applause.*] And this policy, which is erected on the basis of a lifeless scheme and imagined relations, and which takes no account of the special tasks of the proletariat in this revolution, calls itself 'revolutionary realism'.[22]

Let us look at how this realism fits with proletarian tactics in general. In terms of its battle tactics, the Russian proletariat is being urged to avoid prematurely undermining the forces of liberalism and isolating itself. But if this is what is called a 'tactless' tactic, then I am afraid that the whole activity and the entire history of German Social Democracy must be seen as one of continuous tactlessness. From the time of Lassalle's agitation against the 'progressives'[23] right up to the present moment, the entire growth of Social Democracy has occurred at the expense of the growth and strength of liberalism, and every step forward by the German proletariat has undermined the foundations on which liberalism stands. Exactly the same phenomenon accompanies the class movement of the proletariat in all countries. The Paris Commune, which so thoroughly isolated the French proletariat and fatally frightened the liberal bourgeoisie of all countries, must be a case of tactlessness. No less tactless would be the action of the French proletariat during the famous June days,[24] when it finally 'isolated' itself as a class from bourgeois society. In that case, the open action of the proletariat in the great French Revolution was even more tactless: in the midst of the first revolutionary movement of the bourgeoisie, the proletariat's extreme behaviour frightened the bourgeoisie and drove it into the arms of reaction, thereby preparing the epoch of the Directorate and the liquidation of the great revolution itself. And finally, we would surely have to consider the greatest tactlessness to be the historical birth of the proletariat, when it first appeared in the light of day as an independent class [*Applause*], for that was what initiated both its 'isolated position' in relation to the bourgeoisie and also the gradual decline of bourgeois liberalism.

But doesn't the very history of revolutionary development here in Russia demonstrate how it is essentially inconceivable for the proletariat to avoid

---

[22] [See Plekhanov's discussion of 'realism' in RSDRP 1907b, pp. 419–20.]

[23] [The reference is to the *Deutsche Fortschrittspartei*, which emerged in 1861 to promote a liberal parliament and unification of Germany under Prussian leadership.]

[24] [Luxemburg is referring to 22–6 June, 1848, in Paris. See Marx 1850.]

those kinds of 'tactlessness' with which people frighten us lest we become unwilling accomplices in the cause of reaction? The very first action of the Russian proletariat, which formally inaugurated the epoch of our revolution – I mean 9 January 1905 – at once clearly isolated proletarian from liberal tactics and detached the revolutionary struggle in the streets from the liberal campaign of banquets and *zemstvo* congresses, which stalled in a blind alley. Every ensuing step, every demand of the proletariat in the present revolution, is continuing to isolate it. The strike movement isolates it from the industrial bourgeoisie; the demand for an eight-hour working day isolates it from the petty bourgeoisie; the demand for a republic and a constituent assembly isolates it from all shades of liberalism; and finally, the ultimate goal – socialism – isolates it from the whole world. This means that there are no boundary lines here and none can be drawn. If the proletariat were guided by fear of undermining or isolating itself from liberalism, it would have to renounce completely every aspect of its own struggle, its own proletarian policy, its entire history in the West and, above all, the whole of the current revolution in Russia.

The point is that what are seen as special conditions and tasks during a special stage in the history of the proletariat – its position with regard to liberalism in the conditions of struggle against the old autocratic power – are in reality the same conditions that accompany the historical development of the proletariat from beginning to end. They are fundamental conditions of proletarian struggle resulting from the simple fact that the proletariat appears on the historical scene together with the bourgeoisie, grows at its expense, and, gradually emancipating itself from the bourgeoisie in the same process, moves toward finally victory over it. Least of all is it possible for the proletariat to alter this tactic at the present time in Russia. In previous revolutions, class antagonisms appeared only in the course of actual revolutionary clashes. The current Russian revolution is the first to start with the fully matured and conscious class contradictions of capitalist society, and the tactics of the Russian proletariat cannot artificially conceal this fact.

Directly linked with these fundamental views concerning the relation to bourgeois liberalism is the view of conditions and forms of class struggle in general and the importance of parliamentarism in particular. Another of the respected veterans of Russian Social Democracy presented this aspect of the question in a speech to the Stockholm congress of the Party that was, in a sense, classical.[25] The red thread running throughout this speech was the following: let us at least achieve a proper bourgeois system, with some kind of a constitution, a parliament, elections and so on, and then we will be able to wage the class struggle as it ought to be done; then we will take our stand on firm ground in terms of the Social-Democratic tactics that have emerged from long years of experience in the German Party. But, so long as there is no parliament, even the most elementary conditions for class struggle do not exist. And this same respected theoretician of Russian Marxism then painstakingly searched through present-day Russian reality for even the slightest 'hint'[26] of class struggle – 'hints' were a favourite expression in this speech – perceiving them even in the most caricatured hints of parliamentarism and a constitution. This must surely bring to mind the words of Schiller:

> Ein Mensch, der räsonniert,
>
> Ist wie ein Thier auf dürrer Heide,
>
> Im Kreis herumgeführt –
>
> Und ringsumher liegt schöne, grüne Weide.[27]
>
> [A man who ruminates [literally: 'argues'],
>
> Is like a beast in an arid heath
>
> That is being led around in circles –
>
> While all-around there are beautiful green pastures.]

It seems to these philosophisers that no arena exists for the class struggle and that Social Democracy, in the meantime, has neither initiative nor strength and is unable to comprehend the opportunities and broad perspectives provided by history.

---

[25] [Luxemburg is referring to a report from P.B. Axelrod to the IV (unity) Congress of the Russian Social-Democratic Labour Party dealing with approaches to the State Duma.]

[26] [The word used here is 'zatsepka', which literally means 'peg', 'hook', 'catch', or 'snag' – something to which the class struggle might be 'attached'. In the context of Luxemburg's speech, the best translation is probably 'hint'.]

[27] [It appears that Luxemburg was referring not to Schiller but to Goethe's *Faust*, where Mephistopheles says in part I, scene iv:
A chap who speculates – let this be said –
Is very like a beast on moorland dry,
That by some evil spirit round and round is led,
While fair, green pastures round about him lie.
(http://www.levity.com/alchemy/faust05.html)

At the height of a genuine revolution in Russia, there is no possibility of waging the class struggle, only insignificant 'hints'. All of the proletariat's political demands, 'and even a republic' – the speaker notes – are not, strictly speaking, expressions of class struggle, for there is nothing in them that is specifically proletarian. Indeed, in that case – if we look again for evidence in the international workers' movement – we in Germany have not been waging our own class struggle right up to the present time because, as everyone knows, the entire day-to-day political struggle of German Social Democracy is focused on demands of the so-called minimum programme, which comprises almost exclusively *democratic* slogans such as universal suffrage, unrestricted freedom for unions and so forth. And we are defending these demands against the entire bourgeoisie. But even the most formally proletarian demands, such as labour legislation, are not at all specifically socialist because they only formulate the demands of a progressive capitalist society. Therefore, an analysis that does not recognise the character of class struggle in the political slogans of the proletariat in our present revolution is not so much a model of Marxist thinking as a spiritual condition that is commonly characterised by saying: he has reached his wit's end.

Actually, one would have to be stubbornly prejudiced in favour of an exclusively parliamentary form of political struggle in order not to see the grandiose scale of class struggle in Russia at the present moment. One would have to be groping and stumbling, searching for feeble 'hints' of class struggle, in order not to understand that all the political slogans of the current revolution, precisely because the bourgeoisie has repudiated or is repudiating them, are thereby manifestations of the class struggle of the proletariat. Least of all should Russian Social Democracy underestimate these circumstances itself. It is enough for it to look at itself and its own most recent history in order to understand what colossal educational significance attaches to the class struggle at the present moment, even prior to any parliamentarism.

It is enough just to recall what Russian Social Democracy was before 1905, before 9 January, compared with what it is today. The half year of the revolutionary and strike movement that followed January 1905 transformed it from a tiny group of revolutionaries, from a weak sect, into an enormous mass party, and the misfortune for Social Democracy lies not in the difficulty of finding 'hints' of class struggle but, on the contrary, in the difficulty of seizing and making use of the immense field of activity that has been opened up for it by the gigantic class struggle of the revolution. To look for salvation in the midst of this struggle – like a drowning man grasping at straws – in even the slightest hints of parliamentarism, regarded as the sole guarantee of class struggle, which will only come at some future time, after the liberals' victory, means an inability to understand that revolution is the creative period when society breaks apart into classes. All in all, the scheme into which they want to fit the class struggle of the Russian proletariat is a crude one that has never occurred in Western Europe; it is nothing but a crude copy of the immense diversity of reality.

The truth is that real Marxism is as far from this one-sided exaggeration of parliamentarism as it is from a mechanical view of revolution and over-estimation of the so-called armed uprising. This is where I and my Polish comrades disagree with the views of our Bolshevik comrades. At the very outset of the revolution, even when this question was not yet generally topical among Russian comrades, we in Poland had to take into consideration attempts to give the revolutionary tactics of our proletariat the character of conspiratorial speculation and crude revolutionary adventurism. From the very beginning we declared – and it seems to me that we succeeded in fundamentally reinforcing our views in the ranks of the conscious Polish proletariat – that we consider any plan to arm the broad popular masses through underground means to be a purely utopian undertaking, and we think the same of any plan to prepare and organise, in some premeditated way, a so-called armed uprising. We declared from the very beginning that the task of Social Democracy is not a technical one, but rather one involving political preparation of the mass struggle against absolutism. Of course, we think it necessary to clarify for the broad masses of the proletariat that their direct confrontation with the armed forces of reaction, a general popular uprising, is the sole outcome of the revolutionary struggle that can guarantee victory as the inevitable finale of its gradual development, although it is not within the capacity of Social Democracy to prescribe and prepare this outcome by technical means. [*Applause. Plekhanov: 'Absolutely true!'*]

The comrades to my left are declaring that this is 'absolutely true'! I'm afraid, however, that they will not agree with me in the following conclusions. To be precise, I think that if Social Democracy should avoid any mechanical view of the revolution, any view suggesting that it 'makes' the revolution with bayonets and 'specifies' the outcome, then it must also redouble its effort and its determination to point out to the proletariat the broad political line of its tactics, which can be explained only when Social Democracy clarifies for the proletariat in advance the final outcome of this line: to strive to win political power in order to realise the tasks of the present revolution. And this is once again linked directly with a view of the mutual role of the liberal bourgeoisie and the proletariat in the revolutionary struggle.

I see, however, that the time allotted for my report is passing, and I must break off in the middle of my exposition of views concerning the question of our relation to the bourgeois parties. For that reason, I will add just a few general remarks *pro domo sua*[28] that clarify in general terms our position regarding the whole body of questions being debated at this congress.

The comrades who defend the views that I have just been analysing are fond of frequently referring to the claim that they represent true Marxism within Russian Social Democracy, that they enunciate all of these positions and recommend this tactic to the Russian proletariat in the name of Marxism and in a Marxist spirit. From its very first appearance, Polish Social Democracy has taken its stand on Marxist teachings, and in both its programme and its tactics it considers itself to be following the founders of scientific socialism and especially German Social Democracy. For this reason, there is no doubt that references to Marxism are extremely important for us. But when we see Marxist teaching applied in these ways, when we see this kind of shakiness and vacillation in tactics, when we see this melancholy grieving over constitutional-parliamentary conditions and the victory of liberalism, this desperate search for 'hints' of the class struggle in the midst of the grandiose sweep of a revolution, this casting about from one side to the other in search of artificial ways to become 'immersed in the masses', such as workers' congresses,[29] this search for artificial slogans to 'unleash the revolution' at a moment when it is appears temporarily to be receding, together with an inability to take advantage and be decisive when it is once again in full swing – when we see all of this, then we are compelled to exclaim: What a

---

[28] ['For my own part.']
[29] [In response to Lenin's emphasis on a party of professional revolutionaries, Axelrod advocated a broad campaign to form a Workers' League through local organisations that would send elected delegates to a Workers' Congress. The issue was debated at the London congress (RSDRP 1907b, pp. 496–560. For Lenin's view see (CW, Vol. 12: 142–4).]

forlorn mess you comrades have made of Marxist teaching, a teaching that is, indeed, distinguished by its flexibility, but also by its deadly, sparkling blade of Damask steel!

You have turned this teaching, which represents the mighty beat of the proletariat's eagle wings, into the bothersome cackle of a hen that is searching for pearls of grain in the rubbish heap of bourgeois parliamentarism! Marxism, you see, has within it two essential elements: the element of analysis and criticism, and the element of active will on the part of the working class, as the revolutionary factor. But he who personifies analysis and criticism alone represents not Marxism, only a miserable self-corrupting parody of this teaching.

You comrades of the right wing complain at length about narrowness, intolerance, and a certain mechanistic disposition in the views of our comrades, the so-called Bolsheviks. [*Cries: 'Among the Mensheviks'.*] On that matter we agree with you completely. [*Applause.*]

It is possible that Polish comrades, who are accustomed to thinking more or less in ways adopted by the West-European movement, find this particular steadfastness even more startling than you do. But do you know, comrades, where all these disagreeable features come from? These features are very familiar to someone acquainted with internal party relations in other countries: they represent the typical spiritual character of that trend within socialism that that has to defend the very principle of the proletariat's independent class policy against an opposing trend that is also very strong. [*Applause.*]

Rigidity is the form taken by Social-Democratic tactics on the one side, when the other side represents the formlessness of jelly that creeps in every direction under the pressure of events. [*Applause from the Bolsheviks and parts of the Centre.*]

We in Germany can allow ourselves the luxury of being *suaviter in modo, fortiter in re* – gentle and tolerant in form, but firm and unflinching in essential tactics. We can do this because the very principle of the proletariat's independent and revolutionary class policy is with us so firm and unshakeable, and is supported by such an enormous majority of the party, that the presence and even the activity of a group of opportunists in our ranks represents no danger to us; on the contrary, freedom of discussion and diversity of opinion are necessary in view of how enormous the movement is. Unless I am mistaken, it was precisely certain chieftains of Russian Marxism who could not forgive us in the past for *not being rigid enough* because, for instance, we are not throwing Bernstein out of our party ranks.[30]

But if we turn our gaze from Germany to the party in France, there we find completely different relations. At least that was the case just a few years ago. Wasn't the Guesdist party[31] distinguished in its day by its remarkably unique and rigid character? What was the cost, for instance, of our friend Guesde's declaration – which his opponents tried so much to use for their own ends – that in essence it makes no particular difference to the working class whether the republican president Loubet[32] is head of state or Emperor Wilhelm II? Didn't the appearance of our French friends have certain typical attributes of sectarian straightforwardness and intolerance, which were naturally acquired during long years of defending the class independence of the French proletariat against diffuse and 'wide-open' socialism of all varieties? Yet, despite this, we did not waver even for a moment at the time – and Comrade Plekhanov was with us then – nor did we doubt that the Guesdists had essential truth on their side and that every effort must be made to support them against their opponents.

Today we view the one-sidedness and narrowness of the left wing of Russian Social Democracy in exactly the same way, as a natural result of the history of the Russian Party during recent years, and we are convinced that these attributes cannot be eliminated by any artificial means but will moderate of their own accord only after the principle of the proletariat's class independence and revolutionary policy becomes well established and finally wins out in the ranks of Russian Social Democracy. For this reason, we are quite consciously endeavouring to guarantee the victory of this policy – not in its specific Bolshevik form, but rather in the form in which it is understood and implemented by Polish Social Democracy, the form that is most in line with the spirit of German Social Democracy and of true Marxism. [*Applause.*]

---

[30] [An article by Plekhanov 1898 appeared in issues 253, 254 and 255 of the periodical *Sächsische Arbeiterzeitung* (Saxon Workers' Gazette), in which Plekhanov demanded the expulsion of Eduard Bernstein from the German Social-Democratic Party for his revisionist views. An English version appears in Plekhanov 1976, pp. 340–51.]

[31] [Jules Guesde (1845–1922) opposed any participation by socialists in bourgeois governments.]

[32] [Émile François Loubet (*1838–1929*) was president of the French republic from 1889–1906.]

Concluding remarks

I must respond first of all to certain misunderstandings resulting from the accidental circumstance that lack of time compelled me to interrupt my report almost in the middle when discussing basic views concerning the relation of the proletariat to the bourgeois parties. Particularly beneficial to my critics was the fact that I did not get to elucidate in more detail the relation of the proletariat to petty-bourgeois tendencies and especially to the peasantry. So many bold conclusions were drawn from this fact. I spoke only of the relation of the proletariat to the bourgeoisie, and this, according to Comrade Martov,[33] meant simply identifying the role of the proletariat and all other classes, apart from the bourgeoisie, in the present revolution; in other words, it implied the same 'left bloc', effacing the distinctiveness of the proletariat and subordinating it to the influence of the petty bourgeoisie – the same 'left bloc' that the Bolshevik comrades are defending.

In the opinion of the rapporteur from the Bund,[34] the fact that I dealt exclusively with the policy of the proletariat in relation to the bourgeoisie clearly showed exactly the opposite to be the case: that is, that I completely denied any role on the part of the peasantry and the 'left bloc', thereby placing myself in direct opposition to the position of the Bolshevik comrades. Finally, another speaker from the Bund was even more merciless in his conclusions, declaring that to speak of the proletariat as the sole revolutionary class reeks directly of anarchism. As you see, the conclusions are rather divergent and concur only in one respect, and that is that they must all be equally fatal for me.

Strictly speaking, I have to be rather surprised by my critics' agitation over the fact that I dealt primarily with the mutual relation between the proletariat and the bourgeoisie in the present revolution. After all, there is no doubt that precisely this relation, and precisely the determination, above all else, of the proletariat's position in relation to its social antipode, the bourgeoisie, is the

---

[33] [Julius Martov (1873–1923) one of the most prominent leaders of the Mensheviks. See Israel Getzler 1967.]

[34] [The Bund, or General Jewish Workers' Union of Lithuania, Poland and Russia, was one of the largest socialist organisations up to 1905. Its claim to speak on behalf of Jewish workers led to a split with Lenin in 1903. The Bund rejoined the Social-Democratic party in 1906 and in most subsequent disputes sided with the Mensheviks.]

essence of the question and the main axis of proletarian policy around which its relations to other classes and groups are already crystallising, including the petty bourgeoisie, the peasantry, and others. And, when we come to the conclusion that the bourgeoisie in our revolution is not playing and cannot play the role of leader of the emancipation movement, and that by the very nature of its policy it is counter-revolutionary; when we correspondingly declare that the proletariat must regard itself not merely as a subordinate detachment of bourgeois liberalism but rather as the revolutionary movement's vanguard, determining its policy independently of other classes and pursuing it exclusively out of its own class tasks and interests; when we say that the proletariat is not the bourgeoisie's groom but is called upon to follow an independent policy – when we say all of this, it would seem also to imply clearly that the conscious proletariat must make use of any popular revolutionary movement and subordinate it to its own leadership and its own class policy. No one can doubt, especially with regard to the revolutionary peasantry, that we have not forgotten its existence and by no means ignore the question of the proletariat's relation to it. The directives to the Social-Democratic Duma group, proposed to this congress a few days ago by the Polish comrades, including me, addressed this question perfectly clearly and precisely.[35]

Here, I will take the opportunity to say just a few words that touch upon this question more closely. The relation of our party's right wing to the question of the peasantry is being determined, as in the case of the bourgeoisie, by a certain ready-made and pre-given scheme to which real relations are being subordinated. 'For us Marxists,' says Comrade Plekhanov, 'the labouring peasantry, as it exists in the current commodity-capitalist circumstances, represents nothing more than one of a variety of types of small, independent commodity producers, and we justifiably include small and independent commodity producers among the petty bourgeoisie.' From this it follows that the peasant, as a petty bourgeois, is one of society's reactionary elements, and anyone who considers him to be a revolutionary is idealising him and subordinating the proletariat's policy to the influence of the petty bourgeoisie.

---

[35] [See RSDRP 1907c, pp. 293, 345.]

This kind of argumentation is once again a classical example of notorious metaphysical thinking, according to formula that 'Yea is yea; nay is nay; whatsoever is more than these cometh of evil'. The peasantry is a reactionary class, and anything more cometh of evil. The bourgeoisie is a revolutionary class, and anything more cometh of evil. The characterisation of the peasantry in bourgeois society, given in the quotation just cited, is true insofar as we are speaking of so-called normal and peaceful periods of that society's existence. But, even within these limits, it tends to be very narrow and one-sided. In Germany, increasingly numerous strata, not only of the agricultural proletariat but also of the small peasantry, are siding with Social Democracy and thereby demonstrating that talk of the peasantry being a single, compact and homogeneous class of the reactionary petty bourgeoisie involves a certain degree of dry and lifeless schematics. And in this still undifferentiated mass of the Russian peasantry, which the current revolution has put in motion, there are important strata that are not just our temporary political allies but also our natural future comrades. To disavow subordinating them even now to our leadership and our influence would be precisely an act of sectarianism that is unforgivable on the part of the revolution's leading detachment.

But, above all, it is certainly a sin against the historical dialectic to carry over mechanically a scheme of the peasantry, as a petty-bourgeois reactionary class, to the role of that same peasantry in a revolutionary period. The role of the peasantry, and the proletariat's relation to it, is determined in exactly the same way as the role of the bourgeoisie – not by the subjective wishes and efforts of these classes but by their objective position. Despite all its spoken declarations and published liberal programmes, the Russian bourgeoisie is an objectively reactionary class because its interests in the current social and historical circumstances demand the fastest possible liquidation of the revolutionary movement through a rotten compromise with absolutism. As for the peasantry, despite all the confusion and contradictoriness of its demands, and despite all the fog and ambiguity of its efforts, in the current revolution it is an objectively revolutionary factor because, by placing on the revolution's order of the day, in the most acute manner, the question of revolutionary land change, it thereby poses a question that cannot be solved within the limits of bourgeois society and points beyond that society by its very nature.

It is highly possible that once the wave of revolution recedes, and once the land question eventually reaches one solution or another in the form of bourgeois private property, major strata of the Russian peasantry will become a clearly reactionary and petty-bourgeois party like the Bavarian *Bauernbund*.[36] But, while the revolution continues, and until the land question is regulated, the peasantry is not merely a submerged political reef for absolutism but also a social sphinx for the entire Russian bourgeoisie, and, for that reason, it represents an independent revolutionary ferment and, through its interaction with the urban proletarian movement, it imparts to the revolution the expansive sweep characteristic of a spontaneous popular movement. This is also the source of the socialist-utopian colouring of the peasant movement in Russia, which is by no means the consequence of artificial cultivation and demagogy on the part of the Social-Revolutionaries, but rather has accompanied all major peasant uprisings in bourgeois society. It is enough to recall the peasant wars in Germany and the name of Thomas Münzer.[37]

But precisely because they are utopian and incapable of fulfilment by their nature, peasant movements are completely unable to play any independent role and are subordinated in every historical context to the leadership of other classes that are more energetic and more clearly defined. In France, the revolutionary bourgeoisie in the cities enthusiastically supported the peasant uprising, the so-called *jacquerie*. If leadership of the peasant wars in medieval Germany fell into the hands of reactionary malcontents of the petty gentry rather than those of the foremost bourgeoisie, this was because the German bourgeoisie, due to Germany's historical backwardness, achieved the first phase of its class emancipation only in the still distorted ideological form of religious reformation and, because of its weakness, was frightened by the peasant wars rather than welcoming them and thus rushed into the embrace of reaction, just as Russian liberalism is now frightened by the proletarian and peasant movement and is rushing into the embrace of reaction. It is clear that political leadership of the chaotic peasant movement in Russia today, and the exercise of influence over it, are the natural historical responsibility of the conscious proletariat.

And if it were to refuse this role out of concern for the purity of its socialist programme, then it would find itself once more at the level of a doctrinaire

---

[36] [Peasants' League.]

[37] [Thomas Münzer (1490–1525) was a leader of the German Anabaptist movement during the Reformation and an advocate of utopian communism who was executed for his beliefs. See Frederick Engels 1850b, pp. 397–482.

sect rather than rising to the height of being the natural historical leader, in the spirit of scientific socialism, of all the masses who are the deprived victims of the bourgeois system. Let us recall Marx when he said that the proletariat is summoned to fight on behalf of all those who are deprived.

But let us return to the question of relations to the bourgeoisie. Of course, I will not stop to give a serious reply to the complaints and criticisms coming from the members of the Bund. As it turns out, the entire wisdom of the Bund can be reduced to one extraordinarily simple position: begin with no firm and definite principles and adopt the best aspects of every available position. With this petty political wisdom, the comrades from the Bund want to determine relations with all the fractions within our party and with all the different classes in the Russian revolution. In terms of internal party relations, this position properly leads not to the role of an independent political centre but to a policy that counts in advance on the existence of two different fractions. Carried over to the wide ocean of the Russian revolution, it leads to completely deplorable results. This policy, defended by the Bund's representatives, leads to the well-known classical slogan of the German opportunists, to a policy of 'von Fall zu Fall', from case to case or, if you will, from collapse to collapse.[38] [*Applause.*] This clearly displayed physiognomy of the Bund is important and interesting not so much in terms of revealing its own character as in the fact that by its alliance with and support of the Mensheviks at this congress the Bund underscores the political tendency of the Menshevik comrades.

Comrade Plekhanov reproached me for representing some kind of evanescent Marxism that reigns over the clouds.[39] Comrade Plekhanov is polite even when he has no intention to be, and in this case he has paid me a genuine compliment. In order to orient oneself to the flow of events, a Marxist must survey relations not by crawling among daily and hourly conjunctures, but from a certain theoretical height, and the tower from which the course of

---

[38] [The editors of the transcripts of the Congress report that at this point Rosa Luxemburg compared the members of the Bund to petty 'shopkeepers', provoking an uproar that nearly disrupted the proceedings. The Bund demanded that Luxemburg retract her words, but with the support of Polish comrades she refused. Following lengthy discussions, it was decided to excise from the record this section of Luxemburg's speech.]

[39] [A delegate to the Congress asked Rosa Luxemburg what stool she was sitting on. Plekhanov remarked: 'What a naïve question! Comrade Rosa Luxemburg sits on no stool. She is like one of Raphael's Madonnas, floating on clouds…of comfortable dreams.' RSDRP 1907b, p. 422.]

the Russian revolution must be surveyed is the international development of bourgeois class society and its level of maturity. Comrade Plekhanov and his friends bitterly rebuked me on the grounds that I am describing such alluring and brilliant prospects for the present revolution as to imply that limitless victories await the Russian proletariat. This is completely untrue.

My critics in this case are attributing a view to me that is completely foreign to my own, namely, that the proletariat can and should expand its battle tactics as widely and decisively as possible but only on condition that victories are guaranteed to it in advance. I believe, on the contrary, that it is a poor leader and a pitiful army that goes into battle only when it knows in advance that victory is in its pocket. To the contrary, I not only have no intention of promising the Russian proletariat a series of certain victories, but am more of the belief that if the working class, true to its historical duty, steadily expands its battle tactics and makes them all the more determined in line with the continuously developing contradictions and expanding perspectives of the revolution, then it might find itself in situations that are extremely complex and rife with difficulties. What is more, I even think that if the Russian working class rises completely to its task, that is, if through its actions it carries revolutionary developments to the most extreme limit permitted by the objective development of social relations, then what will almost inevitably await it at this limit will be a major temporary defeat.

But I think that the Russian proletariat must have the courage and determination to confront everything that historical development has prepared for it, that it must, if necessary, and even at the price of losses, play in this revolution the role of vanguard in relation to the world army of the proletariat, revealing new contradictions, new tasks and new ways of class struggle – the same role that the French proletariat played in the nineteenth century. I believe that in its tactics the Russian proletariat must be led overall not by calculations of defeat or victory but exclusively by its own class and historical tasks, remembering that defeats of the proletariat, resulting from the revolutionary scope of its class struggle, are only local and temporary manifestations of its worldwide movement forward, taken as a whole, and that these defeats are the inevitable historical steps leading to the final victory of socialism. [*Applause.*]

Chapter Twenty-Two

'The Driving Forces of the Russian Revolution and Its Prospects' (November 1906)

Karl Kautsky

In late 1906, Plekhanov addressed three questions to a number of foreign socialists: 1) What is the 'general character' of the Russian revolution: bourgeois or socialist?; 2) What should be the attitude of Social Democrats towards the bourgeois democrats?; and 3) Should the Social-Democratic Party support the opposition parties in the Duma elections? The responses have been summarised as follows:

> Plekhanov's questionnaire was answered by the Italians Turati and Ferri, the Frenchmen Lafargue, Vaillant and Milhaud (an associate of Jaurès), the Belgian Vandervelde and the British Marxist and editor of *Justice*, Quelch – in short, by a fairly representative selection of left and right within European socialism. Of course their answers were not identical, but more or less amounted to the same thing. They implied cautious support for the Menshevik point of view. Most Western socialists were modest and did not want to play the role of armchair critic. But they all thought that the Russian revolution could not be a socialist one, and only at best a bourgeois revolution with socialist elements.

> They all considered the Duma boycott a mistake, and cooperation with the bourgeois opposition in any form was essential. There was, however, one important exception and that was Kautsky.[1]

Karl Kautsky's response[2] to Plekhanov appeared in four separate Russian editions, one of them with a preface by Lenin[3] and another with a preface by Trotsky,[4] both of which are included here together with Kautsky's article. In a review published in the Bolshevik journal *Proletarii*, Lenin described Kautsky's essay as 'a brilliant vindication of the *fundamental principles* of Bolshevik tactics. He added: 'Kautsky's analysis satisfies us completely. He has fully confirmed our contention that we are defending the position of revolutionary Social Democracy against opportunism, and not creating any "peculiar" Bolshevik trend.'[5] Despite his differences with Lenin, Trotsky was no less enthusiastic. His commentary on Kautsky's work expressed warm praise; and in August 1908 he wrote to Kautsky that his response to Plekhanov's inquiry was 'the best theoretical statement of my own views, and gives me great political satisfaction'.[6]

The fact that Lenin and Trotsky could equally claim Kautsky's support attests to Kautsky's deliberate ambiguity. Since he was unable to read Russian and acquaint himself at first hand with the political life of the country, Kautsky's primary concern was to make clear that a bloc of the workers with the Cadets, representing bourgeois liberalism, was out of the question. Agrarian reform was at the heart of the democratic revolution, and the bourgeoisie was too closely linked with the landlords, and too frightened by the workers, to support confiscation of the landed estates without compensation. The urban petty bourgeoisie, in turn, was too weak to play the role it had assumed during the French Revolution. On these grounds, Kautsky concluded that Social-Democratic workers would be forced to seize power together with the peasants to carry out the democratic revolution.

---

[1] Naarden 1992, p. 221.
[2] Kautsky 1907a, pp. 184–90, 324–33.
[3] Lenin's preface to the Russian edition of Kautsky 1907e), pp. 1–7, is available as Lenin 1906b.
[4] Reprinted in N. Trotsky 1907, pp. 122–48.
[5] Lenin 1906c, pp. 372–3, emphasis in the original.
[6] L. Trotsky 1908. Quoted in Donald 1993, p. 91.

This edition of Kautsky's reply to Plekhanov's questionnaire includes, for the first time in English, a translation of Trotsky's passages from his 1907 book *In Defence of the Party*, where he repeatedly refers to Kautsky's work as a vindication of his views on permanent revolution as developed in his *Results and Prospects*. This will, we hope, help to overcome the stereotypical and mistaken view of Kautsky as an apostle of quietism and a reformist cloaked in revolutionary phraseology. This view – an over-generalisation drawn from Kautky's anti-Bolshevik polemics after 1917 – was first developed by the ultra-left philosopher Karl Korsch in his reply to Kautsky's work *Die materialistische Geschichtsauffassung* (1927)[7] and became established in academic circles after the publication of Erich Matthias' book, *Kautsky and Kautskyanism*.[8] Kautsky's main biographer, Marek Waldenberg, provides abundant material to refute this thesis, which was shared by neither Lenin nor Trotsky, both of whom always recommended the writings of Kautsky's revolutionary period to communist workers. Unfortunately, Waldenberg's work is available only in Polish and Italian.[9] We will therefore refer here to one of the polemical brochures of Karl Radek, which was translated into English in an anthology edited by the late Trotskyist historian Al Richardson.

In *The Paths of the Russian Revolution* (1922) Radek described the renaissance of the theory of permanent revolution in 1902–7 as the work of an international Marxist tendency in which Kautsky played a leading role and was actually to the *left* of the traditional positions of Bolshevism. After the 1917 revolution in Russia, Kautsky himself wanted to create the impression, Radek noted, 'that he had been a Menshevik, so to speak, from birth'. But, by means of a series of quotations from Kautsky's early works (the ones included in this anthology) Radek showed that Kautsky, under the influence of Rosa Luxemburg,

> was not only solidly with the Bolsheviks on the *decisive question of the understanding of the role of the bourgeoisie in the Russian Revolution*, but where he departed from the Bolsheviks *he went even further than they did by estimating as possible the passing over of the Russian Revolution to a direct struggle for Socialism.*

[7] Korsch 1929. Sonderausdruck aus: *Archiv für die Geschichte des Sozialismus und der Arbeiterbewegung*, 1929, Bd. 14, H. 2.

[8] Kautsky 1927. Matthias 1957. Sonderausdruck aus: *Marxismusstudien*; Folge 2, S. 152–97.

[9] Waldenberg 1980, 2 vols. Polish original: Waldenberg 1972.

Radek further commented that

> Kautsky's arguments of 1906 were the reflection of a tendency which had its representatives as the time of the first revolution in Trotsky, Parvus and Rosa Luxemburg, a tendency which, as we have said, [was] outside both of the factions of Russian Social Democracy.

The documents collected in this volume clearly prove this argument, though they also show that Radek should have added the names of David Ryazanov and Franz Mehring. 'The representatives of this tendency,' Radek concluded

> pointed out that even if the peasantry represented a great revolutionary force which the working class must by all means attempt to develop and on whom it had to rely, it was not capable of carrying out an independent policy because of its social atomization, its dispersion, and the low level of its development. Whereas Lenin and the Bolsheviks *talked about the dictatorship of the proletariat and the peasantry*, the above-mentioned Marxists laid down the formula of *the dictatorship of the proletariat supported by the peasantry* [that is, the formula adopted by Lenin in his 1917 April Theses, which historically became the summary expression of the theory of permanent revolution.][10]

* * *

Introduction to the anthology *In Defence of the Party* (1 January 1907)[11]
Leon Trotsky

The last item … is the translation of an article by Kautsky: 'The Driving Forces of the Russian Revolution and Its Prospects'. This article proved to be an unexpected blow for some comrades who contented themselves with cut and dried, utopian conceptions about the course of the Russian Revolution – conceptions that were a far cry from any serious analysis whatever of its real content. They dreamed about a bourgeois-democratic (Jacobin) dictatorship that would be given the finishing touches here by the 'union of unions', there by the Cadets. Poor 'union of unions'! Poor Cadets!

---

[10] Radek 1995, p. 40, emphasis in the original.
[11] Trotsky 1970, pp. 142–3.

Some friends told me – jokingly of course – that a very poetic legend was invented to weaken the effect that Kautsky's article could have: Parvus, after fleeing from the district of Turukhansk [Siberia] and on his way to the election campaign in the Rhine, [is said to have begun] his activity in Fridenau, Berlin, by confusing Kautsky's clear thinking. The authors of the legend prove, by referring to the journal *Nachalo*, that Parvus is a dangerous emissary of the idea of permanent revolution.[12]

That is of course just a witty joke. A completely unintelligent joke, on the other hand, is the attempt, dictated by spiritual laziness, to deny the competence of Kautsky on questions of the Russian revolution. It is especially remarkable that such an attempt was sometimes made by precisely those comrades who contented themselves with the general definition of our revolution as bourgeois, and who identified it as a matter of principle with the old bourgeois revolutions of Western Europe. That would imply that the European theoreticians of Social Democracy are unable to grasp the traditional bourgeois character of the Russian revolution because it is…too peculiar to be understood.

We apologise to our readers for dedicating some lines to these inanities. Kautsky's article is such an outstanding phenomenon that it must be regarded apart from such anecdotal trifles.

* * *

'Kautsky on the Russian Revolution' (23 December, 1906)[13]
Leon Trotsky

…To many comrades [Kautsky's article] will seem completely unexpected and incongruous, perhaps even as just some kind of passing notion. But this is not the first time he has expressed such thoughts. The difference is that now he has put them together in response to the inquiry from Plekhanov. In his

---

[12] [Kautsky, who did not read Russian, obviously could not have been converted to permanent revolution by reading *Nachalo*.]

[13] N. Trotsky 1907. On pp. 122–39 Trotsky provides a summary of Kautsky's essay by way of detailed excerpts. Trotsky's commentary comes in pp. 139–48, which we have translated here for the first time into English.

work last year on the American proletariat,[14] Kautsky already provided a brief but meaningful analysis of class relations in the Russian revolution, which he now uses as the foundation for his [present] study....

After providing a general outline of the social-historical conditions that account on the one hand for the political insignificance of the Russian bourgeoisie, for the absence of any serious movement of bourgeois democracy and, on the other hand, for the might of the revolutionary proletariat, Kautsky wrote the following:

> The struggle for the interests of the whole of Russia falls on the shoulders of the only strong modern class it possesses: the industrial proletariat. In this way, the Russian workers are able to exert a strong political influence, and the struggle for liberation of the land from the strangling octopus of absolutism has become a duel between the tsar and the working class; a duel in which the peasants provide indispensable assistance but in which they can by no means play a leading role.[15]

As for the prospect of world revolution in connection with the revolution in Russia, in 1904 Kautsky wrote: 'A revolution in Russia (which at the time was only anticipated) cannot establish a socialist regime at once. The economic conditions of the country are not sufficiently developed for that.'[16] But the Russian revolution must inevitably provide a powerful impulse to the proletarian movement in the rest of Europe, and the result of a rekindled struggle in Germany could be that the proletariat will come to power. 'Such an outcome,' Kautsky continued,

> would inevitably have a powerful effect upon the whole of Europe and bring with it the political supremacy of the European proletariat, thus creating for the East-European proletariat the possibility of abbreviating the stages of its own development and, by imitating the German example, of *artificially creating socialist institutions*. A society cannot, as a whole,

---

[14] [Karl Kautsky, 'The American Worker' (February 1906). For thematic reasons we have taken this article by Kautsky out of chronological sequence and placed it at the end of this anthology.]

[15] Kautsky 1906, pp. 4–5. See p. 625 below.

[16] [Karl Kautsky, 'Revolutionary Questions'. See this anthology, p. 216. Trotsky omitted Kautsky's next sentence: 'The best it can do is to bring about a democratic government behind which would be a strong, impetuous and progressive proletariat that would be able to demand important concessions.']

> artificially leap over the different stages of its development, but this can be done by its particular elements, which are able to accelerate their own delayed development by imitating the leading countries, and thus they might even come to the forefront of developments because they are not carrying the ballast of tradition with which an old country must deal.... This *might* happen [Kautsky continues] but, as we have already said, here we leave the realm of *inevitability* and enter that of *possibility,* which means that everything could also turn out quite differently.[17]

This was written prior to the outbreak of the Russian revolution. Since then, almost three years have gone by. And no matter how cautiously Kautsky spoke in the concluding part of the foregoing article, it is clear that in terms of international perspectives the course of events during these years has taken the direction that he characterised as an historical 'possibility'. But that is not the essential point. Whether the Russian revolution will *directly* evoke a social-political upheaval in Europe, and just how this might reflect back on the development and outcome of the Russian revolution – these are questions that, however important, for now can be answered only provisionally. At present, the central issue concerns domestic relations and the further course of the Russian revolution. And, as far as this question is concerned, Kautsky's views could not be clearer. We must be extremely grateful to Comrade Plekhanov, whose inquiry prompted a careful and deeply thoughtful socialist to speak so categorically; we must be all the more grateful because the inquiry addressed to Kautsky was so ideologically impartial and because Plekhanov must have known, from all that Kautsky had previously written about the Russian revolution, that the answer could scarcely provide any support for the current views of Plekhanov himself.[18]

Kautsky, who very rarely speaks of dialectical materialism but always uses the method excellently in analysing social relations, answered comrade Plekhanov's first question by refusing to call the Russian revolution bourgeois. The epoch of the bourgeois revolution has passed, and this is also true for Russia. We have no bourgeois-democratic movement that is independent and

---

[17] Kautsky 1906a. [The Russian translation that Trotsky cites differs slightly from Kautsky's original text in German. See above, p. 219.]

[18] [For Plekhanov's self-serving interpretation of Kautsky's response, see Plekhanov 1926a, pp. 295–7.]

revolutionary. Nor will we have one, for the fundamental social-economic precondition of such a movement is lacking; that is, a powerful urban middle stratum, a petty bourgeoisie with an historical past and also an historical future. The peasantry represents an enormous source of revolutionary energy, but it is unable to play an independent historical role. The proletariat will have to lead the peasantry and, to a certain degree, play the same role in relation to it that the petty bourgeoisie of the cities in past revolutions played in relation to the proletariat. 'The Russian bourgeoisie will surrender all its revolutionary positions to the proletariat. It will also have to surrender revolutionary hegemony over the peasants.'[19] Kautsky carries his analysis up to the time when a deep social antagonism opens up between the proletariat in power and the influential strata of the peasant masses on whom proletarian power relies. What is the way out of this antagonism?

It is not fully clear to me just what the comrades from the majority[20] mean by the term '*democratic* dictatorship of the proletariat and peasantry'. I would not want to misrepresent them by incorrectly describing the content of this coalition 'dictatorship'. But if they mean that Social Democracy enters into a formal alliance with a peasant party to form a government, possibly one in which the latter is numerically predominant, and that this government then creates a democratic régime, after which time one of the partners, the proletariat, peacefully goes over into opposition, then in response to such a view I can only repeat what I have already written in my *Results and Prospects*.

> The political domination of the proletariat is incompatible with its economic enslavement. Under whatever political banner the proletariat has come to power, it will be *obliged* to take the path of socialist policy. It would be the greatest utopianism to think that the proletariat, having been raised to political domination by the internal mechanism of a bourgeois revolution, will be able, *even if it so desires*, to limit its mission to the creation of republican-democratic conditions for the social domination of the bourgeoisie. The political supremacy of the proletariat, even if it is only

---

[19] [L. Trotsky 1969, pp. 69–74.]
[20] [The Bolsheviks, led by Lenin, proposed the 'democratic dictatorship of the proletariat and peasantry'.]

temporary, will weaken to an extreme degree the resistance of capital, which always requires the support of the state, and will give the economic struggle of the proletariat tremendous scope. The workers cannot but demand support for strikers from the revolutionary government, and a government relying upon the proletariat will not be able to refuse such support. But this means paralysing the effect of the reserve army of labour and making the workers dominant not only in the political but also in the economic field, and converting private property in the means of production into a fiction. These inevitable social-economic consequences of proletarian dictatorship[21] will reveal themselves very quickly, long before the democratisation of the political system has been completed.[22]

[…]

From the very first moments after taking power, the proletariat will have to find support in the antagonisms between the village poor and village rich, between the agricultural proletariat and the agricultural bourgeoisie. While the heterogeneity of the peasantry creates difficulties and narrows the basis for a proletarian policy, the insufficient degree of class differentiation will create obstacles to the introduction among the peasantry of developed class struggle, upon which the urban proletariat could rely. The primitiveness of the peasantry turns its hostile face towards the proletariat.

The cooling-off of the peasantry, its political passivity, and all the more the active opposition of its upper strata, cannot but have an influence on a section of the intellectuals and the urban petty bourgeoisie.

Thus, the more definite and determined the policy of the proletariat in power becomes, the narrower and more shaky will the ground beneath its feet become.[23]

[…]

But how far can the socialist policy of the working class be applied in the economic conditions of Russia? We can say one thing with certainty – that it will come up against political obstacles much sooner than it will

---

[21] Kautsky refuses to call this political domination of the proletariat a *dictatorship*, and I likewise normally avoid using this word; in any case, my understanding of the social content of proletarian rule is exactly the same as Kautsky's.

[22] [L. Trotsky 1969, pp. 100–6).]

[23] [L. Trotsky 1969, pp. 75–81).]

stumble over the technical backwardness of the country. *Without the direct State support of the European proletariat the working class of Russia will not be able to remain in power and convert its temporary supremacy into a lasting socialistic dictatorship.*[24]

Kautsky says that the limits to the possible use of a proletarian victory will lie in the social interests of the peasantry, which supports the revolutionary régime. But this, of course, must not be understood in the sense that the proletariat, by virtue of some explicit agreement with its ally, must not cross over some particular line. The question is not one of an agreement. The 'limits' that the proletariat will encounter will be purely external and objective obstacles, which at some point in its rule it will not be able to overcome. It goes without saying that the proletariat in power will do everything possible to avoid a premature conflict with the peasantry. But since the possession of power will not change its [the proletariat's] class nature – indeed, it will do the opposite and force that nature to become all the more visible – and since the proletariat cannot help but support agricultural workers in their struggle for a human life, the result is that conflict between the proletariat and the 'strong' peasantry is ultimately inevitable. But this will be the beginning of the end. How can this conflict be resolved? Of course, it will not be resolved through having representatives of the proletariat move from ministerial benches to those of the opposition. The issue will be much more complex than that. The conflict will end in civil war and the defeat of the proletariat. *Within the confines of a national revolution,* and given our social conditions, there is no other 'way out' for the proletariat's political domination. That is why the proletariat will face, from the very first period of its rule, a colossal task with life-or-death implications, namely, to burst through the national limits of the Russian revolution and to bring into motion all the resources of its temporary power in order to transform the national upheaval into an episode of the European revolution. This is the route that follows from the entire revolutionary situation as Kautsky describes it, and the closing lines of his article point to exactly this conclusion.

How does Kautsky respond to Plekhanov's second question, concerning the proper relation to bourgeois democracy, 'which is struggling in its own way for political freedom'? Kautsky replies by asking: What do we mean by

---

[24] [L. Trotsky 1969, p. 105).] These words dramatically emphasise the difference between temporary domination and a socialist dictatorship.

democracy? The kind of revolutionary democracy that wrote its name into history does not exist in Russia. All that remains is bourgeois liberalism on the one side, which is anti-revolutionary to the very marrow of its bones, and the popular masses on the other, above all the peasantry. These are two completely different entities. Comrade Plekhanov poses his question in terms of an 'algebraic formula' of bourgeois democracy. Essentially this means that he thinks in terms of assimilating the Cadets with the popular masses. In reality, however, no such assimilation has occurred and, according to Kautsky, it *will not* occur.

In order to resolve the agrarian question, it will be necessary to renounce all liberal doubts and prejudices and adopt a bold revolutionary position. However, this again requires finding support in the cities, in the centres of political life. Apart from the proletariat there is no such support, and only a socialist party can rely upon the proletariat. Kautsky expects us to focus our tactics on the struggle for direct and immediate influence over the peasantry. Will liberalism be able to compete with us in this sphere? The moment the peasantry comes forth in the form of the Trudovik group,[25] the liberals will be completely discouraged.

A great deal has been written about the diffuse character, the instability and the indecision of the Trudoviks, and all this is beyond dispute. But does this alter the extremely important fact that the Russian peasantry, which has just been wakened by the thunder of revolution and has been called upon for the first time to formulate its demands, nevertheless sent deputies to the Duma who turned out, for the most part, to be patented *left* 'democrats' from the *zemstvos*, the universities and the journalists? And when did this happen? – at a time when it is still deprived of any opportunity to hear freely voiced agitation and still remains confused by the details of a complex electoral system, at a time when the so-called Constitutional Democrats were in the middle of their honeymoon of contact with the people.

Of course, there is no point in idealising the Trudoviks, for they are certainly not the last word in the political evolution of the peasantry. But to brush them

---

[25] [In April 1906, a group of peasant deputies in the *Duma* began separating from the *Cadets* to form an independent party. The Trudovik program endorsed peasant demands for land ownership and an end to all traces of feudalism. The Trudoviks never fully separated from the Cadets, vacillating instead between the latter and the Social Democrats as Trotsky predicted they would do.]

off contemptuously or lump them together with the Cadets would be a grave political mistake. Of course, the left wing of the Cadets has occasional ties with the peasantry, and in the practical determination of our position in the localities we must consider this. But as a whole the peasantry has no ties with liberalism in general. It is difficult to say how far the peasant deputies in the second Duma will actually represent the peasantry, and just who those deputies will be is difficult to predict. There is no doubt, however, that the peasantry has moved to the left at the same time as the Cadets have turned to the right. Kautsky speaks of Social Democracy in terms of revolutionary leadership of the peasantry. In that respect he merely describes the situation that already exists in the Caucasus. Guriya[26] is the finished model of revolutionary relations between the peasantry and the party of the proletariat.

In response to the third question, concerning tactics in elections to the Duma, Kautsky replies that 'Joint action with liberalism is only possible where and when it does not affect joint action with the peasantry'. This cautious formulation is perfectly appropriate. It allows for limited practical agreements with the Cadets while neither treating them as central to the electoral campaign nor, still more importantly, regarding them as the starting point for a coalition campaign. I have considered elsewhere in this volume the political motivation for electoral agreements. Here I will say only that the motivation for agreements with the liberals remains completely within the limits of our direct *struggle against liberalism* for influence over the popular masses.

I repeat: the question now is not what stage our revolution is in, but rather the path by which it will develop. The issue, of course, is not what to *call* our revolution – whether it is bourgeois or socialist – the real issue is to establish its actual direction by analysing the forces involved. Meanwhile, we too often replace a materialistic analysis with a formalistic deduction to the effect that our revolution is a bourgeois revolution; a victorious bourgeois revolution transfers power to the bourgeoisie; the proletariat must help the bourgeois revolution to victory; therefore, it must promote the transfer of power to the bourgeoisie; the idea of a workers' government is therefore incompatible with proletarian tactics in the epoch of the bourgeois revolution, etc., etc.

---

[26] [An historic district of western Georgia.]

Such a series of scholastic syllogisms is mere litter. The construction may be elegant, but one must take care that none of the propositions presupposes 'what has to be proven'. Kautsky refuses to call our revolution bourgeois because the bourgeoisie is not its leading force – although we might provisionally accept this designation in the sense that our revolution is still struggling to achieve the 'normal' conditions for existence of a bourgeois society. But does this really answer the question of *what* forces are actually struggling for these 'normal' conditions or just *how* they are doing so? We know that at one time the 'plebeian' example of the victorious *sans-culottes* (according to Marx) created conditions for the rule of the capitalist bourgeoisie. Are there not grounds for thinking that today those conditions will be prepared by the class example of the victorious proletariat?

Whereas the *sans-culottes* provided support to the Jacobins, however, the proletariat will obviously bring Social Democracy to power. The point is that a general definition or, to be more accurate, a label, can neither pose nor resolve such questions. This requires analysis, and the analysis must answer such questions as these: Is our revolution developing? Does it have any chance of victory, that is, of transferring power to an opposition class? If so, which class? Which party is or might become its political representative? Whoever acknowledges that the revolution has every chance of decisive victory, yet simultaneously denies the inevitability or the probability of rule by the working class, obviously has in mind some other claimant to power. Where is this claimant and who is it? Obviously, it is bourgeois democracy. What classes does it depend upon? Where is its army of fighters?

Since the proletariat has hitherto been the leading force of the revolution, the kind of army that could ensure its representatives a completely independent position will necessarily also be opposed to any bourgeois-democratic government. The fundamental question is not whether bourgeois democracy in our country has or has not played out its historical role – of course, it has not – the real issue concerns the possible limits of this role. With us there is no Third Estate, which primarily means a strong, cultured and revolutionary petty bourgeoisie. This is a fundamental fact. Amongst our urban population, the industrial proletariat takes the place of petty-bourgeois democrats. And who will replace the petty-bourgeois democrats in terms of power? I have heard no definitive answer to this question, although it has been discussed in our party literature for about two years – ever since the time of Parvus's foreword to my pamphlet *Up to the Ninth of January*.

Personally, I have frequently had to return to this question. If the reader will take the trouble to consider my article 'Results and Prospects' (in *Our Revolution*, pp. 224–86),[27] then he will see that I have no reason whatever to reject even a single one of the positions formulated in the article I have translated by Kautsky, because the development of our thinking in these two articles is identical. I find this circumstance all the more gratifying since one reviewer – a person respected by all shades of Marxists, although one who is also too inclined to give voice to common prejudices – recently dismissed my work with sovereign contempt on the grounds that however noble my intentions, I have constructed a pure fantasy. There was nothing more to say because the worthy reviewer did not take the trouble to think through my analysis. Although Kautsky's article introduces virtually nothing new in terms of argumentation, it seems that his work is more appropriate and to the point. Of course, this is not because it scandalised the exponent of common prejudices but rather because the author, in the case of Kautsky's article, carries such authority that he compels comrades, even those with a different point of view, to speak more precisely and concretely of the social relations involved in the revolution. This is exactly what I am waiting so impatiently to hear. Notwithstanding all my hopes [for such clarification], thus far I have been able to learn nothing in this regard from my critics.

*   *   *

Preface to the Russian translation of Kautsky's 'The Driving Forces of the Russian Revolution and Its Prospects'[28]
V.I. Lenin

K. Kautsky has long been known to the progressive workers of Russia as *their* writer who is able not only to substantiate and expound the theoretical teaching of revolutionary Marxism but also to apply it with a knowledge of

---

[27] [The page reference is to the Russian edition of Trotsky 1906, in which *Results and Prospects* was first published.]

[28] [This translation of Lenin's preface and the following translation of Kautsky's essay first appeared in Harding 1983, pp. 352–403. The editors of this anthology express gratitude to Neil Harding and Richard Taylor (who translated Kautsky's work from German) for their kind permission to reproduce the documents here. Non-bracketed footnotes are those provided by Neil Harding.]

affairs and a thorough analysis of the facts to the complex and involved issues of the Russian revolution. But now, when the attention of Social Democrats is sometimes almost entirely taken up with the idle prattle of the liberal Petrushkas[29] and of their conscious and unconscious yes-men, when for many people petty 'parliamentary' technicalities overshadow the fundamental questions of the proletarian class struggle, and when despondency often overwhelms even decent people and impairs their intellectual and political faculties – now it is trebly important for all the Social Democrats of Russia to pay close attention to Kautsky's view of the fundamental problems of the Russian revolution. And not so much to pay attention to Kautsky's view as to reflect on the way he poses the question – for Kautsky is not so thoughtless as to hold forth on the specific issues of Russian tactics with which he is not well acquainted, and not so ignorant of Russian affairs as to dismiss them with commonplace remarks or an uncritical repetition of the latest fashionable pronouncements.

Kautsky is answering the questions that Plekhanov addressed to a number of foreign socialists[30] and, in answering these questions, or, more accurately, in selecting from these poorly formulated questions the points that *can* be useful subjects for discussion among Socialists of all countries, Kautsky begins with a modest reservation – 'I feel like a *novice* vis-à-vis my *Russian* comrades when it comes to Russian affairs.' This is not the false modesty of a social democratic 'general' who starts off grimacing like a petit bourgeois and ends up with the demeanour of a Bourbon. Not at all, Kautsky has *in fact* confined himself to answering only those questions through an analysis of which he can *help* the thinking Social Democrats of Russia to work out for themselves the concrete tasks and slogans of the day. Kautsky has refused to be a general issuing orders: 'Right turn!' or 'Left turn!'. He has preferred to preserve his position as a comrade standing at a distance, but a thoughtful comrade pointing out where we ourselves should look for an answer.

---

[29] [Petrushka was a serf-valet in Gogol's *Dead Souls* who read books by spelling out each word with no regard to their meaning.]

[30] In the hope that leading European Marxists would bolster his position by agreeing with him that the Russian revolution was a democratic revolution which ought therefore to be led by the bourgeoisie, Plekhanov sent them a list of (rather leading) questions. Kautsky cites the three most important of these on p. 369 [of the volume edited by Neil Harding and on pages 604-5 of this anthology].

Plekhanov asked Kautsky: 1. Is the 'general character' of the Russian revolution bourgeois or socialist? 2. What should the attitude of the Social Democrats towards bourgeois democracy be? 3. Should the Social Democrats support the opposition parties in the elections for the Duma?

At first sight these questions would seem to have been chosen with great 'finesse'. But, as the saying goes, 'If a thing is too fine, it breaks.' In fact, any more or less competent and observant person will see straight away the fine…*subterfuge* in these questions. Subterfuge, firstly, because they are fine specimens of the metaphysics against which Plekhanov is so fond of declaiming pompously, although he cannot keep it out of his own concrete historical judgements. Subterfuge, secondly, because the person questioned is artificially driven into a small and excessively narrow corner. Only those who are completely, one might even say virginally, innocent in questions of politics can fail to notice that Plekhanov deliberately starts out from a remote position and gently pushes the person he is questioning into the position of justifying…blocs with the Cadets![31]

To drive a simple-minded interlocutor into justifying blocs with a certain party, without naming that party; to talk of a revolutionary movement without distinguishing the revolutionary democrats from the opposition bourgeois democrats; to imply that the bourgeoisie is 'fighting' *in its own way*, i.e. differently from the proletariat, without saying plainly and clearly what the difference really is; to trap the interlocutor like a fledgling jackdaw with the bait of the Amsterdam resolution[32] which is bound to *conceal* from the foreigner the real bones of contention among the Russian Social Democrats; to declare concrete rules relating to specific tactics in a specific case and to the attitude to be adopted towards the various parties among the bourgeois democrats, from a general *phrase* about the general character of the revolution, instead of deducing this 'general character of the Russian revolution' from

---

[31] The Constitutional Democratic Party (whose members were known as Cadets) was a radical liberal grouping formed in October 1905 with a view to fighting the elections for the forthcoming First Duma in which they emerged as the largest party.

[32] At the Amsterdam Congress of the Second International in August 1904 the SPD and the French Marxists had combined to move a forthright condemnation of revisionism and of socialist participation in bourgeois governments. Plekhanov had invoked the authority of this resolution, which insisted 'that Social Democracy…cannot *aim at* participating in governmental power within capitalist society' against the projects of Bolsheviks and permanent revolutionists alike.

a precise analysis of the concrete data on the interests and position of the different classes in the Russian revolution – is not all this a subterfuge? Is it not an open mockery of Marx's dialectical materialism?

'Yea, yea – nay, nay, and whatsoever is more than these comes from the evil one.' Either a bourgeois revolution or a socialist one; the rest can be 'deduced' from the main 'solution' by means of simple syllogisms!

Kautsky performs a great service in that, in answering such questions, he grasps the point immediately and goes to the root of the mistake contained in the very way they were formulated. Kautsky *essentially* answers Plekhanov's questions by *rejecting* Plekhanov's formulation of them! Kautsky answers Plekhanov by *correcting* Plekhanov's formulation of the question. The more gently and carefully he corrects the questioner, the more deadly is his criticism of Plekhanov's formulation of the question. 'We should do well', writes Kautsky, 'to realise that we are moving towards completely new situations and problems for which none of the old patterns are suitable.'

This hits the nail on the head with regard to Plekhanov's question: is our revolution bourgeois or socialist in its general character? Kautsky says that this is the old pattern. The question must not be put in this way, it is not the Marxist way. The revolution in Russia is not a bourgeois revolution because the bourgeoisie is not one of the driving forces of the present revolutionary movement in Russia. And the revolution in Russia is not a socialist revolution for there is *no way* in which it can possibly lead the proletariat to *sole* rule or dictatorship. Social Democracy is capable of victory in the Russian revolution and *must* strive towards it. But victory in the present revolution cannot be the victory of the proletariat alone, without the aid of other classes. Which class then, in view of the objective conditions of the present revolution, is the ally of the proletariat? The *peasantry*: 'a substantial common interest for the whole period of the revolutionary struggle exists however only between the proletariat and the peasantry'.

All these propositions of Kautsky are a brilliant confirmation of the tactics of the revolutionary wing of Russian social democracy, i.e. the tactics of the Bolsheviks. This confirmation is all the more valuable because Kautsky, setting aside concrete and practical questions, has concentrated all his attention on a systematic exposition of the *general principles* of socialist tactics in our revolution. He has shown that Plekhanov's threadbare notion of an argument that 'the revolution is a bourgeois revolution so that we must support the bourgeoisie' has nothing in common with Marxism. He thus recognises the principal error of our social democratic opportunism, i.e. Menshevism, which the Bolsheviks have been fighting since the beginning of 1905.

Further, Kautsky's analysis, which proceeds not from general phrases but from an analysis of the positions and interests of specific classes, has reaffirmed the conclusion that the yes-men of the Cadets within our ranks considered 'tactless', namely that the bourgeoisie in Russia fears revolution more than reaction; that it despises reaction because it gives birth to revolution; that it wants political liberty in order to call a halt to revolution. Compare this with the naïve faith in the Cadets professed by our Plekhanov who, in his questions, has imperceptibly identified the struggle of the opposition against the old order with the struggle against the government's attempts to crush the revolutionary movement! Unlike the Mensheviks, with their stereotyped views of 'bourgeois democracy', Kautsky has shown its revolutionary and non-revolutionary elements, has demonstrated the bankruptcy of liberalism and shown that, as the peasants become more independent and more aware, the liberals will inevitably move rapidly to the right. A bourgeois revolution, brought about by the proletariat and the peasantry despite the instability of the bourgeoisie – this fundamental principle of Bolshevik tactics – is wholly confirmed by Kautsky.

Kautsky demonstrates that in the course of the revolution it is quite possible that the Social Democratic Party will attain victory and that that party *must* inspire its supporters with confidence in victory. Kautsky's conclusion completely confounds the Menshevik fear of a social democratic victory in the present revolution. Plekhanov's laughable efforts to 'tailor' the tasks of our revolution 'to fit the Amsterdam resolution' seem particularly comical when compared to Kautsky's clear and simple proposition that 'It is impossible to fight successfully if you renounce victory in advance'.

The basic difference between Kautsky's *methods* and those of the leader of our present opportunists, Plekhanov, is even more striking when the former states: to think that 'all the classes and parties that are striving for political liberty have simply to work together to achieve it' means *'seeing only the political surface of events'*. This sounds as though Kautsky is referring directly to that small band of Social Democrats who have deserted to the liberals: Messrs Portugalov, Prokopovich, Kuskova, Logucharsky, Izgoev, Struve and others, who are committing precisely the error that Kautsky refers to (and who in the process are dragging Plekhanov with them). The fact that Kautsky is not acquainted with the writings of these gentlefolk only enhances the significance of his theoretical conclusion.

Needless to say, Kautsky is in *complete* agreement with the fundamental thesis of *all* Russian Social Democrats that the peasant movement is *non-socialist*, that socialism cannot arise from small-scale peasant production, etc. It would be very instructive for the Socialist Revolutionaries, who are fond of asserting that they 'also agree with Marx', to ponder over these words of Kautsky.

In conclusion, a few words about 'authorities'. Marxists cannot adopt the usual standpoint of the intellectual radical, with his pseudo-revolutionary abstraction: 'no authorities'.

No, the working class, which all over the world is waging a hard and persistent struggle for complete emancipation, needs authorities but, of course, only in the same sense that young workers need the experience of veteran warriors against oppression and exploitation, of men who have organised a large number of strikes, have taken part in a number of revolutions, who are versed in revolutionary traditions and who have a broad political outlook. The proletariat of every country needs the authority of the world-wide struggle of the proletariat. We need the authority of the theoreticians of international social democracy to enable us properly to understand the programme and tactics of our party. But this authority naturally has nothing in common with the official authorities in bourgeois science and police politics. It is the authority of the experience gained in the more diversified struggle waged in the ranks of the same world socialist army. Important though this authority is in broadening the horizon of those involved in the struggle, it would be impermissible in the workers' party to claim that the practical and concrete questions of its immediate policy can be solved by those standing a long way off. The collective spirit of the progressive class-conscious workers immediately engaged in the struggle in each country will always remain the supreme authority in all such questions.

This is our view of the authoritativeness of the views held by Kautsky and Plekhanov. The latter's theoretical works – principally his criticism of the Narodniks and the opportunists – remain a lasting asset for Social Democracy throughout Russia and no 'factionalism' will blind any man who possesses the least bit of 'physical brain power' to such an extent that he might forget or deny the importance of this asset. But, as a political leader of the Russian Social Democrats in the bourgeois revolution in Russia, as a tactician, Plekhanov has proved to be beneath all criticism. In this sphere he has displayed an opportunism that is a hundred times more harmful than Bernstein's opportunism is to the German workers. It is against this Cadet-like policy of Plekhanov, who has returned to the fold of Prokopovich[33] and Co. whom he expelled from the Social-Democratic Party in 1899–1900, that we must struggle most ruthlessly.

That this tactical opportunism of Plekhanov is a complete negation of the fundamentals of the Marxist method is best demonstrated by the *line of argument* pursued by Kautsky in the essay here presented to the reader.

*   *   *

'The Driving Forces of the Russian Revolution and Its Prospects'
K. Kautsky

1. The agrarian question and the liberals

The Russian revolution can be looked at in two ways: as a movement for the overthrow of absolutism and as the awakening of the great mass of the Russian people to independent political activity. The former only scratches the surface of events: from this standpoint it looks so far as if the revolution has failed. But we can only speak of real failure if the movement runs aground when seen from the second standpoint as well. If the Russian people are once again pushed back into their old political indifference, then absolutism will certainly have won and the revolution will have lost its game. But, if that does not happen, then the victory of the revolution is assured, even if absolutism attempts to prolong for a while the illusion of its dominance by murdering its own people, squandering its own wealth and laying waste its own country.

The mass of the Russian people consists, however, of peasants. What disturbs them is the agrarian question. Hence this question comes increasingly to the fore: the fate of the revolution depends upon its resolution. This is the case at

---

[33] Prokopovich, at one time a leader of the young opposition to the Emancipation of Labour Group, had, by this time, emerged as a publicist of the Cadets.

least with the mass of Russia proper, which is all we are dealing with here, but not perhaps with Poland, Finland and the Caucasus.

The peasants in Russia do not merely constitute the enormous mass of the population: the whole edifice of the economy and the state rests upon agriculture. If agriculture were to collapse, so too would this edifice. Of the Western European bourgeois observers of the revolutionary situation in Russia Martin has clearly recognised this in his work on the future of Russia and it is on this premise that the certainty of his prophecy of the bankruptcy of the Russian state rests, the prophecy that has recently caused such a sensation in Germany, albeit only in bourgeois circles that knew nothing of the socialist critique of Russian economic policy.[34]

The peasants must be satisfied and agriculture put on a sound economic basis – these are the conditions that must be fulfilled before the population of Russia becomes quiescent again and abandons revolutionary paths.

Almost all the parties in Russia recognise this now. But they do, of course, differ considerably in the way in which they would help the peasants. A recently published essay, *On the Agrarian Movement in Russia*,[35] will give the German reader a very good explanation of the attitude of the liberals: it contains translations of two Russian articles, one by Petrunkevich, the well-known 'Cadet' politician, and one by the Moscow Professor A.A. Manuilov, and a collection of the agrarian programmes of the different Russian parties.

Like everyone else the liberals admit the backwardness and decline of Russian agriculture. Manuilov writes:

> Our largest harvests seem to be half the size of average harvests in other countries. If we take the average yield of all forms of grain in Russia as 100, the yield in other countries will be: rye 230, wheat 280, oats 277, etc. The net yield of grain and potatoes for the average sowing area of the Russian peasant (0.74 desyatin) is on average 20.4 poods[36] whereas in other countries a similar area would produce 56.9 poods, more specifically in Belgium 88, in the UK 84.4, in Japan 82.8 poods, etc....

---

[34] Note in original: 'Rudolf Martin, *Die Zukunft Russlands*, Leipzig: Dieterich, 1906.'

[35] Note in original: 'Zur Agrarbewegung in Russland' (Teutonia-Verlag, Leipzig, 1905). These essays are included in the Russian collection *Agrarnyi Vopros*, eds. P.D. Dolgorukov and I.I. Petrunkevich (2 vols., Moscow, 1905).

[36] Note in original: 'One desyatin is slightly more than a hectare and one pood slightly more than 16 kilograms.' (In imperial measurements, 2.7 acres and 36 pounds respectively.)

Professor A.I. Chuprov has also shown that harvests on our peasant lands with their 35-40 poods of rye per desyatin are so low that even the most primitive improvements, available to all, would be enough to raise the yield by 50% above its present level. [Numerous studies by agronomists suggest that a single improved choice of seed would be almost enough to achieve this result.] But technology disposes of incomparably more powerful resources. A yield of 30 metric hundred-weight of rye to the hectare or 200 poods to the desyatin is considered to be rather low in countries with a developed technology.[37]

And things are getting steadily worse, not better. Manuilov continues:

At the present time as the Department of Agriculture has noted in its report, the peasants have the absolute minimum number of cattle necessary for the existence of agriculture. . . . In the fifty provinces of European Russia the number of horses in the ten years 1888 to 1898 fell from 19.6 million to 17 million, and of large horned cattle from 34.6 million to 24.5 million. . . . Local committees have furnished evidence in support of what I have said in their *Transactions*. It seems, for instance, that in the Nizhny Novgorod province the supply of manure amounts to between one fifth and one third of the demand and, as a result, the average yield, regardless of the fact that the soil is suitable, is extremely low: 38 measures of rye and 49 measures of oats. In the Mikhailov district of Ryazan province only one tenth to one eighth of the surface area is manured. In the Klin district of Moscow province manuring is done at two and a half times below the normal level.[38]

Liberals and socialists are in complete agreement in recognising the significance of these facts. But liberal half-heartedness becomes immediately apparent as soon as it comes to laying bare the *reasons* for these phenomena and proposing remedies for them. Their half-heartedness in the latter case stems from their class position, but it necessarily engenders a similar half-heartedness in the former case. A man who is not determined to root out evil by radical means must also be afraid to lay bare its deepest roots.

---

[37] Note in original: A.A. Manuilov, in P.D. Dolgorukov and P.P. Petrunkevich, *Agrarnyi Vopros*, I, p. 43.
[38] Note in original: *Ibid.*, p. 46.

The liberals see the causes of the decline in Russian agriculture in the manner in which the serfs were emancipated in 1861.[39] The peasants were then tricked out of a part of their land: they did not receive enough and what they did receive was mostly bad land. If their share then was inadequate, since then it has declined further because the population has grown considerably. On this Manuilov writes:

> In 1860 the rural population consisted of 50 million souls of both sexes, but by the end of 1900 it had reached about 86 million....At the same time the average size of a plot was reduced. According to figures produced by the Commission of Enquiry into the impoverishment of the Centre, the average plot for an emancipated serf in 1860 was equivalent to 4.8 desyatins; in 1880 the average size of a plot for a man had been reduced to 3.5, and in 1900 to 2.6 desyatins.[40]

The facts cited here are true but they are only half the truth that is necessary to understand the causes of the decline in agriculture.

When the feudal yoke was lifted the peasants elsewhere were treated in just the same way as in Russia and they were tricked out of their property. In other states this frequently led to the collapse of peasant businesses but it never led to the decline of agriculture, to a deterioration in business overall, to an increase in harvest failures. On the contrary, the pauperisation of the peasantry created the rural proletariat whose existence at that particular stage of commodity production constituted one of the preconditions of capitalist agriculture based on wage labour. This pauperisation led to a situation in which one section of the peasantry descended into the proletariat, while another section rose to prosperity at its expense. From the ruins of the shattered peasant economy there arose a new and higher mode of production. Only the bare beginnings of all this are discernible in Russia. Why is this? This is the decisive question.

There is no way in which we can accuse village communism of having made the advent of capitalist agriculture impossible. Village communism rapidly fell into a decline and it did not have the strength to prevent the emergence

---

[39] [In his 1903 debate with Ryazanov over 'remnants' and 'rudiments, this was also Plekhanov's principal contention. In this volume, see G.V. Plekhanov, '"Orthodox" Pedantry'.]

[40] Note in original: *Ibid.*, pp. 24–5.

among the villagers of landless proletarians on the one hand and profiteers on the other, or the development of the relations of capitalist exploitation of many dreadful kinds. For this reason village communism is nowadays in Russia no longer a real bulwark against the growth of capitalist methods in agriculture.

All the conditions for capitalism had already been in existence for decades, except for two and these were the two most important: the agricultural population had not hitherto had the necessary *intelligence*, the capacity, to break the bonds of tradition and to select with certainty from all the new things pressing in on it those which were most suitable and efficacious. This requires a range of knowledge and methods which it is impossible to acquire without a good school education. But the *capital* itself, the necessary money, was also not to hand. Thus the two conditions which have the greatest importance for the development of capitalist production were absent. It is precisely the latter factor, the accumulation of sufficient sums of money in individual hands, that is the most indispensable of all if higher modes of production, the application of science to production, are to develop on the basis of commodity production.

Next to the lack of *intelligence* it is the lack of *capital* that is the decisive factor in the agricultural crisis in Russia. The shortage of land explains why the peasants are pauperised, but it does not explain why the peasants nevertheless carry on in ever more miserable conditions, why a class of prosperous farmers does not emerge to replace them, a class that would buy out the impoverished smallholdings and manage them rationally with adequate resources; why also the majority of larger businesses are still managed irrationally and with inadequate resources and do not displace the ruined peasant holdings.

Why does this happen? This question must be answered.

2. The shortage of capital in Russia

The question of the reasons for Russia's economic and intellectual backwardness cannot simply be answered by reference to the fact that the modern mode of production had its origin in Western Europe and is only slowly spreading to the East. That is because this immediately raises the further question of why it is spreading so slowly to the East. At the time when Russia was coming into closer contact with Western Europe its agriculture was already at almost the same level as it is today and the Empire was full of numerous hard-working peasants. North America, on the other hand, was then a wilderness in which a few meagre tribes of savages and barbarians were submerged. Despite that it has become the greatest capitalist power in the world.

The reasons for this difference are manifold, but they all stem from the contrast between the political organisation of each country. North America was colonised by farmers and petit bourgeois who had led the struggle for democracy against the rise of absolutism in Europe and who preferred freedom in the American wilderness to subjugation to the absolute state in European civilisation. Russia was a mass of countless village communities which were concerned only with their own affairs and satisfied with democracy in their own community and which had only a very hazy conception of the power of the state and passively left it to the absolute rulers whose armies had freed them from the Mongols and were obliged to protect them against any external enemy.

In America there was unlimited political liberty which gave the individual the fullest freedom of action. The need to come to terms with, and to master, completely new conditions required of the colonists who came from Europe an enormous amount of individual spiritual and physical exertion, complete freedom of action, extreme ruthlessness and the overcoming of countless prejudices.

In Russia there has for centuries not only been no trace of political liberty but there has been police supervision of every move that the citizen makes outside the confines of his village community and only a very limited desire for freedom of movement. There has been a 'healthy arboreal slumber', a dozing in modest inherited conditions which have not changed for generations and which have allowed all sorts of prejudices to grow deeper roots and crippled all forms of energy.

While the conditions for the European population of North America bred all the spiritual characteristics that give man the upper hand in the capitalist mode of production, conditions in Russia bred precisely those characteristics that make the captives of capitalist competition succumb and that hamper capitalist development.

In addition, since Peter the Great, Russia has adhered to a policy whose results I have already referred to in my series of articles on the American worker in the chapter that deals with Russian capitalism (*Neue Zeit*, XXIV, 1, pp. 677ff.).[41] I can only reiterate here what I said there.

Peter I opened Russia to European civilisation, i.e. to capitalism, but he also led Russia into the ranks of Europe's Great Powers, involved it in their conflicts, forced it to compete with them in military armaments on sea and on land and to measure itself against them in military terms. That occurred at a time when capitalism was already very strong in Western Europe and the forces of production were well developed. Despite this, even in Western Europe military rivalry led a number of powers into bankruptcy, e.g. Spain and Portugal, and hindered economic development in many others, with the exception of England, which was preserved by its insular position from the need to exhaust itself in continental wars, and could devote all its resources to the navy through which it ruled the seas, made a rich profit from piracy, the slave trade, smuggling and the plunder of India, and thus made war into a highly profitable business, a means of accumulating capital, just as the Revolutionary Wars later did for France by allowing the victorious armies of the Republic and the Empire to plunder the richest countries of the European continent, Belgium, Holland and Italy, and to extract rich booty from other countries as well.

Russia has never waged such profitable wars. There were a number of serious obstacles to its development as a sea power but on land it borders only on poor neighbours. Had it succeeded in defeating Japan and tapping the riches of China, it would, for the first time in history since its emergence as a European Great Power, have been able to draw considerable economic benefit from a war. But the irony of history willed that it was precisely this war that put the seal upon its bankruptcy.

As Russia was, in economic terms, the weakest and most backward of the European Great Powers, tsarism has since the eighteenth century had, in order to maintain its position among them, to plunder its own poor people on an increasing scale and to render it impossible for them to accumulate any wealth. The state debt soon joined with militarism so that this plundering could be increased.

There is no country in the world, not even the richest, where the yield from taxation is enough to cover the large expenditure that militarism from time

---

[41] [See the next document in this anthology.]

to time requires and that is colossal in time of war but still considerable in periods of armament, rearmament and the like. In such instances state debts have for a long time been the tried and tested way of immediately producing the resources for these large expenditures. The interest payment on state debts is always a heavy burden on the tax-paying population but it can be a means of enriching the capitalist class of a country when it is the state's creditor. The state then expropriates the working classes, in order to enrich the capitalist class, multiplies its wealth and simultaneously increases the number of proletarians at its disposal.

But in Russia there was no capitalist class capable of covering the state's capital requirements and the constant pressure of taxation made it much more difficult for such a capitalist class to emerge on a sufficient scale. Thus money had to be borrowed mainly from *foreign* capitalists who were called upon to fill the state's coffers which had been drained by the unquenchable thirst of militarism. These capital outlays were not deployed productively: they were used only for playing soldiers and for the splendour of the court. The interest on them flowed abroad and, next to militarism, this interest soon formed an ever-widening second open wound sapping the life-blood of Russia.

The Crimean War and its consequences brought home to the Russian government after the 1860s the fact that the colossus of its power rested on feet of clay, because the display of diplomatic and military power is impossible in the long term without economic power. In modern society, however, this derives far less from agriculture than from capitalist industry, and it certainly does not derive from primitive and impoverished agriculture – that is why Russian absolutism seized on the idea of closing the gap as rapidly as possible. It sought to create large-scale capitalist industry by guaranteeing energetic state aid. But, as the state lived off agriculture, that merely meant that industry was to be supported by imposing a heavier burden on the agricultural population. Hence the peacetime policy of industrialisation became, like the wartime policy of conquest, a means of plundering and oppressing the farmers and above all the peasants.

This peacetime policy led, as the wartime policy had done, to a growing indebtedness to foreigners. The growth of domestic capital progressed too slowly for the Russian government's purposes; it wanted to achieve a rapid independence from foreign countries in those branches of industry which are most important for military armaments, which produce cannons and guns, ships and railways and which supply equipment. Since domestic capital was growing too slowly to found the necessary large-scale enterprises, the government in recent decades has tried increasingly to attract foreign capital and that capital is particularly strongly represented in the coal, iron and petroleum industries in Southern Russia. It was, however, not increased independence but dependence on abroad that resulted from this hot-house cultivation of modern large-scale industry.

The existence of credit does of course provide a powerful lever for the development of capitalist industry. When the feudal nobleman borrows money from the usurer and pays interest on his debt, his income is reduced as a consequence and he finally goes to the wall, but the industrial capitalist achieves an increased profit if he borrows money and pays interest on it because he utilises this money productively, not like the nobleman in unproductive consumption, so that, in addition to the interest on the capital, it brings him a profit. If he borrows money at 4% and invests it so that it brings him 10%, then he is gaining 6%. In this form, as finance capital, foreign capital can easily accelerate the emergence of a capitalist class in economically backward countries.

But, to acquire finance capital, you need *credit*, you must already have a going concern, and on that score Russia had nothing to offer. Foreign capital certainly flowed in thousands of millions into Russia to develop its industry but only a minute percentage of this was lent to *Russian* entrepreneurs as capital to establish and extend large-scale industrial plants. On the contrary these plants were mostly established directly by foreign capitalists and remained in their hands so that not just the interest on the capital but the whole profit accrued to them and only the wages remained in Russia. This method of attracting foreign capital resulted only in the development of a strong proletariat, but not of a strong capitalist class, inside Russia. It encouraged, rather than hindered, the impoverishment of Russia.

This tendency, however, emerged at its clearest and most decisive in agriculture which is the one great branch of earnings that is the last and least to partake of the effects of capitalist modes of production that enhance the productivity of labour and which, more than any other, requires an intelligent population if it is to take advantage of modern expedients and methods of production. Capitalism in Russia brought the peasants not improved schools, not the money to obtain artificial fertiliser or improved tools and machinery, but only increased exploitation. Whereas in Western Europe the increased exploitation of the peasant by both state and capital went hand in hand with a growth in the productivity of agricultural labour, in Russia on the contrary the increased exploitation of the peasant, which arose from the increasing competition between Russia and the developed capitalist nations, brought with it a steady decline in the productivity of agriculture. The number of harvest failures grows but in every famine the cattle are of course slaughtered before people succumb to hunger. Thus every famine leaves a reduction in the cattle stock which in turn leads to a shortage of fertiliser, a less efficient order of cultivation, and thus to a further deterioration in agriculture and new and greater harvest failures. But the whole nation descends into misery with the peasant, for with him the domestic market for Russian industry goes under and that is the only market it supplies because it is not competitive on the world market; but with the peasant's demise the state too comes face to face with its own bankruptcy despite that enormous natural wealth that the stockbrokers of Western Europe enthuse over when they are willing to lay more thousands of millions at the feet of the bloody tsar. Yes, if only these millions were used to extract this wealth and not to oppress and butcher those who through their labours are alone capable of turning that natural wealth into items of value that can be exchanged on the world market for money!

The decay of agriculture is, after the rise of the industrial proletariat, the principal cause of the present Russian revolution. It has brought the state to the verge of financial bankruptcy and created conditions that are unsatisfactory, even intolerable, to all classes, conditions that they cannot bear and from which they must try and escape, once they have started to move.

3. The solution to the agrarian question

The most obvious way to help the peasant is to increase his share of the land. Almost all parties are agreed on that. But is it enough? What use is more land to the peasant when he does not even have enough livestock or tools to work his present share properly? It might provide him with temporary relief but the old misery will soon prevail again. If the peasant is to be helped on a longer-term basis then provision must be made for him to go over to more intensive and more rational methods of cultivation. He must have livestock, tools and fertiliser at his disposal, a first-rate system of elementary education must be established: in short, the peasant must be given, as quickly and as fully as possible, what for decades has been withheld or taken away from him in the wake of the progressive mortgaging of the state, its continuing increase in taxation and its growing inability and unwillingness to carry out any kind of cultural task.

Only a régime that is capable of doing this can put Russia's peasant agriculture, and with it the whole state, back on a sound economic footing and thus put an end to the revolution.

Is absolutism capable of doing that? If it were then it could still master the revolution. If the tsar had the intelligence and the strength to become a peasant emperor like Napoleon I he would be able to secure his absolutist régime once more. In the main the peasant has no great interest in the political liberty of the nation. Normally his interest revolves around the affairs of the village. If he saw that the tsar was looking after his economic requirements he would rally round him once again.

But fortunately that is impossible. Even the first Napoleon was only in a position to betray France's political liberty with the help of the peasants and the army recruited from among them because he was *the heir to the revolution* and because the revolution had already met the peasants' demands and he simply appeared as the protector of the gains they had made in and through the revolution.

Even the most energetic and far-sighted monarch cannot defeat a political revolution by himself bringing about its economic goal. To do this he would have to be not only more far-sighted but also more powerful than the entire ruling class in whose midst he lives and at whose expense the economic goal of the revolution can alone be achieved. Even if it were possible for a single individual to think and feel in what is clearly and distinctly a completely opposite manner from that of the entourage that he has known since childhood, there is no single individual, however much feared, who is capable of defying his whole entourage single-handed. The Russian tsar has less power to do this than anyone else. As soon as he showed the slightest inclination to come to terms with the revolution the faithful servants of absolutism would do away with him.

But from Nicholas II we cannot even expect any attempt ever to break significantly with his entourage over any question.

Hence his government energetically rejects anything that could relieve the miserable lot of the peasants even to a limited degree. It offers them nothing but empty promises, swindling and miserable botching. But the time is past when the peasant would allow himself to be deceived by all this. The revolution has already achieved so much in the country that the peasant wants action and he judges each party by its actions. But what has he come to expect from the actions of the government, which he equates with the tsar? Taxes are raised but the provinces where the failure of the harvest has caused famine are offered no support. Schools and hospitals close for lack of resources, the railways deteriorate because their equipment is not replaced, while the tsar needs more money than ever for the soldiers he uses to wage war against his own people. Since the Napoleonic invasion the Russian peasant has not seen an enemy soldier in his country and he has felt secure against foreign enemies thanks to the power of the tsar. Now it is the soldiers of the tsar himself who lay waste the countryside as the Mongols did before them. Thus all the promises that have been made to the peasant and that have from time to time filled him with fresh hopes for final salvation prove to be a miserable deception and this discovery makes his position seem doubly infuriating and his concealed anger twice as strong. The Duma, which was presented to him as a saviour in his time of need, has been dissolved and the right to vote for the second Duma, which is currently being elected, has been taken from under his nose. In view of all this it is no wonder that the peasant's former limitless respect for the tsar has turned into an equally limitless hatred for the tsar.

But do the liberals have a chance to win the peasant over in the long term?

They are certainly offering him what he wants more than anything else: more land. At least, many of them are demanding the expropriation of the large estates and their redistribution among the peasants. But at what price? Property should be treated with consideration in as far as this is possible and that means that the landowners should be fully compensated. But who should compensate them? Who else but the peasant, either directly if he pays interest on the purchase price of the land ceded to him, or indirectly if the *state* compensates the landowner. But then the interest on the purchase price falls once more on the proletarians and the peasants indirectly in the form of new taxes. What would the peasants have gained by increasing their share of the land? Nothing at all, because the increased net proceeds would return in the shape of interest or taxation to the former owners of the large estates. Often not even external appearances would change because many peasants already work parts of the large estates on leasehold to increase their own share. If they were to own the leasehold and, instead of interest on the lease, they had to pay a new tax, how would they be better off?

It is only through the *confiscation* of the large estates that the peasant's share of the land can be significantly increased without new burdens being imposed upon him. The expropriation of a single stratum of the ruling class without compensation is of course a harsh measure. But there is no choice. The pauperisation of the peasantry has gone so far that it is no longer possible to require it to pay compensation. If the liberal landowners had possessed the energy and selflessness to accomplish in good time both the political forms and the policy that would have facilitated an amicable discussion with the peasantry while it was still solvent, they could have preserved their property interest in one form or another. Now it is too late. Moreover they have little to complain about. Their forefathers understood perfectly how to cheat the peasants most productively when serfdom was abolished: ever since then they have taken advantage of their desperate position for the worst kind of profiteering and they have never shown the peasantry the least consideration or respect.

The confiscation of the large estates is unavoidable if the peasant is to be helped. But the liberals are striving resolutely against it. It is only the socialist parties that do not recoil in fear.

But an increase in the peasant's share of the land is still a long way from solving the Russian agrarian question. We have seen that the peasant is not just short of land, but of know-how and money as well. The decay in Russian agriculture will not be arrested in the slightest because the land and soil are divided somewhat differently. On the contrary. If the large estates, where agriculture is frequently conducted on a much more rational basis, are broken up and replaced by ignorant peasants with no resources, the decline of Russian agriculture will only be accelerated if energetic measures are not taken at the same time to increase the peasants' intelligence and their working capital.

That is, however, impossible without a thorough-going upheaval in the whole of the present political system that has been bringing about the present misery at an increasing rate for 200 years. The more deeply this misery, which absolutism is still visibly increasing even now, is rooted, the more energetic the attacks on existing institutions and property relations that will be required if we are to bring this misery under any kind of control.

Without the dissolution of the standing army and the cancellation of naval armaments, without the confiscation of all the property of the imperial family and the monasteries, without the bankruptcy of the state and without the sequestration of the large monopolies still in private hands – railways, oil wells, mines, iron works – it will not be possible to raise the enormous sums that Russian agriculture requires if it is to be snatched from its terrible decay.

But it is clear that the liberals recoil before such gigantic tasks, such decisive upheavals in current property relations. Basically all they want is to carry on with present policy without touching the foundations of Russia's exploitation by foreign capital. They adhere firmly to the standing army, which alone, in their eyes, can secure order and save their property, and they want to acquire new resources for Russia through new loans, which is impossible if the interest on the old ones is not paid on time.

The interest on the national debt and Russian militarism are now costing *two thousand million marks*. The liberals want to go on squeezing this colossal sum from the Russian people year in and year out and yet they imagine that they will be able at the same time to perform all the great cultural tasks that tsarism has neglected and has *had* to neglect in order to pay for militarism and for the national debt. They believe that the establishment of a Duma is enough to conjure up thousands of millions from the land.

They often recall the great French Revolution. Not always correctly. The relations in present-day Russia are in many ways quite different from those of France in 1789. But the difference does not lie in the fact that Russian conditions require less decisive measures than the French. On the contrary. France was not indebted to foreign countries, it was not suffering from the same kind of shortage of capital, its education, agriculture and industry were not as backward as those of Russia when compared with the rest of Europe. Nonetheless even the National Assembly could not save France from national bankruptcy and confiscations. And, if France was able to maintain its militarism, it could only do this because of its victorious revolutionary wars which put it in a position where it could plunder half Europe and thus pay for the costs of the wars. The Russian revolution has no prospect of meeting its financial requirements in this manner. It must put an end to the standing army if it is to satisfy the Russian peasant.

Liberalism is just as incapable of doing this as is tsarism. It may recover again temporarily but it must soon fade away. It will do this all the more rapidly since it is deprived of energetic democratic elements because the only class of any significance upon which it can rely is that of the large landowners, a class whose liberalism is naturally diluted as the agrarian question comes increasingly to the fore.

4. Liberalism and Social Democracy

Russia's liberalism is of a different order from that of Western Europe and for that reason alone is it quite erroneous to portray the great French Revolution simply as the model for the present Russian one.

The leading class in the revolutionary movements of Western Europe was the *petty bourgeoisie* and, above all, that of the large cities. Because of its hitherto frequently mentioned dual position as the representative of both property and labour it became the link between the proletariat and the capitalist class, and it joined them both for common struggle in bourgeois democracy which drew its victorious strength from it. The petty bourgeois saw himself as a budding capitalist and to that extent advocated the interests of rising capital. But he himself created the model for the proletarian, who usually originated from petty-bourgeois circles, had as yet no independent class consciousness and asked for no more than the freedom and the opportunity to be elevated to the petty bourgeoisie.

In addition the petty bourgeoisie in the towns was the most numerous, most intelligent and economically most important of the classes constituting the popular mass. But the towns themselves had become the seats of the ruling powers since the Middle Ages. The towns ruled the open country and exploited it and the petty bourgeoisie played a large part in this rule and exploitation: they succeeded in oppressing the rural craftsmen and yet at the same time asserting their position as a powerful force against the nobility and the aristocracy of the towns.

Nothing like this occurred in Russia. The towns there, weak, few in number and mostly very recent in their development, have never achieved the powerful position they achieved in Western Europe and the popular mass has never known how to distinguish itself from, and raise itself above, the rural population, as it had done there.

The mass of urban craftsmen consisted of peasants and numerous forms of handicraft were pursued more in the country than in the town. Serfdom and oppression, political helplessness and apathy were the same there as here.

It was only after the abolition of serfdom that the seeds of political interest began to germinate among the urban masses, but this occurred in the last decades of the nineteenth century at the time when in Western Europe itself the revolutionary leading role of the petty bourgeoisie had finally been played out. On the one hand the proletariat had become independent and had been powerfully strengthened while on the other hand an enormous gulf had opened up between the petty bourgeoisie and capital. The petty bourgeois no longer sees the capitalists as the class he aspires to be elevated to, but as the class that is oppressing and ruining him. But he sees wage-labourers as the element whose demands are accelerating this process. He no longer constitutes the leader of democracy who joins the capitalist and worker in a common political struggle but the unprincipled malcontent who, disappointed in democracy, rages simultaneously against both proletarian and capitalist and falls into the clutches of every reactionary swindler who promises him something attractive.

In this way the petty bourgeoisie of Western Europe is becoming steadily more reactionary and unreliable in spite of its revolutionary traditions. Russia's petty bourgeoisie enters the political movement without any similar tradition and under the complete influence of the economic situation that is also making itself felt in Eastern Europe. It is, therefore, much more inclined than its Western-European class comrades to anti-Semitism and reaction, to weak-kneed vacillation that can be bought off by all comers, to the role that the *Lumpenproletariat*[42] played in the Western European revolution: it is

---

[42] The *Lumpenproletariat* was, in Marx's account, that section of the class of non-owners of the means of production which, through deficiencies of organisation, articulation and consciousness fell easy prey to the bribery and demagogy of dictators like Louis Bonaparte. In unusually graphic vein Marx described this dangerous, if colourful, group thus:

> Alongside decayed roués with dubious means of subsistence and of dubious origin, alongside ruined and adventurous offshoots of the bourgeoisie, were vagabonds, discharged soldiers, discharged jailbirds, escaped galley slaves, rogues, mountebanks, *lazzaroni*, pick-pockets, tricksters, gamblers, *maquereaus* [pimps], brothel keepers, porters, *literati*, organ-grinders, rag-pickers, knife grinders, tinkers, beggars – in short, the whole indefinite, disintegrated mass, thrown hither and thither, which the French term *la bohème*. (MECW, 11, p. 149).

that *Lumpenproletariat* to which in spirit it becomes more and more closely related and with which, even in Russia, it willingly collaborates. Through the progress of the revolution it may eventually become increasingly involved in an opposition movement but it will not constitute a secure support for the revolutionary parties.

Thus, Russia lacks the firm backbone of a bourgeois democracy and it lacks the class that, through its common economic interest, might forge bourgeoisie and proletariat together in the democratic party in the common struggle for political liberty.

Even before the revolutionary struggle began, the capitalist class and the proletariat in Russia stood in direct opposition to one another. Both had learned from the West. The proletariat came straight on to the political arena, not as part of a purely democratic party, but as Social Democracy, and the capitalist class has allowed itself to be intimidated by the slightest stirring on the part of the proletariat: its principal concern is for a strong government.

The nucleus of the liberal party in Russia was formed by the large-scale landowners, as distinct from the latifundia owners, i.e. precisely that class against which liberalism in Western Europe directed its principal efforts. But in Russia, in contrast to Western Europe, absolutism has recently sacrificed agriculture to capital. The same process that had been completed in Western Europe at the end of the Middle Ages and in the beginnings of absolutism, the exploitation of the country by the town, was practised increasingly by Russia's absolutist régime in the nineteenth century, and it manifestly drove the landed gentry into the opposition. This oppositional stance was made easier for the gentry because it came into direct conflict with the proletariat, the other opposition class, less frequently than did industrial capital in the towns. As long as the peasantry remained calm, the Russian landowner could afford the luxury of liberalism, just as the English Tories and some Prussian Junkers had permitted themselves the aura of friendliness towards their work force at the beginning of industrialisation.

And it remained calm for a long time. Agriculture could visibly decay, the peasant sink into misery, famine after famine decimate his ranks and ruin his business – and he remained devoted to God and the tsar. Certainly, he rose in revolt from time to time but the cause of these disturbances was taken to be particular grievances rather than the entire ruling system, which was not recognised as the source of these grievances.

But the transformation of economic relations was of course gradually preparing a change in the peasant's outlook and his sentiments in the second half of the nineteenth century. The village was linked to world trade which brought its products on to the world market. The isolation of the village came increasingly to an end. General conscription took its sons to the big city where they were exposed to new impressions and learned new demands. In the end large numbers of peasants or peasant children who had lost their land turned to the factory and the mine and thus joined the proletarian class struggle and they conveyed their impressions of it to their comrades left behind in the villages back home.

This is how the foundations on which Russian absolutism rested were gradually undermined, but it needed a powerful blow for these foundations to collapse completely. That happened as a result of the war in Manchuria and the ensuing rebellion of the urban proletariat. The events which thirty years before would have passed the Russian peasant by imperceptibly are now provoking a lively response from him. He has woken up and realised that the hour has come at last to put an end to his misery. It no longer oppresses him: it provokes him. All of a sudden, he sees himself in a completely new light: he regards the government, to whose control he has hitherto trustingly submitted, as the enemy that must be overthrown. He will not allow others to think for him again, he must think for himself, must use all his wits, all his energy, all his ruthlessness and abandon all his prejudices if he is to hold his own in the whirlpool that he has been sucked into. What caused the Anglo-Saxon peasant and petty bourgeois from the seventeenth to the nineteenth centuries to migrate will bring for the Russian peasant at the beginning of the twentieth century, more rapidly and more violently, revolution and the transformation of the easy-going, sleepy and unthinking creature of habit into an energetic, restless and inexhaustible warrior for the new and the better.

This amazing transformation is developing a firm basis for the new Russian agriculture that will arise from the rubble of the old but it also furnishes the most secure guarantee for the ultimate triumph of the revolution.

In the meantime, the more revolutionary the peasant becomes, the more reactionary is the large landowner. The more that liberalism loses in him its previous supporter, the more unstable the liberal parties become and the more the liberal professor and lawyers of the towns swing to the right so that they will not completely lose touch with their previous support.

This process might lead temporarily to a strengthening of reaction but it cannot suppress the revolution in the long term. It only accelerates the bankruptcy of liberalism. It must drive the peasants increasingly into the arms of those parties that protect their interests energetically and ruthlessly and that do not permit themselves to be intimidated by liberal doubts: the socialist parties. The longer the revolution lasts, the more this process must continue to increase the influence of the socialist parties in the country as well. It can ultimately lead to a situation in which Social Democracy becomes the representative of the masses of the population and thus the victorious party.

5. The proletariat and its ally in the revolution

It is perhaps appropriate here, as a conclusion to this study, for me to express my view on an inquiry that my friend Plekhanov has conducted among a number of non-Russian comrades on the character of the Russian revolution and the tactics that the Russian socialists should pursue. That is, I should like to make only a few observations on these questions and not answer them precisely. While I believe that my almost three decades of intimate contact with prominent leaders of the Russian revolutionary movement puts me in a position to provide my *German* comrades with some information on this movement, I also feel like a *novice* vis-à-vis my *Russian* comrades when it comes to Russian affairs. But it is, of course, urgently necessary for us Western-European socialists to form a definite view of the Russian revolution for it is not a local, but an international, event, and the way we assess it will exert a profound influence on the way we view the immediate tactical tasks of our own party. But I also have no reason to hold my own view back when Russian comrades ask me for it.

The questionnaire contains the following three questions:

1. What does the general character of the Russian revolution appear to be? Are we facing a bourgeois or a socialist revolution?
2. In view of the desperate attempts by the Russian government to suppress the revolutionary movement what should be the attitude of the Social Democratic Party towards the bourgeois democratic parties, which are struggling in their own way for political liberty?

3. What tactic should the Social Democratic Party pursue in the Duma elections in order to utilise the strength of the bourgeois opposition parties in the struggle against our *ancien régime* without violating the Amsterdam Resolution?

Neither part of the first of these questions seems to me to be easy to answer. The age of *bourgeois* revolutions, i.e. of revolutions in which the bourgeoisie was the driving force, is over in Russia as well. There too the proletariat is no longer an appendage and tool of the bourgeoisie, as it was in bourgeois revolutions, but an independent class with independent revolutionary aims. But wherever the proletariat emerges in this way the bourgeoisie ceases to be a revolutionary class. The Russian bourgeoisie, insofar as it is liberal and has an independent class policy at all, certainly hates absolutism but it hates revolution even more, and it hates absolutism because it sees it as the fundamental cause of revolution; and insofar as it asks for political liberty, it does so above all because it believes that it is the only way to bring an end to the revolution.

The bourgeoisie therefore does not constitute one of the driving forces of the present revolutionary movement in Russia and to this extent we cannot call it a bourgeois one.

But we should not use this as a reason to call it a socialist one without further ado. There is no way in which it can bring the proletariat alone to political dominance, to dictatorship. Russia's proletariat is too weak and backward for that. In any case it is very possible that in the course of the revolution victory will fall to the Social Democratic Party and social democracy does very well to hold out this prospect of victory to its supporters because you cannot struggle successfully if you have renounced victory in advance. But it will not be possible for social democracy to achieve victory through the proletariat alone without the help of another class and as a victorious party it will not be able to implement any more of its programme than the interests of the class that supports the proletariat allow.

But which class should the Russian proletariat rely on in its revolutionary struggle? If you take only a superficial look at politics you may come to the view that all the classes and parties that are striving for political liberty will just have to work together to achieve it and their differences should only be settled after political liberty has been won.

But every political struggle is basically a class struggle and thus also an economic struggle. Political interests are a result of economic interests; it is to protect these, and not to realise abstract political ideas, that the masses are in revolt. Anyone who wishes to inspire the masses to the political struggle must show them how closely linked it is to their economic interests. These must never be allowed to fade into the background if the struggle for political liberty is not to be blocked. The alliance between the proletariat and other classes in the revolutionary struggle must rest above all else on a *common economic interest*, if it is to be both lasting and victorious. The tactics of Russian social democracy must also be based on that kind of common interest.

A substantial common interest for the whole period of the revolutionary struggle exists, however, only between the proletariat and the peasantry. It must furnish the basis of the whole revolutionary tactic of Russian social democracy. Collaboration with liberalism should only be considered when and where co-operation with the peasantry will not thereby be disrupted.

It is on the common interest between the industrial proletariat and the peasantry that the revolutionary strength of Russian social democracy is founded, as is the possibility of its victory and, at the same time, the limits to the possibility of its exploitation.

Without the peasants we cannot win in the near future in Russia. We must not, however, anticipate that the peasants will become socialists. Socialism can only be constructed on the basis of big business – it is too incompatible with the conditions of small businesses for it to be able to emerge and assert itself in the midst of a predominantly peasant population. It might perhaps be possible, should it come to power in large-scale industry and agricultural big business and, through its example, convince the poorer peasants and incite them to imitation, but it cannot do without them. And in Russia, more than elsewhere, the intellectual and material conditions for it are lacking. The communism of the Russian village lies in ruins and in no way signifies community of production. It is also impossible to convert modern commodity production on the basis of the village community into a higher mode of production. For this you need at least the framework of the large state, but Russian agricultural producers are in no way capable of production on a national basis.

The present revolution can only lead to the creation in the countryside of a strong peasantry on the basis of private ownership of land and to the opening up of the same gulf between the proletariat and the landowning part of the rural population that already exists in Western Europe. It therefore seems unthinkable that the present revolution in Russia is already leading to the introduction of a socialist mode of production, even if it should bring social democracy to power temporarily.

Clearly, however, we may experience some surprises. We do not know how much longer the Russian revolution will last and the forms that it has now adopted suggest that it has no desire to come to an early end. We also do not know what influence it will exert on Western Europe and how it will enrich the proletarian movement there. Finally, we do not yet have any idea how the resulting successes of the Western European proletariat will react on the Russians. We should do well to remember that we are approaching completely new situations and problems for which no earlier model is appropriate.

We should most probably be fair to the Russian revolution and the tasks that it sets us if we viewed it as neither a bourgeois revolution in the traditional sense nor a socialist one but as a quite unique process which is taking place on the borderline between bourgeois and socialist society, which requires the dissolution of the one while preparing the creation of the other and which in any case brings all those who live in capitalist civilisation a significant step forward in their development.

Chapter Twenty-Three

'The American Worker' (February 1906)
Karl Kautsky

Karl Kautsky's series of articles on the Russian and American workers[1] was originally written as a reply to the bourgeois sociologist Werner Sombart's famous study *Why Is There No Socialism in the United States?* As a young man, Werner Sombart (1863–1941) was a correspondent of Engels and something of a Marxist scholar.[2] But, already by the time of Engels's death (1895), Sombart began to turn against Marxism and its organisational standard-bearer in Germany, the Social-Democratic Party, resulting in a series of furious polemics with some its most prominent theoreticians, notably Franz Mehring and especially Rosa Luxemburg.[3] In her classic study *The Mass Strike, the Political Party and the Trade Unions*, written against the new opportunism spearheaded by the

---

[1] Kautsky 1906, pp. 676–83, 717–27, 740–52 and 773–87.

[2] In a supplement to Volume III of Marx's *Capital*, Engels wrote:
In Braun's *Archiv fur soziale Gesetzgebung*, Vol. VII, No. 4, Werner Sombart gives an outline of the Marxian system which, taken all in all, is excellent. It is the first time that a German university professor succeeds on the whole in seeing in Marx's writings what Marx really says, stating that the criticism of the Marxian system cannot consist of a refutation – 'let the political careerist deal with that' – but merely in a further development. (Marx 1981, p. 1031). See also Krause 1961, pp. 636–40.

[3] Mehring 1895, pp. 26–32, Mehring 1896, pp. 135–43, Mehring 1902, pp. 222–8, Mehring 1904, pp. 628–33, Mehring 1905c. Luxemburg 1903, pp. 5–10; reprinted in *Gesammelte Werke* (Berlin: Dietz, 1972), Band 1, Nr. 2, pp. 382–90, Luxemburg 1899–1900, pp. 740–7 and 773–82; reprinted in Ibid., Band 1, Nr. 1, pp. 767–90.

Social-Democratic trade-union apparatus (the General Commission of the Free Trade Unions of Germany), Luxemburg summarised some of the main lessons of the 1905 Russian Revolution and made the following reference to Sombart:

> From the concealment of the objective limits drawn by the bourgeois social order to the trade-union struggle, there arises a hostility to every theoretical criticism which refers to these limits in connection with the ultimate aims of the labor movement. Fulsome flattery and boundless optimism are considered to be the duty of every 'friend of the trade-union movement.' But as the social democratic standpoint consists precisely in fighting against uncritical parliamentary optimism, a front is at last made against the social democratic theory: men grope for a 'new trade-union theory,' that is, a theory which would open an illimitable vista of economic progress to the trade-union struggle within the capitalist system, in opposition to the social democratic doctrine. Such a theory has indeed existed for some time – the theory of Professor Sombart which was promulgated with the express intention of driving a wedge between the trade-unions and the social democracy in Germany, and of enticing the trade-unions over to the bourgeois position.[4]

In his path-breaking book on the Jewish question, Karl Kautsky denounced and refuted one of the most unpleasant aspects of Sombart's nationalism – his anti-Semitism – which led him to become a fellow traveller of the Nazis during the last decade of his life (he died in 1941).[5] Abram Leon also dedicated a whole section of his work on the Jewish question to a refutation of Sombart's thesis, advanced in his book *The Jews and Modern Capitalism*, to the effect that the Jews were 'the founders of modern capitalism'.[6] But, for all their faults,

---

[4] Luxemburg 1896, Chapter VIII: Need for United Action of Trade Unions and Social Democracy, pp. 79–92.

[5] Sombart's 1912 book *The Future of the Jews* already includes gems such as this: 'Who would want to miss the racy Judiths and Miriams? To be sure, they must be racy and ready to remain so. We cannot tolerate this black-blond mix-up.' Sombart, *Die Zukunft der Juden*, Leipzig, 1912, p. 72. Quoted in Kautsky 1921a, Chapter IV: Differences and Oppositions between the Races of Man, p. 80. Sombart would be glad to know that his opposition to the 'black–blond mix–up' is staunchly supported by a certain political tendency in modern Jewry.

[6] Abram Leon 1970, Chapter 4, Section A: The Jews in Western Europe after the Renaissance: The Thesis of Sombart, pp. 175–82.

Sombart's works, because of their wealth of historical data and the insights he gained from his acquaintance with Marx's work, always remained a subject of deep interest for Marxist theoreticians. That is especially true in the case of his massive *magnum opus, Der moderne Kapitalismus*. When the first part appeared in 1902 Rudolf Hilferding reviewed it at length,[7] and 37 years later Leon Trotsky still considered it important enough to criticise it in one of his last books.[8]

The essay translated here was not Kautsky's first work on America. His earlier writings on American socialism include a critical review of Edward Bellamy's famous utopian novel *Looking Backward, 2000–1887*. Kautsky considered Bellamy's novel worthless as a work of art. The plot was absurd, the characters foolish, and the author had no understanding whatsoever of the modern labour movement: the commonwealth of the future was full of housewives, preachers and rich people no longer anxious about losing their fortune. But the book was nevertheless significant because

> Socialism has until now been an exotic growth in America; it was considered a German product. And in fact the socialist movement, if not composed exclusively of Germans, was an outgrowth of German socialism. The task of creating, on the foundation of international scientific socialism, a truly American labour party, with its own literature, program and tactics, is just now beginning to be undertaken. In view of this situation, Bellamy's book has a great symptomatic significance. It shows the power of the American labour movement; the fact is that it forces even bourgeois circles to deal with social problems that are neither theoretically nor practically under the influence of European socialism.[9]

Kautsky's other writings on the United States include a defence of Friedrich Sorge – whose history of the American labour movement was then being serialised by *Die Neue Zeit*[10] – against the sectarian attacks of Daniel De Leon's Socialist Labor Party,[11] and a review of Algie Martin Simons's book *The American Farmer*, published in 1902.[12] Kautsky also wrote at least one other

---

[7] Hilferding 1903, pp. 446–53. Reprinted in Vom Brocke (ed.) 1987, pp. 147–60.
[8] L. Trotsky 1939, pp. 24–51.
[9] Kautsky 1889a, pp. 268–76.
[10] For an English version see Sorge 1977, and Sorge 1987.
[11] Kautsky 1895, pp. 183–5.
[12] Simons 1902. Kautsky 1902a, pp. 148–60.

major item on the United States, namely, his article on the president of the American Federation of Labor, Samuel Gompers, on the occasion of the latter's visit to Germany, a critical edition of which was published by the journal *Historical Materialism*.[13] That article was part of a long series of polemics with the German Social-Democratic union bureaucracy.

Leon Trotsky mentions Kautsky's 'The American Worker' in the 1922 introduction to his book *1905*, describing it as one of the works by Kautsky that constituted 'a merciless rejection of Menshevism and a complete theoretical vindication of the subsequent political tactics of the Bolsheviks' – that is to say, of the theory of permanent revolution as adopted *de facto* by Lenin in his 1917 April Theses.[14] Kautsky's work was immediately translated into Russian and printed in *seven* separate editions, usually under the title *The American and Russian Worker*, one of them with a preface by the future Bolshevik People's Commissar of Education, Anatoly Lunacharsky.[15]

In the fourth chapter of his book *Results and Prospects*, summing up the lessons of the 1905 Revolution, Trotsky included extensive references to 'The American Worker', remarking that 'Kautsky, in his recent book on the American proletariat, points out that there is no direct relation between the political power of the proletariat and the bourgeoisie, on the one hand, and the level of capitalist development on the other', and that 'Germany, to a certain extent, may learn its future from Russia'. Trotsky recommended Kautsky's study 'to our Russian Marxists, who replace independent analysis of social relations by deductions from texts, selected to serve every occasion in life. Nobody compromises Marxism so much as these self-styled Marxists.' He added that 'according to Kautsky, Russia stands on an economically low level of capitalist development, [but] politically it has an insignificant capitalist bourgeoisie and a powerful revolutionary proletariat', and he concluded that under these conditions 'the Russian "man" will take power sooner than his "master"'.[16]

---

[13] Karl Kautsky 1909a. See also Kautsky 1910a, pp. 132–7.

[14] L. Trotsky 1971a, p. VIII.

[15] Kautsky 1906m; Kautsky 1906k; Kautsky 1906g; Kautsky 1906j; Kautsky 1906h; Kautsky 1906i; Kautsky 1907b, See Donald 1993, pp. 296, 300, 301.

[16] L. Trotsky 1969, Chapter IV: 'Revolution and the Proletariat', note 2, pp. 65–6. Although *The American Worker* was never cited explicitly as a source, it seems that Lenin's analysis of the 'American path of bourgeois development' (on which he based the entire strategic perspective of the Bolshevik program from the aftermath

The *Proceedings of the Founding Convention of the Industrial Workers of the World* (27 June to 8 July, 1905),[17] clearly showed the influence of the first Russian revolution on American events. To quote one of the brightest stars in this galaxy of revolutionary leaders, the famous African-American anarchist-communist Lucy E. Parsons:

> You men and women should be imbued with the spirit that is now displayed in far-off Russia and far-off Siberia where we thought the spark of manhood and womanhood had been crushed out of them. Let us take [an] example from them. We see the capitalist class fortifying themselves to-day behind their Citizens' Associations and Employers' Associations in order that they may crush the American labor movement. Let us cast our eyes over to far-off Russia and take heart and courage from those who are fighting the battle there, and from the further fact shown in the dispatches that appear this morning in the news that carries the greatest terror to the capitalist class throughout all the world – the emblem that has been the terror of all tyrants through all the ages…the red flag has been raised.[18]

A resolution was adopted expressing solidarity with the 'mighty struggle of the laboring class of far-off Russia' whose outcome 'is of the utmost consequence to the members of the working class of all countries in their struggle for their emancipation'.[19] In his closing speech at the ratification meeting, delivered on 8 July 1905, Bill Haywood, General Secretary of the Western Federation of Miners and a future leader of early American Communism, who presided at the Founding Convention of the IWW, called on the American workers to become 'organized industrially as the workers in Russia are organized [*Applause.*] – organized into an organization that takes in every man, woman and child working in an industry'. Haywood hoped to see the new movement 'grow throughout this country until it takes in a great majority of the working

---

of the 1905 revolution up until the 1917 April Theses) was inspired by Kautsky's study, especially section 'V. Capitalism in the United States'. *The American Worker* was published in February 1906, while Lenin's analysis appears in his books Lenin 1907e and Lenin 1915. For a detailed analysis of Lenin's theory of the American path of capitalist development, see Gaido 2006, pp. 28–48.

[17] IWW 1905.
[18] IWW 1905, Third Day, Afternoon Session (Thursday, June 29).
[19] IWW 1905, Fifth Day's Session.

people, and that those working people will rise in revolt against the capitalist system as the working class in Russia are doing today'.[20]

The main shortcoming of 'The American Worker', besides its almost total lack of analysis of the significance of the black question for the American labour movement (blacks constituted more than 10 per cent of the American population in 1910 – almost 10 million out of 92 million), is the scant attention Kautsky paid to the issue of imperialism and its impact on the labour movement, especially by furthering the development of a labour aristocracy and trade-union bureaucracy in the imperialist countries. That was due to the fact that, although the term *imperialism* began to be used in socialist circles to designate the latest stage of capitalist development as far back as 1900, the European Marxist theoreticians only began to deal with the issue in depth at the time of the Stuttgart Congress of the Second International, which took place on 6–24 August 1907, i.e., a year and a half after the publication of Kautsky's article.[21] As a contribution to the debate on imperialism, Parvus published his work *The Colonial Policy and the Collapse of Capitalism*,[22] and, immediately after the Congress, Kautsky issued his own brochure on socialism and colonialism, which Bebel called 'his best work'.[23]

For an overview of the history of American socialism, see Morris Hillquit's *History of Socialism in the United States*.[24] Kautsky probably consulted the first edition of Hillquit's work for the study translated here. For a description and critical evaluation of the two major socialist organisations of the United States at that time – the Socialist Party of Eugene Debs and the International Workers of the World – see the essays by the historic leader of American Trotskyism, James P. Cannon.[25] For an extensive analysis of Kautsky's study, including Kautsky's own subsequent political evolution, which led him ultimately to

---

[20] IWW 1905, Appendix, Part I: Speeches at Ratification Meeting.

[21] See Lenin 1907d.

[22] Parvus 1907a. See the laudatory review of this book by Hilferding 1907, pp. 687–8.

[23] Kautsky 1975.

[24] The German version of Hillquit's *History of Socialism in the United States* was the main source on the history of American socialism for European continental Marxists: *Geschichte des Sozialismus in den Vereinigten Staaten*, autorisierte Übersetzung von Karl Müller-Weinberg (Stuttgart: J.H.W. Dietz, 1906).

[25] Cannon 1955b. Also Cannon 1955a.

turn against his former comrades in the left to become the ideologist of the SPD 'centre' faction, see the November 2003 issue of the journal *Historical Materialism*.[26]

In conceptual terms, the major significance of Kautsky's 'American Worker' was that it effectively concluded the debate over *permanent revolution* for the period of the first Russian revolution. Since Kautsky had initiated this debate, it is fitting that he should also be the one to summarise its outcome. In 1902, Kautsky had first predicted in 'The Slavs and Revolution' that the Slavs might be 'the tempest that will break the ice of reaction and irresistibly bring a new, blessed springtime for the peoples'. Impressed by the heroism of the Narodnik tradition, and convinced that the emerging Russian proletariat would rise against a regime that plundered the country in the service of foreign capital, Kautsky thought the centre of revolutionary activity was moving from Western to Eastern Europe and that the coming storms in Russia would reinvigorate Social Democracy in Germany.

In his critique of the draft *Iskra* programme, David Ryazanov was the first to work out the implications of Kautsky's early thinking and to formulate a preliminary theory of *permanent revolution*. If 'backward' Russia was to initiate the revolutionary reawakening of Europe, it was imperative to understand how a 'peasant' country, which of all the major capitalist powers was the least developed, could possibly leap from the smothering institutions of semi-feudalism into a revolution that would clear the path to a socialist future. Ryazanov answered with the audacious argument that Russia was an exception to 'the pattern'. In 'The Draft Programme of "Iskra" and the Tasks of Russian Social Democrats', Ryazanov systematically explored the 'peculiarities' of Russian history, much like Trotsky did almost three decades later in his *History of the Russian Revolution* (the first chapter of Trotsky's book carries the title 'Peculiarities of Russia's development'). Ryazanov noted that unlike Europe, Russia had seen the rise of a native social-revolutionary tradition coincident with the emergence of capitalism; because capitalism was in large part financed by capital imports, and, to that extent, transplanted from Europe, the domestic bourgeoisie was also too weak to support an effective

---

[26] Gaido 2003, pp. 79–123.

liberal opposition to the autocracy; and the combination of accelerating capitalism with impotent liberalism necessarily left the organised workers responsible for Russia's revolutionary future.

In his critical commentary on the work of Lenin and Plekhanov in *Iskra's* draft programme, Ryazanov effectively anticipated all of the major arguments that Leon Trotsky subsequently incorporated into his famous *Results and Prospects*, which has conventionally been regarded as the initial and definitive statement of the theory of *permanent revolution*. Trotsky's comrade, Parvus, provided the immediate inspiration for Trotsky's own assessment of Russia, but in conceptual terms Trotsky's most famous theoretical work owed at least as much to Kautsky and Ryazanov as to Parvus and even to Marx himself. Kautsky and Ryazanov created the theoretical atmosphere from which Trotsky could appropriate and radicalise the conviction that 'backward' Russia might in fact be in the forefront of world-historical developments.

If it was Trotsky whose rhetorical and literary genius captured the idea of *permanent revolution* most dramatically for his own and future generations, it was nevertheless Karl Kautsky, in 'The American Worker', who finally answered the riddle posed by Ryazanov's reference to 'the pattern'. Kautsky's conclusion was elegantly straightforward: *there was and is no single 'pattern'*. Kautsky compared Russia, England and the United States in the belief that world capitalism is the contradictory whole that explains the *necessary peculiarities* of all the parts. Anticipating later theories of imperialism, he related particular histories to the international movement of peoples and capital to account for the dynamic interconnections of world history. Within this larger framework, he saw no one 'pattern' that would uniformly explain class relations in terms of abstract 'levels' of capitalist development; rather 'Each extreme can be present in one country only to the extent that the opposite extreme exists in another country.' Russia and America were the extremes of capitalism that jointly portended the future of world socialism:

> Today there is a whole series of countries in which capital controls the whole of economic life, but none of them has developed all the aspects of the capitalist mode of production to the same extent. There are, in particular, two states that face each other as extremes, in which one of the two elements of this mode of production is disproportionately strong, i.e., stronger than

it should be according to its level of development: *in America, the capitalist class; in Russia, the working class.*

Disputing the notion of any single pattern of capitalist development, Kautsky simultaneously rejected any idea of unilateral economic determinism. Revolutionary 'spirit' was at least as significant as the mundane movement of economic history. In this essay, as in 'The Slavs and Revolution', Kautsky looked to Russia as the exemplar of 'revolutionary romanticism'. If the American intelligentsia was spiritually deadened by 'capitalism of the soul', the Russian intelligentsia, at the opposite extreme, brought to workers 'the theoretical clarity and solidity of their revolutionary *élan*'. That *élan* came from beginning with the whole in order to conceptualise the parts:

> Nothing is more suitable to the spiritual development of the people than revolutionary thought because nothing can give them a more lofty purpose. The revolutionary thinker always has the *whole* state and society in view; he does not need to be blind to the little details of everyday life, but he does not expend all his forces on them; he sees in them only part of a greater whole, and assigns them to their proper places; he inquires above all how these particulars affect him and how he can exert an influence on them; he therefore learns to appreciate them correctly and keeps himself free from any illusion about their effects.

In 'The American Worker', Kautsky captured this spirit of revolution as a significant force in economic and political history. Answering the riddle of the 'pattern', he concluded that revolutionary spirit, as both a cause and an effect of particular histories, was the decisive force in accounting for the Russian revolution:

> It is above all thanks to it that the Russian industrial workers, unorganised, uncultured, and deprived of democratic rights, were able, in a predominantly peasant country, to keep in check the absolutist régime before which all the possessing classes humbled themselves not only in Russia but also in Europe.

* * *

Foreword to K. Kautsky, *The Russian and the American Worker*[27]
Anatoly Lunacharsky

This work by Karl Kautsky, which we are now bringing to the attention of Russian readers, was published in the first 1906 issues of *Die Neue Zeit*, the theoretical organ of German Social Democracy.

Although it was written for the German reader, it will also be very interesting to those in other countries, and it especially speaks to the contemporary *Russian* reader.

Until now, no one has shown with such clarity and precision the fundamental course of our economic development. The autocracy, while expanding its armed forces and anxiously caring for its political power – which ultimately took us to Tsushima[28] – has surrendered the country to the West-European *bourse*, to which the Russian people pay a tribute each year of 300 million roubles. This tribute is still rapidly growing at an astounding rate. Western capital is doing everything necessary to preserve a social order in which the Russian worker and the Russian peasant, reduced to a state of humiliation and dire necessity, labour in hellish conditions to ensure a constant flow of gold into the pockets of the gentlemen bankers and their associates. Russia will never raise itself up or put an end to its hunger, its high rate of mortality, or its unbearable poverty, so long as it carries this monstrous burden on its shoulders. *State bankruptcy* is the real, although still unarticulated, slogan of the broad masses in the movement for liberation. But, in order to end the blood-sucking activity of the *bourse*, it is first necessary to overthrow its henchmen and faithful servants who still rule Russia. Russia's rulers are merely the unpaid bondsmen and mindless mannequins of European bankers. Our weak bourgeoisie has never been determined to wage the liberation struggle to its conclusion and thus to put an end to the entire system of oppression and exploitation of the people, which in our country goes by the name of 'financial policy'. Only the popular masses, upon whom the financial burden falls a hundred times more heavily – the masses with no privileges or rapacious interests to protect – have the ability to liberate the nation from its enslavement to the bourse. The Russian proletariat, with the sympathy of an enormous majority of the nation, must

---

[27] Kautsky 1906m.

[28] [In the Battle of Tsushima, in the spring of 1905, two-thirds of the Russian fleet was destroyed by the Japanese navy.]

and will inevitably stand at the head of these masses and in fact already does so.

Let us not be deceived by the illusory achievements of the liberals. They might be rejoicing, but in reality they are sick at heart. When Rodichev[29] was asked what they plan to do in their famed Duma, he replied: 'How can a young man, who has waited a very long time to meet his beloved young lady and then finally does so, possibly know what he will babble to her in the first moment?' Wouldn't one call the young man a *carp*, and his beloved young lady a *pike*?[30]

So long as the pike remains strong, fine words are of no avail. One must break the pike's power.

We have no intention of losing the 'revolutionary romanticism' that Karl Kautsky speaks of so highly in this pamphlet, or of replacing it with imaginary and clever sobriety or petty 'realism'. We shall look boldly to the future, discern the general character of the movement and the great opportunities it presents, and not stumble over mere bricks on the road or allow them to preoccupy us just because they happen to be in our 'field of view' – we shall have nothing to do with any revisionist short-sightedness. We leave it to our timid bourgeoisie to scold the workers for their 'impracticality' and to cite the example of the 'practical' German worker. K. Kautsky calls upon the German worker to learn *revolutionary romanticism* from his Russian brother. The unique political circumstances that bring the Russian proletariat to the forefront as natural leader of the 'bourgeois' revolution also give it a unique opportunity to take positions that are most beneficial for continuing the struggle and to realise its class ideals.

What Kautsky has to say about Russian capitalism and the Russian proletariat is especially interesting for us. But there is no doubt that his information and conclusions about America are also extremely instructive. They strike a major blow against the position taken by revisionists, and they open up excellent perspectives for the entire international revolutionary workers' movement.

*   *   *

---

29 [Fyodr Ivanovich Rodichev was a landowner, a lawyer, a Zemstvo liberal, and a member of the Cadet Party who sat in each of the state Dumas.]

30 [Pikes are known to eat carps.]

'The American Worker'

I. Two models for the development of Germany

In his 'Studies on the Historical Development of the North American Proletariat', which Sombart published in the *Archive for the Social Sciences* (Vol. XXI, Nos. 1–3),[31] he remarks:

> The United States is the country with the most advanced capitalist development, so that its economic structure represents our future. What Marx correctly stated about England in 1867, we may now apply to America: *De te fabula narratur, Europa* [About you, Europe, is the story being told], when we are reporting about conditions in America, at least as far as capitalist development is concerned.[32]

This assertion can be accepted only with great reservations. A country like England, which in the sixties [of the nineteenth century] could serve in every respect as a classical model of capitalist society and all its tendencies – such a country does not exist anymore. When Marx studied England, it had not only the most highly developed capitalist class but also the most advanced proletariat; that is why it showed in the most consummate way not only the tendencies of capitalist exploitation and organisation but also the counter-tendencies of proletarian rebellion and organisation. Thus, England was the first state to develop, in the most definite way, a socialist party (Chartism), a trade-union movement, a proletarian co-operative movement, and legislation for the protection of the workers.

Today, there is a whole series of countries in which capital controls the whole of economic life, but none of them has developed all the aspects of the capitalist mode of production to the same extent. There are, in particular, two states that face each other as extremes, in which one of the two elements of this mode of production is disproportionately strong, i.e., stronger than it

---

[31] [Editorial note: Sombart first published his series of articles under the title 'Studien zur Entwicklungsgeschichte des nordamerikanischen Proletariats' in the *Archivs für Sozialwissenschaft und Sozialpolitik*, Band XXI, Heft 1–3. In 1906 he republished them in book form under the title *Warum gibt es in den Vereinigten Staaten keinen Sozialismus?* All quotations are taken from the English translation: Sombart 1976.]

[32] Sombart, op. cit., p. 23.

should be according to its level of development: *in America, the capitalist class; in Russia, the working class.*

In America, more than anywhere else, we can speak about the dictatorship of capital. In contrast, nowhere has the fighting proletariat reached such significance as in *Russia*, and this significance must and will increase because this country has just now begun to take part in the modern class struggle.

Germany's *economy* is closest to the *American* one; its *politics*, on the other hand, are closest to the *Russian*. In this way, both countries show us our future; it will have a half-American, half-Russian character. The more we study Russia and America, and the better we understand both, the more clearly we will be able to comprehend our own future. The American example alone would be as misleading as the Russian.

It is certainly a peculiar phenomenon that precisely the Russian proletariat should show us our future – as far as the rebellion of the working class, not the organisation of capital, is concerned – because Russia is, of all the great states of the capitalist world, the most backward. This seems to contradict the materialist conception of history, according to which economic development constitutes the basis of politics. But, in fact, it only contradicts that kind of historical materialism of which our opponents and critics accuse us, by which they understand a *ready-made model* and not a *method of inquiry*. They reject the materialist conception of history only because they are unable to understand it and to apply it fruitfully.

II. Russian capitalism

The extraordinary force of the Russian proletariat must be ascribed to two reasons: the lack of a strong native capitalist class and the need to carry out a political revolution in Russia.

Capitalism developed in the Russian empire on a different basis from that in Western Europe. In the West, a strong urban bourgeoisie developed even before princely absolutism. With the help of the bourgeoisie, royal absolutism from the beginning had to wage a struggle against the independent landowning aristocracy and the clergy. The bourgeoisie and absolutism grew stronger together. The surplus from the work of the productive classes, which under commodity production increasingly assumed the form of surplus-value, could not be pocketed only by monarchs, aristocrats and priests; they also had to leave a portion for the urban bourgeoisie. What monarchs and aristocrats swallowed was wasted in military campaigns and ostentation. What the church took was either spent on luxuries or accumulated as treasure. The bourgeoisie, however, transformed its share of the plunder of the native and foreign working classes into capital, which it accumulated more and more. The less the power of monarchs, aristocrats and priests, the greater was the power of the bourgeoisie in the country, the more rapid (all other conditions being equal) was the accumulation, the self-expansion of capital. On the other hand, the more rapidly the accumulation proceeded, the greater was – to a certain extent – the number, and above all the power, of the capitalists vis-à-vis not only the propertyless and the dominated, but also the property-owning and dominating non-capitalist classes, and the greater was the power of the capitalists in the state.

The development of Russia was different. The power of tsarism did not grow simultaneously with the strengthening of a bourgeoisie or as a result of it. The Russian state rather came into being as a purely agrarian state, as a régime of Asiatic despotism tightly connected with Western Europe precisely at a time when absolutism there had succeeded in subjugating the church and the nobility, had created its own organs of government in the standing army and the bureaucracy, and was becoming increasingly distrustful, even hostile, towards the rising bourgeoisie. Russian despotism recognised immediately how valuable the means of government of West-European absolutism, a standing army and a bureaucracy, could be, and it introduced them into Russia as rapidly as possible. That was, above all, the famous civilising role of Peter the Great. The tools that were first and best employed to strengthen the oriental despotism of the tsars in order, with the help of the means of coercion of capitalist civilisation, to make it the equal of Western-European absolutism, were supplied by Frenchmen and especially Germans. In terms of internal politics, however, this meant that in order to increase the power of the tsar the surplus of the productive classes had to be taken away, and the number of unproductive expenditures that had to be defrayed from that surplus, especially the expenses of soldiers and bureaucrats, increased. Peter I raised the burden of taxation by *five times*. The civilising of Russia thus meant a strengthening of the means to plunder it, not an increase of its capitalist wealth as in Western Europe. A substantial capitalist class like the West-European bourgeoisie could not develop under these circumstances.

The economic development of the country was therefore extraordinarily slow, whereas to the extent that the tsars continued with their 'civilising' process and tightened their connection with Western Europe, their share in the politics of the great European states grew. The Russian Empire had to keep pace in arms expenditure with the rapidly growing large capitalist states, while the economic distance between them increased continuously. The result was an incredible financial mismanagement already in the eighteenth century. The two methods used by the governments of capitalist countries to obtain money were profusely employed: loans and currency forgery (the printing of irredeemable paper money is nothing else). If credit was scarce and nobody wanted to lend money, then the printing press was brought into use. If the state found creditors, the fabrication of counterfeit money could pause for a while. If no other alternative was feasible, then a little state bankruptcy was tried, as in 1843, when the old paper money was taken out of circulation and replaced by a new one – with this proviso, however, that only one new rouble was received in exchange for three and a half old rouble notes.

The mortgaging of the state thus grew uninterruptedly. It is true that the growth of the national debt is not a Russian peculiarity, and there are even some bourgeois economists who believe that a big national debt is the basis of national prosperity. Under certain conditions there is a grain of truth in this assertion. The interest of the national debt is in fact an eternal payment of tribute from the state to the capitalists. It means that the state exploits the productive classes in order to increase capital. The growth of the national debt thus means a growth of the proletariat on the one hand and of capital on the other hand. If the capitalists, to whom the state is indebted, reside within its own boundaries, the national debt can become a means to promote the development of capitalist production, whose elements (proletarians and capitalists) increase because of the payment of interest. This impoverishes the working people, but it enriches the capitalist class and develops capitalist production.

The effects of the national debt are, however, completely different when the state creditors reside outside the country. The payments of interest on the national debt are in this case only a constant drain of money abroad. To the extent that the interest payments become capital, they enrich foreign countries but impoverish the indebted country. In these conditions, the public debt produces indeed local proletarians but only foreign capitalists.

That is what happened in Turkey and, to a no lesser extent, in the Russian Empire.

There is, however, a difference between these two countries. Turkey has become so helpless that it must involuntarily submit to the dictate of foreigners. It exists as an independent state only thanks to the jealousy of the different powers, none of which can have the whole booty alone. They all agree, however, in plundering the unlucky land and forcing their own products onto it, thus hindering the development of any local industry. Because of this, we see in the Turkish economy, as in the Russian, a progressive decay of agriculture and a growth in the number of proletarians, but, in Turkey, these proletarians can find no employment in capitalist industry. The most passive among them turn to begging; the most energetic become bandits and rebels, who never die out in Turkey no matter how many of them are executed.

But Russia was not as helpless as Turkey. As soon as the Russian government realised what power capitalist industry confers upon the state, it tried to promote the industrial development of the country. It certainly did not lack proletarians: the land had millions of beggars and peasants looking for jobs. But where was the necessary capital to be found? It was impossible to find it in Russia. Foreign capital had to be attracted in order to build railways, open mines, erect blast furnaces, spinning mills, weaving mills, sugar refineries, etc. And, since surplus capital in Western Europe, the surplus-value fleeced from the local workers and the foreign possessions, had grown so much by the eighties [of the nineteenth century] that it could not find enough investment possibilities at home and was being sent at serious risk to such places as Portugal, Greece, Turkey, Venezuela: why not send it to Russia? Thus, with mostly foreign capital, a heavy industry was developed in Russia, which grew with special rapidity in the last two decades. This transformed a great part of the Russian proletarians from lumpenproletarians or indigent small peasants into wage-workers, from timid and servile beggars and servants into decided revolutionary fighters. But this growth of a strong fighting proletariat was not paralleled by the growth of a similarly strong Russian capitalist class. These facts gave the class struggle of the proletariat in the empire of the tsars an altogether peculiar character.

When the Russian proletariat fights against capital, it fights largely against the foreigners, against the exploiters who impoverish and weaken the whole of Russia, who take out all the surplus-value that the land produces. The proletariat is thus the champion of the common interests of Russian society.

On the other hand, the tsar, with his whole paraphernalia of soldiers, Cossacks and *chinovniks* [bureaucrats], appears as the representative of the interests of the foreigners who exploit the whole of Russia. The modern government is everywhere the weapon of the capitalists, but Russian absolutism is the weapon of foreign capital. It is the representative of the interests of European finance against the Russian people, whom it plunders in order to hand over meekly the lion's share of the booty. That is, in a sense, one of the sources of strength of the present Russian government. The international usurers know what a servile representative of their interests they have in absolutism, and therefore they support it with all their might even though they know the kind of swindlers they are dealing with. But for precisely this reason the politically conscious population of Russia knows very well that it cannot escape from this state of pauperisation and misery without overthrowing absolutism; and since the country has no strong capitalist class able to oppose the ruinous policy of the government, the struggle for the interests of the whole of Russia falls on the shoulders of the only strong modern class it possesses: the industrial proletariat. In this way, the Russian workers are able to exert a strong political influence, and the struggle for liberation of the land from the strangling octopus of absolutism has become a duel between the tsar and the working class; a duel in which the peasants provide indispensable assistance but in which they can by no means play a leading role.

III. Native and foreign capital[33]

The analysis of the social and political effects of capital coming from abroad, as distinguished from capital locally accumulated, never occupied a prominent place in classical political economy or even in the works of Marx. Ricardo indicated, in the seventh chapter of his *Principles of Political Economy and Taxation*, how difficult it was for capital to overcome the barriers to the export of capital. These barriers have almost completely disappeared only in modern times.

Theory must investigate the problem of the effects of capital in its most simple form, leaving aside, for instance, the existence of foreign countries, and

---

[33] [See Rudolf Hilferding's comments on this 'penetrating analysis' in Hilferding 1981, Book Five: 'On the Economic Policy of Finance Capital', Chapter 22: 'The Export of Capital and the Struggle for 'Economic Space', p. 431, note 17.]

proceeding under the assumption that there is only one capitalist community – much as it distinguishes between capitalists and wageworkers and abstracts from the presence of other classes that are of great significance for social and political praxis. Only after these capitalist relations are comprehended in their most simple form is it possible to investigate and understand their more complex manifestations.[34]

The power of capital over wage-labour is evident. The more capital accumulates and large-scale enterprise develops, the more the means of production will be the monopoly of the capitalist class, the more numerous will be the propertyless masses, and the more impossible will it be for them to win their livelihood in any other way but through the sale of their labour-power to the sole owners of the means of production. All that is well known.

But the more the capitalist mode of production develops and the mass of capital grows, the more dependent on capital will be also the non-capitalist, property-owning and dominant classes, which are able through their positions of power to appropriate part of the surplus-value and often even of the value of labour-power. That is the origin of the ground-rent of the landlords, of the taxes of the princes, etc. Their feudal traditions and their social and political functions in contemporary society induce these classes to spend as much money as possible – one has only to think, for instance, about the arms race.[35] They therefore find themselves in constant need of money, and they must repeatedly borrow from those classes that accumulate capital and under whose sway they consequently fall, no matter how much hatred and contempt they feel towards their creditors.

Finally, the power of capital in society rests upon the position of dependence in which every unproductive class is placed – not only those who live a useless parasitic life like the landlords, but also those who are very active and play an exceptionally useful, sometimes even indispensable role in society.

The personal consumption of the members of the dominant and exploiting classes is usually insignificant; and it is relatively smaller, the more the rate of exploitation grows. A large part of the surplus generated by the productive

---

[34] [In *Capital*, Marx's reproduction schemes began with the assumption of 'pure' capitalism and only subsequently reintroduced other kinds of production together with foreign trade.]

[35] [Possibly a reference to the role of the Junkers as officials in the Prussian army.]

classes and appropriated by the exploiters has always been used to maintain a stratum of unproductive workers. On this stratum rests to a great extent the social and political power of the exploiters. For instance, what the medieval landlords squeezed out of the peasants was not consumed by them alone but was used to maintain vassals and subordinates, buffoons and prostitutes, troubadours and astrologers, chaplains and stable-hands, etc. Since all these lived from the produce of the exploitation of the productive classes, they faced the people as partners in the exploitation and as defenders of the exploitative system.

The more the capitalist mode of production develops, and the more capital comes to the fore as a means of exploitation, the greater will be the number of unproductive workers employed by it. Accumulation is the main aim of the capitalists, to which they subordinate all others. As long as capital is scarce and its profit small, the capitalist is stingy in his personal consumption; he is puritanical and full of contempt not only for senseless luxury and pomp but also for serious art and science. But the more capital and the rate of exploitation grow, the easier it becomes for the capitalists not only to let accumulation go ahead at full speed but also to increase their personal consumption and feed an army of unproductive workers, lackeys of all sorts, learned and unlearned, aesthetic and unaesthetic, ethical and cynical.

These unproductive workers play a crucial role in the defence of exploitation, in which they have themselves an indirect interest. They diminish the number of productive, directly exploited workers, of the fighters against exploitation. To them belongs also a large part of the intelligentsia, who influence the thoughts and feelings of the people through their oratory, writings, and works of art. Finally, these strata constitute the ladder most easily accessible to the exploited in order to rise above the reach of exploitation to a position closer to that of the dominant classes. The wider these strata, the greater the possibilities of entering into them from below, the more numerous will be the elements among the exploited that will attempt to better their position in that way instead of doing it through an energetic class struggle, and the more powerful will be the influence that the unproductive workers exert on the views of the productive workers.

How do these relations turn out in those places where capital does not come from within the country but from abroad, so that the surplus-value that it extracts also goes to foreign countries?

The opposition between entrepreneurs and wageworkers, as well as between usurers and debtors, will become more evident, will be more easily understood and more oppressively felt, when both parts belong to different nations lacking any cultural community. But that is only true where both parts come into *personal* contact, and therefore usually where both live in the same country. Thus, for instance, in Russia the factory owner or the factory director may be a Jew as opposed to a gentile, or a German as opposed to a Slav. But, in the case of *non-personal* capital, such as state loans or joint-stock companies, this personal antagonism is from the outset excluded.

On the other hand, as we have already remarked, the drain of surplus-value to foreign lands leads to an impoverishment of the whole country, of all classes, not only of those productively occupied. But at first that may go unnoticed. The first effect of capital coming from abroad is to increase the amount of capital in the country, to expand the demand for means of production and the number of workers employed in their production, and consequently also to increase the consumption of objects of personal consumption. Only gradually do the effects of the growing drain of surplus-value abroad make their appearance, until they finally become so massive that they can, at most, be only temporarily concealed by extensive capital imports.

The effect of foreign loans that bring practically no capital into the state, and whose function is, for instance, the payment of interest owed to foreign creditors or the unproductive purchase of products of foreign industry, such as cannons or warships, is, as a matter of course, to impoverish the land.

At first, the growing indebtedness of Russia to foreign countries, in the eighties [of the nineteenth century], seemed to inaugurate an era of economic growth. And there are still people foolish enough to believe that if peace and order are restored in Russia they will bring with them general prosperity – without having to make the slightest alteration in the present bureaucratic-military régime or in the rising indebtedness to foreign countries resulting from it.

But what must be evident from the outset in a land with a capitalist industry, where the capital was supplied chiefly from abroad, is the lack of a significant stratum of unproductive workers (servants and intellectuals) dependent on capital. The number of unproductive workers may be quite large in absolute terms, but capital will have less influence on them. If they perform personal services, they will mainly depend on other classes – on landowners, for instance. If they are intellectuals, they will live in poverty but they will be more independent of capitalist feelings and ideas.

The capitalists have an influence only on those strata where they spend their surplus-value, not on those from whom they draw it. A French financier bold enough to spend his money on Russian government securities or on Russian industrial or railway shares, will employ not Russian but French servants; will amuse himself with French, not with Russian actresses; will be the Maecenas[36] of French musicians, painters, poets; will receive in his salons French, not Russian politicians and scholars; and will patronise, if he is pious or wants to preserve religion for the masses, French instead of Russian cloisters; he will bribe French, not Russian journalists. The surplus-value produced in Russia will thus serve to increase his influence in France, not in Russia.

That is an important reason why the majority of the intelligentsia nowhere has, on the one hand, a lower standard of living and, on the other hand, a greater independence from capital, a stronger antagonism to it, a greater understanding of the proletariat and a more ardent devotion to its cause, than in Russia.

Those strata whose profession in Western Europe is to put to sleep and mislead the class consciousness of the proletariat, in Russia mostly work untiringly to enlighten the proletariat about its class position. Nowhere is the number of theoretically educated socialist agitators greater that in the land of the illiterates.

If the Russian proletariat, in its struggle against capital and its tool, absolutism, represented the vital interests of the entire society more than the proletariat of any other country, it was also led, more than the proletariat of any other country, by a large army of representatives of modern scientific thought and research, and was taught and inspired by modern artistic sensibility.

IV. English capitalism

Completely different from Russia are the effects of capitalist development in a country like England, where, in recent decades, the market for industry and

---

[36] [Gaius Maecenas was a counsellor of the Roman emperor Augustus and a wealthy patron of literature and the arts.]

even industry itself have expanded slowly, but where, on the other hand, the mass of surplus-value that flows into the hands of the capitalist class, and therefore also the accumulation of new capital, are colossal; where, year after year, a constantly growing mass of capital, instead of becoming industrial capital at home, flows to foreign countries as money capital in order to assume there the form of unproductive state loans or of industrial or mercantile capital.

The number of capitalists in such a country will be disproportionately much greater than what would correspond to its degree of industrial development. Under certain circumstances, their numbers can increase even more quickly than the number of proletarians, but one must be careful not to take this case as typical of all capitalist societies. Each extreme can be present in one country only to the extent that the opposite extreme exists in another country.

To a disproportionately large number of capitalists there also corresponds a disproportionately large number of servants as well as members of the so-called liberal professions.... If the members of these social strata are especially numerous in England, they are also dependent on capital to the highest degree. Leaving aside the domestic servants, the English artists, scholars and writers are more than anywhere else within the sphere of influence of capitalism; first, because a much larger proportion of them are economically dependent on the capitalists as clients or entrepreneurs, and secondly, because an unusually large part of the members of the liberal professions are directly interested in capitalist exploitation.

In contradistinction to the industrial or commercial entrepreneur, the money-capitalist – for instance the owner of state bonds or shares – is in the agreeable position of having to dedicate virtually no time to the administration of his property. A bank demands a minimal amount of administrative work from its owners. Next to the landowners, the money-capitalist is the most idle and superfluous person in capitalist society. That gives him the opportunity, of which he generally makes extensive use, to kill his time in the most stupid ways. To employ their fortunes with taste and intelligence, as did many landowning aristocracies in lands of ancient culture such as Athens or France, is beyond the capabilities of the modern capitalists, something the American financial magnates especially have shown in the most striking manner. But, where the number of money-capitalists is large, there will always be some who will use their leisure time to carry out artistic and scientific work or who will take an interest in its promotion.

Moreover, the development of impersonal money-capital invested in bank, railway or industrial shares, and in federal, state or city bonds, creates the possibility of transforming even the smallest amounts of money into money-capital. That makes little impression on the wageworkers because their opposition to the capitalist class that exploits them is too strong to be overcome by the interest that they can receive from their meagre savings. But it does have a strong influence on the members of the intelligentsia, who often obtain large amounts of surplus money, and who stand much closer to the capitalist class in their standard of living and social connections and usually do not feel exploited by it.

All these circumstances mean that capitalist ideas and feelings are highly developed in the English intelligentsia. While Russian intellectuals still preserve a strong communist sensibility so that, for instance, the sharing of momentary surpluses with their comrades seems natural to them, among the English intelligentsia, just as in the capitalist class, the bourgeois striving to accumulate every surplus and turn it into capital prevails. No wonder there are very few English intellectuals from whom the proletariat can get a deeper insight about its class position and its class interests and tasks than the insight it can gain by itself from its everyday experience.

But not only are the servants and members of the intelligentsia more numerous and more dependent on capital in England than anywhere else; the large capital exports, which give rise to a strong influx of surplus-value into the country, also make the opposition of the proletariat to the capitalist system weaker than it should be according to the degree of industrial development. While, in a country like Russia or India, capitalist exploitation leads to constant impoverishment of the country, in England it is a means of enriching the country, of accumulating a perpetually growing booty that was won through plundering the whole world. Even the propertyless classes benefit in many ways from this plunder. The greater the surplus-value coming from foreign lands, the larger will be the amounts of money flowing into the state and the communities in the form of taxes, and the greater will be the possibilities of treating the poor with consideration or of increasing the number of public works. If England is still the land of free trade, this is partially due to the growing exploitation of foreign countries. The same is true of Holland. Protective tariffs are also financial tributes, taxes on the consumption of the great masses of the people. In England, the mass of surplus-value flowing yearly to the capitalist class from abroad is so enormous that it can relinquish use of this means of bleeding the people. For money-capital as for merchant-capital, protective tariffs are not a means of increasing its profits as they are for industrial capital. Thanks to the preponderance of money- and merchant-capital, England retains its free-trade policy and rejects the modern policy of protectionism that sharpens considerably the class antagonism between proletarians and capitalists.

The mass of surplus-value that flowed into the country also facilitated the practice of charity, which is nowhere as highly developed as in England. To be sure, the lion's share of this money fell into the hands of the scions of the possessing classes and the members of the intelligentsia; the administrative costs of the philanthropic institutions in England are enormous. What remained for the actual poor was relatively little and was totally inadequate to check, even to some extent, the frightful poverty, as shown clearly by the data on unemployment. But it was sufficient to blunt the opposition of many workers to the capitalist system.

To be sure, the opposition between the proletariat and *industrial* capital in England has been growing since the 1880s. Since that period, British industry has lost its predominance in the world market and has been exposed to the bitter competition of ever more powerful, growing industrial states. But the English workers find it difficult to widen their struggle against the industrial entrepreneur into a struggle against the whole capitalist system of exploitation. They turn against particular manifestations of it, such as the sweatshops or unemployment, without asking themselves to what extent these are connected with the whole of capitalist society and without opposing this society in all its manifestations, without assaulting all its fortified positions. During the Boer War, chauvinism found no energetic opposition in their ranks.[37] Even some socialists paid tribute to imperialism on that occasion. The lamentations of India fall on deaf ears among them. It is true that the new Labour Party wants to remain independent from both Liberals and Conservatives, but, until now, it has refused to adopt a definite programme out of fear that it might be a socialist one. And even Keir Hardie felt compelled to polemicise against the idea of the class struggle a year ago.[38]

---

[37] [During the South African, or Boer, War (1899–1902), Great Britain fought against the Dutch colonists in the Transvaal and Orange Free State.]

[38] [James Keir Hardie (1856–1915), a British labour leader, was elected to Parliament in 1892 as an Independent and in 1906 led the Labour Party in the House of Commons.]

Hence, contrary to Russia, nowhere is capitalism stronger, nowhere did socialist ideas find more obstacles in the working class itself, than in that country in which *two-thirds* of the gainfully employed persons are industrial or railway workers.

To be sure, English capitalism will suffer a frightful collapse when the oppressed lands rebel and refuse to continue paying tribute. If England loses India, Egypt, and South Africa, a mass of surplus-value, which today goes to enrich the country, will remain abroad; the workers will have to pay higher taxes; industrial capital will again have the decisive voice; and the antagonism between capital and workers will be sharpened to the highest degree. If it does not come even sooner, socialism will then become inevitable in England. Till then, however, it will wage a more difficult struggle there than in much more backward countries.

V. Capitalism in the United States

The United States represents yet another special kind of development. As a capitalist country it is not older than Russia. According to Bryce, in the period between 1830 and 1840 there were in America few great fortunes and almost no poverty. In 1845, there were for the first time in Philadelphia 10 millionaires; in New York in 1855 there were only 28. It was the Civil War of the 1860s that suddenly brought the capitalists to power in the United States. Since then, capitalism has developed with tremendous speed. The accumulation and concentration of capital have made rapid progress. In 1892 there were, according to Cleveland Moffett's report in *Wilshire's Magazine*, 200 millionaires in Philadelphia and 2,000 in New York. 'In terms of her capital base – that is, the amount of her capital accumulation,' says Sombart in his already mentioned article, 'the United States (despite her comparative youth) is today beyond all other countries.'

The concentration of capital comes to light clearly in the extent of the American trusts. Sombart gives an overview of them based on Moody's work on the trusts, published in 1904,[39] and summarises its results with these words:

---

[39] [Moody 1904.]

> If one adds together all these giant combinations, within which by far
> the largest part of American economic life is included, one arrives at the
> enormous total of 8,664 'controlled' subsidiaries and $20,379,000,000 in
> capital assets. Just think! Eighty-five thousand billion marks concentrated in
> the hands of a few capitalists.[40]

Comrade Simons, in his recently published excellent work, which offers a
short synopsis of the socio-economic development of the United States from
its origins, estimates the contemporary fortunes of the trusts to be even greater:
thirty billion dollars, i.e., 120 billion marks.[41]

The personal fortune of the richest of the magnates of finance, John D.
Rockefeller alone, was estimated at one billion dollars, as much as the war
compensations that France in 1871 had to pay to Germany [as a result of
the Franco-Prussian War] – a sum then unheard of and that many doubted
wealthy France would be able to raise.

True, John Rockefeller's fortune far surpasses those of his fellow magnates.
The nine richest among them (Andrew Carnegie, Marshall Field, W.R.
Vanderbilt, J.J. Astor, J.P. Morgan, Russell Sage, J.J. Hill, William A. Clarke,
and William Rockefeller) only possess together about as much as he does. But
the capital that they can command or 'control' is much greater than the capital
they own.

---

[40] Sombart, op. cit., p. 6.

[41] Simons 1906b, p. 116. A German version was published in 1909 as a supplement
to *Die Neue Zeit*: Simons 1909. When an enlarged edition, 320 pages in length, was
published by Macmillan two years later under the title *Social Forces in American History*,
Kautsky praised it as follows:

> It is not necessary to offer a description of the contents of this book to the
> readers of the *Die Neue Zeit*. We have already published as a supplement,
> in 1909, a work by comrade Simons called *Class Struggles in America*, which
> contained the main ideas of the present work. He has now expanded and
> polished that short overview, making it more clear and persuasive. It is
> to be hoped that it will also appear in German. It is valuable both as an
> illustration of the fruitfulness of the materialist conception of history and
> as a new building stone for the construction of a single universal materialist
> history, which is gradually reaching its completion. In its present form,
> the book presupposes that the reader is already acquainted with the most
> important facts of American history. But it should not be difficult for German
> readers to add by themselves the necessary information. They will receive
> therewith a quite clear overview of the history of the United States. (Kautsky
> 1912, p. 63.)

Kautsky's praise for Simons's book should not be interpreted as an unqualified
endorsement of its theses, which for a contemporary reader are clearly marred
by racist and Populist prejudices – notably in the analysis of the Civil War and
Reconstruction.]

Where did that fabulous growth of capital come from?

Above all, it came from the fact that in the United States there was no significant power with which capital had to share its surplus-value and which would squander its portion unproductively. Thanks to the enormous tracts of unoccupied land, there was until recently no ground-rent of any consequence in the United States, no class of landowners able to appropriate for themselves a part of the surplus-value in order to waste it as the European feudal landowners did. I am abstracting here from the Southern planters, whose régime ended when that of the capitalists began. Besides, the United States was in the agreeable position of being so far from European affairs and so free from the threat of any invasion that it did not have to sacrifice much for militarism. Its navy and army were small. The American Army in 1870 had only 35,000 men, in 1903, 60,000. This army, composed of conscripts, was relatively expensive, but the country was spared the bloodletting caused in Europe by the unproductive occupation of so many millions of its best workers. In the German Empire alone, there are at present more than 600,000 men who are withdrawn from the production process in that way. If we assume that each one of them could have produced an annual value of 2,000 marks (wages and surplus-value in its different forms), that means that the German people lost every year as a result of militarism, next to the billions that the army cost, more than two additional billions in wasted productive capacity.

If one adds to that the sums, about which there are virtually no statistical data, that are squandered each year by the feudal landowners as ground-rent (the ground-rent flowing each year to the landowners in England was estimated at 300 million pounds sterling, i.e. six million marks), one gets for Germany alone – though the same is true of the other European states – a huge sum that was taken away every year from the economy owing to the existence of private property in land and militarism, and which could have been employed either to increase the personal consumption of the working class or the accumulation of capital.

No wonder that, in the United States, where burdens of that kind did not exist, capital grew far more quickly than in Europe, and Europe was increasingly outstripped by the United States.

But, in opposition to England, this capital remained in the country and served mainly for the development of industry because while the expansion of the home market for English industry was constantly slowing down, the market for American industry grew. This was due once again to the quantity of free land still not appropriated by private owners, as well as to the insignificance of the burdens that weighed upon the American farmers. Thanks to the high rates of natural demographic growth as well as to immigration, one had only to make these lands available for cultivation in order to increase quickly the number of farms and therefore the size of the home market.

This was done through construction of railways in deserted wildernesses.[42] The railroads in America have had an entirely different significance for the expansion of industry and its home market than in Europe.

The whole of Europe had 296,000 kilometres of railways in 1902; Germany, 53,700; by contrast, the United States alone had 326,000.

The number of people gainfully occupied in agriculture grew in the United States [from almost 6 million in 1870 to more than 10 million in 1900. In England, by contrast, it declined, as it has also done recently in Germany].[43]

The agricultural population of America therefore grew in a way entirely different from that of Europe. Moreover, not only its rate of growth but also its consumption capacity differentiated it from the European agricultural population. The American farmer is totally different from the English agricultural labourer as well as from the Russian or even the German small peasant. Until now, he usually had at his disposal at least as much land as he could cultivate, and from the value that he produced he usually had to pay no ground-rent (either in the form of rent [*Pachtzins*] or of mortgage payments) just two decades ago. To a large extent, that is still true even today. He also had to give less money than the European peasant did to the state and was free from the tribute in labour-power represented by compulsory military service. Thus most of the value that he produced remained with him and served either for his personal consumption or to renew and improve his technical apparatus: in both cases, he supplied a market for industry. Moreover, the railways, with their immense needs, also constituted an ever-growing clientele for industry. The railways, however, were intimately linked to agriculture since their profitability depended mostly on the transportation of agricultural produce.

---

[42] [The 'wilderness' only became 'deserted' after the genocide of the Native Americans by the European settler colonialists.]

[43] [Kautsky here provides statistics, which we have omitted, to illustrate the point. These and all the following statistical tables are reproduced in full in the English version of Kautsky's article published in the November 2003 edition of the journal *Historical Materialism*.]

These peculiar American conditions not only were especially favourable for the accumulation of capital; they also enabled this enormous mass of accumulated capital to find employment at home and particularly in industry – including the railways.

The entire capitalist class of the country therefore had, directly or indirectly, the highest interest in the greatest exploitation of the working class, because on it depended the extent of its profits. It was more united and hostile toward the working class than was the capitalist class of England, where money and merchant capital often have interests different from those of industrial capital, and where the capitalists partly draw their profits from sources other than exploitation of the local workers.

VI. The national divisions of American workers

If the capitalists in America are a much more homogeneous class than in England, nowhere is the working class more heterogeneous than in the United States.

That is also a result of the surplus of land that until recently existed in the Union. Without great expenditure, every healthy [white] American with some knowledge of agriculture was able to become an independent farmer and thus avoid being exploited by capital as a wageworker. The American-born population therefore supplied only few workers; and since capital and the market for industry both grew quickly, the demand for wageworkers was large while its supply from the ranks of the native-born population remained small.

From the beginning, the wages of American workers had to be high because the above-described social relations enabled the farmers to produce and keep for themselves a considerable mass of products. In his analysis of the value of labour-power, Marx remarked in *Capital* that 'in contradistinction to other commodities, there enters into the determination of the value of the labour-power a historical and moral element'.[44] But this element has a natural basis, and that is the national average yield of the small peasant estate. The small peasantry is the great supplier of additional labour-power for the capitalists;

---

[44] [Marx 1956, Part II, Chapter VI: 'The Buying and Selling of Labor-Power', p. 190. By 'the historical and moral element' Marx refers to the conventionally accepted minimum standard of living, which varies between times and places.]

it produces in most countries a numerous progeny that cannot find its livelihood in agriculture and ends up in industry; so that wages for simple, unskilled industrial work are determined by the living standards of the sons of the small peasants who flow into industry and of the farm hands of the rich peasants. The work of peasants and farm hands is by no means simple. On the contrary, it is very complicated and requires a long apprenticeship. But, for industry, this apprenticeship is worthless; in industry, the wageworkers coming from agriculture are, as a rule, employed at first only as unskilled workers.

The living standards of the peasant, in turn, depended on the quantity and quality of land at his disposal, the efficiency of his tools and methods of labour and, finally, on the share that he had to hand over to the landowners, the clergy, and the state.

In the last analysis, these social relations determine the foundation of wages in a given country. That they were nowhere more favourable than in America requires, after what has been said, no further explanation. The American farmer had plenty of land at his disposal, fertile land, burdened with few taxes, and without the drain of labour-power represented by military service. He produced a surplus large enough for the acquisition of efficient tools that, in turn, increased agricultural production; and popular education was universal and good enough to make possible their intelligent employment. The living standards of the small farmer, which were determinant for the entire working class, therefore had to be quite high.

But, even when the capitalists were ready to pay the corresponding wages, in America they had no prospects of receiving from the peasantry a sufficient number of workers. Since there was so much free land, it lured successive generations to set up new farms instead of falling into dependence in the cities. Despite its fertility, the rate of natural growth of the urban proletariat is very low and frequently negative – because its mortality is also very high. And with high wages it was not difficult to save enough money to set up a new farm because the price of land was practically nominal. In that way, numerous elements from the urban proletariat repeatedly left their class in order to turn to agriculture.

Under these circumstances a mass proletariat, without which industrial capital cannot thrive, could not have developed; and capital would have retained the form of merchant and money capital had not a powerful factor come to its rescue: the massive *immigration* of foreign labourers. Though the Southern planters compulsorily imported numerous bound workers from Africa, free labourers came of their own will in huge numbers from Europe; at first especially from England, Ireland and Germany, but later also from Italy, Austria, Russia. They were attracted by the prospect of settling as independent farmers or of earning high wages in the cities. The first group increased the number of farmers and therefore the market for industry and the clientele for the railways; the second, lacking the means or the agricultural knowledge, supplied industrial capital with the necessary labour force.

Thus, foreign immigrants have always played a large role in the American economy, and they form an especially large percentage of the wageworkers....[45]

Accordingly, the gainfully employed white persons of American parentage, which for the sake of brevity we will call Anglo-Americans, do not represent even half of the total number of gainfully employed persons. They constitute a third of those employed in domestic and personal service, and only two-fifths of the industrial workers....[46]

[The data] show clearly that whites of American parentage are only weakly represented in the industrial proletariat. In many important branches of industry they constitute only a quarter, and sometimes as little as a fifth or a tenth of the gainfully employed persons.

Especially small is the number of Anglo-Americans in New York. Out of 1,102,471 gainfully employed males, only 195,205 are whites of American parentage; out of 419,594 industrial workers, only 52,827; out of 56,095 textile workers, only 580. For that reason, New York is considered over there as a European suburb.

The workers within the particular groups are, however, by no means a homogeneous mass. The immigrants, above all, present a most variegated picture. The largest groups among them are the Germans, who constitute 29.5% of the immigrants, the Irish (21.7%) and the English (9.3%). The immigrants of each nationality are distributed among the different occupations in very different proportions....

---

[45] [We have here omitted Kautsky's statistical data from the 1900 census elaborating this point and indicating the numbers of American- and foreign-born workers in different occupations.]

[46] [Here, too, Kautsky provides statistical evidence that we have omitted.]

Austrian Social-Democracy experienced many difficulties due to the multiplicity of nations from which the proletariat of that land is recruited. But at least these nations are not strangers; they have developed under the same government, the same laws, sometimes even the same cultural traditions – so that, for instance, a Bohemian German is distinguished from a Czech by nothing more than his language. In America, on the contrary, the immigrants are so different from one another as well as from the native population in their race, religion, and cultural peculiarities, that they are barely able to understand each other even if they have learned to speak the same language. Nowhere is it more difficult to unite the masses in a centralised movement.

While in Russia a very large part of the capital comes from abroad, making the population weaker and the proletariat stronger than they should be according to the degree of industrial development of the country, in America a very considerable section of the industrial proletariat comes from abroad, indeed from the four corners of the world, whereas its capital is totally indigenous and almost completely confined to the circle of interests of industrial capital. Here, capital is stronger and the proletariat weaker than they should be according to the degree of industrial development of the country.

VI. The lack of revolutionary romanticism in America

One of the most important reasons for the relative weakness of the American and the relative strength of the Russian proletariat is the different extent to which capital and the proletariat come from abroad, but it is not the only one. A further reason is that a larger section of the Russian workers are filled with what some of our comrades now like contemptuously to call 'revolutionary romanticism', whereas most American workers are still actuated by that spirit of 'healthy *Realpolitik*' that deals only with proximate and tangible things – a characteristic that fills the above-mentioned comrades with admiration.

These different worldviews did not originate in the different racial characteristics of Russia and America but in the dissimilarities in the historical development of both nations.

The Russian worker developed in a state that united the barbarism of Asiatic despotism with the means of coercion developed by modern absolutism in the eighteenth century: it is within this framework that the capitalist mode of production developed in Russia. As soon as the proletariat began to move, it immediately came across almost insuperable obstacles in every direction, experienced in the most painful way the insanity of the political situation, learned to hate it, and felt compelled to fight against it. It was totally impossible to reform this situation; the only possible course was a complete revolution of the established order. Thus, the Russian workers developed as instinctive revolutionaries who enthusiastically adopted conscious revolutionary thought because it only articulated in a clearer and more precise way what they had already obscurely felt and suspected. And they found a strong stratum of intellectuals who, like them, suffered under the existing conditions, like them were mostly condemned to live a wretched existence, like them could only exist in a constant struggle against the existing order of things and, like them, could only hope for deliverance through its complete revolution. These intellectuals brought to the workers the theoretical clarity and solidity of their revolutionary *élan*. Nothing is more suitable to the spiritual development of the people than revolutionary thought because nothing can give them a more lofty purpose. The revolutionary thinker always has the *whole* state and society in view; he does not need to be blind to the little details of everyday life, but he does not expend all his forces on them; he sees in them only part of a greater whole, and assigns them to their proper places; he inquires above all how these particulars affect him and how he can exert an influence on them; he therefore learns to appreciate them correctly and keeps himself free from any illusion about their effects.

Since his aims are so vast, he learns to consider events in terms of the historical periods in which they can be achieved; he does not let himself be discouraged by defeats or blinded by partial successes. Because he examines every particular aspect in connection with the whole, he does not let himself be confused with panaceas that promise to free the whole state and the entire society from all its wrongs, quickly and painlessly, simply by changing a single phenomenon. Finally, because he always has the whole of society in view, he recognises more clearly the great lines of demarcation that separate the different classes despite particular points of contact; he understands the significance and problems of the class struggle more clearly and is able to infuse greater resolution and unity of purpose in the struggles of his own class.

The revolutionary worldview thus bestows on the proletariat greater force and steadiness of development; revolutionary 'romanticism' is of the greatest practical utility for the workers. It is above all thanks to it that the Russian industrial workers, unorganised, uncultured, and deprived of democratic rights, were able, in a predominantly peasant country, to keep in check the absolutist régime before which all the possessing classes humbled themselves not only in Russia but also in Europe.

Things are different in America. If Russia is the most unfree, America is the freest country of the capitalist world; freer even than England and Switzerland, where a medieval aristocracy sank strong roots and where, as late as the nineteenth century, political equality and the right of association had to be achieved through fierce struggles. The Northern states of the Union, founded by peasant and petty-bourgeois fugitives during the period of the religious wars that followed the Reformation, for a long time bore the burden of European traditions but eventually developed, in correspondence with their economic conditions, state constitutions granting the greatest freedom and equality.[47] And the prevailing social relations, above all the existence of an inexhaustible reserve of land, which made this first and most important means of production available to all[48] and for a long time, prevented the formation of a mass proletariat, made sure that this freedom and equality did not remain on paper only. The scarcity of educated persons opened up the doors of the state administration, the practice of law and journalism, in short, all the most important domains of the intelligentsia. Every intellectually energetic citizen was able to acquire without great difficulties the knowledge necessary for the fulfilment of these roles. That was made relatively easier by the popular system of education, which was universal and very good. Under these conditions, an intellectual aristocracy could not develop, and even less a closed state bureaucracy, because the party momentarily in power, which changed frequently, disposed of the state posts. Every intelligent worker, no matter from which social stratum he came, could expect to step up to a higher social position or at least to rise above the ranks of the exploited.

---

[47] [Kautsky should have added: for white settler colonialists only. Native Americans and black slaves were granted no political and almost no civil rights. Even white women were deprived of political rights and severely handicapped in their civil rights (for instance the right to own real property).]

[48] [That is, to all whites.]

Thus, for a long time, all the conditions were lacking that could suggest to the exploited classes the necessity of a decisive transformation of the state institutions; even the exploited classes themselves, as a mass phenomenon, were missing. And the mentality arising from these conditions has continued to exist to the present day. It is true that, in the meantime, a strong proletariat and the strongest capitalist class in the world have appeared in the United States but, despite that, to this day the mass of the people can be divided according to their feelings not between capitalists and proletarians but between those who are already capitalists and those who want to become such.

Of course, between the two classes in America – in fact, especially in America – there is also the deepest antagonism of interests. But, during the whole course of his historical development, the American worker has never, until now, been forced to enquire into and oppose the *totality* of the existing social order. He always turns against particular institutions that annoy him. Any analysis of the origin of these particular phenomena, or of their connection with the entire political and social organism, appeared to him as idle rumination. In his contempt for any theory, our *Praktiker*[49] could find true happiness.

The American intelligentsia strengthens this worldview of the workers. While in Russia the intelligentsia, because of its social position, became the indispensable agency through which revolutionary consciousness was brought to the proletariat, which it resembled in so many aspects, in America it represented the connecting link between the proletariat and the capitalist class. Many proletarians enter politics, journalism, and the legal professions, which, because of the vastness of the country, constitute sources of enrichment, ladders by means of which a person can escape from the ranks of the propertyless and become part of the capitalist class. The American intelligentsia is therefore completely dominated by the desire to get rich and is filled with the most unscrupulous capitalism of the soul.

From this intelligentsia, the worker can receive no enlightenment about his interests and the historical tasks of his class. The American intellectuals

---

[49] [*Praktiker*: a reference to the 'practical' trade-union revisionists with whom Kautsky was engaged in a fierce controversy at that time.]

themselves know nothing about these matters and, even when they do know, they hide it carefully.

Conditions in the United States are therefore very unfavourable for the development of a resolute proletarian class consciousness and for setting great goals involving the transformation of the entire society.

These circumstances do not, to be sure, bridge over the opposition of interests between capital and labour. In fact, it is perhaps more glaring today than in Europe because the American capitalists, unhindered by any petty-bourgeois or ideological traditions, pursue their interests much more ruthlessly; and the American workers, thanks to the democratic traditions of the country, likewise fight back in a most determined and resolute manner. But all these numerous conflicts as a rule turn around some momentary demands. To the extent that these comprise a more far-reaching aim, it is generally an isolated one by means of which the workers hope to defend themselves from some particular opponent or correct some particular wrong in the state or in society without transforming them radically.

The main point, however, is that even this somewhat far-reaching demand must be 'practical', i.e. attainable in the short term and within the framework of the existing social relations – because the American, whether capitalist or proletarian, is a *Reapolitiker* in the capitalist sense of the word. The *Praktiker* of the Middle Ages believed that they worked for eternity. They built their domes and castles, created their paintings and even produced their tools and materials as if they were to last forever. In the same way, they established their urban and political organisations believing that they would last eternally. Capitalism, which undergoes continual revolutions and which, in order to create new surplus-value, continually depreciates all existing values, is only interested in the profit of the moment, because whatever does not produce an immediate profit can be rendered obsolete next year by a new invention. The *Realpolitiker* of capitalism therefore always aim at momentary results, and this mentality also infects the proletarian politician when he has not freed himself from bourgeois ideas and learned to think as a revolutionary, i.e., to have in view the vast and great future.

For that reason, the American *Realpolitiker* of the proletariat also always limit themselves to 'practical' demands. They easily become very enthusiastic about them, but if they are not attained quickly, they are just as easily given up.

But such particular demands always find supporters among isolated bourgeois politicians because the irreconcilable opposition between capitalists and workers becomes evident not in the particular momentary demands of the proletariat but in its collective endeavour to expropriate the capitalist class. Isolated and momentary demands of the proletariat, such as the mitigation of unemployment, limitation of the power of the trusts, protective legislation for the workers, etc., will always find the support of many bourgeois politicians, even of those who are decidedly hostile to the revolutionary class struggle. Though this may look like a strengthening of the power of the proletariat by bourgeois elements, and therefore an indication of the merits of *Realpolitik*, that is by no means the case. An isolated demand rarely interests the whole proletariat and unites all its forces. It also usually secures for the bourgeois elements who support it a pernicious influence over the proletariat because they are either impotent ideologists without influence, who awaken false illusions in the workers, dim their class consciousness and weaken their struggles without making any real contribution, or else mere demagogues who seek to win the support of the proletariat by means of promises in order to exploit its strength in their own interest.

Thus, we see that the popular reform movements in the United States are only created around particular demands, often of the most fraudulent nature; for instance, the movements that promised to liberate the oppressed classes by issuing paper or silver money (the 'cheap money' movement) or by reforming the fiscal system (the 'single tax' movement of Henry George). These movements developed from time to time very quickly and collapsed even more rapidly, and they have practically no other effect than to serve as springboards for some quacks and swindlers.

It is precisely because all 'revolutionary romanticism' was lacking, because it proceeded from the most insipid *Realpolitik*, that the political activity of the working masses in the United States until now has been so unsteady in its intensity and direction and more than anywhere else in the world has been misled by demagogues and clowns.

VII. Sombart on the American workers

A. *The alcohol consumption of German and American Workers*

[At this point Kautsky gives a critical analysis of Werner Sombart's comments concerning household expenditures and relative alcohol consumption in Germany and America. According to Sombart, German workers had greater disposable income than Americans after the purchase of necessities, but 'The entire difference – and more – between the "free" income of the American worker and that of the German is absorbed by expenditure on alcoholic drinks!' Kautsky shows that despite repressive American attitudes, alcohol consumption was steadily increasing.]

B. *Proletarian ministerialism*

Sombart acquaints us with many other peculiarities of the American worker….He raises, for instance, the question of what benefits accrue to the proletariat when its struggles and growing might result in persuading the ruling parties to offer government posts to some of its leaders. It is well known that when Millerand[50] entered the bourgeois government of Waldeck-Rousseau, our revisionists were enraptured beyond measure and declared that this was the only way in which the proletariat could come to power – any striving to conquer the whole of political power being sterile and foolish 'revolutionary romanticism'. The experience with the Millerand experiment has somewhat cooled down our revisionist statesmen, and when John Burns[51]

---

[50] [Alexandre Millerand (1859–1943), a socialist member of the French Chamber of Deputies from 1885 and leader of the socialist Left until 1896, in 1899 joined the bourgeois 'government of republican defence' of René Waldeck-Rousseau as Minister of Commerce, (together with the butcher of the 1871 Paris Commune, general Gallifet) using as an excuse the Dreyfus trial, in an early application of Stalin's 'popular front' policy. Millerand later filled a series of governmental posts in bourgeois governments and was elected president of the French Republic from 1920 to 1924.]

[51] [John Elliot Burns (1858–1943). A labour leader of working-class origin, Burns was originally a member of the Social Democratic Federation and played a distinguished part in the organisation of mass strikes, which led to his arrest in 1888. In 1892, he was elected chairman of the Trades Union Congress and a socialist member of the House of Commons. On 10 December 1905, Burns followed Millerand's example and entered Sir Henry Campbell-Bannerman's Liberal Cabinet as president of the Local Government Board.]

recently got a ministerial post it was received with an embarrassed silence until the *enfant terrible* of German revisionism declared his enthusiasm for this triumph of the British proletariat.[52] The Prussian professor knows how to assess the value of this piecemeal method of conquering political power better than the Social-Democratic member of the Reichstag – at least for America.

Sombart writes about 'the case of the leading trade-unionists, who are the workers' leaders and to whom a richer reward is held out if they swear loyalty to the ruling party':

> They will be given a well-paid job, perhaps as a factory inspector or even as an Under-Secretary of State, depending on the significance attached to the person to be provided for. The practice of rendering influential workers' leaders harmless by bestowing on them a lucrative post is a thoroughly established one, and for years it has been used with the greatest success by the ruling parties. We can follow this *castration process* among a whole series of the best-known leaders. At the moment the President of the American Federation of Labor [Samuel Gompers], whose equivalent in Germany would be Karl Legien, is said to have been selected to succeed Carroll D. Wright as Commissioner of the Bureau of Labor, while John Mitchell, the victorious leader of the miners and thus roughly equivalent to Hermann Sachse or Otto Hue in Germany, is supposed to be receiving a post as Under-Secretary of State in Washington.
>
> It has been ascertained that in Massachusetts thirteen workers' leaders have obtained political positions in this way within the space of a few years, while in Chicago thirty have done so....
>
> However, when influential leaders betray a really oppositional workers' movement in this way every time they have achieved power and esteem among their fellows, this means a direct gain for the major parties not only in so far as the person of the leader and the group of workers who trusted him are concerned. In a far wider sense capitalism is strengthened indirectly, because a possible independent workers' party experiences a damaging loss when its leader is lured away by the bait of office. In other words, on

---

[52] [A reference to the SPD right-wing leader Eduard Bernstein (1850–1932). For a detailed analysis of the revisionist controversy (the so-called *Bernstein–Debate*) see the main introduction to this anthology.]

every occasion the major parties snatch the officers of the Socialist party organizations from under the noses of the latter while they are still being formed.[53]

One would assume that this is clearly grasped by anyone who has understood that there is a fundamental difference between Social Democracy and the 'large' – that is to say, in America, the bourgeois – parties. Only those who have forgotten the fundamental difference between Social Democracy and liberalism can be of the opinion that a trade-union leader, or any other leader of the proletariat, can represent its interests from a post that he owes to the liberals.

C. *The democratisation of capital*

A second illusion of socialist revisionism is that the workers can become partners of the capitalists through the acquisition of shares, and that this represents a democratisation of capital. Sombart knows very well how this issue must be regarded.

> The capitalists seek to buy off the worker by granting him a share of their profits. The method of doing this is by offering stock on advantageous terms. In certain circumstances the capitalists thereby kill two birds with one stone. Firstly, they draw the worker into the hurly-burly of running the business and arouse in him the base instincts both of acquisitiveness and of morbid excitement in speculation, thus binding him into the system of production that they champion. Secondly, however, they dispose of their inferior stock, averting an impending fall in prices and perhaps at the same time influencing the stock market momentarily in such a way as to secure extra pickings for themselves.[54]

We wish every Social Democrat could see through the gross fraud of the 'democratisation of capital' as clearly as the liberal professor does.

…Sombart points out that, 'at least temporarily', the result of such a policy is that 'the worker becomes steeped in the capitalist mentality'.[55]

---

53 Sombart, op. cit., pp. 36–7.
54 Ibid., p. 113.
55 Ibid., p. 114.

D. *Capitalist trade-union policy*

A third illusion of revisionism is the efficacy of the Trade Alliances, unions of workers' organisations and employers' organisations formed with the purpose of keeping up prices, in which both sides pledge mutual support for the organisation. Just as in the possession of shares by the workers and the granting of state posts to workers' leaders, our revisionists see in the Trade Alliances a way of gradually 'undermining' capitalism, of imperceptibly – indeed very imperceptibly – turning it into socialism without any of those detestable catastrophes. Sombart assesses these Trade Alliances very well. He says:

> This politics of business (of the guild-like-minded trade unions) finds its purest expression in the combinations of the monopolistic trade union and the monopolistic employer in the so-called 'Alliances,' which are organizations aimed at the common exploitation of the public through the union of the employers and workers of a particular sector of the economy. One can describe these sorts of trade unions as capitalist and contrast them with the Socialist trade unions; the former are carved from the same wood as capitalism itself and, in both their inclinations and their effects, they are directed to the *maintenance and strengthening of the capitalist economic system*, rather than to its overthrow. The politics of the *Socialist trade unions* are also tailored to success in the present, but at the same time they do not lose sight of the proletarian class-movement against capitalism.[56]

As a rule, Sombart offers many sensible opinions about the trade-union movement. Many trade-union leaders seem to believe that the aim of the labour movement is not the abolition of private property in the means of production but rather the 'constitutional factory'. Many hold this to be a transitional stage towards socialism and believe that they have largely reached it when the employer abandons his dictatorial attitude and deals with the workers as equals, regarding them not as servants but as sellers of commodities even if that commodity is their labour-power.

That the workers should strive to be treated by their employers not as slaves having no will of their own but as persons with equal rights is obvious. But they must not deceive themselves because the higher, more civilised *form of intercourse* with them changes the *content of their exploitation* very little if at all.

---

[56] Ibid., pp. 21–2.

Sombart discerned this fact very well:

This stress on 'equality of rights,' to which social and public life in the United States is geared, is even to be found inside capitalist businesses. Even here the employer does not confront the worker as the Lord who demands obedience, which was and is the usual case in old Europe with its feudal traditions. From the beginning a purely business standpoint became the prevailing rule in the bargaining of wage agreements. There was no question of the worker having first to engage in long conflict with the employer for the 'equality' between them to be formally recognized. The American woman was treated with great tenderness because she was scarce; similarly, the employer took the trouble to behave towards the labor force, which was not originally available in the quantity he wanted, in a polite and accommodating manner that found strong support in the democratic atmosphere of the country. Today even English workers are still astonished at the respectful tone that employers and foremen in the United States adopt towards the worker, and they are astonished at the license given to the American worker even in his workplace; he is 'freed from what one may call vexatious supervision.' They are surprised that he can take a day or two off, that he can go out to smoke a cigar – indeed, that he smokes while working – and that there is even an automatic cigar-vending machine for his use in the factory. It is also characteristic of the American manufacturers that they fail to put into effect even the simplest protective measures in their plants and that they are not in the least bit concerned that the set-up of the place of work be good when objectively assessed. (Quite frequently places of work are overcrowded and have similar deficiencies). On the other hand, they are most eager to provide anything that could be perceived subjectively by the worker as an amenity; in other words, they take care of 'comfort': bathtubs, showers, lockers, temperature control in the workrooms, which are cooled by fans in the summer and are preheated in the winter....

These are certainly all trivialities, but the saying that 'small gifts preserve friendship' is applicable even here. Later I shall try to show that – when the matter is considered objectively – the worker in the United States is more exploited by capitalism than in any other country in the world, that in no other country is he so lacerated in the harness of capitalism or has to work himself so quickly to death as in America. However, this is irrelevant if one is engaged in explaining what working-class sentiments consist of. To account for their character all that is important is what individuals perceive as being pleasure or pain and what they assess as being valuable or worthless. It is one of the most brilliant feats of diplomatic artifice that the American employer (in just the same manner as the business-oriented politician) has realized how to keep the worker in a good mood despite all actual exploitation, and that the latter is a long way from achieving consciousness of his real position.[57]

Some people could object that, if equality of rights and political freedom have such a deleterious effect on the class consciousness and the class struggle of the American proletariat, while the lack of such conditions in Europe (especially in Eastern Europe) gives greater impetus to the proletarian class struggle, it is absurd to demand equality of rights and political freedom and to make so many sacrifices on their behalf. Not at all. Without equality of rights and political freedom the proletariat cannot develop its whole strength; the worker needs them as he needs air and light; they are vital elements for him. But their effects are different where the workers found them from the beginning as self-evident rights, about which they did not have to worry, as distinct from the case where the proletariat itself had to fight for them. Just as the striving after the truth is much more valuable than the effortless possession of a truth discovered by others, so the struggle for freedom is much more uplifting than the passive possession of a freedom that others have won before.

Last but not least, owing to the possession of these rights inherited from their fathers, the American workers were until now weaker *as a class* than the European workers – though only because each one of them was stronger *as a citizen*. And they possessed not only political freedom, not only social equality of rights; no, in addition the most important means of production, the land, had not become the monopoly of one class but stood at everyone's disposal. Why then become a socialist, why struggle for a distant future, if a very considerable part of the socialist aims had become a reality in America, or rather remained a reality until quite recently?

All the causes that have until now prevented the American worker from becoming as conscious of his class opposition to capital and as conscious of his class solidarity as the European proletarians are now disappearing.

---

[57] Ibid., pp. 111–12.

Sombart therefore closes his 'Studies on the Historical Development of the North American Proletariat' with the promise to show in a forthcoming book how

> all the factors that till now have prevented the development of Socialism in the United States are about to disappear or to be converted into their opposite, with the result that in the next generation Socialism in America will very probably experience the greatest possible expansion of its appeal.[58]

I do not know whether this means that our liberal professor – liberal, that is, with regard to contemporary Germany – has the intention of embracing socialism for America and for the future generations, and whether he will also reject for Germany the revisionist illusions whose futility in America he has recognised so well. In any case, we will look forward to that book with expectation. But we do not have to wait for it in order to recognise that the preconditions for socialism are developing rapidly in America and that we can assist their blossoming not only among future generations but perhaps within a few years.

The last census has published some data on this point, which we would like to examine in our next section.

VIII. The pauperisation of the American worker

A. *The decline of petty-bourgeois agriculture*

When the revisionists set out either to refute or 'develop' Marxist theory, i.e., to break its backbone in order to make it submissive, it was the demand for the conquest of power by the proletariat and the theory of the constant intensification of class antagonisms that made them especially angry. In order to refute them, the revisionists gave them an absurd form, arguing that the demand for the conquest of political power resulted from 'speculation' about 'catastrophes', which in turn was supposedly based on a special theory of catastrophes, and that the theory of the necessary sharpening of class contradictions was derived from a theory of the pauperisation of the workers –

---

[58] Ibid., p. 119, emphasis in the original.

as if Marx had expected that the strength of the proletariat to remodel the social organism would grow out of its increasing degeneration.[59]

The Russian Revolution [of 1905] and the especially strong sharpening of class struggles in the whole of Europe during the last few years have meanwhile condemned the criticism of the so-called 'theory of catastrophes [*Zusammenbruchstheorie*]' if not to complete silence at least to complete meaninglessness. But economic development had even before reduced *ad absurdum* the criticism of the 'pauperisation theory', i.e., the theory of the sharpening of class contradictions between capital and labour.

The American conditions provide new materials on these issues because there the development has been especially rapid in recent decades, making its tendencies clearly visible. They show that the Golden Age for the American worker within the capitalist mode of production lies not *before* but *behind* him; that his social position in relation to capital – and that is the decisive thing – has worsened continuously.

The main cause of the superiority in the situation of the American worker vis-à-vis the European worker was the fact that the decisive means of production, the land, was not the exclusive monopoly of a caste of landowners but was accessible to everybody. However, the American worker has increasingly lost that superiority. In his article on the United States in *Die Neue Zeit*,[60] Comrade Simons has already alluded to the remarkable fact that the agricultural population of the state of Iowa is decreasing. This indication was complemented by a note that appeared in the German press in the last week. It reads:

> ...The reason is, first of all, to be found in the *rapid growth in farmland prices*. In Iowa, where cattle-breeding and dairy farming are pre-eminent, the preservation of the old family property is becoming more and more impossible, and farming is being carried out more and more by capitalist farmers. The traditional farmers must therefore either emigrate to neighbouring Canada or to the South- or Northwest, where land is even cheaper....

---

[59] [See Kautsky 1900a, II. – Le Programme, a) La théorie de l'écroulement et la société capitaliste, and f) La théorie de la misère grandissante.]

[60] Simons 1906a, p. 623.

These developments were not completely unexpected. *In relative terms*, the agricultural population of the United States has been declining for a long time. Despite the abundant free land available, the number of farmers is not increasing as quickly as the number of people employed in other occupations. From 1880 to 1900, the number of gainfully employed people in agriculture grew indeed from 7,713,875 to 10,381,765, but it diminished in relative terms from 44.3 per cent in 1880 to 35.7 per cent in 1900.…[I]n the North-Atlantic states, the reduction in the number of gainfully employed people in agriculture is not only relative, but also *absolute*.…But even in two of the real 'wheat states' [Ohio and Indiana] a reduction of the agricultural population began to take place in 1890, while in the others the increase is minimal.…

Why this peculiar phenomenon in regions so scarcely populated? I intend to deal with this question in more detail as soon as I have additional data at my disposal. For the time being, it is enough to say that this decline must be ascribed to the exhaustion of the soil. This does not mean that there is not enough land available in the United States but that there is no more fertile, uncultivated and well-situated land available, able to supply abundant yields with the extensive and superficial agricultural methods employed till now. A new, more intensive sort of cultivation has to be introduced, but it requires money and capital, i.e., things unavailable to propertyless people. The poor farmers fall into debt and either go bankrupt or have to bear such a burden of labour that the more mobile members of the young generation flee whenever possible from agriculture and turn to industry or commerce. The migration from the countryside to the towns has also begun in America. That does not prove the decline of its agriculture but its transition to capitalist management. It will become a business carried on with capital and exploited by capitalists, and it will cease to be the great escape valve through which the discontent and desperation of large layers of the American proletariat was diverted.…

B. *The decline of wages*

While the proletariat became less and less capable of working in agriculture, which entered increasingly into its *capitalist stage*, industry and commerce, which were already capitalistically managed, are more and more entering the *stage of private monopoly*, of the trusts.…With the trust system, however, arises a capitalist feudalism that gives to a few families absolute dominion over the whole capitalist economy and oppresses more and more even the small capitalists, making completely hopeless any aspiration to rise above the proletariat into the ranks of the bourgeoisie.

At the same time, these developments make the situation of the proletariat progressively more oppressive.

That was clearly shown by an interesting work of the Washington Commissioner of Labor, who surely did not give an exaggeratedly negative view of the situation in a Bulletin of July 1905. It contains a detailed analysis of wages and working hours in industry from 1890 to 1904, as well as of the average foodstuff prices in retail trade during that period....[61] This [report] clearly shows [a decline of real wages due to rising prices].

...The evolution of wages, however, is very dissimilar in different occupations. Next to a few privileged strata of workers, who obtained very considerable rises in wages, there are many others whose rise in money wages fell behind the average, and even others who experienced an absolute fall in money wages.[62]...[I]t is...clear that the purchasing power of wages must have fallen in a whole series of occupations that did not experience any similar rise in money wages and that, especially since 1896, a decided pauperisation, i.e., a considerable absolute worsening in the standard of living, must have taken place where money wages remained stable or even declined.

C. *Child and female labour*

Clear evidence of the increasing deterioration in the situation of broad strata of the American population is provided by the *increase in the number of child and female labourers.*

The number of gainfully employed children in the ten to fifteen year old age group...represented in 1880 16.8 per cent, and in 1900, 18.2 per cent....

Female labour is also growing alongside child labour – and not as a result of the women striving for independence. In America, because of immigration, which brings in more men than women, the latter have always been a minority. In 1900, there were in the United States 39 million men and 37 million women. Like the wage-labourers, women in the United States had a scarcity value that

---

[61] [We omit here Kautsky's statistical data.]
[62] [Here, too, we omit statistical data.]

gave them a higher position than in Europe. And, just as people employed in America as many machines as possible in order to make wage-labourers unnecessary, they also tried to organise their households so as to employ the smallest possible amount of labour-power. Women were in that way relieved from many household duties, but, thanks to their privileged position and the usually good income of men, they did not need to spend their greater leisure time working outside their homes. American women were not emancipated through the independence that their occupations granted them. Nowhere is the woman treated more like a *dame*, like a luxury, than in the United States.

Sering, for instance, gives the following account of the women of the American farmers:

> In her dress and behavior, the farmer's woman looks like a *perfect lady*,[63] and in no way differs from the urban ladies. The farmers' daughters usually receive in college a higher education than the sons, who must pursue a money-making occupation earlier. It is rare to find an American woman working on the fields, and in those cases one can almost always be sure that the woman belongs to a family of immigrant farmers.[64]

With such views, the force of necessity must be especially strong before a woman decides to turn to wage-labour.

Even today, wage-labour is much less common among the women of the native white population than among the foreign-born whites and the blacks. In general, 18.8 per cent of the gainfully employed persons in 1900 were women. But this percentage falls in the case of the native white population to 13 per cent, while it rises to 21.7 per cent among second-generation white Americans, to 19.1 per cent among immigrants, and to 40 per cent among coloured people.

Nevertheless, that 13 per cent already represents a considerable increase of female labour among the native whites, who in 1890 constituted only 11 per cent of the gainfully employed persons....[65]

---

[63] [In English in the original.]
[64] Sering 1887, p. 180.
[65] [Statistics deleted.]

D. *Unemployment*

Next to the evolution of the purchasing power of wages and of child and female labour, there is a third criterion to measure the increase or diminution in the social misery of the working class: *unemployment*. The last American census offers valuable data on this issue as well. It shows [that][66]…more than a *fifth* of the entire number of gainfully employed people – in industry, the liberal professions and domestic service, more than a *quarter* – were unemployed between 1899 and 1900. And unemployment is clearly growing quickly.…The immigrants were the group most badly hit.…The situation of the unlucky Russians was in every respect the worst.…[67]

We gladly concede that the data are incomplete. But, to the extent that they show anything, they reveal a growth and intensification of unemployment, and with complete certainty they show an unheard-of extent of unemployment precisely in 1900, which was a year of *prosperity* in America.…

Taken together with the unemployment, the…data showing a decline in the purchasing power of wages since 1896 reveal an even worse picture. The statistics on wages give the weekly income of the workers, calculated in hourly wages. The decisive question for the well-being of the worker, however, is not his *weekly* but his *yearly* income, and that will evidently be lower (his weekly wages remaining the same), the greater the number of weeks in the year that he must spend without work and without wages.

In view of all these figures, we have the right to speak about a *very considerable* decline in the prosperity of the American worker since 1896. His money wages have declined, while at the same time the purchasing power of money has diminished.

IX. The rise of capital

The decline of the American worker described here took place in a decade of colossal economic growth, of really dazzling prosperity, which witnessed an enormous advance of the capitalist class and a massive accumulation of capital. In heavy industry alone, the value of the invested capital grew during

---

[66] [Statistics deleted.]
[67] [Statistics deleted.]

this period from \$6,524 million to about \$9,857 million – a growth of about \$3,333 million, i.e. 14 billion marks!

And this accumulation was not achieved through anxious thriftiness and Puritan simplicity of lifestyle. The growth of capital rather went hand in hand with a mad drive to spend money, which surpassed everything concocted up to now by the great European exploiters in centuries of idle enjoyment and extravagant waste.

On this issue we can also refer to Sombart:

> It may be said indisputably, that the absolute contrasts between poor and rich are nowhere in the world anything like as great as they are in the United States. Above all, this is because the rich over there are so very much richer than the same group in Germany. In America there are certainly more people who own 1,000,000,000 marks than there are people owning 100,000,000 marks in Germany. Anyone who has ever been in Newport, the Baiae of New York, will have picked up the impression that in America having a million is commonplace. There is certainly no other place in the world where the princely palace of the very grandest style is so obviously the standard place of residence, while anyone who has wandered once through Tiffany's department store in New York will always sense something akin to the odor of poverty in even the most splendid luxury business of large European cities. Because Tiffany's also has branches in Paris and London, it can serve excellently for drawing comparisons between the extravagance and therefore the wealth of the top four hundred families in the three countries concerned. The managers of the New York head office told me that most of the merchandise they offer for sale in New York comes from Europe, where it is made especially for Tiffany's of New York. However, it is completely out of the question that a store in Europe – even Tiffany's own branches in Paris and London – would stock merchandise at prices such as it would fetch in New York. Only in New York are the dearest items said to be brought in for the woman shopper.[68]

So, fabulous wastefulness goes hand in hand with fabulous accumulation in a country whose bourgeoisie, both economically and ideologically, left the stage of severe Puritanism only a few decades ago! What an enormous growth

---

[68] Sombart, op. cit., pp. 8–9.

of exploitation, in both extension and intensity, this sudden transformation implies!

On the one hand, a gigantic growth of wealth, on the other hand, a no less gigantic growth of poverty – truly, the revisionist dogma about the gradual weakening of class contradictions has nowhere been more clearly reduced *ad absurdum*; and the doctrines of our Erfurt Programme, which our revisionists wanted to throw onto the scrap heap, have nowhere been more clearly illustrated than in the great republic on the other side of the ocean....[69]

X. Trade unions and socialism

Nowhere were the conditions more fully developed, under which our revisionists think the economic progress of the working class within the capitalist mode of production would have been guaranteed, than in the United States: complete democracy, the greatest freedom of organisation and freedom of the press, and a high social equality of rights.[70] Though the reserve of free land has shrunk, it has not yet been completely exhausted. And, on top of that, came also a strong development of the trade unions.

We have seen that the deterioration in the living standards of the working class dates from 1896. Precisely since that year there has been a rapid growth of the trade-union organisations. The most important among them, the American Federation of Labor, to which most of the trade unions belong, had 272,315 members in 1896 and 1,672,200 members in 1904. Since then, union membership has decreased a little: in 1905 it was only 1,513,200, a decrease of almost 10 per cent from the previous year.

Many of my good friends will surely distort my statements in order to make them appear as if I had declared that the trade unions are useless or even responsible for the deterioration in the situation of the workers. Of course, that is not my opinion. But the development showed that a force must have appeared that is able to paralyse the effects of a trade-union movement begun with so much energy. And one did not need to search much in order to find that force: it is the *trusts*, whose rise in the United States began simultaneously

---

[69] [(See Kautsky 1892. English edition: Kautsky 1910); reprinted (New York: Norton, 1971).]

[70] [For white Americans.]

with the above-mentioned strengthening of the trade unions, but whose power has grown even more rapidly than the power of the unions in the United States. They are the force that directly or indirectly drove up the prices of all products while they hindered the corresponding rise in wages and sometimes even reduce them absolutely.

The trade unions have not lost their significance for that reason; on the contrary, they have become an absolute necessity for the working class, but they have ceased to be an instrument able by itself to drive back capital, to diminish its exploitation, to undermine its power. These illusions can no longer be maintained. When the employers' combinations are well developed, the working class as a whole cannot get any further through the trade unions alone. To be sure, without the unions the working class would not only fail to make headway but would be driven back: it would have rapidly lost all its conquests and sunk into hopeless, absolute pauperisation.

If the employers' combinations more and more took away from the trade unions the capacity to drive back capital, they also made them indispensable for the proletariat in order to avoid being completely crushed by capital. If the isolated worker is already at a strong disadvantage vis-à-vis the individual capitalist, he would have sunk into hopeless slavery vis-à-vis the employers' combinations from which only the unions can protect him.

But the trade unions have not only become indispensable for preserving the position that the worker has already conquered; in present American conditions they can also become important means for constructing a great workers' party with socialist aims.[71]

It is clear that the American workers must, in the above-described circumstances, become more and more accessible to socialist ideas. True, socialist propaganda in the United States will find difficult obstacles in its way. We have already indicated some of them, such as the large number of immigrants in the American proletariat, who not only hardly understand each other but have grown up under political and social conditions that differ completely from those of their new country, so that they find their way to the tactics demanded by the special American conditions only with great difficulty – and this difficulty increases the more those immigrants had already been politically active in their country of origin and acquired over there firm rules

---

[71] [For a later elaboration of this idea by Kautsky see Kautsky 1909c.]

of political praxis. Besides, the complete lack of 'revolutionary romanticism', in the theoretical sense, makes the average American in many respects quite crippled in terms of socialist propaganda and action and opens a wide field of activity for quacks and swindlers.

But, on the other hand, economic development nowhere proceeds more rapidly than in America, and the capitalist class is nowhere so little hindered by intermediate strata and traditions from developing all its exploitative tendencies; nowhere are class contradictions sharpening more rapidly than in America.

The masses will be forced to rebel against capitalist tyranny in the United States more than anywhere else. Even if this rebellion still temporarily assumes quite peculiar forms, even if it brings to the fore all sorts of demagogues, even if the growth of the Social-Democratic party is still temporarily slow and interrupted by momentary reverses, the American proletariat, like the European proletariat, must finally come to the conclusion that only the realisation of the Social-Democratic programme, only the expropriation of the expropriators, can free them from their yoke that weighs upon them ever more oppressively.

Whoever ponders upon the facts presented above must reach with us the conclusion that within a generation we must also necessarily expect a flourishing of socialism in America, indeed, even considerably earlier. In America, everything happens more rapidly and more forcefully than in Europe. If Russia has shown us, as we expected, the first example of a proletariat constituting the most powerful driving force in the political revolution of a whole country, perhaps America will show us, even before Europe, the example of a proletariat conquering political and economic power from the capitalist class in order to establish a socialist society.

References

Adler (ed.), Friedrich 1954, *Briefwechsel mit August Bebel und Karl Kautsky: Sowie Briefe von und an Ignaz Auer Eduard Bernstein, Adolf Braun, Heinrich Dietz, Friedrich Ebert, Wilhelm Liebknecht, Hermann Müller und Paul Singer,* hrsg. vom Parteivorstand der Sozialistischen Partei Österreichs, Vienna: Verlag der Wiener Volksbuchhandlung.

Anneke, Fr., K. Schapper, K. Marx, H. Becker, and W. Wolff 1849, 'Statement', *Neue Rheinische Zeitung,* No. 273, 15 April, in Marx and Engels, *Collected Works,* Volume 9, London: Lawrence & Wishart.

Aref'eva (ed.), I.G. 1995, *Tragicheskie sud'by: repressirovannye uchenye Akademii nauk SSSR,* Moscow: Nauka.

Ascher, Abraham 2004, *The Revolution of 1905: A Short History,* Stanford: Stanford University Press.

Aulard, Alphonse 1902, *Politicheskaya istoriya Frantsuzskoi revolyutsii,* Moscow: Izdatel'stvo Skirmunta.

Aveling, Eleanor Marx and Edward Aveling (eds.) 1969, *The Eastern Question: A Reprint of Letters Written 1853–1856, dealing with the Events of the Crimean War,* London: Frank Cass.

Baron, Samuel H. 1963, *Plekhanov: The Father of Russian Marxism,* Stanford: Stanford University Press.

Beer, Max 1905, 'Der Kampf um den Stillen Ozean', *Die Neue Zeit,* 23, 1.

Beer, Max 1935, *Fifty Years of International Socialism,* London: G. Allen & Unwin.

Belfort Bax, Ernest 1896a, 'Our German Fabian Convert; or, Socialism According to Bernstein (November 1896)', *Justice,* 7 November.

Belfort Bax, Ernest 1896b, 'The Socialism of Bernstein', 21 November, *Justice.*

Bernstein, Eduard 1893, *Ferdinand Lassalle as a Social Reformer,* London: Swan Sonnenschein.

Bernstein, Eduard 1896, 'Amongst the Philistines: A Rejoinder to Belfort Bax', *Justice,* 14 November.

Bernstein, Eduard 1907, *Evolutionary Socialism,* London: Independent Labour Party.

Bernstein, Eduard 1963 [1895], *Cromwell and Communism: Socialism and Democracy in the Great English Revolution,* London: George Allen & Unwin.

Bernstein, Eduard 1993, *The Preconditions of Socialism,* edited and translated by Henry Tudor, Cambridge: Cambridge University Press.

Bömelburg, Theodor 1905, 'Die Stellung der Gewerkschaften zum Generalstreik', in *Protokoll der Verhandlungen des fünften Kongresses der Gewerkschaften Deutschlands, abgehalten zu Köln am Rhein, vom 22. bis 27. Mai 1905,* Berlin: Verlag der Generalkommission der Gewerkschaften Deutschlands. Reprinted in Grunenberg (ed.) 1970.

Bougeart, Alfred 1865, *Marat, l'ami du peuple,* Paris: A. Lacroix, Verboeckhoven & cie.

Cannon, James P. 1955a, 'The I.W.W.: The Great Anticipation (On the Fiftieth Anniversary of the Founding Convention)', *Fourth International,* 16, 3, Summer.

Cannon, James P. 1955b, 'Eugene V. Debs and the Socialist Movement of his Time', *Fourth International,* 16, 1, Winter.

Day, Richard B. 1973, *Leon Trotsky and the Politics of Economic Isolation,* Cambridge: Cambridge University Press.

Day, Richard B. 1979–80, 'Rosa Luxemburg and the Accumulation of Capital', *Critique*, 12: 81–96.

Day, Richard B. 1981, *The 'Crisis' and the 'Crash': Soviet Studies of the West, 1917–1939*, London: NLB.

Day, Richard B. 2004, 'Introduction' to *Pavel V. Maksakovsky: The Capitalist Cycle – An Essay on the Marxist Theory of the Cycle*, Leiden: Brill Academic Publishers.

Deborin, A. 1930, *Na boevom postu: Sbornik k shestidesyatiletiyu D.B. Ryazanova*, Moscow: Gosudarstvennoe izdatel'stvo.

Deutscher, Isaac 1965, *The Prophet Armed: Trotsky, 1879–1921*, New York: Vintage.

Donald, Moira 1993, *Marxism and Revolution: Karl Kautsky and the Russian Marxists, 1900–1924*, New Haven: Yale University Press.

Engelhardt, A.N., *Iz derevni*, translated by Cathy A. Frierson as *Aleksandr Nikolaevich Engelgardt's Letters from the Country, 1872–1887*, Oxford: Oxford University Press, 1993.

Engels, Frederick 1849, 'The Magyar Struggle', *Neue Rheinische Zeitung*, No. 194, 13 January, in Marx and Engels, *Collected Works*, Volume 8, London: Lawrence & Wishart.

Engels, Frederick 1850a, 'The Campaign for the German Imperial Constitution', in Marx and Engels, *Collected Works*, Volume 10, London: Lawrence & Wishart.

Engels, Frederick 1850b, *The Peasant War in Germany*, in Marx and Engels, *Collected Works*, Volume 10, London: Lawrence & Wishart.

Engels, Frederick 1874, 'On Social Relations in Russia', in Marx and Engels, *Collected Works*, Volume 24, London: Lawrence & Wishart.

Engels, Frederick 1884a, 'Marx and the *Neue Rheinische Zeitung*, 1848–49', *Der Sozialdemokrat*, 13 March, in Marx and Engels, *Collected Works*, Volume 26, London: Lawrence & Wishart.

Engels, Frederick 1884b, 'Letter to August Bebel', London, 11 December, in Marx and Engels, *Collected Works*, Volume 47, London: Lawrence & Wishart.

Engels, Frederick 1885, 'On the History of the Communist League', *Sozialdemokrat* (12–26 November), in Marx and Engels, *Collected Works*, Volume 26, London: Lawrence & Wishart.

Engels, Frederick 1887, 'Preface to the Second German Edition of *The Housing Question*', in Marx and Engels, *Collected Works*, Volume 26, London: Lawrence & Wishart.

Engels, Frederick 1889, 'Letter to Karl Kautsky', 20 February, in Marx and Engels, *Selected Correspondence*, Moscow: Foreign Languages Publishing House, 1953.

Engels, Frederick 1891, 'Introduction to Karl Marx's *The Civil War in France*', in Marx and Engels, *Collected Works*, Volume 27, London: Lawrence & Wishart.

Engels, Frederick 1892, 'Engels to N.F. Danielson', 15 March, in Marx and Engels, *Collected Works*, Volume 49, London: Lawrence & Wishart.

Engels, Frederick 1894, 'Afterword to *Social Relations in Russia*', in Marx and Engels, *Collected Works*, Volume 27, London: Lawrence & Wishart.

Engels, Frederick 1895, 'Preface to Karl Marx, *The Class Struggles in France, 1848–50*', in Marx and Engels, *Collected Works*, Volume 27, London: Lawrence & Wishart.

Engels, Frederick 1969, *Revolution and Counter-Revolution in Germany*, London: Lawrence & Wishart.

Engels, Friedrich 1884, 'Marx und die *Neue Rheinische Zeitung*, 1848–49', *Der Sozialdemokrat*, Nr. 11 vom 13. März. Reprinted in: Marx and Engels, *Werke*, Berlin: Dietz Verlag, 5, 1975. For the English translation, see *Collected Works*, Volume 26, London: Lawrence & Wishart.

Gaido, Daniel 2001, 'The Populist Interpretation of American History: A Materialist Revision', *Science & Society*, 65, 3: 350–75.

Gaido, Daniel 2003, '"The American Worker" and the Theory of Permanent Revolution: Karl Kautsky on Werner Sombart's *Why Is there No Socialism in the United States?*', *Historical Materialism*, 11, 4: 79–123.

Gaido, Daniel 2006, *The Formative Period of American Capitalism: A Materialist Interpretation*, London: Routledge.

Gazette Nationale, ou Le Moniteur universel, trans. Laura Mason in *The French Revolution: A Document Collection*, edited by Laura Mason and Tracey Rizzo, New York: Houghton Mifflin, 1999.

Getzler, Israel 1967, *Martov, A Political Biography of a Russian Social Democrat*, Cambridge: Cambridge University Press.

Grunenberg (ed.), Antonia 1970, *Die Massenstreikdebatte: Beiträge von Parvus, Rosa Luxemburg, Karl Kautsky und Anton Pannekoek*, Frankfurt: Europaische Verlagsanstalt.

Harding (ed.), Neil 1983, *Marxism in Russia: Key Documents 1879–1906*, Cambridge: Cambridge University Press.

Hilferding, Rudolf 1903, 'Werner Sombart, *Der moderne Kapitalismus*', *Zeitschrift für Volkswirtschaft, Sozialpolitik und Verwaltung*, 12: 446–53.

Hilferding, Rudolf 1905, 'Letter to Kautsky', in *Zwischen den Stülen, oder über die Unvereinbarkeit von Theorie und Praxis: Schriften Rudolf Hilferdings 1904–1940*, edited by Cora Stephen, Berlin: J.H.W. Dietz, 1982.

Hilferding, Rudolf 1907, 'Review of Parvus, *Die Kolonialpolitik*', *Die Neue Zeit*, 25, 2: 687–8.

Hilferding, Rudolf 1981 [1910], *Finance Capital: A Study of the Latest Phase of Capitalist Development*, London: Routledge and Kegan Paul.

Hobson, John A. 1902, *Imperialism: A Study*, New York: James Pott.

Hudis, Peter and Kevin B. Anderson (eds.) 2004, *The Rosa Luxemburg Reader*, New York: Monthly Review Press.

Ilyin, Vladimir 1899, *Razvitie kapitalizma v Rossii*, Moscow:Tipo-litografiya A. Leiferta. For the English translation see Lenin 1899.

Iurenev, I. 1924, 'Mezhraionka', *Proletarskaya Revolyutsiya*, 1, 24: 109–39 and 2, 25: 114–43.

IWW 1905, *Proceedings of the Founding Convention of the Industrial Workers of the World: Founded at Chicago, June 27–July 8, 1905*, Stenographically reported by W.E. McDermut; Revised and approved by William E. Trautmann, Secretary of the Convention, New York: Labor News Company.

Joll (ed.), James 1974, *The Second International 1889–1914*, London: Routledge & K. Paul.

Katayama, Sen 1918, *The Labor Movement in Japan*, Chicago: Charles H. Kerr & Company.

Katkov, George 1967, *Russia 1917: The February Revolution*, London: Longmans.

Kautsky (ed.), Karl 1906, *1649–1789–1905*, St Petersburg: 'Luch'.

Kautsky, Karl 1889a, 'Der jüngste Zukunftsroman', *Die Neue Zeit*, 7: 268–76.

Kautsky, Karl 1889b, *Die Klassengegensätze von 1789: Zum hundertjährigen Gedenktag der grossen Revolution*, Stuttgart: Dietz. Originally published in *Die Neue Zeit*, 1889, 7: 1–9, 49–56, 97–108, 145–57. A second edition appeared in 1908: *Die Klassengegensätze im Zeitalter der Französischen Revolution: Neue Ausgabe der Klassengegensätze von 1789*, Stuttgart: Dietz.

Kautsky, Karl 1892, *Das Erfurter Programm: in seinem grundsätzlichen Theil*, Stuttgart: Dietz. English edition: *The Class Struggle (Erfurt Program)*, translated by William E. Bohn, Chicago: C.H. Kerr & Company, 1910; reprinted, New York: Norton, 1971.

Kautsky, Karl 1895, 'Unsere amerikanischen Berichte', *Die Neue Zeit*, 13, 2: 183–5.

Kautsky, Karl 1898, 'Kiaotschau', *Die Neue Zeit*, 16, 2: 14–26.

Kautsky, Karl 1899, *Bernstein und das sozialdemokratische Programm. Eine Antikritik*, Stuttgart: Dietz.

Kautsky, Karl 1900, 'Die Neutralisierung der Gewerkschaften', *Die Neue Zeit*, 18, 2: 388–94, 429–33, 457–66, 492–7.

Kautsky, Karl 1900a, *Le Marxisme et son critique Bernstein*, Paris: P.V. Stock.

Kautsky, Karl 1901, *La Lutte des classes en France en 1789*, translated by Édouard Berth, Paris: G. Jacques, Bibliothèque d'études socialistes, No. 3; reprint: *Les cahiers du CERMTRI*, No. 95, Paris: Centre d'Études et de Recherches sur les Mouvements Trotskyste et Révolutionnaires Internationaux, 1999.

Kautsky, Karl 1902a, 'Socialist Agitation among Farmers in America', *International Socialist Review*, 3: 148–160.

Kautsky, Karl 1902b, 'Slavyane i revolyutsiya', *Iskra*, No. 18. Reprinted in Kautsky 1959.

Kautsky, Karl 1902–4, *Die soziale Revolution*, 2 vols. in 1: I. *Sozialreform und soziale Revolution*, 1902; II. *Am Tage nach der sozialen Revolution*, 1904, Berlin: Vorwärts. First English edition: *The Social Revolution and The Day after the Revolution*, translated by A.M. and May Wood Simons, Chicago: Kerr, 1902.

Kautsky, Karl 1904a, 'Allerhand Revolutionäres', *Die Neue Zeit*, 22, 1: 588–98, 620–7, 652–7, 685–95, 732–40.

Kautsky, Karl 1904b, 'Vorrede zur polnischen Ausgabe der Kommunistischen Manifestes u.d.T.: Wie weit ist das *Kommunistische Manifest* veraltet?', *Leipziger Volkszeitung*, Nr. 169, 170, 172; July 23, 25, 27; *Freie Presse*, Elberfeld-Barmen, Nr. 175, 176, 177; July 28, 29, 30.

Kautsky, Karl 1904c, 'Prefatory Note to Luśnia's "Unbewaffnete Revolution?"', *Die Neue Zeit*, 22, 1: 559.

Kautsky, Karl 1905a, 'Sledstviya Russko-Yaponskoi voiny i sotsial-demokratiya', *Proletarii*, 1905, Nr. 9.

Kautsky, Karl 1905b, 'Alte und neue Revolution', in *Festschrift 1649–1789–1905*, Berlin: *Buchhandlung* Vorwärts.

Kautsky, Karl 1905c, 'Der Kongress von Köln', *Die Neue Zeit*, 23, 2.

Kautsky, Karl 1905d, 'Der Parteitag von Jena', *Die Neue Zeit*, 24, 1: 5–10.

Kautsky, Karl 1905e, 'Die Agrarfrage in Russland', *Die Neue Zeit*, 24, 1: 412–23.

Kautsky, Karl 1905f, 'Die Folgen des japanischen Sieges und die Sozialdemokratie', *Die Neue Zeit*, 23, 2: 460–8, 492–9, 529–37.

Kautsky, Karl 1905g, 'Eine Nachlese zum Vorwärtskonflikt', *Die Neue Zeit*, 24, 1: 313–26. Reprinted in Stern (ed.) 1961, Volume 4.

Kautsky, Karl 1905h, 'Posledstviya pobedy Yapontsev i sotsial-demokratiya', *Iskra*, Nr. 108.

Kautsky, Karl 1905i, 'Staraya i novaya revolyutsiya', *Evreiskii Rabochii*, St. Petersburg, Nr. 1, 9 December.

Kautsky, Karl 1905j, 'To What Extent is the *Communist Manifesto* Obsolete?', *Social Democrat*, 15 March, 9, 3: 155–64.

Kautsky, Karl 1905k, *Sledstvyia Russko-Yaponskoi voiny*, Tr. Lemberk, St. Petersburg: Molot.

Kautsky, Karl 1906, 'Der amerikanische Arbeiter', *Die Neue Zeit*, 24, 1: 676–83, 717–27, 740–52 and 773–87.

Kautsky, Karl 1906a, 'Allerhand Revolutionäres' *Revolyutsionnye Perspektivy*, [Russian translation], Kiev.

Kautsky, Karl 1906b, 'Ancienne et nouvelle Révolution', *Russia Rivoluzionaria* (Lugano) Nr. 1.

Kautsky, Karl 1906c, 'Ein Buch über den Generalstreik', *Könisberger Volkszeitung*, Nr. 138, 15. June.

Kautsky, Karl 1906d, 'Genossin Luxemburg über die Gewerkschaften', *Vorwärts*, No. 89 (18 April). Reprinted in Stern (ed.) 1961, Volume 6.

Kautsky, Karl 1906e, 'Partei und Gewerkschaft', *Die Neue Zeit*, 24, 2: 716–35, 749–54.

Kautsky, Karl 1906f, 'Revolutions, Past and Present', *International Socialist Review*, 6.

Kautsky, Karl 1906g, *Amerikanskii i Ruskii rabochii*, Kiev: Biblioteka sotsialisticheskovo znanii.

Kautsky, Karl 1906h, *Amerikanskii i Ruskii rabochii*, tr. E. and I. Leont'ev, St. Petersburg: Slovo.

Kautsky, Karl 1906i, *Amerikanskii i Ruskii rabochii*, tr. Lurie, foreword and ed. Avilov, St. Petersburg: Znanie.

Kautsky, Karl 1906j, *Amerikanskii i Ruskii rabochii*, tr. S. and M. L-ch, St. Petersburg: Amiran.

Kautsky, Karl 1906k, *Amerikanskii rabochii*, St. Petersburg: Biblioteka obshchestvennaya nauka.

Kautsky, Karl 1906l, *Na sovremennye temy: revolyutsionnye perspektivy*, Kiev: Pravda.

Kautsky, Karl 1906m, *Ruskii i Amerikanskii rabochii, (predislovie, primechaniya i redaksiya A. Lunacharskovo)*, St. Petersburg: Tipografiya Spb. T-va 'Trud'. Fontanka, 86.

Kautsky, Karl 1907a, 'Triebkräfte und Aussichten der russischen Revolution', *Die Neue Zeit*, 25, 1: 184–90, 324–33.

Kautsky, Karl 1907b, *Amerikanskii rabochii*, St. Petersburg: L'vovich.

Kautsky, Karl 1907c, *Na sovremennye temy: revolyutsionnye perspektivy*, St. Petersburg: Znanie.

Kautsky, Karl 1907d, *Sledstviya Russko-Yaponskoi voiny*, St. Petersburg: L'vovich.

Kautsky, Karl 1907e, *Dvishushchie sily i perspektivy russkoi revolyutsii*, Moscow: Novaya epokha.

Kautsky, Karl 1909a, 'Samuel Gompers', *Die Neue Zeit*, 27, 2: 677–85. English edition in Daniel Gaido, 'Marxism and the Union Bureaucracy: Karl Kautsky on Samuel Gompers and the German Free Trade Unions', *Historical Materialism*, 16, 3, 2008: 115–36.

Kautsky, Karl 1909b, *The Road to Power*, Chicago: Samuel A. Bloch.

Kautsky, Karl 1909c, 'Sects or Class Parties', *Die Neue Zeit*, 13, 7: 316–28.

Kautsky, Karl 1910–11, 'Krieg und Frieden. Betrachtungen zur Maifeier', *Die Neue Zeit*, 29, 2: 97–107.

Kautsky, Karl 1910a, 'Die Civic Federation', *Die Neue Zeit*, 28, 1: 132–7.

Kautsky, Karl 1910b, 'Eine neue Strategie', *Die Neue Zeit*, 28, 2: 332–41, 364–74, 412–21.

Kautsky, Karl 1910c, 'Was nun?', *Die Neue Zeit*, 28, 2, reprinted in Grunenberg (ed.) 1970.

Kautsky, Karl 1910d, 'Zwischen Baden und Luxemburg', *Die Neue Zeit*, 28, 2, reprinted in *Materialien zum politischen Richtungsstreit in der deutschen Sozialdemokratie, 1890– 1917*, Volume I, edited by Peter Friedemann, Frankfurt am Main: Ullstein, 1978.

Kautsky, Karl 1911, *Parlamentarismus und Demokratie*, Stuttgart: J.H.W. Dietz Nachf.

Kautsky, Karl 1912, 'A.M. Simons, *Social Forces in American History*', *Die Neue Zeit*, 30, 2: 631.

Kautsky, Karl 1913, 'Nachgedanken zu den nachdenklichen Betrachtungen', *Die Neue Zeit*, 31, 2: 532–40, 558–68, 662–4.

Kautsky, Karl 1914, *Der politische Massenstreik: Ein Beitrag zur Geschichte der Massenstreikdiskussionen innerhalb der deutschen Sozialdemokratie*, Berlin: Buchhandlung Vorwärts.

Kautsky, Karl 1919, *Terrorism and Communism: A Contribution to the Natural History of Revolution*, London: National Labour Press.

Kautsky, Karl 1921a, *Are the Jews a Race?*, London: Jonathan Cape.

Kautsky, Karl 1921b, *Von der Demokratie zur Staats-Sklaverei: eine Auseinandersetzung mit Trotzki*, Berlin: Verlagegenossenschaft Freiheit.

Kautsky, Karl 1927, *Die materialistische Geschichtsauffassung*, 2 vols., Berlin: J.H.W. Dietz.

Kautsky, Karl 1959, *Put' k vlasti: politicheskie ocherki o vrastanie v revolyutsii/Slavyane i revolyutsii* edited by A.V. Romanov, A.M. Rumyantsev, N.V. Tropkin, P.N. Fedoseev, Moscow: Gosudarstvennoe izdatel'stvo politicheskoi literatury.

Kautsky, Karl 1964, *The Dictatorship of the Proletariat*, Ann Arbor: University of Michigan.

Kautsky, Karl 1969, *Le Chemin du pouvoir*, Paris: Éditions Anthropos.

Kautsky, Karl 1972, *Der Weg zur Macht*, hrsg. und eingeleitet von Georg Fulberth, Frankfurt am Main: Europaische Verlagsanstalt.

Kautsky, Karl 1975, *Socialism and Colonial Policy*, London: Athol Books.

Kautsky, Karl 1983, 'The Driving Forces of the Russian Revolution and its Prospects', in Harding (ed.) 1983.

Kautsky, Karl 1988, *The Agrarian Question*, Volume II, London: Zwan Publications.

Keep, J.L.H. 1963, *The Rise of Social Democracy in Russia*, Oxford: Oxford University Press.

King, Bolton 1901, *A History of Italian Unity*, Volume I, Russian translation as *Istoria ob'edineniya Italii*, Moscow: publisher unknown.

Korsch, Karl 1929, *Die materialistische Geschichtsauffassung: Eine Auseinandersetzung mit Kurl Kaulsky*, Leipzig: Hirschfeld.

Krause, Werner 1961, 'Ein unveröffentlicher Brief von Friedrich Engels über die Werttheorie', *Beiträge zur Geschichte der Deutschen Arbeiterbewegung*, 3, 3: 636–40.

Kukushkin (ed.), Yu. S. 1996, *Gosudarstvo russkoe: vlast' i obshchestvo. S drevneishikh vremen do nashikh dnei. Sbornik dokumentov*, Moscow: Izd-vo Mosk. Universiteta.

Larsson, Reidar 1970, *Theories of Revolution: From Marx to the First Russian Revolution*, Stockholm: Almqvist & Wiksell.

Lassalle, Ferdinand 1905, *Rech' pered sudom prisyazhnykh' (Rol' proletariata i burzhuazii v 1848 godu v Germanii): Perevod s nemetskovo pod redaktsiei i s predisloviem N. Trotskovo*, S.-Peterburg: Tsentral'naya Tipo-Lit. M.Ya. Minkova.

Lenin, Vladimir I. 1897, 'The Heritage We Renounce', in *Collected Works*, Volume 2, Moscow: Progress Publishers.

Lenin, Vladimir I. 1899, *The Development of Capitalism in Russia*, in *Collected Works*, Volume 3, Moscow: Progress Publishers.

Lenin, Vladimir I. 1900, 'Preface to the Pamphlet *May Days in Kharkov*', in *Collected Works*, Volume 4, Moscow: Progress Publishers.

Lenin, Vladimir I. 1901, 'The Persecutors of the Zemstvo and the Hannibals of Liberalism', in *Collected Works*, Volume 5, Moscow: Progress Publishers.

Lenin, Vladimir I. 1902a, 'Material for the Preparation of the Programme of the R.S.D.L.P.: Draft Programme of the Russian Social-Democratic Labour Party', in *Collected Works*, Volume 6, Moscow: Progress Publishers.

Lenin, Vladimir I. 1902b, 'Notes on Plekhanov's First Draft Programme', in Lenin 1902a.

Lenin, Vladimir I. 1902c, 'Notes on Plekhanov's Second Draft Programme', in *Collected Works*, Volume 6, Moscow: Progress Publishers.

Lenin, Vladimir I. 1902d, 'A Letter to the Zemstvoists', *Iskra*, No. 18, 10 March, in *Collected Works*, Volume 6, Moscow: Progress Publishers.

Lenin, Vladimir I. 1902e, 'On the Bor'ba Group', *Iskra*, March, in *Collected Works*, Volumes 5 and 6, Moscow: Progress Publishers.

Lenin, Vladimir I. 1902f, 'Political Agitation and the Class Point of View', in *Iskra*, no. 16, 1 February, in *Collected Works*, Volume 5, Moscow: Progress Publishers.

Lenin, Vladimir I. 1902g, *The Agrarian Programme of Russian Social-Democracy*, in *Collected Works*, Volume 6, Moscow: Progress Publishers.

Lenin, Vladimir I. 1902h, *What Is to Be Done?: Burning Questions of Our Movement*, in *Collected Works*, Volume 5, Moscow: Progress Publishers.

Lenin, Vladimir I. 1905a, 'Draft Resolution on the Attitude of the R.S.D.L.P. Towards the Armed Uprising', in *Collected Works*, Volume 8, Moscow: Progress Publishers.

Lenin, Vladimir I. 1905b, 'Friends Meet', in *Collected Works*, Volume 9, Moscow: Progress Publishers.

Lenin, Vladimir I. 1905c, 'On the Provisional Revolutionary Government', in *Collected Works*, Volume 8, Moscow: Progress Publishers.

Lenin, Vladimir I. 1905d, 'Playing at Parliamentarism', in *Collected Works*, Volume 9, Moscow: Progress Publishers.

Lenin, Vladimir I. 1905e, 'Social-Democracy and the Provisional Revolutionary Government', in *Collected Works*, Volume 8, Moscow: Progress Publishers.

Lenin, Vladimir I. 1905f, 'Social-Democracy's Attitude Towards the Peasant Movement', in *Collected Works*, Volume 9, Moscow: Progress Publishers.

Lenin, Vladimir I. 1905g, 'Socialism and the Peasantry', in *Collected Works*, Volume 9, Moscow: Progress Publishers.

Lenin, Vladimir I. 1905h, 'Speech on an Agreement with the Socialist-Revolutionaries', in *Collected Works*, Volume 8, Moscow: Progress Publishers.

Lenin, Vladimir I. 1905i, 'The Beginning of the Revolution in Russia', in *Collected Works*, Volume 8, Moscow: Progress Publishers.
Lenin, Vladimir I. 1905j, 'The Revolutionary Army and the Revolutionary Government', in *Collected Works*, Volume 8, Moscow: Progress Publishers.
Lenin, Vladimir I. 1905k, *Two Tactics of Social Democracy in the Democratic Revolution*, in *Collected Works*, Volume 9, Moscow: Progress Publishers.
Lenin, Vladimir I. 1905l, 'The Revolutionary-Democratic Dictatorship of the Proletariat and the Peasantry', in *Collected Works*, Volume 8, Moscow: Progress Publishers.
Lenin, Vladimir I. 1906a, 'Lessons of the Moscow Uprising', in *Collected Works*, Volume 11, Moscow: Progress Publishers.
Lenin, Vladimir I. 1906b, 'Preface to the Russian Translation of K. Kautsky's Pamphlet: *The Driving Forces and Prospects of the Russian Revolution*', in *Collected Works*, Volume 11, Moscow: Progress Publishers.
Lenin, Vladimir I. 1906c, 'The Proletariat and its Ally in the Russian Revolution', December 10 (23), in *Collected Works*, Volume 11, Moscow: Progress Publishers.
Lenin, Vladimir I. 1906d, 'The Stages, the Trend and the Prospects of the Revolution', in Lenin 1906e.
Lenin, Vladimir I. 1906e, 'Revision of the Agrarian Programme of the Workers' Party', in *Collected Works*, Volume 10, Moscow: Progress Publishers.
Lenin, Vladimir I. 1907a, 'Concluding Remarks on the Report on the Attitude towards Bourgeois Parties', 14 (27) May, in *Collected Works*, Volume 12, Moscow: Progress Publishers.
Lenin, Vladimir I. 1907b, 'Draft Resolutions for the Fifth Congress of the R.S.D.L.P.', in *Collected Works*, Volume 12, Moscow: Progress Publishers.
Lenin, Vladimir I. 1907c, 'Speech on the Attitude towards Bourgeois Parties, May 12 (25)', in *Collected Works*, Volume 12, Moscow: Progress Publishers.
Lenin, Vladimir I. 1907d, 'The International Socialist Congress in Stuttgart', *Proletarii*, Nr. 17, 20 October, in *Collected Works*, Volume 13, Moscow: Progress Publishers.
Lenin, Vladimir I. 1907e, *The Agrarian Programme of Social Democracy in the First Russian Revolution, 1905–1907*, in *Collected Works*, Volume 13, Moscow: Progress Publishers.
Lenin, Vladimir I. 1907f, 'Speech on the Attitude Towards Bourgeois Parties', 25 May, in *Collected Works*, Volume 12, Moscow: Progress Publishers.
Lenin, Vladimir I. 1907g, 'The Fifth Congress of the Russian Social-Democratic Labour Party, April 30–May 19 (May 13–June 1), 1907', in *Collected Works*, Volume 12, Moscow: Progress Publishers.
Lenin, Vladimir I. 1909a, 'Letter to I.I. Skvortsov-Stepanov', in *Collected Works*, Volume 16, Moscow: Progress Publishers.
Lenin, Vladimir I. 1909b, *The Aim of the Proletarian Struggle in Our Revolution*, in *Collected Works*, Volume 15, Moscow: Progress Publishers.
Lenin, Vladimir I. 1915, 'New Data on the Laws Governing the Development of Capitalism in Agriculture', in *Collected Works*, Volume 22, Moscow: Progress Publishers.
Lenin, Vladimir I. 1917a, 'The Tasks of the Proletariat in the Present Revolution', *Pravda*, No. 26, 7 April, in *Collected Works*, Volume 24, Moscow: Progress Publishers.
Lenin, Vladimir I. 1917b, *The State and Revolution*, in *Collected Works*, Volume 25, Moscow: Progress Publishers.
Lenin, Vladimir I. 1918a, Preface to 'Karl Marx: A Brief Biographical Sketch with an Exposition of Marxism (Moscow, 14 May)', in *Collected Works*, Volume 21, Moscow: Progress Publishers.
Lenin, Vladimir I. 1918b, *The Proletarian Revolution and the Renegade Kautsky*, in *Collected Works*, Volume 28, Moscow: Progress Publishers.
Lenin, Vladimir I. 1920, 'The Right of Nations to Self-Determination', in *Collected Works*, Volume 20, Moscow: Progress Publishers.
Lenin, Vladimir I. 1974, *Collected Works*, Volume 35, Moscow: Progress Publishers.
Lenin, Vladimir I. 1993, *Left-Wing Communism, an Infantile Disorder*, London: Bookmarks.

Leon, Abram 1970, *The Jewish Question: A Marxist Interpretation*, New York: Pathfinder Press.

Liebknecht, Karl 1973 [1907], *Militarism and Anti-Militarism*, Cambridge: Writers and Readers.

Looker (ed.), Robert 1972, *Rosa Luxemburg: Selected Political Writings*, London: Cape.

Luśnia, Michał 1904, 'Unbewaffnete Revolution?', *Die Neue Zeit*, 22, 1: 559–67.

Luxemburg, Rosa 1899–1900, 'Die "deutsche Wissenschaft" hinter den Arbeitern', *Die Neue Zeit*, 18, 2: 740–7 and 773–82; reprinted in *Gesammelte Werke*, Volume 1, Nr. 1, Berlin: Dietz Verlag.

Luxemburg, Rosa 1900, *Social Reform or Revolution*, in Waters (ed.) 1970.

Luxemburg, Rosa 1902, 'Aus dem Nachlass unserer Meister', *Vorwärts*, Nr. 263, 9 November, reprinted in *Gesammelte Werke*, Volume I/2, Berlin: Dietz.

Luxemburg, Rosa 1903, 'In Rate der Gelehrten', *Die Neue Zeit*, 22, 1: 5–10; reprinted in *Gesammelte Werke*, Volume 1, Nr. 2, Berlin: Dietz Verlag.

Luxemburg, Rosa 1905a, 'Die Debatten in Köln', *Sächsiche Arbeiter-Zeitung*, Nr. 140, 21 June, reprinted in *Gesammelte Werke*, Volume I/2, Berlin: Dietz Verlag.

Luxemburg, Rosa 1905b, 'Die kommenden Männer in Rußland', *Sächsische Arbeiter-Zeitung*, Nr. 140, 21 June, reprinted in *Gesammelte Werke*, Volume 1, Nr. 2, Berlin: Dietz Verlag.

Luxemburg, Rosa 1905c, 'Die Revolution in Rußland', *Die Neue Zeit*, 23, 1: 572–7, reprinted in *Gesammelte Werke*, Volume 1, Nr. 2, Berlin: Dietz Verlag.

Luxemburg, Rosa 1905d, 'Die russische Revolution', in *Festschrift 1649–1789–1905*, Berlin: *Buchhandlung Vorwärts*, reprinted in *Gesammelte Werke*, Volume 2, Berlin: Dietz Verlag.

Luxemburg, Rosa 1905e, 'In revolutionärer Stunde: Was weiter?', *Czerwony Sztandar* (Cracow), Nr. 26, May, Beilage, reprinted in *Gesammelte Werke*, Volume 1, Nr. 2, Berlin: Dietz.

Luxemburg, Rosa 1905f, 'Nach dem ersten Akt', *Die Neue Zeit*, 23, 1; 610–14.

Luxemburg, Rosa 1905g, 'Parteitag der Sozialdemokratischen Partei Deutschlands vom 17. bis 23. September 1905 in Jena', reprinted in Gesammelte Werke, Volume I/2, Berlin: Dietz Verlag.

Luxemburg, Rosa 1906, 'Parteitag der Sozialdemokratischen Partei Deutschlands vom 23. bis 29. September 1906 in Mannheim', *Gesammelte Werke*, Volume II, Berlin: Dietz Verlag.

Luxemburg, Rosa 1907a, 'Address to the Fifth Congress of the Russian Social-Democratic Labor Party', in Hudis and Anderson (eds.) 2004.

Luxemburg, Rosa 1907b, 'Die zwei Methoden der Gewerkschaftspolitk', *Die Neue Zeit*, 25, 1, reprinted in *Gesammelte Werke*, Volume 2, Berlin: Dietz Verlag.

Luxemburg, Rosa 1910a, 'Die Theorie und die Praxis', *Die Neue Zeit*, 28, 2: 564–78, 626–42, reprinted in *Gesammelte Werke*, Volume 2, Berlin: Dietz Verlag.

Luxemburg, Rosa 1910b, 'Ermattung oder Kampf?', *Die Neue Zeit*, 28, 2, reprinted in *Gesammelte Werke*, Volume 2, Berlin: Dietz Verlag.

Luxemburg, Rosa 1910c, 'The Next Step', in Looker (ed.) 1972.

Luxemburg, Rosa 1910d, 'Was Weiter?', *Dortmunder Arbeiterzeitung*, 14–15 March, reprinted in Gesammelte *Werke*, Volume II, Berlin: Dietz Verlag.

Luxemburg, Rosa 1911, 'Friedensutopien', *Leipziger Volkszeitung*, Nr. 103–4, May, reprinted in *Gesammelte Werke*, Volume 2, Berlin: Dietz Verlag.

Luxemburg, Rosa 1913, 'Das Offi ziösentum der Theorie', *Die Neue Zeit*, 31, 2, reprinted in *Gesammelte Werke*, Volume 3, Berlin: Dietz Verlag.

Luxemburg, Rosa 1915, *The Junius Pamphlet: The Crisis in the German Social Democracy*, in Waters (ed.) 1970.

Luxemburg, Rosa 1918, 'The Russian Revolution', translated by Bertram Wolfe in *The Russian Revolution & Leninism or Marxism?*, Ann Arbor: University of Michigan Press, 1961.

Luxemburg, Rosa 1971, 'Blanquismus und Sozialdemokratie', in *Internationalismus und Klassenkampf: Die polnischen Schriften*, edited by Jürgen Hentze, Neuwied: Luchterhand.

Luxemburg, Rosa 1986, *The Mass Strike, the Political Party and the Trade Unions*, London: Bookmarks.

Luxemburg, Rosa 1989, *Reform and Revolution*, London: Bookmarks.

Martin, Rudolf 1906, *Die Zukunft Russlands*, Leipzig: Dieterich.

Martow, Julius and Th. Dan 1926, *Geschichte der russischen Sozialdemokratie*, Berlin: Dietz. In Italian: Martov, Julij and Fjodor Dan 1973, *Storia della socialdemocrazia russa*, Milano: Feltrinelli.

Marx, Karl 1844, 'On The Jewish Question', *Deutsch-Französische Jahrbücher*, February, in Marx and Engels, *Collected Works*, Volume 3, London: Lawrence & Wishart.

Marx, Karl 1847, *The Poverty of Philosophy*, in Marx and Engels, *Collected Works*, Volume 6, London: Lawrence & Wishart.

Marx, Karl 1848a, 'The Bourgeoisie and the Counter-Revolution', *Neue Rheinische Zeitung*, No. 169, Cologne, 11 December, in Marx and Engels, *Collected Works*, Volume 8, London: Lawrence & Wishart.

Marx, Karl 1848b, 'A Decree of Eichmann's', *Neue Rheinische Zeitung*, No. 147, 19 November, in Marx and Engels, *Collected Works*, Volume 8, London: Lawrence & Wishart.

Marx, Karl 1848c, 'The Crowing of the Gallic Cock in Paris Will Once Again Rouse Europe', 12 November, in Marx and Engels, *Collected Works*, Volume 8, London: Lawrence & Wishart.

Marx, Karl 1848d, 'The Downfall of the Camphausen Government', in Marx and Engels, *Collected Works*, Volume 7, London: Lawrence and Wishart.

Marx, Karl, 1849, 'Two Political Trials', in Marx and Engels, *Collected Works*, Volume 8, London: Lawrence & Wishart.

Marx, Karl 1849a, 'The First Trial of the *Neue Rheinische Zeitung*', in Marx and Engels, *Collected Works*, Volume 8, London: Lawrence & Wishart.

Marx, Karl 1849b, 'Camphausen', *Neue Rheinische Zeitung*, 4 February, in Marx and Engels, *Collected Works*, Volume 8, London: Lawrence & Wishart.

Marx, Karl 1849c, 'The Summary Suppression of the *Neue Rheinische Zeitung*', *Neue Rheinische Zeitung*, No. 301, 19 May, final issue, in Marx and Engels, *Collected Works*, Volume 9, London: Lawrence & Wishart.

Marx, Karl 1849d, 'The Trial of the Rhenish District Committee of Democrats', in Marx and Engels, *Articles from the Neue Rheinische Zaitung 1848–49*, Moscow: Progress Publishers.

Marx, Karl 1850, *The Class Struggles in France, 1848–50*, in Marx and Engels, *Collected Works*, Volume 10, London: Lawrence & Wishart.

Marx, Karl 1851, 'Letter to Engels', London, 13 July, in Marx and Engels, *Collected Works*, Volume 38, London: Lawrence & Wishart.

Marx, Karl 1853, 'Revelations Concerning the Communist Trial in Cologne', in Marx and Engels, *Collected Works*, Volume 11, London: Lawrence & Wishart.

Marx, Karl 1856, 'Letter to Engels', London, 16 April, in Marx and Engels, *Collected Works*, Volume 40, London: Lawrence & Wishart.

Marx, Karl 1859, 'Preface to *A Contribution to the Critique of Political Economy*', in Marx and Engels, *Collected Works*, Volume 29, London: Lawrence & Wishart.

Marx, Karl 1871, 'Address to the General Council of the International Working Men's Association on the Civil War in France, 1871', in Marx and Engels, *Collected Works*, Volume 22, London: Lawrence and Wishart.

Marx, Karl 1877, 'Letter to the editor of *Otechestvennye Zapiski* [*Notes on the Fatherland*]', in Marx and Engels, *Collected Works*, Volume 24, London: Lawrence & Wishart.

Marx, Karl 1881, 'First Draft of the Letter to Vera & Zasulich', in Marx and Engels, *Collected Works*, Volume 24, London: Lawrence & Wishart.

Marx, Karl 1951, *The Class Struggles in France, 1848–50*, in Marx and Engels, *Selected Works*, Moscow: Foreign Languages Publishing House, Volume 1.

Marx, Karl 1956, *Capital: A Critique of Political Economy*, Volume I, New York: The Modern Library.

Marx, Karl 1961, *Capital*, Volume I, Moscow: Foreign Languages Publishing House.

Marx, Karl 1973a, 'The Bourgeoisie and the Counter-Revolution', *Neue Rheinische Zeitung*, No. 169, Cologne, 11 December, in *The Revolutions of 1848*, London: Penguin.

Marx, Karl 1973b, *The Eighteenth Brumaire of Louis Napoleon*, in *Surveys from Exile*, London: Penguin.

Marx, Karl 1974, *The First International and After*, London: Penguin.

Marx, Karl 1976, *Capital*, Volume I, London: Penguin.

Marx, Karl 1981, *Capital* Volume III, London: Penguin.

Marx, Karl and Frederick Engels 1845, *The Holy Family*, in Marx and Engels, *Collected Works*, Volume 4, London: Lawrence & Wishart.

Marx, Karl and Frederick Engels 1847, 'Rules of the Communist League' (December), in Marx and Engels, *Collected Works* Volume 6, London: Lawrence & Wishart.

Marx, Karl and Frederick Engels 1848a, *Manifesto of the Communist Party*, in Marx and Engels, *Collected Works*, Volume 6, London: Lawrence & Wishart.

Marx, Karl and Frederick Engels 1848b, 'The Government of the Counter-Revolution', *Neue Rheinische Zeitung*, No. 110, 23 September, in Marx and Engels, *Collected Works*, Volume 7, London: Lawrence & Wishart.

Marx, Karl and Frederick Engels 1850, 'Address of the Central Authority to the League', in Marx and Engels, *Collected Works*, Volume 10, London: Lawrence & Wishart.

Marx, Karl and Frederick Engels 1954, *Selected Correspondence*, Moscow: Foreign Languages Publishing House.

Marx, Karl and Friedrich Engels 1906, *Das kommunistische Manifest*. Siebente autorisierte deutsche Ausgabe. Mit Vorreden von Karl Marx und Friedrich Engels und einem Vorwort von Karl Kautsky, Berlin: Verlag Buchhandlung Vorwärts.

Marx, Karl and Frederick Engels 1972, *Articles from the 'Neue Rheinische Zeitung' 1848–49*, Moscow: Progress Publishers.

Marx, Karl and Friedrich Engels 1977, *Marx-Engels Gesamtausgabe (MEGA)*, Erste Abteilung, Band 10, *Berlin*: Dietz.

Matthias, Erich 1957, *Kautsky und der Kautskyanismus: Die Funktion der Ideologie in der deutschen Sozialdemokratie vor dem ersten Weltkriege*, Tübingen: Mohr (Paul Siebeck).

McNeal, R.H. (ed.) 1974, *Resolutions and Decisions of the Communist Party of the Soviet Union*, Volume 1: *The Russian Social-Democratic Labour Party: 1898–1917*, Toronto: University of Toronto Press.

Mehring, Franz (ed.) 1902, *Gesammelte Schriften von Karl Marx und Friedrich Engels, 1841 bis 1850*, Bd. III: *Von Mai 1848 bis Oktober 1850*, Stuttgart: J.H.W. Dietz Nachf.

Mehring, Franz 1895, 'Einiges über den jungen Engels', October, reprinted in *Aufsätze zur Geschichte der Arbeiterbewegung, Gesammelte Schriften*, Volume 4, Berlin: Dietz, 1963.

Mehring, Franz 1896, 'Politik und Sozialismus', December, reprinted in *Politische Publizistik, 1891 bis 1904, Gesammelte Schriften*, Volume 14, Berlin: Dietz, 1964.

Mehring, Franz 1899, 'Eine Nachlese', *Die Neue Zeit*, 17, 2: 147–54, 208–15, 239–47.

Mehring, Franz 1902, 'Ein französischer Sombart', March, reprinted in *Politische Publizistik, 1891 bis 1904, Gesammelte Schriften*, Volume 14, Berlin: Dietz, 1964.

Mehring, Franz 1904, 'Marx in Hühnerhof', January, reprinted in *Politische Publizistik, 1891 bis 1904, Gesammelte Schriften*, Volume 14, Berlin: Dietz, 1964.

Mehring, Franz 1905a, 'Die Bergarbeiterstreik', *Die Neue Zeit*, 23, 1: 169–72, reprinted in *Politische Publizistik, 1905 bis 1918, Gesammelte Schriften*, Volume 15, Berlin: Dietz, 1966.

Mehring, Franz 1905b, 'Die Revolution in Permanenz', *Die Neue Zeit*, 24, 1: 169–72, reprinted in *Politische Publizistik, 1905 bis 1918, Gesammelte Schriften*, Volume 15, Berlin: Dietz, 1966.

Mehring, Franz 1905c, 'Recht so!', reprinted in *Politische Publizistik, 1905 bis 1918*, in *Gesammelte Schriften*, Volume 15, Berlin: Dietz, 1966.

Mehring, Franz 1905d, 'Sozialer Krieg', *Leipziger Volkszeitung*, Nr. 6, 9 January, reprinted in *Politische Publizistik, 1905 bis 1918, Gesammelte Schriften*, Volume 15, Berlin: Dietz, 1966.

Mehring, Franz 1907, 'Blut und Eisen', *Die Neue Zeit*, 26, 1: 374–6, reprinted in *Zur Kriegsgeschichte und Militarfrage*, Berlin: Dietz, 1967.

Mehring, Franz 1935, *Karl Marx: The Story of His Life*, London: Covici, Friede.

Mehringer, Hartmut 1978, *Permanente Revolution und russische Revolution: Die Entwicklung der Theorie der permanenten Revolution im Rahmen der marxistischen Revolutionskonzeption 1848–1907*, Frankfurt a.M.: Peter Lang.

Moody, John 1904, *The Truth about the Trusts: A Description and Analysis of the American Trust Movement*, New York: Moody Publishing Company; reprint: New York: Greenwood Press, 1968.

Naarden, Bruno 1992, *Socialist Europe and Revolutionary Russia: Perception and Prejudice, 1848–1923*, Cambridge: Cambridge University Press.

Naoroji, Dadabhai 1901, *Poverty and Un-British Rule in India*, London: Swan Sonnenschein.

Novack, George 1957, 'The Rise and Fall of Progressivism', *International Socialist Review*, 18, 3, Summer.

Parvus (Alexander Helphand) 1896a, 'Der Weltmarkt und die Agrarkrisis', *Die Neue Zeit*, 14, 1: 197–202, 276–83, 335–42, 514–26, 621–31, 747–58, 781–8, 818–27.

Parvus (Alexander Helphand) 1896b, 'Staatsreich und politischer Massenstrike', *Die Neue Zeit*, 14, 2: 199–206, 261–6, reprinted in Grunenberg (ed.) 1970.

Parvus (Alexander Helphand) 1898, 'The Peasantry and the Social Revolution', in Tudor and Tudor (eds.) 1988.

Parvus (Alexander Helphand) 1904a, 'Der Generalstreik', *Aus der Weltpolitik*, Munich, 16 August.

Parvus (Alexander Helphand) 1904b, 'Voina i revolyutsiya', *Iskra*, No. 59 (10 February) and No. 61 (5 March).

Parvus (Alexander Helphand) 1905a, 'Foreword to Leon Trotsky's *Do Devyatovo Yanvarya*', Geneva: Tipografiya Partii; republished in Parvus 1907b.

Parvus (Alexander Helphand) 1905b, *V chem myi raskhodimsya?*, Geneva: Tipografiya Partii.

Parvus (Alexander Helphand) 1907a, *Die Kolonialpolitik und der Zusammenbruch*, Leipzig: Verlag der Leipziger Buchdruckerei Aktiengesellschaft.

Parvus (Alexander Helphand) 1907b, *Rossiya i revolyutsiya*, St. Petersburg: Izdanie N. Glagoleva.

Parvus (Alexander Helphand) 1910, 'Letter to Kautsky', 10 June, Kautsky Archive, IISG (International Institute of Social History, Amsterdam); quoted in Donald 1993.

Pearce (ed.), Brian 1978, *Second Ordinary Congress of the R.S.D.L.P., 1903: Complete Text of the Minutes*, translated and annotated by Brian Pearce, London: New Park Publications.

Perrie, Maureen 1973, 'The Socialist Revolutionaries on "Permanent Revolution"', *Soviet Studies*, 24, 3: 411–13.

Petit, Irène 1969, 'Kautsky et les discussions autour du problème de l'impérialisme dans le parti social démocrate allemand de 1907 à 1914', *Revue d'Allemagne*, I, January–March: 325–37.

Petrunkewitsch, J.J. & A.A. Manuilow & Bernhard Braude 1905, *Zur Agrarbewegung in Russland*, Leipzig: Teutonia-Verlag. These essays are included in the Russian collection *Agrarnyi Vopros*, edited by P.D. Dolgorukov and I.I. Petrunkevich, Moscow, 1905.

Plekhanov, Georges 1926, *Introduction a l'histoire sociale de la Russie*, Paris: Editions Bossard.

Plekhanov, Georgy V. 1883a, 'Socialism and the Political Struggle', in *Selected Philosophical Works*, Volume 1, Moscow: Progress Publishers, 1974.

Plekhanov, Georgy V. 1883b, 'Programme of the Social-Democratic Emancipation of Labour Group', in *Selected Philosophical Works*, Volume 1, Moscow: Progress, 1974.

Plekhanov, Georgy V. 1883c, 'Programme of the Social-Democratic Emancipation of Labour Group', in Harding (ed.) 1983.

Plekhanov, Georgy V. 1884, 'Our Differences', in *Selected Philosophical Works*, Volume 1, Moscow: Progress Publishers, 1974.

Plekhanov, Georgy V. 1887a, 'Second Draft Programme of the Russian Social-Democrats', in Harding (ed.) 1983.

Plekhanov, Georgy V. 1887b, 'Second Draft Programme of the Russian Social-Democrats', in *Selected Philosophical Works*, Volume 1, Moscow: Progress Publishers, 1974.

Plekhanov, Georgy V. 1889, 'Speech at the International Workers' Socialist Congress in Paris (14–21 July, 1889)', in *Selected Philosophical Works*, Volume 1, Moscow: Progress Publishers, 1974.

Plekhanov, Georgy V. 1898, 'Wofür sollen wir ihm dankbar sein? Offener Brief an Karl Kautsky', *Sächsische Arbeiterzeitung*, 253, 254 and 255.

Plekhanov Georgy V. 1903, 'Ortodoksal'noe bukvoedstvo', in *Sochineniya*, Third Edition, Volume 11–12, Moscow: Gosudarstvennoe izdatel'stvo, 1928.

Plekhanov, Georgy V. 1920–7, *Sochineniya*, Second Edition, Petrograd: Gosudarstvennoe Izdatel'stvo.

Plekhanov, Georgy V. 1926a, 'Pis'mo pyatoe', in *Sochineniya*, Volume 15, edited by D. Ryazanov, Moscow: Gosudarstvennoe izdatel'stvo.

Plekhanov, Georgy V. 1926b, *Sochineniya*, Volume 13, Moscow: Gosudarstvennoe Izdatel'stvo.

Plekhanov, Georgy V. 1928, *Sochineniya*, Third Edition, Volumes 11–12, edited by D. Ryazanov, Moscow-Leningrad: Gosudarstvennoe Izdatel'stvo.

Plekhanov, Georgy V. 1974, *Selected Philosophical Works*, Volume 1, Moscow: Progress Publishers.

Plekhanov, Georgy V. 1976, *Selected Philosophical Works*, Volume 2, Moscow: Progress Publishers.

Radek, Karl 1912a, 'Unser Kampf gegen den Imperialismus', *Die Neue Zeit*, 30,2: 194–9, 233–41. Reprinted und in *In der Reihen der deutschen Revolution, 1909–1919: Gesammelte Aufsätze und Abhandlungen von Karl Radek*, München: K. Wolff, 1921.

Radek, Karl 1912b, 'Wege und Mittel im Kampfe gegen den Imperialismus', *Bremer Bürger-Zeitung*, 216 (14 September). Reprinted in *In den Reihen der deutschen Revolution, 1909–1919: Gesammelte Aufsätze und Abhandlungen von Karl Radek*, Munich: K. Wolff, 1921.

Radek, Karl 1922, *The Winding up of the Versailles Treaty: Report to the IV. Congress of the Communist International*, Hamburg: The Communist International.

Radek, Karl 1995, 'The Paths of the Russian Revolution', in *In Defence of the Russian Revolution: A Selection of Bolshevik Writings, 1917–1923*, edited by Al Richardson, London: Porcupine Press.

Ratz, Ursula 1966, 'Karl Kautsky und die Abrüstungskontroverse in der deutschen Sozialdemokratie, 1911–12', *International Review of Social History*, 11, 2: 197–227.

Reichard, Richard W. 1953, 'The German Working Class and the Russian Revolution of 1905', *Journal of Central European Affairs*, 13, 2: 136–53.

Riazanov, David 1928a, 'Zur Frage des Verhältnisses von Marx zu Blanqui', *Unter dem Banner der Marxismus*, 2: 140–9.

Riazanov, David 1928b, 'The Relations of Marx with Blanqui', *Labour Monthly*, August: pp. 1–2, 4–5.

Riazanov, David 1937, *Karl Marx and Frederick Engels: An Introduction to Their Lives and Work*, New York: International Publishers.

Rjazanoff, N. 1917, *Gesammelte Schriften von Karl Marx und Friedrich Engels 1852 bis 1862*, 2 volumes, Stuttgart: Dietz.

Rogge, Walter 1872, *Österreich von Vilagos bis zur Gegenwart*, Volume 2, Leipzig: A. Brockhaus.

Rogovin, Vadim Zakharovich 1993, *Vlast' i oppositzii*, Moscow: Tovarishchestvo 'Zhurnal Teatr'.

Rokityanskii, Ya. G. 1991, 'Neukrotimyi akademik: Novye arkhivnye materialy o D.B. Ryazanove', *Vestnik Akademii Nauk SSSR*, 7: 145–9.

Rokityanskii, Ya. G. 1992a 'Tragicheskaya sud'ba akademika D.B. Ryazanova', *Novaya i noveishaya istoriya*, 2: 201–21.

Roland-Holst, Henriëtte 1905, *Generalstreik und Sozialdemokratie*, with a foreword by Karl Kautsky, Dresden: Kaden.

RSDRP 1907a, 'Ob otnoshenii k burzhuasnym partiyam: Proekt Menshevikov', in RSDRP 1907b.

RSDRP 1907b, *Protokoly i stenografi cheskie otchety s'ezdov i konferentsii Kommunisticheskoi Partii Sovetskovo Soyuza: Pyatyi Londonskii s'ezd RSDRP Aprel'–Mai 1907 goda: protokoly*, Moscow: Gosudarstvennoe Izdatel'stvo Politicheskoi Literatury, 1963.

Ryazanov, N. 1902, *Materialy dlya vyrabotki partiinoi programmy, vyp. 1. Novaya programma 'Rabochevo dela'*, Geneva: Izdanie gruppy 'Bor'ba'.

Ryazanov, N. 1903a, *Materialy dlya vyrabotki Partiinoi Programmy. Vypusk II: Proekt programmy 'Iskry' i zadachi Russkikh Sotsial-Demokratov*, Geneva: Izd. gruppy 'Bor'ba'.

Ryazanov, N. 1903b, *Nasha programma; proekt programmy Gruppy 'Bor'ba' i kommentarii k nei*, Geneva: Izdanie gruppy 'Bor'ba'.

Ryazanov, N. 1904, *Razbitya illyuzii: K voprosu o prichinakh krizisa v nashei partii*, Geneva: n.p.

Ryazanov, N. 1905, *Ocherednye voprosy nashevo dvizheniya*, Geneva: Rossiiskaya Sotsialdemokraticheskaya Partiya.

Salvadori, Massimo 1979, *Karl Kautsky and the Socialist Revolution 1880–1938*, London: NLB.

Schirokauer, Arno 1932, *Lassalle: The Power of Illusion and the Illusion of Power*, New York: Century.

Schneider, Michael 1991, *A Brief History of the German Trade Unions*, Bonn: J.H.W. Dietz.

Schorske, Carl E. 1970, *German Social Democracy, 1905–1917: The Development of the Great Schism*, New York: Russell & Russell.

Schulz, Hugo 1906, *Blut und Eisen: Krieg und Kriegertum in alter und neuer Zeit*, Berlin: Buchh. Vorwärts.

Schwarz, Solomon M. 1967, *The Russian Revolution of 1905*, Chicago: University of Chicago Press.

Serebryakov, E. 1894, *Obshchestvo 'Zemlya i Volya'*, Geneva.

Sering, Max 1887, *Die landwirtschaftliche Konkurrenz Nordamerikas in Gegenwart und Zukunft*, Leipzig: Duncker and Humblot.

Shanin, Teodor 1981, 'Marx, Marxism and the Agrarian Question: I. Marx and the Peasant Commune', *History Workshop Journal*, 12, 1: 108–28.

Simons, Algie Martin 1902, *The American Farmer*, Chicago: C.H. Kerr; reprinted, New York: Arno Press, 1975.

Simons, Algie Martin 1906, 'Die Lage in den Vereinigten Staaten', *Die Neue Zeit*, 24, 1: 622–7.

Simons, Algie Martin 1906b, *Class Struggles in America*, Second Edition, Chicago: Charles H. Kerr & Company.

Simons, Algie Martin 1909, 'Klassenkämpfe in der Geschichte Amerikas', *Die Neue Zeit*, 28, 1, Heft 7. Original English version: 'Class Struggles in American History'.

Smaldone, William 1998, *Rudolf Hilferding: The Tragedy of a German Social Democrat*, DeKalb: Northwestern Illinois University Press.

Smirnova, V.A. 1995, 'D.B. Ryazanov' in *Tragicheskie sud'by: repressirovannye uchenye Akademii nauk SSSR*, edited by I.G. Aref'eva, Moscow: Nauka.

Snyder, Timothy 1997, *Nationalism, Marxism, and Modern Central Europe: A Biography of Kazimierz Kelles-Krauz, 1872–1905*, Cambridge, MA.: Harvard University Press for the Ukrainian Research Institute, Harvard University.

Sombart, Werner 1976, *Why Is there No Socialism in the United States?*, Bristol: Macmillan.

Sorge, Friedrich A. 1977, *Friedrich A. Sorge's Labor Movement in the United States: A History of the American Working Class from Colonial Times to 1890*, edited by Philip S. Foner and Brewster Chamberlin, Westport: Greenwood Press.

676 • References

Sorge, Friedrich A. 1987, *Friedrich A. Sorge's Labor Movement in the United States: A History of the American Working Class from 1890 to 1896*, translated by Kai Schoenhals, Westport: Greenwood Press.

SPD 1905, 'Auszug aus dem Referat Bebels zum politischen Massenstreik', in *Protokoll über die Verhandlungen des Parteitages der Sozialdemokratischen Partei Deutschlands, abgehalten zu Jena vom 17. bis 23. September 1905*, Berlin: Buchhandlung Vorwärts. Reprinted in Grunenberg (ed.) 1970.

SPD 1906, *Protokoll über die Verhandlungen des Parteitages der Sozialdemokratischen Partei Deutschlands: abgehalten zu Mannheim vom 23. bis 29. September 1906*, Berlin: Buchhandlung Vorwärts.

Steenson, Gary P. 1978, *Karl Kautsky, 1854–1938: Marxism in the Classical Years*, Pittsburgh: University of Pittsburgh Press.

Steinigans, Emil 1903, *Kautsky und die soziale Revolution: Eines Arbeiters Kritik der Kautsky'schen Broschüren 'Die soziale Revolution' und 'Am Tage nach der sozialen Revolution'*, Solingen: Genossenschafts-Buchdruckerei.

Stern (ed.), Leo 1961, *Die russische Revolution von 1905–1907 im Spiegel der deutschen Presse*, Berlin: Rutten & Loening.

Struve, Pyotr Berngardovich 1894, *Kriticheskie zametki k voprosu ob ekonomicheskom razvitii Rossii*, St Petersburg: Skorokhodov.

Trotsky, Leon 1902, 'Bobchinskie v oppositsii', in *Sochineniya*, Volume 4, Moscow and Leningrad: Gosudarstvennoe Izdatel'stvo.

Trotsky, Leon 1904, *Our Political Tasks*, London: New Park, 1979.

Trotsky, Leon 1905, 'Open Letter to Professor P.N. Miliukov', August, in N. Trotsky 1906.

Trotsky, Leon 1908, 'Letter to Kautsky', 11 August, Kautsky Archive, International Institute of Social History, Amsterdam; quoted in Donald 1993.

Trotsky, Leon 1910, 'Letter to Kautsky', 21 July, Kautsky Archive, International Institute of Social History, Amsterdam; quoted in J.P. Nettl, *Rosa Luxemburg*, Oxford: Oxford University Press, 1966.

Trotsky, Leon 1917, 'The Paris Commune', *Novy Mir*, 17 March, translated in *New Militant*, 21 March 1936.

Trotsky, Leon 1918, *Our Revolution*, edited and translated by Moissaye J. Olgin, New York: Henry Holt.

Trotsky, Leon 1919, 'Preface', in L. Trotsky 1969.

Trotsky, Leon 1920, *Terrorism and Communism*, London: New Park, 1975.

Trotsky, Leon 1921, 'The Lessons of the Commune', *Zlatoost*, 4 February, translated in *The New International*, April 1935; reprinted in L. Trotsky 1955.

Trotsky, Leon 1925, *Sochineniya*, Volume 2, part I, Moscow and Leningrad: Gosudarstvennoe Izdatel'stvo.

Trotsky, Leon 1926, *Sochineniya*, Volume 4, Moscow and Leningrad: Gosudarstvennoe Izdatel'stvo.

Trotsky, Leon 1931, 'The Case of Comrade Ryazanov', 8 March, translated by Max Shachtman in, *The Militant*, New York, 1 May.

Trotsky, Leon 1932, 'Hands off Rosa Luxemburg', in *Writings 1932*, New York: Pathfinder Press, 1973.

Trotsky, Leon 1936, *History of the Russian Revolution*, New York: Simon and Schuster.

Trotsky, Leon 1938, 'Karl Kautsky', 8 November 1938, in *Writings, 1938–39*, New York: Pathfinder Press, 1974.

Trotsky, Leon 1939, 'Marxism in Our Time', introduction to *The Living Thoughts of Karl Marx*, Greenwich, Conn.: Fawcett Publications, 1963.

Trotsky, Leon 1955, *The Paris Commune*, Ceylon: Star Press.

Trotsky, Leon 1960, *My Life*, New York: Grosset and Dunlap.

Trotsky, Leon 1962, *Permanent Revolution & Results and Prospects*, London: New Park.

Trotsky, Leon 1969, *Results and Prospects*, in *Permanent Revolution and Results and Prospects*, New York: Pathfinder.

Trotsky, Leon 1970, 'Vorwort', in *Zur Verteidigung der Partei*, in *Schriften zur revolutionären Organisation*, edited by Hartmut Mehringer, Reinbek bei Hamburg: Rowohlt.

Trotsky, Leon 1971a, *1905*, London: Penguin.

Trotsky, Leon 1971b, 'The Party of the Proletariat and the Bourgeois Parties in the Revolution', annex to Trotsky 1971a.

Trotsky, Leon 1977, *The History of the Russian Revolution*, London: Pluto.

Trotsky, Leon 1987, *In Defence of October*, London: Militant.

Trotsky, N. 1905a, *Up to the Ninth of January*, in N. Trotsky 1906.

Trotsky, N. 1905b, *Do Devyatovo Yanvarya*, Geneva: Tipografiya Partiin Rue de la Coulouvrenière, 27; republished in L. Trotsky 1925.

Trotsky, N. 1906, *Nasha revolyutsiya*, St Petersburg: Glagolev.

Trotsky, N. 1907, *V zashchitu partii*, St Petersburg: Tipografiya t-va 'Delo', Fontanka, 96.

Tscherewanin, F.A. [pseud. of Fedor Andreevich Lipkin] 1908, *Das Proletariat und die russische Revolution*, Mit einer Vorrede von H. Roland-Holst und einem Anhang vom Übersetzer S. Lewitin, Stuttgart: J.H.W. Dietz.

Tudor, H. and J.M. Tudor (eds.) 1988, *Marxism and Social Democracy: The Revisionist Debate 1896–1898*, Cambridge: Cambridge University Press.

V[orontsov], V. 1882, *Sud'by kapitalizma v Rossii*, St. Petersburg; quoted in Walicki 1980.

Venturi, Franco 2001, *Roots of Revolution: A History of the Populist and Socialist Movements in 19th Century Russia*, London: Phoenix.

Volksstimme (Frankfurt) (Hrsg.) 1904, *Aus der Waffenkammer des Sozialismus: eine Sammlung alter und neuer Propaganda-Schriften*, Frankfurt a.M.: Verlag der Union-Druckerei.

vom Brocke (ed.), Bernhard 1987, *Sombarts 'Moderner Kapitalismus': Materialien zur Kritik und Rezeption*, Munich: Deutscher Taschenbuch Verlag.

Wada, Haruki 1981, 'Marx, Marxism and the Agrarian Question II: Marx and Revolutionary Russia', *History Workshop Journal*, 12: 129–50.

Waldenberg, Marek 1972, *Wzlot i upadek Karola Kaustky'ego*, Cracow: Wydawnictwo literackie.

Waldenberg, Marek 1980, *Il papa rosso: Karl Kautsky*, Rome: Editori Riuniti.

Walicki, Andrzej 1969, *The Controversy Over Capitalism: Studies in the Social Philosophy of the Russian Populists*, Oxford: Clarendon Press.

Walicki, Andrzej 1980, *A History of Russian Thought from the Enlightenment to Marxism*, translated from the Polish by Hilda Andrews-Rusiecka, Stanford: Stanford University Press.

Waters (ed.), Mary-Alice 1970, *Rosa Luxemburg Speaks*, New York: Pathfinder.

Wolfe, Bertram D. 1966, *Three Who Made a Revolution*, Harmondsworth: Penguin.

Yaroshevsky (ed.), M.G. 1991, *Repressivnaya nauka*, St. Petersburg: 'Nauka'.

Zeman, Z.A.B. and W.B. Scharlau 1965, *The Merchant of Revolution: The Life of Alexander Israel Helphand (Parvus), 1867–1924*, Oxford: Oxford University Press.

Zinoviev, Grigory 1973, *History of the Bolshevik Party: A Popular Outline*, London: New Park Publications.

Index